D1795157

The Essential
HITLER

Speeches
and
Commentary

Max Domarus

Edited by Patrick Romane

Foreword by Charles W. Sydnor, Jr.

Bolchazy-Carducci Publishers, Inc.
Wauconda, Illinois USA

General Editor
Marie Carducci Bolchazy

Contributing Editor
Alex MacGregor

Foreword by
Charles W. Sydnor, Jr.

Cover Design & Typography
Adam Phillip Velez

Cartography
Margaret W. Pearce

**The Essential Hitler
Speeches and Commentary**

Max Domarus
Edited by Patrick Romane

© **2007 Bolchazy-Carducci Publishers, Inc.**
All rights reserved.

Bolchazy-Carducci Publishers, Inc.
1000 Brown Street
Wauconda, IL 60084 USA
www.bolchazy.com

Printed in Canada
2007
by Friesens

Paperback: ISBN 978-0-86516-627-1
Hardbound: ISBN 978-0-86516-665-3

Library of Congress Cataloging-in-Publication Data

Hitler, Adolf, 1889-1945.
 [Reden und Proklamationen, 1932-1945. English. Selections.]
 The essential Hitler : speeches and commentary / Hitler ; [edited with commentary by] Max Domarus
; [abridgment] edited by Patrick Romane. -- 1st ed.
  p. cm.
 Includes index.
 ISBN 978-0-86516-665-3 -- ISBN 978-0-86516-627-1 (pbk. : alk. paper)
 1. Germany--Politics and government--1933-1945--Sources. 2. Hitler, Adolf,
1889-1945--Translations into English. 3. National socialism--Sources. 4. Nationalsozialistische
Deutsche Arbeiter-Partei--History--Sources. I. Domarus, Max. II. Romane, Patrick. III. Title.

DD247.H5A575132 2006
943.086092--dc22

2006036890

Contents

Photographs:

Maps:

Foreword

He was the dominant figure of the twentieth century. Adolf Hitler qualified for this role and stature because he was a unique conjunction of personal and historical forces. The enormity of what he attempted and achieved, the unprecedented conflict, mass murder and inhumanity he unleashed, and the political and demographic upheavals he planned and launched affected the entire globe for over a decade, and set in motion historical forces that persist to this day. No other figure in modern history had such a profound, and profoundly malevolent, influence upon humankind, or came nearly as close to achieving the destruction of civilization as he did. Sixty-two years after his squalid suicide in the shattered ruins of Berlin, we still live in a world that struggles with forces, conditions, and consequences that persist from the costs incurred by the massive Allied effort to destroy Adolf Hitler and crush Nazi Germany.

Adolf Hitler rose from complete obscurity, as "the unknown corporal of the Great War," to exercise unlimited dictatorial power in the German Third Reich he created. He was the first German ruler to be idolized and obeyed through an unbroken and unprecedented wave of genuine public popularity that proved as vital to sustaining the Nazi state as the great tyranny directed from Berlin through his SS and police terror apparatus, which after 1938 was used even more ruthlessly in brutalizing the populations in the German conquered and occupied regions of Europe than in the Hitlerian motherland itself.

An odyssey as improbable as Adolf Hitler's could not have begun, much less succeeded, in a politically and economically stable Germany set within a normal and settled European order. The German society and European system into which Adolf Hitler emerged and rapidly rose after the Great War of 1914–1918 were anything but stable and normal. The First World War had exhausted and then overturned and shattered the European and world order of the nineteenth century. Millions of young men from the belligerent states—for example, France, Great Britain, Russia, and Germany—had been lost in the trenches, cut down in history's first conflict of mechanized, technically feasible mass slaughter. At the end of the conflict, in the autumn of 1918, Germany collapsed militarily into a defeat as rapid and complete as it was incomprehensible to the German people—and to the German soldier Adolf Hitler.

Hitler had served for four years in the trenches and was a decorated combat veteran, in a German army that became his home, in a war that shaped his character and his views, and for a cause with which he identified his whole existence. Germany's defeat devastated both Adolf Hitler and the world Adolf Hitler had known, destroying the meaning and purpose of his life. Postwar revolution, Communist-directed violence, spreading political chaos, and the onset of hardship and privation, set against the backdrop of the humiliating Allied peace terms imposed on Germany in the Treaty of Versailles, led millions of Germans—like Hitler—to look for answers, find explanations, search for scapegoats, and seek out individuals and groups—above all alien, minority groups—to blame for the catastrophe cf defeat and Germany's despair and ruin. Postwar political instability bred new political parties and radical fringe groups—a few on the political left, most on the political right—where old resentments, new hatreds, racist doctrines, and xenophobic proposals for German resurgence and national revenge all coalesced around the common elements of intolerance and hatred—vehement, unremitting hatred of those identified as the criminals who stabbed the German army in the back and were responsible for defeat—liberal and left-wing politicians, union leaders and labor agitators, military mutineers and Communist insurgents, intellectuals, and Jews. Operating in this miasmic postwar cauldron as a spy and informer for the German army, reporting on the new extremist splinter groups on the radical right until he was discharged from the army on March 31, 1920, Adolf Hitler discovered personal gifts and instincts that suited him perfectly for the turbulent abnormalities of German politics. His radical German nationalism and his extreme hatred of Jews, Socialists, Communists, and all those who supported the new postwar German Republic, burst forth in a talent for public speaking and demagoguery that was to grow, over the next two decades, into a genius for compelling, overpowering oratory. Hitler had an uncanny ability to sense the moods of his audiences and to tailor the pitch and tone of his speeches to the prejudices, grievances, and resentments the crowds harbored. He had the capacity to connect with individual listeners with such passion and power that he could move huge, open-air crowds of hundreds of thousands to frenzy, and mesmerize spellbound radio audiences of millions of listeners throughout Germany and beyond. Adolf Hitler was history's first media tyrant, sensing the advantages and exploiting the potential modern mass communications offered in amplifying his oratorical powers.

Hitler's rise to power in Germany, while built upon the political skills and alliances he developed, and propelled by his uncanny instincts for seizing opportunities and capitalizing on luck, ran straight through his vocal cords—his rise would have come to nothing without his hypnotic oratory. Until well into his dictatorship, and after he began the Second World War, the essential medium of Hitler's power was the spoken word. No other figure of the twentieth century mastered or deployed public oratory to the results and effects Adolf Hitler did. He wrote all his own speeches, the important orations requiring days of elaborate preparation. He developed and rehearsed exaggerated but powerfully effective techniques that included operatic gestures, alternating cadences of speech, levels of voice, sarcasm and irony, and the uncanny timing that charged his performances with electrifying tones of menace, fury, and hatred. Like an organ virtuoso, Hitler played upon the hypnotic power in the timber and emotional range of his voice to break down the resistance of audiences and sweep them along with him to the frenzied oratorical climax that ended all his public speeches—leaving both Hitler and his audience spent and emotionally exhausted.

In all his public oratory, as in all his public life, the raw force of hatred, depending upon the occasion or the subject of the speech, was either the central theme or a barely disguised undercurrent to what Hitler said and did. Hatred was the emotion most natural to Hitler, the staple of his character. His capacity for hatred was unlimited and was never satiated by any triumph, achievement, political victory, or military conquest throughout his entire political career—before and after he came to power as the Führer.

At the nadir of his inhumanity, Hitler harbored a murderous, limitless hatred of the Jews. Once his dictatorship was established, his power unchallenged, and his war against the world launched, he gave increasing vent to this all-consuming hatred and his murderous intentions in the rhetoric of annihilation and extermination—in public speeches, in harangues to his Nazi Party cronies and satraps, and in the rambling monologues he inflicted on his dinner guests and his inner circle at his headquarters.

Throughout his political life, Hitler's gifts for oratory also served to establish and embellish the cult of the Führer and the myth he consciously created of himself as an historic figure. Hitler cast his public speeches, his proclamations, his remarks at ceremonial occasions, and his participation in the great public spectacles of the Nazi calendar to perpetuate the aura of himself as a legendary figure, a "world historical genius," as he often referred to himself. Before the end of his life, Hitler completely subsumed his private identity into his public persona—the one, all-powerful historic Führer, with whom Germany and its fate were inextricably tied. Thus, the surviving records of what he said in public and in private, what he published as proclamations and issued as decrees, what he acknowledged in interviews and revealed in conversations represent an authentic reflection of the real Adolf Hitler—the public Adolf Hitler.

For four decades, scholars and students seeking fresh insights or new perspectives through research in collections of Hitler's speeches—his spoken and written words—could turn to the definitive, four-volume German edition *Hitler, Reden und Proklamationen, 1932 bis 1945*, edited with commentary by the late Professor Max Domarus, a German historian and medieval specialist who heard Hitler speak many times, and in 1932 began collecting copies of the Führer's speeches, and Hitler's public comments interviews and letters, knowing then they would become important historical materials. After more than a decade of labor, Domarus' first German edition of *Reden und Proklamationen* appeared in 1963, subsequently reprinted in several German editions down to 1988.

Until the last decade the Domarus collection of Hitler's speeches remained unavailable to English-reading audiences. Then, beginning in 1990, and continuing until 2004, Bolchazy-Carducci Publishers of Wauconda, Illinois, commissioned and completed an English translation from the German of the entire four-volume Domarus edition, *Hitler, Speeches and Proclamations, 1932–1945: The Chronicle of a Dictatorship,*—a staggering undertaking. As a result, English-speaking scholars, students, and interested lay readers now have access to one of the most important historical sources documenting the public life of Adolf Hitler and the history of Nazi Germany. Both the German and English four-volume sets contain a running commentary Domarus wrote on the historical context and events Hitler referred to in his speeches, and what consequences developed as a result of what Hitler said.

To complete this enterprise in accessibility, Bolchazy-Carducci Publishers has now finished a one-volume English abridged edition of the complete four-volume set of their English translation. *The Essential Hitler: Speeches and Commentary* includes both the preface and introduction Domarus wrote originally for the four-volume German work, as well as Domarus' observations about Hitler as a personality and political leader, and the event summaries Domarus penned for each of the four volumes for the years 1932–1945. Even though many of the Domarus observations and conclusions are now long superseded thanks to more recent scholarship, they are nonetheless invaluable as a companion historical source, enabling the reader to see Hitler as observed by a first-hand witness, from a time closer to Hitler's era and to the events described in the speeches, proclamations, and other pronouncements.

The main text in this abridged edition centers upon the speeches and documents selected by the editor, which are complemented by Domarus' commentary. Chapters are organized topically, each with a particular focus relating to an important aspect of Hitler's public life and role as the Führer of Nazi Germany—what Hitler believed, how he governed, Hitler and the Nazi Party, the German economy in the 1930's, Hitler and the churches, life in Hitler's Germany, Hitler as a strategist and military commander, Hitler and the Jewish question, and chapters on how Hitler fought and lost the war. Edited by Patrick Romane, *The Essential Hitler: Speeches and Commentary* serves as both a reliable and useful introduction to Hitler the orator and to Hitler's use of the spoken and written word. The result is a volume of general interest that should find a prominent place on the reference shelf of any student or specialist interested in any phase of the life and career of the most complex, destructive, and central historic figure of the twentieth century.

CHARLES W. SYDNOR, JR.
Emory & Henry College
Former president,
Commonwealth Public
Broadcasting Corporation

For information on the German and English four volume editions (*Hitler: Speeches and Proclamations, 1932–1945*) and for CD versions, go to www.bolchazy.com

The Might of the Third Reich

Editor's Preface

Dr. Max Domarus published the first edition of his book, *Hitler, Reden und Proklamationen 1932 bis 1945*, in 1963. Reviewers consider the final edition, a four-volume set, to be one of the most significant primary sources for the history of the Third Reich. Professor Alan Bullock, author of *Hitler, a Study in Tyranny*, called it "an indispensable reference work for the history of our age." In 1990, Bolchazy-Carducci Publishers initiated publication of the English language edition of Domarus' four-volume set, completing the final volume in 2004. Both the German original and the English translation are designed for history students and professionals. There remained a pressing need for an edition accessible to the public because non-historians need to understand Hitler and the Nazi regime so as to avoid any reoccurrence of the most heinous events of the twentieth century.

This is the basic idea behind *The Essential Hitler, Speeches and Commentary*. The importance of this material lies in the fact that these documents represent the official and public positions of Hitler and his government regarding what he saw as important issues. Hitler did not have speechwriters; he constructed each statement of his speeches himself: he simply did not trust anyone to speak for him, although at times, he had people read his speeches to an audience. Moreover, Hitler wrote much else besides speeches and proclamations. Military orders, letters, laws, even an article on architecture came from his hand and these demonstrate Hitler's thoughts and attitudes. Domarus, as a young man in 1932, began collecting Hitler's statements and continued throughout the duration of the Third Reich to its collapse in 1945. Domarus despised Hitler and the Nazis and points out the flaws and miscalculations of the Nazi administration. Nevertheless, the panoramic whole he presents is the most vivid and detailed view of Hitlerism made by a German contemporary.

At the same time, we need to understand that Domarus' work is a primary source itself in that he not only presents Hitler's words and actions but also presents the understandings of a perceptive, involved observer to explain those events. Some of Domarus' statements of interpretation and a few facts (essential items so noted in the text) are at variance with subsequent scholarly consensus. For instance, while Domarus recounts Hitler's initiation of and involvement in the events of the Holocaust, later research emphasizes a much closer relationship of the Second World War to the Holocaust and, indeed, the documentation of Holocaust events have doubled since the fall of the USSR.

Further, we should add that Domarus used text sources for most of Hitler's words. The Nazis had the material published in pamphlet form or, most often, in the party press. Often, films of the speeches have minor but noticeable differences from Domarus' text. Hitler was very particular about his public words and would "correct and extend his remarks" as he saw fit. While the speeches may not be exactly as delivered they do represent what Hitler wanted people to believe he said.

It is important to state that there is no other work that shows the nature of Hitlerism as concisely and as clearly as this book. Hitler wrote both *Mein Kampf* and the *Second Book* before he came to power. They represent theory. Here is practice.

This book consists of selections from Domarus' four volumes. Of the original 3,272 pages of the English language text, we present some 880 pages of material. Domarus' original work is a day-by-day chronicle of Hitler's actions; here the material is topical. The topical arrangement allows the exploration of significant themes that gave Hitlerism its unique character. We start with Domarus' "Preface and Introduction," followed by his year-to-year event summaries compiled into a connected section, giving a chronological overview. Then come sections on major topics. The different topics represent significant areas of Hitler's policies. Each section's materials demonstrate the type of action and explanation characteristic of Hitler and offer deep insights into his methods and attitudes. The topics are: Hitler's beliefs, how he ran his government, the Nazi Party, Hitler's economic ideas, the Jews and the Holocaust, Hitler and the Christian churches, Domarus' essay on how Hitler became supreme commander of the German army, aspects of life in Hitler's Germany, Hitler and the press, the expansion of the Reich, the United States and Hitler, Hitler's war, the war's end, and, last, Domarus' epilogue. Each topic is self-contained but relates to the picture generated by the whole.

There are a number of points regarding style. Hitler spoke only German and often used German words in idiosyncratic ways. In the presentation of his words, we have attempted to capture meaning and flow rather than simple word for word translation. While we have attempted to keep German words at a minimum, at times we have a translation followed by the German in parenthesis so that the German connotations remain. One word that Hitler constantly used and misused is Volk. The English word most often used to represent Volk is "people" in that word's original sense of members of a political or cultural group of like-minded and self-identifying individuals. In some ways, the English cognate "folk" is very close to Volk except in its informality. However, Volk may take on a "racist" quality in its German usage in the sense that membership in such a group is considered a matter of biology. But the English word "race," translated into German as *Rasse*, is not a good equivalent for Volk because, even with biological implications, Volk retains strong cultural or social implications as well; this is something which "race" does not. Hitler used the word Volk to identify those Germans of "pure race" who were culturally "orthodox" Germans—Germans of Jewish background, no matter how culturally German in behavior and outlook, could not be members of the German Volk. In his sense, *das deutsche* Volk, as used by Hitler, is quite different from simply "the German people." Similarly, the Hitlerism *Volksgenossen*, having the meaning of "racial and cultural fellow comrade in the fight for German freedom," was Hitler's usual form of address to his German audience. Hitler spoke in a fast-flowing cadence, the meaning and especially the psychological connections of which was usually understandable to his audience, even if his words, at times, became jumbled. We have attempted to replicate some of this style in the English renderings.

In the presentation of our material, we use the following conventions: standard type for Dr. Domarus' words, standard type indented for Hitler's words; and italics for the editor's comments. There are appendices at the end that contain significant dates and events, a glossary containing specific Nazi and German terms of the time, maps to illustrate events, an article index, and a subject index.

This work is much improved by the diligent labor and perceptive comments of Dr. Charles Sydnor, Jr., of Emory & Henry College and former president of the Commonwealth Broadcasting Corporation and Dr. Ronald Smelser of the University of Utah, both gentlemen true experts in a field often crowded with confusion. Thanks are due to Art and Olga Ladenberger for their help with the German in the text. This work benefited greatly because of their efforts. I also want to thank Dr. Peter Black, head historian at the Holocaust Museum in Washington, DC, for his help. I especially want to thank Dr. Alex MacGregor, Professor at the University of Illinois (Chicago), for the generous input of his profound knowledge of language and the history of the twentieth century. He made clear much that was hazy. Dr. Albert Devine, always insightful and a fount of knowledge, brought clarity to difficult passages as he examined the manuscript. Remaining errors are mine.

In conclusion, I must thank Dr. Marie Carducci Bolchazy for her expert and perceptive editorial work. The ever-present and patient technical assistance of Jody Cull made a difficult task easier. I must express profound gratitude to Dr. Ladislaus Bolchazy for his vision in bringing Domarus to an English-speaking audience through twenty years of labor and sacrifice. Nor can I neglect to thank my patient wife, Judith O'Dell, for putting up with my work on Hitler far too long.

A Note on Casualties Caused by Hitler's Actions and Policies

Hitler caused more deaths than any other person in history, surpassing the deaths caused by Stalin or Mao. Because of his hatred of the victors of the First World War, Hitler decided to solve each problem he saw as a result of that victory by intimidation and force. Clearly, a very large number of deaths were the result of Hitler's drive to supreme power through aggressive war. While the Second World War combined a number of smaller regional conflicts that had no relation to the German question initially, it was Hitler's push to attack countries on all sides of Germany that drove those smaller conflicts into one massive catastrophe. Stalin had no immediate plans to attack Poland or Czechoslovakia in 1938; indeed, those countries had support and aid from western European nations just because they could and did isolate the Soviet Union from the west. Only when Hitler enticed Stalin into the Fourth Partition of Poland, after the destruction of Czechoslovakia, did the Soviet dictator begin to look west. Mussolini, a brutal dictator himself, was unimpressed with Hitler whom he regarded as a junior imitator until Hitler's spectacular string of victories made Mussolini fear that Italy would not have a place at a new victor's congress. Only then did he recognize Hitler's abilities and join the Nazi march of conquest. Japan had been fighting a major war in China for a decade but not until

Hitler attacked the Soviet Union did the Japanese decide that they could seize the British and Dutch possessions in the Far East. To accomplish this, however, they had to eliminate the United States from the area and so attacked Pearl Harbor. The constellation of forces thus grew together and created the great catastrophe of the Second World War.

However, while Hitler excelled at the age-old game of intimidation and conquest, he invented a new type of war, a campaign of destruction against people who did not fit into his schemes of social reconstruction. Hatred of people based on fear of differences underlay Hitler's gross inhumanity and emerged clearly in the list of his victims. At the top of his list were the Jews who were central to his perverted concepts of historical development, not because of what they did but because of who they were. Included in this list were not just those who opposed him—leftists, Communists, traditionalists, and conservatives, those whom he might have a reason to hate—but those who were congenitally unable of meeting social functions he deemed important—the chronically sick, the lame, the deformed, the insane. They too were slated for elimination. While Hitler was fighting to gain power, the fact that many SA and others in the Movement were homosexual bothered him not at all. After the Night of the Long Knives, he sent them to concentration camps. Confessional Christians, Church critics, and pacifists were sent to the camps too. To be a gypsy was a capital offense. After the war started, Hitler continued the slaughter, only to find even more subjects of his attention. Here, battle or collateral damage was not the issue, as bad as it was, but above and beyond that, just wanton savagery against Poles, Serbs, Russians, French, and any other group that Hitler despised, even his erstwhile allies the Italians. The number of Hitler's victims is staggering: millions upon millions suffered death because of him.

Presenting the statistics of death for World War II is difficult. On one hand, the official numbers are patently inaccurate because so much was lost in the disruption and chaos of combat and social upheaval with the result that any comprehensive figures are but estimates. On the other hand, the figures themselves are so large that they lose concrete meaning. Yet, the loss was real. Violence ended all those lives.

There have been many estimates of the total. Gerhard Weinberg (*A World at Arms*, 2nd ed. 2005, page 894) bases his estimates on new evidence from Eastern Europe. He concludes that the number ". . . probably reached 60 million." This figure combines both military and civilian deaths, the civilian number being considerably larger than the military.

First, military deaths: Micheal Clodfelter, (*Warfare and Armed Conflicts, Statistical Reference to Casualties and Other Figures, 1618–1991,* 1992, pages 955–56) gives these figures:

Axis	7,100,000
Allies (not including Soviets)	9,700,000

There is a question, however, about Soviet deaths during the war. Clodfelter's figure is 7,000,000 military deaths. A study by the Russian Republic, *Soviet Casualties and Combat Losses in the Twentieth Century*, gen. ed. Colonel General G. F. Krivosheev, 1997, (page 84) gives a figure for Soviet military "irrecoverable" loses during World War II as 11,444,100, some 4,444,100 more than Clodfelter's figure. Allied deaths then become 14,144,100.

The total, including the new Russian figures, is:

Military deaths	21,244,100

Second, civilian deaths: These are harder to calculate. If we consider Clodfelter's military deaths to be reasonably accurate but modified by the new Russian evidence, then looking at the figure for total deaths we can find the civilian figure.

Civilian deaths	38,755,900

While these figures can be only best estimates, they do give a clear picture of the order of magnitude of the destruction caused by the Second World War.

No less important are the figures of the deaths caused by Hitler's personal efforts beyond the violence of combat. These are included in the figures for civilian casualties, for the most part, but are indicative of Hitler's utter inhumanity.

At the top of Hitler's list were the Jews. The figure of 6,000,000 killed is most generally accepted based on close investigation of the records. This may be conservative. Clodfelter (page 898) gives the figure 5,933,900 killed out of a total 1939 population of some 8,861,800 Jews, the entire Jewish community in Europe at that time.

Hitler thought that handicapped people were needless mouths to feed. To eliminate these "genetically weak" people, starting in 1934 and continuing to the end of the regime, the Nazi government sterilized 300,000 to 400,000 people. However, Hitler had no intention of stopping at that. From 1939 through 1945, the Nazis killed some 200,000 to 250,000 people whom they viewed as unfit.

Hitler and the Nazis saw the "Gypsies," the Siniti and Roma, as both asocial and racially inferior. The Nazis rounded up as many as they could find and sent them to the camps where significant numbers were gassed. The numbers are not reliable, but at least 220,000 and maybe up to 500,000 were killed.

Among the many groups Hitler found obnoxious were the Jehovah's Witnesses. At least they could gain release from the camps if they signed a document renouncing their faith. Some 10,000 were imprisoned, mostly Germans; some 2,500 to 5,000 perished. While in the camps, these people continued their efforts at conversion.

After the invasion of Poland, to clear the land for *Lebensraum*, Hitler and his Nazis butchered some 1,800,000–1,900,000 Poles. Any potential opponents, in Germany, allied, and occupied countries were simply shot, hanged, or sent to concentration camps. Having deployed their available man-power on the battle fronts and in support of their forces, the Nazis imported millions of people from the occupied countries and used them as slave labor, "expending" these people through brutal working conditions, and starvation. Most died. After Italy surrendered to the Allies in 1943, thousands of Royal Italian soldiers in proximity to German troops were killed out of hand by them.

More information about these events are available from the United States Holocaust Memorial Museum (*www.ushmm.org*) from which much of the above material is taken.

Finally, there are indications that the Nazi medical establishment even killed severely wounded *Wehrmacht* and *Waffen SS* troopers whose injuries were permanently disabling so that they would not be a burden to the New Order.

PATRICK ROMANE

Young Hitler, a German Soldier in World War I

I
Domarus' Preface and Introduction

Domarus introduced his collection with an analysis of Hitler as a leader and as a man. This material is significant for two reasons: one, Domarus experienced many of the events he covered in his work and so he imparts a true vividness to his portrait of Hitler; two, in certain matters, he falls short of our subsequent understanding of Hitler's Germany and these specific points are instructive regarding attitudes in Germany following the Second World War.

 We need to point out a number of specifics. One, in his discussion of Hitler's supposed "supernatural powers," case 2, Domarus indicated that the bomb which exploded at the Nazi celebration on November 8, 1939 was part of a eleborate plot concocted by Nazi leaders to unite the German people even more firmly behind Hitler. Subsequent research upholds the interpretation that the bomb was a serious assassination attempt by Georg Elser, now regarded as a resistance hero. In case 3, it appears that a staff officer moved Stauffenberg's briefcase bomb away from where Hitler was standing and so Hitler received protection from the blast by the heavy wooden table.

 Two, Domarus states that some Germans felt that Hitler's rule was a good thing—a view Domarus clearly did not share. This view is no longer acceptable in Germany after decades of nasty revelations and works such as Domarus' books.

 Three, Domarus implies that Hitler's obsessive anti-Semitism came out of his early experience in Vienna, which was a common predjudice in the 1920s and 1930s. Current opinion holds that Hitler invested his entire ego in Germany's fight in World War I and the loss of the war necessitated finding a scapegoat.

 Four, investigating sources of Hitler's inspirations has long been a minor industry. Hitler's Vienna acquaintance, Reinhold Hanisch's story about Kellerman's film and novel Tunnel *is only one of many such stories. Domarus uses the story to describe Hitler's oratory method but the actual influence of Kellerman's work has long been open to doubt.*

This publication of the speeches and proclamations of Adolf Hitler is the final product of records I compiled during the years 1932 to 1945 and supplemented by sources and publications made available after World War II. Such in-depth study of materials documenting the very recent past may first appear unusual for a historian who had, until then, specialized in the 19th century. There are, however, certain parallels between the two fields. My own avid interest in English history led me to concentrate my scholarly research on Napoleon I and William II. When, in 1932, Adolf Hitler became the most important political figure in Germany, I became interested in his public words for, in terms of foreign policy, they reminded me of these two historical predecessors. There could be no doubt that this man, once in power, would perforce come into marked conflict with the Western world, above all with Great Britain. Hence I began to collect all of Hitler's speeches, interviews, proclamations, letters, and other statements available, convinced that they would one day be of documentary value, should this demagogue be allowed to pursue his course.

During my university studies and as a journalist, I had the opportunity to travel widely in Germany from 1932 to 1939 and to gain a close view of many significant aspects of the Third Reich. I personally heard Hitler speak and was able to interview public figures who had direct contact with him. In this way I was able to witness for myself Hitler's astonishing power and influence as an orator. The enthusiasm his speeches prompted was not confined only to easily-aroused mass audiences but also infected, perhaps even more strongly, individuals belonging to Germany's leading circles.

At that time I was aware that Hitler's arguments were most persuasive with the German people and with peoples in neighboring countries or those who had some link to the German mentality and culture. Citizens of the Anglo-Saxon nations were unimpressed by Hitler's oratory, just as the Soviets and Japanese were unimpressed, although they did make certain concessions to Hitler for diplomatic and tactical reasons. My own observations of the events and the comparisons I drew with historic parallels soon taught me how to assess accurately and soberly both the real and alleged accomplishments of the Third Reich and to anticipate the reactions they would elicit abroad.

I became a particularly attentive and critical listener, studying the various phases and methodology of his oratory and making my own notes of key phrases either during his speeches or shortly thereafter. Thus I was able to immediately spot changes and deletions in texts of the speeches subsequently published. As a soldier from 1939 to 1945, I no longer had the opportunity to personally attend speeches and visit mass rallies. However, this was less of a handicap than might have been expected, for Hitler's public appearances became increasingly infrequent during World War II, and the few speeches he did deliver were broadcast on the radio. When I had leave, I updated my collection and supplemented it with such military orders, proclamations and directives as were available to me. After 1945, I was able to further complement the documents I had compiled with archive material.

Friends and fellow historians at home and abroad urged me to publish the collection in the form of a day-to-day chronicle, accompanied by a detailed commentary providing the historical background. This would then serve to make the most anomalous and terrifying phenomenon of our century more accessible and comprehensible and—by revealing the sharp contrast between the Führer myth and reality—act as a corrective to an incomplete or false interpretation of the Nazi regime. Much research on the history of the Third Reich has perhaps viewed its subject in too complicated a fashion. The initiator and driving force behind the fatal events was Adolf Hitler. While he did not necessarily reveal his innermost thoughts, he never made any significant distinction between what he poured forth before mass audiences and what he said in more intimate circles. He readily disclosed most of his views to the public eye, albeit not always at the same time he took action. The advantage in studying his public statements lies in their authenticity, for memoirs and even personal records are inherently prone to error.

The present study is confined to the years 1932 to 1945—but not only for reasons of length. Inarguably, many of Hitler's speeches in the years preceding 1932 also present interesting and valuable sources of information, but his activities as a minor party leader and failed Putschist are of lesser importance for German and European history. He did not become a major factor until he began gaining influence and exercising power, first as leader of the largest party in Germany, then as head of government, head of state, and supreme commander of the German armed forces. This decisive epoch commenced with Hitler's dramatic struggle for control of the government in 1932 and ended with the total collapse of his foreign and military policies in 1945.

I would like to take this opportunity to express my sincere gratitude to all those who, by their inspiration and their assistance, have promoted the publication of this work. First of all, I would like to thank Professors Hugh

Trevor-Roper (Baron Dacre of Glanton), Oxford; Alan Bullock, Oxford; Fridolin Solleder, Erlangen-Nuremberg; and Hugo Hantsch, Vienna, for their encouragement and support. I would further like to thank the following for their expert assistance: Professor Heinz Lieberich, Munich, Director-General of the Bavarian State Archives; Hofrat Gebhard Rath, Vienna, Director-General of the Austrian State Archives; and Dr. Fritz de Quervain, Bern, head of the Swiss Military Library.

I am especially indebted to the Institut für Zeitgeschichte, Munich, particularly to Secretary-General Helmut Krausnick, Professor Thilo Vogelsang and Dr. Anton Hoch; the Bundesarchiv, Koblenz, particularly to Director Karl G. Bruchmann and former Colonel G.S. D.H. Teske (Bundesarchiv, Militärarchiv, Freiburg im Breisgau); the Staatsarchiv, Nuremberg, the Staatsarchiv, Munich, and the Monacensia-Division of the Munich City Library; the Stadtarchiv, Würzburg; the Würzburg University Library; the Stuttgart Military Library; and the Militärgeschichtliches Forschungsamt, Freiburg im Breisgau.

A debt of gratitude is owed to my assistant, Dr. Gerhard G. Drexler, Würzburg, who not only spent years with me working through the voluminous material and reading the proofs, but who also, as a member of the young generation, contributed his valuable assistance in keeping the commentary succinct and to the point. My particular thanks are due to my wife, Gertrud, for her interest and patience throughout.

MAX DOMARUS

INTRODUCTION
Hitler's Personality, Manner, and Mental State

Prominent figures on the rise to power or in the act of seeking aggrandizement have frequently employed the spoken word to attain their ends. They have chosen this vehicle because it not only facilitated their ascent but also satisfied their passion for public speaking. They were intoxicated by both the applause of their audiences and by the demonstration of their power of suggestion and the potential influence they could exert. The history of mankind contains various examples of this phenomenon. In retrospect, Napoleon I and William II are particularly illustrative cases in point for their respective eras at the turn of the 19th and 20th centuries. The speeches and proclamations of the emperor of France, for example, that were first published at a relatively late date, undoubtedly convey the most forceful impression of his personality. The German Kaiser's public addresses appeared in published form prior to World War I but were eclipsed when war broke out. They, however, had been instrumental in nurturing a false impression of the international balance of power in the minds of the German people.

Adolf Hitler's speeches and proclamations played a considerably more formative role in the rise and fall of the so-called Third Reich. The greater part of his theories and plans were expounded in public, and these statements rarely deviated—if at all, only in a chronological sense—from those he made to the few persons with whom he was intimate.

Politicians and statesmen can be granted the privilege of discussing certain topics comprehensively in a private sphere without instantly weighing each phrase as an expression of personal—and public—conviction. Thus, the remarks of such personages made within a limited circle cannot be considered unequivocal evidence of their actual intentions.

While records of Hitler's private conversations are no doubt interesting and revealing, the fact that these reports are second-hand means that they are inevitably flawed by the absence of the verbatim wording and tainted by the possibilities of error and misinterpretation—a product of the unavoidable subjectivity inherent in such studies. Conversely, Adolf Hitler's public speeches and proclamations ring true; they are his own words, and there is no doubt as to their documentary authenticity. Regardless of the circumstances and political necessities that led to their genesis, Hitler judged it fitting to make them available to the public in the form and at the time cited. It is the commentator's duty to place them in a historical perspective.

Adolf Hitler was born on April 20, 1889 in Braunau am Inn (Upper Austria), the son of the minor customs official Alois Hitler and his wife Klara, née Pölzl. Following the collapse of the German empire in November 1918, he resolved to become a "politician," and on January 30, 1933, he became chancellor of Germany. Even before this date, 13 million eligible voters had cast their ballots for him in the hope that he would bring about a better political and economic future.

This insignificant member of the petty bourgeois class, a mere corporal in World War I, rose to become the sole head of government, German head of state, and supreme commander of the armed forces. He deprived his domestic political opponents of power across the board, filling key public offices with his loyal party-liners. In an open breach of the Treaty of Versailles, he called a new national conscription army into existence and then shifted his attention beyond Germany's borders. Without firing a single shot, he annexed Austria and the Sudeten German territories as part of the National Socialist Reich, exploiting the people's right of self-determination to his own ends and finally procuring the stamp of international approval for his actions.

When Hitler used force to invade and annex Poland, the Western powers put their foot down and declared war. The German dictator had neglected to provide for this contingency, and it ultimately was to seal his fate. With the powerful German army, he was still able to conquer a number of weaker countries and invade the Soviet Union, and the swastika flag he had designed flew intermittently from North Africa to the North Pole and from the Atlantic to the Caucasus while he was in power. However, nothing could avert the ultimate consequence that had been mapped out from the very onset. Hitler had started a war he could not finish; he and his politics suffered a total collapse. When the sum of his prophecies and foreign policies had been proven false, he chose to shoot himself on April 30, 1945 in the Reich Chancellery bunker, leaving behind devastation in Germany and Europe unparalleled in the history of mankind. After his death, high-ranking staff branded him a murderer on millions of counts.

In both his private and public life, Hitler cultivated the image of a hero and superhuman being: bursting with energy, of great foresight, never erring, ever courageous, intrepid and endowed with a profound sense of purpose. Was this his real personality? Before Hitler launched his career as a political agitator, he exhibited little evidence of being extraordinary. As a boy, he had been interested solely in doing and learning what he liked, early enjoying the role of "ringleader," although this certainly was not a consequence of any striking individuality on Hitler's part.

Even in the course of the years he spent in Vienna and Munich as a young man, he did not exhibit behavior that would have made him stand out among his peers but was introverted and moody. He retained his childhood aversion to systematic application and regular work. Consequently, he was incapable of assuming a normal profession and, given the frequently disagreeable daily demands of a household, even less inclined or able to establish a homestead or marry. Only dire necessity drove him to enter service as a bricklayer's laborer and a painter and to market his hand-drawn postcards. He preferred dreaming of "great" times, i.e., times marked by the upheavals of war and revolution and found it depressing that the Germany and Europe of the early twentieth century seemingly no longer afforded any room for events of extraordinary import. His public addresses to German youth as Führer and Reich Chancellor repeatedly revolved around the memory of his own pathetic and miserable youth, when he had never been allowed to experience anything "great." Conversely, he stressed how lucky modern youths could consider themselves, having been endowed with his generous gift of "great" times.

In Vienna, the young Hitler avidly followed the chauvinistic speeches and utopian programs of the *Alldeutschen* and the anti-Semitic agitation of crank eccentrics, albeit without taking any active part in their doings. It was only within his own circle of acquaintances that he was fond of voicing loud support for nationalistic theories. Overall, however, he in no way stood out from his fellow workers or the other lodgers at the hostel for the homeless where he roomed. At that time, he was only one of many political ruminators ranging from the café intellectuals to the populist apostles who preached the coming of a Greater German Reich and blamed the Jews for every misfortune ever suffered by the German people.

Hitler had nothing but disdain for the "prophets of populist apocalypse," condemning them as weaklings able to defend themselves only with "spiritual weapons." Hitler was, of course, anything but a heroic personality himself; all those who encountered him before World War I unanimously described him as a reserved man who seemed more insecure and awkward than self-confident or in any way superior. Handwriting samples have served to further document that he was essentially a pessimist and a doubter, prone to vacillation. His lifelong *pathophobia* and his later fear of potential assassins were also characteristic. Similarly, the manner in which he postponed his military service in Austria, opting instead to leave for Munich, is hardly indicative of a pronounced martial nature. Moreover, this decision was also influenced by his contempt for the declining "Danubian monarchy."

The fact that Hitler proved a good soldier and demonstrated a certain amount of courage in World War I does not qualify as evidence to the contrary but illustrates that he had the willpower, when he applied himself, to accomplish feats above and beyond the scope of his natural disposition. When he judged a task worthwhile or sensed imminent danger, Hitler undeniably commanded extraordinary energy reserves and was powered by a veritably supernatural force. Like a second self, this force stood behind him, later propelling him from speech to speech, from plan to plan, and from victory to victory; ultimately, it plunged him into ruin. It remains an open question whether this "force" originated in his subconscious or can be interpreted in psychopathological terms; Hitler himself believed in a mission from a supernatural sphere.

Hitler's own staff and followers as well as his political opponents at home recoiled in the face of his sinister, compelling energy—the almost demonic force he exuded. Even the few assassins who rose against him did not dare to challenge him openly, hiding instead behind the anonymity of a bomb. When he was in a good mood and among people he liked, Hitler could be charming, witty, and gracious. Nevertheless, whenever the demon "willpower" arose in him, he struck his pose and took on the role he felt called upon to play before history and the German nation—or merely before the altar of his own dogmas. The sentimental dreamer then metamorphosed into a cruel despot, more ruthless than a person with a basically brutal disposition could ever have been.

At times like these, Hitler cast off his irresolution and worked himself up to personify "inalterable determination" (*unabänderliche Entschlossenheit*). In a similar fashion, Hitler, the chronic pessimist and doubter, could embody—and project—unbounded optimism. Even in his last days, he was capable of instilling a sense of confidence in many German listeners—albeit a confidence totally lacking any foundation in reality and amounting to nothing but a figment of his imagination. He acted his part somewhat overdramatically but nonetheless with such vehemence that he convinced not only those around him but himself as well that his emotional outbursts were genuine. Yet, in such moments, the slightest interruption—the appearance of a stranger, an unexpected remark—would suffice to disconcert him. Then, instead of countering with a magnanimous gesture or a quick-witted retort, he would be betrayed by the uncertainty in his expression, and his only reply would more often than not be an embarrassed stock phrase.

As a rule, he needed to rehearse important speeches and his public performances on the political stage. Thus prepared, he was able to appear convincing, whether he was inspecting a guard of honor at the front, shaking a king's hand, or acting the part of children's favorite and ladies' man. Hitler was plainly not "normal" within the bourgeois sense of the term. Even as a child, he had lacked the ability to apply himself with any consistency; later, he found it difficult to hold a steady job and lead a well-ordered life. For the most part, his attitudes and habits were in open or disguised conflict with those of his environment. Eminent physicians who came into contact with him termed his character as being that of a psychopath, confirming in their findings the reports of those who witnessed his fits of temper and abnormal behavior.

It is nonetheless difficult to pass conclusive judgment, for Hitler consciously acted the part of a madman on selected occasions and could quite convincingly feign outbursts of rage. This conduct was designed to lend his speeches added emphasis or impress and intimidate his visitors. As soon as they had taken their leave, he, who had only shortly before foamed at the mouth in frenzy, was then instantly able to appear calm and normal. Now and then, he even expressed amusement over the scene he had just succeeded in bringing off. Hitler viewed himself as exempt from commonly accepted standards, believing himself to be one of the heroes of world history, the likes of whom were "bestowed" upon mankind only rarely in the course of millennia, and he frequently intimated in his speeches that he was a "genius." Among those "world historical personalities" whose roads to greatness were not be obstructed by moral considerations were, according to Hegel, Alexander the Great, Caesar, and Napoleon. Hitler was actually able to match and even surpass these men in his hunger for power, his cruelty, in his unquenchable thirst for conquest, and his almost pathological underestimation of facts and eventualities.

Considered from this vantage point, one can doubtless label Hitler a lunatic. However, this does not in fact mean that he was mentally ill to such an extent that he was incapable of thinking and acting clearly and consistently. The mental condition of these "world historical personalities," who in the course of their doings generally caused undue suffering to their contemporaries, is described perhaps most accurately by the English historian Arthur Weigall. In his work *Alexander the Great*, he takes the following stance on the question of Alexander's soundness of mind:

> The question of his sanity has often been discussed by scholars; but I take the view that, while many of his actions, such as his march across the Gedrosian desert, were so insensate that he may well be described colloquially as a "lunatic," he was not actually mad, nor can the descriptions of him as the "Macedonian Madman" be taken literally. In any assembly of men—in a regiment of soldiers, for example—there is usually some dare-devil whom we loosely describe as a lunatic; in any army in wartime there is some general who uses up his men in a way which is criticized as insane; in any realm of adventure there is some foolhardy hero, who, we say, is crazy; in any gathering of statesmen there is some rash visionary whose ideas are too grand to be thought sane; in any group of intellectuals there is some eccentric genius who may be described with no unfriendly intent as being "as mad as a hatter"; in any religious body there is some fanatic who, without real reproach, may so be termed; in every age and every society there is some abnormal man with a mission who, often because his views are so disconcerting to the complacently sane, is named either in vexation or in admiration a lunatic. In all these senses Alexander was a lunatic; and, indeed, the fact seems to have been recognized, for towards the end of his life he was identified with the god Dionysos, who was definitely the divine lunatic made mad by his father Zeus.

This characterization could readily be applied to Adolf Hitler.

Some of his contemporaries uphold the opinion that Hitler, enfeebled by various illnesses, underwent a steady mental deterioration in his later years. In a physical sense, there is indeed evidence of a certain decay (stomach pains, insomnia, tremors, etc.), although his external posture revealed only slight changes toward the end of the war: his shoulders caved in somewhat; his tendency to stoop grew more pronounced; his hair turned gray. However, these physical disorders and signs of aging in no way infringed upon his mental powers. Newsreel shots through March 1945 showed him in the then-familiar poses: smiling and greeting the public, giving Hitler Youth boys a paternal pat on the back, etc.

In the end, Hitler's appeals, telegrams and other official statements breathed the same spirit that had pervaded them from the very beginning: he had retreated not an inch. Adolf Hitler was no more insane in April 1945 than he had been in the year 1919.

Were one to attempt to discern symptoms of mental illness in his public statements, one might well cite Hitler's *gigantomania* and *arithmomania*, obsessions far exceeding the normal scope of like quirks. In nearly every major speech, Hitler produced random arrays of the oddest figures. Tens of thousands of party comrades, for instance, were cited; hundreds of thousands of *Volksgenossen* or prisoners, millions of peasants and workers, millions of tons of foodstuffs, sunken holds, or bombs dropped; billions of letters dispatched, etc., ad infinitum.

Although fond of reveling in figures of such magnitude, he also regarded smaller numbers as sufficiently impressive to warrant endless repetition, e.g. the "seven men" who founded a movement, "thirteen years of struggle and thirteen million followers," "twenty-one replies to Roosevelt" (designed to surpass Wilson's Fourteen Points, at least numerically), etc. Only in a marginal sense did this *idée fixed* originate from a knowledge of real numerology or the causal relationships between specific dates, fate, numbers and so-called coincidences. The demagogue Hitler doted on figures, adding to and subtracting from columns and sums for their own sake alone. One had the impression that Hitler positively intoxicated himself with the sheer sound of the figures, using them as a stimulant and attempting to hypnotize his listeners into a state of rapture with his litanies. But more often than not, Hitler's juggling with figures was thoroughly pointless, for the numbers alone proved nothing; moreover, the real figures added up very differently.

Closely linked to the question of Hitler's mental state is the problem of his soundness of mind. Taken in a certain sense, no criminal is normal, for his thoughts, reactions, and deeds do not conform to those norms fixed by law and convention. Systematically disposing of all internal restraints recognized and respected by what are regarded as normal members of human society, Hitler silenced the voice of his conscience, albeit gradually and with perceptible initial hesitation. Ultimately, however, it is always the initial act in a criminal career that requires the most effort, while ensuing steps become progressively easier. Hitler cold-bloodedly murdered his own comrades and followers on June 30, 1934, merely because, in his view, they obstructed his path to power; thus it comes as no surprise that he was unable or unwilling to use more moderate methods in dealing with his real opponents or those he regarded as such. He believed himself to be the sole judge of right and wrong.

The principle "Whatever benefits the German Volk (i.e., Hitler) is right," which was openly propagated during the Third Reich, gave free rein to criminal instincts. In times of war, moreover, this way of thinking necessarily brought with it particularly harrowing consequences. How could one expect that Hitler, markedly reluctant as he was to comply with laws in times of peace and unscrupulous about violating them when circumstances were opportune, would be willing to abide by legal norms in wartime? It is a sorry fact that the most gruesome consequences of Hitler's self-styled concept of what was right became evident in the course of World War II. Until then, he had oppressed and persecuted only his political opponents in Germany; now, in order to save his "racially valuable" soldiers from dying in vain, he felt justified in literally exterminating (*ausrotten*) entire "enemy" peoples and races—his openly declared intention.

However, World War II represented merely the final phase of a course set as early as 1933–34. Even at this initial stage, Hitler had viewed himself as exempt from all legally established rules, regardless of whether they were designed to preserve the constitution or curb criminal behavior. Numerous laws promulgated by Hitler's cabinet in 1933 went far beyond the scope of the Enabling Act and were clear infringements of the constitution, e.g., the governor law and the party law. Even an alleged national emergency would not have constituted sufficient grounds for the murders carried out on June 30, 1934, at Hitler's orders, let alone justified their commission. This crime was nevertheless declared, in an ex post facto national law to have been "legal." It is worthy of note that there is no official record, even from this early stage, that Hitler was ever called upon to account for such actions or even reprimanded in any way.

One cannot dismiss this fact by reasoning that Germany was governed at the time by a dictatorship tolerating no resistance. There were still quite enough opportunities to register protest or to resign, both within and outside of the cabinet, without risking life and limb. The truth of the matter is that Hitler had already convinced Germany's prominent figures that everything he did was within his given rights, even if his actions conflicted with the laws in force. This conviction was held not only by his party comrades, whom he had early inoculated with these dogmas, but also by non-National Socialist cabinet and Reichstag members and even Reich President von Hindenburg. With his outstanding powers of rhetoric, Hitler had succeeded in mesmerizing even high-ranking, well-educated Germans of flawless personal integrity to such an extent that they gave him carte blanche—and did so in a country that takes great stock in the letter of the law.

It has been said that Hitler had a "sixth sense" that he could, for instance, actually sense when danger was looming and adjust his behavior so as to extricate himself at the last minute. Needless to say, this concept of Hitler as "supernaturally" endowed cannot stand up to scrutiny. The circumstances surrounding the events in which he allegedly escaped imminent danger by some mysterious means were in fact by no measure extraordinary. His behavior on these occasions was normal, and he made no changes in his itinerary—something he certainly would have done had he anticipated any real threat.

No one can seriously claim that Hitler's "supernatural" powers were so keen that, for instance, the mere fact of his presence was sufficient to deactivate a hidden bomb. In the light of reason, there remain only three such incidents that have unusual attendant circumstances:

1. Hitler's flight over the Baltic on November 6, 1933, in which the plane lost its bearings. Allegedly, Hitler suddenly ordered the pilot to change course by 180 degrees against the pilot's will, thus rescuing the aircraft from certain destruction.

2. Hitler's conduct at his speech on November 8, 1939, in Munich. He left the *Bürgerbräukeller* earlier than scheduled; half an hour later, a bomb exploded there.

3. Hitler's deliverance from the assassination attempt of July 20, 1944, in the Führer headquarters, Wolf's Lair (*Wolfsschanze*), in East Prussia.

The real circumstances surrounding these incidents are as follows:

Case 1: The legend of Hitler's aeronautic adventure on November 6, 1933 was based upon a report by the English journalist Ward Price, who was not personally present but gathered his information from reports of those close to Hitler. The aircraft's pilot, Hans Baur, tells a completely different—and by no means mysterious—story. The plane lost its orientation because of limited visibility and a malfunctioning radio direction finder. Due to the length of time already spent in the air, Hitler feared that the plane might have passed Schleswig-Holstein and already be flying over the North Sea. Baur decided to set his course south in search of land; when he sighted a city on the coast, he made a futile attempt to decipher its name on the railway station sign. Hitler, however, recognized a meeting hall where he had once spoken and was thus able to identify the place as Wismar. That was the sum total of his contribution toward "rescuing" the plane.

Case 2: It is an undisputed fact that Hitler vacated the *Bürgerbräukeller* in Munich half an hour earlier than planned on November 8, 1939. But his actions on that date indicate that the detonation of the bomb could easily have been nothing more than a bogus assassination attempt staged with Hitler's knowledge. This interpretation is lent further credence by a number of other peculiarities not only in Hitler's behavior but in that of the Nazi Party security squads (SS) as well.

Case 3: There is nothing supernatural about the fact that Hitler was bending over the table that saved his life in order to study a map on July 20, 1944, when the Stauffenberg bomb exploded. He certainly had no idea that an explosive would detonate under the table at that moment! Moreover, he did nothing on July 20 prior to this attempt on his life that deviated from his usual routine.

It warrants mention that the conference took place that day in a barracks, in which the force of the explosion would necessarily have caused less damage than in the underground bunker that was closed for repair work at the time. Failing to consider this factor was the would-be assassin's mistake; Hitler's escape was thus not the result of any counteraction he had taken in wise anticipation of the danger. Furthermore, Hitler was not the only survivor of the explosion: of a total of 21 persons present, only four suffered mortal injuries. Afterwards, he naturally exploited his "salvation" of July 20, 1944, for propaganda purposes, insisting it had been a miraculous act of Providence; however, this case offers as little evidence as the others for his supposed "supernatural" ability to sense danger in the offing. He once claimed that he had "provided for every eventuality from the start," but the facts of history prove the opposite: his pronounced lack of foresight in foreign policy is only one example.

By contrast, in regard to matters of domestic policy Hitler was constantly on his guard. Unwilling to tolerate the slightest display of power outside his own sphere of influence, he nipped many developments in the bud that, left on their own, might have grown to present a threat. These moves, however, were not motivated by anything faintly resembling supernatural inspiration; they were the result of sober calculation on his part.

From "Artist" to "God-man"

Hitler took pleasure in describing himself in conversation as an artist even when his thoughts were occupied with matters of a completely different nature, such as in the last days of August 1939, when he was attempting to explain German policy in Poland to the British ambassador. In *Mein Kampf,* Hitler narrates in detail his youthful aspirations to become a painter, a career cut short by his failure to pass the entrance examinations to the academy in Vienna. He was barred from studying architectural drawing as well, for he lacked a middle school diploma. These failures served only to intensify his desire to become an architect. The obstacles to this route lay both in financial considerations and in his strong aversion to any type of methodical application requiring attention to detail.

Without means from the very beginning, he had no choice but to earn his living some way or another. He was not happy working as an unskilled construction laborer, and during this time he began to paint postcards, as a "beginning artist and watercolor painter," as he referred to himself, and to sell his attempts or have them sold in inns. Later, when he was a soldier and no longer needed to concern himself with the problem of earning his daily bread, he sketched and painted watercolors for his own enjoyment. His subjects were mainly landscapes and milieu scenes of occupied France. It must be conceded that Hitler did have a certain talent for watercolors. While the products of these artistic efforts are not overwhelming, there is nothing repulsive about them, notwithstanding claims to this effect.

Similarly, the desire to mirror his own greatness and the greatness of the German Volk in gigantic monuments was not the sole motivation for his propensity for architecture. There is little doubt that Hitler could have made a passable architect had he devoted his intelligence and extraordinary willpower to this end. He had a genuine sense of proportion and favored, in his architectural plans, the classical forms which characterized Munich's cityscape in the 19th century. The paintings he later commissioned and sponsored reflected the naturalist style of that period as well. It was one of his pet ideas to erect a huge art gallery in the city of Linz, where he had gone to school. This plan occupied his thoughts even on April 29, 1945, when he was drawing up his last will and testament.

"I think I am one of the most musical people in the world," Hitler once noted in jest to the English journalist Ward Price, claiming to have heard Wagner's *Meistersinger von Nürnberg* a hundred times. Hitler's affinity for Richard Wagner went beyond purely musical considerations. He was at least as impressed by the concepts of heroic saga, mystic mission, and redemption manifested in the master's works, as by the self-assurance of a man whose chosen epitaph was his own name and who deemed the veneration of mere men unable to even approximate a true appreciation of his genius. All the same, Hitler did exhibit a bent for music. Claims that, aside from Wagnerian operas, he attended only Lehar's *Lustige Witwe*, are unsupportable. While it is true that he whistled melodies from this and other operettas to himself when in a good mood, he was equally fond of attending operas by Verdi, Puccini, and Mozart. Less enthralling to him were orchestral and chamber works, but at official functions or in small circles he nevertheless listened to them without becoming bored.

These interests in painting, sculpture, architecture, and music constitute the sum of Hitler's cultural leanings. Although he did occasionally attend theater performances, he was never able to develop any liking or real comprehension of German literature, philosophy, or the humanities in general. At most, he accepted the ideas of Nietzsche, Hegel, Schopenhauer, and Oswald Spengler, but only insofar as they appeared to lend support to his theories of power and struggle. Spengler instantly fell out of his favor when, upon Hitler's seizure of power, he ventured to voice doubts as to the future development of National Socialism. The sole intellectual discipline that held any attraction for Hitler was technology. He was interested primarily in motorization, road building, and the construction of fortifications, armaments, and other military aspects of technological science.

Hitler's personal library was pitiful, a fact even his secretaries noticed, for it was confined to technical manuals and popular-science volumes of a general nature. Although he claimed to have read an "infinite number of books" during his time in Vienna, his reading was in general haphazard and hasty, and the bulk consisted primarily of political and pseudo-historical volumes with a nationalistic slant. Literature as a valuable and significant source of education for the intellect as well as for the understanding of what the world is all about were alien concepts to one as autodidactic as he was. His tremendous powers of retention and recall enabled him to store whatever he had read and reproduce it whenever a fitting opportunity arose. His speeches illustrate the skill with which he could adjust style and content like a chameleon to suit his respective audience.

In his opinion, the spoken word or the printed record of an oral proclamation completely eclipsed the impact of the "written word" in books. Not surprisingly, Hitler's own works *Mein Kampf* and *Zweites Buch* were tedious in comparison to his oratory. Notwithstanding the fact that millions of copies of *Mein Kampf* were printed, the book itself had no widespread impact. Not even his closest staff actually read it, let alone any significant number of his lesser party comrades. And even those of his followers who claimed to have applied themselves to the volume, admitted, if pressed, that they had not proceeded much further than the descriptions of Hitler's youth in the opening chapters.

The speeches on art and culture that he delivered faithfully at the party conventions in Nuremberg and art exhibitions in Munich left much to be desired. With pedantic verbosity, he characteristically held forth at length, attempting to instill in his remarks the character of ageless wisdom. He personally detested modern art, holding it to be "degenerate" (*entartet*), and did not hesitate to make a virtue—and a law—of his private dislike, ordering that this style be banned and artwork exhibiting it be confiscated by the state. Hitler loathed "intellectuals," scorning them and castigating their human weaknesses, their arrogance, their penchant for finding fault, and their lack of heroism—all the while instinctively sensing that, if anyone, it was most likely to be intellectuals who would not succumb to his power and would be more discriminating with regard to his hysterical nationalistic slogans that, from a sober historical perspective, very soon revealed themselves as miscalculations and unreal visions.

Hitler's battle against intellectual critics and the "upper class" persisted throughout his rule. Again and again, he directed his tirades against these groups in helpless rage, never managing to bring them completely under his control. His railings included the following:

> One thing I cannot bear is people whose sole activity consists of criticizing the activities of others. (August 17, 1934)

I want to differentiate here between the Volk, i.e. the healthy, full-blooded mass of Germany loyal to the Volk, and a decadent, so-called high society, unreliable because only conditionally linked by blood. It is sometimes casually referred to as the "upper class," being, however, in reality no more than the scum produced by a societal mutation gone haywire from having had its blood and thinking infected by cosmopolitism. (September 6, 1938)

When I take a look at the intellectual classes we have—unfortunately, I suppose, they are necessary; otherwise one could one day, I don't know, exterminate them (*ausrotten*) or something—but unfortunately they're necessary. So, when I take a look at these intellectual classes and imagine their behavior and take a closer look, in comparison to myself, and to our work, then I almost get scared. For since I have been politically active and particularly since I began to lead this Reich, I have experienced only successes. And all the same, this mass is floating around, often in such a positively repulsive, nauseating way. What would happen if we ever suffered a defeat? It is a possibility, gentlemen. Can you imagine how this race of chickens would act then, given the chance? (November 10, 1938)

The open animosity Hitler had for intellectuals was more than merely the resentment of the half-educated man in the face of the trained thinker —it was a virtual admission of his own inadequacy.

Hitler had conceived of his lifelong goals as early as 1919 and rigidly adhered to them until his death, regardless of how glaringly they clashed with reality. On matters of principle, i.e., with respect to these preconceived ideas, he was unwilling to accept even the best advice and staunchly refused to pay the slightest attention to the existence of other views or to irrefutable facts not consistent with the standpoints he had adopted in 1919.

In order to comprehend his aims and the manner in which he attempted to achieve them, one must bear in mind Hitler's theory of the "man at thirty." He upheld the conviction that a man could change his views on the world only prior to that age; thereafter, these would become irrevocable, and there would be no necessity to "learn anything anew." At most, only minor additions might be made to the existing structure. He summed up his feelings on this point as follows:

It is my conviction that, in general, aside from cases of exceptional talent, a man should not become publicly involved in politics before his thirtieth year. He should not do this because as a rule, until this time, a general platform is being constructed from which he then examines the various political problems and ultimately determines his own position on them. Only after arriving at this, an understanding of the world, and the resultant constancy of his own point of view in regard to the questions of the day should or may he, now at least inwardly matured, take part in the political leadership of the general public.

Even a thirty-year-old will have, in the course of his lifetime, much more to learn, but this will be merely to supplement and fill out the framework given him by the perspective he has adopted. In principle, his learning will no longer consist of new materials but rather of supplements to his basic philosophy, and his followers will not be forced to stifle the anxious feeling that they have been misinformed by him prior thereto; on the contrary: the visible, organic growth of the Führer will give them a sense of satisfaction, for his learning is a reinforcement of their own theories. This in their eyes is proof that their views hitherto have been correct.

A Führer who is forced to depart from the platform of his general *Weltanschauung* as such because he has recognized it to be false only then acts decently if, upon realizing the error of his prior view, he is willing to draw the final consequence. In such a case, he must at the very least forego the public exercise of any further political activities. Because he was once mistaken in his basic beliefs, it is possible that this could happen a second time. (*Mein Kampf*)

These remarks also explain Hitler's fear of having to admit even a single mistake, a fear which would accompany him throughout his life, for under no circumstances would he have been willing to draw the "consequence" he himself proposed. Hitler had reached the milestone of thirty in 1919, and all of the ideas he had conceived of and judged correct prior thereto were to endure as his incontrovertible basic principles. Remaining within this logic, Hitler claimed that he had, in the course of the preceding years, laid a "philosophic foundation of granite," and asserted "in addition to what I

once created, I have had to learn little and needed to change not a thing."
Mein Kampf was the forum for his fixed views on the world, valid for all
time. Not only did he intend never to amend them; he intended to make
them reality one step at a time.

Refusing to the very last to retreat an inch from these preconceived
ideas, he adamantly rejected even first-hand reports if they did not appear
to confirm his opinions.

> I have only been able to score these successes . . . because
> I have never allowed weaklings to talk me out of or lead me
> away from an opinion I had once formed and . . . because I
> have always resolved under any circumstances to respond to a
> necessity once recognized. (September 14, 1936)

What was his premise for this peculiar theory of the "man at thirty"?
It would be safe to assume that its roots lay in the Bible. Christ had begun
teaching only after he had reached the age of thirty, and considering that
Hitler perceived himself a heaven-sent messiah, he doubtless believed to
have come of age for this role at thirty. Furthermore, his participation
in World War I from 1914 to 1918 concluded shortly before the end of
his thirtieth year, and he may well have regarded this experience as a last
anointing prior to taking on his mission in a new life untainted by human fallibility.

With respect to Hitler's views on religion, it should be noted that he was
baptized and raised as a Roman Catholic, and the attitudes instilled in him
early on had a lasting impact upon his thinking. He greatly admired the
colossal organization of the Catholic Church and was impressed by both
the psychic power it exercised over its followers and the strict and devoted
adherence to its dogmas. Although he did not abide by the Church's commandments, he remained personally attached to Catholic ways of thinking
even into the initial years of his rule. As late as 1933, he still described himself publicly as a Catholic. Only the spreading poison of his lust for power
and self-idolatry finally crowded out the memories of childhood beliefs,
and in 1937 he jettisoned the last of his personal religious convictions, declaring to his comrades, "Now I feel as fresh as a colt in the pasture." In his
speeches, Hitler nonetheless continued to invoke "God," "the Almighty"
and "Providence" (*Vorsehung*), doing so not merely as a means to an end

or in a blasphemous sense. He actually believed in a god, but it was not the same God who has been worshipped by the peoples of this planet for millennia as the preserver and protector of all life: it was even less the God whose highest commandment requires one to love one's neighbor.

The god in whom Hitler believed was the peculiarly German god whose name was inscribed on the belt buckles of both the old and the new German army. It was the god who "let iron grow" and wanted "no slaves," who therefore armed the Germans with "saber, sword, and spear." Hitler once noted to the English journalist, Ward Price:

> I believe in God, and I am convinced that He will not desert 67 million Germans who have worked so hard to regain their rightful position in the world.

On another occasion, he stressed in a public speech:

> I, too, am religious; that is, religious deep inside, and I believe that Providence weighs us human beings, and that he who is unable to pass the test of Providence but is destroyed by it has not been destined for greater things. (November 8, 1943)

Hitler's god sat enthroned somewhere above the clouds, looking down and taking note of whether the Germans were indeed united, strong, and truly willing to persevere; he sent down test upon test in which the Germans were to demonstrate their firmness and resolution. And were they to prevail, this god would finally bestow upon them—the best Volk—the crown of supremacy over all other peoples in fulfillment of Geibel's prophecy, "And the essence of what is German shall one day heal the world."

This was to culminate in the establishment of a tremendous, utopian Reich, comparable to a new Atlantis, in a world ruled by super-human Aryans, the legitimate heirs of the Holy Grail. Hitler exposed this National Socialist aim not only in his inner circle, but stated it unequivocally in *Mein Kampf*:

> A state that is dedicated, in this age of racial poisoning, to cultivating its best racial elements must one day become master over the earth. (*Mein Kampf*)

This objective bears a striking similarity to the drive for world suprema-cy Hitler so often ascribed to the "International Jewry" in his book.

Hitler believed in his mythical god with unshakable fervor and was firmly convinced that this being had chosen him from among the millions of German soldiers of World War I as the best, the most unyielding, and the most courageous of all, the one man capable of raising Germany from out of its humiliation to new glory, destined to ultimately redeem the entire world. Thus the Reich Hitler had created, having once passed the scrutiny of Providence, would never again wane. He stated on various occasions:

> I believe that it was also God's will that from here [Aus-tria] a boy was to be sent into the Reich, allowed to mature, and elevated to become the nation's Führer. (April 9, 1938)

> I follow the path assigned to me by Providence with the instinctive sureness of a sleepwalker. (March 14, 1936)

> When I look back on the five years behind us, I cannot help but say: this has not been the work of man alone. Had Providence not guided us, I surely would often have been un-able to follow these dizzying paths. (June 27, 1937)

> The Almighty will always help those who help themselves. (March 20, 1936)

> God formed this Volk, and it has become what it should according to God's will, and according to our will, it shall re-main, nevermore to fade! (July 31, 1937)

> Work such as ours that has received the blessings of the Omnipotent can never again be undone by mere mortals. (June 6, 1937)

> God helped us. (March 25, 1938)

> Where will and faith so fervently join forces, Heaven can-not withhold its approval. (October 6, 1936)

Hitler construed "faith" to mean nothing other than the German Volk's faith in himself. He declared:

> German Volk, I have taught you to have faith, now give me your faith! (March 20, 1936)

> What has happened in these past weeks is the result of the triumph of an idea, a triumph of will, and even a triumph of persistence and tenacity, and above all it is the result of a miracle of faith, for only faith could have moved these mountains. I once went forth with my faith in the German people and took up this immeasurable struggle. With faith in me, first thousands, then hundreds of thousands, and finally millions have followed after me. (March 25, 1938)

His many victories and triumphs were, he felt, visible proof sent down from this god, confirmation that he was on the right path; every danger he withstood and surmounted became yet further evidence of divine approval. In each decision, he was guided by the will of Providence.

His own doubts he drowned out by claiming absolute infallibility. He deemed his judgment irreproachable, not only in respect to the present and the future (he had, it will be remembered, "provided for every eventuality from the start"), but also in view of the past. In his speeches, Hitler was always able to find or manufacture some mysterious reason explaining that even glaringly inaccurate prognoses and false decisions had in retrospect been right after all. Toward the end of his rule, this insistence upon his own flawlessness was to become increasingly grotesque as the gulf between what he had predicted and what had come to pass grew more unbridgeable with each passing day. The image of the god-man that Hitler wished to personify was, of course, incompatible with human fallibility, making him anxious to conceal from the German people anything that he construed as a weakness. For example, Hitler never appeared in public wearing eyeglasses; nor did he ever allow any pictures of him wearing them to be published.

He also took great pains to ensure that no details of his scarce love affairs leaked out to the public. Except for a chosen few, the Germans at large were kept in ignorance, first hearing, for instance, the name of Eva Braun only subsequent to Hitler's death. The god-man Hitler fancied himself to be was a more or less sexless creature, above and beyond the paltriness of human emotions and passions. His heart belonged, not to the female sex, but exclusively to the German Volk. A superior entity of this kind therefore would have no need of hedonic pleasures or stimulants. He held that this monastic being should partake of neither alcohol nor tobacco and even denied himself the consumption of meat.

While Hitler did not take the precept of sexual abstinence all too seriously and was unable to completely dispense with wearing glasses despite his use of oversized letters (1 cm) on the so-called *Führermaschine* typewriter, he did abstain quite strictly from alcohol, tobacco, and meat. There is, however, speculation that these last habits were in truth manifestations of his hypochondriac *pathophobia*. The projected image of the ascetic is further incompatible with Hitler's frequent use of the stimulating drugs increasingly administered to him by his personal physician, Dr. Theo Morell, from the late 1930's onward.

The god-man, in Hitler's view, also comprised the court of final judgment, the supreme judge endowed with a veritably supernatural authority comparable to that which Christ bestowed upon Peter ("Whatsoever you bind on earth shall be bound also in heaven"). The god-man therefore had a divine right to determine the fate of all Germans, the fate of non-Germans hardly qualifying for his consideration. Whomever he deemed worthy of death was destined to die. Conversely, whomever he deemed worthy to live was allowed to do so and even—given good behavior—granted special privileges. According to Hitler's view of the world, the devil incarnate that represented a threat to the divine plan and designed to rob the German people of their rightful reward was Jewry. Infiltrating every corner of the world, it existed for the sole purpose of draining the peoples of the world economically, of corrupting their moral integrity and bringing about their physical destruction.

The Jews, as Hitler presented it, were particularly bent upon destroying the German people. Every enemy of Germany and—since Germany and Hitler were synonymous—every opponent of the Führer was deemed Jewry's accomplice, whether these parties were Freemasons, Bolshevists, gypsies, or members of a foreign race. To ban this evil was to "fulfill the work of the Lord," as Hitler wrote in *Mein Kampf*. The dictator was indeed adept at drumming up credence for such beliefs: "Providence has preordained me to be the greatest liberator of humanity"—he ultimately had taken on the role of savior himself.

POLITICAL AIMS
"Patriotism"

In the main, Hitler's political aims involved foreign affairs. He viewed his domestic policies as the necessary prerequisites for a "strong" foreign policy, i.e., mere tools for concentrating power in a single hand. From the time of his youth, Hitler had been accustomed to equating his own personal happiness with Germany's welfare and power. He took the collapse of the imperial regime and the military defeat of 1918 to heart, perceiving Germany's fate as a personal injustice to himself. Upon hearing the news of the Armistice, he wept bitterly. Hitler was not alone in feeling that a world was falling apart at the end of World War I. Many Germans had deluded themselves into believing in a strong and unconquerable Germany and this illusion was blasted in the face of harsh reality.

Just as Hitler categorically refused to admit a mistake or assume the slightest responsibility for any errors on his part, he made no attempt to understand the catastrophe of 1918 in terms of the imperial government's own policies or as a result of poor judgment with regard to Germany's military and economic potential; moreover, he simply chose to disregard the enemy's overwhelming numerical superiority. Instead, he believed the reasons for the defeat lay in betrayal and in the doings of secret forces, among them the Jews and the Freemasons. Those directly to blame, in his opinion, were the German politicians who had signed the Armistice, although in reality they had had no control over Germany's political and military leadership. Hitler became a zealous advocate of the *Dolchstosslegende* (the "legend of the stab in the back"), and vowed to become a politician so that he might finally wreak revenge upon the Social Democrats and the Marxists. He labeled them the "November Criminals," making public threats that he would bring them to court when he seized power and "let their heads roll."

When he finally took office as Reich chancellor after fourteen years of domestic "struggle," he was unable to prosecute the guilty parties as planned for the simple reason that there had been no "November Criminals" and the imperial army had not been "stabbed in the back." But other heads began to roll: the heads of those who were not willing to submit to Hitler's rule. In the initial years of Hitler's government, his patriotism proved somewhat one-sided, in essence nothing other than a vehicle for his own display of power. When all was said and done, he was thoroughly indifferent to the fate of the German people, viewing them merely as the instrumental Volk that played a subordinate and narrowly defined role in his despotic drama. If they refused to acquiesce and resisted his plans, he was determined to use brute force and stated so quite openly:

> We perceive in this historical evidence of Teutonism the unconscious mandate vested in us by fate: to unite this stubborn German Volk, if necessary by force. This was historically just as necessary then as it is today. (January 25, 1936)

Above all, in the course of World War II, the German dictator unhesitatingly sacrificed millions of Germans for the mere sake of proving his "perseverance" theory. Accordingly, the "last battalion" on the battlefield would be "a German one." Hitler once declared, "I believe I have a right to say that, had fate put me at the helm [in 1918], this collapse would never have come about." In World War II he did in fact stand at the helm, but he steered Germany into a political and military catastrophe far graver than that of 1918. In 1945 he not only had no intention of allowing himself to be "beaten to pieces for this German Volk," he was not even willing to bear the same burden he had foisted upon the shoulders of his fellow countrymen, as he had promised:

> Today I am as willing as I was before to make any personal sacrifice. Germans should not be asked to make any sacrifices I myself would not make without an instant's hesitation! (September 1, 1939)

He was even less willing to assume the responsibility for how he ran the government, let alone allow the German people to "crucify" him: a retaliation he had proposed should he ever fail. Of his various vows in this vein, he kept not one. They included the following:

> German Volk, give us four years, and I swear to you, just as we, just as I have taken this office, so shall I leave it. (February 10, 1933)

> The German Volk shall then form its judgment, take its decision, and pass sentence upon me, and then, for all I care, it can crucify me if it finds that I have not done my duty. (February 24, 1933)

If ever I were to err here, or should the Volk ever be of the opinion that it cannot agree with my actions, then it may have me executed. I will calmly stand firm. (October 24, 1933)

No action will take place for which I will not vouch with my life, as this Volk be my witness. (August 17, 1934)

I wish to bear the entire responsibility. (January 30, 1942)

We are responsible for that which we shall one day leave behind to those who come after us. For Germany must not end with us. (March 4, 1933)

Hitler would never assume this highly touted responsibility to the German people but would abruptly take his leave by pressing a trigger when the sum of his foreign policies and military operations proved a grave miscalculation. The suffering of the German people interested him only insofar as he was able to turn it to a profit at home or abroad. When he himself had caused the hardships, they were declared an unavoidable sacrifice that had to be made for the glory of Germany.

Mussolini, the senior among the European dictators of the time, reacted differently to defeat, accepting his dismissal in 1943—when Italy's imminent collapse was evident—and refraining from appealing to the Italians to continue fighting for the regime. He had remained human. The "god-man" Hitler, however, showed no mercy for the German people. "Were I given the gift of continents, I would still prefer being even the poorest citizen of this Volk," he declared, but his sole objective, to which everything else was subordinated, lay in the exercise of naked power. As a "German," he was initially confined to establishing his supremacy in his own country. But he doubtless would have attempted to realize his visions of unbounded power in any other nation offering prospects of success. He would not, for instance, have been averse to using France as a base for the international empire of the future, for Hitler believed himself capable of motivating the French to comparable, if not even greater accomplishments than those of the Germans. Particularly characteristic of this attitude is a remark he made in 1933, when he exclaimed, "If I were propaganda minister for France—poor Germany!" Three years later, he went so far as to deny any aspirations to military supremacy, stating:

I can only say that my ambition is directed toward other triumphs. It is my ambition to establish a memorial to myself within the German Volk. But I am also aware that it would be better to erect this memorial in peacetime rather than in times of war. My ambition is aimed at creating the best possible institutions for training our Volk. It is my will that we in Germany have the greatest stadiums; that our road network be expanded; that our culture become elevated and refined; I want our cities to become beautiful; I want to put Germany at the top in every field of human cultural life and cultural aspiration. That is my ambition! (March 1, 1936)

The memorial Adolf Hitler erected to himself "within the German Volk" bears no resemblance to this vision.

Anti-Semitism

In Germany, one is occasionally confronted with the opinion that Hitler's rule was basically a good thing—he had only gone too far in persecuting the Jews and starting the war. This viewpoint does little justice to reality, however, for both the holocaust of the Jews and the outbreak of the war were no more than the—albeit ghastly—end sum of Hitler's politics and particularly the logical consequences of his foreign policy. Moreover, the final form each of these aspects took did not match Hitler's original plans, or at least he had envisioned a different chronology of events.

In his public and private speeches prior to 1939, Hitler had not announced in so many words his intention to annihilate all Jews, nor had he disclosed the means he would use to do so. Even during the war when his machinery of destruction was running at top capacity, he confined his remarks on a massacre of the Jews to threats within the scope of his foreign policy, knowing only too well that such an openly propagated program of extermination was certain to meet with resistance from the majority of the German people and the bulk of his party followers.

Anti-Semitism had existed in Germany for centuries—at times open, at times latent—serving always as tinder when the flames of revolution and war swept the country, and often erupting into pogroms and other similar forms of persecution. However, these were phenomena not peculiar to Germany alone but in evidence to greater and lesser degrees in many other

European countries. One of the more obvious causes for such hostility lay in the fact that many—and naturally above all the orthodox—Jews were, in terms of daily life, a group apart, easily isolated as the alien and incomprehensible "other" due to a different physiognomy, distinctive dress, and a foreign cultural heritage characterized by traditions and habits in contrast to their environment.

The Dutch historian Louis de Jong has argued conclusively that in wartime a person need only have an outer appearance differing from that of the normal citizen to be suspected, with no further substantiation, of being a spy and a traitor or to fall prey to the lynch law of an aroused mob in search of a scapegoat. In both world wars, countless members of almost all of the European peoples were arrested, persecuted and even killed as spies, traitors, enemy collaborators, etc.—although they were completely innocent, and had aroused suspicion only by their appearance.

Throughout the course of centuries, anti-Semitic tendencies had been reinforced in the German population by government measures, such as segregation of the Jews in ghettos, restrictions on their gainful employment, and other special and discriminatory laws. They were barred from certain civil service posts and military careers, and this form of social injustice persisted even into the First World War. The two Christian churches in Germany had made it a practice of branding Jews as the infidels who had nailed Christ to the cross. The devil as depicted in Christian publications more often than not exhibited Jewish facial features.

One of the few professions open to the Jews from the very beginning was that of banking. Jews were more generous in granting credit than the other banking institutions, often providing funds to customers who had long been declared unworthy of credit. Yet, when Jewish bankers demanded repayment plus interest and initiated the standard enforcement measures, they were rewarded with ill repute and decried as profiteers and sharks.

When the Jews were finally granted admission to academic professions in the nineteenth and twentieth centuries, German lawyers, physicians, journalists, etc. were suddenly confronted with the competition of large numbers of Jewish colleagues. As long as the economy remained intact, this did not present a problem. However, when the crises of the 1920s and 1930s hit, the cry arose in academic circles that the Jews should be ousted or their numbers in these fields limited to their percentage in the population as a whole.

At the time National Socialism was beginning to take hold, it was widely held that the Jews were responsible for every mishap in Germany from the early Middle Ages to the twentieth century. By 1918 at the latest, anti-Semitism was playing an integral and open part in nationalist circles and parties throughout the country. The extreme right-wing *Freikorps*, returning home from the Baltic, established the swastika—which had been in existence for millennia—as a popular symbol of anti-Semitism in Germany. In Austria the swastika was first introduced as an Aryan symbol by Guido von List at the beginning of the twentieth century. He and Lanz von Liebenfels, the founder of the *Ordo Novi Templi* and editor of the *Ostara* pamphlets, formed the core of a mystical anti-Semitic movement in Vienna that had a major influence on Hitler and during the formative phase of National Socialism.

Anti-Semitism and the Germanic cult were closely related to esoteric doctrines. These less tangible roots of National Socialism remained largely hidden from the public eye, notwithstanding the penchant for the occult displayed by *Reichsführer SS* Heinrich Himmler and the National Socialist ideologist, Alfred Rosenberg. Hitler, too, had been exposed to occult sciences, and in more intimate circles, he occasionally remarked on the esoteric goals of National Socialism. As was the case with other leading National Socialists, Hitler upheld ties to the Thule Society in the early 1920s, which cultivated a mystical Teutonic and anti-Semitic image but whose inner circle was devoted to the study of the occult.

Hitler's own antipathy toward the Jews was a combination of innate dislike, induced hatred, and vague racial ideas preconditioned by the doctrines of Gobineau and Houston Stewart Chamberlain. In reality, neither he nor any members of his family had ever had any unfavorable experiences with Jews. Hitler even wrote that, in his youth, he had been outraged by anti-Semitic remarks and got along well with his Jewish peers. This changed when he was first confronted with immigrants from Galicia with their curls and black kaftans: he regarded these Jews as alien creatures, and they aroused his aversion. Had there been a larger percentage of blacks in Germany, this race would also certainly have prompted his response of innate, primitive antagonism. The gypsies, another people that did not disguise its different cultural traditions, met with nearly the same fate as the Jews during the Third Reich.

Every subject with which Hitler could find fault in Vienna served only to aggravate his hostility toward Jewry: the internationally oriented Marxist organizations, the parliament, the press, and modern art.

When he further concluded, from the anti-Semitic tracts circulating at the time and the invective he heard at pseudo-political meetings, that the Jews upheld an organization which surreptitiously ruled the world and planned to undermine Germany's international standing, he made of his convictions a holy crusade: the Jews were indeed to blame for Germany's tragedy and the catastrophe of 1918. They were none other than devils in disguise, and combating them was but doing the work of the Lord. In *Mein Kampf,* Hitler conjured up an apocalyptic vision of this satanic world conspiracy:

> If, with the aid of his Marxist creed, the Jew triumphs over the peoples of this world, then his coronation will be the dance of death for humanity, and this planet will once more drift through the ether devoid of human life, as it did millions of years ago. Eternal nature is relentless in avenging transgressions of her laws.
>
> Hence, I believe I am acting in accordance with the wishes of the Almighty Creator: by defending myself against the Jew, I am fighting for the work of the Lord.

At the time Hitler and his infant Nazi Party were beginning to play a role in the Germany of the 1920's, his anti-Semitic slogans were not taken seriously by the bulk of the population. Phraseology of this type belonged, as a rule, to the basic vocabulary of the various racist and nationalistic groups that flourished at the time. After Hitler took power, a practical solution to what was regarded as the Jewish problem was promised. Both the German people and the National Socialists entertained such solutions as, for instance, removing Jews from public office, curbing their influence in the economy, and, as a last resort, bringing about their emigration from Germany. The application of pinprick tactics was to render staying in Germany so difficult for Jews that they would soon resign of their own volition and leave the country. "Out with the Jews!" was the refrain of one National Socialist fight song, and this was also the aim presented first to party members and then to the German people as Hitler's ultimate goal. For years there was talk about shipping the Jews to some obscure location such as the island of Madagascar. And while this type of forced emigration would have been unjust and hard, it would not have been the first time in the history of mankind—nor in the short space of the early twentieth century—that similar events had taken place: one need only recall the deportation of 1.5

million Greeks from Asia Minor following the war between Turkey and Greece in 1922. In any case, this fate would by no means have been comparable to the massacre and extermination Hitler ultimately inflicted on millions of Jews during the Second World War.

From the very onset, he did not seriously consider evacuating the Jews as a viable alternative. Initially, Hitler wanted to continue to utilize this group as the enemy personified. Later, he had a further motive: exploiting the Jews as hostages within the scope of his foreign policy and as a means of exerting pressure on foreign countries. His belief in the existence of a secret Jewish world government was genuine, as is evident in his various remarks to this effect in *Mein Kampf.* In fact, Hitler held so fast to his conviction of the strong lobby of "international Jewry" on western governments that he actually expected them to react favorably to his policies of expansion to the east. It was his firm belief that Jews worldwide would successfully influence the governments to exhibit restraint in dealing with Germany in the hope of saving the "Jewish hostages" if he threatened to annihilate them.

As is illustrated in this work, the actions taken against German Jews on April 1, 1933 and November 9–10, 1938 were motivated by foreign policy considerations, and similarly the mass extermination program put into practice from 1941 to 1945 grew out of the same logic.

As early as March 29, 1933, Hitler had declared:

> However, *Judentum* must realize that a Jewish war against Germany would hit *Judentum* in Germany itself with full force.

In addition, on January 30, 1941, he had stated:

> I would not like to forget the promise I made previously on September 1, 1939 before the German Reichstag, that is, that if the Jews should succeed in plunging the rest of the world into a world war, then the entire Jewish race will have played out its role in Europe.

As 1941 came to an end, bringing with it—despite Hitler's prophecies—neither the defeat of the Soviet Union nor peace with England, he once more foisted the blame onto the Jews and promised retaliation:

> I predicted on September 1, 1939, before the German
> Reichstag—and I am careful to refrain from rash prophe-
> cies—that this war will not end the way the Jews would have
> it, namely with the extermination of all European and Aryan
> peoples, but that the result of this war will be the annihilation
> of the Jewish race. (January 30, 1942)

These were reprisals Hitler had announced early on. Ultimately, he
made good his threats, ordering his SS henchmen to liquidate millions of
Jewish men, women and children. The success he had hoped to achieve—
i.e., the willingness of the West to make peace on his terms—had failed to
materialize and left him with the consequences of yet another irrational
estimation of reality.

Domestic Policy

The German people as a whole generally expressed as little interest in Hitler's foreign policy aims as in his anti-Semitic slogans. One must bear in
mind that his domestic policies were instrumental in persuading the populace to elect him. Circumstances played into Hitler's hands in the years
1920 to 1923, when postwar misery, inflation, and economic ruin had shattered Germany, and once more ten years later when the world depression
had taken its toll and there were millions of unemployed.

In the interim years of economic prosperity, Hitler made little impact.
His ideas were dismissed as the folly of a failed Putschist and eccentric, a fact
best illustrated in the election results of 1928, in which the National Socialists won only twelve seats in the Reichstag. Two years later, on September
14, 1930, their number skyrocketed to 107, to increase on July 31, 1932, to a
total of 230 deputies—an election in which thirteen million Germans cast
their ballots for Adolf Hitler. At the time, Reich Chancellor von Papen had
declared, "Herr Hitler, you are only here because there is a crisis!" Hitler
countered in a public assembly with the words, "if good fortune were here,
I would not be needed, and I would not be here either!"

What was Hitler's persuasive cure for the ailing times? What was behind the domestic goals he used to mesmerize millions of Germans? An
ostensible answer to this question lies in the 25 points comprising National Socialist policy at home and abroad that Hitler expounded in the Munich *Festsaal* of the Hofbräuhaus on February 24, 1920. However, Hitler

himself set no great stock in this party program, a fact he frankly admitted in *Mein Kampf.* The main thing, so he argued, was that the 25 points had been declared "inalterable." The form in which they were later to be put into practice was contingent upon the provisions passed for their implementation. In fact, however, numerous points were never tackled after Hitler's seizure of power, among them many domestic policy programs as, for instance, the abolition of large department stores. The item professing belief in positive Christianity, to cite another, had most likely been a purely rhetorical claim from its very inception.

In his speeches, Hitler rarely mentioned the official party program, with the noted exception of his intention to abrogate the peace treaties of Versailles and St. Germain, which received more attention. For his battle on the home front Hitler had another, more tangible program in store. He propagated the belief that the source of all misfortune suffered by the German Volk lay solely in its lack of unity. The population, he contended, was split into classes, stations, religions, parties, etc. and thus hindered from fully developing its inherent potential. The movements of Nationalism and Socialism and their respective adherents represented two warring factions. It was his main objective to join these forces, and he predicted, "On that day when both ideas are fused into one, they will become invincible!" Democracy as a form of government was doomed to extinction, he expounded, for it put only weaklings in power. Parliaments were nothing but talk-shops; their longwinded debates made swift and reasonable decisions impossible. A single, authoritative will was called for. One people, one state, one will (*Ein Volk, ein Reich, ein Wille*) was the only feasible solution. The system that had been governing Germany since 1918 was, composed, in his eyes, of traitors (the so-called "November Criminals") and "fulfillment politicians" in the thrall of the enemy: incompetent, inferior weaklings across the board. Were this system not eliminated without delay, the sorry fate of the German Volk would be sealed, and it would ultimately drown in "Bolshevist chaos." From a modern vantage point, these ideas may well appear wild and absurd, but in the troubled years of the early 1930s, they seemed to hit the nail on the head in Germany.

Just as the German governments of the Weimar Republic were not, contrary to Hitler's unfair accusations, responsible for the economic plight of the time, they were likewise in no position to eliminate or even relieve it. Moreover, they were not even capable of placating the public by adequately explaining that the international economic situation would improve of its own accord as it had in 1923 and thus relieve the suffering, at least in a psychological sense.

As of 1930, the Social Democrats no longer took an active part in politics and restricted their activities to tolerating bourgeois cabinets. The party had become sterile, and it is a fact that many of the leading Social Democrats of the time cared less about alleviating the misery at large than protecting their positions and status in the face of the surging ranks of National Socialists. They did not even consider climbing once more the barricades to defend the rights of the working people; instead, they gladly deserted their posts on July 20, 1932 on the occasion of von Papen's coup in Prussia, just as they were willing to return in the spring of 1933 under Hitler in exchange for their retirement pensions.

Empowered by Article 48, Reich Chancellor Heinrich Brüning of the Center Party was free to rule with an iron hand—an unsatisfactory state of affairs for a government purporting to be democratic. His "emergency decrees" did not suffice to bring unemployment under control. Brüning held the opinion that Germany must "starve itself into shape," but his deflationary measures served only to aggravate the situation. By repeated and drastic cuts of up to more than twenty percent in civil servant salaries, pensions, and retirement payments, and by reducing government spending, he succeeded only in provoking the rage of the powerful civil service sector and the middle class; to compound matters, the buying power of the people had been sharply reduced, resulting in the stagnation of the German economy as a whole. Increasing numbers of factories were forced to shut down, and farmers were hard put to sell their produce and ultimately sank into debt. Hitler stood out of the direct line of fire and prophesied that, unless he was given the chance to rule the nation, matters were certain to worsen steadily.

Hitler's economic program was the exact opposite of Brüning's. With a supreme disregard of money matters—a trait he also exhibited in his private affairs—he categorically refused to consider the objections of orthodox economists to his measures, insisting that it was ridiculous to back up German currency with gold or foreign exchange funds:

> Neither gold nor foreign exchange funds, but work alone is the foundation for money! (June 6, 1937)

> The salvation of our Volk is not a financial problem; it is exclusively a problem of utilizing and employing the available work force on the one hand and exploiting available soil and mineral resources on the other. The national community (*Volksgemeinschaft*) does not subsist on the fictitious value of

> money but on actual production, which gives money its value.
> This production is the primary cover for a currency, not a bank
> or a vault full of gold! And when I increase this production,
> I am actually increasing the income of my fellow citizens; if
> I decrease production, I decrease income, regardless of what
> salaries are being paid out. (January 30, 1937)

In Hitler's view, Germany had at its disposal sufficient workers, raw materials, and foodstuffs to solve its economic problems on its own. His slogan
was, "German workers, begin!" (*Deutsche Arbeiter, fanget an!*). The millions
of Germans unemployed at the time were suffering less from material need—
particularly as unemployment aid preserved them from the worst—than
from the fact that they did not know what to do with their time and loitered
aimlessly on street corners and squares. A popular newspaper quip had it that
the cry for work was louder than the groans of the slaves in ancient Rome.

Hitler had a remedy: he invited the unemployed to join his storm trooper formations. There they would find what they were lacking: something to
do and an ideal for which they could fight. He elevated himself to be their
savior, declaring that he had given them a new faith and a new hope, and allowed himself to be worshiped like a god by his storm troopers. Perceptive
of the more primitive instincts of the masses, he generously accommodated
the German people's affinity for disciplined behavior, uniforms, decora-
tions, parades, and military spectacles.

Not surprisingly, the number of Hitler's supporters grew proportionate-
ly to economic need: on July 31, 1932, their forces amounted to 13 million
Germans, i.e., approximately 37 percent of the voting public. Nearly the
entire middle class (*Mittelstand*), including most civil servants, cast their
votes for Hitler, as did the peasants (excepting those who were staunch
Catholics) and naturally the right-wing extremists, the former members
of the volunteer forces (*Freikorps*), and the bulk of the retired officers. Of
the workers, the only ones who voted for Hitler were those who wanted a
radical change in the existing power structures at any cost and, depending
upon the situation at the moment, supported either the Communists or
the National Socialists.

In spite of all his oratorical efforts, Hitler did not succeed in swaying
the organized Social Democratic workers to support his rise to power. Although his arguments were not completely unjustified, he was unable to
make any headway with this group by claiming that the higher echelons of

the Social Democratic Party (SPD) and the trade unions (i.e., the *Bonzen*—"big shots"—as they were pejoratively referred to at the time) were taking little interest in the workers' plight. The Social Democrats adherents countered with the equally not unwarranted argument that they had always been betrayed in the past and always would be in the future. They preferred "being betrayed by their own kind," as a popular slogan put it. Hitler also did not fare well with members of the Center Party before he took power, for they were under the close guardianship of the clergy, the majority of whom rejected Hitler, albeit not for reasons of foreign policy.

This lack of success with Center Party and Social Democratic Party voters did not discourage Hitler: they could wait until after he seized power. At the time, he was more interested in persuading as many right wing and Communist voters as possible to join his ranks with the aim of overcoming the 50 percent hurdle.

Communism and the extreme right were the only two potential adversaries Hitler took seriously. The Communist methods impressed him; he admired their conformity to one will, their obedience to a single command, and their readiness to fight their enemies in the streets if necessary. Bolshevism itself he dismissed as a primitive philosophy, perhaps just right for the Russians he so despised. Any further critical debate on its precepts he considered a waste of time:

> Communism is not a higher evolutionary stage but the most primitive basic form of shaping peoples and nations. (September 2, 1933)

> It is an ideology founded on a fear of one's neighbor, on a dread of somehow standing out, and is based upon a spiteful, envious cast of mind. This code of regression to the primitive state leads to cowardly, anxious acquiescence. (September 20, 1933)

Hitler had a simple recipe for contending with Communism: brute force, a method with which he achieved great success in Germany. As he saw it, Communism presented no danger whatsoever. On the contrary, the more Communists there were, the easier it was for him to intimidate the bourgeoisie and the reactionaries with the bogy of an impending Bolshevist revolution.

Personally, he believed that the "primitive" German Communists had neither sufficient force nor intelligence to stage a successful rebellion in the critical years between 1930 and 1932, although he would not have begrudged the "Reds" a certain amount of success in doing away with the "upper ten thousand" and the "worthless Philistines" plaguing Germany. He declared quite openly:

> Had Communism really intended nothing more than a certain purification by eliminating the rotten elements from among the ranks of our so-called upper ten thousand or our equally worthless Philistines, one could have sat back quietly and looked on for a while. (September 14, 1936)

In the turbulent years following World War I, the Communists in fact did launch several attempts to overthrow the government, in Munich, Saxony, and the Ruhr District. The bourgeoisie still shuddered to think of the attendant horrors, the slaughter of hostages and other acts of violence, although today it is difficult to determine which atrocities were worse: those committed by the Communist insurgents or those of the right-wing groups and their rampaging militias. However, the period from 1930 to Hitler's takeover held no real danger of a Bolshevist coup. Moreover, Communist voters never made up more than seventeen percent of the population. And this, Hitler argued, had been his doing. He threatened that, were the Nazis not finally allowed to take power, his following would desert en bloc to the ranks of the German Communist Party, and the country would be plunged into what he described as Bolshevist chaos.

With the aid of this sophistry, he ultimately prevailed in convincing the reluctant German Nationalists, the reactionary Junkers, the leaders of industry, and the generals of the *Reichswehr* that it was imperative that he be placed at the head of government. Finally, made weary by financial need and the surfeit of successive elections, the German people could no longer resist the cry, "Put Hitler in power, and bad times will end!" Hitler had outlasted his reactionary opponents, but now he was called upon to demonstrate whether he could really provide the "work and bread" he had promised in dozens of speeches. And Hitler did prove that his economic theory was indeed the more effective, at least in the short term, given the circumstances at the time. A few months after he had seized power, unemployment figures dropped sharply; soon they ceased to be significant. Some observers have claimed that the increasing orders Hitler gave to the armament industry constituted the sole reason behind this accomplishment, but in those first decisive years, this factor played only a minor role. It is more correct to say that he boosted all sectors of the economy. Building owners were forced to have their dilapidated properties repaired; the construction industry was given work. The building of streets and bridges was commissioned; motorization was accelerated. Although the bulk of these measures consisted of government commissioned jobs, private enterprise was also stimulated. Millions regained their means of existence. The farmers expressed their satisfaction with the new "autarky program." The workers were prospering, earning well and even receiving public acclaim for their efforts and being sent on vacations by the recreational organization Strength through Joy (*Kraft durch Freude*).

This miracle was naturally accomplished with the aid of the printing press, using the method of excessive creation of currency by the so-called *Mefo-Wechsel* System devised by Hitler's "financial wizard," Hjalmar Schacht. By simultaneously enforcing strict price controls, the Reich government seemed able to finance arms production while bolstering the German mark even after gold coverage had been abandoned and foreign exchange control instituted. However, these artificial achievements were short-lived. The damage done to the currency in financing unrestrained arms production was knowingly accepted as unavoidable, for, as the gambler Hitler expected, victorious campaigns would bring about a solution before inflation would break out.

All the same, Hitler did demonstrate a certain talent for economic policy in the years following his takeover and this fact alone would have earned him recognition from the German people and tolerance from the rest of the world. But Hitler planned to go down in history as much more than a politician with a keen grasp of economic realities: he wanted to exercise power—power over Germany, and power over the world.

He might have been satisfied with the position of power he had achieved in Germany by 1933. For, in addition to the 13 million Germans who had voted for him in 1932, now both the Social Democratic workers and the adherents of the Center Party pledged him their support in considerable numbers.

In light of the National Socialist manipulations of the votes obvious since the plebiscite of November 12, 1933, it is difficult to accurately ascertain the percentage of Hitler's following in 1933; however, it unquestionably exceeded 50 percent.

But to Hitler, all this was not enough. His lust for power was so great that he was unwilling to allow anyone else even the slightest political influence. He used every opportunity—above all, every genuine or construed crisis—to eliminate persons who had fallen into his disfavor, thereby appropriating their powers himself or seeing to it that these were played into the hands of loyal adherents. He used this recipe within his own party, in government, and later in the armed forces. Even during the war, Hitler never ceased his efforts to enlarge the sphere of his domestic power.

When the storm troopers threatened to mutiny in 1930, Hitler dismissed its leader, the retired Captain Pfeffer von Salomon, declaring himself *"Oberster SA Führer"* (OSAF) and the devoted Ernst Röhm, a retired captain, its new chief of staff. When Gregor Strasser, head of Political Organization, advocated a policy of alliance with Schleicher, Hitler branded him a traitor and proceeded to take over the leadership of the entire party organization.

In 1941, when Rudolf Hess flew off to Britain, Hitler personally took over his vacated position and called upon the servile Martin Bormann to assume the leadership of the party office. When Reich President von Hindenburg was hovering near death in 1934, Hitler made certain of one thing: he alone would succeed the Old Gentleman as head of state and supreme commander of the armed forces.

When Reich Minister of War von Blomberg opposed Hitler's wishes in 1938, the Führer assumed his functions without further ado and simultaneously dismissed the unpopular commander in chief of the army, Freiherr von Fritsch. When in 1941 the German army failed to take Moscow, Hitler used Field Marshal von Brauchitsch as a scapegoat, dismissing him in order to take on the post of commander in chief of the army himself. In 1942, Hitler had the Reichstag empower him to dismiss any judge he chose and take on the function of supreme judge (*Oberster Gerichtsherr*). When the commander of the replacement army (*Ersatzheer*), Friedrich Fromm, adopted an ambivalent attitude on July 20, 1944, Hitler placed him under arrest and appointed in his stead the loyal *Reichsführer SS,* Himmler.

Hitler's thirst for power knew no bounds, and he was continually on his guard against those who refused to recognize his absolute supremacy. His control was so complete that there is little or no doubt that Germany could not have liberated itself from this dictatorship during Hitler's lifetime. Had the dictator not ultimately become the victim of his own foreign policies, neither the people, the churches, the armed forces, nor the National Socialist Party would ever have succeeded in removing him from his seat of power.

After his death, Hitler's empire would have collapsed not unlike that of Alexander the Great. For all his talk of the future *Führer*-state, racial selectivity, etc., he naturally could not bring himself to train or even name a genuine successor, fearing that he might thereby risk sacrificing some—no matter how small—part of his power.

Foreign Policy

When Hitler turned 30 in 1919, he already had a clear picture of his foreign policy plans and refused to the end to relinquish or revise these aims. He had set forth his concepts in *Mein Kampf* for all time:

> The demand for a reestablishment of the 1914 borders is a political absurdity. The borders of 1914 mean nothing at all for the future of the German nation.
>
> In face of this, we National Socialists must keep an unshakable hold on our political aims, namely of securing the land and soil rightfully belonging to the German Volk on this earth. And this action is the only one which, before God and our German posterity, would allow an investment of blood to appear justified.
>
> In this context, I must attack most sharply those "patriotic" pen pushers who pretend to perceive in such an acquisition of soil a "violation of sacred human rights."
>
> Thus, we National Socialists are intentionally closing the chapter on the direction which foreign policy took in our pre-war period. We are taking up where we broke off six centuries ago. We are stopping the endless stream of Germans moving to the south and west of Europe and setting our sights on the land in the east.

Hitler's plans could hardly have been fixed more clearly, but the pseudo-historical deliberations in which they were embedded reveal the naiveté characteristic of his foreign policy as a whole. Except in respect of the time of the fall of the Roman Empire, the myth of an "endless stream of Germans moving to the south" has no basis in fact. The only—admittedly meager—support for the idea of German expansion to the west lies in Bismarck's campaign of 1870–71 and the annexation of Alsace-Lorraine. It would be more correct to speak of a French drive towards the east and to the Rhine.

In contrast, the German drive to the east was indeed a reality that had not slumbered in the 600 years Hitler so flippantly dismissed. The conquests of the Teutonic Order marked the beginning of an eastern policy consistent with that of the Hohenzollerns and the Habsburgs, which persisted up to the Treaty of Brest-Litovsk in 1918.

However, what did Hitler care about the facts of history? He was determined to realize his foreign policy goals at any price. The only debatable question was whether Germany's military potential sufficed to execute his expansionist plans, and how the West would react to his crusades. With regard to the latter point, Hitler had long devised a solution. "In Europe there will be only two allies for Germany in the foreseeable future: England and Italy," he had predicted in *Mein Kampf*. Hitler's foreign and military policies actually did have a common denominator, for they were all ultimately aimed at the establishment of a new German continental empire stretching to include the entirety of Eastern Europe and the Soviet Union all the way to the Ural Mountains. In addition, to put this plan into effect, he needed alliances with Great Britain and Italy, followed by war with the Soviet Union. This was a program of positively Napoleonic dimensions, and the attempt to translate it into action ended no differently from the Corsican's plans 130 years before.

It seems difficult to comprehend why Hitler should have believed his goal for German hegemony in Europe was anything but a foolhardy illusion coming so shortly after Wilhelm II had failed with his ambition for world supremacy and in his colonial and naval policies. World War I had conclusively shown that the world was not willing to tolerate expansionist policies on the part of Germany or Austria, not even in the Balkans. It had further established that Germany's military power fell drastically short of being able to match the united forces of the Western powers. However, German statesmen—and first and foremost Hitler—turned a deaf ear to these so obvious lessons of the First World War.

The discussions regarding the meaning of history, which have been carried on in West Germany for some time, deals with the question of failing to come to terms with the past, where the "past" in this context refers to the Third Reich and the catastrophe of 1945. However, this term might apply more accurately to the German attitude between the two world wars. The majority of the German population, above all the influential bourgeoisie, was taken completely by surprise at the defeat of 1918 and was unable to fathom that the German army, touted for decades as invincible, could have been forced to capitulate.

The statesmen and generals responsible did their utmost to hide the real reasons behind the military catastrophe from the German people.

A legend was called to life blaming the defeat on a "stab in the back of the German army."

On the other hand, the measures taken by the Allies after 1918 were neither wise nor justified. Independent of the perspective one takes, they were half-measures at best and bore the seed of new conflicts. The ill-chosen borders to Germany's east are a case in point, for while they were not actually the immediate cause for the outbreak of war in 1939, they did constitute a major factor. Other problematic points included the military and economic clauses in the Treaty of Versailles and the occupation of the Rhineland. An added burden was the attitude of certain Western circles which indirectly promoted the reactionary parties in Germany for their own gain while obstructing the work of the genuinely pacifist governments of the Weimar Republic.

In the minds of many Germans, Hitler among them, there was no doubt that the catastrophe of 1918 was a result not of any numerical or technical supremacy on the part of the Allies, but of treason in their own ranks. Hitler spoke of the "laurel wreath" which had been "craftily snatched from the German soldier in 1918" and became a spokesman for the unity theory:

> As long as the German Volk was unified in history, it has never been vanquished. It was only the disunity of the year 1918 which led to the collapse. (September 3, 1939)

Hitler honestly believed that the German front had been broken also by virtue of the enemy propaganda dropped behind the lines. He put no stock in the basic lesson that the history of war has taught to all peoples: the military resources constitute the single crucial factor, and they depend in turn upon the number and quality of the available troops, upon the capacity for producing arms and upon the store of foodstuffs. Exhortations to hold out and even new weaponry can, at best, prolong a war, but they cannot influence its outcome.

Hitler also chose to ignore another basic insight that has been reinforced by the events of history: propaganda is effective only with one's own people or vis-à-vis dependent or inferior states; it is powerless in the face of equally strong or superior peoples. The foreign policy concepts Hitler adopted in

1919 were inconsistent with reality with respect to both Great Britain and the Soviet Union. Moreover, they were his inevitable ruin: his view of history was distorted and he refused to correct it. He once claimed:

> There is no excuse before history for an error; no excuse, for instance, to the effect that one explains afterwards: I didn't notice that or I didn't take it seriously. (October 3, 1941)

These words were Hitler's self-pronounced death sentence: persisting in his erroneous assumptions of 1919 could never change reality, and the hard facts caught up with him in the end.

In terms of his preconceived notions of foreign policy, an alliance between Germany and Italy seemed most feasible. Such a tie could be reinforced by drawing parallels in history—not only the alliance which Bismarck had entered into with Cavour's young Italy, but also the close relations between Italy and Germany during the Holy Roman Empire. However, Hitler was less interested in historical precedents than in the simple fact that the manifestation of Fascism and the phenomenon of Mussolini presented themselves as sufficient grounds for an alliance.

In contrast, Hitler's completely unrealistic fantasy of a possible Anglo-German alliance was void of any basis in fact or history. The alliances which had been established in the past—for instance, that between Great Britain and the House of Habsburg during the War of the Spanish Succession, or that between Britain and Prussia during the Seven Years' War—had been formed not as the basis for a new German expansionist drive, but for the sole purpose of defeating France. In Hitler's opinion, the Hohenzollerns would have been well advised to have formed an alliance between imperial Germany and Great Britain, using the latter as protection to the rear for conquering new "living space" (*Lebensraum*) in Russia. He wrote in *Mein Kampf*:

> If one's goal were more land in Europe, this could only be accomplished, broadly speaking, at Russia's expense, meaning that the new Reich [of 1871] would once again join the march on the road of the Teutonic Knights of old, to gain by the German sword sod for the German plough and daily bread for the nation. For this kind of policy there could be but one ally in Europe: England.

These words suffice to illustrate that the German dictator—as the majority of his countrymen—had no understanding of the British mentality, British history, or British statecraft. What did impress him were the British wars and concentration camps, for Hitler conceived of power purely as brute force. In contrast to his ideas, British statecraft propagated a healthy balance: in times of peace, it instilled in the populations of those countries dominated by Britain a sense of individual satisfaction, while during wartime it awakened the will to demonstrate undivided solidarity with the mother country.

As a consequence of World War I, Hitler harbored a strong feeling of hatred for France and viewed it as dependent upon Great Britain. Were Britain to become a German ally, France would be checkmated in any case. In *Mein Kampf,* Hitler mentioned the United States only seldom and in passing. He was nevertheless aware that the United States was closely allied with Britain and reasoned that, were he to win over the latter, he would simultaneously win over its closest ally. The converse sequence, i.e., that war with England would mean war with the United States, apparently did not occur to him. So great was his obsession with the idea of an Anglo-German alliance, that he strictly ruled out the possibility of war with Britain.

There was absolutely no historical basis—and there were no logical arguments whatsoever—for the assumption that Britain would support or even tolerate a German drive against the Soviet Union; it was purely a figment of Hitler's imagination. But it was a theory he did not hesitate to propound over and over again for the sake of his listeners and, above all, himself. Hitler perceived himself as the great simplifier and once stated: "Our problems seemed complicated . . . But I simplified the problems and reduced them to the lowest common denominator."

Applied to his foreign policy, this meant that he simply projected concepts of domestic German policy onto international relations, believing to have thus cut the Gordian knot. The Soviets, for instance, he equated with the "primitive" German Communists, holding that they could be crushed with brute force. The British he placed in the same pot with the backward German Nationalists: once successful, they had now become incapable of rousing themselves to any firm stand. In Hitler's ill-considered opinion, they were best brought into submission—or out of the way—by being either reminded of their common "Germanic-Anglo-Saxon" past and instilled with fear of the Bolshevist threat, or simply left to their own frivolous devices. It was not worth the trouble to fight them, for they would ultimately fold on their own. In light of these views, it is not surprising that Hitler could boldly state, "I do not doubt for a second that we will secure our vital rights outside the country in exactly the same way as we were able to lead it onwards within." Even during the Second World War, he boasted, "I am firmly convinced that this [external] battle will end not a whit differently from the battle I once waged inside Germany!"

From their very beginnings, Hitler's attempts to convert his *idée fixe* of an alliance between Germany and Great Britain were nothing but grotesque. True to his theory of identical procedures in his "struggles" at home and abroad, he accorded the British the same treatment as he had the German Nationalists in the past, comparing them with the "Hugenbergers." When Chamberlain visited Germany three times in 1938, Hitler sincerely believed he was meeting with the equivalent of a German Nationalist privy councilor. Speaking to a gathering of German generals, he said, "These insignificant worms, I came to know them in Munich." And at a public rally in 1942, he pronounced, "The English have simply been ossifying for too long."

Hitler made a habit of snubbing British statesmen, and his offers to form an alliance were the height of insult. He would slap them in the face, as François-Poncet once aptly noted, and at the same time make a pretense of offering them his hand in friendship. Hitler was puzzled over England's manifest lack of interest in becoming a part of the German New Order (*Gleichschaltung*). Moreover, they surprisingly declined to accept his "generous offer" (*grosszügiges Angebot*) to protect the British Empire with his very own divisions. Addressing a visitor from Sweden in 1939, he demanded: "Herr Dahlerus, you know England so well, can you give me any reason for my perpetual failure to come to an agreement with her?"

While Hitler's consternation over such matters by no means moved him to reconsider his rigid preconceptions, Great Britain's declaration of war on September 3, 1939, did jar him into speechless shock for several minutes, according to reports of the interpreter Paul Schmidt. Britain's unexpected step struck a deathly blow to the very roots of his theories on foreign policy and, as such, would have prompted any normal-thinking statesman to step down immediately—at the very least. It had certainly not been Hitler's intention to wage war with England; his primary interest lay merely in conducting a small-scale conquest of Poland. He was completely taken aback when Great Britain actually sounded the call to arms.

However, a few hours later he had regained his composure—and his hold on the view that an alliance with England continued to be a possibility. During the entire course of the war, he thus staunchly refused to take any vigorous action against Britain that might unnecessarily irritate his prospective future ally.

He upheld the belief that he need only pursue his other goals, above all the conquest of the Soviet Union, to bring the British to their knees and to the realization that Hitler was the only ruler in the world to whom they should pay homage—just as Hugenberg, von Papen, and von Hindenburg had done by allowing themselves to be persuaded that Hitler was Germany's savior. If all else failed, he would only have to conjure up the bogy of Bolshevism once again—as he had at home—to bring his reactionary opponents in the West into line.

The attack on the Soviet Union that Hitler launched midway during the war with England originated not only in his old and cherished hope of one day taking over this enormous territory in the East, but also in the irrational hope that the Western world would look up to him as its champion in the fight against Bolshevism. The German newspapers from June 23, 1941 created the impression that the entire world, including the United States, warmly welcomed Germany's treatment of the Soviet Union, and that Britain was certainly no exception. Little did the German dictator suspect that the British welcomed a very different aspect of Germany's endeavors in the East. It was not difficult for them to surmise how much bloodletting this foray would cost the Germans. Even if Hitler were to succeed in conquering the Soviet Union, he would be so weakened as to make it easier for the Western powers to defeat him in turn.

Hitler's hope of overtaking the Soviet Union with a single sweep revealed itself to be a tragic fallacy. His concept of the primitive Russians who were most easily crushed by brute force—just like their supposed counterparts, the German Communists—proved a glaring underestimation. What had been demonstrated in the aftermath of the French Revolution once more became apparent: changes in the world outlook of a regime have no influence upon the willingness of a country's populace to protect itself and its country. Bolshevist Russia defended itself against Hitler's armies just as bitterly as the Czarist regimes had withstood the invasions of Charles XII and Napoleon I. Even the brutal tactics Hitler demanded of the German *Wehrmacht* were to no avail in accomplishing his goals of capturing Leningrad, Moscow, and Stalingrad and forcing the Russian army to capitulate.

The course of the war ran contrary to Hitler's prophecies in every way and in respect to Germany's friends as well as foes. He had once ridiculed the policy of the German Empire vis-à-vis its allies, stating:

> At that time, a few semblances of states grown old and impotent were drummed together and the attempt was made, using this junk destined for destruction, to show a bold front to an enterprising world coalition. (*Mein Kampf*)

However, the allies he mobilized during World War II did not differ markedly from these "semblances of states": the Hungarians, as well as the Finns to whom they were related, the Croatians and the Bulgarians, the Romanians, the Italians, and ultimately the Japanese. Hitler was not even capable of persuading his allies to regard all of Germany's enemies as their own foes as well.

It became evident that German power politics made an impression only upon the weak Balkan peoples and, to a limited degree, upon Italy. There it seemed that Hitler's theories on forming alliances might well prove true. Initially, Mussolini had shown extreme reserve in response to Hitler's attempts to curry his favor. However, his reserve thawed when, during the Italian occupation of Ethiopia, he unwillingly became dependent upon Germany and was increasingly forced to be an audience to Hitler's torrent of words. Being an impulsive Italian, the Duce was impressed by the disciplined conduct of the German military and party organizations. So enthused was he by the German goosestep at his visit to Munich and Berlin in 1937 that he immediately introduced it as the *"Passo Romano"* in his own country. Mussolini—a loquacious man in his own right—was so fascinated by Hitler's oratorical talent that he was soon converted into a patient and interested listener. Given sober consideration back in Italy, some of the German ruler's ideas were less persuasive, and Mussolini only reluctantly agreed to the Italo-German military alliance of May 22, 1939, known as the Pact of Steel.

Hitler's first disappointment dawned only a few months later: in violation of its obligations as laid down in the Pact, Italy refused to side with Germany when war broke out, insisting on remaining neutral. When it did enter the war in 1940, it soon became evident that this had more negative than positive consequences for Germany. After three years of warfare,

Italy collapsed in 1943 and Fascism disappeared without a trace. Mussolini was happy to have escaped with his life, but Hitler had the Italian leader brought to Germany in order to preserve the appearance of an intact alliance. Hitler's irrational preconceptions on foreign policy had been proven false across the board, from the alleged Jewish world government and the potential for an alliance with Great Britain and Italy, to his plans for easy conquest and annihilation of the Soviet Union. However, he refused to acknowledge defeat until the foreign enemies he himself had made had occupied nearly his entire Reich and were literally knocking at the door of the Reich Chancellery. It was not Hitler's prophecy that his warfare abroad would end "not a whit differently" from his domestic struggle—but Churchill's predictions that came to pass:

> And when the final signal is given, the whole circle of avenging nations will hurl themselves upon the foe and batter out the life of the cruelest tyranny that has ever sought to bar the progress of mankind.

It would be wrong to claim that Hitler's war and foreign policy goals met with unanimous approval and support within the party, the state and the army. Even the staunchest chauvinists and militarists strove for a reestablishment of the borders of 1914 and, at the utmost and if circumstances were conducive, the annexation of the coal-mining areas of Brie, the Baltic States and the Ukraine. The German people were, for the most part, extremely cautious and skeptical of any measures that could lead to war, for the shock of World War I was still too vivid.

Hitler, well aware of this, took care in his speeches not to state his military objectives in any certain terms and sought instead to blur and disguise his intentions. Even as late as 1939–1940, he avoided the term "war" in official legislation and directives, preferring to speak in euphemisms, citing for instance a "special task force" (*besonderer Einsatz*), police actions, etc. To the Germans who attempted to warn Hitler of the unavoidable consequences of his fateful foreign policy, he pointed out that he had attained his domestic goals despite all predictions and warnings to the contrary and would thus similarly prove right with his ideas on this external struggle, a mere counterpart to his domestic triumph. Speaking publicly in 1937, he had declared:

I have no desire to concern myself with those who know only the one well-worn objection to all major decisions: "It won't work." I do not need to assure you that a man who has succeeded in rising from an unknown soldier of the World War to be the leader of the nation will also succeed in solving any problems to come. May no man doubt my determination to put my plans once conceived into action, no matter how. (February 20, 1937)

By 1938–1939 and, at the latest, with the occupation of the rest of Czechoslovakia, it had become apparent even to the uninitiated where Hitler's course was headed. Nevertheless, it was already too late for any legal action; his position within Germany had become unassailable. In 1933, he had sworn never to relinquish control of German government during his lifetime. Before switching what he called his "train of government" onto the steeply declining track of war, he had meticulously dismantled every brake that could have brought it to an emergency halt. Hence, with an ever-increasing tempo, Hitler raced onward toward destruction and ruin. A few of the passengers attempted to leap to safety, but few succeeded. The first to abandon the train was Fritz Thyssen; another was Rudolf Hess.

The extent of the catastrophe could have been checked had one of the men riding the "train of government" possessed the courage to stand up to the mad engineer face to face, take over the helm, and turn the course of the train and the tide of events.

But there was no such man to be found in Germany.

The Methodology of Hitler's Oratory

Even prior to World War 1, Hitler had cherished hopes of appearing on the public stage as an orator. The possibility of exercising power by means of the spoken word always held a strong fascination for him. Reinhold Hanisch, one of Hitler's acquaintances from the Vienna hostel for the homeless, reports:

> One evening, Hitler happened to go to a movie theater—a rare occasion—in which Kellermann's *Tunnel* was being shown. There is a public speaker in the film who throws the working masses into turmoil with his speeches. Hitler was beside himself. The impression was so strong that he spoke of nothing except the power of oratory for days.

It was not the film alone that impressed Hitler but also the novel upon which it was based. Apparently, he bought it shortly thereafter. A great part of the vocabulary Hitler later built into his own speeches was doubtless drawn from this source. The language Kellermann used to describe events of fantastic import and persons of extraordinary magnetism left its mark, above all the bold superlatives and the ultimate flourish, "of all time," which grew to become one of the dictator's favorite expressions. The actors in Kellermann's story captivated Hitler's attention as much as the rhetoric. Mac Allan, the main character in the book, is a small-time engineer, able to carry through the idea for building a tunnel—a plan initially ridiculed as folly. He invents an amazingly strong steel drill and, bursting with energy, devotes himself to the task of drilling a tunnel under the Atlantic. His oratorical genius enables him to win over the giants of finance, convince reluctant industrial magnates, and instill in the construction workers the belief that the tunnel rightfully belongs to the people; he is able to overcome every crisis by his circumspect action in emergencies and succeeds in completing the "gigantic" project within twenty-five years. This was the kind of hero Hitler longed to be. In his case, the power of oral persuasion would not be lacking if similarly "gigantic" projects could be found.

S. Woolf, who came from a lower-class background but memorized an enormous number of details and had them constantly at his fingertips, was another character in the story who certainly also commanded Hitler's admiration, even though he was a Jew.

In any case, Hitler began training his memory and learning facts by rote with which he later impressed technical and military experts. Contempt for money and mistrust of the militia, later characteristic of Hitler's attitude, are also reflected in the themes of Kellermann's novel. When Hitler launched his political career in 1919, there appeared to be little chance that he would ever achieve the political power to which he aspired. He had neither assets nor any schooling to speak of; he could claim neither influential friends nor membership in any powerful organizations within a party or a given social class. Nonetheless, he had two reasons to believe himself capable of mounting the steep ladder to political success. One reason lay in the chaotic circumstances gripping Germany in the wake of its total defeat in World War I and in the transition that had taken place in the system of government after 1918. Only when chaos reigned both at home and abroad were the people perhaps sufficiently receptive to the ravings of an unknown agitator. Astute in his estimation of the masses, Hitler did everything—in the years preceding his accession to power—to prevent calm from setting in. He supported every action at home designed to hinder the respective government, while at the same time endeavoring to thwart any stabilization abroad. The second asset Hitler intended to exploit in his bid for power was his extraordinary talent for public speaking. He knew well how dangerous a weapon demagogical speech could be in times of turbulence; in *Mein Kampf,* he had elaborated upon this theme *in extenso*:

> However, the power which has always started the great religious and political avalanches in history has been, from time immemorial, none but the magic power of the spoken word.
>
> Above all, the broad masses of a people have always been subject to the force of oratory. And all great movements are national movements, are volcanic eruptions of human passion and inner emotions, aroused either by the cruel goddess of need or by the torch of the spoken word hurled into the masses, and not soda-sweet outpourings of too shrewd litterateurs and drawing-room heroes.
>
> A change in a people's fortune can be prompted only by a storm of burning passion, but he alone can arouse such passion who harbors it within him. This passion alone can bestow upon him whom it has chosen the words that, like the blows of a hammer, are capable of opening the gates to a people's heart.

Hitler ridiculed the "helpless stammerings of someone like Bethmann-Hollweg" and wrote:

> The oratory of a statesman to his people is not something I judge by the impression it leaves upon a university professor, but rather by the effect it has on the people.

Hitler did succeed in proving, in his domestic climb to power, that a gifted orator can indeed harness the support of a people muddled by times of confusion and chaos. However, events have also shown that the weapon of oratory can become blunted or useless when brandished in foreign politics against an equally strong or superior opponent. Indeed, it can even be turned against the aggressor.

Hitler admired the speeches of Anglo-Saxon statesmen during World War I, above all those of Lloyd George, rating them as "psychological masterpieces for influencing the soul of the masses," and completely overlooking the military and political power from which these speeches drew their force. Similarly, Hitler was firmly convinced that the Western powers had conquered the German army in 1918 not by numerical superiority and better weaponry, but with handbills and other types of propaganda. He also held the opinion that Wilson had won international recognition primarily for the elegant wording of his Fourteen Points. In reality, the united forces of the western powers stood behind this program, and without them, even a man like Wilson—whom Hitler dismissed as a "would-be world savior"—was powerless. When Hitler attempted to repeat the success of his domestic oratory on the stage of foreign politics after taking power, it soon became evident that he was every bit as ineffectual with his outpourings as Bethmann-Hollweg had been with his "helpless stammerings."

However, nothing could have been further from Hitler's thoughts in 1919 at his first appearance at a public gathering in the small Hofbräuhauskeller in Munich, where he was exhilarated by the impact of his oratory. He describes this, his first experience as a demagogue, in *Mein Kampf*:

> What I had before simply sensed inside, without really knowing it, was now proven by reality: I could speak! After 30 minutes, the people in the small room were electrified, and the enthusiasm was first expressed in the fact that my appeal to the willingness of those present to make a sacrifice resulted in a donation of 300 marks.
>
> However, the success of this first major gathering was also significant in another way. During my many years of military service, I had become acquainted with a great number of loyal comrades who now gradually began to join the Movement due to my persuasion. They were all energetic young men, accustomed to discipline and rose, throughout their service, on the principle: nothing is impossible, and if there is a will, there is always a way.

Thus, Hitler set upon the path of rhetorical rabble-rousing, with varying degrees of success depending upon the situation. If times were bad, he spoke to full houses; if matters were stabilizing, his eloquence was powerless to shake the masses out of their complacency. Trusting nonetheless in his luck, Hitler initially put his powers of oratory to the test not in front of mass audiences, but before small select and influential circles and organizations. On January 30, 1933, he achieved his goal and became Reich chancellor.

During the 14 years he strove for political power at home, he had only once relied upon means other than his persuasive public speaking. Intending to repeat the success of the Fascist "March on Rome," he launched his own German variation on November 8, 1923. While he was initially able to win over those holding power in Munich at the time—General State Commissar Gustav von Kahr, as well as the officers responsible for the *Reichswehr* and police—as soon as he turned his attention to other affairs and relaxed his hold upon them, they began to waver, released from the spellbinding power of his oratory, and ultimately resumed their responsibilities to the lawful government in Berlin. Hitler had learned a lesson he would never forget: German generals were not revolutionaries in any sense of the word. They preferred, as the Kapp Putsch (a coup attempt in 1919 protesting the Versailles Treaty that the army did not support but would not put down) had also illustrated, to adhere to the lawful regime—even if they detested it—rather than follow a revolutionary, even if the latter's goals coincided with their own. In later years, after he had become supreme commander of the armed forces, Hitler exploited these tenets of the German military for his own purposes, which cost German soldiery its reputation and was to take many a German general to the gallows after the lost war.

Hitler subtly tuned his speeches to suit the audience he was addressing. Although his remarks rarely varied in content, he enjoyed giving them a local flavor and expressing them in an idiom peculiar to his listeners. When speaking before intellectuals, professors or university students, for instance, he employed the convoluted and abstract style in vogue in such circles. In many of his speeches, he made extensive use of uncommon words and phrases of Latin and Greek origin, and he did in fact use them correctly. Apparently, he believed they sounded impressive and established a sense of familiarity with experts present in the audience. His command of difficult forms of address and ceremonial titles was as perfect as that of a diplomatic *chef de protocol*.

In the years 1932 and 1933, when considering it useful, Hitler pronounced the initial "st" separately as "s" and "t" as though he were from Hanover or Hamburg and had never heard of the German sound shift. His use of set phrases and anomalies was calculated to favorably impress northern German listeners, and it apparently did not miss its mark. When he addressed southern Germans, there was no need for such artifice for he usually spoke an idiom close to Bavarian German. Adolf Wagner, the local Nazi leader in Munich, spoke with a similar intonation and was hence regularly appointed to read Hitler's opening address at the Nuremberg party congresses, while Hitler himself sat behind the lectern among the high-ranking party functionaries and listened to his speaking "double."

Hitler's natural voice was rather high-pitched. Particularly when he commenced a speech, he forced his voice into a lower range to make it sound more resonant and masculine. In other situations, he intentionally allowed his voice to become shrill and overstrained for dramatic effect. He even took the opportunity of dictating his speeches to rehearse the accompanying accents at great volume, and occasionally his voice carried throughout the building. Uninitiated persons within earshot were caught by surprise and assumed he was admonishing his assistants. This constant modulation naturally took its toll on his vocal cords, and in 1935 he had to undergo surgery. Following the operation, performed by Professor Dr. von Eicken, Hitler feared for some time that he might lose his voice, but the ailment proved temporary and his fears groundless.

In moments of excitation, Hitler's voice often took on a threatening, subdued tone; he rolled his "r's" harshly and punctuated his speech with idiosyncratic pronunciations. His intonation became a monotone, his phrasing a series of volleys. This manner of speaking was particularly pronounced when Hitler extolled outstanding feats of National Socialism, Germany's far superior weaponry, and similar supposed accomplishments, i.e., when he spoke on martial subjects or indulged in his penchant for megalomania. Then he appeared in an auto-suggestive, trancelike state—regardless of whether he was delivering a public address or speaking to an audience of one.

Certain figures of speech peculiar to Hitler have given rise to the claim that he spoke incorrect and distorted German. This is, however, an unfounded allegation, for the phrases in question belong to the Austrian idiom that Northern Germans in particular are likely to find alien. Had he, in fact, consistently spoken bad German, neither the German industrial magnates, the German diplomats, nor the German generals, etc. have been so taken by his oratory. There is no doubt that his rhetoric and his command of even the finer nuances of the German language were exceptional. To determine the specific methodology used in each speech, Hitler first considered the external parameters of the situation: the time, the place, the temperature of the hall, etc. In *Mein Kampf*, he explains how significant, for instance, the time of day can be in terms of a speech's impact. He felt that it was psychologically less advantageous to speak in the morning than in the late afternoon or evening when the mental resistance of his listeners had ebbed. The "twilight of the Catholic churches," the "mysterious magic of the Festspielhaus (the Wagnerian opera house) in Bayreuth," and similar local settings were more conducive, he found, to manipulating the masses.

He viewed oratory as "a wrestling match between two diametrically opposed forces," and concluded:

> The outstanding oratorical art of a commanding Messi-
> anic figure will more easily succeed in winning over for a new
> cause people whose powers of resistance have already been
> weakened in the most natural way, than those who are still in
> full possession of their spiritual and mental resilience.

It was the calculated aim of each of his major speeches to break this "resilience" in his audience. The first part of his usual 90–120-minute speeches—some lasted up to several hours—was dedicated to long-winded narrative abounding with endless historical or pseudo-philosophical disquisitions designed to tire his listeners and, like hypnosis, break down their mental resistance. When they had become dulled and lethargic, he bombarded them in the second half of his speech with demagogical phrases, nationalist slogans and the like in order to "electrify" them, goading them on to ever more thunderous applause and indiscriminating mass response.

In his "party narrative," the initial phase of each of his longer speeches, Hitler metaphorically commenced with "Adam and Eve," tracing the annals of the party from its inception in 1919, through the struggles of its early years, and up to the present, in minute detail and including every aspect of its triumphs as a party and a force in the nation to be reckoned with.

In using this method of captivating the attention of his audience, Hitler once again made use of a custom he had borrowed from the Catholic Church, where the sermon is preceded by a lengthy reading from the Bible. In his opinion, the stereotypical repetition of well-known texts transported his listeners into a mild state of trance, making them more receptive to new information to follow. Hitler spoke slowly and in measured words in this first part of his speeches, almost hesitantly and ponderously, not unlike a lecturing professor. Then, when he moved into the second part, the tempo of his speech increased while he pushed the pitch of his voice to its limit.

Even the most agitated theatrical gestures and fervent dramatic phrases that appeared to burst forth spontaneously were, more often than not, carefully cultivated and rehearsed techniques. Both Hitler's valet, Heinz Linge, and his friend and photographer, Heinrich Hoffmann, witnessed the dress rehearsals for such performances in which Hitler stood before a mirror reflecting a full-length image and recited the speech sentence by sentence, all the while observing his reflection. He studied his every movement, his every facial expression. He repeated the sentences and gestures until he was satisfied with his performance. Occasionally he turned to his friends and asked, "Am I good, Hoffmann?" or "Does it ring true, Linge? Do you think I can step before the crowd now?"

In view of such sober reflections and calculated technique, Hitler's speeches might be judged to have been nothing other than cheap comedy—laughable and grotesque charades. But this would serve to neither explain their enormous impact and almost magical effect nor do justice to the facts. Hitler was a natural actor, i.e., he actually became the role he wished to act. In fact, he came to believe what he said or—at least created that impression in Germans and, to some extent, in foreigners—not unlike a great character actor capable of evoking tears of sadness or putting the fear of God into his audience.

Hitler was actually capable of working himself up into a state of intense agitation that left him completely exhausted. His rhetorical talent far surpassed that of any other National Socialist party leader. Even Goebbels, whose role in the Third Reich is greatly overestimated today in both Germany and abroad, did not come near rivaling Hitler's talent as an orator. Goebbels claimed of himself that he was capable of "playing on the psyche of the people as if it were a piano," but in reality the sparks his speeches ignited never grew into any real flame. Although he was able to arouse a non-critical crowd, he did not understand the art of calling forth real enthusiasm. Goebbels was a successful propagandist only when he received his directives from Hitler or was enthralled by his Führer's ideas. The bulk of the people recognized that Goebbels' own arguments were often mere figures of speech, doubtless presented with a certain amount of pathos but flawed by a lack of conviction on his part.

This was definitely not true of Hitler. His charismatic personality and oratory struck a genuine resonance within the German people. In the initial years of his rule, his speeches met with enthusiastic applause, and later, when his theatrical ravings, unrestrained outbursts of temper, and loud-mouthing invective became disagreeable even to the indiscriminating masses, it was fear of the demon that made even these specimens of histrionic oratory outwardly successful. The English journalist Ward Price early recognized Hitler as "the first German demagogue since Luther."

While Hitler conceived of oratory as a "wrestling match," he did ensure that his was the better position from the onset. True discussion and debate were ruled out, both in personal conversation and in the setting of a public meeting. He could not stand criticism, he once exclaimed, and the interjections of hecklers were a thing he abhorred. As he himself admitted, his storm troopers, the SA (*Sturmabteilung*), originally served the sole function of dealing out blows to hecklers and forcibly ejecting anyone disrupting Hitler's performance. Only when absolute silence reigned could he exert his spellbinding power upon his audience.

Only on one occasion did Hitler take part in a debate in the Reichstag—on March 23, 1933. Then, too, he called out to the Social Democratic deputies who interjected their comments (as was common parliamentary practice): "Would you please let me finish; I didn't interrupt you!" The impromptu speech Hitler made on this occasion convinced doubters that he did in fact compose his own speeches and did not require a prompter. When the Social Democrat Wels delivered his unexpected speech against the Enabling Act, Hitler made a few notes on a piece of paper and then dismissed Wels and his arguments so thoroughly as to move even the skeptical Privy Councilor von Hugenberg to avid enthusiasm.

Hitler can be viewed in many ways but certainly not as a bad speaker or one who needed an intellectual crutch to formulate well thought-out speeches. He even declined to use the official drafts of government speeches drawn up by his staff, of which several are on file at the Federal Archives in Koblenz, at the most drawing from statistical material compiled therein.

Schacht's remark that Hitler had never uttered a rash or ill-considered word and had "never made a mistake or a slip of the tongue," may apply to many private discussions but not to his speeches as a whole. Occasionally, Hitler became carried away by the dramatic torrent of his own rhetoric and later regretted certain language as having been too strong. Hence, when he became chancellor, he insisted upon checking all speeches before they were published and he modified or deleted such wording. However, this was only infrequently the case. In general terms, the reprints of his speeches in the *Völkischer Beobachter* and the reports of the official German news agency (*Deutsches Nachrichtenbüro*, DNB) constituted verbatim accounts of what he had said. This also applies, with few exceptions, to the special editions of certain speeches published (in pamphlet form) at a later date by the Nazi Party's official party publishing house, Franz Eher Nachf., in Munich.

During World War II, Hitler doubtless would gladly have withdrawn or erased certain of his past statements and slogans. To cite a case in point, posters containing a "Proclamation to the Soldiers on the Eastern Front" issued on October 2, 1941 had to be taken down by special commandos a few weeks later. The text had announced the imminent collapse of the Soviet Union, and every soldier at the German eastern front was acutely aware of how premature this announcement was. It was characteristic of Hitler to speak only if he had real or alleged triumphs of which to boast. In the wake of defeats or after having initiated measures capable of arousing public antipathy, he shrouded himself in silence and, instead of delivering the expected or even fervently hoped-for speech, he issued a written proclamation, thus avoiding any direct contact with the public.

It is for this reason that his public speeches grew more and more infrequent in the course of the Second World War. Only once was he forced to deliver an address after he had suffered a devastating defeat: on November 8, 1942, when the landing of the Allied Forces in North Africa coincided with his traditional commemorative speech on the occasion of the Munich Putsch in 1923. Predictably, the speech he delivered that day ranks among his weakest. The portentous event weighed heavily in the hall and preoccupied the thoughts of the older party comrades; they even occasionally forgot to applaud at the places in Hitler's speech that normally would have prompted an automatic response.

One might have expected Hitler to refrain from comment on the assassination attempt of July 20, 1944, for it did prove that strong opposition pervaded even the ranks of those closest to him. He chose instead to interpret his escape as a sign from Divine Providence, a triumph tantamount to a miracle and interrupted long months of silence to report the news of his "victory." Demonstrating by this public appearance that he had survived unscathed was secondary only to his pose of triumph.

When speaking in smaller circles or to his friends, Hitler made use of the same techniques he employed when addressing public gatherings: he made certain that he was given undivided attention and complete silence, initially tiring his listeners with repetitious and circumlocutory narrative, and then striking the tone he had chosen from his repertoire: sentimental reminiscence, incensed anger, plaintive self-pity, or fanatical fervor. Ward Price, who witnessed Hitler's behavior in countless situations, wrote in 1938: "When more than two people are present, even though they are of his most intimate circle, there is no general discourse. Either Hitler talks and they all listen, or else they talk among themselves and Hitler sits silent."

So great was Hitler's oratorical power over many Germans that, even into March and April of 1945, he was still capable of instilling new faith in normally quite levelheaded people in a situation that was devoid of hope. Albert Forster, local Nazi leader in Danzig, reported to the Reich Chancellery bunker in March of 1945 in despair that 4,000 Russian tanks were approaching Danzig. The German tanks available could not halt their progress. Forster consulted with Hitler and returned in a completely altered state of mind. "He told me that he will save Danzig," he cried, "so there can be no doubt about it!"

Colonel General Ritter von Greim, whom Hitler had dispatched to Berlin after Göring had been dismissed, arrived at the chancellery bunker on April 26, 1945 completely demoralized, as his pilot Hanna Reitsch reports. When he emerged from Hitler's room, he was convinced of the possibility of an ultimate German victory. Hitler had painted a rosy picture of the dismal situation and subsequently appointed von Greim field marshal and commander in chief of an air force that effectively no longer existed.

On the other hand, there can be no doubt that Hitler's speeches mainly impressed those Germans who were witnessing his performance for the first time or for whom the spectacle was a rare occasion. Even the highest-quality blade will dull with repeated use, just as the most beautiful melody can become unbearable when heard too often. Grand Admiral Erich Raeder noted before the International Military Tribunal in Nuremberg that Hitler's arguments lost much of their impact with those who were forced to hear them frequently and even daily, particularly during the course of World War II.

The generals at the Führer headquarters, who came to know Hitler's tirades nearly by heart, had no qualms about nodding off to sleep during his monologues unless, of course, Hitler's remarks were directed at themselves. Foreign visitors to Germany were struck by the fact that, during Hitler's most frenzied outbursts when he ranted like a madman, his closest advisors—Göring, Ribbentrop and others—looked on in utter indifference or gazed out of the window.

Hitler's attempts to repeat the oratorical triumphs he had scored within Germany in the scope of his foreign policy and to impress foreign statesmen by impassioned delivery and radio speeches were completely ineffectual when parried by representatives of comparable or superior nations. Behavior with which he could humble Schuschnigg, Hácha, Horthy, and many of the politicians from the Balkans, and convince Mussolini and Ciano, was useless when practiced upon British, American, and Russian statesmen. Hitler's oratorical art made as little impact on Chamberlain, Churchill, Halifax, and Henderson as on Roosevelt and Sumner Welles. And even the "enthusiastic" newspaper articles published by Lloyd George and Lord Rothermere on their respective visits to see Hitler were in reality nothing more than amused, ironic commentaries. When Hitler received Molotov in 1940, his raptures on a fantastic future did not evoke a like response from the Russian, who kept steering the discussion back to topics in the present that were more to the point. Even Franco, who was indebted to the German dictator for his military support in the Spanish Civil War, remained immune to Hitler's impassioned rhetoric in 1940 in Hendaye and persisted in upholding his policy of neutrality.

The years 1932 to 1938—during which Hitler brought Germany under his control and set up the Greater German Reich—were studded with triumphs; the years 1939 to 1945—during which he struggled with the same means to bring the world under his control—were pierced by defeat upon defeat. The contrast between what Hitler had prophesied and what actually came to pass grew increasingly stark, and the speeches he delivered as blows to foreign powers ultimately worked against him. The wild threats with which Hitler intended to force the British into submission during World War II had the opposite effect. Churchill declared as early as November 1939:

> "If words could kill, we should be dead already. But we are not disturbed by these blood-curdling threats. Indeed, we take them as a sign of weakness in our foes."

The BBC adopted the practice of broadcasting segments of Hitler's speeches and contrasting his allegations with the true facts. The difference was a fatal one for Hitler. He had attempted to measure the world in terms of domestic German standards, and this basic miscalculation ultimately brought about his ruin.

MAX DOMARUS

Himmler inspects a concentration camp.

II

Major Events in Hitler's Germany 1932–1945

Domarus divided his book into yearly sections and introduced each section with a summary of the year's events. Here, we present those yearly sections along with his end-of-year conclusions in consecutive order. Domarus empha- sized certain points which in this format might seem repetitious but we think that Domarus' ideas are too important as a primary source themselves to alter these sections. Writing as a German who experienced Hitler and the Second World War, Domarus makes the point a number of times: Germany did not lose the war because of mismanagement or bad strategy or lack of resources, although all of that occurred; rather, once Hitler invaded Poland, the United Kingdom and her allies would never stop until Hitler and his Nazis were defeated. Also typical of the time in which he wrote, Domarus has no emphasis on the violence and destruction wrought on Germany's Jews before the Second World War. He writes of Kristallnacht *(November 1939) in one paragraph and then returns to the subject only when he covers the events of 1942. Nev- ertheless, Domarus' narrative of the Hitler years is a thought-provoking and spirited recounting of the setting for the words of Hitler that follow in the suc- ceeding parts of this book.*

THE YEAR 1932
Major Events in Summary

The year 1932 marked the climax of Hitler's domestic struggle. To a certain extent, the events of these twelve months reflect the entire course of his endeavors to gain control of the government of Germany since 1919. Thus, the year 1932 as mirrored in this work is an accurately drawn miniature of the fourteen years of struggle for power that preceded it. Three alternative paths could lead Hitler to the power he so coveted. The first possibility was a violent coup that would necessitate, in all probability, bloodshed and an open confrontation with the armed forces of the *Reichswehr* and the police—a path that Hitler was hesitant to take now and had attempted to avoid at his Putsch in November 1923. Nevertheless, he kept this possibility in mind as a last resort and made certain preparations for a possible coup during this major year of struggle, 1932.

The second path was that of legal accession to power by means of a popular vote, i.e., by achieving an absolute majority or a "right-wing majority" in the Reichstag and the *Landtage* (provincial legislatures) or else with the election of a National Socialist Reich president. Under normal circumstances, the Weimar Constitution provided for the latter only every seven years.

In both cases—either a right-wing majority in the Reichstag or the election of a National Socialist Reich president,—nothing could have prevented the legal constitution of a cabinet chosen by Hitler. The year 1932, given Hitler's rhetorical prowess, appeared to fulfill all of the prerequisites for this solution: domestic chaos had reached a peak due to the worldwide economic crisis; six million unemployed were demanding work and bread. The middle class, the civil servants, and the peasants were less than satisfied with the German government. The Reich president and the Reich chancellor had been governing since 1930 with what amounted to dictatorial powers by virtue of Article 48 of the Weimar Constitution and had nevertheless been unable to alleviate the economic depression. Hitler's extraordinary demagogical talents dominated no less than fifteen election campaigns in 1932 (two presidential elections, two Reichstag elections, nine *Landtag* elections, and two local elections). He was nonetheless able to score only partial successes in relatively small *Länder*. In the more decisive elections, the requisite 50% of the votes cast eluded his grasp despite his tireless efforts and unrivaled oratorical campaigns.

The third path to power led through the "back door." It was essential to exert sufficient influence on both the private and public counselors of the Reich president in aristocratic, *Reichswehr*, and economic circles to the extent that they would, in turn, attempt to sway the Reich President to form a presidential cabinet under Hitler composed of ministers enjoying his presidential confidence.

This path that ultimately took Hitler to his goal also gave him many opportunities to make use of his powers of oral persuasion. He who had long been the butt of ridicule as a minor party leader and failed Putschist had become socially acceptable by 1932. The Reich president received him several times. Ministers in and out of office, leaders of industry, former generals, and active officers of the *Reichswehr* met to confer with him; party leaders from the German Nationalists to the Center made appointments to see him. Some were attempting to consolidate their forces with his, others to pacify him with insignificant ministerial posts. As the "drummer" of the national uprising, he had served their purpose well; now they wanted to exercise the power he had gained.

Nevertheless, Hitler outplayed them all. Under the very eyes of the government, he had established a "state within a state" with his National Socialist Party and now declared publicly that he and the Nazi Party were the true representatives of Germany, not the existing Reich government. His national and local party leaders conducted themselves as though they were Reich ministers and district presidents. Countless party "offices" (Agrarian Policy Office, Army Policy Office, Labor Service Office, etc.) made public statements on the events of the day and interfered with genuine "official" matters. Hitler dispatched his own observer—retired General Franz Ritter von Epp—to the Disarmament Conference in Geneva.

In 1932, he issued a proclamation to the German peasants admonishing them to finish harvesting their crops in good time. The "Reich press chief" of the Nazi Party conducted press conferences as though he were the press chief of the Reich government. Uniformed men of the SS, the Nazi Party security squads, assumed the task of erecting roadblocks at mass meetings and rallies as though they were the regular police. Tens and even hundreds of thousands of the SA, Nazi Party storm troopers in uniform, marched and paraded in spectacular performances through the former German garrison towns. Their formation numbers were the same as the former imperial army troops. When Hitler later acceded to power, he did not hesitate to appoint his party friends to the same positions in the state that they had held within the party, with the exception of the SA, as would become dramatically evident in 1934.

When attending negotiations in Berlin in 1932, Hitler resided at the Kaiserhof Hotel across the street from the chancellery. He intended that those in power there see that he was really standing "before the gate" and hear the cries of the many thousands from the Wilhelmsplatz demanding that Hitler take power. Asked by a journalist whether one might indeed witness a march on Berlin, as did Mussolini, Hitler replied: "Why should I march on Berlin? I'm already there!"

In reality, Hitler was not as certain of victory as he pretended to be. He knew very well that, were he not successful in exploiting the extraordinary circumstances of the year 1932 (i.e., the economic and political crises and the presidential and parliamentary elections), his accession to power would become a thing of the distant future. By the end of 1932, the worst of the world economic crisis had passed, the unemployment rates had already begun to decline, and there were endeavors in Lausanne and Geneva to close the book on the Treaty of Versailles and the reparations. To some of Hitler's voters, the struggle for power had already taken too long: they would no longer cast their ballots for him. Party leaders here and there began to lose heart and became restless. Hitler declared at that time: "If the party ever falls apart, I will take a gun and end it all in a minute."

But Hitler mastered these crises. His talent for oratory and his persistence won out. In the end, he was able to persuade not only his vacillating party comrades, but also those in power at the time—above all von Papen and Hindenburg—that he alone was able to lead Germany onwards to an age of new greatness.

The triumph Hitler achieved over his domestic opponents in 1932 continued to affect him throughout his lifetime. He believed himself capable of attaining his foreign-policy goals by using the same methods and expected that the outcome of this second struggle would not deviate "by a hair's breadth" from the first.

THE YEAR 1933
Major Events in Summary

On January 30, 1933, Hitler finally achieved the success he had been denied throughout the year 1932: he was made Reich chancellor and head of a presidential cabinet. Unlike his two predecessors, von Papen and Schleicher, he was able to secure a majority in parliament by insisting upon new Reichstag elections. The experiences of the preceding months had shown that the support of the Reich president alone was not a sufficiently reliable basis for governing the country. However, as Hitler had pledged repeatedly in October 1932, he was determined, come what may, not to relinquish control of the government he had finally taken over. To "take power swiftly and with a single stroke," was his declared goal. The post that Hitler had assumed was that of responsible leader of German politics as defined by the Weimar Constitution. Now that he was in power, he intended, without further delay, to set aside those parts of this same constitution that limited the scope of his power and granted other public figures and groups a basis for claiming their own constitutional rights and exercising political influence.

"We will amend the constitution in a strictly constitutional manner," Hitler had still claimed in 1932, warning his opponents to refrain from seizing power by force or violating the constitution. In practice, he now proved rather lax in observing constitutional rules. Indeed, there was little reason to abide by the law, for his predecessors had already demonstrated the extent to which Article 48 could be exploited to defeat the constitution's own purposes. The decree of the Reich president for "Restoring Order to the Government in Prussia," promulgated on February 6, constituted one such flagrant breach of the constitution and moreover an open contravention of the judgment of the Constitutional Court of October 25, 1932. Hitler was careful to have this decree—which dissolved the Prussian legislature—counter-signed by von Papen: one of the few cases in which Hitler allowed von Papen to act as his proxy in exercising the functions of Reich chancellor. The next step was the "Decree for the Protection of the Volk and the State" promulgated on February 28. This law provided that, if law and order were jeopardized, all of the articles of the Weimar Constitution could be rescinded (e.g., inviolability of the individual and the home, privacy of postal communications, etc.). Moreover, the Reich government (in reality, the Reich minister of the interior) was delegated the right normally held by the Reich president alone to appoint Reich commissars in the German *Länder* and assume the authority vested in public offices. After March 5, Hitler made use of this opportunity in all the states not governed by the National Socialists.

The next breach of the Reich Constitution followed on March 12, 1933. Article 3 provided that the colors of the Reich were black-red-gold. Hindenburg and Hitler decreed on March 12 by virtue of an edict of the Reich president that the black-white-red and the swastika flag were to fly jointly "until the question of the Reich colors has been definitively settled."

With the majority required to amend the constitution, the Reichstag passed the "Law for Removing the Distress of the Volk and Reich" on March 23 (the "Enabling Act") which provided that, in the future, the Reich government was empowered to enact laws and the chancellor, not the president, was to draw up and promulgate new legislation. Government decree could amend the constitution insofar as the amendment did not concern the institutions of the Reichstag or the *Reichsrat* as such. Allegedly, the rights of the Reich president were to remain inviolate, but the fact that it was now the Reich chancellor who drew up legislation alone substantially limited the president's powers. Furthermore, whereas the question of succession to the office of Reich president had been anchored in the constitution, the Enabling Act contained no such guarantees.

Two new laws passed by the Reich Government deprived the regional states (*Länder*) of power: the "First Coordination (*Gleichschaltung*) Law of *Länder* and Reich" of March 31 vested the law-making powers of the regional legislatures (*Landtage*) in the administration of the regional state governments and established the party representation in the administration in the same proportions as those resulting from the Reichstag election of March 5. The "Second Coordination (*Gleichschaltung*) Law of *Länder* and Reich" of April 7 introduced Reich governors (*Reichsstatthalter*) in all of the *Länder,* who were empowered to appoint the regional administrations. In Prussia, the largest state, Hitler personally assumed the office of *Reichsstatthalter.* This served to abolish the *Reichsrat* as well, the upper house composed of representatives of the states in the national Reich government that was allegedly to remain inviolable pursuant to the Enabling Act.

The next step was the elimination of trade unions, political parties, and leagues. The union offices had already been closed on May 2, and on May 10 Hitler decreed the formation of a new National Socialist organization for the workers, the *Deutsche Arbeitsfront*, DAF (German Labor Front), and appointed Robert Ley as its head.

The Communist Party (KPD) had participated one last time in the election of March 5. However, the deputies elected were prohibited from taking office. A law passed on May 26 seized the assets of the KPD. Although a decree banning the KPD was never officially issued, the Social Democratic Party (SPD) was abolished by decree on June 22. The assets of the SPD and its paramilitary organization, the *Reichsbanner*, had already been seized on May 10.

On June 21, the German National Fighting Leagues (*Kampfverbände*) were dissolved. A section of the *Stahlhelm* was integrated into the SA and the rest placed under Hitler. On June 27, the German National People's Party (DNVP; in the 1933 elections it campaigned as the *Kampffront Schwarz-Weiss-Rot*) dissolved; Hugenberg resigned as Reich minister. The remaining parties announced their own dissolutions in short succession: the German State Party (former German Democratic Party, DDP) on June 28; the Christian Socialist People's Service (*Christlich-Sozialer Volksdienst,*

CSV) and the German-Hanoverian Party (*Deutsch-Hannoversche Partei*) on June 30; the Party of People's Justice (*Volksrechtspartei,* VRP) on July 1; the German People's Party (DVP) and the Bavarian People's Party (BVP) on July 4; and the Center Party on July 5.

On July 14, Hitler passed a law stipulating that the National Socialist German Workers' Party constituted the only political party in Germany and that any attempt to establish a new party was punishable with penal servitude of up to three years. Hitler could have been well pleased with his success in having taken power "swiftly and with a single stroke." But subsequent developments showed that he was in no way satisfied with what he had achieved and continued his inexorable labors to expand his power.

By comparison, his methods were much more lax in the economic sector. He granted the economists and departmental ministers a relatively free hand while strictly prohibiting any currency manipulation. The long-accumulated energy of German labor quickly regained its momentum in Hitler's economic program of repairing buildings, constructing roads, boosting private enterprise with government commissions, promoting motorization, etc. This and the waning Depression united to end quickly the economic misery which had plagued Germany for so many years. The majority of the Germans, who had long been victimized by poverty, was thus quite satisfied with Hitler's government and paid little attention to his legislative measures to eliminate dissenting political parties and suppress political opponents.

Abroad, the developments inside Germany were naturally viewed with concern. The foreign press openly criticized Germany's evolution to a one-party system or, more precisely, to a dictatorship under Hitler. Infuriated by this criticism, Hitler decreed a boycott of all Jewish businesses in Germany. He regarded a measure of this sort as an appropriate means for bringing pressure to bear on his foreign opponents, and its success seemed to justify his expectations.

The Concordat with the Vatican, concluded on July 8, not only helped Hitler to move the Center Party to proclaim its dissolution but also strengthened his position abroad. On the other hand, he desired to avoid any consolidation in Germany's foreign policy. Domestic chaos had brought him to power; chaos abroad would allow him, so he hoped, to attain his foreign policy goals. If the world or, more specifically, the League of Nations accepted Germany's claims for equality, revision of the Treaty of

Versailles, etc., he would no longer be able to make demand upon demand, armed with the demeanor of injured innocence that he used to justify both his aims and his methods.

Hitler was thus assiduous in his efforts to put into practice the equality of rights for Germans resolved by the major powers on December 11, 1932. On October 14, he kept the promise made in his foreign policy speech to the Reichstag on May 17 and declared Germany's withdrawal from the League of Nations and the Disarmament Conference. As usual, he succeeded in killing two birds with one stone. He had long been irked by the Reichstag elected on March 5, for it still contained deputies of the German Nationalists, the Center Party, etc., albeit only as guests of the Nazi Party. Now he had the Reichstag dissolved, allegedly in order to obtain the people's mandate on a possible withdrawal from the League of Nations. Of course, a plebiscite would have served this purpose just as well, if not better.

But Hitler wanted a Reichstag composed solely of National Socialists, and this he achieved in the new elections of November 12. 1933 was a successful year for Hitler in every way. Unlike Mussolini, he was not forced to either fight for the absolute domination of his party or to negotiate with the Vatican for compensation. Within a few short months, Hitler was able to take over every major position of power with the exception of head of state and supreme commander of the armed forces. But in order to achieve this, he had had to spend five times as long combating much stronger resistance until he, like Mussolini, ultimately became head of government.

THE YEAR 1934
Major Events in Summary

Hitler entered the year 1934 less triumphantly than might have been expected after the many successes he had scored in 1933. He was preoccupied with the question of succeeding Hindenburg, for it was obvious that the 86-year-old president would hardly live out the year. To Hitler, it was equally apparent that he was the only conceivable choice to take the Old Gentleman's place. At first glance, there was no real reason for Hitler's apprehension. The wording he had chosen in the Enabling Act of March 23/24, 1933 gave him every right to assume the functions of the Reich president's office at Hindenburg's death. In addition, Hitler had at his disposal a Reichstag that would pass any constitutional amendment he chose. Thirdly, there could be no doubt that, even in the event of a regular presidential election, he would win an absolute majority on the first ballot.

Even if Hindenburg were to designate his successor in his will and thus influence the outcome of an election, Hitler was convinced that he was capable of swaying the Reich president to designate him as his heir. Hitler's fears had less to do with the office of head of state than with the corresponding position of supreme commander of the armed forces. He had no desire to hold this position merely as a figurehead, as Ebert had done, but wanted to actually exercise supreme military command in the planned expansion. The key question was whether the generals would accept a former corporal as their superior. At the time, Hitler still regarded the upper echelons of the German Army as some sort of Olympian gods. Although the experiences of 1923 had taught him that the German generals were not political personages but loyal servants of the head of state and the government, in a military sense he perceived them in 1933 and 1934 as burning with desire to enter into Valhalla as war heroes and, not unlike bloodhounds straining on their leashes, eager to sink their teeth into the next enemy. As was often the case in fundamental matters, Hitler was greatly mistaken in his assessment of the military attitude of the generals.

In 1934, in any case, he was primarily interested in impressing them and winning their unreserved support for his cause in view of his plans to institute general conscription with a two-year term of service immediately after the Saar referendum. Hitler detested the type of paramilitary training practiced in the militias and paramilitary organizations. It was his belief that a two-year military service constituted the sole instrument with which he could translate his military aims into reality. Thus, he was strongly disinclined to accept the plans for a militia drawn up by the SA chief of staff Röhm and the former leaders of the *Freikorps*. Hitler and the generals were united in rejecting Röhm, albeit for different reasons. The German army (*Reichswehr*) was afraid of the very thing Röhm intended: that the coordination (*Gleichschaltung*) of the party and the state would be extended to include its own ranks. This *Gleichschaltung* had been carried through in nearly every other area in 1933: the national Nazi leaders (*Reichsleiter*) had become Reich ministers; the local Nazi leaders (*Gauleiter*) became district presidents (*Reichsstatthalter*); the Nazi youth leaders had risen to become youth leaders of the German Reich; the *Reichsführer SS* was gradually advancing to become the chief of police of all of the German *Länder*; and various leaders in the SS were taking over high positions in the police hierarchy. What could be more logical than that the SA units that already bore the regiment numbers of the former imperial army, would become regiments in a new militia—unless they were completely absorbed in the national socialist armed forces.

It was very understandable that Röhm was eyeing the post of Reich Minister of Defense and wanted at least to achieve the rank of general. After all, he too had been a captain like Göring, who had advanced from this rank to general of infantry, and had even become a lieutenant colonel in Bolivia. Hitler believed it necessary to prove his solidarity with the *Reichswehr* by drastic measures. He compensated for his feelings of military inferiority by committing an act of horrendous brutality: he resolved to cold-bloodedly murder his closest friends, the best known of the SA leaders, for the sake of appeasing the German generals. He did not even flinch at having his chief of staff, who had used his connections to greatly aid Hitler's ascent to power, executed without trial. It was only a few months before that he had reassured Röhm of his "proud friendship".

Admittedly, he also made practical use of the occasion to do away with a number of men who had become too loud in their opposition: Gregor Strasser, General von Schleicher, General von Bredow, the former general state commissar, Dr. Kahr, the leader of Catholic Action, *Ministerialdirektor* (undersecretary) Dr. Klausener; von Papen's associates, Herbert von Bohse and Dr. Edgar Jung, and many others.

"I have given them a rap on the knuckles which will smart for quite some time," Hitler declared to his confidant Rauschning in connection with these measures.

The incidents of June 30, 1934 marked a decisive turning point in the history of the Third Reich, for with them the former concept of a constitutional state was now not only practically but also formally dismissed and superseded by the precept that whatever Hitler demanded or executed now constituted what was legal. The *Reichswehr* was not alone in giving its consent to Hitler's elimination of the SA leaders by its actions and lack thereof. The Reich president, the cabinet, and the Reichstag were also accomplices who demonstrated that they accepted whatever Hitler pronounced as right without criticism or opposition.

Having once entered the vicious circle of using violence as a political weapon, Hitler logically kept to the same means in dealing with domestic problems and, consistent with his policy of what worked at home would work abroad, in his dealings with other countries as well. He was given the first chance to put this into practice scarcely a month later. In Danzig a National Socialist government had been installed in the last election, and in the Saar a German front under National Socialist leadership had been established by agreement. In Austria, however, playing the legal card had not enabled him to win the trick. In July 1934, he judged it high time to gain a foothold there by force.

However, the attempted coup in Vienna on July 25, 1934, proved a dismal and bloody failure, and Hitler left his comrades to their fate—for which he was directly responsible—without batting an eye. A few days later Hindenburg died, and Hitler became head of state in Germany. Once more, he declared that the struggle for power had now ended.

Hitler had triumphed yet again, but at the same time had struck a blow to the very roots of his own authority and, for the first time, done permanent damage to the confidence placed in him by his followers. Neither the party nor the state would ever completely recover. Hitler's flow of words, which had constituted a veritable torrent in 1932 and 1933, slowed noticeably in 1934. It was as though, now that he had let his mask fall, he was reluctant to appear in public unless it was absolutely necessary.

Thus, the year 1934—a year that had seen the National Socialists achieve their domestic goal—closed not in triumph, but in a mood of crisis. Crises at home and abroad were indeed characteristic of the Third Reich in the years 1934 to 1939, when they followed in a nearly uninterrupted sequence. For the most part, Hitler deliberately provoked them, while others were caused by his typical impatience. He could not tolerate waiting for a matter to ripen gradually on its own but was driven onward by his inner demon. Although initially he had seemed to race breathlessly from one triumph to the next, his behavior increasingly came to resemble a precarious balancing act. Indeed, he himself had once spoken of the "instinctive sureness of a sleepwalker" with which he trod the "path assigned to him by Providence."

This sureness abandoned him abruptly in September 1939: colliding with reality, he lost his balance and fell.

THE YEAR 1935
Major Events in Summary

The last crisis of the preceding year—in particular rising tensions between the German army and the SS—cast its shadow over the early months of 1935. Hitler was able, however, to play down this friction in a speech to "the German leadership."

The overwhelming outcome of the Saar plebiscite on January 13 then catapulted the entire population into such a mood of nationalistic euphoria that domestic problems seemed, at least temporarily, a thing of the past. On the heels of the triumphant return of the Saar to the German Reich came measures instituted by Hitler that shattered the illusions many Germans had had. As early as March 9, the existence of a new German *Luftwaffe* was openly proclaimed, and on March 16, the day before "Heroes' Memorial Day," general conscription was reintroduced by means of a "Declaration to the German Volk."

The Germans had barely begun to nourish hopes that, with the return of the Saar, things would settle down and a peaceful future was dawning. Hitler's actions brought them up short. One must bear in mind that the dominant tendency in Europe at the time was to do away with regular armies and introduce defense-oriented militia systems in their stead. Standing armies based upon conscription service of several years' duration were frowned upon. Rumor had it at the time that general conscription— which existed in Great Britain, for instance, only during wartime—was also to be abolished in other countries. The German population at large regarded itself as particularly fortunate in this sense, for not only did the Treaty of Versailles not provide for conscription but it, moreover, stipulated only a professional army of 100,000 men, which meant that there were no obstacles to the introduction of a militia system based upon voluntary service. Because of what Hitler had been saying in his speeches, the introduction of compulsory labor service was anticipated but certainly not general conscription, for the latter was viewed as a clear indication of a country's intention to conduct aggressive warfare. Hitler was perfectly aware of the blow this measure had dealt to the German people and thus did not dare to schedule any elections or plebiscites during 1935—notwithstanding his repeated claim that a statesman's appointment should be confirmed anew each year by the people in elections. As late as August of 1934, he had stated to Ward Price, "Every year I take one opportunity or another to submit my powers to the German Volk."

The reintroduction of general conscription caused less consternation to the western powers than had been expected. As noted above, they displayed a willingness to allow Hitler free rein as long as his actions could be justified as a claim to equal rights or as a principle of the general rights of nations; they would act, however, immediately as soon as he fired the first shot. Great

Britain condoned the reinstitution of general conscription in Germany by dispatching its foreign secretary, Sir John Simon, and Lord Privy Seal Anthony Eden to Germany in March and subsequently concluding a naval pact in June that fixed German tonnage at one-third that of Great Britain's.

Hitler was hence in a position to legally step up rearmament. In the autumn of the year, those born in 1914 commenced their military service, the first to be drafted for duty.

At the Reich Party Congress in Nuremberg, three laws were proclaimed: the notorious anti-Semitic racial laws and—less known but at the time the most important one for Hitler—the "Reich Flag Act." The compulsory labor service Hitler had propagated so enthusiastically in 1933 and 1934 finally did become law on June 26 but was limited to a mere six months. In the course of time, it was revealed to be what Hitler had always envisioned, namely a preliminary stage to military service, which was thus extended, for all practical purposes, to two and a half years. The SA was also assigned its new function in 1935: that of preparing German youth for military duty by training them for the SA sports and defense badges. The *Stahlhelm*, whose function as a militia-like organization had always irked Hitler, was finally dissolved on November 8, 1935.

THE YEAR 1936
Major Events in Summary

In 1936, Hitler intended to surpass the victories of the previous year with new triumphs of a military nature. He set himself the goal of extending the military sovereignty of the Reich to the Rhineland. In addition, he planned to prolong the one-year compulsory military service to two years. He had earlier chosen the shorter term of service only to make its introduction politically and psychologically more acceptable.

Hitler attained these goals on March 7 and August 26. He took full advantage of the staging of the 1936 Winter Olympic Games in Garmisch-Partenkirchen and the summer games in Berlin. Through the games, he was able to divert the attention of the German public and the international community as a whole from his military and political activities.

Further, by means of the German participation in the Spanish Civil War, Hitler gained a magnificent training ground for German troops and armor. For the next three years in Spain, the new German combat planes, tanks, etc., would be put to the test. For them, it was a valuable hands-on "live" training experience. In Austria as well, Hitler could claim a significant interim victory for himself. Italy's backing of the Austrian government had waned because of the substantial moral and economic support Hitler had accorded Mussolini's aggression in Abyssinia. Austrian Chancellor Kurt von Schuschnigg was forced to reach an understanding with Hitler. On July 11, von Schuschnigg found himself cornered into accepting an ill-disguised National Socialist as a member of his cabinet, namely the director of the Austrian War Archives, Edmund Glaise-Horstenau. Agreements with Italy (Rome-Berlin Axis) and Japan (Anti-Comintern Pact) in November strengthened Germany's position; they were not in the main aimed—as pretended—against Bolshevism but to impress the western powers.

THE YEAR 1937
Major Events in Summary

The year 1937 marked an important turning point in the years of Hitler's rule. It was in 1937 that Hitler's deeds and ambitions turned to an aggressive stance in matters of foreign policy and military strategy. That year also was a crucial one in Hitler's personal development as he began to reassess his relationship to questions of a religious nature. In the course of the previous four years, Hitler had secured nearly all positions of power within Germany that he deemed worthy of his effort. Naturally, there were controversies still outstanding with those leading men of the military who could not reconcile themselves to accepting Hitler's word as the sole truth. Furthermore, the tedious problem of the *Soldatenbund* remained. This veterans' organization openly advocated transforming the Third Reich into a military dictatorship. Hitler realized that in one way or another he would have to come to terms with this particular interest group. Yet Hitler was in no hurry to resolve either of these issues. As Supreme Commander of the German army of the Third Reich (*Wehrmacht*), he could force compliance with his wishes if need be. It was an entirely different matter with regard to his intellectual critics. They were not organized in a manner that would allow Hitler to resolve the affair by simply eradicating members of a social circle. Even if he forbade discussion or outlawed the voicing of critical remarks, there was no way in which he could silence his opponents' unspoken disagreement. He sensed their silent criticism, and it drove him to near insanity. He simply could not deal with the intellectuals.

Within the borders of the German Reich, Hitler had achieved everything he could in matters of military policy. The military provisions of the Treaty of Versailles had been reversed and general conscription had been reintroduced to Germany. Once again, the military sovereignty of the Reich encompassed the Rhineland. Nevertheless, if Hitler indeed insisted upon pursuing further goals in matters of foreign and military policy it was reasonably clear that he would have to wage a war abroad. The time had come for decision. Before the year 1937 was over, Hitler revealed to his generals and to the pertinent ministers that he intended to carry through the foreign policy goals he had set for himself in 1919. This, in turn, meant only one thing—war!

Hitler also resolved to take decisive action with regard to a question that may also have been closely linked to his decision about war. He made a clear break with his previous values and norms, still rooted in a Catholic worldview, and declared: "Now I feel as fresh as a colt in a pasture." For religious inspiration, he now looked to a mysterious martial deity, who challenged the German Volk's strength and courage. He understood himself to be the executor of this divine will.

Judging by outward appearances, 1937 was a tranquil, quiet year. Hitler was preoccupied with his own personal concerns. Neither plebiscite nor election was called for, and Hitler refrained from "tilling" his Volk "as the peasant tills his field." The sole excitement 1937 afforded was the German naval attack on the Spanish port of Almería on May 31. Further glamour was lent to that year by the grand ceremonies on the occasion of Mussolini's visit in September. Outside of these two events, the year passed by quietly, its flow barely disturbed by the customary celebration of state or party holidays. The dates were the usual ones: January 30, February 24, April 20, May 1, the Day of German Art, the Harvest Festival (*Erntedankfest*) to be celebrated one last time that year, and finally the commemoration of the November Putsch.

Nevertheless, outward appearances can be deceiving, and matters were not as calm as they appeared to be; much was brewing beneath the surface. Numerous secret meetings and talks were held behind closed doors. Of the latter, the most important address was the one of November 5, in which Hitler chose to reveal his immediate military ambitions to the Reich foreign minister and to the heads of the *Wehrmacht*.

Thus in many respects the year 1937 passed by like the lull before the storm.

THE YEAR 1938
Major Events in Summary

Hitler had set his mind to making 1938 a year of activity and advancement once again. The months of restraint and caution had ended. With the singular exception of the bombing of Almería, 1937 conspicuously lacked any great event, both within Germany and abroad. There had not even been one plebiscite. Nothing at all had happened that Hitler would have deemed worthy of such "great times" as these. Now he felt himself obliged to make up for the lack of excitement in 1937. The "period of so-called surprises," that he pronounced dead on January 30, 1937, had come again.

First, Hitler sought to consolidate his domestic support to give himself freedom to maneuver in foreign affairs. Thus, he turned upon the only remaining opposition still functioning within Germany: the reactionary generals. On February 4, after elaborate intrigues in preparation, Hitler relieved the minister of war, Field Marshal von Blomberg, and the commander in chief of the army, Freiherr von Fritsch, of their posts. Hitler himself assumed control of the *Wehrmacht*. Göring, still his "best man," was promoted to the rank of field marshal. This made Göring the highest-ranking officer in the *Wehrmacht*. In addition, Hitler had the remaining generals "move." No less than sixty of them were either assigned new responsibilities or completely removed from active duty through forced early retirement. In order not to push his luck, Hitler decided to refrain from destroying the conservative veterans' organization (*Soldatenbund*), the group that aimed to transform the Third Reich into a pure military dictatorship. However, in only six weeks an opportunity to dissolve the *Soldatenbund* arose. Within a week following March 10, this organization ceased to exist.

On February 4, Hitler also got rid of Foreign Minister von Neurath, whose unreliability had displeased him. Hitler named the German ambassador in London, Joachim von Ribbentrop, to fill the vacancy created by von Neurath's dismissal. The appointment of a man so obviously subservient to his Führer signaled that in the realm of foreign affairs Hitler also intended to take personal control. To make matters perfectly clear, Hitler simultaneously recalled Ambassadors Hassel from Rome, Dirksen from Tokyo, and von Papen from Vienna. In particular, von Papen's removal from office left little doubt as to Hitler's intent to treat Austria more severely. Schuschnigg immediately grasped the foreboding significance of von Papen's dismissal. He declared himself willing to see Hitler at the Obersalzberg to make a plea for the maintenance of good relations between the two states.

On February 12, Hitler seized upon the occasion of Schuschnigg's visit to admonish the Austrian for his "un-German" (*undeutsch*) behavior. After hours of reproof, Hitler handed Schuschnigg a three-day ultimatum. The document demanded that the Austrian federal chancellor release all Austrian National Socialists. Further, it instructed him to appoint a second National Socialist minister to his cabinet and to restore legality to the National Socialist Movement in his country. Schuschnigg had no choice but to agree to comply. In the event that he failed to do so, Hitler threatened to invade Austria. This threat was all the more significant since Mussolini could no longer be relied upon for support.

Nonetheless, behind the scenes, Schuschnigg actively searched for a way out of this dilemma. Misjudging the possibilities that lay before him and underestimating the support a union with Austria (*Anschluss*) enjoyed within the Austrian populace, he decided to call for a plebiscite on March 13, a fateful step, as time would prove. He announced this in Innsbruck on March 9. The plebiscite was to rally Austrians in the defense of a free, independent, and Christian Austria. However, this undertaking backfired completely on Schuschnigg, as Mussolini had predicted. After Schuschnigg's attempt to step out of line, Hitler decided to go ahead with the military intervention. As early as March 12, the entire *Vaterländische Front* had collapsed in Vienna. The Austrian National Socialists assumed power for one day, awaiting the arrival of Hitler and the German troops to take over. By the next day, the annexation of Austria to the German Reich was a *fait accompli*. At the same time, Hitler called for a new election to the Reichstag. All went according to plan and the election on April 10 was a complete success, with the Austrian annexation providing Hitler with a great deal of popular support.

Still, Hitler did not allow himself to rest on his laurels. He quickly focused his energies on staging his masterstroke of 1938: the war against Czechoslovakia. As early as April 21, he instructed the military to prepare for an assault upon the country. Returning from a visit to Italy in May and perceiving an escalation in the Sudetenland crisis, Hitler resolved to do away with this unloved neighbor once and for all before winter set in. A line of fortification to the west was to ensure that no foreign power intervened in his Czechoslovakian enterprise. Yet, events proved to be not quite as simple as Hitler had envisioned. To anyone aware of the true power structures at the time, it was clear that if indeed Hitler set out to do battle he would end up fighting both Great Britain and France. This Hitler refused to acknowledge. To him, the senility of the British was a self-evident truth that could be shaken by no considerations. In his eyes, events at the height of the crisis only proved the validity of his hypothesis.

The British had resolved to comply with Hitler's demands with regard to Czechoslovakia, on the basis that this was by some stretch of the imagination congruent with the principles of international law and provided that Hitler would agree to abide by treaty obligations. However, nearly seventy years old at the time, the British Prime Minister Neville Chamberlain repeatedly flew to Germany to discuss the issue of the Sudetenland. The British statesman offered Hitler his services in an effort to resolve the Sudeten German question by means of negotiation. Repeatedly in his speeches, Hitler had clamored for a resolution of the issue at hand, justifying the Reich's claims by referring to the principles of international law. As he later admitted, Hitler himself had never seriously considered a scenario in which his demands would actually be met. Indeed, from the outset Chamberlain's behavior reinforced his belief in the decrepitude of British statesmanship to an extent Hitler himself had not thought possible. As a result, he treated Chamberlain—"that little worm"—with even less respect than he had the German Nationalists in the early 1930s.

Pressured by Mussolini, Hitler finally agreed to a conference in Munich. However, he remained convinced that agreement on the promised territorial cessions was not possible. If indeed he was correct in his assessment, then at least the failure of negotiations could serve as a pretense for him to rush to the rescue of the oppressed Germans in the region. In the process, his march to Prague would transform all of Czechoslovakia into a sea of flames. Yet his appraisal of the situation turned out to be a faulty one. Both the British and the French statesmen yielded to every single one of his demands with regard to the Sudetenland. In the end, Hitler found himself cornered and grudgingly signed the treaty.

The entire world held its breath and stood in awe of what it considered to be Hitler's most astounding victory yet. Without firing a single shot, he had brought three-and-a half million Germans of Czechoslovakian citizenship "home to the Reich." Moreover, he had gained valuable territory upon which stood the entire fortification system of the Czechoslovakian state. However, there was still one man who was not at all content with the situation—Hitler. Quite to the contrary, he was furious. He felt himself outwitted, if not to say outright duped. In his eyes, the Sudeten German territories were of little use if he was precluded from laying his hands on the entirety of the Czechoslovakian territory as he had planned.

After all, the country played a pivotal part in the most decisive of his envisioned future conquests. He had intended to launch these campaigns from its territory in his drive towards the east. He was incensed by what he considered to be a great embarrassment for him: he had not been allowed to conquer the territories in question himself. Instead, he had only an international forum to thank for them. The agreement in Munich appeared to be an accurate re-enactment of what had infuriated Hitler so much in the case of the Saarland, where international bodies ceded territories to him without according him the opportunity to act independently prior to the transfer of property.

Hitler did have a point—given his perception of the developments at the time. It was true that he had stumbled into a trap at Munich. For the first time he had been maneuvered into voluntarily signing an international agreement. In 1936, he had solemnly vowed to abide by all treaty agreements that he had signed. He had claimed that, after all, his signature carried with it the weight of sixty-eight million people. As long as one of these men and women remained alive, he or she would uphold the treaty. Furthermore, Hitler had repeatedly pledged never to place his signature on a treaty if he was not completely certain that Germany was capable of complying with its exigencies. However, by signing the agreement of September 29 he had subjected himself to the manipulation of foreigners. The treaty not only ran contrary to his schemes, it also made their realization impossible.

Yet fate had still other rainy days in store for Hitler. In Munich on the next day, Chamberlain called at the Führer's private apartment at the Prinzregentenplatz. The interpreter Schmidt immediately noticed Hitler's disconcerted demeanor. In a rotten mood and absent-minded, he passively submitted to the civilities of the British prime minister. Then Chamberlain procured a piece of paper, which proved to be an already polished statement by Great Britain and Germany enjoining consultation between the two states. The draft amounted to a non-aggression pact. In this instance as well, Hitler uncharacteristically yielded to Chamberlain's urging and signed the document.

Reading the newspapers the next morning, Hitler must truly have felt as though he had been duped once again. In particular, the manner in which Chamberlain had been received back in London and the prime minister's comments on the British-German declaration helped foster this impression. In Hitler's opinion, the British had just demonstrated at Munich that they neither desired nor were able to wage a war against him. To this end, no separate declaration would have been necessary, since the farthest thing from Hitler's mind was to become entangled in an armed conflict with England. Nonetheless, not only had Chamberlain dared to propose mutual consultations on all topics that pertained to both states, but also Hitler had even agreed to this proposal. This occurred despite the fact that as a matter of principle, Hitler never discussed his decisions with anyone. He did not consult even the most intimate of his co-workers; and he did not ask his friend Mussolini's opinion. Least of all would he stoop to ask the advice of a decrepit old Englishman.

However, far worse in Hitler's view was the fact that the British now held two documents bearing his signature to which they most certainly would point accusingly the minute he undertook any step of an aggressive nature. Nevertheless, he was determined to show these British and the world Jewry standing behind them who was the master at this game! Just how incensed Hitler was by the manner in which Chamberlain, "that cheeky fellow," had gotten the better of him in Munich was apparent repeatedly in many of his speeches and actions during the latter months of 1938. On October 9, barely two weeks after the Munich Agreement, Hitler vented his anger at the British in a speech at Saarbrücken, furiously raging, "We will no longer tolerate any schoolmarm patronizing us!" To lend credence to his statement with regard to the military, Hitler announced the construction of a new line of fortification to the west. Clearly, Hitler had reverted to his tactics of "slaps in the face." On October 21, Hitler issued an ordinance to the *Wehrmacht* to prepare for the military liquidation of the "remainder of Czechoslovakia" (*Rest-Tschechei*). Again, in the Bürgerbräukeller on November 8, Hitler expressed his genuine displeasure with the British and cried out: "We will not stand for being supervised as if by a schoolmaster!"

The night of November 9, 1938, ushered in the Jewish pogrom in Germany. A young Jew of German origin, Herschel Grynszpan, had assassinated the German legation counselor in Paris, Ernst vom Rath. This time Hitler reacted in a completely different manner from the way he had in the remarkably similar case of Wilhelm Gustloff over two years earlier. In the Gustloff case, Hitler had been forced by tactical considerations to content himself with a funeral oration protesting the incident. However, in the case of vom Rath, he resorted to far more drastic measures. On the one hand, he wanted to teach the Jews a lesson for their malevolent attitude during the Sudetenland crisis. More important was Hitler's desire to spread terror among the members of the supposed secret Jewish world government. He wanted them to have good reason to pressure the Anglo-Saxon powers to embrace a more favorable stance toward him, for the sake of the German Jews.

On November 10, Hitler advised the representatives of the German press in a "secret speech" to prepare the German people for war. They were to instill the masses with a fervent belief in the final victory. The journalists were no longer to advocate concern for peace. As 1938 drew to an end, Hitler resolved to make up for the "setback" suffered at Munich the next year. Never again would the British keep him from claiming hold of the remainder of Czechoslovakia. Neither would they prevent him from waging his war to the east in the struggle for new *Lebensraum*.

The year 1938 was to be the last year of Hitler's great speeches. For one last time, the year 1938 afforded him the opportunity to pour forth monstrous speeches at the Party Congress and in the course of his speech-making campaigns. Early that year, the union with Austria (*Anschluss*) and the spring Reichstag election had provided opportunities for speeches. Later in the year, Hitler again spoke publicly in the aftermath of the occupation of the Sudetenland and the retroactive Reichstag election conducted there in autumn. These were to be his last great speaking appearances at mass rallies. Especially in Austria and the Sudetenland, there still existed large population groups that would flock to his speeches and would submit themselves without reservation to Hitler's verbose oratory. They had not yet learned to differentiate between Hitler's words and actions.

After five years of his rule, most people living in the old Reich territory had grown increasingly skeptical. At speaking engagements, Hitler was beginning to feel that the tide had turned against him. Therefore, he chose to speak only at carefully orchestrated and staged mass rallies in the old Reich. Nevertheless, in the newly annexed regions he eagerly took advantage of spontaneously appearing before genuinely enthusiastic crowds. As in his earlier days, he would literally become intoxicated at the opportunity to exhibit his rhetorical prowess. Once again, he basked in the exalting thunderous applause, relishing the enraptured expression on the faces of his audience.

With the year 1938, Hitler's series of successes ended. From 1939 onward, the German train of government, whose wheel the Führer had sworn never to abandon, set out on a journey to destruction.

THE YEAR 1939
Major Events in Summary

Hitler focused on additional territorial annexations in the east in the first months of 1939. In his eyes the city of Danzig, the Memel territory, and the remainder of Czechoslovakia were rightful possessions of the Reich. In complete disregard of the actual situation, he speculated that the western powers would remain silent or, at most, would launch formal protests when confronted with persistent aggression on Germany's part. Blinded by the successes scored in 1938 with the *Anschluss* and the return of Sudeten German areas to the Reich, he adhered to his earlier perceptions that these achievements were due to nothing other than the display of the Third Reich's military potential. He failed to realize the importance of international law that invalidated Germany's territorial claims in the case of the Sudetenland.

On the contrary, he felt humiliated at the thought that he had placed his signature on so odious a paper as the Munich Agreement. He perceived this as the gravest error in his political career to date. In his mind, it greatly detracted from the other achievements of 1938. The eager acquiescence of the British at Munich he interpreted as proof of Britain's declining power and status. Instead of paying heed to Chamberlain's and Mussolini's offers to mediate, he should have followed his instincts and—this thought enormously troubled him—he ought to have taken the entire Czechoslovakian state in late 1938. This would have spared him the disgraceful signature of the Munich papers, and he would not have been humbled by accepting that an international body had secured territorial concessions for him. Had he proceeded by the use of force, he would also have avoided placing himself at the mercy of the same despicable forum. He worried little about his actions eliciting a negative response from abroad, as he was certain that neither France nor Great Britain would have declared war on him in either event.

Given this mind-set, it was not surprising that at the onset of this most fateful year in Germany's history, Hitler's thoughts rested foremost with atoning in some manner for his "lapse of presence of mind" at Munich. No matter under what pretext, the Third Reich simply had to swallow the remainder of Czechoslovakia and lay hold of Slovakia militarily. He attached little importance to the fact that such moves would present a grave affront, not only to the other parties to the Munich Agreement but also to his friend Mussolini and even the Poles, indeed the whole world. The thought that this would clearly expose him as a man not to be trusted before the eyes of the world apparently never entered his mind. That breaking his word so blatantly might backfire and discredit his regime was a consideration alien to him. The decrepit English, the decadent French, and the depraved democracies worldwide meant nothing to him. He would show them once and for all that it was he, Adolf Hitler, who ruled Europe. All other heads of government would have to bow to the Reich's might and submit to his arbitrary reign. That these statesmen would ultimately come under his spell, as the German Nationalists once had, was something he never questioned.

Among the many peoples and states in Europe, Slovakia was the most to Hitler's liking. Having grasped the exigencies of the hour, Tiso and other Slovak statesmen like Tuka, Mach, and Durcansky nearly fell over each other in their quest to please and flatter the German dictator. They were only too eager to comply with his implicit request and to deal a fatal blow to the fragile Czechoslovakian federation by becoming vocal in their demands for more autonomy for their ethnic group. Their requests were deliberately such that Prague could not possibly satisfy them without the federation self-destructing. The upheaval and turmoil thus created in Czechoslovakia prepared the ground for a German military intervention. Officially, this represented an effort to re-establish the rule of law and order in the area. Once the Slovak politicians had accomplished their mission, Hitler was more than willing to grant them an autonomous state for their people. In fact, however, this state's freedom of action was severely limited by Hitler's reservation that it remain subject to the military sovereignty of the Reich.

The easternmost reaches of the Czechoslovakian state were situated in the Carpatho-Ukraine, an area for which Hitler had special plans as well. Magnanimously, he intended to cede the area to Hungary in an effort to divert attention from his other territorial ambitions. Much as he had handled the transfer of the Olsa region to Poland the previous year, Hitler was set on currying favor with the Hungarians this time and luring them into an alliance with Germany. Unaware of the German head of state's ultimate designs, an autonomous, pro-German government had already formed in the Carpatho-Ukraine. They promoted the cause of incorporating in their envisioned new state those parts of their homeland that had fallen prey to the Soviet Union and Poland in earlier years. They unwittingly counted on Hitler's active support for their dream of a reunited "Greater Ukrainian Empire." While Augustin Vološin served officially as the autonomous region's minister-president, behind the scenes the hand of Hetman Skoropadskyi was at work. He had already served as chief-of-state of the

Ukrainian territory that the Central Powers had annexed in 1918, under the tutelage of Wilhelm II. The Carpatho-Ukrainians were the first foreign people, though by no means the last, to experience how quickly and mercilessly Hitler could turn against former supporters and allies once these had served their purpose. The Poles, Yugoslavs, and Russians were the next in line for this realization.

In March 1939, Hitler embarked on the realization of his ambitious ventures in connection with the remainder of Czechoslovakia and the Slovak peoples. Encouraged by Hitler's alluring promises and backed by him, the Slovaks stirred up civil unrest and involved themselves in intrigues against the central government in Prague to such an extent that the newly appointed Minister-President Hácha felt compelled to ask for the resignation of the Tiso cabinet and replaced it with a government headed by Sivak. This represented the cue for a massive German intervention in Pressburg (Bratislava). All of a sudden, dubious men, such as Hitler's expert for annexations, *Gauleiter* Bürckel, haunted the halls of administrative buildings in the capital. This veteran of the Austrian *Anschluss* and the repatriation of the Saarland strode down hallways accompanied by other suspicious characters such as Seyss-Inquart, along with numerous highly decorated German generals. Deployed on numerous similar missions in the course of his career, Hitler's special plenipotentiary Wilhelm Keppler reinforced their ranks. Together these so-called envoys set out to convince the Slovak regime that the time had come for them to sever ties to the central government in Prague. History demanded of them that they create an "independent" Slovak state under the guidance of National Socialist Germany. Should they be unwilling, the consequences for their people would be grave ones. The German faction in Slovakia, suddenly armed, made sure with its daily demonstrations that everybody understood what Hitler wanted.

On March 13, Hitler consented to seeing Tiso and Durcansky at the chancellery in Berlin. He lectured them on the importance of immediately proclaiming Slovakia an independent state. Upon his return to Pressburg the following day, Tiso did indeed read to the Slovak Parliament a "declaration of independence of the Slovak State" that Hitler had drawn up for him. This pulled the "Slovak" pillar out from beneath the increasingly unsteady Czechoslovakian federation. It also signaled the renewal of a German propaganda campaign directed against Prague. Once again, newspapers carried story after story of alleged Czech atrocities, of violations of the civil rights of ethnic Germans, and of renewed unrest in Bohemia and Moravia. Despite the turmoil created, reserve troops in Germany received no orders to march. This corresponded with a projected assessment of the situation as discussed in a directive of December 17, 1938, in which Hitler insisted that the German military need not fear encountering resistance of any significance as it moved to occupy the remainder of Czechoslovakia.

In the evening hours of March 14, German troops and armed SS contingents penetrated the area surrounding Moravian Ostrau in order to take this strategically important city in a first strike against Prague. The proximity of this population center to the Polish border was also to deter Poland from resorting to any foolish measures, such as resisting the German occupation of neighboring Czechoslovakia. On the night of March 14–15, Hitler ordered Hácha and the Czechoslovakian Foreign Minister Chvalkovsky to come see him and to sign an agreement, practically at gunpoint, which effected the Reich's annexation of Bohemia and Moravia. To his credit, Hitler once more scored a major success without bloodshed. The Czech army received instructions not to oppose the German soldiers closing in on it from all sides. To ensure this, the Czech soldiers had to hand over their weapons.

After the successful occupation of the territory, Hitler hastily issued two proclamations to the German people. He then rushed on to Prague to enter the Hradcany Castle and finally reap the fruits of his labor that he felt the Munich Agreement had unfairly deprived him of. Nevertheless, the victory was a deceptive one. No glorious warlord was to be honored for his exploits; rather an exploited people were to be raped once more. Moreover, to achieve this dubious victory, Hitler had sacrificed what remained of his credibility in the eyes of the world. In spite of repeated, solemn pledges denouncing intentions of further aggressive actions, like the ones enumerated below, he revealed himself to be a man without scruples:

> I shall never, as a statesman, put my signature on a treaty that I would never sign as a man of honor in private life, even if it were to mean my ruin! For I would also never want to put my signature on a document knowing in the back of my mind that I would never abide by it! I abide by what I sign. What I cannot abide by, I will never sign. (October 18, 1933)

For my part, I declare that I would rather die at any time than sign something that, in my most sacred conviction, I hold to be intolerable for the German Volk. (October 24, 1933)

I will never sign anything knowing that it can never be upheld, because I am determined to abide by what I sign. (November 2, 1933)

Whatever we believe we cannot adhere to, on principles of honor or ability, we will never sign. Whatever we have once signed we will blindly and faithfully fulfill! (February 24, 1935)

The German Reich government does not intend to sign any treaty that it does not feel able to fulfill. It will, however, scrupulously comply with every treaty signed voluntarily, even if the same was drawn up prior to its having taken office and coming to power. (May 21, 1935)

Nowhere in the world today is there a greater guarantee for the security of such a treaty than if it is signed by this [Hitler's] hand. (March 28, 1936)

Hitler had not only pledged to respect treaties he placed his signature on, he had also denied that he had any further territorial claims to make on behalf of Germany. Moreover, the establishment of a Greater German Reich would not entail subjugation of foreign peoples since, after all, as Hitler enjoyed pointing out, the last thing he wanted in this new Germany were Czechs. He pledged himself and his Movement to respect the right to self-determination of other ethnic groups:

We will never attempt to subjugate foreign peoples . . .
We have no territorial claims to make in Europe.

The German Reich government shall thus unconditionally abide by the other articles governing the coexistence of the nations, including territorial provisions, and put into effect solely by means of peaceful understanding those amendments that become inevitable by virtue of the changing times.

It is the last territorial demand I shall make in Europe. I repeat here before you, once this issue [the cession of the Sudeten German territories] has been resolved, there will no longer be any further territorial problems for Germany in Europe!

We do not want any Czechs at all.

He proved all these statements to have been despicable lies by invading what remained of the former Czechoslovakian state within five months after taking part in the Four Power Summit at Munich. His signature was worth less than the paper he scribbled it on. He had succumbed to the temptation of what he perceived to be the decrepitude of the English, the indecision of the French, the servile attitude of Mussolini, and the inferiority of Poland's military. For, in fact, the move of March 15 affected the Poles no less than the peoples of Czechoslovakia, as they strongly suspected Poland to be the next item on Hitler's list for future conquests.

In light of Hitler's deluded view of reality, the move of March 15 was not inconsistent with his previous statements. Given a fundamentally different assessment of the situation, the reaction abroad to the renewed provocation by Germany was entirely different from what Hitler had anticipated. The English were no German Nationalists, and they were not about to let the megalomaniac proceed as he wished. It would take just one additional slight provocation, one more attempt to subdue by force of arms yet another foreign people, and—British sources left no doubt of this—His Majesty's government would be compelled to declare war on Germany as a consequence. Only the fact that no bloodshed had been involved in the March 15 foray spared the German people the horrors of war for another six months. Czechoslovakian troops had received timely orders not to fire on the advancing German units, and this saved Hitler one last time from the wrath of the western powers.

Meanwhile, this latest treaty violation by National Socialist Germany had reinforced Great Britain's decision to wait until Hitler's government had fired the first shot before launching a military intervention. In a radio address aired from Birmingham on March 17, 1939, Chamberlain made the British position clear. The prime minister pointed out that earlier territorial claims by Germany had always been well founded and sustainable in terms of international law. However, this latest undertaking was by no means compatible with the established conduct of affairs between states and represented a violation of all rights known to man:

> Germany, under her present regime, has sprung a series of unpleasant surprises upon the world. The Rhineland, the Austrian *Anschluss*, the severance of Sudeten-land—all these things shocked and affronted public opinion throughout the world. Yet, however much we might take exception to the methods that were adopted in each of those cases, there was something to be said, whether on account of racial affinity or of just claims too long resisted—there was something to be said for the necessity of a change in the existing situation.
>
> But the events that have taken place this week in complete disregard of the principles laid down by the German government itself seem to fall into a different category, and they must cause us all to be asking ourselves: "Is this the end of an old adventure, or is it the beginning of a new?"
>
> Is this the last attack upon a small state, or is it to be followed by others? Is this, in fact, a step in the direction of an attempt to dominate the world by force?

To these remarks, Chamberlain added the warning that no greater mistake could be made than to suppose that Britain would not take part to the utmost of its power in resisting such a challenge.

Hitler failed to take seriously the well-meant admonishment, and instead of paying heed to it, he proceeded to the next items on his agenda for the spring of 1939: the Memel territory and Danzig. The former point was easily dealt with: fortune apparently chose to smile upon him one last time. Lithuania yielded to diplomatic pressure and, on March 22, declared its willingness to return the terrain illegally seized from the German Reich in 1923.

Poland, however, was not willing to make concessions on a similar scale. It refused to cede the Free City of Danzig to the German Reich. It also declined cooperation in the construction of an extraterritorial motorway piercing the Polish corridor. Its reluctance was not a matter of spite but one of well-founded concerns for its own safety. After the most recent forceful annexation of the remainder of Czechoslovakia and the military occupation of Slovakia, Poland found itself surrounded on three sides by

Germany. The Third Reich's troops had positioned themselves to its west, its north and its south, thus effectively encircling Poland, given that the equally antagonistic Russians stood in the east. The Polish government was haunted by the suspicion that any concessions on its part would, at best, keep Hitler at bay for another half a year. A military confrontation had apparently become unavoidable. And the Poles were not about to lend a hand in their own destruction, especially as they knew that Great Britain stood behind them.

Chamberlain unambiguously restated England's commitment to Poland in a speech before the House of Commons on March 31, 1939:

> As the House is aware, certain consultations are now proceeding with other governments. In order to make perfectly clear the position of His Majesty's government in the meantime before those consultations are concluded, I now have to inform the House that during that period, in the event of any action which clearly threatened Polish independence, and which the Polish government accordingly considered it vital to resist with their national forces, His Majesty's government would feel themselves bound at once to lend the Polish government all support in their power. They have given the Polish government an assurance to this effect.
>
> I may add that the French government has authorized me to make it plain that they stand in the same position in this matter as do His Majesty's government.

This declaration left no doubt that the western powers were determined to meet any further armed aggression by Germany with a declaration of war. This was to apply also if German forces attempted to take Danzig, irrespective of the fact that Germans populated the area, and that it had once formed part of the Reich. The British stance was as clear then as it had been in 1914 when Austria set out to annex Serbia by force. Both causes, that of Serbia in 1914 and of Danzig in 1939, ultimately led to a world war, a confrontation pitting England and the Western powers against Germany and Austria. The Reich's invasion first of Belgium in 1914 and later of Poland in 1939 precipitated mortal conflict and open warfare.

After the outbreak of the Second World War, many Germans, and in his lifetime Hitler also, argued that England was to blame for these regrettable developments leading up to the great calamity of September 1939. Germany would not have resorted to arms had England not unduly reinforced the Poles by its lamentable declaration of March 31, 1939. It was only because of the British reassurances that Poland so vehemently denied Germany the construction of an extraterritorial motorway through the Polish corridor and, by the same token, that the Poles refused to return the city of Danzig to Germany.

On the other hand, it is perfectly possible that Poland would have reacted in the same manner regardless of Great Britain's behavior. The issues at stake transcended the immediate dispute concerning the linkage of East Prussia to the Reich and the status of the Free City of Danzig. The existence of the Polish state was no more the subject of the dispute in 1939 than either Serbia or Belgium had been the cause of disagreement in 1914. The crux of the matter was Germany's forcible annexation of neighboring territories and the support lent by Austria. Great Britain and the western powers were no more willing to tolerate such militant expansionism in 1939 than they had been in 1914. Persistent denial of the serious nature of the warnings by the west clearly places the responsibility for the ensuing tragedy on the shoulders of the German and Austrian statesmen of both periods. Had the politicians involved acknowledged that Great Britain and the world community had severe misgivings about the route chosen by the Reich, they could easily have prevented the outbreak of hostilities if they had ceased the pursuit of territorial expansion by brute force. By refusing to consider this option, in a sense the politicians in Berlin and Vienna might as well have signed the British declaration of war themselves.

Refraining from the pursuit of his goals was not a subject to be discussed with Hitler. He was determined to set out on "the road of the Teutonic Knights of old, to gain by the German sword sod for the German plough . . ." And in this quest, he argued there was "but one ally in Europe: England." That it was possible that Great Britain did not share his enthusiasm for such a policy apparently never entered his mind.

Thus, it was not surprising that the Führer was shocked by Chamberlain's address to the House of Commons on March 31, 1939. England's willingness to support Poland was inexplicable to him. He was at a loss trying to understand the rapid developments and the reactions they had elicited abroad in the course of the preceding two weeks. The annexation of the remainder of Czechoslovakia had provoked Chamberlain's sharp criticism. Then Poland had indignantly rebuked Germany's demand for a return of Danzig. To top this off, Great Britain announced the existence of a mutual assistance pact it had evidently concluded with Poland earlier. This series of developments shook the very foundation of Hitler's beliefs and the great stock he had placed in the decrepitude of the British mind. Obviously, English perceptions had not been dulled to the degree Hitler had counted on. Not surprisingly, Hitler was outraged at the impertinence of the British move when the news of Chamberlain's statement of March 31, 1939, reached him. He shouted: "I shall brew them one Devil's brew!"

The main ingredient for this potion was not difficult to divine: entry into an alliance with Bolshevist Russia. This was to disquiet the Western powers and to entice them to greater indulgence toward Germany. That this strategy would achieve its ends, Hitler was certain: had not the National Socialist and Communist cooperation in the 1932 transportation workers' strike in Berlin forced von Papen and his reactionary German Nationalists to embrace his politics? Apparently oblivious of his previous proclamations that he would never collaborate with tainted men such as the Bolshevists and risk exposure to this mind-poisoning ideology, he pursued these tactics to the end, albeit one quite different from what he had anticipated.

From April through August 1939, Hitler was busily adding other ingredients to the "potion" he was developing especially for the English. In his mind, they richly deserved his vengeance. It was the British government's recalcitrant behavior that had brought this misfortune upon them and forced him into an alliance with its archenemy. As of this time, however, he was still willing to grant England—magnanimously—one last chance to redeem itself. He would hold his anger in check and, at first, would deal it a few obvious slaps in the face. Should it fail to react to this in the desired manner, then, just like his conservative opponents in Germany, his "Hugenbergers," England would have in fact dealt its last card and he would carry through on the envisioned alliance with the Soviet Union.

The Reichstag speech of April 28, 1939, appeared to Hitler a splendid occasion to affront the British government once more and to test its reaction. First, he unilaterally abrogated the naval agreement on the size of the respective fleets arrived at in 1935. In one bold stroke of a pen, he then proceeded to declare null and void the 1934 Mutual Non-Aggression and Friendship Pact with Poland which, albeit many years ago, the party press had once celebrated as a masterpiece of National Socialist statesmanship.

Behind these two moves was Hitler's megalomaniacal desire to prove to Poland that Germany was free to move politically as he saw fit, despite the British avowal of support for the Polish state.

All in all, Hitler did himself more damage than good as he terminated agreements he himself had labored so long to realize. And the twenty-one insolent responses to Roosevelt with which he laced his speech made him appear far more ludicrous than serious. Throughout the summer of 1939, he staged military parade after military parade in an effort to display the prowess and might of Germany's *Wehrmacht* in a transparent effort to intimidate the English. Already at a speech in Wilhelmshaven on April Fool's Day 1939, the Führer had dedicated all his efforts to raise the specter of an overpowering German fleet before the eyes of the spectators, not to mention the British, at the christening of the battleship *Tirpitz*. The name was to remind London of the none-too-successful early stages of its struggle against the German navy in the First World War. When he appointed Admiral General Raeder commander in chief of the navy, Hitler hoped the English would begin to wonder whether a new *Tirpitz* was to head Germany's naval forces. If all went according to plan, he would cause the British to marvel at the apparent might of a navy that once more felt confident enough to face off Great Britain's own legendary naval power.

For his 1939 birthday celebration in Berlin, Hitler had columns of soldiers file by in front of him for hours, one of the most extensive military parades to date. In May, Hitler reserved several days for a thorough official inspection of the fortifications in the west in an attempt to underline the military's importance and might. Amidst much ado on May 22, he placed his signature beneath the so-called "Pact of Steel," a military alliance conclusively binding Italy to Germany. In the weeks to follow, a multitude of minor statesmen, mostly from the Balkans, came to call on the German dictator in Berlin, who rejoiced at these repeated opportunities to stage yet further impressive military parades. Between visits, Hitler busily attended maneuvers, issued directives to the military, and spoke frequently before Germany's generals. A special SS force took up quarters in Danzig, while Hitler called up reserve units and ordered a concentration of German troops along the eastern frontier of the Reich, primarily in East Prussia and Slovakia.

Still the English failed to react as Hitler desired; they showed little inclination to be bluffed by military displays and paid little heed to Germany's obvious preparations for war against Poland. On the other hand, they repeatedly insisted on earlier statements that, should Berlin launch an armed aggression against Warsaw, even on as peripheral a topic as Danzig, an immediate declaration of war by England would be the consequence. The English took notice of the developments in Germany, and realized that the time for military confrontation would soon arrive. What was at stake was not the fate of one small country but "larger issues," a topic Chamberlain had already expounded in a radio broadcast on September 27, 1938. Speaking on the eve of the Sudetenland crisis, he had alluded to the likelihood of such a confrontation, while maintaining that the time for this was not yet ripe.

> However much we may sympathize with a small nation confronted by a big and powerful neighbor, we cannot in all circumstances undertake to involve the whole British Empire in a war on her account. If we have to fight, it must be on larger issues than that.

The atmosphere that summer recalled one not so long ago when the Kaiser had still made pretenses about the glory to be gained for the Germany of 1914 in the then pending conflict. National Socialist rhetoric and Hitler's outrageous pronouncements in 1939 sounded remarkably similar. The German public had been systematically divorced from reality, had no access to unbiased information, and hence had become easy prey for an exuberant propaganda apparatus. Few Germans had the resources necessary to recognize the true political and military power structure in Europe. This was as true in 1939 as it had been in 1914 on the eve of the First World War.

In England that summer, to the contrary, the air was heavy with forebodings. In a radio broadcast addressed to the American people and aired on August 8, 1939, Churchill described the situation in Europe in the following manner:

> Let me look back—let me see. How did we spend our summer holidays twenty-five years ago? Why, those were the very days when the German advance guards were breaking into Belgium and trampling down its people on their march towards Paris! Those were the days when Prussian militarism was—to quote its own phrase—"hacking its way through the small, weak, neighbour country" whose neutrality and independence they had sworn not merely to respect but to defend.

But perhaps we are wrong. Perhaps our memory deceives us. Dr. Goebbels and his propaganda machine have their own version of what happened twenty-five years ago. To hear them talk, you would suppose that it was Belgium that invaded Germany! There they were, these peaceful Prussians, gathering in their harvests, when this wicked Belgium—set on by England and the Jews—fell upon them; and would no doubt have taken Berlin, if Corporal Adolf Hitler had not come to the rescue and turned the tables. Indeed, the tale goes further. After four years of war by land and sea, when Germany was about to win an overwhelming victory, the Jews got at them again, this time from the rear. Armed with President Wilson's Fourteen Points they stabbed, we are told, the German armies in the back, and induced them to ask for an armistice, and even persuaded them, in an unguarded moment, to sign a paper saying that it was they and not the Belgians who had been the ones to begin the war. Such is history as it is taught in topsy-turvydom.

Churchill's insistence that the fate of Belgium was of paramount importance to the developments in 1914 has to be taken with a grain of salt. "Larger issues" were at stake, to use Chamberlain's terminology of September 27, 1938. And, as Chamberlain expressed it, England would not go to war for the sake of one small nation alone, no matter how great its sympathy for the country.

Nevertheless, Churchill hit the nail on the head when he spoke of "topsy-turvydom" and its false prophets. The legend of the stab in the back, the myth of an invincible German army losing the First World War in 1918—all this bore evil fruit two decades later. Advocated by outspoken men such as Ludendorff and Hitler in conservative circles and served up, these theories led to a dangerous overestimation of Germany's military might and a no less perilous underestimation of the fighting power of the British and their staying power in battle. Hitler was among those who seriously believed that the Englishmen of this century were past their prime, and hence he did not anticipate encountering such a determined stance on their part.

Despairing of the ineffectiveness of repeatedly slapping the British in the face, Hitler had maneuvered himself into a position where he could only resort to serving up his fabled "Devil's brew." A non-aggression and mutual assistance pact with the Soviet Union came about quickly and was ready for signature in Moscow by August 23, 1939. By entering into a pact with the devil, so to speak, Hitler was certain to achieve his ends, since a similar strategy had proved most effective against domestic opponents in the early years of his political career.

It took the English two full days to react to this obvious provocation. On August 25, Great Britain and Poland signed a formal mutual assistance agreement. Contrary to Hitler's expectations, Great Britain did not stumble after this renewed slap in the face, and the "potion" administered failed in its purpose. This left Hitler ill at ease. He halted preparations already underway for a strike against Poland on August 26 to gain time to win England's favor. If London was not willing to enter into friendly relations with National Socialist Germany, perhaps assurances of its neutrality could at least be secured before a military move against Poland. Once more, he pinned all his hopes on his oratorical prowess, his ability to persuade his opponents under almost any circumstances. He truly believed he could bring about a decisive change in the British stance this late in the game.

The approach he took was an old one: he was going to transmit a renewed "offer of friendship" to the British Government through the good offices of Göring's friend, the Swede Dahlerus. This was to signal his willingness to tie Germany to Great Britain—anything to secure England's good will. To this end, he stood prepared to antagonize his friend Mussolini, whom he had just gravely affronted by entering into the Non-Aggression Pact with the Soviets without informing Italy or asking for its consent. These new allies he also willingly would have sacrificed on the altar of England's friendship, albeit only after a conquest or, at the very least, a renewed partition of Poland.

The absurdity of Hitler's thoughts became all the more obvious when he seriously offered to deploy German military forces in order to protect the British Empire. At first, in the far east, this would have entailed facing off with Japanese troops, although an earlier alliance bound Germany to Japan and its interests in the region. Moreover, Hitler was completely unaware that, by making this clumsy attempt, he was affronting the English in nearly the worst manner conceivable. All English-speaking countries regarded it as a great privilege and honor to be allowed to contribute to the defense of the English motherland and the outreaches of the commonwealth in times of danger. According to the public opinion in Germany, at least ever since the times of the Kaiser, the British Empire was always on the verge of collapse. And even if this were the case—to think the British would accept the help of Hitler's army divisions was veritably ridiculous.

By the asphyxiation of the truncated Czechoslovakian state, Hitler had clearly demonstrated that any compromise reached with him was ultimately doomed to fall victim to his megalomania. Granted that Downing Street would perhaps have been able to make the Poles step down and yield to the German demands for Danzig and the Polish corridor, it had far less incentive to do so after the willful annexation of the remaining territory legally ruled by Prague as an outcome of the Munich Agreement a year earlier.

Rescinding his order to attack Poland on August 25, Hitler had been certain that he could secure Great Britain's benevolent neutrality within a few days. Roused by the British failure to react in the manner anticipated, Hitler proceeded to ignore Britain's very existence and its opposition to his envisioned undertakings. The conceptions formed in 1919 clouded his view. As in so many earlier instances, the English would assuredly come around. If London chose not to support Germany's campaign against Russia, it would at least not hinder Berlin's pursuit of territorial expansion in the east. Irrespective of the time frame involved, so he believed, London would desist from any rash actions, issue protests for the record, and maintain benevolent neutrality when faced with the accomplished fact of the German incursion into Poland.

His chest swelling with confidence, he ordered the military move against Poland to begin at 4:45 a.m. on September 1, 1939. That morning, he dressed carefully in his field-gray tunic for the first time, proudly bearing the Third Reich's emblem on the left sleeve. He then formally announced to the Reichstag that the German army was to "return fire" on Polish troops. Initial reactions by Great Britain and the Western powers appeared to vindicate Hitler's tactics. Ambassadors of both Great Britain and France called on the German foreign minister in the late evening hours of September 1, 1939. They protested the German move on behalf of their respective governments and stated that this represented "an act of aggression" against Poland. The ambassadors brought to the foreign minister's attention the import of certain obligations binding their states to the fate of Poland. Their governments would feel compelled to act on these, should German military forces not withdraw from the sovereign territory of the Polish state immediately. Such statements were precisely the type of reaction Hitler had anticipated: diplomatic gestures void of any real significance in light of the impotence of the western powers' military forces, of which he was so firmly convinced.

While Great Britain's response was subdued that first day, a British declaration of war on Germany lay on the Chancellor's desk by the third day of the conflict. Stunned by this unexpected turn of events, he was—for once—at a loss for words. For several minutes he could only stare at the floor. The man who prided himself on having provided for every contingency imaginable had been taken by surprise. "What now?" was all he could say. When presented with a similarly unexpected declaration of war by the English on August 4, 1914, Bethmann-Hollweg had become no less despondent. In spite of Hitler's haughty disdain for his predecessors in office, the Führer cut a no less miserable figure in the chancellery a mere quarter of a century later.

Thanks to Hitler's remarkable resilience, he regained his composure and confidence within a matter of hours. Undaunted by the recent breakdown of his conception of a foreign policy based on a tacit alliance with Great Britain and incompatible with the present British position, he carried out neither of the measures he himself had once required of any other politician who failed on a comparable scale. He neither stepped down nor committed suicide. Instead, he issued a multitude of proclamations to the German Volk, the *Wehrmacht,* and the National Socialist Party. Through these he hoped to deflect blame from his own person to the British, who were solely responsible for the calamitous situation at hand, at least in his opinion.

Defiantly, he told his supporters, "We have nothing to lose but everything to win!"

Speedily he set out to inspect the state of preparations along the eastern front, in part undoubtedly to escape the disquieting situation in Berlin. He consoled himself by not taking the British declaration of war too seriously. He attributed it to a desire by the British to publicly satisfy the letter, not the spirit, of the English guarantee extended to Poland. Once the German military had conquered Poland with lightning speed, the English would undoubtedly resign themselves to the fact, whether they liked it or not. In time, they would realize that reconciliation with Germany and acceptance of its hand extended in friendship represented the only realistic approach for British foreign policy on the continent.

Hence, it was imperative that the Polish campaign be brought to a successful conclusion as soon as possible under the circumstances. This in turn meant that Hitler had to concede parcels of territory in eastern Poland to Russia. One month after he set out to eliminate the Polish state, it had indeed disappeared from the political map. While this first "blitzkrieg" had lasted a mere twenty-eight days, official sources in Germany shortened it considerably to eighteen days to emphasize the supposedly unequaled swiftness of the strike. A more decisive factor in the conflict had, however, been the numerical superiority of the German forces. Population figures were unmistakable here: 76 million Germans against 25 million Poles.

Goebbels' propaganda apparatus heralded this great military achievement as indicative of the intrinsic worth of National Socialism and its policies. Hitler's so-called "Leadership Principle," that is, the prompt "blind" execution of all commands from above and the elimination of any delay in the lower echelons, could certainly expedite the measures of the German government and of the military leadership, respectively, but it could not render soluble the problems which overwhelmed the German forces. Hitler's quick victories over Poland; later over Denmark, Norway, Belgium, Holland, Luxemburg; over a France that at the time—compared with Germany—was only half as strong; and over Yugoslavia and Greece, were achieved against smaller states and with overwhelming force. Hitler's dictatorial methods had only one result: a victory that was assured in any case could be achieved more quickly than would have been the case under a different form of government. Against states of equal or greater strength— Russia, England and America—Hitler could not achieve decisive results with his dictatorial and brutal methods.

This baffled Hitler, as these measures had proved most useful in domestic politics. For example, when he ordered the construction of a large segment of the Autobahn, he could be assured of its immediate implementation. To construct a relatively small section of this Autobahn to cross the Polish corridor, for some inexplicable reason, proved to be more of a task than he had imagined. That this was the case because of the determined opposition by the western powers to this particular project was a fact he was either unaware of or simply refused to accept.

Thrilled by the rapid conquest of Poland, Hitler determined the time had come to end the senseless confrontation with Great Britain. After all, the war between the two countries had not yet really begun. Nowhere had German troops actually faced off with their British counterparts, and already Hitler expected the British to back down without putting up a fight. In a speech before the Reichstag on October 26, 1939, he challenged the English to regain their senses, to accept the *fait accompli* of the Reich's annexation of Poland and to enter into negotiations for a settlement with Germany. Apparently, he sincerely believed that London would gratefully grasp the hand he extended in friendship as a splendid opportunity to end the war with Germany. This was a grotesque assumption.

In light of the peace proposal to Great Britain by the German resistance movement in 1941, it is tempting to consider Hitler's 1939 offers with greater leniency. While Hitler's conception was undeniably divorced from reality, Goerdeler's bid for peace was even more absurd because of its late date. It seemed as though Goerdeler felt compelled to outdo Hitler in requesting the impossible. If this was indeed the case, he certainly realized his ambition by asking for a restoration of the German Reich within its borders of 1914, retention of the lands overrun by Hitler's troops, and a return of the colonies lost to Great Britain in the First World War. These outrageous demands lent further credence to Churchill's caricature of the Third Reich as "topsy-turvydom." Apparently, many of the Reich's citizens were convinced that the defeated party was entitled to dictate its terms for peace to its more successful adversary at ceasefire talks, in particular if the former was Germany.

In the last phase of the First World War, the Western powers had already encountered similarly odd convictions in the Germans. These unpleasant experiences made the Allies adhere to a more prudent stance this time. As the war was winding down, they insisted on an "unconditional surrender" by Germany, Italy, and Japan. Popular belief held this demand to have exacerbated the situation for Germany by forestalling an earlier end to the fighting and a possible removal of Hitler. This type of argument was based on the same fallacy as the one asserted about the Munich Agreement. Many officers with the German armed forces maintained that the 1938 Munich Conference had effectively prevented them from launching a successful *coup d'état* to oust Hitler.

There has been much debate on the topic of "unconditional surrender." In fact, any surrender is unconditional as far as the defeated party is concerned. The party to the conflict that lays down its weapons first will always be at the mercy of the conqueror. The vanquished party does not have the prerogative as to whether or not to accept certain proposals, unless it wishes renewed hostilities leading to its ultimate defeat. The term "unconditional" thus refers primarily to the defeated party, although it does not entail a complete liberty of action for the victor either. And as the textbook case of the Second World War shows, the demand for an "unconditional surrender" does not of necessity provoke rights abuses. At the end of this particular conflict, the Allies desired merely to ensure that no doubts arose regarding the defeat of Germany: to avoid questioning that might lead to a repeat of the German military's claim after 1918 that it had been lured into laying down its weapons, despite the preservation of sufficient fighting power to decide the conflict in Germany's favor. Churchill pointedly sketched Great Britain's stance in the matter in a radio broadcast of October 1, 1939, after the onset of open hostilities:

> It was for Hitler to say when the war would begin; but it is not for him or for his successors to say when it will end. It began when he wanted it, and it will end only when we are convinced that he has had enough.

Given this state of events, it is hardly surprising that even the most gracious offers for peace by Hitler met with silence in England. Three days passed after the Reichstag speech of October 6, 1939, without any reaction from Great Britain. Enraged that the British were ignoring his peace proposals, Hitler decided to turn to the last resort at his command: the alliance with the Soviet Union. He would show the British who was the master of the continent. He would break their outpost, France. German tanks would roll over Belgium, Holland, and Luxembourg, countries officially neutral though sympathetic to the English cause and dependent on its protection. He was still reluctant to assault the British mainland, as he still held hopes for a later reconciliation with this people bound to the German Volk by ties of blood. Nonetheless, he would chase the English from the European continent, which ultimately would be his. He would make them "scurry back to the Thames," as he proclaimed in public.

Immediately, he set out to prepare for an offensive in the west. By October 9, 1939, he issued a directive "for the conduct of the war," the opening statement of which was still cautiously phrased in the slowly diminishing hope that he could win the British over at this late date.

> If it should become apparent in the near future that England and, under England's leadership, also France are not willing to make an end of the war, I am determined to act vigorously and aggressively without great delay.

It was October 10 already, and still there were no signs that Great Britain was contemplating entering into peace negotiations with Germany. Again, Hitler felt compelled to expand on the advantages a peace settlement would afford London. On the occasion of the annual drive for the Wartime Winter Relief Organization, (*Kriegswinterhilfswerk*), Hitler spelled out in great detail once more how much London stood to gain by arriving at a settlement with Germany:

> We know not what the future will bring. But one thing we know for certain: No power in this world shall ever wrestle Germany to the ground again! No one shall vanquish us militarily, destroy us economically, or trample upon our souls! And no one shall see us capitulate—under any circumstances.

> I have expressed our willingness for peace. Germany has no reason to do battle against the western powers. It was they who began this war on a threadbare pretext. In the event they decline our offer for peace, Germany stands determined to take up the fight again and to follow through on it—in one way or another!

Not even this threat had any perceptible effect on the English. Chamberlain naturally rejected the peace proposal in his address to the House of Commons on October 12, 1939. Once more he emphasized that Great Britain and he himself judged Germany and Hitler by deeds and not words. Hitler found himself in a situation where he had to put aside his plans for reconciliation with the British and to embark on an offensive along the front in the west.

On October 13, Hitler issued an official declaration by the government admitting that the British had rejected the German peace initiative. Once more he pronounced himself able and willing to fight. And if it was to come to war with Germany's neighboring states, then a conquest of these countries would be carried out quickly. Any additional waste of time would merely allow Great Britain to prepare for war and increase the likelihood that it would embrace a more aggressive policy soon. Secondly, France might finally awaken from the lethargy it had displayed at the time of the campaign against Poland. Above all, swift action was to preclude a change of heart on the part of the Russians, whose alliance with Germany was of a relatively recent vintage and of whose continued support Hitler was not at all certain.

Oblivious of objections to launching a military campaign just before the onset of winter, Hitler resolved to commence the campaign on November 12, 1939. Naturally, he had yet to come up with a plausible immediate motive for propaganda purposes and to justify the venture in the eyes of the public. For one, the move entailed a violation of the neutrality of states such as Belgium, Holland, and Luxembourg, that National Socialist Germany had vowed to respect just as Imperial Germany once had. On the other hand, this was no more a reason to desist for Hitler than it had been for Wilhelm II. In the case of Poland, Hitler had already displayed his ingenuity for coming up with a "propagandistic reason" for unleashing the war, for divining an incident that could be portrayed as an affront sufficiently serious to warrant arousing the public, and to keep it from questioning the true motivation behind this particular military move. However, an incident of border violation like the staged assault on the Gleiwitz radio station was not feasible along the frontier with Holland. Nevertheless, the apprehension of two British secret service agents in the vicinity could be blown up into a sufficiently compromising affair.

When considering such carefully prepared undertakings orchestrated by Hitler and his assistants, it is imperative to keep in mind that any such incident was intended only secondarily as a justification of Germany's aggression abroad, and primarily to rouse the public inside the Reich. Most of its citizens had vivid recollections of the First World War and were understandably reluctant to have those governing them embark on such risky forays as an attack in the west. There was widespread fear of another Verdun and renewed trench-warfare. In Hitler's mind, to overcome this defeatist attitude by the German public, the propaganda experts of the Reich had to provide for an occurrence to outrage it and to set free the Teutonic fury essential to any successful and swift action against any of the countries bordering it. The fact that Holland, Belgium, and Luxembourg served as bases for secret service surveillance of Germany came to the aid of the propaganda department's staff.

The attack was scheduled for Sunday, November 12, 1939. Once more Hitler displayed his preference for a weekend to launch a military strike, a habit discernible in many other instances as well. A provocative act to justify the invasion of Holland had to have taken place by this date. On November 7, because of bad weather, the date had to be postponed for three days.

On November 8, 1939, a mysterious attempt on Hitler's life ended with the explosion of a bomb in the Bürgerbräukeller in Munich, immediately after his delivery of the annual commemorative speech there. In fact, Hitler escaped injury only by departing for the train station earlier than scheduled. To this day, the particulars of this event are not fully understood. The next day witnessed the staging of a more carefully prepared incident, involving English spies at the Dutch border. It had initially been intended to rouse public opinion in Germany, a goal it failed to achieve. An SS *Kommando* abducted two British secret service agents in Holland and brought them across the border in the vicinity of Venlo. The press in Germany tried to establish a connection between the explosion in Munich and the apprehension of the secret agents, which had allegedly occurred on German territory. The general public in Germany, however, did not judge this a plausible link and largely ignored the latter incident.

Far more likely seemed the explanation current in the foreign press: that the kidnapping was a coup staged by Hitler to procure an excuse for aggressive action against the Netherlands. Conspicuous troop movements had been under way on the three days before November 8, and these on such a scale that even uninterested passers-by had to notice that something out of the ordinary was going on. As a precautionary measure, the Dutch flooded the channels and streets on their side of the border.

Under these circumstances, Hitler considered it wise to delay the attack. Orders were rescinded, at first temporarily and then for a lengthier period as the season changed. A winter set in the like of which had not been seen in these latitudes for over a decade. Already in December, thermometer readings recorded minus twenty degrees Celsius and below. In the military compounds, vehicles refused to start. Against this background, even Hitler had to admit it would be rash to engage in any type of new military confrontation at this point.

Another factor that contributed to the considerable delay of the offensive in the West was the outbreak of the Russo-Finnish War on November 28, 1939. Hitler refused to render the Finns any type of assistance and even denied them moral support. Too many times in the past Finland had gravely affronted his regime and had even rebuffed an offer to enter into a mutual non-aggression pact with Germany. On December 7, 1939, the *Völkischer Beobachter* published an article, "Germany and the Finnish Question," in which Hitler reprimanded Finland for its pro-British stance and the anti-German sentiments it frequently expressed. In connection with this, he quoted an old German saying: "As one shouts into the forest, so it echoes back."

This first year of the war closed on a relatively quiet note. The front in the east remained calm and the so-called Phony War (*Sitzktieg*) in the west continued uneventfully throughout the winter months. At sea and in the air, too, both sides remained tentative and avoided engagement for the time being.

THE YEAR 1940
Major Events in Summary

Hitler entertained many ambitious designs in 1940. For one, he stood determined to defeat the Anglo-French field army in the west and thereby to chase the English "back to the Thames." Second, he envisioned taking possession of the Netherlands, Belgium, and northern France to establish operational bases for the navy and the *Luftwaffe*: they would pursue the "economic warfare" that would overcome England. Third, by taking possession of Norway and Denmark, he would expand his "economic warfare" from their coasts. The government in London would undoubtedly perceive the necessity of extending its hand in friendship to Germany once England had been forced to retreat from the continent, German submarines attacked British vessels, and the *Luftwaffe's* raids penetrated the British coastal waters and the mainland. From Hitler's point of view, these arguments made perfect sense. From the standpoint of Britain, however, none of these considerations could induce it to give up its firm stance in opposition to Germany. The United Kingdom was not about to lower its flag at the mere sight of Hitler, no more than it had been willing to do so when Napoleon's specter arose on the continent.

Nevertheless, Chamberlain's insistence that Hitler had "missed the bus" proved premature; for the time being, everything went according to plan for the Führer. The Third Reich was able to launch its surprise invasion of Denmark and Norway on April 9. Denmark was forced to surrender within hours of the attack. The strike was less successful against Norway. The Norwegians mounted an unexpectedly strong opposition to the invading troops along the coastline. This inflicted heavy loss upon the German naval units in particular, a development compounded by the unanticipated intervention of the Royal Air Force and the British navy. A relatively small Anglo-French expeditionary force furthermore interfered with the operations of the German troops. Nevertheless, within eight weeks, the overwhelming might of the German troops eliminated active resistance.

In Germany, the undeniably audacious move against Denmark and Norway was hailed as an unparalleled masterpiece of Hitler's military strategy. Assuredly, he had proved himself a master in conquering smaller states. Already in the Sudeten crisis of 1938, he had boasted that the conflict had pitted "75 million Germans against 7 million Czechs." He pointed to a Germany of "90 million" as having conquered 25 million Poles within little more than one month's time. In a similarly glorious military feat, the Third Reich's numerical superiority brought success in the subjugation of Denmark with its population of 3.7 million and of Norway with its 2.9 million inhabitants. The victories attained proved deceptive ones in the end. They tied down the *Wehrmacht* and hence worked more to the advantage of Great Britain than to that of Germany. The German forces stationed in these areas could not actively participate in the overall war effort. The swift nature of the conquest brought no advantage, as the subsequently necessary occupation of the vanquished territories cost Germany enormous forces. Naval vessels carrying supplies could reach the areas only with difficulty and the re-supplying operations imposed a heavy toll upon the military.

Denmark and Norway were not destined to be the last entries in the roll call of countries Hitler assaulted without any declaration of war. On May 10, the 300,000 inhabitants of Luxembourg, who possessed virtually no military defenses to speak of, became the next to fall victim to his insatiable lust for power, along with the peoples of Belgium and the Netherlands. The 8.4 million strong population of the Netherlands capitulated on May 15. Resistance among the 8.3 million Belgian nationals collapsed by May 28.

In northern France, military operations also went precisely in accordance with Hitler's plans. Once more, a crucial role was played by the strategically located city of Sedan, which had already gained prominence in the Franco-Prussian War of 1870–71. At the time, Bismarck had masterminded the invasion of France, carefully avoiding any violation of Belgium's territorial integrity. Undoubtedly, a repetition of this approach would have been possible in 1940, had the German military received like instructions. As in 1870, France stood isolated and would have had to face Germany largely by itself while Germany was not yet tied down along two fronts as it had been in the First World War. By 1940, as a final consideration, Germany claimed a population nearly twice that of France, and its soldiers were correspondingly more numerous. Given the circumstances, France was bound to collapse if the United Kingdom and the United States failed to come to its rescue.

By May 13, German Panzer armies achieved a breakthrough at Sedan and by May 20, they reached the English Channel. The Anglo-French field army stood isolated. German troops turned to the north to completely cut off the enemy forces. They could easily have dealt a deadly blow to the forces thus encircled. However, Hitler ordered the tanks to halt in order to allow the British divisions to use the gateway of Dunkirk to flee to England just across the channel. While the majority of their equipment had to be left behind, the English were extraordinarily fortunate to escape with their lives. This magnanimous behavior of Hitler's was to demonstrate that he desired no military confrontation with Great Britain and once more was extending his hand to the British in a gesture of genuine friendship. This notwithstanding, caution ought to be exercised in the assessment of this event. Even had the *Wehrmacht* eliminated the British expeditionary force at Dunkirk, this would have meant that His Majesty's armed forces would ultimately have had a few divisions less at their disposal and one to two hundred thousand English soldiers would have languished as prisoners of war in Germany. The outcome of such a scenario would have had a negligible influence upon the future military confrontation on a larger scale. The English escape was of no decisive importance to the outcome of the war. In this sense, it constituted a historic parallel to the 1914 Battle of the Marne; even the remarkable victory scored then by the Imperial troops failed to prevent Germany's ignominious defeat in the First World War. The 1940 campaign in the West was equivalent to a new Battle of the Marne, and its ringing successes no more determined the outcome of the Second World War than the Battle of the Marne prevented ultimate defeat in 1918.

Had the British expeditionary force been annihilated in 1940, had the British Isles been occupied, then, just as Churchill had foretold on November 12, 1939, the United States would have taken up the struggle. Germany would have been laid low, perhaps somewhat later, but inevitably all the same. The occupation of Luxembourg, Belgium, the Netherlands, and northern France signaled the end of the first phase of the war, the successful implementation of "Case Yellow." On June 5, Hitler issued a proclamation that announced that the "greatest battle of all time" had assured Germany's victory. To his great chagrin, the English whom he had just driven "back to the Thames" failed to realize this and refused him the well-deserved capitulation offer. Uncertain of how to proceed, he resolved to punish them indirectly by occupying all of France. Thereby he secured France's Atlantic coast for Germany for future operations against Great Britain. Faced by German troops stationed as far south as the Spanish border, the English would assuredly acknowledge the futility of further resistance and reconcile themselves to Hitler's undisputed reign. Then they would no longer rudely rebuke his peace proposals, but gladly accept these from the hand of the man who ruled virtually the entire continent.

Dawn on June 5 witnessed German troop advances across the Somme and Aisne Rivers in the south and the southwest. These moves heralded the implementation of "Case Red," the actual battle for France. It was not until five days later, on June 10, with the collapse of France imminent, that Hitler allowed the impatient Mussolini to enter the war. The German dictator was not about "to share the victory with anyone." Had Berlin allowed Rome to declare war on the Western powers at an earlier date, this might have created the impression that Italy's entry into the war had contributed substantially to the fall of France.

The German full-scale assault upon the Maginot Line began on June 14, and on this same day, Paris fell into the hands of the aggressor. German troops were crossing the Rhine at Colmar by June 16. One day later, the French government requested an armistice. In the cease fire agreement, Hitler "generously" granted France an unoccupied zone in the south and the southeast. However, the *Wehrmacht* laid claim to the entire Atlantic coastline. German troops occupied northern France as well as the capital city of Paris.

In view of these recent developments, Hitler speculated that he needed just one effective speech to sway the British to seriously consider a peace settlement with Germany. Graciously he extended yet another "generous peace proposal" to England, although he had earlier designated the overture on October 6, 1939 as absolutely the Reich's last offer. In fact, the renewed "peace proposal"—detailed in Hitler's speech before the Reichstag on July 19, 1940—surpassed that of a year earlier in its grotesqueness. At the time, he had audaciously instructed the British to end their involvement in the conflict, as the country at stake in the war no longer existed. By 1940, he had resolved to "appeal to England's reason" to accept the fact that a continuation of the war had become senseless in view of the capitulation of France, Luxembourg, Belgium, the Netherlands, Denmark, and Norway. For his part, Hitler declared: "I see no reason compelling us to pursue this fight." He thought the Axis destined to "infuse new life into Europe." Hitler was at his wits' end when Churchill, "one of the most pitiful glory-seeking vandals in world history," failed to respond in the desired fashion to the rhetoric the Führer had so carefully employed in his speech before the Reichstag.

On July 16, three days before delivering the speech, Hitler had issued a directive for the implementation of "Operation Sea Lion," i.e., the military invasion of the British Isles. Naturally, this was merely a precautionary measure intended primarily to serve as an additional trump card in the unlikely event that Britain felt it had not yet sustained sufficient "blows" to warrant capitulation. Realistically, Hitler no more believed in the feasibility of a like undertaking than Napoleon had as he waited for the response of the English to reach him at Boulogne in 1805. Beyond this, the possibility of a future alliance with Great Britain was indispensable to Hitler's 1919 conceptions. Hence, it was imperative not to anger the British too readily.

Nevertheless, as the British statesmen persistently refused to toe the line, Hitler determined to frighten them into acquiescence. Relying once again upon his fabled powers of oratory, he resolved to severely admonish them at yet another "public speaking engagement" (*Volkskundgebung*). He chose his annual address to the War Winter Relief Organization on September 4 as the setting for this verbal onslaught. There, he threatened Britain with heavy aerial bombardment and even his own appearance on the Isles should the English persevere further.

Actual heavy bombardment notwithstanding, the terror that rained from the skies upon British cities failed to produce the results desired. The "Battle of Britain" (*Luftschlacht um England*) in fact proved a fiasco for Germany's foreign policy. Instead of weakening the English public's support of His Majesty's government, the terror strikes merely reinforced the determination of the English to persist in the struggle. To add insult to injury, the British antiaircraft defenses and the Royal Air Force's fighters, which Hitler had mocked so often, proved more than a match for the *Luftwaffe* squadrons, upon which they inflicted heavy losses. Even a headquarters report by the *Wehrmacht* on September 16 had to concede that the British had downed forty-three German fighter planes on that day alone. The "war in the air" was a debacle of untold proportions both militarily and politically speaking. Soon German planes no longer dared to attack London during daylight hours. As a result, German aerial attacks had to be restricted to nighttime sorties. Infuriated by the "cruel, wanton, indiscriminate bombings of London" in the dark of the night, Churchill announced retaliatory measures.

Faced by such determination on the part of the British, Hitler began a desperate search for allies in his struggle against England. On September 21, the conclusion of a triple alliance comprising Germany, Italy, and Japan was made public. This in turn was to demonstrate to the English that should they refuse to desist from their military engagement in Europe, the Empire's colonial possessions in the Far East might well fall victim to Japanese expansionism. Threats like this stood in striking contrast to Hitler's promise in August 1939 that he would protect England from the Japanese. This so-called Tripartite Pact was also intended to deter the United States from contemplating intervention in the war on behalf of Great Britain. The pact completely failed of its purpose in this respect. Neither America nor England was in the least impressed by this latest political move, while the Soviet Union cast a suspicious eye on this resurrection of the basic structures of the Anti-Comintern Pact of earlier days.

In October, Hitler went on trips to court additional allies in Europe. Two potential candidates were Spain and the French government at Vichy, and separate meetings were arranged, one with Franco at Hendaye and another with Marshal Pétain at Montoire. Neither bore fruit; Hitler's oratorical gift could not sway Franco and Pétain to abandon their states' non-belligerency.

The autumn of 1940 was replete with misfortune upon misfortune for Hitler. To compound the dilemma, his friend Mussolini resolved to strike out daringly on his own and failed to consult his master Hitler before Italy's invasion of Greece. Moreover, the Duce's timing, just before the onset of winter, was most unfortunate for both Rome and Berlin.

In the meantime, Hitler had reflected upon the cause of his persistent failure with the British. They refused his hand extended in friendship time and time again, in spite of the *Wehrmacht*'s driving them "back to the Thames" and Germany's annihilation of Britain's allies Poland, France, and a series of smaller neutral states. Hitler simply could not comprehend why the British treated him so inconsiderately in light of the generosity he had once more displayed in magnanimously allowing for the escape of the British expeditionary force at Dunkirk. No, there had to be another explanation for their insistent refusal to play the role of Germany's ally in Europe that he had assigned them in 1919.

Having arrived at this point in his contemplation, Hitler concluded that all Great Britain was indeed waiting for was the Soviet Union's declaration of war on Germany. However, so he conceived, they were to be quickly disappointed in this hope, because he was inspired to strike out at Russia before it could turn against Germany. This would allow him to conquer the *Lebensraum* in the East essential to Germany's future, in accordance with his thesis of 1919. And in turning against Russia instead of

Great Britain, he would assure the Third Reich of the latter's everlasting gratitude. One must concede to Hitler that the English did their utmost to reinforce this absurd idea in the German chancellor's mind. In nearly every speaking engagement on the topic after September 1939, Churchill had interpreted Russia's behavior with regard to Poland, the Baltic States, etc., as directed against Germany's interests. Supposedly, the Soviet Union was laboring to erect a line of fortification to thwart Germany's expansionist designs in the east. For the English it was only natural to seek to deflect Hitler's fury toward the east, away from their island—a similar strategy had proved its worth already in Napoleon's day. This feat could be easily accomplished once more, as the influential circles in England were only too well aware of Hitler's distorted understanding of world politics and they had known the theses expounded in *Mein Kampf* for a long time. It is, however, more than remarkable that Hitler should start his campaign against Russia in 1941 on exactly the same day as Napoleon did in 1812: on June 22.

Before directly confronting Russia, Hitler launched one last effort to induce the Soviets to share in the "spoils" of the British Empire—perhaps in the Middle East, with a drive toward the Persian Gulf or India. Should the Russians really fall for this trick, then he could graciously turn to England to offer the Third Reich's protection against the Bolshevist onslaught. On a visit to Berlin in November of the previous year, Molotov had listened to Hitler's rambling without batting an eye. Once Hitler had ended, Molotov had immediately returned to the topic of the pending difficulties in the German-Soviet relationship: the question of Finland and the Baltic States, and also the Balkans where Germany apparently intended to gain a permanent foothold. Hitler was indignant. The same day Molotov returned to Moscow, Hitler attended a reception at the Japanese Embassy, as if to signal that his indulgence to the Russians had come to an abrupt end. The future in fact would find him back among his former cohorts of the Anti-Comintern Pact.

Hence, the year 1940 drew to a close on a note quite different from what Hitler had anticipated. Granted, the English had been driven "back to the Thames," and the Third Reich's sphere of influence extended all the way from the North Cape to the Pyrenees. These outward successes were deceptive, however. Hitler felt the British had outmaneuvered him. This suspicion was a well-founded one. England neither had come to conclude peace with Germany nor was the prospect of friendship with England any closer than it had been at the beginning of the year. As always when Hitler was disconcerted or unsure of how to proceed, he resolved to adhere all the more fervently to the ideas he had formed in 1919, as if his unshakable willpower alone sufficed to change magically the course of events. If the dream of conquering new *Lebensraum* in the East came true, why should the friendship of England further elude him? In this context, for Germany, there was and would be "but one ally in Europe: England."

THE YEAR 1941
Major Events in Summary

"The year 1941 will bring about the completion of the greatest victory in our history," declared Hitler in his New Year's order to the *Wehrmacht*. Twelve months ago, on the occasion of the new year, he had said: "May 1940 be decisive!" What were the German *Wehrmacht* and the German people supposed to understand as the completion "of the greatest victory"? Earlier, "the greatest victory" was the defeat of France. At any rate, on June 24, 1940, Hitler announced "the most glorious victory of all times."

If the greatest victory was still to be completed, it should have implied the defeat of England. But Hitler implied something different: specifically, the defeat of Russia! In this way, England would automatically become ready for peace and friendship. Hitler remained almost alone with this theory. There was not a single more or less sensible person to be found in the whole country that would, in that situation in Germany and in the middle of the war against England, have wished to have any military disagreements with the Soviet Union, and would have supported it or at least considered it a necessary evil. Even the members of the party, who had been fed for years with anti-Bolshevik and anti-Russian slogans, knew that a war against Russia would by no means improve Germany's prospects for victory but would most probably make them worse as a result of opening a new front. They considered Hitler's German-Russian settlement of 1939 as a deed of genius, and they based their new plans for victory on it. On September 9, 1939, Göring had confirmed them in these convictions. It is known that military men had been dreaming of German-Russian cooperation since World War I. There were close and friendly relationships between the army of the Reich and the Red army. Many German high-ranking officers had acquired their knowledge of modern weapons in Russian military schools and training grounds.

If Hitler's generals fulfilled Hitler's orders and without any special objections prepared the plans of the Russian campaign, they weren't doing it sincerely; on the contrary, they hoped that it would be another of Hitler's tricks, like Operations Sealion and Felix, with the aim of undertaking a distracting maneuver to disguise other plans. Of all the reasons that Hitler set forth in favor of war against Russia, the generals accepted only one argument: something must be done to engage the German army, because an army that has nothing to do is subject to demoralization, as happened to the "Blue Jackets" in 1918.

On December 27, 1940, Raeder expressed "quite great doubts" concerning the campaign against Russia before the defeat of England. On another occasion, Göring had tried in vain to talk Hitler out of that undertaking, quoting Hitler's own words regarding the dangers of a major second front. Ribbentrop, who had been imbued with sympathy toward the Russians after his visit to Moscow, met them like "old party comrades" and might have wished anything but war against Russia. Hess, who had known Hitler for decades and was able better than anyone else to trace the course of his decline, was determined to disappear from Germany before the campaign against Russia started. Halder, chief of Hitler's general staff, who was to work out the plan of hostilities against Russia, said after World War II that he had considered that project insanity. Wherever one looked in Germany, Hitler's idea of the campaign against Russia was faced disconcertedly and coldly by everyone, except one, and only one, man: Herr von Papen! Hitler's statements about Bolshevik dangers impressed him as much as they had in 1933.

Von Papen, for his part, tried to support Hitler in his attitude against Russia, presenting as dangerous every concession in the Bulgaria-Turkey case, and told him in the middle of November 1940:

> After all, didn't we determine on January 30, 1933, to protect Germany and thus the whole of Europe from Bolshevism?

These words certainly served Hitler's purpose. They confirmed the effectiveness of his old trick about the Bolshevik danger. If it was still possible to impress that idea upon von Papen, a representative of the rigid, conservative, aristocratic stratum of Germany, then it should certainly impress similarly rigid Englishmen. They too would start worshipping him if he attacked

Bolshevik Russia, as once did von Papen, Hindenburg, Hugenberg, and others, when he exterminated the German Communists. The savior and master of Germany will rise to become the savior and master of the whole of Europe and the whole world!

Von Papen fully shared Hitler's idea that war against Russia was the best means of achieving peace and friendship with England. When on June 22, 1941, the German army launched its attack against Russia, von Papen attempted, through intermediaries, to influence the British ambassador in Ankara, proposing "to bury the European discords and to confront jointly the power whose program is the extermination of the West."

Von Papen, just like Hitler, could hardly grasp that the English were absolutely immune to the horrors of Bolshevism, and that on June 22, 1941, Churchill would declare: "We have but one aim and one single, irrevocable purpose. We are resolved to destroy Hitler and every vestige of the Nazi regime. From this nothing will turn us—nothing."

Such was the situation in which Hitler found himself after September 3, 1939, at 11 o'clock, and that would not change at all up to his death on April 30, 1945, even if he had used every possible evasion.

It is therefore out of place to ask whether Hitler's fate might have taken a different turn if he had not attacked Russia, if he had defeated her, or if he had induced Russia to join in Germany's campaign against England. In each of these three cases, Hitler's fate would have been the same, though—at any rate, the war would certainly have lasted longer. But Hitler would never have managed to resist for long the joint pressure of the Anglo–American world, even if he had been able to rely not only on Russia's friendly assistance but also on her active military support. His end had been predestined since September 3, 1939, and he could but slow it down or speed it up. In addition, he obviously speeded it up when he decided to attack Russia.

His decision can be considered incomprehensible, taking into account all the historically well-known defeats suffered by Charles XII and Napoleon I, taking into account the war that had become fateful for Germany on its two fronts in World War I, a policy that had been willfully renewed by Hitler. That decision of his is explained by Germany's centuries-old urge to push east for conquest and expansion. One may point out that Hitler, like Napoleon, also failed to deal with the British navy, that, throughout the whole war history of Germany, the Germans had hardly ever prepared for and even more rarely risked an attempt at naval operations, and, finally, that the campaign against Russia seemed both to Napoleon and to Hitler, with their purely continental, one-sided military thinking, to be an easy undertaking, a convenient plundering raid that would free them from the obligation to admit their weakness in respect to England.

All those factors doubtlessly played a certain role in generating Hitler's Russian adventures. But one should not forget one absolutely decisive circumstance: Hitler had become a prisoner of his own thesis of 1919 that declared: Conquest of new territories in the east—that means war against Russia, and, to that purpose, friendship with England and Italy, Germany's alleged allies in her push to the east.

Hitler managed to arrange and maintain friendship with Italy, in spite of some difficulties. However, he failed to become friendly with England. What else could he do, except to implement his third thesis, war against Russia, in order to realize miraculously, as a sort of reward, the second thesis, friendship with England? Indeed, Hitler felt rather uneasy about his Russian campaign. All the doubts expressed by his subordinates—two fronts, the unsolved problem of England, the United States, Napoleon's fate, a vast territory that would be hard to keep under control even in case of success—all these questions worried him as well, and after the war against Russia had begun, he said: "Every such step opens a door behind which a mystery lies hidden, and only posterity knows exactly how it came about and what happened."

During a long and hard winter, Hitler was almost constantly engaged in preparation for Operation Barbarossa that could not remain hidden from the German public. There were not only the great transfer of the troops to East Prussia, to the General-Government of Poland, and Slovakia, the constant training of reservists, and so on, but also the formation of numerous motorized columns that moved all over Germany and turned even small towns and villages into garrisons and sources of supply. What was the destination of these columns that were being equipped with the help of the entire automobile repair shops of Germany? Clearly not England! The operation was conducted under the acronym STI (probably, the letters stood for *SOW-JETUNION*, Soviet Union). This operation, STI, worried the population more than any other rumor, and the party functionaries themselves did not know what they were to say. Was it possible that Hitler was planning so mad an undertaking as an invasion of Russia? Finally, an explanation was found that, later on, nevertheless turned out to be false. The letters STI must have stood for "Syria, Turkey, Iraq," so it meant a relatively harmless, bloodless operation for eliminating English influence in the Near East!

The party leaders took ever further steps to calm down not only the people, but also themselves. They would declare quite seriously that Russia was going soon, of her own good will, to cede the Ukraine to Germany. Realizing that Russia had too much land and Germany had too little, Russia, as a token of German-Russian friendship, proclaimed herself ready for the step, that might be compensated later and elsewhere from British colonial properties. These ideas may seem funny or unbelievable today, but at that time they were expressed with a confident tone and showed the confusion reigning in party circles. Little Switzerland might just as well have demanded from the great Reich to cede, for instance, a significant part of its territory.

Before Hitler could start his Operation Barbarossa, he had to clean up the Balkans and liquidate his friend Mussolini's Greek adventure. At the end of February, he made King Boris give his consent to German entry into Bulgaria, and on March 1, Boris managed to join the Tripartite Pact. On March 25, in Vienna, representatives of the Yugoslav government signed the Pact. However, Hitler was not destined to rejoice for long over it. On March 27, the Zvetkovitch government was overthrown. The young King Peter replaced Prince Regent Paul.

Hitler understood at once what that revolt meant and decided instantly to crush Yugoslavia. On April 6, German troops attacked Yugoslavia and Greece without warning; German aircraft bombarded Belgrade. This campaign in the Balkans lasted only a few weeks. On May 4, Hitler could once more declare victory in front of the Reichstag. On May 10, Hess secretly fled to England and Hitler made a controversial announcement about that embarrassing incident. On May 20, Hitler launched an exceedingly pointless attack on the island of Crete with airborne divisions. The operation lasted until June 1 and resulted in disproportionately heavy losses. On May 27, the English sank the German battleship *Bismarck,* which had ventured to attack British naval forces in the Atlantic Ocean. Early in June, a revolt in Iraq supported by Germany collapsed, and once again, the English became masters of the situation more than ever. In the meantime, American troops occupied Greenland.

Everything began on June 22: a powerful attack extending from the Arctic Ocean to the Black Sea. It was the same date on which Napoleon had attacked Russia, though Hitler had not the slightest idea of that fact. He chose the day because it was Sunday, and the attack could advance with particular suddenness. A few weeks later, it already became clear that Hitler's prognoses about the nature and duration of the war had been wrong. In spite of the brutality of the combat operations, the armies failed to deal with the "primitive" Russians. Even though hundreds of thousands of prisoners were taken and vast territories were captured, it did not help achieve the cherished goal—to conquer Leningrad or Moscow. In the Ukraine and the Crimea, they also advanced more slowly than had been envisaged. August came, then September, yet no capitulation of Russia presented itself. Gradually Hitler found himself in the situation he had had with England, and, in the end, he had to insist that the war against Russia was won, although the facts clearly proclaimed the opposite.

On October 3, in a speech in Berlin, he said: "I am saying this today because I can say today that the enemy is already broken and shall never rise again." A day before, in spite of the onset of a cold spell, Hitler had given orders to start a new offensive toward Moscow, "the last, great blow" which was to destroy the enemy before winter set in.

But November came, then December, and the German troops had not yet conquered Moscow. On the contrary, the Russians started an offensive from Moscow and threw the exhausted and frozen Germans back to the west. On the Black Sea, too, the Russian troops started an offensive towards Taganrog.

On the night of December 8, Hitler sat worried in his armchair when he received the news of the Japanese air raid upon Pearl Harbor. He jumped up as if electrified and decided that it was a turning point of destiny. He urgently convened a meeting of the Reichstag, and, on December 11, passports were handed to the American envoy "in accordance with the terms of the Tripartite Pact." It was the only formal declaration of war by Hitler, and it was meant particularly for the United States of America.

So ended the year 1941—which, according to Hitler's words, was to bring "the completion of the greatest victory in German history"—with a catastrophic situation in the political and military spheres. Germany found herself in a state of war against nearly everyone, at least against the most powerful states of the world. Her military forces were dispersed and scattered over a vast territory.

Of course, now it was necessary to find a scapegoat on whom to blame all Hitler's failures and it was the commander in chief of the army, Field Marshal von Brauchitsch. Hitler dismissed him on December 19 on the ground of a "heart condition," and took up the duties of commander in chief of the army himself. As during every other crisis of the past—the SA disorders crisis of 1930, the Strasser crisis of 1932, the Blomberg crisis of 1938—Hitler used this opportunity to strengthen his full power. At last, he could be in command of his troops alone. He had been angry with von Brauchitsch when the latter, in the course of the western campaigns, gave orders to some divisions that differed from what the supreme commander in chief had wished. He did not want any advisers or critics: nobody who would understand things better than he would! It was not by chance that he had said:

> I have no experts! My own head is always quite enough for me! I don't need any brain trust to support me!"

THE YEAR 1942
Major Events in Summary

On New Year's Day, Hitler was more cautious in making a forecast for the year 1942 than in previous years. Two years ago, he proclaimed: "May the year 1940 bring us the decision." Then, he had prophesied: "The year 1941 will bring about the completion of the greatest victory in our history." Now, he modestly turned to the Almighty: "Let us ask the Lord to allow the year 1942 to bring a decision for the salvation of our Volk and the allied nations." For the time being, Hitler wanted to obtain a stabilization of the situation on the eastern front. Russia was on the offensive there, especially in the central sector, where it had forced German troops back by up to a hundred kilometers. In retrospect, many commentators have praised Hitler's genius for preventing a complete debacle there at this time. In particular, the Führer himself was greatly impressed by the ingenuity of his policy and believed that he had outdone Napoleon in this respect.

However, a comparison of the situation faced by Napoleon's *Grande Armée* of 1812 with that of the German armies in the winter of 1941–1942 is out of place. There was little similarity, aside from its having been cold in Russia in both instances. Napoleon's *Grande Armée* was marching in a long column, moving rapidly from east to west in order to reach its supply bases at Smolensk and Vilnius. At times, this army on the march was threatened on its flanks by Russian attacks and, as at the Berezina River, its retreat was hindered by natural barriers.

By contrast, the German troops in 1941–1942 formed a more or less connected front from north to south. The more they retreated westward, the shorter their supply lines became, while the Russians, in pursuing them, extended *their* lines of supply farther and farther. At this point, they were not yet able to transform their victories into larger envelopments. Their military potential was still partly in the developmental stage. The battle-hardened

German troops, however, clung to their positions, irrespective of losses, in accordance with Hitler's orders. Only when necessary did they retreat, one step at a time. To regard Hitler's tactics as ingenious is truly inappropriate. It cost the lives of hundreds of thousands of German soldiers, who fell or froze to death. And what did this achieve? The collapse of the Third Reich was postponed for the time being, but the war was nonetheless lost. In the course of the next three years, millions of German soldiers would either perish or fall into an arduous captivity.

Ruthlessness in sacrificing hundreds of thousands of their own men was one characteristic shared by the warlords of the two Russian campaigns (in 1812 and 1941); moreover, both Napoleon and Hitler paid heed only to their personal safety and comfort. Hitler's offensive plans for 1942 remained limited in nature. He realized that he would never again be able to risk a push for Moscow, no more than he would be able to threaten England with a landing, as he had in 1940. On the other hand, he believed that a push in the direction of Stalingrad in southern Russia was still possible, as well as one in the direction of the oil fields at Maikop and Grozny and the Caucasus. He planned to pierce southern Russia in order to reach Turkey. This would secure his right flank and enable him to pose a threat to Iran. Perhaps this would then move the English to consider peace.

In the north, he planned a personal visit to Finland, where he would urge Marshal Mannerheim to move more energetically against Leningrad, that would finally make a linking up with the Finns possible on land. In the Mediterranean, Hitler wanted to paralyze Malta but not to conquer it. He would allow Rommel to drive the British back to Egypt but not to treat them too harshly, as Hitler did not wish to alienate his future "allies" too much.

From a political point of view, Hitler placed great stock in threatening a massacre of the Jews. His forecasts on the imminent collapse of England and Russia had not come true. Who was to blame for this? Surely not he, because his theories of 1919 were right after all! No, the Jews were to blame! Their secret Jewish world government had apparently backed England and Russia. It had not allowed these states to collapse.

In Hitler's opinion, this left only one alternative: to threaten the annihilation of all Jews within the German sphere of influence. This would scare the secret Jewish world government so much that it would urge the governments in London, Washington, and Moscow to acquiesce to Hitler's demands in order to save a few million Jews.

The threatened massacre of the Jews was the last trump card that Hitler believed he held. On January 30, 1941, he had already alluded to it. On January 30, 1942, he made additional massive threats. His gamble was completely utopian, since the secret Jewish world government existed only in the minds of Adolf Hitler, Erich and Mathilde Ludendorff, Julius Streicher, and other similarly profound "philosophers." The Jews simply had no influence on the political and military decisions of importance made in England, America, and Russia.

If the leaders of these states would regret that Hitler killed the several million Jews at his mercy, they were nevertheless unwilling to change their stance on the elimination of Hitler's regime because of the Jews. Churchill made this clear on June 22, 1941:

> We are resolved to destroy Hitler and every vestige of the Nazi regime. From this nothing will turn us—nothing.

Nothing! Not even the threatened massacre of the Jews!

However, Hitler did not believe the "senile" English. Therefore, in the year 1942, he felt compelled to go ahead with his monstrous threat. He had millions of Jews—men, women, children, and the elderly— killed, shot, massacred, gassed in the extermination chambers. Nevertheless, he was still unable to profit politically from this unprecedented crime.

In the military field, Hitler also suffered defeat after defeat in the last quarter of 1942. On the night of October 23, the British Eighth Army under General Montgomery launched an offensive at El Alamein that ultimately led to the annihilation of the German Africa Corps and the Italian armies. On November 8, American troops under General Eisenhower landed in North Africa and quickly gained possession of Morocco and Algeria. Hitler was forced to send troops to southern France, lest he risk the occupation of this part of Europe by Anglo-American forces. On November 19 and 20, the Russian generals Vatutin, Rokossovski, and Yeremenko launched a large-scale offensive that led to the encirclement of the German Sixth Army at Stalingrad.

While Hitler suffered painful military defeats abroad in the year 1942, he was able to increase his power at home. Having taken over command of the army in December 1941, he concluded that the time had finally come to remove the judges, whom he hated and despised, from their privileged positions and to proclaim himself "supreme law lord." On April 26, 1942, he put through a resolution of the Greater German Reichstag that granted him the right to dismiss from office judges, civil servants, and officers as he saw fit "without being bound by existing regulations."

The year 1942 ended. The "decision" in Germany's favor had not come about, despite Hitler's prophecies. Instead, a number of countries had declared war on Germany, for instance Mexico on May 22, Brazil on August 22, and Ethiopia on December 14. The German *Wehrmacht* had been forced to go on the defensive along all fronts. The struggle in the south of the eastern front and in North Africa had become hopeless. Disastrous strikes by the Royal Air Force continued to rain down on major German cities, and the *Luftwaffe* was unable to prevent this. The oceans were no longer ruled by German U-boats but by the Allied fleets. Such was the situation at the beginning of the New Year.

THE YEAR 1943
Major Events in Summary

Three years earlier, Hitler had declared: "May the year 1940 bring about a decision." Twelve months later, he had still prophesied: "The year 1941 will bring about the completion of the greatest victory in our history." Another twelve months after that, he had still felt that a "decision" was imminent and had asked the Lord for His assistance in bringing it about. At the beginning of 1943, he was more modest in his prophecies. This was not a surprise in view of the catastrophic situation in Stalingrad and North Africa. Hitler stated only that National Socialist Germany was "determined to end this fight with a clear victory."

Following the destruction of the German armies in Stalingrad and Tunis, he hardly felt like launching any new offensive. After a number of delays, however, only Operation Citadel with the goal of Kursk was started on June 5. Because of strong Soviet resistance, the operation had to be called off after only one week. Hitler was content that he managed to maintain the front just as it was in the spring of 1942, at least until the fall of 1943. Although Hitler had failed to secure the oil fields of Maikop and Grozny, he was not about "to liquidate the war." Even though he was on the defensive along all fronts, he still intended to fight down to "the last battalion." At home, too, Hitler was eager to remain in power. Therefore, he declined to summon the Reichstag, which had the legal power to demand his resignation. On two occasions in 1943, Hitler ought to have summoned the Reichstag:

1. The extension of the Reichstag's legislative tenure. While the Reichstag had been elected for a four-year period on April 10, 1938, Hitler manipulated it so that its tenure did not officially begin until January 30, 1939. By January 30, 1943, a further extension of the tenure would have required a Reichstag decision with a two-thirds majority.

2. The extension of the Enabling Act, which expired on May 10, 1943.

Hitler proceeded in complete disregard of the constitution in both cases and, in an arbitrary act, extended both the Reichstag's tenure and the duration of the Enabling Act by himself.

Even the "Resolution of the Greater German Reichstag" of April 26, 1942, which had freed him from observing existing laws on the appointment of personnel, did not give him the right to make such highhanded changes in the constitution, especially where the competence of the Reichstag itself was concerned. However, neither the Reichstag president Göring nor any other Reichstag deputy seemed to be disturbed by this. Nevertheless, Hitler continued to be haunted by his fear of a possible Reichstag meeting. When he heard of the vote of no confidence in Mussolini in late July, he ordered Himmler to make sure that "such possibly surfacing dangers are to be prevented through the strictest measures by the police." This meant that all Reichstag deputies were placed under continuous police surveillance.

Hitler was troubled, not only by the Reichstag, but also by the existence of persons who might be considered his potential successors. There was good reason for his concern. Following the disaster at Stalingrad, Field Marshal von Manstein had publicly stated his intention to recommend that Hitler resign as supreme commander of the *Wehrmacht*. At first, Hitler considered removing von Manstein. However, he did not dare to make a move against him at this time. Instead, he tried to defame all his prospective successors in the military or political sphere: Göring, Schirach, and Rommel. He did so indirectly by measures that tended to humiliate them in public and directly by influencing Goebbels, who was responsible for focusing public opinion.

Hitler slowly began to exclude Göring from the conduct of government affairs as "president of the ministerial council." On September 1, 1939, he had thoughtlessly named the *Reichsmarschall* as his successor, although only in the event of his death. Now Hitler took care of day-to-day business with the help of his complaisant secretaries: Lammers, Keitel, and Bormann. In spite of this, he still felt that Göring was a "dangerous man." As president of the Reichstag, Göring had the power to summon the Reichstag at any time. Therefore, Hitler sought to belittle him in the eyes of the public by blaming him for the "failure" of the *Luftwaffe* that was actually due to the superiority of the Allied air forces.

At one point, Hitler had removed Schirach from Berlin because of his alleged ambitions to succeed him. Even with Schirach in Vienna, Hitler still felt that he represented a threat. He constantly criticized him, claiming that he had "gone soft—Viennese style" (*verwienert*) and had become "unreliable." He tried to "force him aside" by suggesting a diplomatic career and even wanted him put on trial before the People's Court.

In March, Rommel, whose popularity had been a thorn in Hitler's side from the start, was recalled from the front in Africa against his will. Hitler sent him on a vacation in order to create the impression with the soldiers and the public that Rommel had abandoned his troops in Tunis and run to safety. Hitler kept himself busy with such tricks and precautionary measures in 1943 and was indifferent to the military catastrophes in Stalingrad and Tunis. He tried to appear in public as little as possible. Only three times did he speak on public occasions: on Heroes' Memorial Day (March 21), at Lutze's funeral (May 8), and at the commemoration of the Munich Putsch (November 8). There was also one radio broadcast about the collapse of the Italian government on November 10, when Goebbels practically had to force him to go to the microphone. In addition, Hitler delivered addresses before Reichsleiters and Gauleiters in February, May, and October, before industrial leaders in June, and before officer candidates in November.

Undoubtedly, the gravest event of 1943 for Hitler was the collapse of Mussolini and Fascism. His theory of 1919—friendship with England and Italy—broke down completely, even regarding his second ally. Of course, this could not be allowed to happen! Thus, Hitler had Mussolini kidnapped in Italy. He wanted to keep the weak Duce and the body of the Fascist Party alive artificially so that his alliance theory of 1919 would not die.

Overall, the year 1943 was a bleak one for Hitler. Since he wished to remain "steadfast in face of the impossible," he was happy that he managed to hang on. In the meantime, the Allies were taking up the positions whence they would deal the decisive blows against Hitler's Reich in 1944 and 1945. On January 14, Churchill and Roosevelt met in Casablanca to discuss future cooperation with Russia, China, and the representatives of "Free France," de Gaulle and Giraud. At a press conference, after ten days of discussions at "Villa No. 2," they emphasized their call for the "unconditional surrender" of Germany, Italy, and Japan.

After the war, there was a tendency, at least in Germany, to attribute too much importance to the Casablanca Conference. Especially the members of the German resistance movement claimed that the call for Germany's "unconditional surrender" had made it impossible for them to move effectively against Hitler. It is not the purpose of this work to investigate whether the German resistance movement ever had the necessary willpower and the opportunity of moving against Hitler. However, the reference to the Casablanca Conference is in much the same vein as the claim that the outcome of the Munich Conference had prevented action by the German generals against Hitler.

As mentioned earlier, from the point of view of the defeated, any type of surrender is unconditional. It is not the defeated who lays down conditions but the victor who dictates them. If the defeated refuses to accept them, then the fight continues until either he surrenders "unconditionally" or he is destroyed.

Following Germany's capitulation in 1918, the Reich government of the Weimar Republic tolerated the official claim by German Nationalists and the military that the German army had been close to securing the final victory in 1918, when the "November Criminals" had committed treason by signing the armistice agreement without being forced to do so. This belief, which virtually became Germany's state doctrine from 1933 on, caused the western powers to insist on "unconditional surrender" from the start. This meant that at the end of the Second World War, the German *Wehrmacht* would publicly have to declare its defeat and place itself at the mercy of the victor. This decision by the western powers did not come about because of the Casablanca Conference. From the start, the statements by Allied statesmen were clear on this point. On October 3, 1939, before the lower house of Parliament, Chamberlain said the following: "We are not willing to accept from the present German government even the slightest promise."

In a broadcast on October 1, 1939, Churchill declared the following:

> It was for Hitler to say when the war would begin; but it is not for him or for his successors to say when it will end. It began when he wanted it, and it will end only when we are convinced that he has had enough.

In another broadcast on June 22, 1941, Churchill stated the following:

But now I have to declare the decision of His Majesty's government—and I feel sure it is a decision in which the great dominions will, eventually, concur—for we must speak out now at once, without a day's delay. I have to make the declaration, but can you doubt what our policy will be? We have but one aim and one single irrevocable purpose. We are resolved to destroy Hitler and every trace of the Nazi regime. From this nothing will turn us away—nothing. We will never parley; we will never negotiate with Hitler or any of his gang. We shall fight him by land, we shall fight him by sea, we shall fight him in the air, until with God's help we have rid the earth of his shadow and liberated the peoples from his yoke. Any man or state who fights against Nazidom will have our aid. Any man or state who marches with Hitler is our foe.

On December 11, 1941, President Roosevelt sent the United States Congress the following message:

The long-known and the long-expected has thus taken place. The forces endeavoring to enslave the entire world now are moving toward this hemisphere. Never before has there been a greater challenge to life, liberty, and civilization.

On December 8, speaking expressly about Japan but implicitly about Japan's allies, Germany and Italy, President Roosevelt had said to Congress the following:

No matter how long it may take us to overcome this premeditated invasion, the American people in their righteous might will win through to absolute victory.

The call for unconditional surrender was not intended to mean that the victors were unwilling to respect the law or grant the defeated their rights or that they would arbitrarily treat the peoples of Germany, Italy, and Japan afterwards. This was also stated in no uncertain terms at Casablanca. The statement to the press there read as follows:

The President and the Prime Minister, after a complete survey of the world war situation, are more than ever determined that peace can come to the world only by a total elimination of German and Japanese war power. This leads to the simple formulation of war objectives in terms of an unconditional surrender by Germany, Italy and Japan. Unconditional surrender by them means a reasonable assurance of world peace for generations. Unconditional surrender means not the destruction of the German populace, nor of the Italian or Japanese populace, but does mean the destruction of a philosophy in Germany, Italy and Japan that is based on the conquest and subjugation of other peoples.

The other claim, that, before Casablanca, there had never been an "unconditional surrender" in world history cannot be substantiated. There is, for example, Hitler's treatment of the states that he conquered. The occupied territories in Poland and Russia were almost literally raped. They were not granted any life of their own. A completely arbitrary rule was instituted in Norway, Holland, and the Balkans, with the intention of incorporating these areas into the German Reich. In May 1940, it was Hitler who explicitly demanded an "unconditional surrender" by the Belgian king Leopold. Keitel told the French intermediaries who came to the Forest of Compiègne in June 1940 that they had to accept "unconditionally" all German demands and sign the armistice. The call for Germany's and its allies' unconditional surrender only repeated the goals that had been articulated earlier. It was not the only or most decisive outcome of the Casablanca Conference. Far more important was the solidarity demonstrated between the Anglo-American powers and the other states fighting against Germany, the Soviet Union, and Free France.

In reality, the Casablanca conference did not change anything, not even for the Germans. Hitler's conduct of the war was not influenced by it. The German generals behaved no differently after the Casablanca conference than they did before it. The German resistance movement grew more active in 1943 and 1944 and made several ill-fated attempts on Hitler's life, even though the Casablanca conference had supposedly tied their hands. It would be more appropriate for members of the former German resistance movement if they simply admitted that they did not have any single man who dared to oppose Adolf Hitler openly.

In Germany, there were hundreds and thousands of people who had no influence, like the Scholl siblings, and who, nonetheless, were ready to lay down their lives and to help in whatever way possible to free Germany of the tyrant. Many low-ranking officers likewise risked their lives in this cause. However, in Germany's leading circles, there was nobody who was willing to place his life on the line, when he met the Führer face to face.

THE YEAR 1944
Major Events in Summary

Whereas Hitler's prognoses for 1943 had already been more modest than in earlier years, his forecasts for 1944 were downright gloomy. On the one hand, he still proclaimed: "In this struggle of life and death, Germany will win in the end!" On the other hand, he also said: "The year 1944 will make heavy and difficult demands on all Germans. The tremendous developments in the war will reach a crisis point this year. We are completely confident that we will successfully ride it out." Hitler desired to "ride out" the year 1944 "successfully"! It was more like scraping by if possible! In the east, he still had some room for eluding the enemy. However, if a landing in the west succeeded, then the "crisis," that is, Germany's collapse, would be a question of only months. Hitler probably realized this, although he still boasted: "No matter where the plutocratic world will undertake the threatened attempt to land in the west, it will fail!" Hitler charged Rommel with an inspection of the coasts in question along the Atlantic, the North Sea, and the Mediterranean. Since the autumn of 1943, Rommel had constantly been on the go: first in the Balkans, then at the Riviera, later in Denmark and France. In the winter of 1943–1944, the German newsreels often presented Rommel on the screen, inspecting the fortifications of the so-called "Atlantic Wall." His otherwise inscrutable face revealed what he thought: if the Allies really undertook a landing, then all measures would have been in vain.

On November 28, 1942, Rommel had already candidly told Hitler, who was greatly angered by this, that the German weapons were not up to the "effectiveness of the British bombers, tanks, and artillery." On December 20, 1943, Hitler had declared: "From mid-February, early March on, the attack will take place in the west." Since this period passed and nothing happened, Hitler felt that he could take his annual spring vacation at the Berghof. Again, all sorts of representatives from the satellite states had to make an appearance either there or at Klessheim Castle. Hitler enjoyed himself so much that it was not until mid-July that he finally returned to the *Wolfsschanze* headquarters. In the meantime, the war continued: the Germans lost the Crimea in May and were forced to give up Rome on June 4. The Allies landed in northern France on June 6 and gained a foothold there, even though Hitler had prophesied that they should consider themselves fortunate if they managed to stay "on land for nine hours."

Hitler's "V-1" rocket bombs, which targeted the British Isles and later Belgium from mid-June on, and even the improved "V-2", gained no successes. Given the state of the technology at the time, their military significance was negligible. They served as an instrument of terror, but terror, like propaganda, works only against an inferior nation, never against one of equal or superior strength.

On June 22, the third anniversary of Hitler's attack on the Soviet Union, the Russians launched a major offensive along the central sector of the eastern front. Within a few weeks, the entire German Army Group Center, consisting of twenty-five divisions, was destroyed. Romania collapsed in the south of the eastern front, followed by Bulgaria. Brute force kept Hungary in line. Finland laid down its arms in the north. On July 20, a few days after Hitler's return to the *Wolfsschanze* headquarters, an attempt on his life was made. Hitler survived with barely a scratch, while a number of innocent men were killed or seriously injured in the explosion. It furnished Hitler with a pretext for hanging thousands of Germans who were under suspicion anyway, or sending them to concentration camps. He also launched a propaganda campaign on his "miraculous rescue" and "the warning finger of God," that had supposedly become apparent here. But all that could not change the fact that the end was drawing nearer and nearer the closer the Allies came to the borders of the Reich.

By September, the Russians were at the border of East Prussia and the Allies were in front of Aachen (*Aix-la-Chapelle*). While Hitler himself had stated, "if they attack in the west, then this attack will (decide) the war," he was nonetheless not about to capitulate after the Anglo-American landing. After all, he had announced earlier that he intended to "remain steadfast in the face of the impossible" and fight down to the "last battalion" in order to stay alive. He hoped that, by some miracle or through his new "wonder weapons," Providence could still bestow the palm of victory on him, if only he "persisted." He did not yield. Instead, he conscripted a militia of all German men, the *"Volkssturm,"* a type of *"levée en masse,"* the very idea of which he had belittled not that many years before. While speaking before a group of *Kreisleiter* gathered at the Vogelsang Ordensburg, he had expressed the following conviction:

> I do not believe, you know, in this so-called *levée en masse*. I do not believe that by mobilizing their enthusiasm, let us say, you make soldiers.

Now twelve-year old boys and women were being trained for defensive battle. The Germans on the western and eastern borders of the Reich had to dig antitank ditches in order to document the "German will to resist." In order to improve the public's mood in Germany, Hitler launched an offensive in the Ardennes shortly before Christmas. However, the victory reports he presented to the German public at Christmas were rather meager. It was obvious that this injection of courage would hardly outlast the holidays.

THE YEAR 1945
Major Events in Summary

At the beginning of 1945, the world and Germany felt that this year would put an end to Hitler, in one way or another. He had four months left; four months, in which the Allies smashed his Reich piece by piece. A flood of enemy armies swept across Germany. At the end of April, only three islands remained above water: Schleswig-Holstein, Berlin, and the Alps. In the midst of the wrecked capital, Hitler dwelled in the bunker beneath his Reich Chancellery, wanting to remain "steadfast in face of the impossible." For nearly these four months, he managed to delude himself that everything was still as in former times and that he was still the head of state, chief of the government, and chief military commander of a functioning powerful state.

It was true that one heard his voice only twice on the radio: once, when he read his New Year's Proclamation to the German Volk and, second, when he delivered before the microphone on January 30, a commemorative address on the anniversary of the seizure of power. Yet Hitler composed more proclamations in 1945 than he had in the same period of the previous year. As though the situation were completely normal, as though no Russian troops stood at the Oder, and as though no Anglo-American soldiers stood at the Rhine, Hitler issued two proclamations, besides the New Year's Proclamations to the Volk and to the *Wehrmacht*, and he did so even on two commemorations that he had canceled in 1944: the remembrance of the party's foundation on February 24 and Heroes' Memorial Day.

Even when, in March and April, the enemy troops in the west and the east engaged the Germans in a last battle, he issued another proclamation to the soldiers on April 15. He announced: "Berlin will remain German, Vienna will again become German." Incessantly, he sent telegrams and diplomatic greetings to the few statesmen in the satellite states who were still in office; the last one he sent to Mussolini on April 21.

It was not until enemy shells literally exploded on the doorstep of the Reich Chancellery that he realized that the end had irrevocably come. On April 29, he wrote his last proclamation: his political testament.

Even in this last statement, he refused to acknowledge authorship of the unheard-of catastrophe into which he had plunged Germany and the entire world. On the contrary, he continued to claim, as always, that the Jews were guilty of everything, together with the German officers and, yes, even *Reichsmarschall* Göring and *Reichsführer SS* Himmler. The reader searches in vain for an official admission by Hitler of the collapse of his foreign policy and military conceptions. All his theories and ideas with which he had operated since 1919 had been wrong without exception: the idea of the *Lebensraum* in the East that he intended to conquer for the German people; the idea of waging war against Russia while preserving the friendship of England and Italy; his thesis concerning the identity of domestic and foreign policy; the conception of the English as being like senile German Nationalists against whom it was not worth fighting, since they would collapse by themselves; the idea of the primitive Bolshevik Russians, with whom you could deal as with the German Communists, namely by using brute force; his thesis concerning the secret Jewish world government that ruled London, Washington, and Moscow, and that could be intimidated by terrorizing and exterminating the Jews; his theory of unity, according to which the German Volk was invincible as long as it was united, and finally his thesis of perseverance, according to which Providence would give the victory to the man who would never capitulate.

With these ideas, Hitler had for decades thrown dust into the eyes of his followers. Not one of these ideas had turned out to be correct in the end. With each of them, he had suffered catastrophic shipwreck. He now faced an unprecedented expanse of ruins, but still he was not about to admit responsibility, no matter how often he had earlier declared that he wished to "bear the entire responsibility," that he would "vouch with his life" for his actions, and that he would "calmly stand firm" should the Volk one day be dissatisfied with him and wish to execute him.

But when had Hitler ever kept a promise he had made? Coward that he had always been, he now dodged responsibility again. On April 30, 1945, he reached for his pistol to end his life.

> It takes only a fraction of a second, and you are relieved of all that, and you can have some quiet and eternal peace.

Hitler ponders.

III
What Hitler Believed

Adolf Hitler presented his ideas in an unsystematic and non-analytic manner as if they grew out of each particular situation. However, he was clear that, at their root, God inspired his ideas and that they rested on the bedrock of absolute divine certainty. As he spoke, he favored an emotional development of ideas intermixing thoughts and themes so that by constant and incessant repetition, he could make his points without obvious contradiction or logical development.

Neither Christian nor conservative, Hitler maintained that God created Germany and put the Germans into conflict, not with similar competitors, but against a predatory and corrupting evil: an evil whose victory meant the destruction of the human world. The Germans were a Volk, as were the other peoples of Europe and the world. Each Volk had unique qualities that differentiated it from any other Volk. When a Volk recognized and emphasized these qualities, it was successful and prosperous; when a Volk neglected these qualities, it broke up into smaller unsuccessful groups. The blood that is the nexus between members of a Volk is not a simple biological fact but is a spiritual connection that transcends the mere material. Indeed, Hitler used the word, Volksgenossen, to address his fellow Germans: the term has the force of "blood-related comrades in life." True Volksgenossen dealt with each other in a manner Hitler described as Volksgemeinshaft indicating an open, cooperative, selfless family, with loving ways. Such a way of life was possible only if a Volk had sufficient Lebensraum, living area for crops and natural resources. Since there was only so much land in the world, different Volk were in fierce competition with other Volk for favorable lands and those peoples who failed to gain and hold good lands would perish and those who did gain the best lands would survive and prosper. Thus, God made the world and this is good, according to Hitler.

However, Hitler saw a further factor influencing human development: there was a corrupting anti-Volk force, an explicit evil. This force appeared to be people but was not human because they were not a Volk. Rootless, without homeland, sophisticated, worldly, intellectual, this group dealt with money rather than goods, facts and figures rather than people. They corrupted and devoured the blood of the Volk, leaving nothing but soulless wreckage in their wake. Hitler saw this force as the Jew. *God, in his grace, offered mankind a solution to this problem. He found a simple man who would awaken people to the evil that faced them and who would help them eliminate this evil. That man was Adolf Hitler.*

I. *At the core of Hitler's political thought was the conviction that strong unity of purpose could emerge only under a forceful leader backed up by a threat of violence.*

▸ October 22, 1933 The motto "One people, one nation, one will" (a perversion of the old imperial motto, *"ein Reich, ein Volk, ein Gott"*) expressed Hitler's basic objective.

> . . . to which we aspire in our struggle: *ein Volk, ein Reich, ein Wille.*

▸ February 24, 1935 *Hitler asserted that power was the basis of political action. In this speech to the party faithful, Hitler castigated those whom he removed from power. His disgust with democracy was clear. The "party narrative" was an hour-long self-serving narrative of his struggles to gain power. This celebration of the formation of the National Socialist German Workers Party (NSDAP—Nazi Party) was held in the hall of the Munich Hofbräuhaus (beer hall).*

The customary festivities commemorating the birth of the Nazi Party were held on February 24 in the Munich Hofbräuhaus. In a markedly aggressive mood, Hitler went through the ritual of the "party narrative" and then turned his wrath upon his domestic foes:

> I have been a prophet so often in my lifetime, and you have not believed but instead ridiculed and mocked me. Once again I will be a prophet and say to you: you will never return!
> All the dimwits who are counting on a return of the past would have to resolve to take the same path I took. That means that one of the nameless would have to come and take up the same struggle I took up, but with one difference: I conquered democracy with its own madness, but no democrat

can conquer us. I was able to eliminate our opponents when they had all the power and we had nothing; so let me say to you: today we have power, and you have nothing! You will surely not eliminate us.

Hitler held the erroneous opinion that foreign powers, too, would never be able to "eliminate" him. He stated:

> The rest of the world will have to change its views. It will have to erase the fourteen years of German history before us from its memory and put in its place the memory of a thousand-year history prior thereto, and then it will understand that this Volk was without honor for fourteen years thanks to a leadership without honor but was strong and brave and honest the thousand years prior thereto. And it can rest assured that the Germany that is living today is identical with the eternal Germany.
>
> The humiliating interim is over! The nation is united in a yearning for peace and determined to defend German liberty. We want nothing but to coexist with other peoples in mutual respect. We do not wish to threaten the peace of any people. But we will tell the world that anyone who would rob the German Volk of liberty must do so by force, and each and every one of us will defend ourselves against force!
>
> Never will I nor any government after me that is born of the spirit of our Movement affix the nation's signature to a document signifying a voluntary waiver of Germany's honor and equality of rights. Conversely, the world can also rest assured that, when we do sign something, we adhere to it. Whatever we believe we cannot adhere to, on principles of honor or ability, we will never sign. Whatever we have once signed we will blindly and faithfully fulfill!

▸ May 1, 1935 *Hitler saw political power as a force that depended on unity of purpose among the Volk. In many ways, Hitler found Oswald Spengler's ideas attractive but the fact that Spengler rejected National Socialism became a problem. Spengler's book, written in 1919, asserted that human societies form an artistic, intellectual, and social unity that progresses through a predetermined development of growth, maturation, and death. These stages of development Spengler called after the seasons: spring, summer, autumn, and winter. Spengler identified the current age of history as the end of autumn and the beginning of winter. Hitler asserted that the new power of National Socialism cut out the winter phase of Spengler's system and initiated a new springtime for Hitler and Germany. When Hitler arrived for this particular speech, it had snowed, but when he began to speak the sun came out. This he took as a sign of divine favor. This May Day speech was given at Tempelhofer Field to some million and a half people. When Hitler referred to specific dates, he was referring to the dates of important events along his path to power.*

Hitler made use of his speech before the assembled masses to vent his anger at Oswald Spengler and his book *The Decline of the West* (*Der Untergang des Abendlandes*), alleging that these critics had now been proven wrong, for his—Hitler's—success was obvious to all; moreover, his "forging anew" of the German Volk constituted "the greatest feat of this century."

The speech began as follows:

German *Volksgenossen*!

The first of May—in days of yore the German spring holiday. And another first of May—a day of strife and discontent, a day of our Volk being torn asunder into classes. And yet another first of May—the day marking the springtime of the nation! The day of the solidarity of a Volk in its work! A great age has thus dawned once again for Germany. We say this knowing that the greatness of an age lies in the greatness of the tasks assigned to it and thereby to us. Great tasks, such as those vested in only a few generations in history.

Yesterday we were still a powerless Volk, for we were strife-torn, falling out and apart in internal discord, fragmented into hundreds of parties and groups, leagues, and associations, ideologies, and religious institutions—a Reich built upon this fragmented Volk, equally weak and powerless, a mere plaything at the mercy of alien despotism! Small states derided it, small states deprived it of its rights and gagged the people of this Volk. The economy was in the throes of death. Disintegration and ruin at every turn. Every principle had been abandoned. What had once seemed good became bad; what had been detestable was suddenly venerable. What was once meant to and able to give life more meaning was now passed off and perceived to be merely a burden to mankind. One author summed up the impressions of this age in a book that he entitled *The Decline of the West*.

Is this then really the end of our history and hence of our peoples? No! We cannot believe or accept it! It must be called not the "Decline of the West," but the "Resurrection of the Peoples of the Western World"! Only what has become old, rotten, and bad dies. And it should die! But new life will generate. The will shall find the faith. This will lies in leadership, and faith lies in the people!

But all must believe in one thing. He who would tackle this great work of reorganization must begin with the Volk itself. First a new Volk, and with it the new age! Great tasks have always been accomplished only by strong leaders; but even the strongest leadership must fail if it does not have a faithful, inwardly steadfast, and truly strong Volk standing behind it.

It is mankind's misfortune that its leaders forget all too often that ultimate strength does not lie anchored in divisions and regiments or in cannons and tanks; rather, the greatest strength of any leadership lies in the people themselves, in their unanimity, in their inner unity, and in their idealistic faith. That is the power that, in the end, can move the mountains of resistance! But this requires a philosophy that the Volk understands, a philosophy that it comprehends and that it loves. When we first set forth in 1919 as preachers of the National Socialist philosophy, we were a tiny little group of idealists or, as they said, dreamers, the object of ridicule. The critics have been proven wrong today. Some of them might also have striven for what has happened since, but they were incapable of bringing it about; in a historical sense, visible success is ultimately decisive for the correctness of a principle. And this here is documentary proof of this success that no one can forge: one Volk in one Reich!

Everything we have achieved would have been impossible; nothing we did could have been accomplished; there never would have been a January 30th; never a 21st nor a 16th of

March; the external success would never have come about if the German Volk had not gone through an inner transition. The fact that we were able to give the German Volk a new philosophy and to lead it to a new type of life by means of this philosophy is the greatest feat of this century for our Volk. The greatest achievement that will outlive by far everything that can be accomplished in day-to-day work, thanks to this unique achievement.

Hitler then gave himself up to sentimental reflections on the poverty of the Germans compared to the wealth of other peoples, building up to the assurance that no one in the world need fear him. Even if he were given the gift of continents, he would still prefer to be the poorest citizen of the German people. The flowing rhetoric in which this noble message was clothed is as follows:

And this united nation—we need it, for when was a leadership confronted with a more difficult task than our German leadership? Bear in mind, my *Volksgenossen*, what our Germany is, and compare it to other countries. How little we have! 137 people per square kilometer, no colonies, no natural resources, no foreign currency, no capital, no foreign assets left, only heavy burdens, sacrifices, taxes, and low wages. What do we have compared to the wealth of other states, the wealth of other countries, the wealth of other peoples, the wealth of possibilities they have? What do we have? Only one thing: we have our Volk! It is either all, or it is nothing. Our Volk is the only thing on which we can depend. The only thing upon which we can build. Everything we have accomplished to date we owe only to its quality, its capabilities, its loyalty, its decency, its diligence, its sense of order. And when I weigh all of that, then it appears to me to be more than everything the rest of the world has to offer us. And that, I believe, is something we can well impart to other peoples on this first of May: you need not fear we will place demands on you. We are proud enough to confess that the utmost—something you cannot give us—is something we have ourselves: our Volk.

As Führer, I cannot conceive of any task on this earth more marvelous and glorious than to serve this Volk. Were I given the gift of continents, I would still prefer being even the poorest citizen of this Volk. And with this Volk it must and will be possible to accomplish the tasks of the future as well.

At the close of his speech, Hitler proclaimed that the demonstration (i.e., *the sun coming out from the clouds*) was the greatest and most glorious in the world and that his will must be the faith of all.

And thus I ask of you: renew on this day of the greatest and most glorious demonstration in the world your vow to your Volk, to our community and to our National Socialist State. My will—and this must be the vow of each and every one of us—is your faith! To me—as to you—my faith is everything I have in this world!

But the greatest thing God has given me in this world is my Volk!
In it rests my faith. It I serve with my will, and to it I give my life!
May this be our mutual sacred vow on the day of German labor, that so rightfully is the day of the German nation!

To our working German Volk: *Sieg Heil, Sieg Heil, Sieg Heil*!

▶ February 20, 1938 *In this speech to the Reichstag, Hitler delineated the unique quality of his National Socialist government. The reference to February 4 was to the removal of von Neurath as foreign minister and his replacement by von Ribbentrop. Many foreign newspapers saw this as a bad sign and it was.*

One of these accomplishments [of National Socialism] is above all the formation of a leadership of the Volk and State that is as far removed from parliamentary democracy as it is from a military dictatorship. In National Socialism, the Volk has been given the leadership that, as a party, has not only mobilized but also organized the nation, and organized it such that the supremely natural principle of selection would appear to indicate that the continued existence of a secure political leadership is guaranteed. And this is perhaps one of the proudest chapters in the history of the past five years. Contrary to what a petty foreign journalist may believe, National Socialism did not conquer the foreign ministry in Germany on February 4; it has possessed Germany in its entirety since that day I emerged from the building on the Wilhelmsplatz five years ago as Reich chancellor, and possessed it totally and without exception. There is not a single institution in this state which is not National Socialist.

In terms of leadership, the greatest safeguard of the National Socialist Revolution at home and abroad lies in the fact that the National Socialist Party encompasses, in a comprehensive sense, the Reich and all its facilities and institutions. The Reich's protection against the world, on the other hand, lies in the new National Socialist Armed Forces (*Wehrmacht*).

▶ February 24, 1940 *On the twentieth anniversary of the founding of his party, Hitler spoke to the party faithful in the Munich Hofbräuhaus. He asserted that his personal leadership was vital to the success of National Socialism. Part of his litany included the supervisory levels of the party from local to national. He indicated his abhorrence of the former Imperial Chancellor Bethmann-Hollweg, who was not sufficiently aggressive in the early days of the Great War, according to Hitler. The "Spartacist gangs" were the way Hitler referred to the far-left effort to gain power in late 1918 and early 1919. Forces from the right crushed them in January 1919.*

I have often told you: I am nothing other than a magnet that, in constantly passing over the German nation, extracts the steel from within this nation. I have often declared the time would come when everyone who counts himself a man in Germany will stand on my side, as he who does not stand on my side is not worth much anyway. I have termed this process the formation of the historic minority. And it came to pass as I predicted. In the course of thirteen years, a sum of personal energies gathered in the National Socialist Party, from the smallest *Blockwart* or *Zellenwart* to the

Ortsgruppenleiter, the *Kreisleiter*, the *Gauleiter*, the *Reichsstatthalter*, the *Reichsleiter*, and so on. Selection took place in all areas. Enormous energies were mobilized and today are positioned in the appropriate places.

If you find it difficult to grasp the whole picture at first glance, just imagine any old national event of the years 1903 or 1905, let us say 1908, 1910, or 1912. And then look at a similar national celebration today. Let us think of the unveiling of a memorial dedicated to a national hero, let us say Bismarck, or the launching of a ship. The first impression: a sea of top hats—only top hats—no real people anywhere. And today there are real people and no top hats. That is the difference! When I speak to you today, my dear old party comrades, you will say to yourselves: our dear old revolutionary Führer!—Sorry, your head of state. And do not forget how all this would look abroad if a head of state were speaking.

Just as it might have looked twenty or fifteen years ago. Look at the picture today. Today we truly have a German Volk and at its head we see leaders all over today, leaders who issued forth from the people, irrespective of descent. It is truly an immense sum of manly energy and determination that leads the German nation today. It is truly worth something when a nation is so well organized that at each post someone stands who issued forth from the Volk itself. He does not stand there by virtue of name or high birth but only due to his ability as a man of action. And one last point: we have a different Volk today. This Volk has straightened itself up, it has found its way back to itself. It has recovered its self-confidence to an unprecedented degree. It knows nothing is impossible in this world. It knows our history. It knows that in our resolve today we are no less than the great heroes of our past.

The German Volk graduated from a school that, in western Europe, no other Volk possesses, with the exception of Italy. It is a school of enlightenment and political education. This Volk is organized through and through. When today one of those English top hats wants to make propaganda, propaganda to work inside our Volk, then I say: Others have tried and have failed faced with us. Mr. Chamberlain might use his phrases for his own people. With us they have no effect whatsoever.

We know these gentlemen; we know their advisors better yet. We know them exceedingly well because only eight years ago they were still among us. We recognize their accents when they speak. They speak German as awkwardly as they probably speak English awkwardly. We had these people living in our midst once when they ruled Germany by force. Today they have no force other than the force of their voices. These find little resonance here in Germany. The German Volk dislikes this jargon. It does not want to hear it. And when it sees the persons hiding behind these voices, the German Volk has already seen more than enough. What these people say is of no import; no one in the German Volk believes a word of it. They lie their heads off—this every German knows.

No, this German Volk has become a different one today. There are no more Bethmann-Hollwegs among its leadership.

No more Spartacist gangs permeate the Volk. All this is over. A new Volk has come and this Volk will wage the war forced upon it. And I am determined to wage this war! Doubtless there will be some who say: "But why not wait a few years?" No, it is better this way since the fight cannot be avoided. These gentlemen forced it upon us now. And, moreover, it is intolerable that, every other decade, one people should say to another, which is eighty million strong: "We do not want you to do this or that. And if we feel like it we will cut you off from imports through a blockade, and then you will get nothing and starve." We will not tolerate this! We will eliminate this organized terror of this despicable clique of world plutocrats! We have routed these sharks of international finance in Germany, and we will not stand for others telling us what to do now. The German nation has the same right to life as other peoples do.

II. *Hitler proclaimed, repeatedly: only through the practice of National Socialism could the German Volk achieve its full potential.*

▶ January 4, 1933 *During 1932, the German government held repeated elections because no cabinet could put together a working majority in the Reichstag. President Hindenburg supported the parties of the right by allowing them to use "emergency presidential power" to ignore the Reichstag but this did not sit well with the electorate. In previous years, the parties of the left had held a Reichstag majority but were split among themselves. The National Socialist Party, that is the Nazi Party, which maintained that it was neither of the right or left (actually the Nazis contained strong elements of both), picked up significant vote totals but never more than about 40% nation-wide. With this total, however, the Nazis became the largest single party, and were unified and disciplined. Hitler then obstructed every political move until he gained power. Hitler's argument was always that the Volk is more than the state and he alone represented the Volk.*

The joint communiqué issued by Hitler and von Papen on January 5, after news of their conference in Cologne had leaked to the press, read as follows:

> In response to the false conjectures widely circulated in the press concerning the meeting between Adolf Hitler and the former Reich Chancellor von Papen, the undersigned hereby state that the discussion was exclusively limited to questions regarding the possibility of a major national and political united front, and that in particular the respective views of the parties in the Reich cabinet presently in office were not discussed in any way, as the talk was of a general nature.

Hitler's contribution to the subject matter discussed at this meeting is most clearly evidenced by the speech he gave on the same evening, i.e., January 4, in Detmold, marking the start of the election campaign to the local legislature in Lippe, for his remarks in political negotiations differed little from his proclamations in public rallies.

He stated in Detmold as follows:

> What brought the National Socialist Movement into being is the yearning for a true community of the German Volk which inspired our nation's best for centuries. This Movement gives us something we cannot express in words, but rather only sense, and it is something we know must be done. Fate has given us the great task of eliminating the disunity of the German Volk, the roots of its misfortune. Simple emergency decrees passed down from above by means of legislation cannot

remedy this plight. The important thing is not that today those in the Wilhelmstrasse imagine that they are governing the National Socialists; what counts is who has conquered the German individual. If today I were given the alternative of becoming Reich Chancellor but not being able to win more workers than hitherto, or on the other hand, not to rule but to win over millions of new working people to the nation within the course of the coming months, I would say: "Keep the government, I am reaching for the Volk! Sooner or later, with this Volk, I will surely unlock the door to the Wilhelmstrasse!"

Yet the Movement can only fulfill this one great mission if it uncompromisingly exterminates the things that tear our Volk apart. And when the bourgeoisie run our Movement down and ask, "Why do you attack the bourgeoisie as well as the Marxists?" then my answer to them is: Because there would be no Marxists, and would never have been any, had the bourgeois parties not existed previously. The bourgeois parties would be happy to have only a fraction of the faith, idealism, and sense of sacrifice our Movement calls its own. Where would the bourgeoisie be today were it not for this brown army, this brown bulwark, this brown wall!

My opponents have had a generation's time. At least they should refrain from criticizing me. I have worked for thirteen years, spent thirteen years in struggle or in prison for Germany and have created the *Volksgemeinschaft* of this Movement. What have my critics—who also could have taken on these tasks—accomplished in this same space of time?

All that is good in the ideas of our opponents in power today was stolen from us, and whatever is not from us is not even deserving of criticism. Schleicher's government will be a continuation of von Papen's government and will end where von Papen's government ended. I have refused to become a minister without portfolio, not because I shy away from the responsibility, but rather because that path does not lead to the goal. In any case, it certainly would have been easier to stand before a microphone every four weeks and read off what an entire ministry has accomplished.

And when people say to me that I should have entered the government and come to power through the back door, then I can only say that I have never learned how to play behind the scenes and I never want to learn it! I will never allow myself and the Movement to be fobbed off with half-measures, and if they say: then we'll dissolve once more. Do it! It doesn't bother us! It is in any case the German individual we have to fight for.

Neither can the threat of exhausting the voters scare us. In the end, it makes no difference what percentage of the German Volk makes history. The only important thing is that we are the last ones to make history in Germany! And by the way, when they talk about decline, they should not deceive themselves: the wave will return! The Movement will continue to present its ideas to the people over and over again until they are under our spell.

We will not tire and will continue resolute on our path until the finish. In the end, with our faith, our sacrifice, and our willpower, we will triumph after all. And thus this election will also take us one step further on the road that leads us upwards to the liberation of Germany!

Hitler's remarks to the effect that he had never learned to "play behind the scenes" and never even known the desire to do so appears rather curious in light of the secret conference he had held with von Papen only shortly before. But the main emphasis of both the Detmold speech and his statements in Cologne lay in the sentence: "The [National Socialist] wave will return!"

▶ February 10, 1933 *Hitler gained power January 30, 1933, and on February 10 he addressed the nation from the Berlin Sportpalast on radio.*

Hitler had something special in mind for the closing of his speech on February 10, 1933. He ended his address, which had lasted for several hours, by paraphrasing the Protestant version of the Lord's Prayer, evidently with the design—as a Catholic—of impressing the Protestants:

For I cannot divest myself of my faith in my Volk, cannot disassociate myself from the conviction that this nation will one day rise again, cannot divorce myself from my love for this, my Volk, and I cherish the firm conviction that the hour will come at last in which the millions who despise us today will stand by us and with us will hail the new, hard-won, and painfully acquired German Reich we have created together, the new German kingdom of greatness and power and glory and justice. Amen.

It appears that Hitler took pains to earn the title of "Nazi Padre" (*Nazi-Feldprediger*) bestowed upon him by the Social Democratic press years before.

▶ September 1, 1933 *In his proclamation to the Nazi Party Congress (Congress of Victory), he described the fanaticism necessary to perpetuate the Movement.*

Power and the brutal use of force can accomplish much, but in the long run no state of affairs is secure unless it appears logical in and of itself and intellectually irrefutable. And above all: the National Socialist Movement must profess its faith in the heroism that prefers any degree of opposition and hardship to even once denying the principles it has recognized as right. It may be filled only by a single fear, namely that one day a time might come when we are accused of insincerity or thoughtlessness. The heroic idea must, however, be constantly willing to renounce the approval of the present if sincerity and truth so require. Just as the hero has renounced his life to live on in the Pantheon of history, so must a truly great movement perceive in the rightness of its concept, in the sincerity of its actions the talisman which will safely lead it from a transient present to an immortal future.

▶ September 3, 1933 *As the Congress of Victory continued, Hitler spoke to his storm troopers (SA) and security troops (SS). The Men of November are the government officials who surrendered Germany in 1918. The community ritual of National Socialist units revolved around the Blood Banner* (Blutfahne).

On September 3, Hitler once again assumed the role of a padre in his address to the SA and SS. He spoke of the community of great faith that had assembled before him and once more granted absolution for the sins of the past.

The party congress of our Movement has always been a great military parade of its men, its men who are determined and willing to not only uphold the discipline of the community of the Volk in a theoretical sense, but to put it into practice. A community with no respect to origin, class, profession, assets, or education. A community that has come together, united in a single great faith and in a single great will, united not only for one rank, not for parties, not for professions, and not for classes, but united for our Germany.

Fourteen years of want, misery and humiliation lie behind us. In these fourteen years, however, a new, miraculous ideal has also asserted itself in our German Volk. We National Socialists have every right to say: when everyone became disloyal, we remained loyal and became truly loyal—an alliance of unswerving loyalty, unswerving comradeship, and if the goddess of fortune turned away from our Volk for fourteen years, we know it was because our Volk had itself to blame. But we also know that she will turn her gaze upon us once more when we have atoned for our guilt. May Heaven be our witness: the guilt of our Volk is extinguished, the crimes punished, the disgrace blotted out! The Men of November have been felled, and their tyranny is over.

In order to lend this rally more mystical force, Hitler consecrated—as he would every year until 1938—the new flags and standards of the SA and SS by touching them with the Blood Banner (*Blutfahne*) which had been carried at the march to the Feldherrnhalle in 1923 and allegedly been drenched in the blood of the martyrs to the cause.

▶ September 13, 1933 *Before the first winter after the National Socialists gained power, the Nazis instituted a new type of welfare system. This was called the Winter Relief Project against Hunger and Cold. Hitler saw the project as a good example of his* Volksgemeinschaft *(mutual sacrifice was the social foundation of the Volk.) A regular charity might have accomplished only so much, but the Nazi Party and the storm troopers supported winter relief. The following is part of Hitler's speech initiating the project.*

We have smashed international Marxist solidarity within our Volk in order to give the millions of German workers another and better solidarity in exchange. It is the solidarity of our own Volk, the indivisible bond not only in good times, but also in bad; a bond, not only with those who are blessed by good fortune, but also with those who are dogged by fate. If we correctly understand this idea of national solidarity, we must understand it as an idea of sacrifice, i.e., if someone says it is too much of a burden that one is constantly required to give, then the only reply is: "But that happens to be the meaning of a true national solidarity." Taking cannot be the meaning of any true national solidarity.

If one part of our Volk has come to suffer hardships due to circumstances for which all are responsible, and the other part, spared by fate, is willing of its own volition to take upon itself only a part of this hardship that has been forcibly imposed upon the other, all we can say is: a certain amount of hardship should be intentionally imposed upon a part of our Volk so that this part may aid in making the hardships of the other more bearable. The greater the willingness to make such sacrifices, all the more quickly will the hardships of the other side be able to be reduced.

Every person must understand that giving has any real value only in the sense of bringing about a true *Volksgemeinschaft*, when the act of giving involves a sacrifice on the part of the giver. This is ultimately the only way to build up the superior solidarity to which we must aspire if we want to overcome the other solidarity. When this Volk has correctly grasped the fact that these measures must mean sacrifice to everyone, then these measures will not only result in alleviating material want but will also produce something much more tremendous—the conviction that this community of the Volk is, not merely an empty phrase, but something that is really alive. We need this community more than ever in the difficult struggle of the nation. Were Germany blessed by good fortune, it might be able to be accorded somewhat less significance. But when we are made to endure difficult times, we must be conscious of the fact that these can be overcome only if our Volk holds together like a single block of steel.

We will be able to achieve this only if the masses of millions who are not blessed by good fortune are given the feeling that those who are more favored by fortune feel with them and are willing to voluntarily make a sacrifice in order to document to the entire world the indivisible solidarity of our Volk.

Whatever the German Volk sacrifices today will—and everyone can be assured of this—be refunded to our Volk in kind, with interest and compound interest; for what are material sacrifices made voluntarily in contrast to the greatest gift, namely the gift of being a joint, unified Volk that feels that it belongs together, that is willing to set upon its earthly path of destiny as one and to fight a united struggle?

The blessing that comes from this mutuality, from this national solidarity, is much greater and much more beneficial than the sacrifice that the individual person makes for its sake. This campaign against hunger and cold must stand under the motto: we have smashed the international solidarity of the proletariat, and in its place we shall build the living national solidarity of the German Volk.

▸ October 1, 1933 *In this speech, Hitler expounded on the nature of the Volk.*

In the afternoon, Hitler delivered a speech to the crowds of peasants gathered on the Bückeberg:

German *Volksgenossen!*

My German peasants! A change of historic dimensions has taken place in Germany since the crops were harvested last year. A state of the parties has fallen; a state of the Volk has arisen. Perhaps only a future age will be able to fully appreciate the extent of the radical change that has taken place in these past eight months. We are all too bound by the spell of this age that is rushing forwards to be able to gauge its progress by drawing comparisons. What seemed impossible but a few years ago has now become possible. What millions held to be a lost cause has today become reality. That which attempted to defy this force has been overthrown. A revolution roared through the German countryside, smashing a system, stirring up our Volk to its innermost depths. It should surprise no one that the class most strongly seized by this powerful movement was the one which constitutes the supporting foundation of our Volk. The starting point for National Socialism's views, positions, and decisions lies neither in the individual nor in humanity. It consciously places the Volk at the center of its entire way of thinking. For it, this Volk is a revelation conditioned by blood, in which it recognizes the God-given building block of human society. The lone individual is short-lived; the Volk is lasting. While the liberal world outlook, by according the individual a god-like status, must of necessity lead to the destruction of the Volk, National Socialism wishes to preserve the Volk as such, if necessary at the expense of the individual. It requires a tremendous educational effort in order to make clear to the people what initially appears to be a difficult lesson in order that they may realize that in the discipline of the individual lies a blessing not only for the whole, but ultimately also for the individual himself.

An undertone of concern was audible in this speech. Hitler feared severe complications and even military action as a result of his planned withdrawal from the League of Nations. Events proved his apprehension unfounded. Without explaining exactly which "difficult decisions" he had to make, he proclaimed:

> Fate has delivered us into a difficult age and thus also assigned us the holy task of making difficult decisions, if necessary. We know how great the misery is throughout the entire German Volk. We are determined to use every means that human intelligence can discover to fight it.

Near the end of his address, Hitler worked himself up into a state of frenzy by dwelling on the colossal dimensions of his flock of peasants on the Mount. He raved:

Thus you, my peasants, have assembled at the largest rally of its kind that has probably ever taken place on earth. However, it should not only be a demonstration of your power but also a visible display of the will of your leadership. By means of the celebration of labor and the celebration of the harvest, we wish to consciously document the spirit that dominates us and the path that we are determined to take. May the size of this demonstration instill in everyone a sense of mutual respect and the conviction that no class alone, but only all united, will be able to survive. May this feeling of solidarity between city and country, between peasants, manual laborers, and intellectual workers continue to swell to become the proud consciousness of a tremendous unity.

We are one Volk; we want to be one Reich.

▶ September 11, 1936 *In a speech to National Socialist political leaders, Hitler made the point that the Volk was an expression of ultimate unity.*

How could we help but feel once more in this hour the miracle that brought us together! Once you heard the voice of a man, and that voice knocked at your hearts, it wakened you, and you followed that voice. For years you pursued it, without ever having even seen the owner of that voice; you simply heard a voice and followed it.

When we meet here today, we are all of us filled with the miraculousness of this gathering. Not every one of you can see me, and I cannot see every one of you. Yet I feel you, and you feel me! It is the faith in our Volk that has made us small people great, that has made us poor people rich, that has made us wavering, discouraged, fearful people brave and courageous; that has made us, the wayward, see, and has joined us together!

Thus you come from your little villages, from your small market towns, from your cities, from the mines and the factories, leaving the plow; one day you come into this city. You come from the limited environment of your daily life struggle and of your struggle for Germany and our Volk, to have for once the feeling: now we are together, we are with him, and he is with us, and we are now Germany!

▸ June 6, 1937 *At a mass rally in Regensburg Hitler revealed the divine nature of the German community.*

For the first time, Hitler himself employed the term *Gottgläubigkeit* (belief in God), evidently in order to indicate that in the future he, too, could be counted among the adherents of this confession.

> I will never allow anyone ever again to tear this Volk asunder, to reduce it to a heap of warring religious camps. We have gone through enough in German history and need not undergo any more such experiences. They have been the sorriest experiences ever. Once our Volk numbered 18.5 million people; after a thirty years' war, a mere 3.6 million were left. It is my belief that some of those who are dissatisfied with the fact that we have finally created one Volk will attempt to reestablish that situation in Germany, but this attempt, too, will fail: they will never, ever destroy the German Volk and the German Reich.
>
> Generation after generation of our Volk will march on thus in our history, with this banner always in mind, this banner that places us under an obligation to our Volk, its honor, its freedom, and our community—to our truly National Socialist fraternity. They will then consider it only natural that this German Volk takes but the one path Providence bade it take by giving these people a common language. We, therefore, go our way into the future with the deepest belief in God (*Gottgläubigkeit*).
>
> Would all we have achieved been possible had Providence not helped us? I know that the fruits of human labor are hardwon and transitory if they are not blessed by the Almighty (*Allmacht*). Work such as ours which has received the blessings of the Almighty can never again be undone by mere mortals. As long as the pillars of the Movement hold this banner fast in their grip, there is not an enemy alive, no matter how powerful, who will ever be able to wrest it from our grasp.

Obviously, Hitler already had arrived at a belief in the divine origin of the Reich he had created. Hence, the empire could not be destroyed by mere mortals.

▸ June 27, 1937 *On the square in front of the Wurzburg Residenz, at a mass rally, Hitler spoke further about the divine nature of the National Socialist Movement.*

What then followed was a type of religious credo, to which Hitler recently had pledged his allegiance. He expressed the essence of his newfound belief with the assertion that his activities in the past five years had not been "the work of man alone." Rather these years had proved the existence of a supreme being, acting through him. How else, he argued, would he have been capable of navigating the "dizzying paths" to which fate had led him.

> And I can tell those doubters something else, too, namely, that I am well aware of what a human being can accomplish and where his limits lie, but it is my conviction that the human beings God created also wish to lead their lives modeled after the will of the Almighty. God did not create the peoples so that they might deliver themselves up to foolishness and be pulped soft and ruined by it, but that they might preserve themselves as He created them! Because we support their preservation in their original, God-given form, we believe our actions correspond to the will of the Almighty.
>
> As weak as the individual may ultimately be in his character and actions as a whole, when compared to Almighty Providence and His will, he becomes just as infinitely strong the instant he acts in accordance with this Providence. Then there will rain upon him the power that has distinguished all great phenomena of this world. And when I look back on the five years behind us, I cannot help but say: this has not been the work of man alone. Had Providence not guided us, I surely would often have been unable to follow these dizzying paths. That is something our critics above all should know. At the bottom of our hearts, we National Socialists are devout! We have no choice: no one can make national or world history if his deeds and abilities are not blessed by Providence.

▸ September 13, 1937 *At this year's party congress, the Reich Party Congress of Labor, Hitler explained how punishment was part of God's plan.*

How often we dwell on the question of what would have happened to Germany if fate had granted us a swift and easy victory in 1914. What we were all striving for at that time with hearts aglow would presumably—seen from a higher vantage point—have been but a misfortune for our Volk. That victory would probably have had extremely grievous consequences. For in the inner sphere, it in particular would have prevented us from gaining the knowledge that today allows us to look back in horror at the path on which that Germany of the past was already making its way. The perceptive few who were preaching caution had lapsed into ridiculousness.

The state, grounded only in the external military means of power which bore it up, would sooner or later have become the annihilator of its own existence and its own means of existence, wholly ignorant of the meaning of the blood-related sources of the German people! Phenomena such as we have had an opportunity to observe in many other countries after their supposed victory would have descended upon us. Instead of being jerked back from the brink of destruction by a disruption of a catastrophic nature, we would all the more surely have gradually succumbed to the insidious poisons of inner decay of the Volk! In our case, the accuracy of a wise saying can be said to have been proven true: there are times when Providence demonstrates the deepest love it has for its creatures in an act of punishment!

▶ October 3, 1937 *At the mass celebration of this year's* Erntedankfest, *Hitler described how national unity and mutual self-sacrifice of the Volk were part of God's plan.*

The German people were soon to catch the brunt of the ramifications of Hitler's grandiose assertions. Hitler's summons of the Almighty, who assuredly would not desert him in the end, proved of little use in the face of the harsh realities to come. The closing words of Hitler's final address on the Bückeberg made clear the extent to which he had already succumbed to these delusions:

If we adhere to this path, decent, industrious, and honest, if we do our duty so bravely and loyally, it is my belief that the Lord will help us again and again in the future. He does not abandon decent people for any length of time! While He may sometimes put them to the test or send them trials, in the long run He will always allow His sun to shine upon them and ultimately give them His blessing.

If we all stick together in the city and the country, if each and every person decently does his duty in the place he occupies and thinks not only of himself but of his fellow humans as well, then you can trust that there is nothing that could break us asunder. We shall prevail! In the year to come, and in the decades to come!

We have a magnificent sun today. A year ago, we had pouring rain. What next year will bring is something I do not know. But that we will be standing here over and over again, that is something I do know, no matter what the weather! When we meet here again after a year has passed, we will once more be able to pledge anew: the year is over, and once again everything has gone well. Everything has become even more splendid. And we are fortunate to be allowed to live in Germany.

To Our German Reich and our German Volk—*Sieg Heil!*

▶ October 5, 1937 *At the opening rally to initiate this year's Winter Relief Project, Hitler spoke to 20,000 volunteers at the Deutschlandhalle in Berlin.*

Sometimes when I see shabbily dressed girls, shivering with cold themselves, collecting with infinite patience for others who are cold, then I have the feeling that they are all apostles of a certain Christianity! This is a Christianity that can claim for itself as no other can: this is the Christianity of a sincere profession of faith, because behind it stands not the word, but the deed!

With the aid of this tremendous society, countless people are being relieved of the feeling of social abandonment and isolation. Many are thus regaining the firm belief that they are not completely lost and alone in this world, but sheltered in their *Volksgemeinschaft;* that they, too, are being cared for, that they, too, are being thought of and remembered. And beyond that: there is a difference between the theoretical knowledge of socialism and the practical life of socialism. People are not born socialists, but must first be taught how to become them.

Now one statement followed that Hitler had already voiced repeatedly, that the contributions made to the *Winterhilfswerk* represented an "insurance program against lack of political common sense."

People in the bourgeois era before us insured themselves against everything: against fire, against theft, against hailstorms, against burglary, etc.—but they forgot one kind of insurance, insurance against political madness, insurance against lack of political common sense, that first tears a Volk asunder and then allows it to become powerless to fulfill its life-tasks. And this one omission made all the other types of insurance pointless.

We, however, place at the fore of all types of insurance the insurance of the German *Volksgemeinschaft!* It is for this we are paying our donation, and we know that it will be reimbursed a thousand times over! For as long as this *Volksgemeinschaft* remains inviolate, nothing can threaten us! Therein lies the guarantee for the future, not only of the life of the nation, but hence of the existence of every individual as well.

Therefore, it is just to demand from each individual a premium corresponding to his income. Wanting to establish a general lump sum for this premium is a sign of an indecent cast of mind. The little old woman who sacrifices five or ten pfennigs in Moabit or somewhere out in the country casts in more than someone who puts in one hundred or one thousand or perhaps ten thousand marks. Had our so-called intellectual classes initiated these premium payments prior to the war, many a later misfortune could have been avoided.

Hitler closed his speech with the remark that there might be additional sacrifices—though of a different nature—that fate might ask of the German Volk in the future.

▶ April 3, 1938 *At a mass rally in the city of Graz, as he campaigned in the election to ratify the union with Austria, Hitler said:*

> The Lord created all peoples. What God has placed to-gether, let no man put asunder. And as a holy symbol of this truth the whole German nation will step forth on April 10! I have called upon the nation to do so not only here, but in the entire Reich. And it will do so.
>
> Today I stand at the fore once more as I did during the times of my struggle and wrestle for the German individual. On April 10, we will jointly pass judgment. For the first time in the history of our Volk, a Reich is being constructed in ac-cordance to the will of the Volk. And I desire to be nothing other than what I have been in the past: the warner of my Volk, the instructor of my Volk, the Führer of my Volk! In the future as well, I will bow to one single commandment only, a commandment that has compelled me ever since I was born: Deutschland!

▶ September 6, 1938 *During the Party Congress* Grossdeutschland *of 1937, Hitler spoke at the cultural convention. While talking about architecture, one of his favorite subjects, he explained that the art of the Volk, in its National Socialist ideal, must be "pure." In the context of the speech, he condemned the neo-paganism that some party leaders advocated.*

At the culture convention that same day, Hitler once again presented his views on the essence of culture and art at great length. He spoke of the "culturally completely unproductive Jews" and of the "blasé attitude" of the pseudo-intellectual upper class. The latter he referred to with great disdain in the following strong words:

> I want to differentiate here between the Volk, i.e. the healthy, full-blooded mass of Germany loyal to the Volk, and a decadent, so-called high society, unreliable because only con-ditionally linked by blood. It is sometimes casually referred to as the "upper class," being, however, in reality no more than the scum produced by a societal mutation gone haywire from having had its blood and thinking infected by cosmopolitism.

There was nothing new about his use of such terminology. In this instance as well, it was clearly Hitler's intent to put an end to the preposterous ideas of Rosenberg and Himmler. Their importunate efforts to revive a Wotan cult had long been a thorn in the side of Hitler. Their attempts consisted of constructing sites for the worship of mystical Germanic cults with the goal of exchanging Christian rituals for "Nordic" consecration ceremonies—including different marriage and burial rites. Such aspirations could only detract from what Hitler believed to be the crucial mission of National Socialism: to expand upon and maintain its power base.

Starting from the assumption of the pernicious "mysticism of Christianity," he announced that the "cultural work of the German Volk" strove to fulfill "one mission" [Hitler's]. This undertaking must perforce be achieved in the pursuit of the commands issued by "one spirit"—which, of course, was again that of Hitler. The "subversion by occult mystics in search of an afterlife" could not be tolerated. Cult facilities, cult sites, cult performances and rituals were dangerous. There must be only one teaching of a *völkisch* and political" nature and the "brave fulfillment of the duties entailed."

While Hitler did not mention the names Rosenberg or Himmler, everyone knew that the admonishment was aimed specifically at these two adherents of mysticism. Hitler detailed the following considerations:

> In this period of the most inward orientation, Christian mysticism demanded an approach to the solution of structural problems and hence to an architecture whose design not only ran contrary to the spirit of the time but also helped produce these mysterious dark forces that made the people increasingly willing to submit themselves to cosmopolitism. The germinating resistance to this violation of the freedom of the spirit and the will of man that lasted for centuries immediately found an outlet in the forceful expression of a new form of artistic design. The cathedrals' mystical narrowness and somberness gave way to more generous room and light, reflecting the increasingly free spirit of the time. More and more the mystical twilight gave way to light. The uncertain and probing transition to the twentieth century finally led to the crisis we face today and that will find its resolution in one way or another.
>
> And in this manner the cultural evolution of a Volk resembles that of the Milky Way. Amongst countless pale stars a few suns radiate. However, all suns and planets are made of the

same one material, and all of them observe the same laws. The entire cultural work of a Volk must not only be geared toward fulfillment of one mission, but this mission must also be pursued in one spirit. National Socialism is a cool and highly-reasoned approach to reality based upon the greatest of scientific knowledge and its spiritual expression. As we have opened the Volk's heart to these teachings, and as we continue to do so at present, we have no desire of instilling in the Volk a mysticism that transcends the purpose and goals of our teachings.

Above all, National Socialism is a Volk Movement in essence and under no circumstances a cult movement! Insofar as the enlightenment and receptivity of our Volk demand the use of certain methods, which by now have become part of its traditions, these methods are rooted in experience and realizations that were arrived at by exclusively pragmatic considerations. Hence it will be useful to make these methods part of our heritage at a later date. They have nothing to do with other borrowed methods or expressions derived from other viewpoints that have to this date constituted the essence of cults. For the National Socialist Movement is not a cult movement; rather, it is a *völkisch* and political philosophy that grew out of considerations of an exclusively racial nature. This philosophy does not advocate mystic cults but rather aims to cultivate and lead a Volk determined by its blood.

Therefore we do not have halls for cults but halls for the Volk. Nor do we have places for worship but places for assembly and squares for marches. We do not have cult sites but sports arenas and play areas. And it is because of this that our assembly halls are not bathed in the mystical twilight of cult sites but rather are places of brightness and light of a beautiful and practical nature. In these halls, no cult rituals take place; they are exclusively the site of Volk rallies of the type that we conducted in the years of our struggle, that we have become accustomed to and which we shall preserve in this manner.

Hence the National Socialist Movement will not tolerate subversion by occult mystics in search of an afterlife. They are not National Socialists but something different, and in any event, they represent something that has nothing to do with us. At the heart of our program you will not find any mysterious presentiments; rather you will find succinct realization and hence open avowal. Since we place the sustenance and securing of a creature created by God at the center of this realization and avowal, we sustain God's creation, and it is in this manner that we serve this will. We do not do so at a new cult site bathed in mysterious twilight but rather in the open for the Lord to see.

There were ages when twilight was the prerequisite for the propagation of certain teachings. In this day and age, however, light is the prerequisite if our work is to succeed. God have mercy on him who attempts to subvert our Movement and our state by insisting upon convoluted orders or introducing vague mystical elements to them. It suffices for this lack in clarity to be contained in words only.

It is already dangerous to order the construction of a so-called cult site because this already entails the necessity of coming up with cult games and rites at a later date. The only cult we know is that of a cultivation of the natural and hence of that which God has willed. We stand in complete and unconditional humility before the divine laws as revealed to man. These laws we respect, and our prayer is one of brave fulfillment of the duties entailed. We cannot be held responsible for acts of worship; after all, that is the domain of the churches!

Therefore, truly great solutions to the problems of architecture today can be found only if architecture is charged with great and timely tasks. To abandon this principle would render the undertaking hideous. The attempts at resolution would become artificial, dishonest, and wrong, and hence would lose their significance for the present and future.

▶ February 24, 1940 *In another excerpt from his speech celebrating the twentieth anniversary of the founding of the party, given at the Munich Hofbräuhaus, Hitler asserted that divine Providence was directing the German nation. The war had begun, Poland was conquered, Britain and France were at war with Germany, and Hitler was planning to attack in the west. The quotation at the end of the excerpt is from Martin Luther's hymn, "A Mighty Fortress is Our God."*

Besides that, I believe one thing: there is a Lord God! And this Lord God creates the peoples. And, as a matter of principle, He accords all these peoples the same fundamental rights. We Germans terribly misbehaved in history some twenty, twenty-two, twenty-three years ago. There came a revolution and hence we suffered a defeat.

Then began the resurrection of our Volk with immeasurable labor. And during this entire period, Providence blessed our work time and time again. The more brave we were, the greater were the blessings accorded us by Providence. And within the last six years, Providence was constantly on our side, believe me: some call it luck, some have another name for it, but in the end such great works cannot be accomplished without its approval. And just a few months ago, I myself bore profound testimony to the workings of Providence which stands by mankind and assigns it missions to be fulfilled. And we serve it through these missions. What we desire, is not the oppression of other peoples, but our freedom, our security, the securing of our *Lebensraum*. It is the securing of our Volk's life itself. For this we fight!

Providence has blessed us in this fight, a thousand times over. Could it have done this, would it have done this, had it harbored the intent now, all of a sudden, to allow this battle to end to our detriment?

Here I believe in a higher and eternal justice. It is imparted to him who proves himself worthy of it. And it was in this belief that I stood up before you here for the first time twenty years ago. Back then I believed: it simply cannot be that my Volk is forsaken. It will be forsaken only if there are no men to be found to rescue this Volk. If, however, someone pledges himself with a trusting heart to this Volk and works for it, who places himself wholly at the disposal of this Volk, then it cannot be that Providence will allow this Volk to perish. Providence has wrought more than miracles for us in the time since.

All I can ask of you now: Firmly take hold of your faith as old National Socialists. It cannot be any different: we must win, and therefore we will win!

And even if our foes so terribly threaten and press upon us, it cannot be any worse than it was once before. Our ancestors were forced to endure all this many times. And thus we all want to bring ourselves to pronounce once more the great avowal of faith once spoken by a mighty German: "And if there were only devils in this world, we would still succeed!"

Hitler's idiosyncratic logic, "We must win, and therefore we will win!" was destined to become the German leadership's main slogan in the war years.

III. *Hitler believed that the unity of the German Volk depends upon their God-given Führer, Adolf Hitler.*

▶ April 9, 1938 *Once Germany had occupied Austria, Hitler was adamant to hold a plebiscite on the question of Austrian independence that had precipitated the Austrian crisis. He campaigned for Austrian acceptance of union with Germany and gave a speech in Vienna, broadcast on radio. His belief in divine selection was clear: God sent Hitler to Germany. Schuschnigg was the Austrian chancellor. He had attempted to assert Austria's will for independence by proclaiming a plebiscite to demonstrate Austrian resolve. Hitler took this very badly, accusing Schuschnigg of breaking his word and decided to occupy Austria immediately.*

I believe that it was also God's will that from here a boy was to be sent into the Reich, allowed to mature, and elevated to become the nation's Führer, thus enabling him to reintegrate his homeland into the Reich. There is a divine will, and all we are is its instruments.

When Herr Schuschnigg broke his word on March 9, at that very instant I felt that Providence had called upon me. And all that happened in the next three days could have come about only because Providence willed and desired it. In three days the Lord struck them down! And it was entrusted to me to reintegrate my homeland into the Reich on the very day of its betrayal. When one day we shall be no more, then the coming generations shall be able to look back with pride upon this day, the day on which a great Volk affirmed the German community. In the past, millions of German men shed their blood for this Reich. How merciful a fate to be allowed to create this Reich today without any suffering!

Now, rise, German Volk, subscribe to it, hold it tightly in your hands! I wish to thank Him who allowed me to return to my homeland so that I could return it to my German Reich! May every German realize the importance of the hour tomorrow, assess it and then bow his head in reverence before the will of the Almighty who has wrought this miracle in all of us within these past few weeks!

IV. *Hitler believed that the Volk must have unity in order to survive and prosper. National Socialism was the only way to complete unity. Those who were against National Socialism were traitors to the German nation.*

▸ August 27, 1933 *At a speech at the Niederwald Monument, commemorating a battle of the Franco–Prussian War (1870–1871) near Rüdesheim, Hitler made the assertion that only through unity is there strength.*

After the successful rally in Tannenberg, Hitler immediately headed west on August 27 and, after a flight of some hours, arrived at another national monument, the Niederwald Monument near Rüdesheim, which had been erected in memory of the triumphant campaign of 1870/71. Several thousand Saarlanders had gathered for the occasion, and Hitler was in the right frame of mind to deliver a nationalistic speech.

German *Volksgenossen!*

My dear Saarlanders! I have come here first of all to bring you greetings from the province that has maintained unshakable loyalty to Germany in the distant east. A tragic and undeserved fate has struck our East Prussia. Separated from the homeland, two million Germans are loyally standing watch to hold, with their will and their basic convictions, the bridge that has been broken off geographically. Today, an uplifting ceremony took place at the Tannenberg Monument, not only in memory of the great past, but also bearing solemn witness to the fact that there exists a will to preserve what is ours, to preserve the sacred memories, but also to preserve the rights of the present. One of these rights of the present is the return of the Saar territory to the Reich!

Of course—and you who are here, my friends, will perhaps know this best—Germany now is no longer the same as the Germany that evolved in a time when the Saar was temporarily taken from the Reich; rather, it is a Germany of honor, a Germany conscious of its national rights and obligations.

When the Battle of Tannenberg was won, it was a symbol for the tremendous power of a unified nation. When the Saar was lost to the Reich, it was as a consequence of the loss of this inner unity. It is our unshakable will to restore this inner unity of the nation that we lost in the collapse of November 1918. For fifteen years this goal has been all at once our wish, our prayer, and our idea, and today we can say that our prayer has been answered, our wish fulfilled. Our will has made reality of what had to come about in Germany in order to preserve our Volk from final ruin. Today those around us are talking about terror in Germany, about violence. That is neither terror nor violence; it is destiny. The whole of Germany is rising up!

We have liberated Germany from the rape of those who did not want a strong Germany! We have liberated Germany from the rape and the terror of those who consciously rent it apart because they were able to control this Volk only by destroying its unity. What you witness now in Germany is one Volk and one Reich no longer experiencing party rule and party strife.

It is not the German Volk who yearn for former conditions but a handful of people who were living off the misfortune of the nation and the inner conflicts of the German Volk.

If we have said it once, we have said it a hundred times: we want peace with the rest of the world. We ourselves have experienced the dreadfulness of war. None of us wants it. None of us wants foreign property. None of us wants to annex foreign peoples. But what God has given to the Volk belongs to the Volk. And if treaties are to be sacred, then not only for us, but also for our opponents. The treaties clearly provide that the Volk of the Saar is entitled to choose its own fate.

I know that, when the hour comes, the voice of the nation will encompass every single individual, and he will go and cast his vote for the German *Vaterland*.

We are gladly willing to discuss all economic matters with France. We are gladly willing to reach compromises with France. But there is one point upon which there can be no compromise: the Reich can neither abandon you, nor can you abandon Germany.

▶ March 29, 1938 *At a mass rally in the Hanseatenhalle in Hamburg, Hitler expounds on the concept of* Volksgemeinschaft. *Hitler was provoking the Austrian crisis. His figures for the alleged suffering of Austrian National Socialists are simply false.*

First of all, domestic political order had to be restored to the Volk. Only then was it possible for the economy to revive. Only then was it possible for the Volk to become a decisive factor once more in foreign policy. Events proved us right.

What could a Volk expect that had neither trust nor confidence in itself? Could it expect that others would rate it more highly than it rated itself? First one had to get rid of all this cronyism and rubbish about an economically bankrupt system just as one had to discard obsolete economic doctrines and terminology. These had to be replaced with simple and fundamental principles and realizations.

Only what a nation produces as a whole will benefit the nation as a whole. What it does not produce, it does not possess. Money can never replace inadequate production, rather—in this case—it becomes merely a means of duping the nation.

Those who base their politics on subversive activities shall be mercilessly exterminated.

Frequently, people abroad have claimed that we were making propaganda, while in truth it was the idea that propagandized itself. It holds great attraction especially for those who are of the same blood. It does not matter whether or not this pleases the democrats.

Ideas cannot be imprisoned. States can be torn apart, but the bonds of a *Volksgemeinschaft* are indissoluble. And once the sparks of these ideas begin to fly, they inflame every man whose blood links him to them as though it were an internal antenna. And this is precisely the case with National Socialism. Austria's National Socialists were persecuted, hundreds of them were murdered, and thousands were shot. They were hanged as though they were murderers lacking any feeling of honor although their only crime had been their belief in their Volk.

And the world remained silent and uttered not a word of condemnation. You can judge for yourselves the meaning the word democracy took on for us. It became the embodiment of lies and injustice, the pinnacle of hypocrisy. But the minute—be it in Berlin or Vienna—we cause one of those Jewish agitators to close his shop for a while and to go somewhere else, then democracy becomes incensed and speaks of an assault upon holy rights.

V. *Hitler believed that criticism led to disunity and that only the disloyal were critical of the regime.*

▶ January 30, 1934 *On this date, Hitler addressed the Reichstag. He had been in power for a year and in this excerpt talked about his critics who were, he asserted, only bitter emigrants and confused intellectuals.*

The fact that our activities during this past year were nonetheless put under fire from countless foes is only natural. We have borne this burden in the past and will also be able to bear it in the future. Degenerate emigrants, who for the most part quitted the scene of their former operations not for political, but for purely criminal reasons because the changed atmosphere had given them cause for alarm, are now attempting to mobilize a gullible world against Germany with truly villainous dexterity and a criminal lack of conscience, but their lies will catch up with them all the faster now that tens of thousands of respectable and honorable men and women are coming to Germany from other countries and can compare with their own eyes the accounts delivered by these internationally "persecuted" parties with the actual reality.

Furthermore, the fact that a number of Communist ideologists believe it necessary to turn back the tide of history and, in doing so, make use of a subhumanity (*Untermenschentum*) which mistakes the idea of allowing criminal instincts free rein for the concept of political freedom will likewise cause us little concern. We were able to deal with these elements when they were in power and we were in the opposition. In the future we will be even more certain of being able to deal with them because they are now in the opposition and we are in power.

A number of our bourgeois intellectuals as well are of the conviction that they cannot accept the hard facts. However, it is much more useful to have this rootless intellectuality as an enemy than as a follower. For these persons turn away from all that is healthy, and all that is diseased awakens their interest and is given their support.

I would also like to add to the ranks of the enemies of the new regime the small clique of those whose gaze is incorrigibly directed backward, in whose eyes the people are nothing other than a rootless proletariat who are only waiting for a master so as to find, under his divine guidance, the only possible inner satisfaction. And last of all, I add that little group of folk ideologists who believe that it is only possible to make the nation happy by eradicating the experiences and consequences of two thousand years of history, to start out on new trails, clad, so to speak, in their "bearskins."

All of these opponents taken together, in numerical terms, scarcely amount to two and a half million people, in contrast to the more than forty million who profess their faith in the new state and its regime. These two and a half million are not to be rated as opposition, for they comprise a chaotic conglomeration of the most diverse opinions and views, utterly incapable of pursuing any type of common goal, and capable only of joining in rejecting today's state.

▸ May 1, 1934 *At a mass rally at Tempelhofer Field in Berlin, with some two million people, Hitler spoke of his critics. He stated that the elimination of all political parties, except the Nazi Party, and abolishment of all unions, replacing them with the Nazi labor organization, increased the freedom of the German people. Those former officials of the abolished parties and unions who supported the Nazis were readily employed in the expanded Nazi organizations.*

Only a person who is better able to solve a problem is justified in criticizing. We have come to terms with the problems in Germany better than our former opponents and current critics. We thus do not intend to allow the necessary authority accorded to the nation's leadership to be attacked by those who perceive nihilism as the only fitting framework for their own futile activities. Whenever criticism becomes an end in itself, chaos must be its ultimate consequence. And just as we defend ourselves against these critics in order to preserve confidence in the nation's leadership, we for our part also want to do everything to reinforce this confidence.

Millions of people who want to take an active part in reconstruction have offered me their support. Millions of our former opponents are today standing in our ranks and, thanks to their work and, thanks to their skill as helpers in our reconstruction, are held in no less regard than our own longstanding party comrades. I may affirm before the German Volk that we do not perceive the nature of our authority in the effectiveness of cannons and machine guns but rather in the actual confidence vested in us.

In this past year, we have thus eliminated all those organizations that we were forced to regard as breeding grounds for phenomena that undermine the self, cause discord in the Volk, and lead ultimately to national and economic ruin. When we initiated the destruction of the German party system on May 2 of last year by taking over the unions, we did so, not in order to rob any Germans of their useful representative bodies, but in order to liberate the German Volk from those organizations whose greatest damage lies in the fact that they were forced to encourage that damage be done in order to justify the necessity of their own existence.

Thus we have delivered the German Volk from an infinite amount of internal strife and discord that was of benefit to no one except those directly interested but was a constant source of fatal harm to the entire Volk.

▶ August 17, 1934 *Two days before the plebiscite to unite the offices of German president and chancellor, Hitler spoke at a state ceremony in the Hamburg City Hall also broadcast over radio. Hitler included comments about his critics.*

I would like to take this opportunity as well to dwell briefly on those who believe that their freedom of criticism has been unjustly encroached upon. In my eyes, criticism is not a vital function in and of itself. The world can live without critics but not without workers. I protest that a profession should exist that consists of nothing but acting the know-it-all without any responsibility of one's own and of telling responsible working people what to do and think. I have spent thirteen years of my life fighting a regime, however not by negative criticism, but with constructive suggestions as to what should be done. And I did not hesitate a second to assume the responsibility when the blessed Old Gentleman gave it to me, and I am now responsible to the entire German Volk. And no action will take place for which I will not vouch with my life, as this Volk be my witness. However, I can at least claim before this Volk the same right that every worker and peasant and entrepreneur can also claim for himself.

What would a peasant say if, while he was laboring in the sweat of his brow, someone kept strolling around on his farm with nothing else to do but go around carping, criticizing, and stirring up discontent? What would a worker do who is standing in front of his machine and is constantly talked at by someone who has no skills and does nothing but incessantly carp and find fault? I know they would not tolerate such creatures for more than a week; they would tell them to go to hell.

The organization of the Movement gives hundreds of thousands of people the opportunity to play a constructive part in shaping our life as a nation. Any serious suggestions and any genuine cooperation are welcomed with gratitude. But people whose only activity is confined to judging and condemning the activities of others without ever assuming any practical responsibility themselves are people I cannot bear.

In this state, everyone is called upon to fight and work in some way or another.

In this state, there will no longer be a right to carp but only a right to do a better job.

We have malicious enemies in the world. Do what we might, a certain international conspiracy will stop at nothing to interpret it as something bad. They permanently subsist on the sole hope that our Volk might once again drown in inner discord. We know our fate throughout the centuries all too well to overlook the consequences.

It has always been Germans who have sacrificed themselves as allies of a foreign design. Ambitious noblemen, greedy merchants, unscrupulous party leaders and parties have repeatedly become the shield-bearers of foreign interests against their own Volk. The hope for such aid has thrown Germany into the most severe misfortune of war more than once. History should be a lesson to us.

VI. *The National Socialist Movement, according to Hitler, represented the will of the German Volk.*

▶ January 27, 1934 *Hitler always understood the use of good press relations. He did very well in interviews. Here, he discussed National Socialism with Hanns Johst and maintained that the Movement was neither left nor right, favoring neither employee nor capitalist.*

On January 27, the *Frankfurter Volksblatt* published a conversation between Hitler and the writer Hanns Johst on the concept of the *"Bürger."* When Hitler took a stand against the so-called *"Bürger,"* or bourgeoisie, he usually had the intellectuals in mind, whose skepticism of his prognoses for the future never failed to enrage him. However, Hitler by no means rejected the bourgeois way of life: his private hopes and expectations and his needs in terms of accommodations and daily life were, in essence, those of the lower middle class or petite bourgeoisie (*Kleinbürgertum*).

According to Johst, the discussion ran as follows:

> Question: The *"Bürger"* is feeling increasingly distressed with respect to the romantic idea of peace of mind, his own peace of mind. So would you, Reich Chancellor Hitler, allow me to ask quite openly: what is your position on the *"Bürger"*?

> Answer: I believe it would be a good thing if we first detach the concept of the *"Bürger"* from the extremely unclear ambiguity which surrounds it and mutually establish an unambiguous definition of what we understand by the term *"Bürger."* I need only cite the *"Staatsbürger"* (citizen) and the *"Spiessbürger"* (Philistine) to name two members of this species.

> Question: Do you mean to say the *"Staatsbürger"* is the man who stands up for his state politically no matter what, and the *"Spiessbürger"* is the type who calls himself apolitical for fear of losing his peaceful existence and, acting the Philistine, uses the well-known practice of sticking his head in the sand to avoid being an eyewitness to political conditions?

> Answer: That's exactly what I mean. One section of the bourgeois world and the bourgeois world view (*Weltanschauung*) enjoys acting the part of being completely disinterested in political life. These people have not progressed beyond the prewar position that politics has its own forms of existence far removed from their normal life in society and is to be practiced by a special caste engaged and predestined for that purpose. These people, armchair politicians, enjoy criticizing you as part of a general mood or motivated by personal interest, but they will never take on any representative, public responsibility. My Movement, as an expression of will and yearning, encompasses every aspect of the entire Volk. It conceives of Germany as a corporate body, as a single organism. There is

no such thing as non-responsibility in this organic being, not a single cell which is not responsible, by its very existence, for the welfare and well-being of the whole. Thus in my view there is not the least amount of room for apolitical people. Every German, whether he wants to be or not, is by virtue of his being born into German destiny, by the fact of his existence, a representative of the form of existence of this very Germany. In upholding this principle, I am turning every class conflict around and at the same time declaring war on every concept of caste and consciousness of class.

Question: That means that you will not tolerate any flight into private life, whereas the bourgeois likes to take refuge in being a private person? You are forcing everyone to take on the position of an active citizen (*Staatsbürger*)?

Answer: I reject shilly-shallying (*Drückebergerei*) about decisions! Every single German must know what he wants! And he must take a stand for what he wants! Since 1914, 1 have devoted my life to fighting. First as a soldier, blindly obedient to the military leadership. When this leadership allowed itself to be locked out of the power sphere of command in 1918, I took a close look at the new political command and recognized in it the true face of Marxism. With that began my fight against the politics of this theory and its practice.

Question: You encountered Marxist parties and the indifference of the middle class. You were regarded as part of the bourgeois right-wing.

Answer: This evaluation of my life's work contains two errors. My entire energy was devoted from the beginning to overcoming the leadership of the state by parties, and secondly—although this is logical and obvious from the origins of my uprising—I must never be understood in bourgeois terms. In the quarrel of the parties, it became evident that the discussion was being conducted under false pretences. It is wrong, you see, that the bourgeois parties have become the employers and for the Marxists to call themselves proles and employees. There are just as many proles among the employers as there are bourgeois elements among the employees. The bourgeois—allegedly for the sake of the *Vaterland*—are defending property, a capitalistic value. Thus from a Marxist point of view, love of one's country is not dumb but rather capital's greed for profit. On the other hand, the international character of Marxism is regarded by the middle class as the first move towards a world economy in which there is only state administration and no longer any private property.

The member of the bourgeoisie avoids this division of the Volk into opposing interest groups by hiding behind the superficial and zealous optimism of his daily paper and allowing himself to be educated "apolitically." The lessons are organized very nicely according to the taste of his majesty, Gullible Fritz (*Majestät Zipfelmütze*), placid and peaceful. People are reverting step by step. The compromise serves over and over again to ban controversy literally from the face—but only the face—of the planet, and the end, the end is a political matter somewhere in the distance which is better left alone to preserve the peace, of course. But the fact that this peace was not a peace at all, but a daily defeat, a daily victory of consciously political Marxism—it is for the recognition of this fact that National Socialism is fighting. National Socialism takes for itself the pure idea from each of these two camps. From the camp of bourgeois tradition, it takes national resolve, and from the materialism of the Marxist dogma, living, creative Socialism.

Volksgemeinschaft: that means a community of all productive labor, that means the oneness of all vital interests, that means overcoming bourgeois privatism and the unionized, mechanically organized masses, that means unconditionally equating individual fate and the nation, the individual and the Volk.

I know that liberal bourgeois concepts are highly developed in Germany; the bourgeois man rejects public life and has a deep-seated aversion toward what goes on in the streets. If he weakens in his resolve for any length of time, this public life, the street, will destroy the ideal of his four walls. In cases like this, attack is the best form of defense.

I am not responsible for the fact that the central command of the German state was taken over by the street mobs in 1918. However, the bourgeoisie does not have the slightest reason to suspect that I was the drummer who sounds the reveille, for if the bourgeoisie had slept through the facts of history, it would have awakened too late, awakened to a political state of affairs that is called Bolshevism and that is the mortal enemy of the concepts of the middle class. The Russian Revolution was up in arms against the middle class as bourgeoisie, and in Germany the decisive battle of this *Weltanschauung* has just been lost. The fact that all of Germany is enlightened as to Bolshevist imperialism, that not a single German can say, "I knew nothing of it," but can resort only to the lame excuse, "I didn't believe it"—that is and always has been my commitment and the basic principle of all of my loyal followers.

Question: Inasmuch as you were forced by the Weimar Constitution to organize along party lines, you called your movement the National Socialist Workers' Party. In my opinion, you are thus giving the concept of the worker priority over the concept of the bourgeoisie.

Answer: I chose the word "worker" because it was more natural and corresponded with every element of my being, and because I wanted to recapture this word for the national force. I did not and will not allow the concept of the worker to simply take on an international connotation and become an object of distrust to the bourgeoisie. In a certain sense, I had to "naturalize" the term worker and subject it once again to the control of the German language and the sovereign rights and obligations of the German Volk. Similarly, I will not tolerate that the correctly used and essentially understood concept of the "*Bürger*" is spoiled. But I believe the "*Bürger*" is called upon to ensure this.

Question: In the world view of National Socialism, there are therefore only the active citizen (*Staatsbürger*) and the worker. And all people are either both or they are neither and thus they are parasites in the life of the State.

Answer: Certainly, I feel this is a significant comparison, for this alone enables us to dispense with the entire superficial vocabulary of unnecessary arrogance caused by parliamentarianism and all of that liberalism. The philistine (*Spiessbürger*) must become a citizen of the state; the Red comrade must become a *Volksgenosse*. Both must, with their good intentions, ennoble the sociological concept of the worker and raise the status of an honorary title for labor. This patent of nobility alone puts the soldier and the peasant, the merchant and the academician, the worker and the capitalist under oath to take the only possible direction in which all purposeful German striving must be headed: towards the nation. Only when everything that happens within the entire German community happens with a view to the whole does the whole, in the changing currents of political effects, in turn become capable of taking on the positive and productive leadership of all of the individual units, classes and conditions.

Leadership is always based upon the free will and good intentions of those being led. My doctrine of the Führer concept is therefore quite the opposite of what the Bolshevists like to present it as being: the doctrine of a brutal dictator who triumphs over the destruction of the values of private life. Thus as Reich Chancellor I am not discontinuing my activities as a public educator; on the contrary: I am using every means provided by the state and its power to publish and make known my every word and deed with the goal of winning the public with this openness for every single decision of my national will by proof and conviction. And I am doing this because I believe in the creative power and the creative contribution of the Volk.

Question: In other words, Herr Reich Chancellor, in the Volk you envision a mythic fusion of the worker and the *Bürger*, just as you envision the state as the malleable instrument of the Volk? If I may state it quite openly, you see the instrument of the state in the hand of the Volk, and you thus see in your own chancellorship the sovereignty of the Volk as consecrated to the name of Adolf Hitler!

Answer: I hope that this dialogue serves as an enlightenment to the broad circles of the bourgeoisie. The bourgeois man should stop feeling like some sort of pensioner of tradition or capital and separated from the worker by the Marxist concept of property; rather, he should strive, with an open mind, to become integrated in the whole as a worker, for he is not a member of society at all in the distorted sense in which he was persecuted as a hostile brother within the ranks of the Volk. He should base his classic bourgeois pride upon his citizenship and, in other respects, be modestly conscious of his identity as a worker. For everything that does not feverishly press for work and affirm its faith in work is condemned to extinction in the sphere of National Socialism.

▸ May 1, 1934 *At a mass rally in Berlin of some two million people, Hitler emphasized that* Volksgemeinshaft *was the foundation of the National Socialist Movement.*

In this past year, we began to establish this *Volksgemeinschaft* not only in a purely theoretical sense; we have also endeavored to secure the practical foundations it requires. For it is not sufficient to overcome unemployment as such, to simply train new workers; rather, it is necessary to gradually enlighten the millions of our *Volksgenossen* as to the nature of the new concept of work. More than one year ago, the National Socialist Party was victorious in Germany. All power and authority in the state is now in the hands of this organization. Millions of people voluntarily subjected themselves to it, and millions of others were brought into line. However, that does not mean that all of them became National Socialists. The purpose of the National Socialist idea—to put together a *Volksgemeinschaft* by overcoming rank, profession, class, and confession—is not fulfilled by simply registering with a party. One can become a party comrade by subscribing, but one can only become a National Socialist by adapting one's perception, by urgently appealing to one's own heart.

The National Socialist State is resolved to build the new German *Volksgemeinschaft*; it will never lose sight of this goal and, even if only gradually, it is certain to reach it. The gigantic organizations of our Movement, its political institutions as well as the organizations of the SA and SS, the structure of our labor front, and the state organizations of our army are all national and social melting pots in which, albeit gradually, a new German individual is being formed. What we do not successfully accomplish with the present generation we will achieve with the coming one. For just as doggedly as we have fought and fought again for the adult man and the adult woman, we shall fight for German youth. It is growing up in a different world and will be the first to do its share to build another world. In our National Socialist Youth Organization, we have created the school for the education of the individuals who will people a new German Reich.

With faith in their hearts and a strong sense of purpose, this youth will one day be a better link in our Volk's genealogical chain than we ourselves were and perhaps can be today.

When you regard the symbol of today's celebration that a German artist created for us, then it should convey to you the following: sickle and hammer were once the symbols of the German peasant and the German worker. The arrogance and lack of reason of a bourgeois age abandoned and lost these symbols. Ultimately, Jewish international litterateurs stole the tools of hardworking people and nearly succeeded in exploiting them for their own designs and purposes. The National Socialist State will overcome this ill-fated development. The hammer will once more become the symbol of the German worker and the sickle the sign of the German peasant, and the intellect must form with them an indissoluble alliance, just as we have been preaching and propagating for a decade and a half.

Therefore we have gathered together this day not only to celebrate German labor but also to celebrate a new German individual. Just as an entire year has been praised in thousands of announcements, articles in the press, and speeches of the intellectual workers, today we wish to partake in celebrating the fame of that army of millions who—as unknown and nameless soldiers of work—have, by the sweat of their brow, made a loyal contribution in the cities and the country, on the fields, in the factories, and in the workshops, to produce those goods that rightfully elevate our Volk to join the ranks of civilized nations in the world and allow it to prevail in honor. And it is thus also our will that, on this day every year for all eternity, the entire German Volk may be conscious of what it has in common and, leaving behind it any disputes, may once more join hands in inner acknowledgement of its common alliance that we call the German *Volksgemeinschaft*.

▶ January 30, 1937 *On the fourth anniversary of gaining power, Hitler spoke to the Reichstag, giving a statement of his accomplishments. His account of the National Socialist Revolution ignored the fact that many people had simply disappeared or somehow ended up dead. Nevertheless, Hitler was clear: the enemies of National Socialism simply faded away—and no one should mention them again!*

Hitler's speech ran one hour longer than had been planned. In his lengthy "party narrative," he paid particular attention to the claim that the National Socialist Revolution had been the "revolution of revolutions," and painstakingly stressed that no blood had been shed in its course.

I can say it with a certain amount of pride: this was perhaps the first modern revolution in which not so much as a window pane was shattered. Yet I do not want to be misunderstood: if the course of this revolution was bloodless, it was not because we were not men enough to stand the sight of blood. For four years, I was a soldier in the bloodiest war of all time. I never once lost my nerve throughout, no matter what the situation or what I was confronted with. This also applies to my fellow workers. But we perceived the task of the National Socialist Revolution not as destroying human life or property but instead as building up a new and better life. It is our greatest source of pride that we carried out this—undoubtedly greatest—cataclysm in our Volk with a minimum of casualties and losses.

Only where the murderous lust of Bolshevism believed itself capable, even after January 30, 1933, of preventing the triumph or the realization of the National Socialist idea by force have we naturally countered with force—and have done so with the speed of lightning. Then again there were other elements.

We recognized their lack of restraint, coupled with the gravest lack of political education, and these we merely took into preventive custody, only to restore to them their liberty after a very short time, generally speaking. And then again there were those few whose political activities served only as a cover for a criminal attitude evidenced in numerous sentences to prison or penal servitude; these we prevented from continuing their devastating work of destruction by urging them to take up a useful occupation, probably for the first time in their lives.

The Führer then claimed that all those persons who remained in the concentration camps were truly hardened criminals, for they had earlier served lengthy terms in prison or a penitentiary. Once more returning to a detailed description of the great National Socialist Revolution of 1933, he continued:

In the space of a few weeks, both the political residues and societal biases of the past thousand years in Germany had been cleared away and eliminated. Germany and the German Volk have overcome several great catastrophes. Naturally, there always had to be certain men—I will be the first to admit—who took the necessary steps and who saw these measures through despite the eternal pessimists and know-it-alls. True, an assembly of parliamentary cowards is most ill-suited to lead the Volk forth—away from destitution and despair!

▸ January 30, 1939 *In the very important speech to the Reichstag on the sixth anniversary of gaining power, Hitler made very clear that loyalty and dedication were far more important qualities of leaders in the new Germany than any question of ability or skill. Moreover, the interests of the German Volk overrode any question of morality.*

The German Volk of earlier decades, politically and socially disorganized, squandered a large part of its inherent strength in an inner struggle as fruitless as it was senseless. The so-called democratic freedom to live to the full according to one's persuasions and instincts leads neither to an evolutionary advancement nor to a freeing of exceptional forces or values. Instead, it leads to a squandering of the existing wealth of the creative potential of the individual and to his ultimate paralysis. By putting an end to this fruitless struggle, National Socialism released the inner strength otherwise suppressed and set it free to realize the vital interests of the nation in the sense of managing the great community tasks in the interior of the Reich and securing the vital necessities for the community with regard to the surrounding world. It is complete nonsense to presume that obedience and discipline are useful only to soldiers and that they have no further application in the life of peoples beyond this. To the contrary: a national community (*Volksgemeinschaft*) instilled with discipline and obedience can far more easily mobilize the forces necessary to secure the survival of its own people, thereby benefiting other peoples and serving the interests of all more effectively. Such a *Volksgemeinschaft* cannot be created by force primarily, however, but by the compelling force of the idea itself, hence, through the toil of a continuing education.

There are indeed men whom neither the greatest of calamities nor earth-shattering upheaval can incite to inner reflection or induce to spiritual action. Their hearts beat no more. They are of no value to the community. They cannot make history and history cannot be made with them. Their blasé decadence and narrow-mindedness expose them as a useless waste product of nature (*Ausschussware der Natur*). They find some consolation, even satisfaction, in considering what they hold to be their cleverness or wisdom elevating them to a lofty height above the events of the day; in other words, in the contemplation of their own ignorance.

Now it is easy to imagine that, without such ignorant men, a Volk may well be capable of the greatest actions and deeds. However, it is impossible to imagine a nation, much less to lead it, that has at its core a multitude of such ignorant men instead of a mass of full-blooded, idealistic, believing, and positive men. They constitute the only valuable elements in a *Volksgemeinschaft*. You will allow them a thousand weaknesses, if only they possess the strength to give all they have, if necessary, for an ideal or for an idea.

My deputies, we still face enormous, gigantic tasks! We must build up a new class of leaders for our Volk. Its composition is subject to racial criteria. Through the educational system and the methods we employ, it is equally necessary to demand and secure valor and readiness to take on responsibility as natural prerequisites to the assumption of public office.

In assigning men to posts of leadership in state and party, attitude and character are to be valued more highly than so-called purely scientific or supposed mental qualifications. For, wherever leadership has to be exercised, it is not abstract knowledge that is decisive but instead the inborn ability to lead and therefore a high degree of readiness to take on responsibility, of determination, courage, and persistence. In principle, we must realize that documented proof of a presumably first-class scientific education can never compensate for a lack of readiness to take on responsibility. Knowledge and leadership abilities, and hence vigor, are not mutually exclusive. In case of doubt, however, knowledge cannot serve as a substitute for attitude, courage, valor, and initiative, under any circumstances. These attributes are the more important ones in terms of the leadership of a *Volksgemeinschaft* in party and state.

When I express this to you, my deputies, I do so under the impression of that year of German history which has taught me, more than my entire previous life, how important and irreplaceable these virtues are and how, in a critical hour, one man of action weighs more than one thousand sophisticated weaklings. As a social phenomenon this new selection of leadership has to be divorced from the numerous prejudices that I can only term phony and profoundly nonsensical social morals.

There is no attitude that does not have its ultimate justification in the resulting advantages for the community. What is unimportant or detrimental to the existence of the community can never be seen as moral in the service of a social order. Above all: a *Volksgemeinschaft* is conceivable only in recognition of laws that apply to all. You cannot expect or demand of one that he abide by principles that seem absurd, detrimental, or merely unimportant in the eyes of another.

I fail to comprehend the endeavors of dying social classes, seeking to hide behind a hedge of withering class laws that have become unreal and divorcing themselves from reality to sustain life artificially. Nothing can be said against it, if it is being done in an effort to secure a calm cemetery where to rest after passing away. However, if it is being done in order to erect a barrier against the progress of life, then the storm of a forward-charging youth will brush away the old scrub.

Today's German people's state (*Volksstaat*) knows no social prejudices. Hence, it knows no special social morals. It knows only the laws and necessities of life, as they reveal themselves to man through reason and knowledge.

VII. *Hitler thought it best to reveal certain of his beliefs to only a few or no people.*

▸ October 31, 1937 *Hitler talked a great deal about what he believed, but he was very reticent about the actual basic concepts that formed the foundations of his beliefs. Because of this, some commentators have assumed that there were no such core beliefs, that Hitler was simply a supremely power-hungry opportunist. However, there have always been rumors of secret speeches and discussions.*

It is no coincidence that in these days as well, Hitler decided to leave the remnants of his former private life behind and to sever all ties to the Catholic faith.

A number of Hitler's "secret speeches" during this time, while not revealing all his inner thoughts, tell us a great deal. The majority of these speeches consisted of little more than hackneyed phrases and concepts Hitler had already presented in earlier speeches and in *Mein Kampf.* Nevertheless, on occasion Hitler dropped certain clues to the "secrets" he harbored, but only when facing the appropriately impressionable audience, such as the political leaders or, typically, a group of workers. The Führer reasoned that those in his audience would feel all the more obliged to remain loyal to him once given the honored role of keeper of his secrets.

However, Hitler kept the true "secrets" to himself. Speaking to his closest advisers, he never attempted to veil this fact. Whenever a conversation touched upon a topic he did not care to discuss, he would shroud himself in a cloak of mystery and end the conversation in a manner similar to Jesus Christ when he had said to his disciples: "I have yet many things to say to you, but you cannot bear them now."

Hitler still proceeded according to his old maxim. In 1932, he had explained it to Lüdecke in the following terms:

> I have an old principle, only to say what must be said to him who must know it, and only when he must know it.

A "basic directive" issued to the *Wehrmacht* in 1940 articulated this even more pointedly:

> No one, no office, and no officer may gain knowledge of secret affairs unless their duty absolutely necessitates this, or be informed of either more or earlier than is absolutely necessary.

Late in October and early in November 1937, Hitler deemed it "absolutely necessary" to reveal to a small group his new religious convictions and his plans for a policy of aggression. He did this in two "secret speeches," one in Berlin before the propaganda leaders of the party, the other before an assembly of the commanders in chief of the branches of the *Wehrmacht* and in the presence of the Reich foreign minister. While speaking before the propaganda leaders, Hitler's topics included the following:

1. He, Hitler, would not live much longer, at least as far as this was accessible to the human mind. In his family, men did not grow old. Also both his parents had died young.

2. It was hence necessary to face the problem of gaining more productive land for the German people (*Lebensraum*). That problem absolutely had to be resolved as quickly as possible—so that this would occur while he was still alive. Later generations would not be capable of accomplishing this. His person alone was in a position to do this.

3. After long and bitter mental battles, he finally had divorced himself from the religious convictions that still existed from his childhood. "Now I feel as fresh as a colt in the pasture."

VIII. *Hitler's solution to all of Germany's social and economic difficulties was the expansion of territory for Germans to occupy and the elimination of current inhabitants* (Lebensraum).

▶ November 19, 1937 *At a speech in Augsburg to celebrate the fifteenth anniversary of a local Nazi Party group, Hitler discussed the need to use force to gain German* Lebensraum.

After yet another recapitulation of the achievements of the past fifteen years ("The National Socialist German Worker's Party is the greatest organization man has ever built!"), Hitler directed his attention to the new tasks faced and addressed the subject of the "too confined *Lebensraum* of the German Volk:"

> I may say so myself, my old party comrades: our fight was worth it after all. Never before has a fight commenced with as much success as ours. In these fifteen years, we have taken on a tremendous task. The task blessed our efforts. Our efforts were not in vain, for from them has ensued one of the greatest rebirths in history. Germany has overcome the great catastrophe and awakened from it to a better and new and strong life. That we can say at the end of these fifteen years. And there lies the reward for every single one of you, my old party comrades!
>
> When I look back on my own life, I can certainly say that it has been an immeasurable joy to be able to work for our Volk in this great age. It is truly a wonderful thing after all when fate chooses certain people who are allowed to devote themselves to their Volk.
>
> Today we are facing new tasks. For the *Lebensraum* of our Volk is too confined. The world is attempting to disassociate itself from dealing with this problem and answering this question. But it will not succeed! One day the world will be forced to take our demands into consideration. I do not doubt for a second that we will procure for ourselves the same vital rights as other peoples outside the country in exactly the same way as we were able to lead it onwards within. I do not doubt that this vital right of the German Volk, too, will one day be understood by the whole world!

I am of the conviction that the most difficult preliminary work has already been accomplished. What is necessary now is that all National Socialists recall again and again the principles with which we grew up. If the whole party and hence the whole nation stands united behind the leadership, then this same leadership, supported by the joined forces of a population of sixty-eight million, ultimately personified in its *Wehrmacht*, will be able to successfully defend the interests of the nation and also to successfully accomplish the tasks assigned to us!

When he delivered his speech in Augsburg, Hitler had already determined to apply force to the effort of resolving the problems faced by Germany in the future. In his address, he once again articulated the principles that had driven him onward ever since his accession to power on January 30, 1933, and that would continue to inspire him up to the last days of the Second World War:

I do not doubt for a second that we will procure our vital rights outside the country in exactly the same way as we were able to lead it onwards within.

In content, this remark corresponded to a statement that Hitler would make later in the course of the war.

I am firmly convinced that this battle will end not a whit differently from the battle I once waged inside Germany!

This assumption that the analysis of problems and situations in the domestic realm could be superimposed upon international affairs, indeed, that both spheres were fundamentally equivalent, would slowly but surely precipitate the fall of Hitler and his regime.

▸ January 30, 1939 *In another excerpt from this important Reichstag speech, Hitler talked about* Lebensraum *as the most critical problem of the German* Volk. *As usual, he was ambiguous in his phrasing of concepts but the National Socialists heard the message clearly.*

For what is the reason for all our economic troubles? Simply the overpopulation of our *Lebensraum*! And in this context, I can only hold out to these critical gentlemen in the west and in the democracies beyond Europe one simple fact and one simple question: The German Volk survives with 135 inhabitants per square kilometer without any exterior assistance and without access to its earlier savings. The rest of the world has looted Germany throughout the past one-and-a-half decades, has burdened it with enormous debt payments. Without any colonies, its people are nonetheless fed and clothed and, moreover, Germany boasts no unemployment. And now to my question: Who among our so-called great democratic powers is in a position to say as much of itself?

To him on whom nature has bestowed bananas for free, the struggle for survival necessarily will appear far easier than to the weary German peasant who, all year round, toils to sow and reap on his plot of soil. And, therefore, we insist that this carefree, internationalist banana-picker refrain from finding fault with the labor of our German peasant.

After endless accounts of the economically unsound policy forced on Germany by the victorious Allies in the aftermath of the year 1918, Hitler intimated that the economic sphere in Germany was soon to undergo radical changes. He insisted that an "expansion of *Lebensraum*" was both necessary and inevitable.

The dilemma we will then face can only be resolved in two ways:

1. through an increase in the import of foodstuffs which necessitates an increase in the export of German manufactured goods in due consideration of the fact that raw materials used in the production process have to be imported initially and hence only a fraction of profit remains for the purchase of foodstuffs, or

2. through an expansion of *Lebensraum* for our Volk, thereby establishing an economic circle to secure the production of sufficient foodstuffs for Germany domestically. Since the second approach is as yet impossible to pursue due to the

persistent delusions of the one-time victorious powers, we are forced to follow along the path of the first proposition. This means we must export in order to be able to purchase food from abroad. Since these exported goods use up raw materials which we ourselves do not possess, this means we must export yet more goods to secure these raw materials for our economy. We are compelled not by capitalist considerations, as this may be the case in other countries, but by dire necessity, the most excruciating which can befall a people, namely, concern for its daily bread.

And when foreign statesmen threaten us with economic sanctions, for what reason I do not know, then all I can do is to assure them that this would lead to a desperate struggle for economic survival. We could far more easily hold our own in such a struggle than those other satiated nations, for our motive for entering into this struggle would be a very simple one: German Volk, either live, i.e., export, or perish! And I can assure all these doubters abroad that the German Volk will not perish; it will live! And, if necessary, this German Volk will place at its leadership's disposal its entire capacity for work realized in the new National Socialist community. It will take up this struggle and it will persevere in this struggle. And as far as its leadership is concerned, I can only assure you that it stands determined to do whatever is necessary.

A final resolution of this problem in a reasonable manner will come about only when the greed of certain peoples has been conquered by the insights of human common sense and reason if one accepts that insistence on injustice is, not only detrimental politically, but also useless economically; indeed that it spells insanity.

IX. *When Hitler spoke to new army officers he was as clear as he ever was explaining his thoughts. The following, first, a summary, and second, a complete speech, illustrates Hitler's beliefs as he expressed them to his followers.*

▸ January 24, 1940 *This summary brings out most of the structure of Hitler's beliefs.*

January 24 marked the anniversary of Frederick the Great's birthday. On this occasion, Hitler spoke before an assembly of 7,000 officer cadets at the Berlin Sportpalast. Already in the previous year, in timely concurrence with the completion of the new Reich Chancellery, Hitler had singled out newly appointed officers and officer cadets for several addresses. Now, in time of war, he wished to conjure up the spirit of Frederick the Great, of his "staying power," to create the impression that he too, Adolf Hitler, would secure victory in the end.

Before the year 1943, Hitler delivered a total of eight such war appeals in front of officer cadets, almost without exception at the Berlin Sportpalast. Naturally these were only a pale reflection of the early grandly staged party or storm trooper (SA) rallies that Hitler had held at this location in the days after his rise to power. Hitler's style had changed as had the size of his audience: five to ten thousand officers as compared to twenty thousand party functionaries or SA men. Hitler's military audience was less likely, due to discipline, to break out in extended exuberant shouts of *"Heil!"* Nor were the officers likely to disrupt Hitler's speech with thunderous applause. They restricted themselves to curt responses: *"Heil, mein Führer!"* when Hitler greeted or bade them leave in a resounding military tone, shouting, *"Heil, Offiziersanwärter!"*

These military roll calls were among the few "mass rallies" that Hitler could afford to stage during the war. He tended to be out of sorts on these occasions, however. Apparently, he no longer took care to prepare himself specially for routine appeals where he usually repeated the same thoughts without giving any attention to current affairs. He evidently thought these repetitions a matter of no import, as the officer cadets appearing before him every year naturally were always different ones.

Thinking he need not come up with anything new, he reiterated the following "philosophical considerations" in the Sportpalast appeals during the war:

1. "Party narratives," more or less lengthy in nature, gave way to reflections upon German history as interpreted by Hitler. Therein he expounded upon Germany's fate throughout the past centuries and millennia much in the manner already employed in *Mein Kampf.* The term "struggle" as the essence of life, its sense and mission, played a central role in these expositions.

2. The relationship between population size and *Lebensraum*, that was to be and had to be resolved through "adaptation." Either population figures "adapted" themselves to the *Lebensraum* available (possible either through starvation or a decline in birth rates), or the *Lebensraum* was "adapted" to an ever increasing population (and this unequivocally meant conquest of new lands).

3. The German Volk in its role as not only the best, but the numerically strongest people in Europe, and, with the exception of China, in the entire world. Hence Germany had to win and would win.

On Hitler's address to the 7,000 officer cadets on January 24, 1940, the following communiqué reached the public:

> The Führer and supreme commander of the *Wehrmacht* assembled officer cadets of the army and *Luftwaffe* at the Sportpalast on Wednesday [January 24]. These candidates await appointment as officers and return to their units along the front after the completion of their training. Junkers of the Nazi Party security squads (SS) *Verfügungstruppen* also participated in the roll call.
>
> In consideration of the meaning and vital necessity of struggle in life, the Führer spoke of the duties and tasks of the officer in the National Socialist *Wehrmacht*. On the anniversary of the great king, the Führer pointed to Frederick the Great and his soldiers as models of the best soldiership. The 7,000 young soldiers enthusiastically reacted to the Führer's words. Field Marshal Göring led them in endless cries of *Sieg Heil* for the first soldier of the Reich.

Some gems from Hitler's speech of January 24 are quoted below:

> We have two states as our enemies: England and France! These two states owe their existence as world powers and as great powers solely to the century-long decline of the German Volk.

We Germans number eighty-two million people in today's Reich. This means that we are the only state, aside from China, to boast such a great number of people of one *Volkstum* in a contiguous setting.

Germany has become a factor again [in world politics] through National Socialism.

This war was an inevitable one! This Europe at the mercy of France and England begrudges the German Volk its existence since it does not want to bear German greatness and power and because it believes it cannot bear this structure. However much we limit ourselves, we shall never be able to appease France and England!

You are soldiers today. I, too, was once a soldier and I remain one today. Though this struggle for my Volk was an inevitable one [historically], I have the absolute will to see this struggle through in my lifetime. Then today's German generation shall take up this great task, and it shall not say it will leave it to its children.

Today, for the first time in German history, the German giant faces only one front and is armed better than ever before. They believed that they would be able to engage us in struggle along several fronts this time, too, but in this they failed because of the alliances and treaties formed.

They [Germany's enemies in the West] are all waiting for action. We decide when these actions will take place. Let no one entertain any doubt, however, that they will indeed take place. No struggle in world history was ever decided by inaction, by staying low or on the sidelines. Rather, any historic struggle is decided only by victory, and any victory is decided only in the struggle.

While undoubtedly there was some truth to Hitler's theory on inaction in war, it was ironically he himself who shied away from engagements with the British by "staying low." When he spoke of struggle or battle, he obviously had only France or small neutral states in mind. He was still convinced that, driven "back to the Thames," the British fighting forces would collapse. Thus, he was surprised anew every time he met with England's determination to pursue victory on the battlefield instead of at the conference table.

▶ May 3, 1940 *This is a complete speech but is rather short compared to most of Hitler's speeches.*

On May 3, in the Berlin Sportpalast, 6,000 officer cadets were summoned to bear witness to an appeal by the Führer. For the occasion, Hitler dressed in riding pants and knee boots as though to underline he was ready for a "fight." The following statement was published on Hitler's appeal to the cadets:

> On Friday [May 3], the Führer and supreme commander once more gathered about him candidates for officer and leadership positions in the army, *Luftwaffe*, and Waffen SS at the Sportpalast. In an impressive address, the Führer outlined the tasks his young comrades would face at the front in the fight to decide the existence or non-existence of our Volk. Field Marshal Göring concluded the appeal with a *Sieg Heil* shout for the Führer. The young soldiers demonstrated that they had understood their supreme commander with enthusiastic shouts of *Heil*.

The speech was typical for the appeals that Hitler enjoyed making to this audience, as it included all major points usually discussed on similar occasions.

Key phrases were: the adaptation of the *Lebensraum* to increasing population; Germany as the most populous nation on earth, with the exception of China; struggle as the essence of life. Hitler's comments were decidedly colored by the imminent launch of the offensive in the west. Hitler spoke of the "second act in a gigantic struggle," referring to the First World War as the "first act," and of a "period of rapidly approaching great decisions of world-historical import." He could not resist mocking "the pitiful leadership of the Great War" that constantly "stumbled over threads" and dared not "step across lines drawn in crayon." Hitler need not have worried himself; he was not the man to be held back by threads, such as those tying

Germany to its obligations under international law or contracts previously entered into with other states. His "philosophy of state" was decidedly less complex in nature. It was steeped in the concept of brute force that he had already set forth in *Mein Kampf.* And he had few qualms about frankly admitting this in various boasts before the young officers sitting in front of him: "The earth is there for him who takes it. It is a challenge cup that is taken from those peoples who become weak," because: "Strength *(Kraft)* determines right on this soil."

Hitler began his speech as follows:

Heil Offiziersanwärter!

The battle in the midst of which Germany finds itself today is the second act of the great, decisive struggle that will determine the future of our race, of our Reich. You often hear the term balance of power these days: the balance of power in Europe. In particular of late, you will have had occasion to read that the cause for this battle lies with the threatened disruption of this balance of power in Europe. Now what is the meaning of this thesis? Germany's racial core consists of a mass of Volk of over eighty million men. Throughout the centuries, albeit in lesser numbers, this mass of Volk formed the center of gravity in Europe. Over the past 300 years, this center of gravity in terms of the Volk's mass has lost its significance in power politics.

At the end of the Thirty Years' War, the political unity of this mass began to disintegrate and to evolve into a conglomerate of small, individual states. With this, it lost its inner value—and, in particular, the impact in terms of power normally attributed to the center of gravity in Europe. The Peace of Münster established at least the vision of the political divisiveness of the German nation. Hence, it created the prerequisites for the rise of other powers to hegemony on the world stage to a degree far beyond the numerical significance and value of these other races. Without this fragmentation of Germany, this political atomization, the rise of England as a world power over the past three hundred years would not have been conceivable. Without this, France would never have become what it became later, after overcoming its political, internal multifariousness, and what it would still like to be today. Broadly speaking, these two world powers are nothing other than the result of the elimination of the German nation as a factor in power politics. By the same token, the political impotence of the German nation remains a prerequisite to their continued existence in the future, as well. Hence, a balance of power has established itself in Europe devoid of a foundation in terms of the masses. The strongest European nation by far has rendered this exaggerated significance possible through its political fragmentation. Without this fragmentation, Germany undoubtedly would still constitute the determining factor in Europe as was the case earlier.

And thus came about a state of affairs called the balance of power in Europe. Its mission is to eliminate the strongest European force as a factor in power politics by fostering its internal fragmentation. For us Germans, the question arises: is a modification of this state of affairs necessary? Today, we need not reply to this any more. Its answer lies in the natural drive of all living beings. Its political answer goes back to the time when at the moment of collapse, or rather when the collapse of the Old Reich was imminent, a rebirth already became evident in the creation of a new nucleus, that of the Brandenburg-Prussia of the day.

He then proceeded in detail to the subject of *Lebensraum.*

Yet, beyond this, there is another compelling reason to seek a modification in this balance of power in Europe. The problem presents itself in the following manner to us Germans. There are two decisive elements in the life of a Volk. One the one hand, there is a variable: the Volk's numbers; and, on the other hand, there is the *Lebensraum* as a given—a fact that does not change by itself. The Volk's numbers and the *Lebensraum* exist interdependently and this interdependence is of fateful significance in the lives of peoples. Man lives not by theories alone. He lives not by phrases, nor does he live by programs. Man lives by what the *Lebensraum* at his disposal affords him in terms of foodstuffs and raw material, and by what he is then able, thanks to his industriousness, to reap from it through his work. Nonetheless, the *Lebensraum* is of primary importance, of course. For while a Volk of great industry may be able to fashion a bearable existence from even the most modest of *Lebensräume*, there will come a time when the discrepancy between the Volk's numbers and the *Lebensraum* becomes too great. This then leads to a restriction of life, even to an ending of life.

And thus, ever since there has been a history of man, this history has consisted of nothing other than the attempt to bring into harmony the naturally increasing numbers of a Volk with the *Lebensraum*. This meant either to adapt the *Lebensraum* to the Volk's numbers or to adapt the Volk's numbers to the *Lebensraum*. These are the two ways of establishing a tolerable relationship here.

I will begin with the first alternative: people adapt to the *Lebensraum*. This can occur naturally as the insufficient *Lebensraum* cannot provide for people. Weak peoples then begin to capitulate in the face of necessity and to abandon the foundation of their existence. This means that they start to reduce their numbers, primarily due to need.

There is yet another way of adapting the Volk's numbers to the *Lebensraum*. It is called emigration. In both ways, Germany has lost human material of immense value throughout the centuries. In centuries past already, need had been great in the German lands. Often this has led to a virtual decimation of men. The second way robbed us of yet more German blood. Throughout centuries, pressured by insufficient *Lebensraum* of their own, German men left their homeland and helped to build up those foreign states that now face us as enemies.

Another third way was found of adapting the Volk's numbers to the given *Lebensraum*. It is called: voluntary reduction of birth rates. After the first way—that of hunger—no longer appeared tolerable and the second way—that of emigration—was blockaded by the Peace Treaties of Versailles, people turned to the third way in increasing numbers. It was even hailed as a virtue to voluntarily limit the strength of one's own Volk, to reduce the Volk's numbers. I need not tell you where this led. In the end, the result of all these attempts was that the potential for natural selection in a people was severely curtailed. And, in the end, it begins to surrender its forces to better peoples. For it is emigration above all that, like a magnet, draws the active element out of a race, a Volk, and leaves behind only the weak, the cowardly, the meek. And if such a state of affairs is allowed to persist over the centuries, then a formerly important people will slowly but surely lose its steel and turn into a weak, a cowardly mass of men, willing to accept any fate.

This is the first way of establishing balance between a Volk's numbers and the *Lebensraum*. This way, no matter what the circumstances, will always lead to the destruction of a Volk. In the future, this will lead to a reduction of such a Volk in comparison to those peoples who choose the second way, namely, not to adapt the Volk's numbers to the *Lebensraum*, but rather to adapt the *Lebensraum* to the Volk's numbers.

This is the way chosen by all vigorous nations of this earth. It is the natural way since Providence has placed man upon this earth and has given him this earth as his playground, as the basis for his existence. Providence has not initiated man into its designs. It has not assigned peoples certain *Lebensräume*. Instead nature has placed these beings on this earth and has given them freedom. He who wants to live asserts himself. He who cannot assert himself does not deserve to live.

He will perish.

This is an iron-clad, yet also a just, principle. The earth is not there for cowardly peoples, not for weak ones, not for lazy ones. The earth is there for him who takes it and who industriously labors upon it and thereby fashions his life. That is the will of Providence. That is why it has placed man upon this earth, along with the other beings, and has paved the way for him, has freed him to make his own decisions, to lead his own struggle for survival.

And should he fail in this struggle, should he become weak in asserting his existence, then Providence will not rush to his aid. Instead, it will sentence him to death. And rightly

so. Other men will come. The space will not remain empty.
What the one man loses, another will take. And life continues in accordance with its own eternal rhythm without consideration for the weakling.

The earth is a challenge cup. It is a challenge cup that passes into the hands of those peoples who deserve it, who prove
themselves strong enough in their struggle for existence, who
secure the basis for their own existence. It is a challenge cup
that is taken from those peoples who become weak, who are
not willing, at the risk of the life of one generation, to secure
the life of later generations. The right to this soil is given
equally to all these peoples. On this earth, no Englishman
has more rights than a Frenchman, no Frenchman has more
rights than a Russian, no Russian has more rights than a German, no German has more rights than an Italian, and so on.
Strength *(Kraft)* determines right on this soil. And strength
is nothing other than an expression of a healthy sense of self-
assertion. Peoples who start to lose this strength are no longer
healthy and therefore lose their right to this earth. And to be
able to exercise this strength that is first of all a question of
will, it is necessary to create certain organizational prerequisites. Foremost amongst these is the inner unity of a Volk. In
Germany, we have witnessed the long, almost tragic evolution
that was necessary to lead us from inner political conflicts
once more to the core, not of a new philosophy of state, but to
that of the creation of a new state.

The core that gave us not only political unity but above
all the foundation of ethnic unity. Thereby it created the prerequisites for the inner unity of the German nation. What
has come to pass in this realm within these seven years is the
greatest of chapters in German history. Not only have countless political forms, old, no longer viable structures, been
broken down, but also, in the realm of society, the birth of a
new *Volksgemeinschaft* and hence of a new German Volk became apparent. In the course of the last years, we were able
to observe how the toughness and the power of resistance of
this new formation passed the test. I do not doubt that it will

hold its own in emerging victoriously from this greatest trial in German history. And hence out of this social and moral revolution grew the new German people's state (*Volksstaat*).

Hitler could not resist the temptation of exaggerating in his "party narrative" either:

Since 1933, this new German *Volksstaat* has undergone change, strengthened its inner formation, through numerous acts of a lawgiving nature. And thus, this *Volksstaat* has now begun to create the elements necessary for its external liberation. What has been attained in this area within these seven years, is one of the greatest chapters in German history. In these seven years—I feel free to avow this openly before history—we have not wasted a single month in securing that power, without possession of which a people is doomed in its search for justice on this earth.

Its lack has shown us how helpless a Volk is when it depends upon the insight or mercy, the compassion or goodwill of other peoples whom it must implore and for which it must beg. And thus the Greater German Reich has fashioned its own arms. And with the increases in its arms and its power, the Greater German Reich itself has been strengthened. And today, we find ourselves in the midst of a great historic conflict, the second phase in a gigantic struggle. The initial phase we once lost not because our arms were bad by themselves; rather we lost it because the leadership failed and the German Volk in its inner formation was not yet prepared to see through such a struggle, as it lacked inner cohesion and strength. I have striven to make up for this within twenty years' time. And, so I believe, I succeeded.

Whereas once the German soldier fought a lonely battle at the front, today he knows behind him the united force of a uniformly led and orientated Volk. This Volk today expects of the German soldier that he fulfill the mission of his life. The German soldier today can rest assured that the Volk standing behind him will recognize his needs and fulfill his wants.

Hitler then reproached the "small skeptic, the apprehensive man," for his misgivings regarding victory in the end:

> And then comes the question that will plague every small skeptic, every apprehensive man, one time or another, and that might well make you ill at ease also in the most trying of hours: "Is it actually possible to win this fight?" And, from the depths of my convictions, I would like to give you the following reply. I give it to you not as a pale theoretician, not as a man who is a stranger to the demands facing you at present. I face them myself. I am acquainted with all the needs, all the worries, all the cares, and all the hardships, that you will encounter and that some of you have already encountered.
>
> I have experienced them all myself. And in spite of this, after the greatest of collapses then suffered, I already immediately knew the answer to this question. I found it for myself. At no moment was there any doubt in my heart that Germany would survive and would win this most difficult of struggles in its history.

Having proved the veracity of his convictions beyond all doubt in this proclamation, Hitler once more focused on the numbers and value of the German Volk and claimed that "there is no Volk better on this earth than the German one."

> Reasons for this belief lie not with some sort of fanatical hope; rather they are founded in recognition. For one, the numbers of the Volk. Even the most expert and most worthy of peoples can fail in their struggle for survival if the discrepancy of their numbers is too great and too obvious in view of the tasks faced and especially, of the forces of the environment. Antiquity furnishes us with two great, tragic examples: Sparta and Hellas. They were both doomed to failure in the end because the world in which they lived was numerically so superior to them that even the most successful of struggles was bound to tax their forces beyond measure.
>
> When we look at today's Germany in light of this consideration, then, my young friends, we recognize a fact which occasions great joy: certainly, there is a British Empire, but there

are only 46 million Englishmen in the motherland. There is a huge American state, but amongst its 130 million inhabitants, there are barely 65 million true Anglo-Saxons, and that's that. The rest are Negroes, Jews, Latins, Irishmen, and Germans, and so on.

There is a huge Russian state. However, it has not even 60 million true Great Russians as its bearers. The rest consists of, in part, greatly inferior races. There is also France, spanning over nine million square kilometers of earth and with more than 100 million men, but amongst them are perhaps at most 37 million true Frenchmen who must uphold this structure.

Well, here we stand, my young friends, a state of a total of 82 million German Teutons (*deutsche Germanen*). At present, we are the ethnically most numerous political structure of one race that exists on this earth, with the exception of China. This fact is not new. In former times as well, the German Volk determined, thanks to the force of its numbers, Europe's destiny.

And now there arises a second question, one of equal decisiveness, namely, that of the value of the Volk. For all of us know that numbers by themselves are not in the final instance decisive. And here, my young friends, we are able these days to proudly acknowledge: there is no Volk better on this earth than the German one. Believe me, in the days and months of the collapse of 1918, one thought uplifted me, put me back on my feet again, and returned to me my faith in Germany. It made me strong internally to begin and to take up this gigantic struggle. It was the conviction that even the Great War had not proven us to be second class. On the contrary, it had proved us to be undoubtedly the best Volk, especially insofar as this was a question of soldierly virtues. And this is apparent again these days. Here is a Volk that in terms of numbers is the strongest state people on this earth. And beyond this, it is also the best Volk in terms of value, for this value in the end becomes apparent in the soldier. A Volk that does not cherish soldierly virtues is like straw on this earth; it will be blown away by the wind. However, a Volk that possesses as much metal as the German one needs only to develop its values and to apply these subsequently. Then no one can take its future from it.

There is yet another factor that must give all of us internal confidence: it is the ability of our Volk, also its economic ability. Here as well, great feats have been accomplished. The German Volk has wrought a miracle economically within these barely seven years. You all know of our great plans. They were inspired but by one thought.

Naturally, Hitler did not forget to mention the *Wehrmacht*, with "the best-equipped soldier of the world."

Above all reigned the thought of the resurrection of the German *Wehrmacht*, the increasing independence of our economy, its freedom from exterior influences, its stability in the event of a blockade. These were the principles that moved us from day one to implement all these plans, that in the final instance found their realization in the Four-Year Plan. We have an economy in Germany today that ranks at the top of the world economy in particular as far as production in realms of vital importance to the war is concerned.

There is something else, too: German organization. It is today's organization growing out of our basic nature, out of our national community (*Volksgemeinschaft*). Said organization that today encompasses the entire German Volk, that reaches into every home, into every village, and there again into every farmstead, into every factory, into every craftsman's shop. There is no German who is not integrated into this gigantic organization. We have created a miracle instrument that enables us to issue a single directive and to drive it home into even the most remote hut within a few hours.

No Volk in the world today possesses a better form of organization than the German Volk; most do not even possess one nearly as good. A state of affairs that is accepted as a matter of course in other countries even today, we have long overcome. You need only think of the parliamentarian theatrics in these states and, as soldiers, apply this mentally to a company or a battalion.

You will laugh at the idea of being able to hold your own in battle with such a lot. With such peoples, you cannot score successes in the long run. And this is better, too: we are the state that has created the most profound harmony between political organization and its military implementation; the state in that soldierly principles have been applied in the build-up of the *Wehrmacht* and that, in turn, have already found their political translation therein. And thus we can say that between the *Wehrmacht* and its principles on the one hand, and the political organization and the constructive elements therein on the other hand, there exists complete harmony. To this we must add the German soldier as a warrior. His equipment—today we have the best-equipped soldier of the world in our army and in our *Luftwaffe*.

And secondly, the German soldier and his training. When today we hear of such low—relatively low—losses across the board, which stand in no relation to the losses that I myself had the opportunity to witness in the Great War, then we owe this to the improved training of the individual soldier. But also we owe it to the leadership experienced in war, the more thorough training. Surely, today we have the best army there is in the world at this time.

The most important factor, however, was the leadership and the trust in this leadership, i.e., Adolf Hitler. In this context, Hitler portrayed himself as the role-model for the young soldiers. He claimed that he had not forgotten the "gnawing fear of death" that had gripped hold of him, too, as he had lain in the trenches. He had compassion for the young officers, but still he insisted: "It is of no import whether the individual among us lives—what must live is our Volk!" Hitler relished playing the role of a Frederick the Great and called upon the soldiers to be "brave and valiant." Other phrases followed, such as "the German is no scoundrel who will ever abandon his company commander," since "he will love him who leads him." Hitler stated in detail:

> And finally, and this ought to be almost at the top of the list, there is one more thing that ought to reinforce us in our belief in victory: trust in the German leadership; in the leadership on top and way down. Trust in a leadership that knows only the thought of winning this battle, that subordinates all other concerns to this, that is suffused with the fanatical will to do everything and to risk everything for success in this

battle, that unlike the pitiful leadership of the World War does not stumble over threads or is unable to step across lines drawn in crayon.

Instead the German Volk and above all you, as soldiers and future officers, must know that at the helm of the Reich there stands a leadership which night and day knows only the one thought: to force victory under any circumstances! And to risk everything for it. And beyond this, you must know that this leadership naturally can only accomplish what is provided for by the highest echelons of leadership. And that you yourselves form part of this total leadership. Every one of you will have to struggle with the same problems that are not spared the supreme leadership of today either.

For when I look back upon the war myself, then I have not forgotten those difficult hours full of worries, the gnawing fear of death, and all those other sentiments that man experiences in face of these most horrendous stresses placed upon nerves and willpower, of physical strain. I have not forgotten these—yet, still, how easy do all the decisions of the soldier then appear to me as opposed to the decisions that one later has to take upon oneself in positions of responsible leadership. How easy all of this is when it is merely a question of one's own life as opposed to holding, in the final instance, the nation's life and destiny in one's hands.

Whatever situation you may encounter individually, never forget one thing: Every decision you make, every action you order, every stand you occupy, all this will not be any more difficult than the same decisions, the same stands, the same willpower asked of those who in other places have to bear the responsibility and have to bear it overall. In this respect, a great community of leadership must take hold in which every one occupies his place, is ready to fulfill his mission, is ready to rejoice in taking on responsibility with the one thought: It is of no importance whether the individual among us lives— what must live is our Volk!

We now stand in the midst of the most decisive struggle for Germany's entire future. Of what importance is it should the individual amongst us, every individual included, leave the stage? What is decisive is that our Volk can assert itself. And it will only then be able to assert itself when its leadership, at every instance, is fanatically willing to do everything for the one goal: to win this struggle. And believe me, my young friends, the individual man is always brave and valiant; the front-line soldier, he is always decent basically, he looks up to his leaders, he sees his company commander before him, his platoon leader. And let no one forget: The German is no such scoundrel (*Hundsfott*) that he will ever abandon his company commander. He would never do such a thing. He will follow his leader, but his leader must make it easy for him through his dedication, his daring, his courage. Such a leader will then always find a following and will chain it to himself—whatever his position may be, at the top or at the head of a group or platoon, or company. It will always be the same. The result: he will love him who leads him!

And even if life is wonderful and the sacrifice of life ever so hard, my young friends, many generations lived before us. That we are here today we do not owe to their peaceful existence but to their placing at risk their own lives in the struggle. For the soil upon which we stand today was not given us by the Good Lord as a gift. It had to be gained in battle. And time and time again, there were Germans to be found who were willing to place their lives at risk in the past so that life might be given to later generations. And it is not as though placing one's life at risk was any easier then than it is today. It was just as bitter and just as difficult.

When we speak of the dead of the World War, then we should never forget that every single one of these two million gave his life for the future of the nation just as this may be asked of us and of you individually at one point. Another thing yet is certain: the more determined a Volk is in taking up a fight, the more ruthlessly it acts, the less the sacrifices will be!

And thus, I expect of you in this era of an approaching great, world-historical decision that you shall first be valiant, courageous, and exemplary officers, that you shall be comradely and loyal not only amongst yourselves, but also with the men placed in your care. Today you have a Volk—not mercenaries, not vagrants caught along country roads. Rather *Volksgenossen* are entrusted to your leadership. And this you may never forget. These *Volksgenossen* will all the more attach themselves to you the more they feel they can see in you true leaders of the German Volk, of the Volk in arms. Expand your horizon, for the soldier needs—beyond heroics and courage and enthusiasm—the true foundations of knowledge. Here, too, knowledge is power. Above all, apply this expertise and knowledge in the care for the *Volksgenossen* entrusted to you. It is because of the absolute authority this state grants you that you are obligated to carefully attend to this authority in the service of the leadership of the men entrusted to you. To be a leader means to truly care for all those with whose care one has been entrusted. Above all, be a man in the hours of great trial. Persevere and above all be persistent.

Such ideas were not far off the mark when one attacked smaller, weaker nations. Hitler remarked that "today Germany fights as the strongest military state against a front of enemies inferior to it in terms of numbers and value." However, with a superior adversary, the same maxims quickly turned against the aggressor. Hitler's beloved metaphor of the "last battalion" did not apply to Germany, no matter how loudly he proclaimed it:

The great victories of world history were accorded to that party that commanded the last battalion on the battlefield, i.e., the men who knew how to carry their heads high to the last minute. It is not as though the dice fell during the first minute of any battle. It is not as though one could say in the first minute already: naturally there will be success for the one side; it will carry the victory, no one can deny it, while on the other side, there will be only destruction. Great world-historical decisions seldom look like successes from the start. Many times the struggle is a difficult one and victory appears elusive. In the end, it will bestow its favors upon him whose persistence, whose fanatical, indestructible stand makes him the more deserving one. And here we Germans can look with pride to one soldier who has entered the halls of history as an immortal.

If there are men who doubt success or the possibility of success, then all we can say to them is: today Germany fights as the strongest military state against a front of enemies inferior to it in terms of numbers and value. Once a man, with a state of 2.7 million, dared to attack the monarchy in the Reich of the day and, after three wars against a European coalition of over 40 million men, he achieved the victory in the end. His were not only victories. What was so wonderful in all this was his attitude in the most critical of situations, his attitude when he faced defeat. Everyone can suffer a defeat now and then. What is decisive is his character, how he takes it, and immediately goes on the offensive again. This, my young friends, must be instilled in your flesh and blood, and this you must instill in your soldiers: we may be defeated once perhaps, but vanquished—never! And in the end, the victory will be ours— one way or another!

Thereupon, Hitler indulged in sentimental reminiscences on his "eventful life," his many "defeats, blows, worries, and setbacks." The masses, however, had failed to recognize these.

I can look back upon a most eventful life. It was not as though this struggle for power in Germany, for the new Movement, had consisted of only victories. You need only read the prophecies of my opponents. Who believed in my ultimate victory? Who believed in the certainty of the outcome of this struggle? It was a question of a great deal of persistence to overcome all these defeats, these blows, to emerge from them only to take power in the end. And in these last years as well—there have been many worries in countless realms. Many setbacks. The mass of the people may well not even have realized all of this, for the leadership has learned to come to terms with these setbacks.

It is one of the most uplifting tasks of leadership to allow one's followers to mark only the victory, and to take upon oneself the entire responsibility at critical moments, to step in front of one's followers to shield them against this responsibility.

And now I ask of you to be aware at every hour that in your hand lies the honor of a great Volk, the honor not only of your generation but that of generations past. At every hour, not only the eyes of millions of your living contemporaries follow you, but also the eyes of those who closed them before us upon this earth. They look upon you through the past and hence through immortality and they will seek to determine whether and to what extent you are fulfilling those duties that other men before us so gloriously fulfilled. They expect of us that posterity should have no more cause to be ashamed of us than we have cause to be ashamed of the great eras of our past. When we hold up this sacred banner of honor and hence of a sense of duty, and when we with faithful hearts follow this flag, then the goal we all pursue can be nothing other than the victory of Greater Germany!

Hitler's conclusion, affirming the certainty of victory for Greater Germany, compelled Göring to pledge himself and the audience once more in an "oath of loyalty" to the Führer. Göring customarily did this at the end of each Reichstag speech. On this day in May 1940, Göring proclaimed: "The force and the strength of the first soldier have now been conferred upon you. May the strength of the Führer uplift you!"

Hitler took great care to stage-manage the sessions of the Reichstag.

Hitler explains.

IV

How Hitler Governed

The political powers of the Weimar Republic made Hitler Reich Chancellor because they believed this would allow the development of an authoritarian regime that would bring peace to Germany by curbing the left and also would trap Hitler into the responsibilities of governing. These political powers believed that Hitler would fail and so they would be rid of him as well as the left. When he entered office, Hitler found a state built of many layers, some going back centuries, some new to meet the challenges of the current time. The Weimar government had a full panoply of civil rights, checks and balances, federal layering, and independent jurists. All this Hitler swept away, rather effortlessly, not by repealing laws but by building new layers that made the old institutions obsolete.

▶ February 1, 1933 *Just after being appointed Reich chancellor, Hitler addressed the German people.*

Late in the evening of February 1, at 10:00 p.m., Hitler spoke for the first time as Reich Chancellor in a radio broadcast. He dressed in his dark blue suit and black tie, as had been his practice in 1932 on the occasion of important speeches. Hitler read his first proclamation as German head of government, a Proclamation of the Reich Government to the German Volk:

> More than fourteen years have passed since that ill-fated day when, blinded by promises at home and abroad, the German Volk lost sight of the most valuable assets of our past and of our Reich, its honor and its freedom, and thus lost everything. Since those days of treachery, the Almighty has withheld His blessing from our Volk. Dissension and hatred have made their way into our midst. In the profoundest distress, millions of the best German men and women from all walks of life watch as the unity of the nation vanishes and dissolves in a muddle of political and egotistical opinions, economic interests, and differences in basic understanding (*Weltanschauung*).

As so often before in our history, Germany has presented
a picture of heartbreaking disunity since that day of revolution. We were never given the promised equality and fraternity, and we have lost our liberty. The disintegration of the
unity of spirit and will of our Volk at home was followed by
the disintegration of its political standing in the world.

Imbued with burning conviction that the German Volk
entered the great fight in 1914 without a thought to any guilt
on its part and filled only with the burdensome care of having to defend the Reich from attack and preserve the freedom and the very existence of the German Volk, we see in
the shattering fate that has plagued us since November 1918
merely the product of our disintegration at home. However,
the rest of the world as well has been shaken no less by major
crises since then. The historical balance of power, which once
played no small part in bringing about an understanding of
the necessity for internal solidarity of the nations, with all its
positive economic consequences, has been done away with.

The insane conception of victors and vanquished destroys
the confidence between nations and with it world economy.
But the misery of our Volk is appalling! The starving millions of unemployed proletarians in industry are being followed by the impoverishment of the entire middle class and
the professions. When this disintegration ultimately reaches
the German peasants, we will be confronted by a catastrophe of unfathomable dimensions. For not only will a Reich
disintegrate at the same time, but also a two-thousand-year-
old inheritance of the most valuable assets of human culture
and civilization.

The warning signs of this approaching disintegration are
all about us. In a single gigantic offensive of willpower and
violence, the Communist method of madness is attempting
to poison and disrupt the Volk, which is shaken and uprooted to its innermost core, with the aim of driving it toward
an age that would be even worse in relation to the promises
of today's Communist spokesmen than the period we have
now left behind us in relation to the promises of those same
apostles in November 1918.

Beginning with the family and ranging through all of the concepts of honor and loyalty, *Volk und Vaterland*, culture and economy, all the way to the eternal foundation of our morality and our faith, nothing has been spared by this negating, all-destroying dogma. Fourteen years of Marxism have ruined Germany. One year of Bolshevism would destroy Germany. The richest and most beautiful cultural areas of the world today would be transformed into chaos and a heap of ruins. Even the suffering of the last decade and a half could not be compared to the misery of a Europe in whose heart the red flag of destruction had been hoisted. May the thousands of wounded, the innumerable dead that this war has already cost Germany serve as storm clouds warning against the coming tempest.

In these hours when we were overcome by a powerful anxiety as to the existence and the future of the German nation, the aged leader of the Great War appealed to us men in the national parties and leagues to fight under him once more as we had at the front, this time at home, in unity and loyalty for the salvation of the Reich. The venerable Reich president has allied himself with us in this noble sense, and therefore we shall vow to God, our conscience, and our Volk as national leaders that we may resolutely and steadfastly fulfill the task thus conferred upon us as the national government.

The inheritance we have taken on is a terrible one.

The task that we must accomplish is the most difficult ever posed to German statesmen within the memory of mankind. But our confidence is unbounded, for we believe in our Volk and in its imperishable virtues. Peasants, workers, and bourgeoisie must all join together to provide the building blocks for the new Reich. The national government will therefore regard it as its first and foremost duty to reestablish the unity of spirit and will of our Volk. It will preserve and defend the foundations upon which the power of our nation rests. It will extend its strong, protecting hand over Christianity as the basis of our entire morality, and the family as the nucleus of the body of our Volk and state. It will reawaken in our Volk, beyond the borders of rank and class, its sense of national and political unity and its resultant duties. It will establish reverence for our great past and pride in our old traditions as the basis for the education of our German youth. Thus it will declare a merciless war against spiritual, political, and cultural nihilism. Germany must not and will not drown in anarchistic Communism.

It will replace turbulent instincts with national discipline as the guiding rule of our life. In doing so, it will devote great care to those institutions which constitute the true guarantors of the power and strength of our nation. The national government will perform the immense task of reorganizing the economy of our Volk with two great four-year plans:

Salvation of the German peasant in order to maintain the food supply and thus the basis of life in our nation.

Salvation of the German worker in an enormous and all-embracing attack on unemployment.

In fourteen years the November parties have ruined the German peasantry. In fourteen years they have created an army of millions of unemployed. The national government will, with iron determination and unshakable persistence, implement the following plan:

Within four years the German peasant must be rescued from impoverishment.

Within four years unemployment must be finally overcome.

At the same time, this will lay the groundwork for the recovery of the rest of the economy. The national government will couple this gigantic task of reorganizing our economy with the task and accomplishment of reorganizing the Reich, the regional states (*Länder*), and the communities, both in administrative and fiscal terms. Only then will the concept of a federal preservation of the Reich become a full-blooded, real-life certainty. The concept of a compulsory labor service and the settlement policy number among the cornerstones of this program. Securing daily bread, however, also includes the performance of social duties for the sick and the aged.

In an austerity administration, promoting employment, maintaining our peasantry, as well as exploiting individual initiative also give the best guarantee for avoiding any experiments which would endanger our currency.

In terms of foreign policy, the national government regards preserving the right to live and thus regaining the freedom of our Volk as its highest priority. By being resolute in bringing about an end to the chaotic state of affairs in Germany, it will assist in restoring to the community of nations a state of equal worth and thus, moreover, also a state with equal rights. The government is impregnated with the immensity of the duty of advocating, together with this free and equal Volk, the preservation and maintenance of a peace that the world needs today more than ever before.

May the understanding of all others assist us in fulfilling this, our most sincere wish, for the welfare of Europe, and more, for the welfare of the whole world. As great as is our love for our army as the bearer of our arms and the symbol of our great past, we would be happy if the world, by limiting its own armaments, would never again make it necessary for us to increase ours. However, if Germany is to experience this political and economic revival and conscientiously fulfill its obligations to the other nations, one decisive step is required: overcoming the Communist infiltration of Germany.

We men of the government feel that we are responsible to German history for reestablishing the great and orderly body politic and thus finally overcoming class madness and class struggle. It is not any one class we look to, but rather the German Volk, its millions of peasants, bourgeois and workers together, either overcoming the problems of these times or succumbing to them. Resolved and true to our oath, we will thus—in view of the present Reichstag's inability to support this work—ask the German Volk itself to take on this task we call our own.

Reich President von Hindenburg has called upon us and given us the order to use our own unity to restore to the nation the chance for recovery.

Thus we now appeal to the German Volk to take part in signing this deed of reconciliation.

The government of the national uprising wants to work, and it will work. It was not this government that led the German nation into ruin for fourteen years; this government wants to lead the nation to the top once more. It is determined to pay the debt of fourteen years in four years. But it cannot make the work of reconstruction dependent upon the approval of those who are to blame for the collapse.

The Marxist parties and their fellow travellers have had fourteen years to prove their prowess.

The result is a heap of ruins.

Now, German Volk, give us four years, and then pass judgment upon us!

True to the order of the field marshal, we shall begin. May Almighty God look mercifully upon our work, lead our will on the right path, bless our wisdom, and reward us with the confidence of our Volk. We are not fighting for ourselves but for Germany!

This was the first time a large segment of the German public outside the National Socialist Movement heard and read one of Hitler's proclamations. The bourgeoisie, which had witnessed Hitler in the non-Nazi press to date as an uneducated, ribald, and proletarian agitator, was visibly impressed. Many Germans, however, refused to believe Hitler capable of such a proclamation and suspected that his advisors had written the text. It proved a fatal error from the very start that those in power in Germany failed to take accurate stock of Hitler's personality. People believed that he was incompetent and totally unintelligent; they assumed his oral and written remarks to be the work of others and believed him to be under the influence of certain important Nazi Party leaders (*Unterführer*), industrialists, and obscure backers.

Thus it must be stressed yet again that Hitler had no need for outside assistance in writing speeches and letters. He even refused to make use of the customary drafts of government proclamations prepared by his staff but, rather, consistently used his own words. Since 1919 he had allowed no one to correct, much less influence, his preconceived ideas. Goebbels, Göring, Hess, Ribbentrop, Strasser, and Röhm had no influence whatsoever on this man, as little as did subsequently, Raeder, Dönitz, Blomberg, Keitel, Jodl, Brauchitsch, Rommel, or any of the other German generals, politicians, or diplomats. Hitler was never at the receiving end; he was the one who influenced others. Thus it is only characteristic of this trait that a great number of the party leaders, diplomats, and generals held completely different personal views of the problems of the day from Hitler and that, when Hitler had spoken with them, they subordinated their own views and adopted his in the belief that Hitler's opinions were more likely the better of the two. It is absurd to assume that von Papen drafted the Reich government proclamation of February 1, 1933. One must bear in mind that Hitler had been doing nothing else but composing these types of proclamations and speeches for years.

The proclamation of February 1 is thoroughly consistent with his style. In any case, prestige considerations would never have allowed him to accept any draft other than his own. He wanted to demonstrate to the cabinet members from the very first that his word was now the only one that carried weight.

▶ February 28, 1933 *Once appointed Reich Chancellor, Hitler faced Reichstag elections on March 5. Already preparing a decree granting him dictatorial powers, Hitler took advantage of the Reichstag fire of February 27.*

As of February 27, Hitler was back in Berlin. The Reichstag election on the fifth of March was nearing steadily. After the election, Hitler planned to take immediate action against the non-National Socialist regional governments. He already had the draft of an emergency decree set aside for the occasion, which would allow him to appoint Reich commissars without having to call upon Hindenburg in each case.

The decree giving Hitler a free hand was the "Decree for the Protection of the Volk and the State," to be enacted in the event of Communist acts of violence. As early as February 2, he had hinted at his intentions in a proclamation to the Nazi Party storm troopers (SA):

> The hour for crushing this [Communist] terror is coming.

On February 27, 1933, the Reichstag building went up in flames, and on February 28, Hindenburg signed the prepared emergency decree. It was short and to the point, suspending all of the articles of the Weimar Constitution that could be rescinded in states of emergency, instituting the death penalty for crimes of high treason, conspiracy to assassinate, and similar plots, and authorizing the Reich government to assume the powers of the regional governments (*Länder*). This authorization was definitely of the greatest importance for Hitler. The other measures could, for the most part, have been derived from prior statutory regulations—particularly considering that Göring was Reich Minister for the police and had appointed tens of thousands of SA and Nazi Party security squads (SS) men as auxiliary police on February 25. He had also filled the most important posts—*Oberpräsident* and chief of police—with loyal National Socialists. The Social Democratic holders of these offices offered as little resistance to Göring as they had to von Papen's dismissal from office on July 20, 1932. They were satisfied to retain their pensions. On February 28, Hitler sent the following letter to the commissar of the Reich for the Prussian ministry of the interior, Reich Minister Göring:

> In yesterday's dastardly attack on the Reichstag building bearing the signature of a criminal Communist hand, the prompt action of the Berlin Fire Department, the circumspect direction of its leadership, and the self-sacrificing duty performed by individual firemen aided in averting, within the space of a few hours, the immediate danger of the complete destruction of the building and in holding the fire in containment. It was also the active initiative of the police that made it possible to go about the work of extinguishing the fire without disruption and to conduct a successful investigation into the crime.
>
> I am glad to take this opportunity to extend my special thanks and my warmest appreciation to all those who took part in the rescue operation, and I request that you, Herr Minister, bring this gratitude to the attention of the Berlin Fire Department and police.
>
> Adolf Hitler

On March 1, Hitler made his report on the political situation to the Reich President. He also received a delegation from the National Socialist workers' organization, the *Nationalsozialistische Betriebszellen Organisation,* NSBO (National Socialist Factory Cell Organization), and declared in his address that the elimination of Marxism was of vital importance for the life interests of German workers.

He judged this reminder appropriate in light of the arrests of "Marxist" Communist Party (KPD) and Social Democratic Party (SPD) working class leaders that had been taking place since February 28, allegedly in order to counter an imminent coup on the part of the Communists. Subsequently, Hitler rejoined the election campaign. He spoke on March 1 in Breslau in the Jahrhunderthalle. This was followed by speeches in Berlin (Sportpalast) on March 2 and Hamburg on March 3. Hitler's March 4 speech in Königsberg was broadcast on the radio as well. Throughout Germany marches and torchlight processions were held on this "Day of the Awakening Nation," culminating in the loudspeaker transmission of Hitler's speech. To the customary "party narrative" and the settlement of accounts with the parties of the Weimar Republic, Hitler added the following words:

> In the end, we do not live for ourselves alone; rather, we are responsible for everything that those who lived before us have left behind, and we are responsible for that which we shall one day leave behind to those who must come after us. For Germany must not end with us.

▶ March 5, 1933 *As part of the emergency powers granted his government, Hitler appointed commissars to run the regional states* (Länder). *This essentially ended regional government in the German state. Hitler now ran both the national administration and all local administrations. The Nazis took the opportunity to intimidate or eliminate enemies. Here, Hitler addresses the SA and SS, extolling their party's victory. Excesses in these actions were caused by "Communist infiltrators," of course. Such a fiction maintained discipline and gave plausible cover to violent acts.*

Neither in Bavaria nor in any other district had there been the slightest resistance to the appointment of the Reich commissars. Hitler was thus finally able to issue the expected triumphant proclamation to his adherents on March 10:

> Party comrades! Men of the SA and SS!
>
> A tremendous upheaval has taken place in Germany! It is the fruit of the most difficult of struggles, the most dogged persistence, and of the utmost discipline. Unprincipled characters, mostly Communist spies, are attempting to compromise the party with individual actions that are not in any way related to the great task of the national uprising and can only damage and belittle the accomplishments of our Movement. In particular,

there are attempts to bring about a conflict between the party, or Germany, and foreign countries by harassing foreigners in cars flying foreign flags. Men of the SA and SS! You must apprehend such creatures yourselves immediately and call them to account for their actions; you must turn them over to the police without delay, regardless of who they may be.

As of today, the national government has the executive power over all of Germany in its hands. This means that the national uprising will continue to be carried out methodically and under control from above. Only in instances when these orders meet with resistance or when, as was the case in the past, surprise ambushes are made on individual men or marching formations, should this resistance be immediately and thoroughly broken. The harassment of individuals, obstruction of cars, and disruptions to business are to be put to an absolute stop.

Comrades, you must make sure that the National Revolution of 1933 does not go down in history as a counterpart to the revolution of the Rucksack Spartacists. And one more thing: never let yourselves be distracted for one second from our watchword, that is, the destruction of Marxism.

Berlin, March 10, 1933 Adolf Hitler

Hitler made reference in this proclamation to the Communist provocateurs who had allegedly infiltrated the SA. He was thus able to dismiss attacks led by party comrades or members of the SA as "Communist" disruptions. If it was not the Jews, then it was the Communists who were the source of all evil.

▶ March 20, 1933 *To demonstrate the union of old traditional Germany with new national socialist Germany, Hitler staged a ceremony in the Potsdam Garrison Church attended by all the leading men of the state. However, Hitler's speech certainly demonstrates that his program was not conservative.*

The ceremonial act of state commenced at noon in the garrison church whose crypt contained the remains of the Prussian kings Friedrich Wilhelm I and Frederick the Great; the church bells played traditional melodies.

Thus it would seem that Hitler was carrying on the best of German traditions and virtues. The Prussian spirit of Frederick the Great and the military tradition of the Kaiser, symbolized by Reich President von Hindenburg in his marshal's uniform, gave their blessings to the new Germany as personified in Hitler. Only Reichstag members of the right-wing parties, the Center Party (with the Bavarian People's Party), and the splinter parties were seated inside the church. The Social Democratic deputies had refused to take part in the ceremony. The rest of the church was well filled with prominent public figures, among them Crown Prince Wilhelm, Field Marshal von Mackensen, Colonel General von Seeckt, and others.

Hindenburg turned the rostrum over to Hitler after his own speech, and Chancellor Hitler, attired in a formal cutaway coat, delivered the following address:

> *Herr Reichspräsident!* Deputies, Ladies and Gentlemen of the German Reichstag!

> For years our Volk has borne a heavy burden. After a period of proud uprising, of rich blossoming and flourishing in every area of our life, now—as so often in the past—need and poverty have again come upon us. Despite industriousness and the will to work, despite drive, wide knowledge and the best of intentions, millions of Germans today are trying in vain to earn their daily bread. The economy is desolate, finances are shattered, millions are without work. The world knows only the deceptive outer appearance of our cities; it does not see the wretchedness and the misery.

> For the last two thousand years these changing fortunes of fate have accompanied our Volk. Again and again ascent has been followed by decay. The causes have always been the same. The German is a victim of internal decay: divided of spirit, fragmented of will, and thus powerless to act, he becomes too weak to assert his own life. He dreams of justice written in the stars and loses his footing on earth. But the more Volk and Reich have become divided and thus the protection and shield of national life weakened, all the more constant has been the attempt to make a virtue out of necessity. The theory of the separate values of our tribes suppressed the realization of the

necessity of a joint will. In the end, the Germans were left only with the path leading inwards. As a Volk of singers, poets, and philosophers, it dreamed of a world in which the others lived, and only when it was inhumanly defeated by need and misery did there spring, perhaps from the arts, the yearning for a new birth, for a new Reich and thus for a new life.

When Bismarck allowed the cultural aspirations of the German nation to be followed by political unification, it seemed to signify an end to the long period of discord and internal war between the German tribes for all time. True to the proclamation of the Kaiser, our Volk participated in multiplying the values of peace, culture, and the human ethos. It has never detached the feeling of its strength from a deeply felt responsibility for the community life of the European nations.

During this period when the German tribes were unified in terms of both politics and power, the dissolution of *the Weltanschauung* of the German national community (*Volksgemeinschaft*) set in, that we are still suffering from today. And this internal disintegration of the nation once again became, as has so often been the case, the ally of the world around us. The November 1918 Revolution marked the end of a struggle that the German nation had taken up in the most sacred conviction that it was protecting only its freedom and thus its right to exist.

For neither the Kaiser, nor the government, nor the Volk wanted that war. It was only the disintegration of the nation, the universal collapse that compelled a weak generation, against its better judgment and against its most sacred inner conviction, to accept the allegation of war guilt.

However, this collapse was followed by disintegration in every sector. Our Volk sank lower and lower in terms of political power, morals, culture, and economy.

The worst thing was the conscious destruction of belief in one's own strength, the disgracing of our traditions, and thus the annihilation of the basic principles of a firm trust. Since then, our Volk has been shattered by crises without end. But the rest of the world has not become happier or richer either by politically and economically dislodging one of the major components of its community of states. The utter folly of the theory of eternal victors and vanquished gave birth to the utter absurdity of reparations and, as a consequence, the disastrous state of the world's economy.

While the German Volk and the German Reich thus became mired in internal political conflict and discord and the economy drifted into ruin, a new group of Germans gathered, Germans who, with faithful trust in their own Volk, wished to form it into a new community. It was to this young Germany that you, General Field Marshal von Hindenburg, entrusted the leadership of the Reich in your magnanimous decision of January 30, 1933.

In the conviction that the German Volk should also give its consent to the new order of German life, we men of this national government addressed a final appeal to the German nation.

On March 5, the Volk made its decision and the majority gave us their vote. In a unique uprising (*Erhebung*), it has restored the national honor within a few short weeks and, thanks to your understanding, Reich President von Hindenburg, consummated the marriage between the symbols of old glory and young strength.

When the national government now, in this solemn hour, makes its first appearance before the new Reichstag, at the same time it professes its unshakable will to take on the great task of reorganizing the German Volk and the Reich and to carry through this task with determination. With the knowledge that it is acting in accordance with the will of the nation, the national government expects the parties in parliament, after fifteen years of German misery, to rise above the confines of a doctrinaire, party-oriented way of thinking and submit to the iron rule imposed upon us all by this misery and its imminent consequences.

For the task that fate requires of us must rise to tower above the scope and basic nature of the petty substitutes of day-to-day politics.

We want to restore the unity of spirit and will to the German nation!

We want to preserve the everlasting foundations of our life: our *Volkstum* and the energies and values inherent therein.

We want to subordinate the organization and leadership of our state once more to those basic principles that have been the prerequisites for the glory of peoples and nations at all times.

We want to combine a confidence in the basic principles of our way of life—which are healthy because they are natural and right—with a consistency of political development at home and abroad.

We want to replace eternal indecision by the steadfastness of a government that shall thus once more give to our Volk an unshakable authority.

We want to take into consideration all the experiences— in both individual and community life as well as in our economy—that have proven useful to the welfare of the people in the course of millennia.

We want to restore the primacy of a policy destined to organize and lead the nation's struggle for existence.

But we also want to include all of the truly living powers of the Volk as the supporting elements of the German future; we want to make a sincere effort to unite those with good intentions and ensure that those who attempt to injure the German Volk receive their due.

We want to rebuild a different community from the German tribes, from the stations, professions, and classes that have existed until now. This community shall have the ability to bring about the just balance of vital interests demanded by the future of the entire Volk. Peasants, bourgeoisie, and workers must once more unite to become one German Volk.

This Volk shall then for all eternity act as custodian of our faith and our culture, our honor and our freedom. To the world, however, in justice to the victims of the Great War, we wish to be sincere friends of a peace that shall ultimately heal the wounds with which all are afflicted.

The government of the national uprising is determined to fulfill the task it has assumed before the German Volk. Thus it is addressing the German Reichstag today in the fervent hope of finding in it a support for the implementation of its mission. May you, ladies and gentlemen, recognize the meaning of these times as elected representatives of the Volk in order that you may contribute to the great task of our new national uprising.

We have today a hoary head in our midst. We salute you, Herr General Field Marshal. Three times you have fought on the battlefield of honor for the existence and the future of our Volk. As a lieutenant in the Royal army, you fought for German unity; in the armies of the old German Kaiser for the glorious creation of the Reich; and in the greatest war of all times as our field marshal for the continued existence of the Reich and for the freedom of our Volk. You were there to witness the evolution of the Reich; you saw before you the work of the Great Chancellor, the miraculous ascent of our Volk, and you have finally led us during the great age that Fate has allowed us to witness and fight in.

Today, Herr General Field Marshal, Providence has given you the privilege of being the patron of the new *Erhebung* of our Volk. And this, your wondrous life, is for us all a symbol of the indestructible vitality of the German nation. Thus the youth of the German Volk and all of us who perceive your consent to the task of the German uprising to be a blessing may thank you. May this power also communicate itself to the new representatives of our Volk now assembled.

And may Providence also bestow upon us the courage and the persistence that we sense all about us in this place sacred to every German, as humans fighting for the freedom and glory of our Volk at the feet of the bier of its greatest king.

After Hindenburg had laid wreaths on the sarcophagi of the Prussian kings, a parade of *Reichswehr* formations and national leagues (SA, SS, *Stahlhelm,* etc.) marched through the streets and past Hindenburg for several hours. Hitler and his ministers stood modestly a few rows behind the military guests of honor.

▸ March 23, 1933 *The passage of the Enabling Act of 1933 marked the formal moment at which Hitler and his National Socialist Party (Nazi Party) seized power. Clearly, Hitler already held power and was not about to give it up, but the speech and opposition to the Enabling Act are instructive. The following recounts the Reichstag meeting that passed the act.*

Clad in a uniform and brown shirt, Hitler submitted the following policy statement on the Enabling Act to the Reichstag on March 23:

Ladies and Gentlemen of the German Reichstag!

By agreement with the Reich Government, today the National Socialist German Workers' Party and the German National People's Party have presented to you for resolution notice of a motion concerning a "Law for Removing the Distress of Volk and Reich." The reasons for this extraordinary measure are as follows:

In November 1918, the Marxist organizations seized the executive power by means of a revolution. The monarchs were dethroned, the authorities of Reich and *Länder* removed from office, and thus a breach of the constitution was committed. The success of the revolution in a material sense protected these criminals from the grips of justice. They sought moral justification by asserting that Germany or its government bore the guilt for the outbreak of the Great War. This assertion was deliberately and objectively untrue. In consequence, however, these false accusations in the interest of our former enemies led to the severest oppression of the entire German Volk, and the violation of the assurances given to us in Wilson's Fourteen Points then led to a time of boundless misfortune for Germany, that is to say the working German Volk.

All the promises made by the Men of November 1918 proved to be, if not acts of intentional deception, then no less damnable illusions. The "achievements of the revolution" were, taken in their entirety, agreeable for only the smallest of fractions of our Volk, but for the overwhelming majority, at least insofar as these people were forced to earn their daily bread by honest work, they were infinitely sad. It is understandable that the survival instinct of those parties and men guilty of this development invents a thousand euphemisms and excuses. An objective comparison of the average outcome of the last fourteen years with the promises once proclaimed is a crushing indictment of the architects responsible for this crime unparalleled in German history.

In the course of the past fourteen years, our Volk has suffered deterioration in all sectors of life that could not conceivably have been greater. The question as to what, if anything, could have been worse than in these times is a question that cannot be answered in light of the basic values of our German Volk as well as the political and economic inheritance that once existed. In spite of its lack of mobility in political feelings and positions, the German Volk itself has increasingly turned away from concepts, parties, and associations that, in its eyes, are responsible for these conditions. The number of Germans who inwardly supported the Weimar Constitution, in spite of the suggestive potential and reckless employment of the executive power, dwindled, in the end, to a mere fraction of the entire nation.

Another typical characteristic of these fourteen years was the fact that—apart from natural fluctuations—the curve of developments has shown a constant decline. This depressing realization was one of the causes of the general state of despair. It served to further a realization of the necessity of thoroughly rejecting the ideas, organizations, and men in which one gradually and rightly began to recognize the underlying causes of our decay.

The National Socialist Movement was thus able, in spite of the most horrible oppression, to convert increasing numbers of Germans in terms of spirit and will to defensive action. Now, in association with the other national leagues, it has eliminated the powers that have been ruling since November 1918 within a few short weeks and, by means of a revolution, transferred public authority to the hands of the national government. On March 5, the German Volk gave its approval to this action.

The program for the reconstruction of the Volk and the Reich is determined by the magnitude of the distress crippling our political, moral, and economic life. Filled with the conviction that the causes of this collapse lie in internal injury to the body of our Volk, the government of the national revolution aims to eliminate the afflictions from our national life that would, in future, continue to foil any real recovery.

The disintegration of the nation into irreconcilably opposite ideologies (*Weltanschauungen*) that was systematically brought about by the false doctrines of Marxism means the destruction of the basis for any possible community life.

The dissolution permeates all of the basic principles of social order. The completely opposite approaches of the individuals to the concepts of state, society, religion, morality, family, and economy opens up differences that will lead to a war of all against all. Starting with the liberalism of the past century, this development will end, as the laws of nature dictate, in Communist chaos. The mobilization of the most primitive instincts leads to a link between the concepts of a political theory and the actions of real criminals. Beginning with pillaging, arson, raids on the railway, assassination attempts, and so on—all these things are morally sanctioned by Communist theory. Alone, the method of individuals terrorizing the masses has cost the National Socialist Movement more than 350 dead and tens of thousands of injured within the course of a few years.

The burning of the Reichstag, one unsuccessful attempt within a large-scale operation, is only a taste of what Europe would have to expect from a triumph of this demonical doctrine. When a certain press, particularly outside Germany, today attempts, true to the political lie advanced to a principle by Communism, to link Germany's national uprising to this disgraceful act, this can only serve to strengthen my resolve to leave no stone unturned in order to avenge this crime as quickly as possible by having the guilty arsonist and his accomplices publicly executed!

Neither the German Volk nor the rest of the world has become sufficiently conscious of the entire scope of the operation planned by this organization. Only by means of its immediate action was the government able to ward off a development that would have shaken all of Europe had it proceeded to its disastrous end. Several of those who fraternize with the interests of Communism both within and outside of Germany, motivated by hatred for the national uprising, would themselves have become victims of such a development. It will be the utmost goal of the national government to stamp out and eliminate every trace of this phenomenon, not only in the interest of Germany, but in the interest of the rest of Europe.

It will not lose sight of the realization that, in doing so, it is not the negative problem of this organization with which it is dealing but rather the implementation of the positive task of winning the German worker for the national state. Only the creation of a real national community (*Volksgemeinschaft*), rising above the interests and conflicts of personal standing and social class, is capable of permanently removing the source of nourishment of these aberrations of the human mind. The establishment of such a solidarity in basic philosophy (*Weltanschauung*) in the German body politic is all the more important, for only this will make it possible to maintain friendly relations with the non-German powers without regard to the tendencies or *Weltanschauungen* to which they are subject, for the elimination of Communism in Germany is a purely domestic German affair. It should be in the interests of the rest of the world as well, for the outbreak of Communist chaos in the densely populated German Reich would lead to political and economic consequences particularly in the rest of western Europe, the extent of which are unfathomable.

The inner disintegration of our *Volksgemeinschaft* inevitably resulted in an increasingly alarming weakening of the authority of the highest levels of leadership. The sinking reputation of the Reich government—that is the inevitable product of unstable domestic conditions of this type—led to ideas on the part of various parties in the individual regional governments (*Länder*) that are incompatible with the unity of the Reich. The greatest consideration for the traditions of the *Länder* cannot erase the bitter realization that the extent of the fragmentation of national life in the past was not only not beneficial, but positively injurious to the world and life status of our Volk.

It is not the task of a superior national leadership to subsequently surrender what has grown organically to the theoretical principle of an unrestrained unitarianization. But it is its duty to raise the unity of spirit and will of the leadership of the nation and thus the concept of the Reich as such beyond all shadow of a doubt. The welfare of our communities and *Länder*—as well as the existence of each German individual—must be protected by the state. Therefore the Reich government does not intend to dissolve the *Länder* by means of the Enabling Act. However, it will institute measures that will guarantee the continuity of political intention in the Reich and *Länder* from now on and for all time.

The greater the consensus of spirit and will, the lesser the interest of the Reich for all time in violating the independent cultural and economic existence of the separate *Länder*. The present habit of the governments of the *Länder* and the Reich of mutually criticizing each other, making use of the modern means of public propaganda, is completely outrageous. I will under no circumstances tolerate—and the Reich government will resolve all measures to combat—the spectacle of ministers of German governments attacking or disparaging each other before the world in mass meetings or even with the aid of public radio broadcasts.

It also results in a complete invalidation of the legislative bodies in the eyes of the Volk when, even assuming normal times, the Volk is driven to the polls in the Reich or in the individual *Länder* almost twenty times in the course of four years. The Reich government will find the way to ensure that the expression of the will of the nation, once given, leads to uniform consequences for both the Reich and the *Länder*.

A further reform of the Reich will only ensue from ongoing developments. Its aim must be to design a constitution that ties the will of the Volk to the authority of a genuine leadership. The statutory legalization of this reform of the constitution will be granted to the Volk itself. The government of the National Revolution basically regards it as its duty, in accordance with the spirit of the Volk's vote of confidence, to prevent the elements that consciously and intentionally negate the life of the nation from exercising influence on its formation.

The theoretical concept of equality before the law shall not be used, under the guise of equality, to tolerate those who despise the laws as a matter of principle or, moreover, to surrender the freedom of the nation to them on the basis of democratic doctrines. The government will, however, grant equality before the law to all those who, in forming the front of our Volk against this danger, support national interests and do not deny the government their assistance.

Our next task, in any case, is to call upon the spiritual leaders of these destructive tendencies to answer for themselves and at the same time to rescue the victims of their seduction. In particular, we perceive in the millions of German workers who pay homage to these ideas of madness and self-destruction only the results of an unforgivable weakness on the part of former governments who failed to put a stop to the dissemination of these ideas, the practical implementation of which they were forced to punish.

The government will not allow itself to be shaken by anyone in its decision to solve this problem. Now it is the responsibility of the Reichstag to adopt a clear standpoint for its part. This will change nothing as to the fate of Communism and the other organizations fraternizing with it. In its measures, the national government is guided by no other factor than preserving the German Volk, and in particular the mass of millions making up its working populace, from unutterable misery.

Thus it views the matter of restoring the monarchy as out of the question at present in light of the very existence of these circumstances. It would be forced to regard any attempt to solve this problem on the part of the individual *Länder* as an attack on the legal entity of the Reich and take appropriate action. Simultaneously with this political purification of our public life, the Reich government intends to undertake a thorough moral purging of German society (*Volkskörper*). The entire system of education, the theater, the cinema, literature, the press, and radio—they all will be used as a means to this end and valued accordingly. They must all work to preserve the eternal values residing in the essential character of our Volk. Art will always remain the expression and mirror of the yearning and the reality of an era. The cosmopolitan contemplative attitude is rapidly disappearing. Heroism is arising passionately as the future shaper and leader of political destinies.

The task of art is to give expression to this determining spirit of the age. Blood and race (*Blut und Rasse*) will once more become the source of artistic intuition.

The task of the government, particularly in an age of limited political power, is to ensure that the internal value of life and the will of the nation to live are given that much more monumental artistic expression in culture. This resolve entails the obligation to grateful appreciation of our great past. The gap between this past and the future must be bridged in all sectors of our historical and cultural life. Reverence for great men must be instilled once more in German youth as a sacred inheritance. In being determined to undertake the political and moral purification of our public life, the government is creating and securing the requirements for a genuinely profound return to religious life.

The advantages in personnel policy that might result from compromises with atheist organizations do not come close to offsetting the results that would become apparent in the general destruction of basic moral values. The national government perceives in the two Christian confessions the most important factors for the preservation of our national life (*Volkstum*). It will respect any contracts concluded between these Churches and the *Länder*. Their rights are not to be infringed upon. But the government expects and hopes that the task of working on the national and moral regeneration of our Volk taken on by the government will, in turn, be treated with the same respect.

It will face all of the other confessions with objective fairness. However, it cannot tolerate that membership in a certain confession or a certain race could mean being released from general statutory obligations or even constitute a license for committing or tolerating crimes that go unpunished. The government's concern lies in an honest coexistence between church and state; the fight against materialist worldviews (*Weltanschauungen*) and for genuine social community (*Volksgemeinschaft*) that equally serves both the interests of the German nation and the welfare of our Christian faith. Our legal institutions must above all work to preserve this social community (*Volksgemeinschaft*). The irremovability of the judges on the one hand must ensure a flexibility in their judgments for the welfare of society on the other.

Not the individual but the Volk as a whole must be the focal point of legislative efforts. In the future, high treason and betrayal of the Volk will be ruthlessly eradicated. The foundations on which the judiciary is based can be none other than the foundations on which the nation is based. Thus may the judiciary always take into consideration the difficult burden of decision carried by those who bear the responsibility for shaping the life of the nation under the harsh dictates of reality.

Great are the tasks of the national government in the sphere of economic life.

Here all action shall be governed by one law: the Volk does not live for the economy, and the economy does not exist for capital, but capital serves the economy and the economy serves the Volk!

In principle, the government protects the economic interests of the German Volk, not by taking the roundabout way through an economic bureaucracy to be organized by the state, but by the utmost promotion of private initiative and a recognition of the rights of property. A fair balance must be established between productive intention on the one hand and productive work on the other. The administration should respect the results of ability, industriousness, and work by being thrifty.

The problem of our public finances is also a problem that is, in no small part, the problem of a thrifty administration. The proposed reform of our tax system must result in a simplification in assessment and thus to a decrease in costs and charges. In principle, the tax mill should be built downstream and not at the source. As a consequence of these measures, the simplification of the administration will certainly result in a decrease in the tax burden. This reform of the tax system that is to be implemented in the Reich and the *Länder* is not, however, an overnight matter, but one to be addressed when the time is judged to be right. As a matter of principle, the government will avoid currency experiments.

We are faced above all with two economic tasks of the first order. The salvation of the German peasant must be achieved at all costs. The annihilation of this class in our Volk would bring with it the most severe consequences imaginable. The restoration of the profitability of the agricultural operations may be hard on the consumer. But the fate that would descend upon the entire German Volk should the German peasant perish would not bear comparison with these hardships. Only in connection with the profitability of our agriculture that must be achieved at all costs can the problems of foreclosures or debt relief be solved. Were this to prove unsuccessful, the annihilation of our peasants would inevitably lead not only to the collapse of the German economy per se, but above all to the collapse of German society (*Volkskörper*).

The maintenance of its health is, however, the first requirement for the blossoming and flourishing of our industry, German domestic trade, and the German export industry. Without the counterweight of the German peasantry, Communist madness would already have overrun Germany by now and thus conclusively destroyed the German economy. What the entire economy, including our export industry, owes to the healthy common sense of the German peasant cannot be compensated by any kind of sacrifice in terms of business. Thus our greatest attention must be devoted to the further settlement of German land in future.

Furthermore, it is perfectly clear to the national government that the removal of the distress in both agricultural and urban economy is contingent upon the integration of the army of unemployed in the process of production. This constitutes the second and most monumental economic task. It can be solved only by a general pacification in implementing sound natural economic principles and all measures necessary, even if, at the time, they cannot expect to enjoy any degree of popularity. The creation of jobs and compulsory labor service are, in this connection, only isolated measures within the scope of the offensive as a whole. The attitude of the national government toward the middle class (*Mittelstand*) is similar to its attitude toward the German peasants. Its salvation can only be effected within the scope of general economic policy. The national government is determined to find a far-reaching solution to this problem. It recognizes its historical task of supporting and promoting the millions of German workers in their struggle for their rights to exist.

As Chancellor and a National Socialist, I feel allied to them as the former companions of my youth. The increase in the consumer power of these masses will constitute a substantial means of reviving the economy. While maintaining our social legislation, the first step to its reform must be taken. In principle, however, every worker shall be utilized in the service of the public. The stagnation of millions of human working hours is madness and a crime that must inevitably lead to the impoverishment of all. Regardless of which values would have been created by the utilization of our surplus work force, for millions of people who today are going to waste in misery and distress, they could represent essential values of life. The organizational capabilities of our Volk must and will succeed in solving this problem.

We know that the geographic position of Germany, with her lack of raw materials, does not fully permit autarky for our Reich. It cannot be stressed too often that nothing is further from the Reich government's mind than hostility to exporting. We know that we need this connection with the world and that the sale of German goods in the world represents the livelihood of many millions of German national comrades (*Volksgenossen*). But we also know the requirements for a sound exchange of services between the peoples of the earth. For years, Germany has been compelled to perform services without receiving counter-services. Consequently, the task of maintaining Germany as an active partner in the exchange of goods is less a question of commercial than of financial policy. As long as we are not accorded any settlement of our foreign debts that is fair and appropriate to our strength, we shall unfortunately be forced to maintain our foreign exchange control policy (*Devisenzwangswirtschaft*). For this reason, the Reich Government is also obligated to maintain the dam built against the flow of capital across the borders.

If the Reich government allows itself to be guided by these principles, one can surely expect the growing understanding of the foreign countries to ease the integration of our Reich in the peaceful competition of the nations.

The first step toward promoting transportation with the aim of achieving a reasonable balance of all transportation interests—a reform of the motor vehicle tax—will take place at the beginning of next month. The maintenance of the national railroad system (*Reichsbahn*) and its reintegration under Reich authority, which is to be effected as quickly as possible, is a task that commits us not only in an economic, but also in a moral sense. The national government will give every encouragement to the development of aviation as a means of peacefully connecting the people to one another.

For all this activity, the government requires the support not only of the general powers in our Volk, which it is determined to utilize to the furthest possible extent, but also the devoted loyalty and work of its professional civil service. Only if the public finances are in urgent need will intervention take place; however, even in such a case, strict fairness shall have the highest priority in governing our actions.

The protection of the frontiers of the Reich, and with them the life of our Volk and the existence of our economy, is now in the hands of our *Reichswehr* which, in accordance with the terms imposed upon us by the Treaty of Versailles, can be regarded as the only really disarmed force in the world. In spite of its small size prescribed therein and its totally insufficient arms, the German Volk can regard its *Reichswehr* with proud satisfaction. This feeble instrument of our national self-defense came into existence under the most difficult conditions. In its spirit, it is the bearer of our best military traditions. With painstaking conscientiousness the German Volk has thus fulfilled the obligations imposed upon it in the peace treaty; what is more, even the replacement of ships in our fleet to which we were authorized at that time has—I may be allowed to say, unfortunately—been carried out only to a small extent.

For years Germany has been waiting in vain for the redemption of the promise to disarm given us by the others. It is the sincere desire of the national government to be able to refrain from increasing the German army and our weapons insofar as the rest of the world is also finally willing to fulfill its obligation of radically disarming. For Germany wants nothing except equal rights to live and equal freedom. However, the national government wishes to cultivate this spirit of a will for freedom in the German Volk.

The honor of the nation, the honor of our army, and the ideal of freedom—all must once more become sacred to the German Volk!

The German Volk wishes to live in peace with the world.

It is for this very reason that the Reich government will use every means to definitively eliminate the separation of the peoples on earth into two categories. Keeping open this wound leads the one to distrust, the other to hatred, and in the end to a general feeling of insecurity. The national government is willing to extend a hand in sincere understanding to every people that is determined to once and for all put an absolute end to the tragic past. The distress of the world can come to an end only if the appropriate foundation is created by means of stable political conditions and if the peoples regain confidence in one another.

To deal with the economic catastrophe, the following is necessary:

1. an absolutely authoritarian leadership at home to create confidence in the stability of conditions;

2. safeguarding peace on the part of the major nations for a long time to come and thus restoring the confidence of the peoples in one another; and

3. the final triumph of the principles of common sense in the organization and leadership of the economy as well as a general release from reparations and impossible liabilities for debts and interest.

We are unfortunately confronted by the fact that the Geneva Conference, in spite of lengthy negotiations, has not yet reached any practical result. The decision to institute a real disarmament measure has repeatedly been delayed by questions of technical detail and by the introduction of problems that have nothing to do with disarmament. This procedure is unsuitable. The illegal state of unilateral disarmament and the resulting national insecurity of Germany cannot last any longer.

We recognize it as a sign of responsibility and good will that the British government has, with its disarmament proposal, attempted finally to move the conference to arrive at speedy decisions. The Reich Government will support any efforts aimed at effectively implementing general disarmament and securing Germany's long-overdue call for disarmament. We have been disarmed for fourteen years, and for the past fourteen months we have been waiting for the outcome of the Disarmament Conference. Even more far-reaching is the plan of the head of the Italian government, which is making a generous and foresighted attempt to ensure the smooth and consistent development of European politics as a whole. We attach the most earnest significance to this plan; we are willing to cooperate with absolute sincerity on the basis it provides in order to unite the four great powers, England, France, Italy, and Germany, in peaceful cooperation to courageously and determinedly approach those tasks upon which the solution of Europe's fate depends.

For this reason we feel particularly grateful for the appreciative warmth that has greeted Germany's national uprising in Italy. We wish and hope that the concurrence of spiritual ideals will be the basis for a continuing consolidation of the friendly relations between the two countries.

Similarly, the Reich government, which regards Christianity as the unshakable foundation of the ethics and morality of the Volk, places great value on friendly relations with the Vatican and attempts to develop them. We are filled with a feeling of empathy for the troubles and distress of our brother Germans in Austria. In all its doings, the Reich government is conscious of the connection between the fate of all German tribes. The attitude toward the other individual foreign powers is evident from what has already been said. But there as well, where the mutual relations are already encumbered with difficulties, we shall endeavor to reach a settlement. However, the differentiation between victor and vanquished can never be the basis of an understanding.

We are nonetheless of the conviction that a settlement of this sort in our relations to France is possible if both governments really attack the problems confronting them with farsightedness. With regard to the Soviet Union, the Reich government is determined to cultivate friendly relations that are productive for both parties. The government of the national revolution above all views itself capable of such a positive policy with regard to Soviet Russia. The fight against Communism in Germany is an internal affair, in which we will never tolerate outside interference. The national political relations to other powers to which we are related by mutual interests will not be affected by this. Our relationship with the other countries shall continue to warrant our most earnest attention in the future, in particular our relationship to the major countries overseas, with which Germany has long been allied by friendly ties and economic interests. We have particularly at heart the fate of the Germans living outside the borders of the Reich who are allied to us by language, culture, and traditions and who fight hard to retain these values. The national government is resolved to use all the means at its command to support the rights internationally guaranteed to the German minorities.

We welcome the plan of the World Economic Conference and approve of its meeting soon. The Reich government is willing to contribute to this conference in order to finally achieve positive results. The most important question is the problem of our short-term and long-term indebtedness abroad. The complete change in the conditions of the commodity markets of the world requires an adaptation. Only by means of trusting cooperation is it possible to really remove the widespread problems. Ten years of honest peace will be more beneficial for the welfare of all nations than thirty years of drawn-out stagnation in the terms of victor and vanquished.

In order to place itself in a position to fulfill the tasks falling within this scope, the government has had the two major parties, the National Socialists and the German Nationalists, introduce the Enabling Act in the Reichstag. Some of the planned measures require the approval of the majority necessary for constitutional amendments. The performance of these tasks and their completion is necessary. It would be inconsistent with the aim of the national uprising and it would fail to suffice for the intended goal were the government to negotiate with and request the approval of the Reichstag for its measures in each case. In this context, the government is not motivated by a desire to give up the Reichstag as such. On the contrary: it reserves the right, for the future as well, to inform the Reichstag of its measures or to obtain its consent.

The authority and the fulfillment of the tasks would suffer, however, were doubts about the stability of the new regime to arise in the Volk. The Reich government views a further session of the Reichstag as an impossibility under the present condition of a far-reaching state of excitation in the nation. Rarely has the course of a revolution of such great magnitude run in such a disciplined and unbloody manner as the uprising (*Erhebung*) of the German Volk during these past weeks. It is my will and my firm intention to provide for this smooth development in future as well.

However, this makes it all the more necessary that the national government be accorded that position of sovereignty that is fitting, in such an age, to put a halt to developments of a different sort. The government will make use of this authorization only insofar as this is requisite for the implementation of vital measures. The existence of neither the Reichstag nor the Reichsrat is endangered. The position and the rights of the Reich president remain inviolate. It will always be the first and foremost task of the government to bring about inner consensus with his aims. The existence of the *Länder* will not be abolished. The rights of the churches will not be curtailed and their position vis-à-vis the state will not be altered. The number of cases in which there is an internal necessity for taking refuge in such a law is, in and of itself, limited. All the more, however, the government insists upon the passage of the bill. Either way, it is asking for a clear decision. It is offering the parties of the Reichstag the chance for a smooth development that might lead to the growth of an understanding in future.

However, the government is just as determined as it is prepared to accept a notice of rejection and thus a declaration of resistance. May you, gentlemen, now choose for yourselves between peace or war!

The gentlemen chose peace, or so they were led to believe. The deputies of all the parties had only domestic policy in mind while they listened to Hitler's remarks on his government. The National Socialists were already accustomed to complying with Hitler's every wish. The German Nationalists and the other right-wing parties were pleased that the Socialists, i.e., the "Marxists," would be prevented from taking any part in government. The Center Party was happy that the indispensable role it had played in bringing about an absolute majority in every government since 1918 had at least prevailed in regard to achieving the two-thirds majority. The democratic German State Party wanted to prove that it took its name seriously and was genuinely supportive of the state. The Social Democrats, on the other hand, were naturally in no position to approve of Hitler's bill, for he had announced their removal from all public offices and even threatened their extermination in countless speeches.

Not a single deputy voiced objections to the Chancellor's foreign policy program. The entire Reichstag, including the Social Democrats, declared its unanimous consent both in this session on March 23 and in a further session on May 17—in spite of the fact that Hitler's foreign policy program represented the largest threat to the nation.

The terms of Germany's domestic policy, i.e., whether or not the Germans engaged in a civil war, whether the country was governed by a dictatorship or a democracy—even whether or not the Jews were persecuted—were questions that received only marginal attention abroad. Never would any of these domestic matters have incited foreign powers to launch a military intervention against Hitler. Conversely, the foreign policy aims of the German Government did indeed command attention abroad.

The flattering words with which Hitler addressed England, France, Italy, and the Soviet Union in his March 23 statement of policy carried no real weight. The real blueprint revealing his future foreign policy was the program he had laid down in *Mein Kampf* and expounded in numerous earlier speeches. Even if one dismissed as unrealistic folly the idea of a new German Reich formed by conquering *Lebensraum* in the east, there still remained Hitler's goal of disposing of the Treaty of Versailles—an all-too-real element of his foreign policy program.

There is a general reluctance in Germany to think an uncomfortable matter through to its final consequences. Hitler's program of abolishing the Treaty of Versailles ultimately meant a restoration of the borders of 1914; this, however, entailed war with Poland; war with Poland also meant war with the western powers—and hence Germany's military ruin. The deputies did not dwell on these unpleasant thoughts on March 23. Spokesmen for party after party, the Social Democrats included, stood up and declared their respective party's consensus with Hitler's statements on foreign policy. After all, no one wanted to seem anti-national. Ever since 1914, the German Social Democratic Party had lowered its colors whenever the talk had turned to nationalism for fear of being judged unreliable in national matters.

The speech denouncing Hitler's Enabling Act delivered by the Social Democratic deputy Otto Wels was remarkably weak. It might have been expected that he would at least take a stand against the "stab-in-the back" legend; for although Hitler had refrained from mentioning it in his policy statement, he had repeated it often enough in other speeches. Wels chose instead to demonstrate how he and the Social Democrats had supported a nationalist program since 1918. His remarks were confined to domestic issues. Wels protested against the persecution suffered by his fellow party members throughout the country. In touching this topic, however, he made himself vulnerable to counterattacks, for the Social Democratic rulers, particularly in Prussia, had not exactly been gentle in their treatment of National Socialists during the preceding years.

Thus Hitler took advantage of this chance to settle this special account with the Social Democratic Party one last time. He took notes during Wels' speech and, at its close, once more stepped to the rostrum. If anyone still harbored the suspicion that Hitler had a ghostwriter prepare his speeches, he now learned the error of his ways. No one could have written a rejoinder to Wels' unscheduled speech in that short time.

Below are the speeches of both Wels and Hitler as recorded in the stenographic minutes of the Reichstag:

President Göring:
Deputy Wels has the floor.

Wels (SPD), Deputy:

Ladies and Gentlemen! We Social Democrats approve of the Reich Chancellor's foreign policy demand of German equality of rights even that much more emphatically because we have advocated it from the very beginning. ("Hear, hear!" from the Social Democrats.)

I may take the liberty, in this context, of making the personal remark that I was the first German to oppose the untruth of Germany's blame for the outbreak of the World War before an international forum, to be precise, at the Bern Conference on February 3, 1919. ("Hear, hear!" from the Social Democrats.)

No basic principle of our party has ever been able or will ever be able to hinder us from representing the just claims of the German nation to the other peoples of the world. ("Bravo!" from the Social Democrats.)

The day before yesterday, the Reich Chancellor made a remark in Potsdam to which we also subscribe. He said, "The utter folly of the theory of eternal victors and vanquished gave birth to the utter absurdity of reparations and, as a consequence, the disastrous state of the world's economy." This statement applies to foreign policy; it applies no less to domestic policy. ("Hear, hear!" from the Social Democrats.)

Here too the theory of eternal victors and vanquished is, as the Reich Chancellor has noted, utter folly. But the Reich Chancellor's remark also recalls another remark that was made on July 23, 1919 in the National Assembly. It was said at that time, "We may be stripped of power, but not of honor." (Calls of approval from the Social Democrats.)

It is clear that the opponents are after our honor, there is no doubt of that. But it will remain our belief to the last that this attempt at divesting us of our honor will one day rebound on those who instigated this attempt, for it is not our honor that is being destroyed in the worldwide tragedy. ("Hear, hear!" from the Social Democrats; shouts of "Who said that?" from the National Socialists.)

That is part of a statement that a government led by Social Democrats submitted before the whole world on behalf of the German people, four hours before the Armistice ran out, in order to block any further enemy advance. This statement constitutes a valuable complement to the remark made by the Reich Chancellor. No good can come of a dictated peace; ("Hear, hear!" from the Social Democrats) and this applies all the more to domestic affairs. (Renewed calls of approval from the Social Democrats.)

A real social community (*Volksgemeinschaft*) cannot be established on such a basis. That requires first of all equality of rights. May the government guard itself against crude excesses of polemics; may it prohibit incitements to violence with rigorousness for its own part. This might be achieved if it is accomplished fairly and objectively on all sides and if one refrains from treating defeated enemies as though they were outlaws. ("Hear, hear!" from the Social Democrats.)

Freedom and life they can take from us but not honor. (Applause from the Social Democrats.)

Considering the persecution the Social Democratic Party has suffered recently, no one can fairly demand or expect of it that it cast its vote in favor of the Enabling Act introduced here. The elections of March 5 have resulted in a majority for the parties in government and thus given them the opportunity to govern, strictly as laid down in the letter and the intention of the constitution. But where this opportunity is given, it is coupled with an obligation. ("Hear, hear!" from the Social Democrats.)

Criticism is beneficial and necessary. Never in the history of the German Reichstag, however, has control over public affairs vested in the elected representatives of the people been eliminated to the extent to which this is now the case ("Hear, hear!" from the Social Democrats) and will be even more so by means of the new Enabling Act. This type of governmental omnipotence is destined to have even more grave consequences due to the total lack of freedom of the press.

Ladies and gentlemen! A devastating picture has often been painted of the state of affairs prevailing in Germany today. As always in such cases, there is no lack of exaggeration. As far as my party is concerned, I wish to state that we did not ask for any intervention in Paris; we did not send off millions to Prague; we did not disseminate exaggerated news abroad. ("Hear, hear!" from the Social Democrats.)

It would be easier to counter such exaggerations if the type of reporting that differentiates between right and wrong were admissible at home. (Calls of approval from the Social Democrats.)

It would be even better if we were able, with a clear conscience, to attest to the fact that the stability of the law has been restored for all. (Renewed calls of approval from the Social Democrats.)

And that, gentlemen, is up to you. The gentlemen of the National Socialist Party call the Movement they have unleashed a national and not a National Socialist Revolution. The only connection between their Revolution and Socialism has been confined until now to the attempt to destroy the Social Democratic Movement that has constituted the pillar of the Socialist body of thought for more than two generations, (laughter from the National Socialists) and will continue to do so in future.

If the gentlemen of the National Socialist Party intended to perform Socialist deeds, they would not need an Enabling Act to do so. ("Hear, hear!" from the Social Democrats.)

You would be certain of an overwhelming majority in this forum. Every motion you made in the interests of the workers, the peasants, the white-collar employees, the civil servants, or the *Mittelstand* would meet with overpowering if not unanimous approval. (Calls of approval from the Social Democrats; laughter from the National Socialists.)

But you nevertheless first want to eliminate the Reichstag to proceed with your revolution. Destroying what exists does not suffice to make up a revolution. The people expect positive achievements. They are awaiting drastic measures to combat the economic distress prevalent, not only in Germany, but everywhere in the world. We Social Democrats have borne joint responsibility in the most difficult of times and have been stoned as our reward. ("Hear, hear!" from the Social Democrats; laughter from the National Socialists.)

Our achievements in reconstructing the state and the economy and in liberating the occupied territories will prevail in history. (Chorus of assent from the Social Democrats.)

We have created equal rights for all and socially oriented labor legislation. We have aided in creating a Germany in which the path to leadership is open, not only to counts and barons, but also to men of the working class. (Renewed assent from the Social Democrats.)

You cannot retreat from that without abandoning your own Führer. (Cheering and applause from the Social Democrats.)

Any attempt to turn back the wheels of time will be in vain. We Social Democrats are aware that one cannot eliminate the realities of power politics by the simple act of legal protests. We see the reality of your present rule. But the people's sense of justice also wields political power, and we will never stop appealing to this sense of justice. The Weimar Constitution is not a Socialist constitution. But we adhere to the basic principles of a constitutional state, to the equality of rights, and the concept of social legislation anchored therein. We German Social Democrats solemnly pledge ourselves in this historic hour to the principles of humanity and justice, of freedom and Socialism. (Calls of approval from the Social Democrats.)

No enabling act can give you the power to destroy ideas that are eternal and indestructible. You yourself have professed your belief in Socialism. Bismarck's Law against Socialists has not destroyed the Social Democratic Party. Even further persecution can be a source of new strength to the German Social Democratic Party. We hail those who are persecuted and in despair. We hail our friends in the Reich. Their steadfastness and loyalty are worthy of acclaim. The courage of their convictions, their unbroken faith—(laughter from the National Socialists; "Bravo!" from the Social Democrats) are the guarantees of a brighter future. (Renewed cheering from the Social Democrats; laughter from the National Socialists.)

President Göring:
The Reich chancellor has the floor. (Thunderous applause and cries of *"Heil!"* from the National Socialists.)

Hitler left his seat on the government bench and strode to the podium for the second time that day; he pointed an accusing finger at the Social Democratic deputies and began:

You came too late, but you came none the less! (*Spät kommt ihr, doch ihr kommt!* – Schiller)

(Calls of approval from the National Socialists.)

The pretty theories that you, Mr. Deputy, have just expounded here have been addressed to world history a little too late. (Amused assent from the National Socialists.)

Perhaps these realizations, put to practice years ago, would have made the complaints you have today superfluous. You declare that the Social Democratic Party subscribes to our foreign policy program; that it rejects the lie of war guilt; that it is against reparations. Now I may ask just one question: where was this fight during the time you had power in Germany? ("Hear, hear!" from the National Socialists.)

You once had the opportunity to dictate the law of domestic behavior to the German Volk. You were able to do it in other areas. It would have been equally possible to infuse in the German revolution, that you played a part in initiating, the same momentum and the same direction that France once infused in its uprising in the year 1870. ("Hear, hear!" from the National Socialists.)

It would have been at your discretion to shape the German uprising into one of true national character, and you still would have had the right, had the flag of the new republic not returned triumphant, to say: we did everything in our power to avoid this catastrophe by a final appeal to the strength of the German Volk. (Calls of approval from the National Socialists and the German Nationalists.)

At that time you avoided the fight; now you suddenly feel an urge to talk about it to everyone around you. You state that being stripped of power does not mean being stripped of honor. You are right; that does not necessarily have to be the case. Even if we were divested of our power, I know we would not be divested of our honor. Thanks to having been oppressed by your party, our Movement had been stripped of power for years; it has never been stripped of honor. (Thunderous applause from the National Socialists.)

It is my conviction that we shall inoculate the German Volk with a spirit that, in view of the Volk's defenselessness today, Mr. Deputy, will certainly never allow it to be stripped of its honor. (Calls of approval from the National Socialists and the German Nationalists.)

Here, too, it was your responsibility, you who were in power for fourteen years, (cries of "Oh, no!" from the Social Democrats) to ensure that this German Volk had set an example of honor to the world.

It was your responsibility to ensure that, if the rest of the world insisted upon suppressing us, at least the type of suppression the German Volk was subjected to would be one of dignity. You had the opportunity to speak out against all of the manifestations of disgrace in our Volk. You could have eliminated this treason just as easily as we will eliminate it. (Cheering from the National Socialists and German Nationalists.)

You have no right to even associate yourself with this claim; for you should never, at that hour when every revolution would have constituted the concurrence of the offenses of treason against the country (*Landesverrat*) and high treason (*Hochverrat*—treason against the government), have given your support, even indirectly, to such acts. And you should have prevented the German Volk from being subjected to a new constitution drawn up at the beck and call of foreign countries. That has nothing to do with honor, allowing the enemy to dictate one's own internal structure. (Cheering and clapping from the government parties.)

And, moreover, at that time you should have professed your faith in the German tricolor and not in the colors on the handbills the enemy threw into our trenches, (renewed cheering from the right) because more than ever in an age of distress and suppression by the enemy must one show one's pride and even more pledge one's support to one's Volk and the symbols of one's Volk. You would still have had the opportunity, even if the circumstances had forced us to surrender everything that had formerly been sacred to us, to allow the national honor to be evidenced to the world in domestic policy. ("Hear, hear!" from the right.)

You say: equal rights! Just as we desire it abroad, we also desire it at home. It was for these "equal rights," Herr Wels, that we fought for fourteen years! You ignored these equal rights as far as national Germany was concerned! So do not talk to us today about equal rights! (Loud cheering from the right.)

You say that the vanquished should not be labelled outlaws. Well, Mr. Deputy, we were outlaws as long as you were in power. (Renewed thunderous applause from the National Socialists; protests from the Social Democrats; a cry of "Severing!" from President Göring—referring to a Social Democratic official who tried to outlaw the Nazis.)

You talk about persecution. I think there are few of us here present who were not forced to pay in prison for the persecution you practiced. Few of us here present who were not made to feel the effects of that persecution in acts of harassment a thousand times over and incidents of suppression a thousand times over! (Calls of approval from the right.)

And in addition to those of us here present, I know a company of hundreds of thousands who were at the mercy of a system of persecution that vented itself on them in a disgraceful, even in a positively despicable manner! You seem to have totally forgotten that, for years, our shirts were ripped off our backs because you did not approve of the color. (Loud jeers from the National Socialists.)

Let us stay within the realm of reality! Your persecution has made us strong! You also said that criticism is beneficial. We will take criticism from anyone who loves Germany. But we will take no criticism from anyone who worships the *Internationale!* (The anthem of the revolutionary left.)

Here too, you have come to your realization a good deal too late, Mr. Deputy. You should have recognized the beneficial power of criticism when we were in the opposition. Back then you had not yet been confronted with these words; back then our press was banned (*verboten*) and *verboten* and again *verboten;* our assemblies were banned; we were not allowed to speak, and I was not allowed to speak—and that went on for years! And now you say criticism is beneficial! (Laughter from the National Socialists; shouts from the Social Democrats; the President's bell calling for order.)

President Göring:
Stop talking and listen to this for once! (Cries of "Bravo!" from the National Socialists.)

Hitler, Reich Chancellor:
You complain that in the end the world is told untrue facts about the state of affairs in Germany. You complain that the world is told that every day dismembered corpses are turned over to the Israelite cemeteries in Berlin. How that torments you; you would be so glad to do justice to the truth! Well, Mr. Deputy, it must be child's play for your party, with its international connections, to find out the truth. And not only that. These past few days I have been reading the newspapers of your own Social Democratic sister parties in German-Austria. No one is hindering you from disseminating your understanding of the truth there. (Cries of "That's already been done!" from the Social Democrats.)

I would be curious as to how effective the power of your international connections really will be in this case as well. (Amusement on the part of the National Socialists; shouts from the Social Democrats.)

Would you please let me finish; I didn't interrupt you! I have read your paper in the Saar, Mr. Deputy, and it does nothing other than commit constant acts of treason against the country (*Landesverrat*), Deputy Wels; (indignant shouts from the National Socialists) it is constantly attempting to discredit Germany abroad, (jeers and cries of "Dirty trick!" (*Gemeinheit*) from the National Socialists) to shed a bad light upon our Volk with lies to the rest of the world.

You talk about the lack of stability of the law. Gentlemen of the Social Democratic Party! I too witnessed the Revolution in 1918. I really do have to say that if we did not have a feeling for the law, we would not be here today, and you would not be here either! (Shouts of "Bravo!" from the National Socialists.)

In 1918 you turned against those who had done nothing to harm you. ("Hear, hear!" from the National Socialists.)

We are restraining ourselves from turning against those who tortured us and humiliated us for fourteen years. ("Hear, hear!" from the National Socialists.)

You say the National Socialist Revolution has nothing to do with Socialism, but rather that its "Socialism" exists only in the sense that it persecutes the "only pillar of Socialism in Germany," the SPD. (Laughter from the National Socialists.)

You are sissies, gentlemen, and not worthy of this age, if you start talking about persecution at this stage of the game. What has been done to you? You are sitting here and your speaker is being listened to with patience. (Cries of "Hear, hear!" and amusement on the part of the National Socialists.)

You talk about persecution. Who has been persecuting you? ("Hear, hear!" from President Goring.)

You say you are the only pillar of Socialism. You were the pillar of that mysterious Socialism of which in reality the German Volk never had a glimpse. (Cries of "Hear, hear!" and amusement on the part of the National Socialists.)

You are talking today about your achievements and your deeds; you are speaking of all the things you intended to do. By your fruits shall ye, too, be known! (Tumultuous approval and applause from the National Socialists.)

The fruits testify against you! (Protest from the Social Democrats; laughter from the National Socialists.)

If the Germany you created in fourteen years is any reflection of your socialist aims, then all I can say is give us four years' time, Gentlemen, in order to show you the reflection of our aims. (Calls of approval from the National Socialists.)

You say: "You want to eliminate the Reichstag to proceed with your Revolution." Gentlemen, if so, we would not have found it necessary to first go to this vote, to convene this Reichstag, or to have the draft of this bill presented. God knows we would have had the courage to deal with you some other way as well! (Thunderous, long drawn-out cheering and applause from the National Socialists.)

You also said that we cannot ignore the Social Democratic Party because it was the first one to clear these seats for the Volk, for the working people, and not only for barons or counts. In every instance, Mr. Deputy, you are too late! Why did you not advise your friend Grzesinski of your views in good time, why did you not tell your other friends Braun and Severing, who accused me for years of being nothing more than a house painter's apprentice! (Enthusiastic assent and indignant jeers from the National Socialists; protest from the Social Democrats; countering cries of "Of course that's what you said!" from the National Socialists.)

For years you claimed that on your posters. (Renewed protest from the Social Democrats; cries of "Quiet!" from the National Socialists; the president's bell calling for order.)

President Göring:
Now the chancellor is getting even! (Approval from the National Socialists.)

Hitler, Reich Chancellor:
And in the end I was actually threatened that I would be driven out of Germany with a dog whip! (Jeers from the National Socialists.)

We National Socialists will now clear the path for the German worker leading to what is his to claim and demand. We National Socialists will be his advocates; you, gentlemen (addressing the Social Democrats), are no longer necessary! (Cries of "Hear, hear!" and long drawn out, thunderous applause from the National Socialists.)

You also state that not power but a sense of justice is crucial. We have attempted to awaken this sense of justice in our Volk for fourteen years, and we have succeeded in awakening it. However, I now believe on the basis of my own political experiences with you—("Hear, hear!" from the National Socialists) that unfortunately, justice alone is not enough—one has to be in power, too! ("Hear, hear!" from the National Socialists.)

And do not mistake us for a bourgeois world! You think that your star might rise again! Gentlemen, Germany's star will rise and yours will fall. (Loud cries of "Bravo!" and "Heil!" from the National Socialists; long drawn out cheering, also from the galleries.)

You say you were not broken during the period of Socialist legislation. That was a period in which the German workers saw in you something other than what you are today. But why have you forgotten to mention this realization to us?! ("Hear, hear!" from the National Socialists.)

Everything that becomes rotten, old, and weak in the life of a people disappears, never to return. (Assent from the right.)

Your death knell has sounded as well, and it is only because we are thinking of Germany and its distress and the requirements of national life that we appeal in this hour to the German Reichstag to give its consent to what we could have taken at any rate. ("Hear, hear!" from the National Socialists.)

We are doing it for the sake of justice—not because we overestimate power, but because we may thus one day perhaps more easily join with those who, today, may be separated from us but who nevertheless believe in Germany, too. (Calls of "Bravo!" from the National Socialists.)

For I would not want to make the mistake of provoking opponents instead of either destroying or becoming reconciled with them. (Cries of "Bravo!" and "Hear, hear!" from the National Socialists.)

I would like to extend my hand to those who, perhaps on other paths, will also come to feel with their Volk in the end, (cries of "Bravo!" from the Center Party) and would not want to declare an everlasting war, (renewed cries of "Bravo!") not because of weakness, but out of love to my Volk, and in order to spare this German Volk all what will perish with the rest in this age of struggles. (Renewed shouts of "Bravo!" from the National Socialists and the German Nationalists.)

That you may never misunderstand me on this point: I extend my hand to everyone who commits himself to Germany. (Cries of "Bravo!")

I do not recognize the precepts of the Internationale. (Cheering from the National Socialists and German Nationalists.)

I believe that you (addressing the Social Democrats) are not voting for this bill for the reason that you, in your innermost mentality, are incapable of comprehending the purpose that thereby imbues us. ("Hear, hear!" from the National Socialists.)

I believe, however, that you would not do this were we really what your press abroad today makes us out to be, ("Hear, hear!" from the National Socialists) and I can only say to you: I do not even want you to vote for it! Germany will be liberated, but not by you! (Long drawn-out, thunderous cries of

"Heil!" and cheering from the National Socialists and in the galleries. Applause from the German Nationalists. Repeated waves of thunderous applause and cries of *"Heil!"*)

It was to be the first and only time Hitler took part in a debate before the Reichstag and, at least from 1932 onwards, before the public. The snub he had delivered to the Chairman of the Social Democratic Party naturally elicited the highest acclaim, both in the right-wing parties and among the members of the Reich government. Even the normally reserved Hugenberg was openly enthusiastic and thanked Hitler at the cabinet meeting on March 24 "on behalf of the other cabinet members for the impressive and successful appearance in the Reichstag, but most of all for the brilliant rebuff of that Marxist leader, Wels."

The further course of the Reichstag session on March 23 brought no other incidents. The deputies Kaas (Center Party), Ritter von Lex (BVP), Reinhold Meier (German State Party), Simpfendörfer (CSV), and Göring (Nazi Party) subsequently declared the consent of their respective parties to the Enabling Act, which was then passed with a total of 441 votes (all of the parties with the exception of the SPD) to the 94 votes of the Social Democrats. The Reichsrat, now composed exclusively of National Socialist *Länder* representatives, passed the bill unanimously the same day.

It is pointless to speculate what Hitler would have done had the Enabling Act not secured the required two-thirds majority. Such a situation would certainly not have presented an obstacle to his plans for governing the country; he had said as much in no uncertain terms on various occasions. As early as August 6, 1932, Goebbels had recorded Hitler's intentions in his diary on the occasion of the then forthcoming government negotiations. He had noted: "If a Reichstag rejects the Enabling Act the Führer demands, it will be sent home."

In all probability, Hitler would have continued governing with the aid of emergency decrees pursuant to Article 48 of the Weimar Constitution. He had no need to fear interference from the Reichstag due to its right-wing majority. At the next opportunity, he would have announced new elections, as he would in November, in order to procure a two-thirds majority in the Reichstag.

► July 6, 1933 *Within six months of being appointed to power, Hitler's authority had become absolute. However, he had to maintain efficiency if he was to keep power. In this talk to National Socialist Party (Nazi Party) officials, Hitler set out his policies.*

After the Center Party had been dissolved on July 5, Hitler regarded the political struggle for power within Germany as settled for the time being. Although he had declared that the revolution would not be ended until a new order had been established both within and without the entire German world, with regard to the economy he felt it was expedient to temporarily shift his focus, as illustrated in an address to the regional authorities (*Reichsstatthalter*) in Berlin on July 6:

> The political parties have now been eliminated in full. The achievement of external power must now be followed by internal education. Care must be taken to avoid making purely formal decisions in a rush and expecting this to bring a lasting solution. People are easily capable of bending an outer form into one bearing the stamp of their own ideas.
>
> A change, of course, can be made only when the persons required for such a change are present. The majority of revolutions are successful in their initial onslaught, but as soon as they succeed they slip up and are brought to a standstill. The revolution is not a permanent state of affairs, and it must not be allowed to develop into any such permanent state. The river of the revolution that has been released must be channeled into the safe bed of evolution. The most important thing in this connection is the education of the individual. Today's conditions must be improved and the people embodying them must be instilled with a National Socialist concept of the state. Thus a businessman may not be dismissed if he is a good businessman but not yet a National Socialist, particularly if the National Socialist appointed in his place does not understand anything about business. In business, ability alone must be the decisive factor.
>
> It is the task of National Socialism to ensure the development of our Volk. However, we should not be searching to see if there is anything left to revolutionize; rather, it is our task

to secure position after position, to hold our positions and to make exemplary appointments to these positions in a gradual process. In doing so, we must focus our actions on the space of many years and think in terms of relatively long periods of time. Theoretical coordination of the nation (*Gleichschaltung*) will not enable us to provide bread to workers. Moreover, history will not judge us according to whether we have dismissed and jailed the largest possible number of businessmen, but rather according to whether we have been able to provide work.

Today we have the absolute power to enforce our will everywhere. But we must also be able to replace those who are dismissed with better people. In the long term, security in terms of power politics will be all the greater, the more we are able to underpin it economically. It is the task and the responsibility of the regional authorities (*Reichsstatthalter*) to ensure that no arbitrary organizations or party offices claim for themselves governmental authority, dismiss individuals or make appointments to offices, for these are matters in which the Reich government—and with respect to the economy, the Reich minister of economics—alone is competent. The party has now become the state. All power lies in the authority of the Reich. It must not come to pass that the main emphasis in German life be transferred back to individual areas or, much less, individual organizations. Authority is no longer anchored in any partial area of the Reich but in the concept of the German Volk itself!

▸ December 1, 1933 *The "Law to Secure Unity of Party and State" became, essentially, the constitution of Germany. The party was the state and Hitler controlled the party.*

For this purpose, a "Law to Secure the Unity of Party and State" (*Gesetz zur Sicherung der Einheit von Partei und Staat*) was passed. The terms "national uprising" and "national revolution" were now replaced by the official title, "National Socialist Revolution." The law provided as follows:

§1 Following the triumph of the National Socialist Revolution, the National Socialist German Workers' Party is now the representative of the German concept of the state and is inextricably bound to the state. It is a corporation under public law. Its statutes are to be determined by the Führer.

§2 In order to guarantee the closest cooperation between the offices of the party and the SA and the public authorities, the deputy of the Führer and the SA chief of staff shall become members of the Reich government.

Hess and Röhm were sworn in on December 4 by Hindenburg as Reich ministers without portfolio.

▸ January 30, 1934 *In his speech to the Reichstag, marking his first year in power, Hitler made it clear that National Socialist Germany would never restore the monarchy.*

Thus at this time I would like to protest against the theory that has been advanced again recently that Germany could only be happy under the rule of its traditional princes.

No! We are one Volk, and we want to live in one Reich.

And those who sinned against this principle so often in the past in German history were not able to credit their mission to God's merciful will but instead, as history has taught us, unfortunately all too often to the expedient favor and support of their worst enemies. In this year, we have thus consciously enforced the authority of the Reich and the authority of the government against those infirm descendents and heirs to the politics of the past who thought that they could still parade their traditional resistance to the National Socialist State.

It was one of the happiest hours of my life when it became clear that the entire German Volk was granting its approval to a policy that exclusively represented its interests.

With all due respect to the values of the monarchy and all esteem to the truly great emperors and kings of our German history, the question of permanently shaping the structure of

the State of the German Reich is completely beyond discussion today. No matter how the nation and its leaders may one
day decide, there is one thing they should never forget: he who
personifies Germany's highest peak receives his calling from
the German Volk and is obligated to it alone!

For my part, I regard myself merely as an agent of the nation engaged to implement those reforms that will one day
enable it to make the final decision on the permanent constitution of the Reich.

Hitler had never seriously advocated the reinstitution of the monarchy.
Now and again, when he judged it opportune in light of his respective audience, he indulged in nebulous allusions to a monarchical constitution for
the Reich, possible perhaps in some distant future. By no means was he
willing, however, to accept the idea that this might come to pass during his
own lifetime. His speech of January 30 made this unequivocally clear to
those who persisted in clinging to this type of "misplaced" hope.

▸ January 30, 1934 *In the same speech to the Reichstag, Hitler indicated how
he would deal with "unproductive elements."*

Hitler then shifted the focus of his offensive to opportunists and the congenitally ill, for whom he announced "genuinely revolutionary measures":

> More dangerous than these, however, are the two catego-
> ries of people whom we must perceive as a genuine burden to
> our present-day Reich and the Reich of tomorrow.
>
> First of all, there are the political birds of passage who alight
> wherever the crops are being harvested in summer. Spineless,
> weak characters—yet true opportunists who pounce on every
> successful movement, and endeavor by overloud clamor and
> more than perfect behavior to avoid or answer from the very
> start the question of their past origins and activities. They are
> dangerous because they attempt to satisfy their purely person-
> al and egotistical interests behind the mask of the new regime
> and, in doing so, become a genuine burden to a Movement for
> which millions of decent people spent years making the most
> difficult sacrifices without ever even having conceived of the

idea that they could ever be repaid for the suffering and deprivation that they had taken upon themselves for their Volk. Purging the state and the party of these importunate parasites will be an important task, particularly for the future. Then many inwardly decent people who were unable to come to the Movement earlier, often for understandable and even cogent reasons, will also find their way to it without having to fear being mistaken for such dubious elements.

And another heavy burden is the army of those who were born into the negative side of our national (*völkisch*) life due to their hereditary predisposition. Here the state will be able to take genuinely revolutionary measures.

The National Socialist Movement deserves great credit for having launched, by way of legislation as early as last year, an initial offensive against this threat of the gradual disintegration of the Volk. When objections are raised—particularly from the religious quarter—and opposition is offered to this legislation, I am forced to reply by saying that it would have been more effective, more decent and above all more Christian not to have stood by those who deliberately destroyed the healthy instead of harassing those who have no other goal but to avoid disease from the very onset.

Apart from that, whatever is allowed to happen in this sphere not only constitutes an act of cruelty against the innocent victims themselves but is also an act of cruelty against the Volk as a whole. If the development were allowed to progress at the rate of the last hundred years, the number of those dependent upon public welfare would one day threaten to approach the number of those who ultimately would be the only support for the preservation of the community.

It is not the churches which must feed these armies of the unfortunate but the Volk. Were the churches to state their willingness to take those suffering from hereditary illnesses into their care and keeping, we would gladly be willing to dispense with their sterilization. But as long as the state is condemned to raise gigantic, annually increasing sums—today already exceeding the level of 350 million—from its citizens toward maintaining these regrettably congenitally ill people in the nation, then it is forced to resort to a remedy that keeps such undeserved suffering from being passed on in the future and also ensures that millions of healthy persons will not be deprived of the bare necessities of life in order to artificially preserve the lives of millions of unhealthy people.

► July 13, 1934 *During the Night of the Long Knives, June 29–30, 1934, Hitler turned on his Nazi Party storm troopers (SA) and eliminated many of their leaders along with numerous other people both prominent and obscure. Here he gave his explanation and clear warning to any who might criticize his rule.*

In his speech of July 13, Hitler cited dozens of reasons why he had been forced to take action against Röhm and the SA leadership which included everything from moral perversion to alleged rebellion. His real motive—that of winning the sympathy of the *Reichswehr*—was naturally not among them.

As the self-proclaimed "supreme justice of the German Volk," he left no doubt as to the maxim that was to govern German affairs from then on:

> Every person should know for all time that, if he raises his hand to strike out at the state [i.e., Hitler], certain death will be his lot.

When the Reichstag session opened on July 13, there were already visible indications of the changes that had taken place since the last session on January 30, 1934. Steel-helmeted Nazi Party SS guards (*Schutzstaffel*)were stationed next to the podium and throughout the auditorium. Apparently Hitler feared assassination attempts by incensed party comrades. Twelve SA leaders who had been Reichstag deputies were absent, having been slain in the purge. Reichstag President Göring had exchanged his SA uniform for the dress of the German Air Sports Association.

The composition of the government bench also reflected the new state of affairs: Röhm was naturally missing; Reich Minister of Economics Schmitt was absent—albeit due to illness; and von Papen was not in attendance. Foreign Minister von Neurath had taken the vice chancellor's place for the time being. Neither Hitler nor Göring took the trouble to explain von Papen's conspicuous absence. Even if the rumors that he had been put under house arrest or received a brutal beating at the hands of the SS were only gross exaggerations, one thing was certain: he would never return to his place next to Hitler on the government bench.

The *Völkischer Beobachter* reported on July 14 that all Reich ministers had been in attendance at the Reichstag session, listing each deputy separately with the exception of von Papen and Schmitt. The party's mouthpiece was well informed: apparently these two men were no longer regarded as ministers.

Strikingly few civilians were in evidence, and those present included General Litzmann who had stood by Hitler so loyally in the Reich Chancellery on July 1.

Hitler began his speech with the following words:

Deputies! Men of the German Reichstag!

Acting on behalf of the Reich government, the president of the Reichstag, Hermann Göring, has called you together today in order to give me an opportunity to enlighten the Volk before this body, the highest appointed forum of the nation, concerning events that will we hope live on in our history for all time as both a sad reminder and a warning. Out of a combination of objective circumstances and personal guilt, of human incompetence and human defects, a crisis arose in our young Reich that all too easily may have brought about truly destructive consequences for an indeterminate period of time. The purpose of my remarks is to explain to you and thus to the nation how they came about and were overcome. The contents of my remarks will be completely frank. Only in respect to scope must I impose upon myself limitations necessitated, on the one hand, by consideration to the interests of the Reich and, on the other, by the boundaries drawn by the feeling of shame.

However, before Hitler proceeded to the stated purpose of his remarks, he warmed up his listeners with a half-hour version of the "party narrative" on his accomplishments since January 30, 1933. He then elaborately described four groups of people composing what he viewed as the opposition in Germany.

Street riots, barricade fighting, mass terror, and an individualistic propaganda of disintegration today trouble nearly all countries throughout the world. In Germany as well, a few isolated fools and criminals of this type are still making repeated attempts to ply their destructive trade. Since the defeat of the Communist Party, we have experienced, albeit growing constantly weaker, one attempt after another to establish Communist organizations with varying degrees of an anarchist character and to put them to work. Their methods are always the same. While portraying the present lot as unbearable, they extol the Communist paradise of the future and, in so doing, are in effect waging war for hell. For the consequences of their victory in a country like Germany could be nothing other than destructive. However, the trial run of their capability and of the consequences of their rule have, in the concrete case, already produced results so clear to the German Volk that the overwhelming majority, particularly of the German workers, has recognized this Jewish-international benefactor of mankind and defeated it inside Germany. The National Socialist state will wage a hundred years' war, if necessary, to stamp out and destroy every last trace within its boundaries of this phenomenon that poisons and makes dupes of the Volk (*Volksvernarrung*).

The second group of discontented is comprised of those political leaders who regard their futures as having been terminated by January 30 but who have never been able to reconcile themselves to the irreversibility of this fact.

The more time veils their own incompetence with the merciful cloak of forgetfulness, the more they believe themselves entitled to gradually reintroduce themselves to the mind of the Volk. However, because their incompetence then was not a matter of time but a matter of inborn incompetence, they are equally unable today to prove their worth by positive, useful work but instead perceive their purpose in life as being fulfilled by voicing criticism that is as underhanded as it is false. The Volk does not belong to them either. They can neither seriously threaten the National Socialist state nor seriously damage it in any way.

A third group of destructive elements is made up of those revolutionaries who were shaken and uprooted in 1918 in regard to their relation to the state and who thus have lost all inner connection to a regulated human social order.

They have become revolutionaries who pay homage to the revolution for its own sake and would like to see it become a permanent state of affairs. All of us once suffered from the horrible tragedy that, as obedient and dutiful soldiers, we were suddenly faced by a revolt of mutineers who actually succeeded in gaining possession of the state. Each of us had originally been trained to abide by the laws, to respect authority and to show obedience to the commands and orders it issues, and instilled with an inner devotion to the representatives of the state.

Now the revolution of deserters and mutineers forced us to inwardly disassociate ourselves from these concepts.

We were unable to muster any respect for the new usurpers. Honor and obedience forced us to refuse to obey; love of the nation and the *Vaterland* obliged us to wage war on them; the amorality of their laws extinguished in us the conviction of the necessity for complying with them—and hence we became revolutionaries. However, even as revolutionaries, we had not disassociated ourselves from the obligation to apply to ourselves the natural laws of the sovereign right of our Volk and to respect these laws. It was not our intention to violate the will and the right of self-determination of the German Volk but to drive away those who violated the nation.

And when finally, legitimated by the trust of this Volk, we drew the consequences from our fourteen-year-long struggle, this was not done in order to unloose a chaos of unbridled instincts, but with the sole aim of establishing a new and better order. For us, the revolution that shattered the Second German Reich was nothing other than the tremendous act of birth that summoned the Third Reich into being.

We wanted to once again create a state to which every German can cling in love; to establish a regime to which everyone can look up with respect; to find laws that are commensurate with the morality of our Volk; to install an authority to which each and every man submits in joyful obedience. For us, the revolution is not a permanent state of affairs. When a deathly check is violently imposed upon the natural development of a Volk, an act of violence may serve to release the artificially interrupted flow of evolution to allow it once again the freedom of natural development. However, there is no such thing as a permanent revolution or any type of profitable development possible by means of periodically recurring revolts.

Among the countless files that I was obliged to read through in the past few weeks, I also found a journal with the notes of a man who was cast onto the route of resistance to the laws in 1918 and now lives in a world in which the law itself appears to provoke resistance; an unnerving document, an uninterrupted sequence of conspiracies and plots, an insight into the mentality of people who, without realizing it, have found in nihilism their ultimate creed. Incapable of any real cooperation, determined to take a stand against any kind of order, filled by hatred of every authority as they are, their uneasiness and their restlessness can be quelled only by their permanent mental and conspiratorial preoccupation with the disintegration of whatever exists at the given time. Many of them stormed the state with us in our early period of struggle, but an inner lack of discipline led most of them away from the disciplined National Socialist Movement in the course of the struggle.

The last remnant seemed to have withdrawn after January 30. Their link with the National Socialist Movement was dissolved the moment this itself, as the state, became the object of their pathological aversion. As a matter of principle, they are enemies of every authority and thus utterly incapable of being converted. Accomplishments that appear to strengthen the new German state only provoke their even greater hatred. For there is one thing, above all, that all of these oppositional elements principally have in common: they do not see before them the German Volk, but the institution of order they so abhor. They are filled not by a desire to help the Volk, but by the fervent hope that the government will fail in its work to rescue the Volk. Thus they are never willing to admit that an action is beneficial but are instead filled by the will to contest any success as a matter of principle and to extract from every success any potential weaknesses.

This third group of pathological enemies of the state is dangerous because, until a new order has begun to crystallize from a state of chaotic conflict, they represent a reservoir of willing accomplices for every attempt at revolt.

I must, however, now devote my attention to the fourth group, that which on occasion—perhaps even unintentionally—nonetheless plies a truly destructive trade. I am speaking of those who belonged to a relatively small class in society, who have nothing to do and thus find the time and the opportunity for word-of-mouth commentaries on everything capable of bringing some interesting—and important—variety to lives that are otherwise completely meaningless. For while the overwhelming majority in the nation is made to earn its daily bread by toilsome labor, in certain classes of life there are still people whose sole activity consists of doing nothing, followed by more of the same to recuperate from having done nothing. The more pathetic the life of such a drone is, all the more avidly will he seize upon whatever can fill this vacuum with some interesting content.

Personal and political gossip is caught up eagerly and passed on even more eagerly. And because these people, as a result of doing nothing, have no living tie to the masses of the nation's millions, their lives are delimited by the scope of the sphere within which they move.

Every bit of prattle that becomes absorbed by these circles throws its reflection back and forth endlessly as between two distorting mirrors.

Because their very beings are filled with a nothingness that they constantly see reflected in those like them, they believe that this phenomenon is universal. They mistake the view of their circle for the view of all. Their doubts, they fancy, constitute the troubles of the entire nation. In reality, this little colony of drones is only a state within the state, without any living contact with life, with the feelings, hopes, and cares of the rest of the Volk. However, they are dangerous, for they are veritable germ-carriers for unrest, uncertainty, rumors, allegations, lies, suspicions, slander, and fear, and thus they contribute to creating a gradually-increasing tension until, in the end, it is difficult to recognize or draw the natural boundaries between them and the Volk.

Just as they wreak their havoc in every other nation, they do so in Germany, too. They regarded the National Socialist revolution as a conversation topic just as interesting as, on the other hand, the fight of the enemies of the National Socialist state.

But one thing is certain: the work of rebuilding our Volk and, with it, the work of our Volk itself is possible only if the German Volk follows its leadership with inner calm, order, and discipline and above all if it trusts in its leadership. For it is only the trust and the faith placed in the new state that have enabled us to take on and solve the great tasks put to us by former times. Even though the National Socialist regime was forced to come to terms with these various groups from the very beginning and has, in fact, come to terms with them, a mood has nonetheless arisen in the past few months that, in the end, could no longer be taken lightly.

The prattle of a new revolution, of a new upheaval, of a new uprising—while at first infrequent—gradually took on such intensity that only a foolhardy leadership of state would have been capable of ignoring it. It was no longer possible to simply dismiss as empty chatter what was put down in hundreds and ultimately thousands of oral and written reports. Even three months ago, the leadership of the Party was convinced that it was simply the foolish gossip of political reactionaries, Marxist anarchists, and all sorts of idlers, completely lacking any substantiation in fact.

Hitler then began to spin his yarns of the purported Putsch planned by Röhm and Schleicher, neglecting to cite a single shred of solid evidence for his fantastic allegations. Indeed, those who could have testified had been silenced forever.

▸ September 15, 1935 *Hitler convened the Riechstag during the 1935 Party Congress (Party Congress of Freedom) so he could introduce important legislation during a high point of world attention. This is some of what he said.*

At 8:00 p.m. the Reichstag convened in the hall of the Nuremberg Cultural Association building in order to pass the three bills introduced by the government. It was to be the first and last time during Hitler's rule that a Reichstag session was held outside Berlin. Nuremberg had last been the site of a German Reichstag (at the time an assembly of the German Empire's estates) in 1543, and the location more than the content of the session made this Nuremberg gathering remarkable.

From a constitutional standpoint, Hitler could have passed the laws himself, but he judged it more fitting to have the tradition-laden, black-white-red flag of imperial Germany discarded by a jointly responsible Reichstag, the legislative body authorized to amend the constitution under Weimar law. The reasons for this were obvious, for had he himself declared the swastika the sole national flag; this may well have prompted resistance at home from followers of the *Stahlhelm* and the more reactionary generals, with whom relations were already strained.

But in terms of foreign policy as well, he considered a resolution of the legislative body to be more effective. The swastika had already become a target of anti-German sentiments abroad, having, for instance, been ripped from the bow of the Lloyd steamer Bremen in New York Harbor, an incident to which Hitler referred in this speech. By virtue of both the flag act and his anti-Semitic *Blutschutz* legislation, Hitler wished to convey to foreign countries that any speculations on a change in course within Germany were completely unsubstantiated.

His September 15 speech to the Reichstag demonstrated anew that he was primarily pursuing foreign policy goals in his treatment of German Jews. Already extremely irritated by criticism in the foreign press, Hitler was also irked by the fact that his relations with the British statesmen were not evolving as he had envisioned in his plans for an Anglo-German alliance. Naturally choosing not to seek the reasons in his own erroneous conceptions, he held "Jewish press agitation" abroad accountable and resolved to exert yet more pressure. In his opinion, this would be conducive toward swaying "world Jewry" to intervene and end the boycott campaign against Germany in the foreign press while at the same time prevailing upon the Anglo-Saxon powers to be more amenable to Germany's wishes. As further developments showed, this was a complete miscalculation, and while the British and the Americans sympathized with German Jews, they were not willing to change their attitude toward Hitler for this reason alone.

In the Nuremberg laws, Hitler employed the same tactics underlying his boycott of April 1, 1933: he persecuted the German Jews but stopped short for the time being of making their lives totally unbearable. At the same time, he threatened to issue further sanctions if the foreign powers continued to refuse to comply with the wishes of National Socialist Germany. This complicated blackmail strategy was based, however, upon false premises; and thus even his drastic measures after 1941 were doomed to fail.

Hitler's September 15 speech to the Reichstag was as follows:

> On behalf of the German Reich government, I have requested Reichstag President Göring to convene for today a session of the German Reichstag in Nuremberg. The place was chosen because, by virtue of the National Socialist Movement, it is closely connected with the laws that will be presented to you today for passage; the time was chosen because the great majority of the deputies are still in Nuremberg in their capacity as party comrades.
>
> I would like to make a few general remarks on these bills that are being introduced on a notice of motion. The first part of the Reich party congress in Nuremberg has come to an end. The *Wehrmacht* Day will mark its final conclusion tomorrow. The picture presented by this celebration of the Movement echoes even more strongly last year's impression. The German Volk has found the way to a unity and discipline such as has never before existed in history. This expression of the stability of the Movement is simultaneously the expression of the strength of the current regime. What the German nation longed for in vain for centuries has now been given unto it: a united Volk of brothers, free of respective biases and the scruples of past epochs. This inner strength will be reflected by the picture the *Wehrmacht* will present to us tomorrow. It will not be a mass demonstration but an exposition of the inner value of our new army. The German Volk can consider itself lucky at the knowledge of having regained this strength after having suffered so terribly and been impotent for so long. And that particularly at a time that seems to be afflicted by formidable crises. Germany has regained its health. Its facilities are back in working order, both inside and out.

All the greater is the responsibility of the leadership of the Reich in such grave times. There can be but one guiding principle for the whole of our actions: our great and unshakable love of peace. It appears to me that such a statement is necessary at this time, for a certain international press will unfortunately persist in its attempts to draw Germany into the circle of its calculating designs.

Before we know it, there will be reports that Germany plans to take action against France; there will be speculation that it is turning against Austria; or the suspicion that it will attack Russia—don't ask me where. These threats are then usually presented as an argument for the necessity of forming various coalitions, depending on the needs of the moment. In no less generous terms does this press give German friendship away and treat it as something given free for the taking to any statesman inclined to reach out his hand for it.

I hardly need assure you, my deputies and men of the Reichstag, that the German government does not base its decisions upon any kind of negative attitude towards anyone but solely on the consciousness of its own responsibility to Germany. The purpose of our work is not, however, to squander what it has achieved in some thoughtless and hence lunatic gamble.

The purpose of building up the German army was not to threaten the freedom of any European people, much less deprive them of it, but solely to preserve the freedom of the German Volk. This viewpoint is the fundamental principle upon that the foreign policy of the German Reich government rests. Therefore we refuse to comment on incidents that do not affect Germany, and do not wish to be dragged into such incidents.

It is with all the more concern, however, that the German Volk is following the incidents in Lithuania. In the midst of peacetime, the Memel territory was stolen from Germany years after the peace treaty. This theft was legalized by the League of Nations and coupled only with the condition that the contractually stipulated autonomy awarded to the Memel Germans be preserved. For years now, the German element in this area has been abused and harassed in violation of law and the treaty. A great nation is forced to look on while, contrary to law and the stipulations of the treaty, its blood relations who were attacked in the midst of peacetime and torn away from the Reich are being subjected to a treatment worse than that to which criminals are subjected in normal states.

Yet their only crime is that they are Germans and wish to remain Germans. Proposals of those responsible in Kaunas have, to date, not progressed beyond mere worthless formalities with no consequences within the country.

The German Reich government views this development with interest and with bitterness. It would be a laudable undertaking were the League of Nations to turn its attention to the respect due to the autonomy of the Memel territory and see to it that it is put into practice, before here, too, the events begin to take on forms that could one day but be regretted by all those involved. The preparations for the election that are now taking place there constitute a mockery of both law and obligation!

Germany is by no means lodging unreasonable claims in demanding that suitable measures be taken to compel Lithuania to comply with the existing treaties. A nation of sixty-five million ought surely to have the right to demand that it at least receive no less consideration than the whims of a country of two million.

Unfortunately, we are witnessing how, although the understanding between peoples is more needed than ever, the Bolshevist International of Moscow has resumed its open and methodical revolutionizing that means whipping up animosity among the peoples. The farce of the Comintern Congress in Moscow is a telling illustration of the sincerity of the "nonintervention" policy this same power demands.

Since we expect nothing to come of protests and remonstrances in Moscow and have learned through our own experience and, as far as we can ascertain, from the experiences of other states as well, we are resolved to combat the Bolshevist revolutionary agitation in Germany with the effective weapons of National Socialist enlightenment.

The party congress has certainly left no room for doubt that National Socialism—if an attempt is made by Moscow-Bolshevism to establish a foothold in Germany or to drive Germany into a revolution—will most definitely put a stop to this plan and such attempts.

We are further compelled to note that here, as everywhere, it is almost exclusively Jewish elements that are at work as instigators of this campaign to spread animosity and confusion among the peoples. The insult to the German flag—which was settled most loyally by a statement of the American government—is both an illustration of the attitude of Jews, even in civil service status, towards Germany and revealing proof of the pertinence of our National Socialist legislation that is designed as a precautionary measure to prevent from the very onset that similar incidents take place in our German administration and in our courts and to prohibit them at any cost. However, should the pertinence of our view require yet further underscoring, this is provided in abundance in the renewed boycott campaign that the Jewish element has just launched against Germany.

This international unrest in the world unfortunately appears to have given rise to the opinion among Jews in Germany that now perhaps the time has come to set Jewish interests up in clear opposition to the German national interests in the Reich. Loud complaints of provocative actions of individual members of this race are coming in from all sides, and the striking frequency of these reports and the similarity of their content appear to indicate a certain method behind the deeds themselves. These actions have escalated to demonstrations in a Berlin cinema directed against a basically harmless foreign film that Jewish circles fancied was offensive to them.

To prevent this behavior from leading to determined defensive action on the part of the outraged population, the extent of which cannot be foreseen, the only alternative would be a legislative solution to the problem. The German Reich government is guided by the hope of possibly being able to bring about, by means of a single secular measure, a framework within which the German Volk would be in a position to establish tolerable relations with the Jewish people. However, should this hope prove false and intra-German and international Jewish agitation proceed on its course, a new evaluation of the situation would have to take place.

I now propose that the Reichstag adopt the bills that the Reichstag president, Party Comrade Göring, will read aloud to you. The first and second laws repay a debt of gratitude to the Movement, under whose symbol Germany regained its freedom, in that they fulfill a significant item on the program of the National Socialist Party. The third is an attempt at a legislative solution to a problem that, should it yet again prove insoluble, would have to be assigned to the National Socialist Party for a final solution by law. Behind all three laws stands the National Socialist Party, and with it and behind it stands the nation. I may request that you adopt the laws for passage.

Before Reichstag President Göring disclosed the wording of the three laws, he took the podium to speak for thirty minutes in support of Hitler's views. True to his adage of July 13, 1934 ("We will all always approve of everything our Führer does"), he merely parroted what his Führer had told him to say. Although he spoke with the "voice of his master," Göring was consistently capable of expressing his own views in a tone of utter conviction; the fact that he spoke almost exclusively of the flag act on this occasion indicated how very important this matter was to Hitler.

In his remarks, Göring stressed that the old black-white-red banner had now been lowered in honor and belonged to a Germany of the past. One had been forced, he explained, to take steps to ensure that this flag was not demoted to a mere "party pennant disguising a conservative sign of victory."

> We wish to prevent the black-white-red banner from being further degraded as not worth a fig and held up as a fig leaf disguising the naked truth about democratic-pacifistic ignorance. For us, the swastika has become a sacred symbol, and thus it is quite self-evident that, if this flag is to fly over Germany in the future, no Jew may be allowed to hoist this sacred insignia. The new flag shall clearly demonstrate to the world that Germany will stand under the swastika for ever and for all eternity.

Göring also made reference to the New York incident involving the swastika flag, stating:

> He who offends this flag insults the nation. We have noted to our regret what happened recently in America, and we feel sorry for the American people for having been forced to witness such an indignity. We frankly declare, however, that we

regard this act merely as an excess and hold that a brazen Jew will never be able to insult us in his profound hatred. The victory of the swastika gave us back our pride and gave us back our might. The *Wehrmacht* yearns for the insignia under which it was resurrected. Had the victory not been won through the fighting and the sacrifices of the brown battalions, had we not had this victory, we know that not a single battalion, not a single ship, not a single new airplane would have been possible. Thus for us the swastika has become for all time the symbol of freedom, and therefore it is only natural that today, at the Party Congress of Freedom, this symbol of freedom be anchored.

At the close of his speech, Göring announced the wording of the three laws. The "Reich Flag Act" and the "Reich Law of Citizenship" were received with the standard applause. The reading of the "Law for the Protection of German Blood and German Honor" elicited hoots of laughter when Göring read the "comical" text of §4: "Jews are prohibited from hoisting the flag of the Reich and the nation and from exhibiting the Reich colors. However, exhibiting the Jewish colors is permitted. The exercise of this right is subject to state protection."

As a matter of course, the three laws were unanimously accepted for passage, whereupon Hitler felt called upon to make yet a further statement in which he stressed how many centuries would be thankful for the Reichstag's work. He declared in his "final appeal:"

My deputies!

You have now approved of a law, the impact of which will become evident only in its full scope after many centuries have passed. See to it that the nation itself does not stray from the straight and narrow path of the law! See to it that our Volk adheres to the path of the law! See to it that this law is ennobled by the most tremendous discipline of the entire German Volk, to whom and for whom you are responsible.

▶ January 30, 1939 *Hitler consolidated his position by simply ignoring legal requirements but he remained fearful of the power of the Reichstag.*

At this particular session, the Reichstag unanimously extended the Enabling Act of March 24, 1933, due to expire in two years' time, to remain effective until May 10, 1943. Technically speaking, there was no pressing reason for such a step at this time. The same legislative body had already passed a decree on January 30, 1937 that had rescheduled the expiration date for April 1, 1941. Hitler was extremely cautious in all questions regarding power politics, as mentioned earlier. The first historic session of the Greater German Reichstag appeared to him an excellent forum for extending the Enabling Act until 1943. After all, so he speculated, there was no telling whether he would still be in a position to see through a like heavy-handed move in 1941. As a precautionary measure, he himself issued the following "Law on the Tenure of the Reichstag":

§1 (1) The Reichstag shall serve for a period of four years.

(2) Tenure shall commence on election day, and shall terminate four years after the first session of the Reichstag.

§2 Within sixty days after the expiration of tenure, a new election shall be held.

§3 The Reich minister of the interior shall issue specific regulations.

Berlin, January 30, 1939

The Führer and Reich Chancellor, Adolf Hitler
The Reich Minister of the Interior, Frick

The emphasis of this particular decree was obviously on Paragraph 1, Section 2. The preceding Reichstag had been elected on April 10, 1938. In violation of the constitution, this Reichstag was not called into session until this January 30, 1939. Hence, its period of service would not expire on April 10, 1942; instead it would remain in office until January 30, 1943, legally.

According to the new regulation, an election to the Reichstag was to be held within sixty days of this date, i.e. before Sunday, March 30, 1943. The law was obviously intended to circumvent the requirements of Article 23 of the Weimar Constitution. The most salient feature of this new regulation was that it contained no stipulation indicating when the new Reichstag was to convene for the first time. Hence, if Hitler so desired, he could easily delay calling on the Reichstag for years and thus avoid a new election. In theory, he could postpone the dissolution of this Reichstag indefinitely as long as he never convened it in the first place.

In view of the extension of the Enabling Act by the Reichstag that day, it would have been only logical had Hitler made use of this same forum to pass the law on the Reichstag. That he refrained from doing so was revealing, because Article II of the Enabling Act provided that governmental laws could deviate from the letter of the constitution only "to the extent that they do not concern the institutions of the Reichstag or Reichsrat as such." Hitler obviously violated the spirit of this provision by issuing the law on Reichstag tenure, as this undeniably jeopardized the institution of the Reichstag as such. But he alone shouldered, as he once put it, the responsibility for this action. In any case, he did not venture to place this law before the Reichstag for a vote, although in all likelihood, it would have passed the law as unanimously as it had assented to the prolongation of the Enabling Act. Probably no one would have noticed the hidden traps that had been set therein.

Hitler's paranoid concern for his position in power politics had proved completely unfounded in the past, but still he lived in constant fear that a stranger might come along and depose him, or capture power in some other manner. Hitler's own rise to power appeared so miraculous to him that he was haunted by the vision, throughout his years in power, of someone else launching a similarly astounding career. After the Röhm Purge, Hitler had grown apprehensive about meeting his Volk face to face. He feared the Reichstag no less, as had already been evident in his address on July 13, 1934. At the time, he had sought to explain the murders of June 30, 1934. Before entering the hall, he had armed SS guards wearing steel helmets positioned around the rostrum and dispersed throughout the hall.

This precautionary measure was to discourage any assassination attempts by any deputies outraged at the bloodbath. In particular, Hitler feared the Reichstag's disposition in the event he should suffer some political setback. Speaking before the leading editors of Germany's press in a conference on the passive opposition by German intellectuals on November 10, 1938, he expressed this anxiety in the following manner: "What would happen if we ever suffered a defeat? It is a possibility, gentlemen."

Hitler's fear of the Reichstag was not completely unfounded, since this parliamentary body represented what might well be termed the Achilles' heel in his system of governance, as, in theory at least, it made steps in opposition to the government legally permissible. An illegal uprising to oust

Hitler was highly improbable. Given the cultural heritage of obedience to authority in Germany, no revolutionary movement could hope for more than initial successes in any such undertaking. Exerting pressure from below, through a mass uprising for instance, was inconceivable. Even in the unlikely event that a protest movement gathered momentum in its early phases, it was doomed to collapse beneath a shower of bullets fired by the members of the armed forces, traditionally loyal to whatever regime was in power. Hitler's 1923 Putsch debacle was a textbook example of this historical reality. Moreover, desertions from the governing elite did not imperil Hitler's reign. Any attempt to overthrow Hitler as the legal head of state and government would have required illegal activities. German bureaucrats and officers were not suitable as candidates for such a venture.

The Reichstag presented an entirely different case, however. As the sole parliamentary body empowered to render null and void Hitler's decrees, it possessed the vested authority to remove Hitler from office. While the Reichstag deputies were members of the National Socialist Party and their appointments to this legal body reflected their ideological reliability, this was no guarantee of their loyalty to Hitler in times of crisis. In the past, this had repeatedly proved to be of concern to him. One has only to think of the case of Gregor Strasser, an early party member who worked with Hitler for years, only to turn on him, so Hitler thought.

Every member of the Reichstag had the right to take the floor, to give a speech, or to propose a motion. Hitler was well aware that there was no telling how such a step by one renegade deputy might affect the Reichstag as an entity. All depended on the overall political and military situation and the arguments employed. Hitler was decidedly more aware of this potential vulnerability than of the entire resistance movement within Germany, as he was decidedly more competent in questions of constitutionality and power politics. His greatest nightmare was that, in the wake of some policy disaster, one of the deputies might unexpectedly rise to speak. With an extensive pool of the Führer's wrongdoings, false prophecies, and fallacies to draw on, the renegade deputy could conceivably conclude his speech with a demand for the impeachment of Hitler.

There was ample reason for Hitler's misgivings, as Mussolini's overthrow on July 25, 1943, proved in retrospect. At a session of the Great Fascist Council, a deputy by the name of Grandi courageously rose to offer this parliamentary body undeniable proof that Mussolini's ill-conceived policies were responsible for the unprecedented debacle Italy now faced.

Thereupon, the Italian equivalent of the Reichstag proceeded successfully to pass a vote of no confidence against the Duce. Its enigmatic leader gone, the entire Fascist Party vanished from the political stage as though it had never existed. Yet no man with the fortitude of Grandi was to be found among the 884 deputies constituting the Reichstag in Germany.

The situation in 1939 and in particular during the years of war to follow was entirely different from the one faced by Reichstag deputy Wels on March 23, 1933 when the Social Democrat sought unsuccessfully to counter Hitler. To effect the removal of Hitler by entirely legal means, it would have sufficed for one of the Reichstag deputies vigorously to challenge Hitler, acting as a sort of counsel for the prosecution on behalf of the German Reich. Any man attempting to parry Hitler would, admittedly, have had to command considerable courage and intelligence, as well as extraordinary oratorical prowess. Moreover, he would have had to boast a familiarity with the constitution and an understanding of its pitfalls, a subject in which Hitler excelled. Had there been such a man among the deputies, he might possibly have risen to request innocently Göring's permission to take the floor. Most likely the president of the Reichstag would have accorded the deputy this opportunity to voice his laudation of the Führer—what else could possibly be his design? Now the fictitious deputy might have reiterated Hitler's assertions of his alleged desire for peace and his loyalty to treaties, of the alleged neutrality of England, of the alleged break-up of Russia, of the alleged invincibility of the German *Wehrmacht,* etc. A rigorous comparison of these claims to the undeniable realities of the day might well have prepared the ground for a motion toward a vote of no confidence in the Führer. A two-thirds majority in favor of such a resolution would have sufficed to remove Hitler and to call for the formation of a new government.

Of course, it is entirely possible that such a motion would have failed. The renegade deputy in this speculative example might have been booed by the audience, arrested, or shot at once. Nevertheless, given careful maneuvering on his part as well as favorable circumstances, he might well have succeeded in the end. After a vote of no confidence, Hitler might have reacted by retreating into some form of exile, followed by a large number of his adherents, to launch his struggle for power at a later date. Or, possibly, he might have committed suicide.

Many of Hitler's early followers had premonitions of his ultimate failure since they had more intimate knowledge of his person than others, such as conservatives and officers for instance. Better acquainted with his ambitious designs, these Nazi Party members had looked with open eyes at Hitler's ruthless determination ever since the events of June 30, 1934. Once the Second World War broke out, they grasped how tragically mistaken Hitler's assumption of British neutrality had been and that from this point onward, Hitler was merely improvising and had lost the assurance flaunted previously. Several members of the Reichstag would flee Germany in the course of the Second World War, such as Fritz Thyssen and Rudolf Hess. Others committed suicide, like *Gauleiter* Josef Bürckel. Even the relatively dense Himmler realized that Hitler's policies heralded disaster and, at the very latest from 1943 on, desperately searched for a way out.

Despite an abundance of good intentions, there were very few outstanding personalities among the deputies who could have mustered the courage necessary to openly oppose so extraordinary a man as Hitler. Not even Graf Helldorff, a high-ranking SA leader and president of the Berlin police, could make any pretense to such a distinction. This intelligent and courageous sympathizer with the resistance movement was not used to speaking publicly nor did he command the legal knowledge required for such a sophisticated attack.

While opposition within the Reichstag was precluded from the start, as no deputy dared to openly challenge Hitler, he was cautious enough not to take this for granted. He took every step imaginable to curtail the Reichstag's ability to take action. The public by and large paid no attention. The press was not allowed to publish anything pertaining to the law of January 30, 1939 concerning the Reichstag. All was well, as long as no deputy bothered to draw the pertinent conclusions on the law's ramifications.

During the war, Hitler approached the Reichstag with utmost caution. He preferred not to call on the parliamentary body to convene, even on as innocuous an occasion as the anniversary of his rise to power.

▸ August 30, 1939 *In effect the Ministerial Council for the Defense of the Reich became the actual government of Germany, empowered by the Enabling Act and serving at Hitler's pleasure.*

Besides the "generous offer" to Poland, Hitler had yet another task facing him on this August 30. Since military affairs would largely take up his time in the months to come, Hitler resolved to charge a deputy with the Reich's internal functioning. The natural choice for such a position was Göring, his "best man." In the past months, he had repeatedly proved his qualifications to represent his Führer. Hitler was content with his choice. Of course, he would not entrust even Göring with the power to make any real decisions. This function would be reserved for the "Reich government" and the "Reichstag," in other words for Hitler himself.

Nevertheless, in spite of these efforts to provide for his anticipated absence from the domestic scene, Hitler had to ensure that the administrative apparatus functioned in the most effective manner possible. He was greatly apprehensive about the internal bickering and inability to perform so characteristic of any bureaucracy. To restrict this potential for delay, Hitler promulgated a "Führer Decree on the Establishment of a Ministerial Council for the Defense of the Reich."

I. For the period of the present foreign policy tension, I order the following in the service of a coherent management of the administration and of the economy:

(A) As a permanent committee, a "Ministerial Council for the Defense of the Reich" shall be formed from the body of the Reich Defense Council.

(B) The following shall serve as permanent members of the Ministerial Council for the Defense of the Reich: Field Marshal Göring, as its president, the deputy of the Führer, the plenipotentiary general for the administration of the Reich, the plenipotentiary general for the economy, the Reich minister and chief of the Reich Chancellery, the chief of the high command of the *Wehrmacht*.

(C) The president shall also be entitled to consult additional members of the Reich Defense Council as well as other persons.

II. The Ministerial Council for the Defense of the Reich is empowered to issue decrees that shall have the force of law, unless I order the passing of a law by the Reich government or the Reichstag.

III. The powers of Field Marshal Göring based on the instructions for the implementation of the Four-Year Plan of October 18, 1936 (RGBl, I, p. 887) shall remain in force, in particular his right to issue directives.

IV. The Reich minister and chief of the Reich Chancellery shall conduct the affairs of the Ministerial Council for the Defense of the Reich.

V. I shall determine the expiration of this decree.

Berlin, August 30, 1939

The Führer Adolf Hitler
Göring, Field Marshal
The Reich Minister and
Chief of the Reich Chancellery, Lammers

Previously, Hitler had placed the title "The Führer and Reich Chancellor" next to his signature beneath governmental decrees, ordinances, and laws. From now on, he began to prefer the abbreviated version, "The Führer," although, along with this, the alternative "The Führer and Reich Chancellor" was still to be found on many official documents.

▶ October 12, 1939 *The following describes the nature of German government in occupied territories.*

On October 12, 1939, Hitler promulgated the following decree on the administration of the occupied territory in Poland:

To restore and to maintain law and order and public life in the occupied Polish territories, I order:

§1 The territories occupied by German troops, insofar as they are not incorporated into the German Reich, are to be placed under the governor general for the occupied Polish territories.

§2 (1) I appoint Reich Minister Dr. Frank as governor general
for the occupied Polish territories.
   (2) I appoint Reich Minister Dr. Seyss-Inquart as deputy
of the governor general.

§3 (1) The governor general is directly subordinate to me.
   (2) All branches of the administration are assigned to the
governor general.

In creating the "General-Government" in Poland, Hitler followed Ludendorff's lead. In the course of the First World War, Ludendorff had set up a similarly short-lived structure by the same name. Hitler, however, in the campaign aiming at the eradication of the Polish intelligentsia, of the Polish Catholic clergy, and of the Polish Jews, went far beyond the measures implemented by his predecessor. This move surpassed anything the world had previously seen.

It was on Hitler's orders that his cohorts in the SS indulged in an unprecedented murder spree among a small people left virtually defenseless. Despite his obvious involvement, Hitler nevertheless refused to "bear all responsibility" in this case. He had equally shied away from assuming responsibility for the events of the 1938 Crystal Night, and he would do so again later in the wholesale extermination of Jews. As in November 1938, Hitler played the innocent before the German public, acting as though he had no connections to the gruesome murders perpetrated in Poland and elsewhere.

The man most closely tied to the liquidation of the Polish upper class, *Reichsführer SS* Heinrich Himmler, Hitler's most diligent and conscientious servant, repeatedly and unequivocally indicated while speaking with the German generals that Hitler had personally issued orders for this campaign. In Koblenz, in March 1940, Himmler declared in this context: "I do nothing of which the Führer is not aware." On a different occasion, Himmler stated: "The person of the Führer must not be mentioned in this context under any circumstances. I will assume all responsibility."

For the record, Reinhard Heydrich, the chief of the Reich Central Security Office (*Reichssicherheitshauptamt,* RSHA), noted on July 2, 1940, that he was acting on "special orders of the Führer." As to the contents of the instructions received, Heydrich remarked: "Order for the liquidation of numerous Poles in leading circles, amounting to thousands."

The governor general of Poland, Dr. Hans Frank, recorded the following in his diary on May 30, 1940, after attending a gathering of police officers: "The Führer told me: 'What we have now determined as the leadership of Poland is to be liquidated; what grows back needs to be secured by us and, after an appropriate period, it is to be removed also.'" On October 2, 1940, Hitler himself stated in a briefing that "all members of the Polish intelligentsia" were to be killed off. Though he admitted this might sound harsh, he claimed it was nothing other than the "law of life."

▸ July 29, 1941 *Critics of Hitler were not always tried in public.*

Also on July 29, General von Schröder died in Hohenlychen. He had commanded the army in Serbia and had formerly been the president of the Reich Air Defense Union (*Reichsluftschutzbund*). He died as the result of a "sudden embolism," caused by an earlier flying accident. Schröder was the first in a series of high-ranking officers, state administrators, and party functionaries to die such a "sudden death."

In the years 1941 through 1945, papers in Germany reported on a multitude of "sudden deaths," usually resulting from heart disease, stroke, or flying accident, and, at the same time, announced a state funeral. In a few cases, it later became known that the persons in question had committed suicide (for example, Air Force General Udet, *Luftwaffe* chief of staff Jeschonnek, Field Marshal Rommel, and *Gauleiter* Bürckel).

The "bad state of health" of high-ranking officers, functionaries in state and party, and the number of state funerals became so alarming that people on the street jokingly began to refer to those who dared to criticize the general situation as "candidates for a state funeral." While it is possible that a number of these deaths truly resulted from illness or accident, on the whole, they do appear odd, especially since the SS leaders apparently enjoyed better health.

▸ December 7, 1941 *Night and Fog Decree (*Nacht und Nebel *became a notorious phrase)*

On December 7, Hitler dictated the so-called "Night and Fog Decree," that provided for punishing offences against the German-occupying power in the conquered territories. The offenders were to be either killed or secretly deported to Germany. The decree read as follows:

In the occupied territories, with the beginning of the Russian campaign, Communist elements and other anti-German circles have intensified their attacks against the Reich and the occupying power. The scope and the danger of these subversive activities force us, for reasons of deterrence, to take most severe measures against the offenders. For the time being, the following guidelines shall be observed:

I. In the occupied territories, offences by non-German civilians that are directed against the Reich or the occupying power, and that threaten their security and ability to strike, in principle always call for capital punishment.

II. In principle, offences under Section I are to be tried in the occupied territories only if it is probable that death sentences will be passed on the offenders, or at least the principal offenders, and that trial and execution can speedily be carried out. If not, offenders, or at least the principal offenders, will be brought to Germany.

III. Offenders who are brought to Germany will be tried by court-martial if special military interests make this necessary. In response to inquiries by German and foreign offices regarding these offenders, it should be said that they have been arrested and that the nature of the trial does not allow one to give further information.

IV. The commanders in the occupied territories and the justices bear personal responsibility for the implementation of this decree within the framework of their jurisdiction.

V. The chief of the high command of the *Wehrmacht* determines in which occupied territories this decree will be applied. He is authorized to issue explanations, supplements, and to implement regulations. The Reich minister of justice decrees the implementing regulations for his jurisdiction.

Hitler thought that he could master the rising unrest and outrage everywhere by such draconian measures. In reality, this decree merely documented his declining power. After all, the assassination attempts and acts of sabotage had become possible because Germany's luck was running out at the front, and the German forces were increasingly less able to control the huge occupied territories.

▶ March 21, 1942 *Hitler, during the great battles of the Second World War, became concerned with the state of justice in Germany. He decided on a program of reform.*

Since Hitler had made himself commander in chief of the army, he felt that it was unbearable that anybody in his Reich should have a different opinion from his. Hitler had always detested public servants and their "well-established rights," "irremovable judges" and their freedom of decision, because they would not unconditionally accept as right whatever corresponded to the Führer's view. He felt that the party jurists were the worst. They always tried to remind him of his own legal provisions, espousing the "naive" view that the laws of the National Socialist Reich must be recognized and maintained. He much preferred the bourgeois legal experts, like Gürtner and Bumke, who had no scruples about publicly declaring his breaches of the law "legal."

The only National Socialist jurist whom Hitler accepted was Lammers. He "took care of things without resorting to legal abstraction." On the other hand, Göring and Goebbels felt that Lammers was a "super-bureaucrat." Understandably so, as Lammers always demanded that Hitler's laws be obeyed in a bureaucratic fashion. Nevertheless, if Hitler desired to commit a breach of the law, topple the law in force, or have some hair-raising injustice legally sanctioned, Lammers was always immediately at hand to draw up the required decree and to countersign it. It was not surprising that Hitler considered Lammers to be the "only acceptable jurist." This splendid cooperation was evidenced by Hitler's decree of March 21 on the simplification of the administration of justice. Among other things, it provided for the following:

> The defense of Volk and Reich necessitates the smooth and swift working of the administration of justice. In order to enable the courts and public prosecutors to continue fulfilling their tasks under the special circumstances of the war, I decree the following:

I. Proceedings in criminal cases, as well as the execution of judgments in civil cases and in matters of voluntary jurisdiction, shall, by the omission of all expendable steps and the deployment of all available forces, be simplified and speeded up insofar as this can still be reconciled with the purpose of the proceedings. In particular in criminal cases, the enforcement of the prosecution by the injured party and the opening of the trial shall be omitted. The penal authority of the judge of the district court (*Amtsgericht*) shall be enlarged, and the permissibility of the order of summary punishment shall be expanded.

II. Bills of indictment and judicial decisions shall be concise and short, restricted to what is absolutely necessary.

III. Participation of full-time assessors in judicial decisions shall be limited.

Undoubtedly, this decree signaled major interference by Hitler with existing law. This would actually have required passing a new law. At the very least, it would have necessitated consulting with the Reich minister of justice, state secretary Dr. Schlegelberger, who had temporarily taken over this function following Gürtner's death. However, he would probably have objected to this, and so Lammers jumped into the breach, simply countersigning as "Reich Minister and Chief of the Reich Chancellery." The state secretaries, judges, and so on, were free to read in the *Reich Law Gazette* what new principles of law Hitler had come up with!

However, these arbitrary decrees did not satisfy Hitler. His immense power was not yet great enough. Within the party, he was the sole authoritative leader; supreme commander of the SA; head of the political organization; and—since Hess's escape—his own deputy.

Within the state, he was head of state (as "Führer," he held the former office of Reich president); head of government (Reich Chancellor); and minister of war. Within the armed forces, he was supreme commander of the *Wehrmacht* and commander in chief of the army. However, why was he not "supreme law lord" and sole authoritative chief of the entire judiciary?

Hitler spent February and March of 1942 preoccupied with the privileges of jurists, including those of the party jurists. Not only did his statements to Goebbels prove this, but also his verbal attacks on jurists with which he pestered his audience at the "table talk." He recounted all sorts of anecdotes from his life in order to prove what "a cancerous sore today's jurisprudence is for the German Volk." Besides this, he wildly attacked jurists in general.

On February 8, he declared for example:

> Our judiciary is not flexible enough. After ten years of imprisonment, a man is a lost cause for the national community (*Volksgemeinschaft*) anyway. Who will give him work then? You either stick a fellow into a concentration camp or you kill him. These days, the latter is more important for the sake of deterrence. If you want to set an example, you must also hit all fellow travelers!
>
> Instead of this, the judiciary dedicates all its love and care to rummaging in the files in order to arrive at a just judgment in line with its peacetime exercises. Such judgments must be quashed under any circumstances.

In a long tirade, Hitler claimed on March 29, 1942:

> No man of reason can comprehend the jurisprudence that the jurists have concocted. In the end, today's jurisprudence is nothing other than one great system of shifting the responsibility onto someone else. He would therefore do everything to disparage as much as possible the study of law, that is, the study of this type of interpretation of the law. Because these studies would not form men who were fit for life and suited to guarantee for the state its natural legal order. These studies meant only an education in irresponsibility.
>
> He would take care that all judges, with the exception of a ten-percent true elite, were removed from the judiciary. The whole swindle of lay assessors would be done away with. He wanted to put an end for good to a judge's getting around taking responsibility for his decision by declaring that the lay assessors had outvoted him.
>
> Today, he was therefore making clear that, for him, a jurist was either someone deficient by nature or someone bound to become so over time.

No matter how much Hitler railed against jurists, it soon became obvious, even during the "table talk," what his actual objective was, namely, the autocracy of Adolf Hitler. He did not want to be restrained by legal norms or supervised by jurists. Characteristic of this attitude was the following "example," with which Hitler sought to make things clear to his audience.

> Further, he [Hitler] noticed that bequests—that were made to him in large numbers and that, for his own person, he waived as a matter of principle, only sometimes assigning them to the NSV—could only effectively be waived by having his signature under the relevant declaration attested by a lawyer. In the opinion of the jurists, the signature of the German Reich chancellor, together with the seal of the Reich, was apparently not as credible as that of a lawyer.

All of Hitler's nice speeches and attacks were in vain as long as he did not have a concrete case, some striking example, that would enable him to tell German jurisprudence "to go to hell" and to make himself supreme law lord.

Soon, a suitable occasion presented itself. On March 19, 1942, the case of Ewald Schlitt was tried by the Oldenburg *Landgericht* (regional court of a *Land*). Ewald Schlitt was a twenty-nine-year-old engineer at the navy shipyard at Wilhelmshaven. He had married in 1937, and this marriage had been far from ideal. In June 1940, the couple had had a violent dispute. In October 1940, Mrs. Schlitt had died in a nursing home. The case was rather unclear. It could not be established by forensic medical tests whether the death of the wife had resulted from an earlier battery by Schlitt or not. Normally Schlitt would have spent several months in jail for assault occasioning grievous bodily harm. The judge, however, who was known for his strictness, sentenced him to five years in prison! Even in the case of battery resulting in death, the sentence could range from six months to five years in prison. Therefore, the sentence in the Schlitt case was called "too harsh," even by superior judges.

The *Berliner Nachtausgabe* reported on the Oldenburg ruling. Hitler read the article on March 21 and decided right away to use this case for his planned move against the judiciary and for seeing his full discretionary powers through the Reichstag. This mild sentence was outrageous: only five years of imprisonment for a man who had beaten his wife to death, while out there at the front thousands of brave soldiers had to die every day! Immediately,

Hitler struck a pose and behaved like a madman. He ranted and raved, demanding immediately to speak to Dr. Schlegelberger, although it was the middle of the night. He shouted into the receiver:

> That's typical again! A violent criminal like this Schlitt gets away with five years of confinement to safe barracks, and this at state expense, while hundreds of thousands of decent men risk their lives at the front for their wives and children! I will tell you and the entire judiciary to go to hell if this sentence is not immediately revised! Immediately! If this does not happen, I will have the whole sentencing process and the whole criminal prosecution handed over to the Reichsführer SS!

Schlegelberger truthfully replied that he had not read the *Berliner Nachtausgabe* and was not familiar with the Schlitt case. And how would the acting justice minister in Berlin have known about so insignificant a case, which had just been tried by a regional court (*Landgericht*) in the province?

Hitler angrily hung up. He then demanded to speak to Freisler, who served as second state secretary in the Reich ministry of justice at the time. Roland Freisler was a man who could not be accused of having any scruples. Nevertheless, he could not tell Hitler either how to go about revising this final sentence. Naturally so, as Freisler was one of those despised party jurists. Hitler continued to rant and rave, as his pilot Baur told the "table talk" assembly the following day:

> He [Hitler] was very angry about this mild sentence for a woman's murderer. He regards the murder of women and children as particularly abominable. If the judiciary continues to produce such sentences, then Hitler wants to tell the ministry of justice to go to hell [*zum Teufel schicken*] via a Reichstag law.

Undoubtedly, Hitler had already toyed with the thought of getting rid of the ministry of justice ever since Gürtner's death in 1941. For this reason, he had not appointed a successor to him. In 1938, the Reich war ministry had been abolished because it was no longer needed under Hitler. Was there a need for the Reich ministry of justice with an Adolf Hitler around? Why maintain the whole administration of justice? Were there not enough policemen and Gestapo officials? Were there not concentration camps that could see to the execution of a sentence?

▸ March 31, 1942 *Hitler's efforts to restructure the legal system continued.*

In the meantime, the responsible men of German jurisprudence had tried to find a way to appease Hitler in the Schlitt case. Schlegelberger and Freisler had met in conference with the president of the national court (*Reichsgericht*), Dr. Bumke. Not surprisingly, this bourgeois legal expert, who had always found favor with Hitler, was better able than the two National Socialist "judicial officers" to find a way out. Since Hitler obviously desired a death sentence, the only remaining question was how to justify such a revision of the earlier sentence. Bumke felt that this called for an "extraordinary objection by the supreme Reich counsel." This would mean a new trial by the Leipzig *Reichsgericht* over which he presided. And that was exactly how things came to pass: without due consideration of the Oldenburg *Landgericht,* Schlitt was transferred to Leipzig.

On March 31, 1942, Schlitt was tried by the "Extraordinary Criminal Division of the Court of Appeal," presided over by Bumke. Of course, he was sentenced to death and executed on April 2 in Dresden. The German judiciary was capable of working quite speedily, if Hitler's favor was at stake!

However, in this instance, the German judiciary failed to recognize the actual issue at stake. Hitler was interested in the Schlitt case only as a means of obtaining "full discretionary powers" from the Reichstag. And Hitler would not budge on this. In his speech before the Reichstag on April 26, he cited the Schlitt case as though nothing had happened in the meantime, and did not even mention the new death sentence!

▸ April 26, 1942 *Hitler increased his power by a super enabling act.*

Afterwards, an insecure and hesitant Göring delivered his address. He informed the deputies of the "resolution" desired and worded by Hitler, that they were to pass as a type of "super enabling act," so to speak. It read as follows:

> There can be no doubt that, in the present time of war in which the German Volk struggle "to be or not to be," the Führer must possess the right claimed by him to do all that serves the struggle for victory or contributes to it. Therefore—without being bound by existing regulations—in his capacity as the Führer of the nation, as supreme commander

of the *Wehrmacht,* head of government, and supreme bearer of the executive power, as supreme law lord, and as leader of the party, the Führer must be able at all times to order every German—whether he is a common soldier or officer, low or high-ranking administrator, or judge, leading or lesser functionary in the party, worker or employee—to fulfill his duties by all means that appear appropriate to him; and if he neglects these duties, the Führer must be able to assign him a suitable punishment following a conscientious examination, irrespective of so-called acquired rights, and, in particular, without initiating prescribed procedures, to relieve him of his office, rank, or position.

Of course, the qualification that the Führer could proceed "without being bound by existing regulations" was crucial in this context.

The sequence in which Hitler listed his various functions, in accordance with their importance, was likewise interesting:

1. "Führer of the nation." This meant head of state, the former office of Reich president.

2. "Supreme commander of the *Wehrmacht.*" This function was connected to the office of Führer or Reich president.

3. "Head of government." This office of Reich Chancellor, that Hitler had once sought so fervently, had apparently lost in significance in his eyes to such an extent that he felt it was not necessary to refer to it by name.

4. "Supreme bearer of the executive power." Hitler had not previously made pretenses to this function. Normally, the head of the government was the bearer of the executive power as well; and this was the case at least since January 30, 1934, when the sovereignty of the *Länder* in police affairs had been suspended. However, Hitler now placed great emphasis on being the supreme chief of the police.

After all, you could never tell when some high Nazi Party official (*Obergruppenführer*) might come up with the idea of appropriating for himself police powers.

5. "Supreme law lord." Hitler had coined this term in a Reichstag session on July 13, 1934, when he had claimed with regard to the Röhm purge: "in that hour, I was responsible for the fate of the German nation and was thus the supreme law lord (*Gerichtsherr*) of the German Volk!" Now, he wanted to be able to carry out such arbitrary killings at any hour.

6. "Leader of the party." The party, this "pillar" of the Third Reich, ranked lowest! It appeared only at the tail end of the list of Adolf Hitler's functions. When it had been a question of seizing power in the state and securing it, the party had been important to him. But now, in the year 1942, the Nazi Party interested Hitler no more than did the German Volk. Soldiers and policemen were all he needed!

The whole Reichstag session of April 26, including Hitler's speech and the—naturally unanimously approved—plenipotentiary law, made a poor impression on the German public and abroad. Partly, it led to the conviction that Hitler was fighting an inner opposition and no longer commanded the necessary power to enforce his decrees. Actually, the converse applied. While the Third Reich was in trouble militarily, this was because Hitler's political and military ideas were false, unrealistic, utopian, and insane. However, disobedience to his orders was not a problem, and, internally, the Third Reich was as stable as before.

The "resolution by the Greater German Reichstag" had been necessary to quench Hitler's thirst for power and to satisfy his pathological desire for a completely arbitrary reign. He could not bear the thought that anyone might be able to claim a right for himself if this did not correspond with his wishes. And he especially hated the Reichstag, which had once again fulfilled his wishes without objection. After all, this Reichstag had more powers than he did, because the almighty Führer had to ask this forum for his juridical powers. The Reichstag could in theory divest him of these special rights again. Completely legally, it could depose him and tell him to go to hell. A terrible thought! Thus Hitler decided now never again to summon the Reichstag.

▸ August 20, 1942 *Hitler extends his powers.*

On August 20, he even named a new Reich minister of justice. Now that he himself was "supreme law lord" and no longer bound by "existing regulations," he no longer feared trusting a "jurist" with the exercise of this office. Of course, he also took care to maintain control of the justice system by conferring "special powers" on the new Reich minister in a simultaneous decree, that—according to Hitler's "guidelines and directives"—empowered him to "depart from existing law."

The following announcement on this topic was published:

Führer Headquarters, August 20, 1942

Official communication: In view of the particular significance attributed to the tasks of the judiciary during the war, the Führer has decided to fill again the post of Reich minister of justice, which has been vacant since the death of Reich Minister Dr. Gürtner. The Führer has therefore appointed the president of the people's court (*Volksgerichtshof*), retired state minister Dr. Thierack, who served as justice minister of Saxony from the seizure of power until the nationalization of the administration of justice, to the post of Reich minister of justice.

At the same time, the Führer has relieved of his duties state secretary Professor Dr. Schlegelberger, who had been entrusted with the conduct of the affairs of the Reich minister of justice, and has approved his request for retirement. The Führer has thanked state secretary Dr. Schlegelberger in a handwritten letter for the excellent services rendered the German Reich during his decades of self-sacrificing work. Further, he has received him at the Führer headquarters to allow him personally to report off duty.

The Führer has appointed the president of the Hanseatic *Oberlandesgericht* Hamburg, Senator Dr. Rothenberger, to the post of state secretary in the Reich ministry of justice; and he has appointed the state secretary in the Reich ministry of justice, Dr. Freisler, to the post of president of the *Volksgerichtshof.*

The Reich Press Bureau of the Nazi Party announces the following:

The previous head of the National Socialist *Rechtswahrerbund,* president of the German Law Academy, and head of the Nazi Party Reich legal office, Dr. Frank, has asked the Führer to relieve him of these duties so that he can dedicate himself fully to his work as Governor-General. The Führer has granted this request. He has appointed the newly named Reich minister of justice, Dr. Thierack, to the posts of president of the German Law Academy and head of the National Socialist *Rechtswahrerbund.* The Führer has dissolved the Reich legal office and the *Gau* and *Kreis* legal offices. He has integrated the former leaders of the *Gau* and *Kreis* legal offices in the *Gau* and *Kreis* staff offices. Within the framework of these offices, the National Socialist legal counseling offices shall continue their work.

Official communication: The Führer has conferred special powers on the newly named Reich minister of justice in the following decree:

Führer decree on the special powers of the Reich minister of justice:

A strong judiciary is necessary for the fulfillment of the Greater German Reich's mission. I order and empower the Reich minister of justice, in accordance with my guidelines and directives and in concurrence with the Reich minister and chief of the Reich chancellery and the head of the party chancellery, to build up a National Socialist judiciary and to take all necessary measures. In so doing, he may depart from the existing law.

The Führer Adolf Hitler

Besides Schlegelberger, Hitler had also received Thierack at the military headquarters. It was interesting in this context that Frank was forced to relinquish his posts as jurist. Hitler again killed two birds with one stone—his old tactics. At first, Thierack did serve Hitler well. In particular, the concentration camps were greatly expanded thanks to his measures. It was Thierack who coined the legal term "extermination through work" (*Vernichtung durch Arbeit*) and who regulated the corporal punishment ordered by Hitler.

▸ January 25, 1943 *Hitler, in essence, eliminated the Reichstag.*

Hitler was more interested in continued elimination of the Reichstag at this point than in Stalingrad. It was high time that he did something. The Reichstag's tenure expired on January 30. On January 25, Hitler signed—with the term "Der Führer,"—the law on the extension of the tenure of the Greater German Reichstag, in violation of the constitution:

> The Reich government has decided on the following law, which is herewith made public:
>
> I.   The tenure of the presently existing Reichstag is extended until January 30, 1947.
>
> II. The Reich minister of the interior decrees the legal and administrative regulations necessary to the implementation of this law.

On January 27, Sauckel ordered, "based on special authorization by the Führer," that all men from sixteen to sixty-five years of age and all women from seventeen to forty-five years of age report to the employment office for work in the defense of the Reich.

▸ May 10, 1943 *Extention of Enabling Act*

Neither in his speech before the Reichsleiters and Gauleiters, nor in the course of his discussions with the above individuals, did Hitler make any mention of his intention to extend the Enabling Act secretly without summoning the Reichstag and announcing it in the press. In Berlin on May 10, Hitler signed this decree that represented a blatant violation of the constitution. It was published in the *Reich Law Gazette* only, under the innocent heading: "Decree by the Führer on Governmental Legislation." It read as follows:

Füher Headquarters, May 10, 1943

In consideration of the formal expiration of the law of March 24, 1933 (*Reich Law Gazette,* I, p. 141) on May 10, 1943, I order the following:

The Reich government will continue to exercise the powers bestowed on it by virtue of the law of March 24, 1933. I reserve for myself the confirmation of these powers of the Reich government by the Greater German Reichstag.

Adolf Hitler

Hitler included the mention of a possible confirmation by the Reichstag in order to silence potential critics, but he had no intention of allowing the Reichstag ever to convene again.

Hitler sets the stage for a party rally.

V

Hitler's Party

Hitler's instrument for gaining power, exercising control, and maintaining his position of supremacy was the National Socialist German Workers' Party (NSDAP). The short form of the name was Nazi. After some ten years of endeavor, the Nazi Party's ideology was Hitler's beliefs; its policies were those policies advocated by Hitler; its leaders were those acceptable and most often chosen by Hitler. There was little difference between Hitlerism and Nazism.

▶ March 15, 1932 *At a rally of some 5,000 party members in the Weimar Goethehalle, Hitler described the difference between common politicians and his style of politics.*

I really did not believe it possible that the great "socialist, revolutionary liberators of the people," the Social Democrats—down to the last man—and even a large part of the German Communist Party (KPD) would really vote for Hindenburg for Reich president. We openly confess that we deceived ourselves on this count. I was aware of the fact that the gentlemen are afraid of me. But that the gentlemen were so afraid of me and that they were so scared stiff that they turned out down to the last man—that I did not expect. Actually, we can all be proud of that. After a struggle of barely twelve years, we have performed this miracle: that they have such an utter respect for a movement and, I am proud to say, for one man, that they abandon principles and pledges and memories and traditions to take up the single cry: It's every man for himself.

If I then turn my gaze to the unequal weapons with which we had to fight: on the one hand the large and powerful representatives of the state—ministers, chancellors, of course only in their capacity as civil servants, not as agitators or, much less, as candidates; when I take a look at the imbalance of arms, with the radio, the cinema, and the power to prohibit everything that is really convincing on the other hand; and when I see the other side at the mercy of this terror; and when I further reflect on this admirable number of opponents: the Center, the Bavarian People's Party, the German People's Party, the Social Democratic Party, the Reichsbanner, the Iron Front, all of the unions, the Christian unions, the free unions, the *völkisch* organizations—if you take a look at this whole bunch of parties, associations, and organizations, then I can be proud that, confronted with this whole jumbled-up mixture, we National Socialists alone summoned up 11.3 million, and now, in a barely thirteen-year-long fight, compared to these "venerable remains" of times past, we have, after all, been able to raise—from nothing—the largest German party that has ever existed. I know very well that this or that person from the ranks of those who do not know me and do not know us has perhaps thought: "Now they'll have had enough."

My fellow German citizens (*Volksgenossen*)! I may make one pledge to you here: throughout my entire life, I have always said that, for me, no one day will ever mark the end of the struggle, but rather that the following day the struggle will continue. And above all, I can promise you one thing: I have sunk my teeth into my opponent and you will not be able to shake me loose from this opponent. And as I have attacked today, so will I attack again tomorrow, and the day after once more. You would have to kill me before you will get me to loosen my grip on this enemy of Germany.

▶ Summer 1932 *This is a transcript of a typical election campaign speech recorded on a phonograph record.*

The great time of decision has now arrived. Fate has allotted those in power today more than thirteen years to be tested and proven. But they hand down their own worst sentence in that they themselves confess to the failure of their efforts by the type of propaganda they use today.

Once it was their desire to govern Germany better in the future than in the past, and they are forced to observe that the only real product of their attempts at government is that

Germany and the German Volk are still alive. In the November days of '18, they solemnly pledged to lead our Volk and in particular the German worker into a better economic future. Today, after they have had nearly fourteen years to keep their promise, they cannot cite a single German professional group as witness for the quality of their actions.

The German peasant has become impoverished; the middle class (*Mittelstand*) is ruined; the social hopes of many millions of people are destroyed; one-third of all German men and women of working age is unemployed and thus without income; the Reich, the communities, and the regional governments (*Länder*) are over indebted; finances are in a muddle across the board; and all the coffers are empty! What more could they possibly have destroyed? The worst thing, though, is the destruction of the faith in our Volk, the elimination of all hopes and all confidence. In thirteen years they have not succeeded in mobilizing in any way the powers slumbering in our Volk; on the contrary!

Out of their fear of the awakening of the nation, they have played people off against one another: the city against the country, the salaried workers against the civil servants, those who work with their hands against those who work with their brains, the Bavarians against the Prussians, the Catholics against the Protestants, and so forth, and vice versa. The activism of our race was entirely consumed at home; outwardly, only fantasies remained: fantastic hopes of a cultural conscience, a law of nations, a world conscience, ambassador conferences, the League of Nations, the second Communist *Internationale*, the third Communist *Internationale*, proletarian solidarity, etc.—and the world treated us accordingly.

Thus Germany has slowly disintegrated, and only a madman can still hope that those forces that first caused this disintegration might now bring about the resurrection. If the present parties seriously want to save Germany, why have they not done so already? Had they wanted to save Germany, why has it not happened? Had the men of these parties honestly intended to do so, then their programs must have been bad. If, however, their programs were right, then either their desire cannot have been sincere, or they must have been too ignorant or too weak.

Now, after thirteen years, after they have destroyed everything in Germany, the time has finally arrived for their own elimination. Whether or not today's parliamentary parties exist or not is of no consequence; what is, however, necessary is that the German nation be prevented from falling completely into ruin. Therefore it is a duty to vanquish these parties, for in order to secure their own existence, they must tear the nation apart over and over again.

For years they have persuaded the German worker into believing that he alone could save himself. Fooled the peasant for years by claiming that only his organization would help him. The *Mittelstand* was to be snatched from the jaws of ruin by parties of the *Mittelstand*; the economy by the parties of business. The Catholic was forced to seek his refuge with the Center, the Protestant, with the Christian Socialist People's Service. In the end even the home owners had their own political representation, just as did the tenants, the salaried workers, and the civil servants. However, these attempts at breaking the nation down into classes, ranks, professions, and religious affiliations and at leading it piece by piece to the economic good fortune of the future have now failed completely.

Even on the day our National Socialist Movement was founded, we were already governed by the conviction that the fate of the German individual is inseparably bound up with the fate of the entire nation.

When Germany disintegrates, the worker will not flourish in social good fortune and neither will the entrepreneur; the peasant will not save himself then; nor will the *Mittelstand*.

No, the ruin of the Reich, the disintegration of the nation, means the ruin and the disintegration of all! Not a single confession and not a single German tribe will be able to escape sharing the same lot. Even on the day our National Socialist Movement was founded, we had already long been certain that it was not the proletariat who would be victor over the bourgeoisie, and not the bourgeoisie who would be victor over the proletariat, but that international big finance must ultimately become the sole victor over both. And that is what has come to pass! Recognizing this disintegration, thirteen years ago I took a handful of people and formed a new movement that in its very name is to be a proclamation of the new national community (*Volksgemeinschaft*).

There is no such thing as a socialism that does not have the power of the spirit at its disposal; no such thing as social good fortune that is not protected by—and even finds its prerequisite in—the power of a nation. And there is no such thing as a nation—and thus no such thing as nationalism—if the army of millions who work with their intellects are not joined by the army of millions who work with their fists, the army of millions of peasants. As long as Nationalism and Socialism march as separate ideas, they will be defeated by the united forces of their opponents. On that day when both ideas are fused into one, they will become invincible!

And who will deny that, in a time when everything in Germany is falling apart and degenerating, when everything in the business world and political life is reaching a standstill or coming to an end, a single organization has experienced an enormous and miraculous upturn?

With seven men I began this task of German unification thirteen years ago, and today over thirteen million are standing in our ranks. However, it is not the number that counts, but its inner value! Thirteen million people of all professions and ranks—thirteen million workers, peasants, and intellectuals; thirteen million Catholics and Protestants; members of all German *Länder* and tribes—have formed an inseparable alliance. And thirteen million have recognized that the future of all lies only in the joint struggle and the joint successes of all.

Millions of peasants have now realized that the important thing is not that they comprehend the necessity of their own existence; rather, it is necessary to enlighten the other professions and walks of life as to the German peasant and to win them for his cause.

And millions of workers have similarly realized today that, in spite of all the theories, their future lies not in some *Internationale* but in the realization on the part of their other *Volksgenossen* that, without German peasants and German workers, there simply is no German power. And millions of bourgeois intellectuals, too, have come to the realization of how insignificant their own illusions are if the masses of millions comprising the rest of the Volk do not finally comprehend the importance of the German intellectual class.

Thirteen years ago we National Socialists were mocked and derided—today our opponents' laughter has turned to tears!

A faithful community of people has arisen which will gradually overcome the prejudices of class madness and the arrogance of rank. A faithful community of people which is resolved to take up the fight for the preservation of our race, not because it is made up of Bavarians or Prussians or men from Württemberg or Saxony; not because they are Catholics or Protestants, workers or civil servants, bourgeois or salaried workers, etc., but because all of them are Germans. Within this feeling of inseparable solidarity, mutual respect has grown, and from this respect has come an understanding, and from this understanding the tremendous power that moves us all.

We National Socialists thus march into every election with the single commitment that we will, the following day, once more take up our work for the inner reorganization of our body politic.

For we are not fighting merely for the mandates or the ministerial posts but rather for the German individual, whom we wish to and shall join together once more to inseparably share a single common destiny.

The Almighty, Who has allowed us in the past to rise from seven men to thirteen million in thirteen years, will further allow these thirteen million to become a German Volk. It is in this Volk that we believe, for this Volk we fight; and if necessary, it is to this Volk that we are willing, as the thousands of comrades before us, to commit ourselves body and soul.

If the nation does its duty, then the day will come that restores to us: one Reich in honor and freedom—work and bread!

► September 7, 1932 *In this speech, given in Munich's Circus Krone, Hitler rejected the idea for any support of von Papen's conservative administration.*

The hour is only ostensibly favorably disposed towards those in power today. The gentlemen in office believe that the German Volk is enduring for their sake alone and has only one fervent desire: "Dear God, please do send us the old excellencies of 1914 again!" They really believe that this German Volk and in particular that part that we have organized and snatched from despair has no other hope than to finally fall under the leadership of the gentlemen's club (*Herrenklub*). They are mistaken! In the meantime we have worked for thirteen years, and by no means do we owe our successes to chance.

We have adhered strictly to legality and have gradually become the determining factor in Germany. And now that it is no longer possible to govern constitutionally without us, suddenly these same gentlemen are stating that the constitution and parliamentarianism have become obsolete; that the party system must be done away with. A new age has dawned, they say, in which these outmoded phenomena must be swept away.

Well, if a new age is really coming, then we want new heads, too; then you can get out! In this case as well, one cannot fill old bottles with new wine. The new age has already come, and we welcome its arrival: the new age is the new German Volk that we have created!

No, I am only holding to the pledge I was forced to make. We want to rule strictly in compliance with the constitution. Mind you, we will amend the constitution some day, too, but we will amend it in a strictly constitutional manner! One has only to look at the government's new economic program. It will serve to rescue, not the German Volk, but at most a few banks!

But, strangely enough, these gentlemen seem not to view the product of our work as so vulgar that it is not worth plundering piece by piece. Piece by piece our work is being exploited now letter by letter, word for word, but not the contents! Today these gentlemen boldly declare: "Who do the National Socialists think they are, presuming to take on this position?" Oh yes, in 1919 and 1920, then it was possible to "presume to take on a position"! Then one had only to begin with nothing, to work hard and slave away. Today we say: there are two types of nobility: one you are born with, and the other you achieve!

To thunderous applause, Hitler pointed down to the arena, where Hitler's storm troopers (SA) and security squad (SS) stood in close ranks.

There stands the nation's new nobility! These are the men who fought and struggled for thirteen years for the freedom of their Volk! If Herr von Papen believes today that half of the National Socialist Party no longer stands behind Hitler but rather behind him, the only thing I can say is: dear Herr von Papen, please call a halt! You are not even capable of speaking well enough to persuade the party to come to you; you would have had to practice for at least thirteen years!

Now, I know for certain that you, Herr von Papen, made an appearance in our party office in Berlin only three months before you took office and asked: what ideas and plans does the National Socialist Party have? But you cannot learn that in three months, you know, especially if you only ask once! When people try to accuse me of identifying myself with murderers, I say: no. I identify myself with my comrades! The men convicted in Beuthen are my comrades, because they fought with us for Germany. And for me, comradeship does not end if someone takes a false step!

The five convicted men have now been granted a "reprieve"—their sentences have been commuted to life imprisonment. Do they really believe that it will take that long until we rise to power in Germany? And I can assure these gentlemen now: we will rise to power! My picture is hanging in the cells of each of the convicted men. I should be the one to betray them? Whatever they have done wrong is something we will one day clarify; we will be fair judges, and they will submit to our judgment. But we will then also make certain that these things cannot happen again—not by inventing draconian punishments, but that we remove elements such as the Polish insurgent Pietrzuch! Poland has expelled more than 900,000 Germans. How many Poles has Germany ever expelled?

Do you think that I would sell the Movement for a few ministerial posts? Do you think that I am wooing a title? One day it will stand in my will that nothing but "Adolf Hitler" shall be inscribed on my tombstone. I am making my own name the title I bear. Even Herr von Hindenburg cannot bestow a title upon me. I am not wooing any title, I am striving only for leadership!

And if people say today: you are not entitled to leadership! Fine, I will take up the gauntlet, you noble rulers!

I have never waited for others to begin the offensive; I myself initiate the attack. If the others say that the constitution has become outmoded, we say: the constitution has only now begun to have a purpose! By virtue of it, the German Volk is getting a chance to speak for the first time in fourteen years. We want to take up the fight and want to see whom the Volk heeds: the order of Herr von Papen, "Everyone, about face!" or our command, "Young Germany, forward march!"

In this Munich speech, Hitler also made a point of the difference in age between himself and Hindenburg, doing so in a manner that evoked little public approval. He declared

There is one advantage I have over my most illustrious opponent: the Reich President is 85 years old, and I am 43 and feel fit as a fiddle. I also have the conviction and the certain feeling that nothing can happen to me, for I know that Providence has chosen me to fulfill my task. My will is tough, unrestrained, and unshakable. And by the time I am 85 years old, Herr von Hindenburg will be long gone. Our turn will come.

Whatever the Government chooses to do, whether it dissolves the Reichstag or not, is of no concern to us National Socialists. In the long run it will not work to govern with bayonets and the army.

▸ January 1, 1933 *Just weeks before gaining power, Hitler explained his political program.*

In his "New Year's Proclamation to the National Socialists and Party Comrades," following the usual recapitulation and forecast, Hitler stressed that under no circumstances would he retreat from his previous demands concerning a formation of the government.

> Today, more than ever, I am determined to the utmost not to sell out our Movement's right of the firstborn for the cheap substitute of a participation in a government devoid of power. That objection by the cautious that we should come from inside and through the back door and gain gradual success is nothing but the same protest that bade us, in 1917 and 1918, to reach an understanding with irreconcilable opponents and then to debate with them peacefully in a League of Nations. Thanks to the traitors from within, the German Volk surrendered itself to this advice. The Kaiser's lamentable advisors believed that they should not oppose him. But as long as the Almighty gives me life and health, I will defend myself to my last breath against any such attempt, and I know that, in this resolve, I have the millions of zealous supporters and fighters of our Movement behind me who did not hope, argue, and suffer with the intention of allowing the proudest and greatest uprising of the German Volk to sell its mission for a few ministerial posts! If our opponents invite us to take part in a government like this, they are not doing it with the intention of slowly but surely putting us in power, but rather in the conviction that they are thus wresting it from us forever!
>
> Great are the tasks of our Movement for the coming year. But the greatest task of all will be to make it as clear as possible to our fighters, members, and followers that this party is not an end in itself but merely a means to an end. They should realize that the organization, with all its greatness and beauty, only has a purpose, and thus the justification to exist, when it is the eternally unforbearing and belligerent herald and advocate of the National Socialist idea of a German *Volksgemeinschaft* to come!
>
> Everything that this Movement calls its own—its organizations, whether in the SA or the SS, in the political leadership, or the organization of our peasants and our youth—all

of this can have only the single purpose of fighting for this new Germany, in that there will ultimately be no bourgeoisie and no more proletarians, but only German *Volksgenossen*.

This is the greatest task with which our Volk has been confronted for more than a thousand years. The movement that accomplishes this task will engrave its name for all eternity in the immortal book of the history of our nation.

Thus in the face of the red flood, the dangers in the east and France's eternal threat; in the midst of need and wretchedness, misery and desperation, we, my party comrades, SA and SS men, National Socialist peasants, and National Socialist youth, shall clench our fists even more firmly about our banner and, with it, march into the coming year.

We shall be willing to sacrifice and fight and would rather pass away ourselves than allow that Movement to pass away, which is Germany's last strength, last hope, and last future.

We salute the National Socialist Movement, its dead martyrs and its living fighters!

Long live Germany, the Volk, and the Reich!

Munich, December 31, 1932
Adolf Hitler

▸ June 26, 1933 *Within a few months of becoming head of government, Hitler eliminated all other political parties, along with unions and all other political organizations.*

As Hitler indicated in this proclamation, he felt it was time to dissolve all of the parties—with the exception, of course, of his own. The Communist Party (KPD) had virtually disappeared; its leadership was in concentration camps, along with numerous leading Social Democratic Party (SPD) members. The SPD's newspapers had been banned and all political activity on the part of the SPD prohibited. When the Social Democratic Party was finally banned as being treasonable and hostile to the state on June 22 by decree of the Reich Minister of the Interior, the act served only to confirm an accomplished fact.

Hitler chose a different procedure to rid the country of the bourgeois parties. In 1933, Germany found itself in a state of intoxication similar to that of 1914, when the exclamation made by Wilhelm II—"I no longer recognize parties: I recognize only Germans!"—was jubilantly received. At that time, this remark had had no further impact upon the existence of the parties as such. In June and July of 1933, however, Hitler was able to exert such influence on the chairmen and members of the bourgeois parties in numerous private meetings that they resolved the dissolution of their parties of their own accord for the sake of the nation.

On June 27, the German National People's Party (*Kampffront Schwarz-Weiss-Rot*) resolved its own dissolution by a 56 to 4 vote of its leadership. On June 28, the German State Party (the former German Democratic Party) announced its dissolution; on July 2, the Christian Socialist People's Service disbanded, followed by the German People's Party and the Bavarian People's Party on July 4 and the Center on July 5. The fact that the Center and the Bavarian People's Party were moved to disband was doubtless the result of Hitler's concentrated powers of persuasion, particularly if one calls to mind the role which the Center had played in the German Empire and the Weimar Republic. Hitler had argued that, in view of the forthcoming concordat with the Vatican, the objectives of the Center had been accomplished and thus the party itself was superfluous.

▶ August 30, 1933 *The massive Nuremberg party rallies, well known from film and photographs, were less pleasant than the pictures might suggest.*

On August 30, Hitler proceeded to Nuremberg to attend what was called the "Reich Party Congress of Victory" (*Reichsparteitag des Sieges*).

In view of the triumphant mood of 1933, this demonstration on the part of the NSDAP was understandable—but Hitler intended to turn it into an annual affair. This congress and those following up until 1938 were yet further occasions for him to experience the intoxication of his power over hundreds of thousands and even millions of people and to indulge in his passion for speaking at mass rallies. The scale of the event grew from year to year; the parades became more and more tremendous; mammoth stone towers were built only to serve as huge flagpoles. An oversized convention hall was to eclipse all existing comparable structures throughout the world. It remained only a torso when the harsh realities of 1939 put an end to Hitler's rhetorical spectacles and shows of numbers.

To the other participants, these rallies were significantly less pleasant than to Hitler. They were housed in tents, stood for hours on end, and marched in endless processions. Although some of them might have regarded the rally as an experience, most of them were more interested in the circumstances surrounding the congress itself—the visit to a big city, the many attractions and amusements, the fireworks, etc.—than in its political contents. Well aware of this, Hitler demonstrated a generosity rivaled only by the Catholic Church on its illustrious pilgrimages.

▸ September 5, 1934 *The Reich Party Congress of 1934 had no title. Hitler's proclamation to the congress usually set forth party policy. This year's theme: the Nazi revolution was the last major event in German history; the consolidation of power was final.*

On September 5, *Gauleiter* Adolf Wagner read Hitler's proclamation in the Luitpold Hall. In addition to the standard retrospective on the past and prophecy for the future, it contained several remarks on the character of the National Socialist Revolution that are noteworthy for their phrasing:

We wish to establish two realizations as historic facts:

1. The year from September 1933 to September 1934 brought with it the final consolidation of National Socialist power in Germany. The Congress of Victory marked the beginning of a battle of pursuit in the course of which we broke up and captured our enemies' positions one after another.

2. For the National Socialist leadership of state, this period at the same time constituted a year of tremendous constructive and productive work.

This inevitably leads to the unquestionable conclusion: the National Socialist revolution has now come to an end as a revolutionary and power-related process! As a revolution, it has completely fulfilled what could be expected of it.

The world does not live on wars, and similarly the Volk does not live on revolutions. Both cases can, at most, provide the basis for a new life. But no good will come of it if the act of destruction is not accomplished for the sake of a better and thus higher idea, but is exclusively subject to the nihilistic drives of destruction and will thus result not in the formation of something better but in unending hatred. A revolution that perceives its sole purpose as the defeat of a political opponent, the destruction of earlier accomplishments, or in the elimination of existing circumstances will lead to nothing better than a world war that will reach its appalling culmination—or rather its logical progression—in a mad *Diktat*. Genuine revolutions are conceivable only as the consummation of a new calling to which the will of the Volk assigns its historic task in this way. And today this leadership of the Volk has the power to do anything in Germany! Who can deny that the National Socialist Movement has become the omnipotent master over the German Reich? The crowning glory of this political development is expressed symbolically in the fact that the armed forces of the Third Reich (*Wehrmacht*) has adopted the sovereign symbol of the Movement; in the fact that the leader of the party has been elected to head of state of the German nation, and the *Wehrmacht* and administration of the Reich subsequently pledged an oath of allegiance to him. Thus we shall crush any and all attempts to instigate acts of violence against the leadership of the National Socialist Movement and of the Reich and nip them in the bud, regardless of whom they originate from.

We all know to whom the nation has given its mandate! Woe betide anyone who does not know this or forgets it! Revolutions have always been rare in the German Volk. The nervous age of the nineteenth century has finally come to an end with us.

There will not be another revolution in Germany for the next thousand years!

▸ September 13, 1935 *At the Reich Party Congress of Freedom, 1935, Hitler made the point: the party exists to follow the leader, Adolf Hitler.*

On September 13, Hitler addressed 100,000 political leaders at Nuremberg Zeppelin Field, christening them the political "officers of the nation" in spite of the pronounced non-military appearance of most of them.

It is good that we are able to see each other like this once a year, you the Führer, and the Führer yourselves. This can also serve as a lesson to all those who would so gladly make a distinction between the Führer and his following, those who are so incapable of understanding that there can be no distinction between us, who would so gladly say: the Führer, yes! But the party—is that really necessary? I do not ask if it is necessary, but if it was necessary! A commander without officers and soldiers—there are those who would gladly welcome that! I will not be the commander without soldiers; I will remain your Führer. For me, you are the political officers of the German nation, bound to me for better or worse, just as I am bound to you for better or worse. Not one man alone conquered Germany; all united conquered Germany. One man won you over, and you have won over the German Volk!

▶ September 16, 1935 *At the same Party Congress of Freedom, Hitler marked September 16 as* Wehrmacht *Day. From that day, the* Reichswehr *became the* Wehrmacht. *Hitler reviewed a march past by the military service heads and then gave a closing address. One of his points: the position of Führer is an office and will continue.*

Following this triumph, Hitler delivered his lengthy closing speech to the assembled Party Congress participants. So engrossed was he in his subject that he even made a few remarks on a future constitution for the Reich and a time when he would no longer dwell among his comrades, announcing that his successor should also personify the combined offices of "*Herr* (leader) of the party, head of the Reich, and supreme commander of the *Wehrmacht.*"

When I will breathe my last breath is something I do not know. But that the party will live on is something I do know, and that it will successfully shape the future of the German nation beyond any individuals, whether they be weak or strong is something I believe and something I know! For it guarantees the stability of the leadership of the Volk and the Reich, and by its own stability it guarantees the authority this leadership requires. The constitution of the new German Reich will grow out of this solid base. It is the duty of the party as the political navigator of German fate to provide the nation and thus the Reich with its Führer. The more naturally and uncontestedly this principle is established and maintained, the stronger Germany will be.

The army as the representative of an organization for the defensive strength of our Volk must always preserve and maintain the organized military strength of the Reich entrusted to it and place the same in loyalty and obedience at the disposal of the Führer given to the nation by the Movement. For when the new Führer is appointed, he shall be *Herr* of the party, head of the Reich, and supreme commander of the *Wehrmacht*. If these principles form the unshakable foundation of the German structures of Volk and state, Germany will be able to withstand any storms that may come its way. But let the two fundamental manifestations of the new Reich both bear in mind that they can only satisfy the demands placed upon them jointly. The party gives to the Volk the army, and the Volk gives to the army its soldiers; both together thus provide to the German Reich the security of internal peace and order and the power to stand up for itself. Today, as Führer of the Reich and the nation, I can still personally offer help and advice. But these principles must lead from the personal to the eternal.

Führers will come and Führers will die, but Germany must live on. And alone this Movement will lead Germany to this life. All of us, though, will one day be judged by the quality and historic permanency of what we are building today!

We, my party comrades, co-leaders of the Volk and the army, have been chosen by fate to make history in the loftiest sense of the word. What millions of people are deprived of has been given to us by Providence. Even most distant posterity will be reminded of us by our work. And it should one day find most noteworthy and distinguished of all the fact that, in an age marked by lack of loyalty and rampant betrayal, it was possible in the Germany of our age to form as never before a mutual league of the most loyal followers. And we know one thing:

One day, a page in world history will be devoted to us, the men from the National Socialist Party and the German army who joined efforts to build and safeguard the new German Reich. One day we will stand then side by side, immortalized in the pantheon of history, immortalized in indivisible loyalty as in the time of the great struggle and the great fulfillment.

▸ September 10, 1937 *At the Reich Party Congress of Labor, Hitler addressed Reich political party leaders. His message: Hitler is the soul of the party.*

On that same September 10 an appeal was issued to the political leaders, whom Hitler increasingly saw as his "disciples," too. Therefore, he addressed them in words similar to those of the Master recorded by St. John, as he had previously done only when speaking before then of the SA or SS: "You once found your way to me and . . . I found you."

Nevertheless, the physical appearance of the political leaders in no way corresponded to the new heroic German man Hitler envisioned for future generations. However, they were completely dependent upon Hitler—nearly every one of them held a position that was in one form or another paid for by the party or the state. It was precisely this dependence that made the political leaders particularly dear to Hitler, even more so than the SA, whose personal ambitions were usually quite modest, the majority of them wishing to be nothing more than true patriots. On September 10, Hitler preached the following "gospel" to his political leaders:

> For us zealous National Socialists, these days are the most splendid celebration of the whole year! How much trouble and sacrifice does it mean for the individual; how difficult and strenuous it is for many of you—but for us, too—to keep coming here! Yet nonetheless, when these days come to their close, we are all struck by a sadness; we are like children who are deprived of a great celebration.
>
> For us, these days comprise a remembrance of the time of our historic struggle for Germany. Among you there are many standing before me who still know the Movement from the time when it was difficult and dangerous to support it. Particularly for these old, true comrades in arms, these days are the

most splendid remembrance and, at the same time, a reward. Once a year we see each other face to face again, just as so often before. Once a year you are again with me, as so often before in the battles for Germany. Back then I could go forth in your districts (*Gaue*), and each of you knew me. Today you must come to me, and here at this place we see each other again and again as the old guard of the National Socialist revolution!

We have chosen the motto of "labor" for the Party Congress of 1937. There are a scattered few who perhaps—particularly outside of Germany— might raise the question: Why such a slogan? After having liberated Germany within four years' time, we have the right to rejoice in our labor!

I am so pleased to have my old fighters before me again once a year. I always have the feeling that, as long as the human being has the gift of life, he should yearn for those with whom he has shaped his life. What would my life be without you! The fact that you once found your way to me and believed in me gave your life new meaning and a new goal! The fact that I found you was the prerequisite for my own life and my struggle!

The German nation, under the leadership of its party, will protect Germany and never again allow it to fade! And our faith is bound up with this knowledge. It was not the point of the actions of Providence that have accompanied and blessed our miraculous path that now, perhaps in the final act, the fruits of this struggle should be lost. The Almighty has allowed us to take this wonderful path and will continue to bless us. For we are fighting here for a higher right, for a higher truth and for a higher human decency. I can look forward to the future so serenely because we have now in effect put our own affairs in order.

Germany shall not be overrun, neither from within nor from without! And I believe that this fact is one of the highest contributions to peace, because it warns all those who attempt, from their base in Moscow, to set the world on fire.

▸ November 22, 1937 *In this "secret speech," Hitler presented his program to his fellow Nazis.*

On November 22, Hitler toured the Messerschmitt Flugzeugwerke in Augsburg. The day subsequent to his tour of the factory, Hitler attended the inauguration of the Ordensburg Sonthofen in the Allgäu, which was the third to open its gates. There, before all the regional and district Nazi Party leaders (*Kreisleiter* and *Gauamtsleiter*) assembled, Hitler delivered a two-hour "secret speech" on "the structure and organization of the leadership of the Volk" (*Volksführung*). The content of this address has been preserved for us.

In the introduction, Hitler presented an overview of his version of German history over the last three hundred to four hundred years. He continuously attempted to substantiate his claims with numbers, carelessly juggling enormous figures (the majority of which were incorrect). Needless to say, he could not resist citing his favorite historical example, the claim that, of the 18.5 million Germans at the outbreak of the Thirty Years' War, only 3.6 million survived. Further "historical observations" on his part culminated in a comparison of the relations between the people of Austria and Prussia and the similar bonds that existed between the English and the German people. He explained these ties in the following manner:

> Since in international life there are only natural, sober interests, it should be based neither on gratitude nor on family connections. Family connections were as useless in preserving Prussia and Austria from war as they were for Germany and England. In Europe, we have more difficult obstacles to overcome than those, for instance, that exist for England—which needed only its naval supremacy to occupy large living spaces with relatively little loss of blood.
>
> Nonetheless: we had Europe once before. We lost it only because our leadership lacked the initiative that would have been necessary to not only maintain our position on a long-term basis but also to expand it.

Then Hitler turned to the "Germanic Empire of the German Nation," the birth of which he himself had proclaimed at the Reich Party congress of September 13.

Now he declared:

> Today a new state is being established, the unique feature
> of which is that it sees its foundation not in Christianity and
> not in a concept of state; rather, it places its primary emphasis
> on the self-contained *Volksgemeinschaft*. Hence it is significant
> that the "Germanic Empire of the German Nation" now puts
> this supremely capable concept of the future into practice,
> merciless against all adversaries, against all religious fragmen-
> tation, against all fragmentation into parties.

This observation was followed by a mystical recollection of the German past:

> If we regard our German history in a very extensive sense
> from our most dim and distant past up to today, we are the
> richest Volk in Europe. And if, with utmost tolerance, we al-
> low our great German heroes to march by, all our great leaders
> of the past, all our great Germanic and German emperors—
> for they were great without exception—England would have
> to shrink before us.

However, Hitler soon returned to the present, that is, to his own claim
to power, and remarked:

> It is this unification of the German nation that gives us
> the moral justification to step before the world with vital de-
> mands. The fact is that ultimate justice resides in power. And
> power, in international life, resides in the self-containment of
> the nations themselves. Today the German nation has finally
> been given what it has lacked for centuries, namely, the organi-
> zation of a leadership of the Volk. Today we are laying claim to
> the leadership of the Volk, i.e., we alone are authorized to lead
> the Volk as such—that means every man and every woman.
> The lifelong relationships between the sexes is something we
> will organize. We shall form the child!

In this context, Hitler also commented on questions of a religious
nature that preoccupied him in particular this year. He addressed the
churches formally:

We are giving you unconditional freedom in your teachings and in your views on what God is. For we are well aware that we ourselves know nothing of these things. Yet let one thing be quite clear: the churches may determine the fate of the German being in the next world, but in this world the German nation, by way of its leaders, is determining the fate of the German being. Only if there is such a clear and clear-cut division can life be made bearable in a time of transition.

At the bottom of our hearts, we National Socialists are religious. For the space of many millennia, a uniform concept of God did not exist. Yet it is the most brilliant and most sublime notion of mankind, that which distinguishes him most from animals, that he not only views a phenomenon from without, but always poses the question of why and how.

This entire world, a world so clear-cut in its external manifestation, is just as unclear to us in its purpose. And here mankind has bowed down in humility before the conviction that it is confronted by an incredible power, an Omnipotence, which is so incredible and so deep that we men are unable to fathom it. That is a good thing! For it can serve to comfort people in bad times; it avoids that superficiality and sense of superiority that misleads man to believe that he—but a tiny bacillus on this earth, in this universe—rules the world, and that he lays down the laws of nature that he can at best but study. It is, therefore, our desire that our Volk remains humble and truly believes in God. Hence an immeasurably large scope is given for the churches, and thus they should be tolerant of one another!

God did not create our Volk so that it be torn apart by priests. This is why it is necessary to ensure its unity by a system of leadership. That is the task of the NSDAP. It is to comprise that order which, beyond the limits of time and man, is to guarantee the stability of the German development of opinion and hence of the political leadership.

It would have been most interesting to hear precisely what magic potion Hitler had in store and how he intended to secure this stability "beyond the limits of time and man." It soon became all too apparent that this cure was none other than the one he always counseled, namely, blind obedience to the absolute authority Adolf Hitler.

The Nazi Party is the largest organization the world has ever seen. All counted, it encompasses a total of twenty-five million people and has 300,000 functionaries. It is quite obvious that an organization that is only eighteen years from its founding cannot be the same as it would be after one hundred years. Yet the important thing is that we equip it with the law according to which it came to power and that it shall retain. Here we have established the basic rule of absolute obedience and absolute authority. Just as the army—the weapon— cannot prevail without this law of the absolute authority of each and every superior to those below him and his absolute responsibility to those above, neither can the political leadership of this weapon prevail. For what is gained by the weapon is ultimately subject to political administration, and what the political administration wants, the weapon is to procure. The leadership of the Volk in former times, the church, also recognized only this one law of life: blind obedience and absolute authority.

At the end of his "secret speech," Hitler expatiated upon the requirement of political leaders in addition to blind obedience: bravery.

Old Germany was overthrown because it did not possess this zealous blind will, did not have this confidence and this serenity. New Germany will be victorious because it integrates these virtues and at present has already integrated them in an extremely difficult struggle. I know quite well that this is independent of the individual. I know quite well that, were anything to happen to me today, the next one would take my place and continue in the same fashion, just as zealously; because that, too, is part of this Movement.

Just as it is not possible to instantly turn a political bourgeois association into a fighting group of heroes, it will be equally impossible to ever turn this Movement, that was built up from the very beginning on courage and initiative, into a bourgeois association. That is also the future task above all of these schools: to conduct this test of courage over and over

again, to break with the opinion that only the soldier must
be brave. Whoever is a political leader is always a soldier too!
And whoever lacks bravery cannot be a soldier. He must be
prepared for action at all times. In the beginning, courage
had to be the basic prerequisite for someone to find his way
to the party—and it really was, otherwise no one came. Today we have to install artificial obstacles, artificial trenches
over which the person has to jump. That is where he now has
to prove whether he is brave. Because if he is not brave, he is
of no use to us.

This truly was an "ingenious solution." All that was asked of future
political leaders was they combine obedience with bravery in order to please Hitler. Mastery of these virtues could be proven simply by
"jumping across artificial trenches." Without doubt the somewhat cor-
pulent Kreisleiters and Gauamtsleiters assembled were relieved that the
Führer did not demand any such "tests of courage" in order to ascertain
their valor.

▸ February 24, 1942 *Hitler addressed the party about the war.*

On February 24, Hitler was absent for the first time from the festivities
in commemoration of the party's foundation in Munich. He claimed that
it was not possible for him to leave his headquarters since he was "preparing
for the final confrontation." Obviously, this was merely an excuse. There
could be no talk of a "final offensive" before May or June. And on other
occasions before and after February 24, it was evidently possible for him to
leave his headquarters.

The truth was that he was afraid of his old party comrades, especially
of the old party leaders (*Obergruppenführer*). He feared that one of them
would stand up and reprimand him for his various false prophecies. From
1939 on, he had made dozens of wrong forecasts, including the claim that
the English would never go to war and that the Russians were "already broken and will never rise again."

Hitler chose to send a "message" instead, which Gauleiter Wagner read
to the audience:

Führer Headquarters, February 24, 1942

Party Comrades!

For the first time in many years, I am unable to participate in the day of commemoration with my oldest comrades in arms. I cannot well leave headquarters at a time when the winter is ending, a winter on which our enemies have placed all their hopes. From June to October 1941, German armies advanced over a thousand kilometers into the empire of an enemy who intended to destroy our Volk and our homeland for good. This winter—the like of which has not been seen in over a hundred years—surprised us as early as late November 1941. Snow and frost temporarily halted the triumphant advance of the German *Wehrmacht* that was unique in history.

Our enemies hoped that the German armies would then suffer the same fate as the Napoleonic retreat. This attempt failed pitifully. Above all, it failed because of the bravery and the willingness of our unique men to sacrifice, who side by side with our allies held out during the icy storms of December, January, and February as staunchly as they had before fought for their unfading victories in the heat of June, July, August, and September.

Now that the worst cold is over, now that the snow is beginning to thaw in the Crimea and in southern Russia, I am unable to leave my post, as preparations for the final confrontation are being made to settle accounts with this conspiracy in which the banking houses in the plutocratic world and the vaults of the Kremlin pursue the same goal: the extermination of the Aryan peoples and races.

This community of Jewish capitalism and Communism is nothing new to us old National Socialists, especially to you, my oldest comrades in arms. As before, during, and after the First World War in our country, so today the Jews and again only the Jews have to be held responsible for tearing apart the nations.

There is a difference, however, if we compare the present world struggle with the end of the war from 1914–1918. In 1919, we National Socialists were a small group of believers who not only recognized the international enemy of mankind but also fought him. Today, the ideas of our National Socialist and Fascist revolution have conquered great and mighty states. My prophecy will be fulfilled that this war will not destroy the Aryan, but, instead, it will exterminate the Jew.

Whatever the struggle may bring, however long it may last, this will be its final result. And only then, after the elimination of these parasites, a long era of international understanding, and therefore of true peace, will come over the suffering world.

Today more than ever, I am with you in spirit, my old National Socialists, since you were already my followers when, as is still true today, being a National Socialist only meant making sacrifices.

On this day, I am personally all the more inspired with the imperturbable confidence and the sacred faith that this mighty fight in which we are engaged today and for which, back then, on February 24, 1920, we set out from this same hall in which you are now assembled, cannot and will not end differently from our own miraculous struggle for power in the German Reich. Just as Providence has blessed our fight in all those years, it will now let us win it for good! What used to be our party program is now the basis of a new and improving world.

Therefore, receive my greetings, which I convey to you through party comrade Adolf Wagner, as though I were standing in your midst. In my thoughts, I am with you anyway in these hours!

Adolf Hitler

In this message, Hitler again expressed his determination to exterminate the Jews. To murder millions of defenseless people was all he had left to offer, a Führer who was too much of a coward to face his old followers at the Hofbräuhaus hall in Munich. Never again would he dare to face them in this hall.

▸ December 12, 1942 *The Nazi Party was removed as an institution of the state. Both party and state depended upon Hitler's will.*

On December 12, Hitler signed a series of domestic ordinances. One decree established an advisory board for the German railroad (*Reichsbahn*), that was made up of eighteen members "to be named by the Reich government." Another decree dealt with appointments to disciplinary courts.

One important decree concerned the legal status of the National Socialist German Workers' Party. It had greatly diminished in significance over the years. As was already apparent in the "Resolution of the Greater German Reichstag" of April 26, the military and police would now take center stage! Hitler's Nazi Party decree of December 12 was not intended to give the party a new lease on life. On the contrary, by becoming a corporation under public law, the Nazi Party was even more at his mercy than before. The decree read as follows:

I.   The rights and duties of the National Socialist German Workers' Party shall derive from the tasks that I shall set for it and its resulting organizational position.

II. Party law shall exclusively determine the inner organization of the party.

III. The party shall participate in legal relations in accordance with the regulations applying to the state, insofar as special arrangements have not been, or will not be, made for it.

IV. I rescind the provisions of Paragraph 1, Section 2, of the law on securing the unity of party and state of December 1, 1933 (*Reich Law Gazette* I, page 1016)

V.   The regulations necessary for the implementation of this decree will be issued by the head of my party chancellery in agreement with the Reich treasurer of the Nazi Party, and the Reich minister and chief of the Reich Chancellery.

The Führer Adolf Hitler

VI

Putting Germany to Work

Hitler always maintained, on his road to power, that National Socialism would quickly improve everyone's material well-being. At the height of the Depression in 1932, there were many skeptics. Indeed, one reason that von Papen and his governing circle allowed Hitler into power was that they assumed his programs would fail and they would then discredit him. Hitler understood this very well and launched programs immediately. Hitler always emphasized economic autarky, *the idea that the nation should produce all necessary commodities by itself without need for trade. Since not all areas had all raw materials, Hitler supported the development of manufacturing processes for artificial goods, such as petroleum and rubber. Nevertheless, the quest for raw materials, including farmland, formed the basis of the concept of* Lebensraum, *the idea of simply seizing the areas needed. Hitler espoused* Lebensraum *and vowed to eliminate anyone who opposed the move.*

▸ January 3, 1933 *At a convention of the Nazi Party on agricultural policies in Munich, Hitler explained that agriculture was the foundation of economic activity. He particularly emphasized the small farmers (peasants) in his "blood and soil" programs.*

The fulfillment of the fundamental idea of national policy reawakened by National Socialism that is expressed in the theory of *Blut und Boden* will be accompanied by the most thorough and revolutionary reorganization that has ever taken place.

Our demand for strengthening the basic racial principles of our Volk, which this term signifies, and that at the same time includes safeguarding the existence of our Volk in general, is also the determining factor in all of the aims of National Socialist domestic and foreign policy. Once we have succeeded in purging and regenerating our Volk, foreign countries will very soon realize that they are confronted with a different Volk from hitherto.

And thus the prerequisites will be given for putting our own land and soil in thorough order and securing the life of the nation on our own for long years to come. The development in world economics and politics that automatically leads to an increasing blockade against our exports in international markets makes a major, fundamental transposition an absolute necessity. Even if today's rulers shut their eyes to this fact, the chronic cause of our grave economic need and appalling unemployment is nevertheless an indisputable reality. Either we eliminate this cause and accomplish the required reorganization with vigor and energy in good time, or fate will bring it about by force and destroy our Volk.

If we succeed in putting the basic principle of *Blut und Boden* into practice at home and abroad, then for the first time we, as a Volk, will not be tossed at the mercy of events but, rather, will then master circumstances on our own.

Just as the peasant who sows each year must believe in his harvest without knowing whether it may be destroyed by wind and weather and his work remain unrewarded, so must we too have the political courage to do what necessarily must be done—regardless of whether success is already in sight at the moment or not. The German peasant in particular will understand even more of our National Socialist struggle in the future than hitherto. But if the German peasant, the foundation and life source of our Volk, is saved, then the entire nation will once again be able to look ahead to the future with confidence.

▶ February 10, 1933 *Within two weeks of assuming office, Hitler gave a speech from the Berlin Sportpalast that was broadcast on radio, explaining his policies: after the usual party narrative Hitler talked about his economic reforms.*

Then they committed the crime of inflation, and after this rampage on the part of their minister Hilferding, a ruinous usury set in. Outrageously exorbitant interest rates, which should never have been allowed to go unpunished in any state, are now part and parcel of the "social" republic, and this is where the destruction of production begins, the destruction wreaked by these Marxist theories of economics as such, and moreover by the madness of a taxation policy that sees to the rest; and now we witness how class upon class are collapsing, how hundreds of thousands, gradually driven to despair, are losing their livelihoods; and how, year after year, tens of thousands of bankruptcies and hundreds of thousands of compulsory auctions are taking place. Then the peasantry starts to become impoverished, the most industrious class in the entire Volk is driven to ruin, can no longer exist, and then this process spreads back to the cities, and the army of unemployed begins to grow: one million, two, three, four million, five million, six million, seven million; today the number might actually lie between seven and eight million.

They destroyed what they could in 14 years of work, and no one did anything to stop them. Today this distress can perhaps be best illustrated by a single comparison—one *Land*, Thuringia. Total revenues from its communities amount to 26 million Marks. This money must suffice to defray the costs of their administration and cover the maintenance of their public buildings as well as everything they spend for schools and educational purposes. This money must cover what they spend on welfare. A total of 26 million in revenues, and welfare support alone requires 45 million.

That's what Germany looks like today! Under the rule of these parties that have ruined our Volk for fourteen years. The only question is, for how much longer? Because of my conviction that we must begin with the rescue work now if we do not want to come too late, I declared my willingness on January 30 to make use of the Movement—which has meanwhile swelled from seven men to a force of twelve million—toward saving the German Volk and fatherland.

Our opponents are asking about our program. My national comrades, I could now pose the question to these same opponents: "Where was your program?" Did you actually intend to have happen what did happen to Germany? Was that your program, or didn't you want that? Who prevented you from doing the opposite? Surely they do not intend now suddenly to recall that they bear the responsibility for fourteen years.

However, we shall both remind and reproach them and thus make certain that their conscience may not rest, that their memory does not fade.

When they say, "Show us the details of your program," then my only answer is this: any government at any time would presumably have been able to have a program with a few concrete points. But after your fine state of affairs, after your dabbling, after your subversion, the German Volk must be rebuilt from top to bottom, just as you destroyed it from top to bottom! That is our program! And a number of great tasks tower before us.

The best and thus the first item on our program is: we do not want to lie and we do not want to swindle. This is the reason why I have refused ever to step before this Volk and make cheap promises. No one here can stand up against me and testify that I have ever said that Germany's resurrection was only a matter of a few days. Again and again I preach: the resurrection of the German nation is a question of recovering the inner strength and health of the German Volk.

Just as I myself have now worked for fourteen years, untiringly and without ever wavering, to build this Movement; and just as I have succeeded in turning seven men into a force of twelve million; in the same way I want and we all want to build and work on giving new heart to our German Volk. Just as this Movement today has been given the responsibility of the leadership of the German Reich, so shall we one day lead this German Reich back to life and to greatness. We are determined to allow nothing to shake us in this conviction.

Thus I come to the second item on our program. I do not want to promise them that this resurrection of the German Volk will come of itself. We are willing to work, but the Volk must help us. It should never make the mistake of believing that life, liberty, and happiness will fall from heaven. Everything is rooted in one's own will, in one's own work.

And thirdly, we wish to have all of our efforts guided by one realization, one conviction: we shall never believe in foreign help, never in help that lies outside our own nation, outside our own Volk. The future of the German Volk lies in itself alone. Only when we have succeeded in leading this German Volk onwards by means of its own work, its own industriousness, its own boldness, and its own perseverance—only then will we rise up, just as our fathers once made Germany great, not with the help of others, but on their own.

The fourth item on our program dictates that we rebuild our Volk not according to theories hatched by some alien brain, but according to the eternal laws valid for all time. Not according to theories of class, not according to concepts of class.

We can summarize our fifth item in a single realization: The fundamentals of our life are founded on values that no one can take away from us except us ourselves; they are founded on our own flesh and blood and willpower and in our soil. Volk and earth—those are the two roots from which we will draw our strength and upon which we propose to base our resolves.

And this brings us thus to our sixth item, clearly the goal of our struggle: the preservation of this Volk and this soil, the preservation of this Volk for the future, in the realization that this alone can constitute our reason for being. It is not for ideas that we live, not for theories or fantastic party programs; no, we live and fight for the German Volk, for the preservation of its existence, that it may undertake its own struggle for existence, and we are thereby convinced that only in this way do we make our contribution to what everyone else so gladly places in the foreground: world peace.

This peace has always required strong peoples who strive for and protect it. World culture is founded upon the cultures of the different nations and peoples. A world economy is conceivable only if supported by the economies of healthy individual nations. In starting with our own Volk, we are assisting in the reconstruction of the entire world in that we are repairing one building block that cannot be removed from the framework and structure of the rest of the world.

And another item reads: because we perceive our highest goal to be the preservation of our Volk, enabling it to undertake its own struggle for existence, we must eliminate the causes of our own disintegration and thus bring about the reconciliation of the German classes. A goal that cannot be achieved in six weeks or four months if others have been laboring at this decay for seventy years. But a goal that we always keep in mind, because we shall rebuild this new community ourselves and slowly eliminate the manifestations of this disintegration. The parties that support this class division can, however, be certain that as long as the Almighty keeps me alive, my resolve and my will to destroy them will know no bounds.

Never, never will I stray from the task of stamping out Marxism and its side effects in Germany, and never will I be willing to make any compromise on this point. There can be only one victor: either Marxism or the German Volk! And Germany will triumph!

In bringing about this reconciliation of the classes, directly and indirectly, we want to proceed in leading this united German Volk back to the eternal sources of its strength; we want, by means of an education starting in the cradle, to implant in young minds a belief in a God and the belief in our Volk.

Then we want to resurrect this Volk on the foundation of the German peasants, the cornerstones of all national (*völkisch*) life. When I fight for the future of Germany, I must fight for German soil and I must fight for the German peasant. He renews us, he gives us the people in the cities, he has been the everlasting source for millennia, and his existence must be secured.

And then I proceed to the second pillar of our national tradition: the German worker—the German worker who, in the future, shall no longer and must no longer be an alien in the German Reich; whom we want to lead back to the community of our Volk and for whom we will break down the doors so that he, too, can become part of the German national community (*Volksgemeinschaft*) as one of the bulwarks of the German nation. We will then ensure that the German spirit has the opportunity to unfold; we want to restore the value of character and the creative power of the individual to their everlasting prerogatives.

Thus we want to break with all the manifestations of a rotten democracy and place in its stead the everlasting realization that everything that is great can originate only in the power of the individual and that everything that is to be preserved must be entrusted once more to the ability of the individual.

We will combat the manifestations of our parliamentary and democratic system, which leads us to our twelfth item—restoring decency to our Volk. In addition to decency in all areas of our life: decency in our administration, decency in public life, and decency in our culture as well, we want to restore German honor, to restore its due respect and the commitment to it, and we want to engrave upon our hearts the commitment to freedom; in doing so, we desire to bestow once more upon the Volk a genuinely German culture with German art, German architecture, and German music, which shall restore to us our soul, and we shall thus evoke reverence for the great traditions of our Volk; evoke deep reverence for the accomplishments of the past, a humble admiration for the great men of German history.

We want to lead our youth back to this glorious Reich of our past. Humbled shall they bow before those who lived before us and labored and worked and toiled so that they could live today. And we want most of all to educate this youth to revere those who once made the most difficult sacrifice for the life of our Volk and the future of our Volk. For all the damage these fourteen years wrought, their worst crime was that they defrauded two million dead of their sacrifice, and these two million shall rise anew before the eyes of our youth as an eternal warning, as a demand that they be revenged. We want to educate our youth to revere our time-honored army, which they should remember, which they should admire, and in which they should once more recognize the powerful expression of the strength of the German nation, the epitome of the greatest achievement our Volk has ever accomplished in its history.

Thus this program will be a program of national resurrection in all areas of life, intolerant against anyone who sins against the nation, but a brother and friend to anyone who has the will to fight with us for the resurrection of his Volk, of our nation.

Therefore I today address my final appeal to my fellow countrymen:

On January 30, we took over government. Devastating conditions have descended upon our Volk. It is our desire to remedy them, and we will succeed in doing so. Just as we have eliminated these adversaries despite all the scorn, we shall also eliminate the consequences of their rule. To do justice to God and our own conscience, we have turned once more to the German Volk. It shall now play a helping role.

It will not deter us should the German Volk abandon us in this hour. We will adhere to whatever is necessary to keep Germany from degenerating. However, it is our wish that this age of restoration of the German nation be associated not only with a few names, but with the name of the German Volk itself; that the government not be working alone, but that a mass of millions come to stand behind this government; that the government have the will, with the aid of this backing, to fortify us once again for this great and difficult task. I know that, were the graves to open today, the ghosts of the past who once fought and died for Germany would float aloft, and our place today would be behind them. All the great men of our history, of this I am certain, are behind us today and watch over our work and our labors.

For fourteen years the parties of disintegration, of the November revolution, have seduced and abused the German Volk. For fourteen years they wreaked destruction, infiltration, and dissolution. Considering this, it is not presumptuous of me to stand before the nation today and plead of it: German Volk, give us four years' time and then pass judgment upon us. German Volk, give us four years, and I swear to you, just as we, just as I have taken this office, so shall I leave it.

I have done it neither for salary nor for wages; I have done it for your sake! It has been the most difficult decision of my life. I dared to make it because I believed that it had to be.

I have dared to make this decision because I am certain that one cannot afford to hesitate any longer. I have dared to make this decision because it is my conviction that our Volk will finally return to its senses and that, even if millions might curse us today, the hour will come in that they will march with us after all, having recognized that we really wanted nothing but the best and had no other goal in sight than serving what is, to us, most precious on earth.

▸ February 11, 1933 *A day after his major economic speech, Hitler demonstrated his interest in and enthusiasm for automobiles and related products.*

On February 11, Hitler made an appearance of a completely different nature. Formally attired in a cutaway coat, he inaugurated the opening of the International Automobile and Motorcycle Exhibition on the Kaiserdamm in Berlin. It was the first time a Reich Chancellor had opened an exhibition of this sort, and the magnates of the automobile industry were flattered by the honor. Their satisfaction increased when Hitler presented himself not only as a respectable and responsible statesman, but as a knowledgeable expert on motorization as well.

His speech commenced with a lengthy perspective on the evolution of the various means of transportation in general and Germany's outstanding contribution to this field in particular.

Proceeding to more practical questions, he declared:

> As I am today given the honor of speaking to you at the request of the Reich president, my dear gentlemen of the [automobile] industry, I would not want to neglect conveying to you my opinion regarding what I believe to be necessary toward promoting what is probably today's most important industry.
>
> 1. Separation of the state motor traffic syndicate from the present realm of transportation. The automobile, by its very nature, is more closely affiliated with the airplane than with the railroad. Automobiles and airplanes have a common basis in the motor industry. Without the development of, for instance, the diesel engine for motor traffic, it would have been practically impossible to lay the necessary groundwork for its utilization in aviation.
>
> 2. Gradual reduction of the tax burden.

3. Institution and implementation of a large-scale road-building program.

4. Promotion of sports events.

Just as the horse and cart once cut their trails and the railroad built its required track network, so must motorized traffic be supplied with the requisite roads. In the past, one attempted to measure a people's standard of living in terms of track kilometers; in the future, road kilometers for motorized traffic will replace this yardstick.

These are momentous tasks that are also part of the program for the reconstruction of the German economy!

Now I would like to thank you on behalf of the Reich president and the Reich government for everything you have accomplished in the meantime on your own initiative. We are able to view this attractive exhibition today thanks to three factors which I would like to recall here:

You businessmen and leaders of industry and commerce have possessed the boldness not to abandon the struggle even in these troubled times, but to take up the fight against the foreign automobile industry, that is, in part, so much better situated.

But I would also like to thank the countless German designers and technicians whose genius is creating wondrous works of human invention. It is regrettable that our Volk is rarely given the opportunity to become acquainted with these nameless men who, by designing our cars, not only make hundreds of thousands of individuals happy, but have also opened up new and comfortable means of transportation for millions across the board of motorized traffic.

And I would also like to take this opportunity to pay tribute to that great army of our German workers, whose industriousness and ability and tremendous conscientiousness in their work makes it possible to transform technological ideas into machines that can be described as real masterpieces of precision as well as aesthetic beauty.

Lastly, I wish to commemorate the German Volk. May it, as well, fully appreciate the work, industriousness, and genius of so much effort. May it here, as well, revere its German masters of brain and brawn, and may it never forget that many tens of thousands of our *Volksgenossen* are without work and have the right to expect that the entire Volk remember these comrades and, out of solidarity with their need, recognize their brotherhood with German workers.

With this hope, I hereby with proud confidence declare this automobile exhibition on behalf of the Reich president open to the public.

▶ September 20, 1933 *Hitler emphasized consumer economy. By starting massive public works programs, Hitler brought full employment. But he was aware of the fact that money needed to circulate if the employment level were to remain high. The reference to the Brüning government is about some of the responses of that government to the depression.*

On September 20, Hitler spoke to the members of the newly established General Council of the German Economy (*Generalrat der deutschen Wirtschaft*) in Berlin and explained his economic policy, which greatly differed from Brüning's system of educating the people to exercise modesty in their needs.

The economy is now once again able to make long-range plans, because with this government there is no danger that it will be gone tomorrow or the day after. Two million people have been reintegrated in the production process. The Reich government is convinced that this success can only be permanent if unemployment is combated by a continuous series of vigorous offensives and fanatical persistence. If we succeed in halting the seasonal remigration of the masses of workers in fall and winter, a new general attack can be launched in spring with every hope of success.

In order to achieve this, new and more extensive measures are required. It is the task not only of the Reich government but of the economy as well to accomplish the educational work that is of primary importance here.

It is most necessary to combat the ideology of modesty of needs, the systematic reduction of demand, i.e., the cult of primitivism stemming from Communism. This Bolshevist ideal of the gradual regression of civilization's claims must inevitably result in the destruction of economy and of life as a whole. It is an ideology founded on a fear of one's neighbor, in dread of somehow standing out, and is based upon a spiteful, envious cast of mind. This code of regression to the primitive state leads to cowardly, anxious acquiescence and thus presents a tremendous threat to mankind.

The decisive thing is, not that all limit themselves, but rather that all endeavor to make progress and improve their lot. The German economy can exist only given a definite rate of demand and a definite cultural requirement on the part of the German Volk.

▶ September 23, 1933 *The Autobahn was one of the main public works emphasized by Hitler. While plans for the roads had developed in the late twenties, and other countries had started building a few such roads, no other country threw its resources into the project as much as Germany. And Hitler was always out in front.*

In a speech on September 23 before a gathering of German Autobahn workers near Frankfurt am Main, he made an effective presentation of his theory, which was doubtlessly correct at the time, of creating work and increasing consumption. When the first sod was turned in preparation for the initial Autobahn connecting Frankfurt and Heidelberg, Hitler exclaimed: *"Deutsche Arbeiter, ans Werk!"* (German workers, get to work!) The program he developed exhibited parallels to the embankment project in Goethe's *Faust*:

Ministers, Presidents of the Reichsbahn and the Reichsbank! Statthalters, Gauleiters, Party Comrades, and German Workers!

Today we stand at the threshold of a tremendous task. Its significance not only for German transportation but in the broadest sense for the German economy, too, will come to be appreciated in full only in the course of future decades. We are now beginning to build a new artery for traffic! Aspects of modern traffic will be given deserved and necessary consideration in the development of the German motorway system. In future decades, transportation will be coupled with these great new roads that we now plan to build throughout Germany. The first step toward this goal is 6,400 kilometers long. I know that this gigantic project is only conceivable given the cooperation of many; that this project could never have evolved had the realization of its greatness and the will to turn it into reality not seized hold of so many, all the way from the cabinet and the Reich government to the German *Reichsbank* and the German *Reichsbahn*.

At the same time we are fighting the most severe crisis and the worst misfortune that has descended upon Germany in the course of the past fifteen years. The curse of unemployment, which has condemned millions of people to a degrading and impossible way of life, must be eliminated!

It is quite clear to us that the battle against unemployment cannot become a complete success overnight, but we are also aware of the fact that this battle must be waged under any circumstances. We are determined to take it up, for we have taken a vow to the nation to resolve this crisis.

Back then we asked for four years, and we plan to turn these four years to the benefit and advantage of our German Volk and, above all, of the German worker. Workers, I myself was often attacked for my origins during the period of my struggle for power in Germany by those who pretended to represent the interests of the workers. At that time people were fond of saying: what does that ex-construction worker and painter want? I am happy and proud that fate forced me to tread this path. In this way perhaps I have gained a greater understanding for the German worker, for his character, for his suffering, but also for that which makes up the vital necessities of his life.

In beginning this project today, I am acting on these feelings, on these experiences from my own life; therefore I also know that what is beginning today with a celebration will mean toil and sweat for many hundreds of thousands. I know that this day of celebration will pass and that the time will come when rain, frost, and snow will make the work trying and difficult for everyone. But it is necessary: this work must be done, and no one will help us if we do not help ourselves.

In my view, the most productive way of leading the German Volk back into the process of work is to once again get German industry going by means of great and monumental projects. In taking on a difficult task today that you must continue in the hard times that fall, winter, and spring will bring, you are ensuring that hundreds of thousands more will receive work in the factories and workshops by virtue of your increased buying power. It is our goal slowly to increase the buying power of the masses and thus to provide orders to the centers of production and get German industry off the ground again.

Therefore I ask you to constantly bear in mind that today it is not at our discretion to choose the work to be done. I ask you to bear in mind that we are living in an age that perceives its very essence in work itself; that we wish to build up a state that values work for its own sake and holds the worker in high regard because he is fulfilling a duty to the nation; a state that aims, by means of its labor service, to educate everyone— even the tender sons of high-born parents—to hold work in high regard and to respect physical labor in the service of the *Volksgemeinschaft*.

I know that this great process of inwardly welding our Volk together cannot be completed overnight. Even we are incapable of doing away with what has gradually disintegrated, become deformed and distorted in the course of thirty, forty, fifty, or a hundred years within a few months. The biases have been too deeply implanted in the people to be forgotten overnight. But they will forget. It is our task to build this resolve on the concept of respecting work, no matter what it may be. Fate has not allowed us the freedom to pick and choose the type of work that fits our fancy.

We want to educate the Volk so that it moves away from the insanity of class superiority, of arrogance of rank, and of the delusion that only mental work is of any value; we want the Volk to comprehend that every labor that is necessary ennobles its doer, and that there is only one disgrace, and that is to contribute nothing to the maintenance of our *Volksge-meinschaft*, to contribute nothing to the maintenance of the Volk itself. It is a necessary transposition that we will effect not with theories, not with declarations or with wishes and hopes, but that we will effect only by life itself, in that today we are setting millions of people to the task of restoring health to the German economy.

In setting hundreds of thousands to work that is great, monumental, and of—I would like to say, eternal—value, we shall ensure that the product is no longer separated from those who have created it. In the future one should not think only of those who have planned or drafted it as engineers but rather also of those who, by their industry, by their sweat, and by work that was just as hard, have translated the plans and the ideas into reality for the benefit of the entire Volk. Thus, in this hour I cannot hope for anything better than that it be not only the hour when the construction of this, the greatest road network in the world, was initiated, but that this hour also be, at the same time, a milestone for the construction of the German *Volksgemeinschaft*, a community that will bestow upon us as Volk and as state all that we may rightfully de-mand and expect from this world.

And so I ask of you: go to work now! Construction must begin today! Let us commence the task! And before many years have passed, a gigantic work shall bear witness to our service, our industry, our capability, and our determination: German workers, get to work! (*Deutsche Arbeiter, ans Werk!*)

▶ September 5, 1934 *At the Reich Party Congress of 1934, local Munich party leader, Gauleiter Adolf Wagner, read Hitler's policy proclamation. In this document, Hitler's efforts to achieve high employment remained a prior-ity; however, much of this activity was cover for the secret arms industry that began to take up a great deal of labor.*

Speaking on National Socialist economic policy, Hitler disclosed a number of future projects including road-building, a new national railway station, and a restructuring of the major cities.

Tremendous, above all, was the work that had to be done in the areas of decay that manifested itself most evidently at the time. He who finds fault with the economic policy of these past twelve months can be only malicious or have taken leave of his senses.

When we took power, Germany's economy was in what seemed to be an unstoppable process of shrinking. Fear and distrust, despondency and despair comprised the breeding ground for a development whose collapse could be clearly foreseen. These successes are the convincing proof of the effectiveness of our economic policy and the German Volk's confidence in it:

1. The destruction of German peasantry by mortgage foreclosures was not only stopped but fully eliminated.

2. The measures taken to create work have, on a large scale, been attended with tremendous success.

3. The number of unemployed has decreased by an estimated four-and-a-half million.

4. The German Mark has remained stable and that in spite of the many export problems.

5. Savings deposits have grown tremendously.

6. The volume of traffic has undergone enormous increases on the railroads, in terms of motorized traffic, and in the air.

7. The receipts from contributions and taxes have far surpassed estimates with respect to all voluntary, non-state, and state organizations, as well as to all public funds.

When, two years ago, we predicted that this development would take place if we took power, this was, not only challenged and denied, but claimed to be impossible and even dismissed with scorn. And today these same people who did nothing but ruin Germany by their own labors now dare to claim that our achievements are trivial and insignificant. But where would Germany be had these destructive elements governed for even one year longer?

This year that lies behind us has accomplished the tremendous preliminary work for projects that will only become visibly evident to the nation in the course of the next few years. The gigantic road building plans could not be pulled out of a hat from one day to the next but required a certain amount of time alone for their conception and design.

But the German Volk will see what preliminary work has been accomplished during these twelve months in what will be carried out in the years to come. In addition to the national network of roads, tremendous new national railway stations have been completed in the conceptual and design stages. Revolutionary construction programs are being drawn up for a whole series of major German cities, the magnitude of which will only be able to be fully and finally appreciated after decades have passed.

Some industries have been broken up, new industries have been founded; the housing policy was consolidated in order to be more effective in general. In order to combat the world boycott, the substitution of raw materials was begun and the initial preparations undertaken to make Germany independent of this need. Constantly guided by a single belief: no matter what happens, National Socialism will never capitulate!

The proclamation closed with the following words:

> Posterity shall one day say of us: never was the German nation stronger and never its future more secure than at the time when the ancient Germanic people's old mystical symbol of salvation (*Heilszeichen*) was rejuvenated in Germany to become the symbol of the Third Reich.
>
> Long live our German Volk, long live the National Socialist Party and our Reich!

▶ February 14, 1935 *Hitler was not only interested in the Volk's new roads but also in the Volk's automobile, the Volkswagen.*

On February 14, Hitler opened the International Automobile and Motorcycle Exhibition in the Berlin Exhibition Halls on Kaiserdamm with a lengthy speech. As in preceding years, he first discussed general aspects of transportation and then focused his attention on government measures promoting motorized traffic. In respect to the Autobahn and Volkswagen projects, he stated:

> When the Reich Autobahn network is completed, Germany will be able to call its own the most modern system of roads in the world by far. Tremendous evidence of peaceful progress! These measures are to be complemented by the task of creating a car for the people at large. I am happy to say that a brilliant designer has succeeded, with the cooperation of his staff, in completing preliminary plans for the German Volkswagen and will finally be able to test the first models beginning in midyear.

Hitler closed his speech by pointing out that producing synthetic rubber and synthetic gasoline was now theoretically possible and stated, "Not only are our automobiles and motorcycles the fastest in the world; they are also, we can proudly say, the best."

▶ September 11, 1935 *At the Reich Party Congress of Freedom, 1935, Hitler's policy proclamation set out his economic policies at that time. There was to be no inflation because his administration controlled currency with strict wage and price controls. Enforcement was harsh and judgment swift.*

Turning to economic problems, Hitler once again took up his crusade against any type of currency manipulation. He would by no means tolerate salary and price increases, and this would rule out the possibility of inflation such as that of the twenties. Although the dictator admittedly entertained quite sound economic views, he failed—as did many others—to realize that the inflation of 1920–23 was not due to unwise economic policy but was the inevitable consequence of the destruction that the economic structure had undergone during the First World War; a phenomenon that was not limited to this war and not only to the defeated. However, in 1935 he could still boast:

> Today we can admit it openly: the year 1934 was unfortunately a bad harvest year. We are still suffering from the aftereffects. But it was nevertheless possible to secure the German Volk's supply of vitally important foodstuffs. The fact that this was possible, in spite of the many restrictions, is an achievement of which the broad masses of our Volk have perhaps not been sufficiently aware. The difficulties connected with this harvest led many a time to a temporary shortage of this or that foodstuff.
>
> We were nonetheless determined that under no circumstances would we capitulate as a certain international press was ardently hoping. And we overcame the crisis. We were forced, in this context, to repeatedly halt, with every means available, attempts to compensate for the bad harvest by partly understandable but also partly unjustified price increases.
>
> In this year we were—and will likewise be in future—motivated by the unshakable desire to prevent the German Volk from stumbling unawares into a new inflation. But this would still be the unavoidable result of any increase in salaries or any increase in prices at present. So if today, too, irresponsible egoists or unthinking fools fancy that any kind of shortage—that can always arise—gives them the right to increase prices, this behavior would, if the government were to let it, set the well-known vicious circle of 1921 to 1923 in motion, leaving the German Volk with inflation on its hands for the second time around. For this reason we will attack such elements from now on with brutal ruthlessness and—if good intentions fail—will not shrink from using concentration camps to make them conform with and adapt to the national interest as a whole.

▶ February 15, 1936 *Hitler continued to emphasize the automobile and related industries.*

Hitler inaugurated the International Automobile and Motorcycle Exhibition in Berlin by delivering a lengthy speech. The first part of his talk consisted once again of a lecture on "economics and philosophy." In this particular instance Hitler's rendition of his theory on the primitive nature of Bolshevism does merit attention. Of all of Hitler's theories, the economic ones were the best. However, accurate realizations on his part were distorted by his political preconceptions, which had haunted him ever since 1919.

Examples of these included the idea that the English were becoming increasingly more senile and that the Bolshevists were of a primitive nature. Hitler simply projected his own personal experiences with the German Nationalists and the German Communists onto the international arena, and he characteristically saw the motorization question in a similar way.

Indeed, the government of the Weimar Republic had not done much for traffic motorization, doing more to impose restraints upon it than to seek its advancement. In Hitler's eyes, this was the obvious outcome that the misbegotten conception of the equality of all men had led to. In the end, all it had brought about was an equally low standard of living for all. As Hitler maintained, the percentage of cars per person in Germany had been so low in 1932 that only the Russians possessed fewer automobiles. He regarded the low level of motorization in the Soviet Union as proof of the primitive nature of Bolshevism. Imagine his surprise when in World War II, the supposedly primitive Russians threw column after column of motorized vehicles and tanks at the German lines.

On February 15, 1936, however, Hitler was still undaunted in voicing the following "profound" insights in a speech to representatives of the German automobile industry:

> I believe it is particularly fitting on a day such as this, if merely to counter the forgetfulness of mankind, to stress those factors that have been psychologically responsible for the sorry decline of our automobile industry and thus of our transportation industry as a whole, that is to say, of that industry that can currently be described as the single most powerful industry and that is thus called upon to put its unique and characteristic stamp on today's age.

1. One factor responsible for this decline on the part of the consumer was the view originating in the social-democratic theory of equality, that it was necessary for the human race to become a race of primitives, which was to be accomplished by proletarianizing the standard of living for all so as to arrive at a level shared by as many as possible. This more than primitive idea proceeded on the limited assumption that human progress was rooted in the collective masses and was therefore to be valued or rejected as a collective manifestation.

   The fact is, however, that every act of human progress, seen from a mental and objective point of view, originates with a very few individuals; from a mental viewpoint, because the invention is born only of the imagination of individuals and not of the cross-section of a collective endeavor; objectively, because each human invention, regardless of whether its value is recognized or underestimated, always appears initially to be an additional pleasure in everyday life and thus a luxury article for a more or less limited circle. It is not an isolated incident, but rather unfortunately quite often the case, that this circle is regarded by the amiable collective of fellow mankind as being crazy—as this was, in fact, the case with our great inventors Benz and Daimler.

   Thus a truly progressive development is only possible given respect for individual creative power and for the similarly unique mental receptivity and actual marketability. It is not proof of the falseness but rather proof of the accuracy of this statement that the Marxist state, in order to limp along after mankind on its collective mental crutches, practically borrows the individual engineers, draftsmen, managers, inspectors, chemists, etc., from individually organized economies to enable it to cultivate its original Marxist economy with their generous assistance. This merely serves, of course, to show that just as the rest of the world was able to achieve culture without Bolshevism; Bolshevism itself would be unable to survive as a Communist entity all of its own without the help of the rest of the world.

This insight is significant because concentrated support particularly for our modern transportation industry is dependent upon the complete liberty of a Volk to make use of it, not only in terms of legislative liberty, but above all in terms of psychological liberty. It is just as antisocial to buy oneself an automobile as it once was to insert a piece of modern glass in one's window instead of using the traditional oiled hide. The evolution of such an invention necessarily proceeds f:om a very few persons, also its being put into practice, to then spread to increasingly larger circles, ultimately reaching everyone. Thus it was no coincidence that the lowest percentage of automobiles—after Communist-Marxist Soviet Russia—was seen in Germany which, at that time, also had a Marxist government.

2. Due to the fact that, in the long term, the ideology of the masses cannot and will not forever stand in opposition to the ideology of those in government and vice versa, it was only too natural that, originating from this common root of ignorance and irrationality, those in government acted on the Marxist theory of primitiveness, and for their part, also regarded the automobile as something unnecessary—and thus as something superfluous— and set taxes accordingly.

A capital error, I might add, that served to show how badly our own bourgeois economic views were already failing. For the theory of so-called luxury tax articles is absurd wherever and whenever in all human probability the luxury article promises to become an article of general use. Above all, one should not tax those products that are in the process of development but rather those whose development can clearly be deemed to be finished.

It goes without saying that, on the basis of such false thinking, all those specific steps that could be conducive toward promoting the development of this so incredibly promising and propitious industry were neglected or even completely ignored. Fiscal authorities and police headquarters cooperated to choke off and stamp out the development of German road traffic and with it the transportation

industry as thoroughly as possible, and—this is one com-
pliment that must be paid to the Marxist-Centrist governments—they succeeded brilliantly in their joint attack.

Whereas in America approximately 23 million automobiles were on the roads and three to four million were being
manufactured annually, the combined efforts of the leadership of Volk and state succeeded in limiting the number of
automobiles in Germany to barely 450,000 and in reducing the number produced in the year 1932 to 46,000.

3. The economy itself. It was bad enough that the leadership
of Volk and state, under the influence of such ideas, had no
comprehension of the development of motorization; it is at
least as bad that the German economy, albeit perhaps un-
consciously, gave in nonetheless to quite similar thoughts.
Thus the economy was likewise incapable of understanding
that the automobile must become a tool for the general public, for otherwise the broad potential for development slumbering therein will not be realized. The automobile is either
a costly luxury object for very few and thus of no particular
consequence in the long term for the economy as a whole,
or it should truly give the economy the enormous impetus
of which it is intrinsically capable, and then it must evolve
from a luxury object for very few to an object of use for all.
And this is where the German automobile industry—and
I fear this is still a general view—was not yet fully aware of
the fact that the development of German automobile production as a whole can only truly be successful only if its
pricing is commensurate with the incomes of the customer
groups it is to reach. The question as to the number of automobiles Germany can absorb is very easy to answer.

a) The desire for automobiles in our Volk is at least as lively
as in any other country; I would almost like to say that
the yearning for automobiles is so strongly in evidence
here because our Volk has been deprived of them. And
gentlemen, you can see the best proof of this in the enormous, incomparable numbers of visitors, particularly at

these exhibitions. They are the most pointed disproof of the view held by those who believed, only a few years ago, that they could completely dispense with these exhibitions as being merely insignificant and uninteresting. The German Volk has exactly the same need to use automobiles as, for instance, the American people.

It is superficial to regard a quantity of twenty-three or twenty-four million automobiles in America as natural and understandable and 500,000 or 600,000 as natural in Germany, although in terms of numbers the German Volk makes up somewhat more than half of the population of the North American Union. No, the popular demand is clear in Germany, too.

b) The prerequisite for the fulfillment of this desire can, however, be no different from the rest of the world. That means that the price of an automobile must correspond to the income of its potential buyer. And that means that there will be people who are in a position to sacrifice 20,000 Marks and more for an automobile because their income is proportionate. But the number of these people will not be large. Lowering the cost to 10,000 Marks will result in a much greater number of respective able buyers. And lowering the cost of a car to 5,000 Marks will mobilize an even greater group with corresponding incomes. All this means:

If I hope to achieve a volume of three or four million automobiles in Germany, then the price and maintenance costs for these automobiles must be graded to correspond to the incomes of the three or four million potential buyers. I advise the German automobile industry to proceed on the basis of these ideas and gather information on the income situation of the four or five million best-situated Germans, and you will then understand why I am so ruthlessly determined to have the preliminary work for producing the German Volkswagen carried on and brought to a conclusion, and, gentlemen, I am talking about a successful conclusion.

I do not doubt that the genius of the designer entrusted with the task as well as the subsequent manufacturers, in connection with the highest insights into national economy on the part of all those involved, will succeed in putting the costs of acquisition, operation, and maintenance for this car in a ratio acceptable to the income of this broad mass of our Volk, as we can see has successfully been accomplished in the brilliant example of America.

It is a regrettable error for anyone to believe in this context that such a development will move the buyers of better and more expensive cars to drop down to the Volkswagen. No, gentlemen, this car will act to mobilize millions, of whom hundreds of thousands will all the more easily find their way to better and more attractive cars as a result of their continuously rising standard of living. The Ford car did not displace better and more expensive American automobiles—on the contrary: it served initially to loosen up and mobilize the enormous masses of American buyers, from whom particularly the more expensive models later profited.

Hence, in finding two or three million buyers for a new German Volkswagen, there will be some who, in the course of their lives, will quite naturally switch to better and thus more expensive cars of their own accord. A great number will never be in a position to purchase an expensive car. Not because these people have no desire to do any Mr. Manufacturer a favor, but because they are unable to do so because of their modest income. Yet to simply exclude these millions from the pleasure of this modern means of transport because one is unwilling to run the risk that, of the two or three hundred thousand better-situated people, perhaps a few would buy the cheaper car, would be not only humanly unprincipled, but also economically unwise. For this would mean nothing but artificially bringing to a halt the most tremendous economical development for our Volk and our country out of both selfish and short-sighted considerations.

I know that I am thus assigning an extremely large task to the German economy, but I also know that Germans are no less capable than anyone else in the world. And matters that have been solved in one corner of the globe can and must be solved in Germany as well.

After this forceful appeal to the industry to advance the production of a "true car for the people" (*Volkswagen*), Hitler announced that, thanks to the "wonders the German chemists and inventors have truly accomplished," it had become possible to create synthetic gas and synthetic rubber. Without doubt this was a great step toward Hitler's goal of self-sufficiency, designed to make Germany independent of imports from foreign countries. However, these successes misled both Hitler and the German people to believe that wonders could be achieved, given the true spirit of invention, as for example, infinitely increasing the production of war goods during a conflict whenever the need arose. Hitler declared:

1. The crisis of Germany's fuel supply, whose paramount significance we can gauge particularly at the present time in political terms, can be considered overcome. Our chemists and inventors have truly accomplished wonders, particularly in this sector as a whole. And trust in our determination to put this theoretical solution into practice!

2. In this exhibition, you will find for the first time tires made of German synthetic rubber. And it is my pleasure to inform you and the German Volk at this time that the performance tests that have been conducted by the *Wehrmacht* for nearly a year now have shown that this synthetic rubber surpasses natural crude rubber in terms of life and durability by ten to thirty percent.

▸ October 4, 1936 *Hitler separated German currency from the world monetary market indicating that, rather than gold or other countries' opinions, his currency was backed by "the productive capacity of the Volk." The devaluation of most of the major currencies in 1936 led Hitler to ignore international monetary requests for similar action, thus causing conversion problems. This was just as well for Hitler, who looked forward to economic autarky.*

On October 4, an *Erntedankfest* celebration took place on the Bücke-berg near Hamelin. For once, there was no sunny "Hitler weather;" rather, it was raining, and Hitler had a hard time accounting for the fact in his speech. The currency problem, much debated by economists, could not be avoided in this speech. Following the lead of the Anglo-Saxon powers, most countries bordering on Germany had agreed to devalue their currencies. If Germany did not follow suit, German exports would be endangered. Hit-ler was opposed to such measures. In his opinion, the backing of a currency was determined by the productive capacities and the "working power of the Volk." He preferred to accept economic difficulties rather than follow the other European countries in matters of financial and currency politics. His "proof," however, that a currency not backed with either gold reserves or foreign currency as well as wages and prices could remain stable in spite of gigantic armament expenses, was a short-lived illusion built on hidden money-creating measures by the *Reichsbank*. When war broke out—the money circulation had already been out of all proportion to real produc-tivity reflected in the balances of trade, payments, etc.—not even the Nazi government could prevent a considerable inflation. No government ever has been able to do that, not since the first days of the monetary system. On that 4th of October, however, Hitler believed he had decisively resolved the currency problem, and confidently declared on the Bückeberg:

> I believe that reason is to be the sovereign in our state and that the German Volk has sufficient insight and disci-pline to grasp the necessities this reason entails. And there-fore we recognize:
>
> First of all, that we can only prevail if we have social peace, i.e., if not, everyone can do what he wants to. The individual must subordinate himself to the whole, to a higher common interest. Hence the worker cannot look after only his own in-terests, just as the peasant and the urban dweller cannot look after only their own; rather, each is called upon to show mu-tual consideration to the others!
>
> Secondly, that we must keep our wage policy and thus our pricing policy stable and steady. And if anyone believes he can violate that policy, believe me, as long as I live and remain standing at the head of the Reich, I will successfully defend the cause of general, national self-preservation against these few lunatics!

I am thereby doing something that in fact brings great good fortune to millions upon millions of people in Germany. We could make maneuvers like those others are making: today I grant a worker a fifteen or twenty-percent wage increase; tomorrow I raise prices by fifteen or twenty percent; then I raise wages and then prices again, and two months later we devalue the German Mark and betray the savers, and then we increase wages again, and so on—do you think that would make the German Volk happy? I am directing an appeal to all of you: gauge the good fortune of our inner German economic, social, and political peace!

How splendid it is indeed in Germany today! Take a look at other nations that have lost this power of reason! We must never allow this good fortune and this peace to be taken from us, and I know that this will never come to pass!

Where in the world would it be possible that, on a day such as today—on a day so cold that the wind whips the clouds over the mountains and one expects it to rain again any minute—where else would it be possible that hundreds of thousands and hundreds of thousands—nearly a million people—flock together on such a day to profess their unity?

▶ May 26, 1938 *Hitler continued to emphasize the automobile industry. At the same time, many "automobile" plants were producing armaments.*

Beforehand, however, Hitler had to attend the placing of the cornerstone at the new Volkswagen factory in Fallersleben on May 26. On this occasion, he announced that the new Volkswagen car was to be christened the "KdF car." In addition, he declared: "I hate the word 'impossible.' It has at all times been the distinguishing mark of the coward who does not dare to realize great ideas." Hitler's speech on the occasion of the dedication of the new Volkswagen factory was the following verbatim:

As the National Socialist Movement came to power in 1933, it seemed to me that this area was particularly well suited to open the campaign against unemployment: the problem of motorization! Here the German Volk was the most in arrears. Not only by comparison to production figures in America, but also in comparison to those of other European countries, the production of automobiles in Germany had remained at a ludicrously low level: barely forty-six thousand cars a year! This did not correspond in the least to the motorization needs of the German Volk. It is only logical therefore that, in a time when seven million unemployed weighed down our life, there would have to be radical and immediate change in this area.

The first step toward motorization was a divorce from those precepts that claimed that a car was a luxury. Of course, this is true in a country where there are no more than two, three or four hundred thousand cars. However, the German Volk does not need two or three hundred thousand cars; it needs six or seven million! The crucial point is to adjust the costs for buying and maintaining this means of transportation—the most modern there is—to the income level of the Volk.

At the time, I was told, "This is impossible!" My only reply to this is, "What is possible in other countries is also possible in Germany." I hate that word "impossible" since it has always been the mark of people not daring enough to make and to implement great decisions. The automobile must become the means of transportation for the Volk! Since this ambition could not be realized given the price range of automobiles to date, I had already resolved, even prior to our takeover of the government, to use the precise moment in which we rose to power to push for production of a car at a price that would make it accessible to the broad masses. Only then would the automobile cease to be a distinction of class.

There was yet another reason why I looked to motorization in particular. Given the limits imposed upon the production of foodstuffs in a country with 140 persons per square kilometer, a catastrophe would ensue if the German Volk invested its earnings in foodstuffs only. Therefore it is necessary to divert the buying power of the German Volk in other directions. In former times, our political economists never bothered themselves with such questions. We, however, have to face the facts and solve the problems that result from them.

The Volkswagen forms part of a series of measures aimed at channeling the buying power of the German Volk toward other products of equal value. Every year hundreds of thousands of Marks will be invested in pursuit of this goal. These needs can be satisfied based on our work alone, on our own raw materials, our iron ore and our coal, and so on. Few today realize the true significance of this project and its consequences. The Volkswagen will not enter into competition with the cars produced by the automobile industry to date. After all, a man who buys this car and not a Mercedes does not do so simply because he might be an opponent of the Daimler factory but because he cannot afford to buy a Mercedes.

What forces the buyer to turn to cheaper goods are simple and level-headed considerations. Whoever can afford the more expensive goods will buy it anyway! For the broad masses, however, this is not possible! It is for these broad masses that this car has been designed. It is to correspond to their need for transportation, and it is in this context that it is to bring enjoyment to the people.

Hence, I believe there is only one name that can be given to this car, a name I shall give to it on this very evening. It shall bear the name of that organization that strives to instill both joy and strength in the masses. The name shall be: Strength through Joy Car ! (*Kraft durch Freude-Wagen*)

As we build this greatest of Germany's automobile factories, we shall also build an exemplary German worker settlement. It shall also serve as a prototype for the future of social housing projects and city design. We wish to demonstrate how National Socialism sees, approaches, and resolves such problems. It is at this point that I wish to thank those men who deserve recognition for their efforts in planning and hence in implementing this project, in particular to a man from the automobile industry who has labored to represent and implement my views and who has loyally stood by me in these past years: our old party comrade Jakob Werlin.

And further let me thank those men who shall join forces with him in the practical implementation of this project: our great idealist party comrade Robert Ley, the brilliant engineer Porsche and finally Dr. Lafferentz. Those are the men to whom we will owe, in a large part, the realization of this enormous project! Hence I proceed to lay the cornerstone for this factory that, I am certain, shall become a symbol of the National Socialist national community (*Volksgemeinschaft*)!

After the speech, Hitler took a seat in a Volkswagen convertible and had himself chauffeured for an honorific ride.

▸ September 6, 1938 *At the Reich Party Congress,* Grossdeutschland, *Hitler's policy proclamation repeated his objective of gaining real autarky.*

Speaking on the subject of the "Ostmark," (*the name given to Austria as part of Nazi Germany*), Hitler turned to economic issues. He announced the elimination of unemployment in Austria, and proclaimed that he sought the guarantee of sufficient nutrition "under any circumstances." He argued that, in the case of war, an economic blockade of Germany would be "a dead issue":

> The unemployment crisis in the Ostmark of the Reich will, as well, have been completely resolved by the end of next year. Today, we have only two real economic concerns:
>
> a) the concern over manpower, in particular that of skilled laborers for industrial work, and
>
> b) the concern over manpower in the countryside.
>
> If other states regard these concerns as certain evidence for a supposedly persistent economic weakness of the Third Reich, then we shall gladly compare the criticism of our lack of manpower at home to the unemployment in the democracies.
>
> If today I can point to the lack of manpower as the sole economic concern in Germany, then this is so because of two facts:
>
> 1. The grace of the Lord has bestowed upon us a bountiful harvest this year. Despite crop failures during the past years, it was possible nonetheless to stock up considerable reserve supplies for the new year—thanks to the unrelenting steps taken by our party comrade Göring. We shall not have to fear for our food stocks for many years to come thanks to these reserve supplies and thanks to this year's bountiful harvest. Nevertheless, we will proceed with economy. It is our will to accumulate large reserves in wheat so that we shall be spared destitution under any and all circumstances.

2. The fruits borne by the Four-Year Plan are becoming increasingly noticeable. What I believed and forecast in earlier years has come true: once the national economic prerogatives were pointed out to the leaders of Germany's economy and to our inventors in particular, the ingenuity and expertise of our chemists, physicists, mechanical engineers, technicians, foremen, and organizers have achieved a success that no one had anticipated and that—I may assuredly say—has been simply astounding.

Here, too, Hitler entertained the deluded notion that, with the assistance of German inventors, he could achieve anything, perform miracles, and overcome all boundaries imposed by nature upon man. He continued:

We are building up Germany's economy in such a fashion that it can, at any given time, function independently of other countries and stand on its own feet. And this we have achieved. An economic blockade against Germany has become a dead issue. With its own peculiar energy, the National Socialist state has drawn the ultimate consequence from the World War. We will remain true to our principle rather to limit ourselves in one domain or another, should this be necessary, than to ever again become dependent upon other countries. Above all, one resolution will reign supreme in all our economic enterprises: the security of our nation has priority.

Hence its material existence must be completely secured within the confines of our *Lebensraum* and our capacity for self-sufficiency. Only then can the German *Wehrmacht* guarantee the protection of the Reich, its interests, and freedom of action, under any and all circumstances. And only then does Germany become of interest and value to others as a friend and ally.

When I pronounce this on the occasion of the tenth Reich Party Congress, then I do this in the confident knowledge that the time of Germany's political and economic isolation has come to an end. The Reich has befriended strong and great world powers.

Naturally, he loaded his speech with platitudes on the Bolshevist threat to the world, and heaped praise upon Italy's new anti-Semitic stance:

Party Comrades!

More threatening than ever, the danger of Bolshevist destruction of all peoples looms on the horizon. A thousand times
over we have witnessed the activities of the Jewish agitators
prodding this global pestilence.

I believe that this is the time and place, on my own behalf
and the behalf of you all, to pronounce with great inner movement how we rejoice at the fact that another great European
power has realized this, too. On the basis of its own experiences, its own reflections, and its own approach, it has arrived
at the same conclusions as we have and has drawn the consequences with a truly admirable determination.

▸ January 19, 1939 *When the* Reichsbank *began getting nervous about the
precarious state of the currency, Hitler took over the bank.*

One of the consequences of this realization was Hitler's decision to
dismiss Schacht, who occupied the position of *Reichsbank* president and
who was particularly opposed to a further increase in the creation of money. Simultaneously, Hitler resolved to deal also with the other bourgeois
economists who had approached him with their misgivings regarding the
stability of the currency and other petty concerns.

On January 7, Schacht had placed before Hitler a memorandum on the
intricate nature of Germany's finances. He had pointed out the strain of
the armament process on the economy. Other directors with the *Reichsbank* had countersigned the policy paper, too. Of course, Hitler paid no
heed to the memorandum. Instead, he made it clear to Schacht that he regarded him as an obstacle to the implementation of the National Socialist
economic policy. Hence, he effected Schacht's dismissal on January 19.

Berlin, January 19, 1939

Dear Herr Minister!

I wish to take advantage of the occasion of your leaving the office of president of the *Reichsbank* board of directors to express
to you the sincere and cordial appreciation of your services in
this position throughout long and difficult years on behalf of

Germany and my own person. Your name will remain tied to the initial period of the epoch of our national restoration. I am glad to know you are at my disposal and to assign you new responsibilities in your capacity as Reich minister.

With the German salute, Adolf Hitler

Precisely what type of "new responsibilities" Hitler had in mind for Schacht remained a secret for the time being. Perhaps Hitler was speculating on making use of Schacht's services at a later date, as he was to do with the deposed Neurath just a few weeks later. For appearances' sake, both men stayed on as members of the cabinet, whose reputation and presence were to create the illusion of national unity. The new *Reichsbank* president, Funk, received the letter reproduced below:

Dear Herr Minister!

I take advantage of the occasion of your appointment as president of the *Reichsbank* to congratulate you on assuming this new position. It shall be your task:

1. to secure the absolute stability of wages and prices in your position, that is to combine the two important realms, and thereby secure the value of the Mark,

2. to develop and augment the private lender's access to funds in the money market,

3. to bring to a conclusion the process initiated by the law of February 10, 1937; in defiance of the Dawes Plan, to reclaim the German Reich's uncontested sovereignty over the former *Reichsbank* and to place it unconditionally under the sovereignty of the state as a German bank of issue, in accordance with National Socialist principles.

With the German salute, Adolf Hitler

Judging from these lines, it was not difficult to divine that Schacht, the previous *Reichsbank* president, simply no longer fit into the mold of the "National Socialist principles." At an earlier date, Schacht had been deemed a good man and a "well-tried" National Socialist. Needless to say, Hitler also removed those directors of the *Reichsbank* who had placed their signatures beneath Schacht's memorandum. The official announcement read as follows:

Berlin, January 21

The Führer has relieved the following members of the *Reichsbank* Board of Directors of their duties: Vice President Dreyse and *Reichsbank* Director Hülle. Simultaneously, the Führer has appointed the state secretary in the Reich Ministry of Economics, Rudolf Brinkmann, as member of the *Reichsbank* Board of Directors. He shall retain his title as state secretary. The Reich minister of economics and *Reichsbank* president, Funk, has named State Secretary Brinkmann Vice President of the *Reichsbank* Board of Directors.

Having removed the dissenters from the *Reichsbank*, Hitler took immediate control of the bank. He decreed that the *Reichsbank* was to extend to the state whatever credit he deemed necessary. Hitler openly acknowledged his intentions in his speech before the Reichstag on January 30, 1939, stating:

I stand determined to bring to its conclusion the transformation of the German *Reichsbank*—a path pursued ever since January 30, 1937—from an internationally controlled bankers' enterprise to the institution of monetary issue of the German Reich.

If the rest of the world laments the loss of the international character of yet another German institution, may we point out that it is our inexorable decision (*unerbittlicher Entschluss*) to impart to all institutions affecting our lives predominantly German, i.e., National Socialist, characteristics.

> I now hold it to be the duty, my *Reichstag* deputies, of every German man and every German woman to comprehend the conduct of the Reich's economic policy. In the cities and in the countryside you have to consider in particular that Germany's economic policy is not based on some sort of financial theory, but rather on a very fundamental understanding of production, i.e., on the realization that the sole determining factor is the quantity of goods produced.
>
> That we are faced with numerous other tasks, such as the necessary deployment of a high percentage of manpower to the armament—by itself unproductive—of our Volk, is regrettable, yet unalterable. After all, the economy of the present Reich hinges on its external security. It is best to arrive at this realization early rather than too late. I hence see it as imperative for the National Socialist leadership of this State to do everything humanly possible to strengthen our defenses.

This explanation signaled that Hitler had abandoned the formerly highly praised National Socialist economic policy. He thought such a development "regrettable, yet unalterable." Finally, the bank of issue could strive to fulfill its supreme purpose: to fuel the armament production to the point of no return. Carelessly, Hitler tossed aside the very economic policy that had carried him to power in the first place by successfully fighting unemployment. No longer did he pay any heed to the relationship between production and the circulation of money, nor to the "backing of the currency by means of national productivity." What was crucial to the war effort was to keep prices and wages stable, even though this stability was clearly an artificial one. Small matter if this meant that in the end the money earned by the workers did them little good, since they could not buy anything with it.

It was Hitler's firm belief that once the new *Lebensraum* in the east had been conquered, the economy would take care of itself. Should the conquest fail—well, that would be the end in any event! Therefore, Hitler began to improvise, both in foreign affairs and military policy. "The economy of the present Reich hinges on its external security"—this motto best sums up his new-found economic faith.

After all was said and done, Hitler's assessment of this relationship proved to be correct in the end. The Third Reich would indeed ruin both the economy and the people. Once Hitler's reign was finally over for good,

Germany awoke, not only to an unparalleled military and political fiasco, but also to an economy in shambles. This collapse was far worse than the catastrophe of 1918.

▶ February 17, 1939 *By this time, the German economy had begun to slip out of control and foreign affairs were reaching a boiling point. Hitler's speech to the International Automobile Exposition was far less confident than previously.*

On February 17, he gave a lengthy speech at the festivities opening the annual International Automobile and Motorcycle Exhibition in the Berlin Exhibition Halls on Kaiserdamm. This particular address was the last he could deliver on such an occasion, as it was the last exhibition of this kind to take place in the Third Reich.

Although the setting was as elaborate as the year before, if not more so, the affair lacked the ebullience of previous ones. Though Hitler expounded upon the significance and potential of motor vehicle production at great length and in great detail, his words failed to convey the enthusiasm he had earlier displayed on this particular topic. Hitler barely mentioned his favorite project, the Volkswagen, and referred to the construction of the Autobahn as an aside only.

Indeed, the tone was a subdued one in 1939. The forced armament production was already overshadowing the automobile industry as well as other branches of the economy that relied heavily on the infrastructure, traffic, and transportation. Raw materials and fuel supplies were becoming increasingly scarce, and Hitler admonished the public to exercise economy in the consumption of these goods: "Every kilogram of steel needlessly tacked onto an automobile not only raises its costs and its retail price, but also maintenance expenditures. This in turn leads to more gas being used up, tires wearing out more quickly, and street surfaces needing more frequent replacement."

These new insights imparted by Hitler to the audience in his appeal for economy were intended to challenge the automobile industry to construct new car models, weighing no more than 2,000 kilograms instead of the customary 3,000 kilograms. Hitler further argued that the Autobahn highways had not been built "for speeds from 120 to 140 kilometers per hour, but rather for average speeds, let us say, of 80 kilometers." This speed limit soon became law.

Ironically, after the National Socialists' rise to power in 1933, one of the first pieces of legislation enacted had been a repeal of earlier speed restrictions that allegedly had inhibited the development of motorization. At the time the Nazis had claimed that high speeds even reduced the number of accidents on the road! A change of heart on this subject now turned speeding into "un-National-Socialist behavior."

Hitler began his speech at the International Automobile and Motorcycle Exhibition with the following remarks:

> For the seventh time, I have the pleasure of opening an exhibition that affords us insight, not only into the workings of one of the most important branches of industry in our country, but also of a large part of the world.

Hitler then indulged in sentimental reminiscences of the great "victory" celebrated by the automobile in the days of Gottfried Daimler and Carl Benz. He proceeded, in a five-point overview, to enumerate the measures taken by the National Socialist administration to promote the development of the motorcar. The first four points concerned the evolution in society's attitude toward the automobile: "The automobile is not a luxury article; it is an article of general use." Furthermore, National Socialists had succeeded in lowering costs and prices: "adaptation of price policy to the group of buyers in question." This would lead to an increase in "the confidence of the German Volk in its own car." In fact, the transport infrastructure the National Socialist state had built up over the years was far superior to "the attainments of the past." The most important aspect of Hitler's speech was no doubt contained in the fifth item concerning the creation of "an independent raw material base." A discussion of additional goals to be pursued in the future followed:

> Within the framework of the Four-Year Plan, we sought to free motorization in Germany from dependence on factors abroad and to establish our own independent raw material base. After only a few years, the results of this effort may today already be called gigantic. In part, they have led to revolutionary new inventions whose superiority renders

it unnecessary to use raw materials formerly [involved in the production process], even should they be abundantly available once more in the future.

In an overview of these facts, that in themselves reveal to us the greatness of the results attained, we note the striking evidence of the gigantic increase in production, the extraordinary rise in exports, the lowering of prices for certain models of automobiles and motorcycles, and above all, the excellent work in detail. I open an exhibition today that will splendidly demonstrate these achievements.

In spite of this, along with a few smaller tasks and current problems, there remain great tasks yet to be accomplished:

1. It was understandable that, in times of grave concern for sales, each individual firm, more or less nervously, tried to scan the market and its requirements. Hence, as I already pointed out in my last speech, each firm seized that model that apparently held the greatest promise, without considering how many other factories were already involved with this particular model, or the potential size of the series already in production at any one factory. The resulting competition precluded a potential decrease in prices for certain models. Furthermore, it was understandable that, under the circumstances, a relentless competition for customers ensued that led to an exaggeration of the mechanical element. This meant the incorporation of any type of innovation in the car, no matter how insignificant its practical application, simply because of the belief that one had to oblige a highly selective customer. The conditions that led to this technically and economically undesirable phenomenon no longer exist today. It is less the task of today's German automobile industry to seek potential customers than to satisfy the demands of existing customers. The demand for automobiles is overwhelming. The following are necessary in order to satisfy this demand:

a) Lower prices. This is possible in the long run only if one instills order in the types of models produced. This means that individual firms must achieve a consensus on the type of models to be produced and restrict the overall number of models. Indeed, there must be a simplification of the production program to very few models. It is crucial to augment the total production of automobiles instead of increasing the number of models offered. The multitude of these would ultimately lead to a splintering off into an infinity of models, encumbering the production process and possibly lowering total output.

b) Justice can be done to this call for lower prices only if the weight of cars, particularly of those in mass production, is significantly lowered. Every kilogram of steel needlessly tacked onto an automobile, not only raises its costs and its retail price, but also maintenance expenditures. This in turn leads to more gas being used up, tires wearing out more quickly, and street surfaces needing more frequent replacement. Moreover, a 3,000-kilogram automobile performs no better than one in a 2,000-kilogram category but needlessly taxes the raw materials at our disposal. Two cars in such a heavy weight class simply rob us of the materials needed to produce a third one. I do understand that, in the end, the industry was not capable of arriving at such an ordering of its production on its own. Therefore, I appointed Colonel von Schell as plenipotentiary to see to these tasks being carried out. He is presently issuing binding directives to all appropriate offices within the framework of the Four-Year Plan. His activities have already resulted in exceptional results and hold great promise. He will be in a position to account for his activities for the first time at the 1940 exhibition. The resulting further decline in prices for our automobile industry will undoubtedly have a positive effect on exports.

2. Let the new Volkswagen represent an enormous, real avowal of these principles. All those concerned are called on to devote the greatest energy to press forward the construction of its factory. I sincerely rejoice in being able to afford you a look at the car for the first time in this exhibition. The Volkswagen's ingenious designer has bestowed an object of extraordinary worth on the German Volk and the German economy. It is up to us now to persevere in our efforts to shortly begin mass production of this car.

3. The pending increase in the flow of motorized traffic, due to the Volkswagen and the introduction of a series of low-price trucks, now forces us to take steps necessary to ensure traffic safety. In a period of six years, the German Volk sacrifices nearly as many men to automobile-related accidents as it did in the Franco-Prussian War of 1870–71. This cannot be tolerated. Though the beneficial cooperation of state and party offices and the deployment of traffic police patrols has already brought some relief, these results can neither be regarded as satisfactory nor can the situation be regarded as tolerable.

Above all, there are certain principles and duties all those who participate in traffic on German roads must be aware of: When someone causes a railroad accident today, whether he be the engineer or the switchman, then the responsible party will be regarded as an unscrupulous criminal who is indifferent to the lives of his contemporaries, and he will be punished accordingly. The driver of a private vehicle bears similar responsibility not only regarding his own life, to which he may be indifferent or which may be of little value, but for those of other participants in traffic. Whoever nonchalantly endangers these lives acts in a criminal manner and without any scruples.

Those who cause the nation to lose 7,000 men annually, in addition to imparting to it the care of 30,000 to 40,000 injured, are parasites on the Volk. They act irresponsibly.

They shall be punished as a matter of course, provided they do not escape the national community's (*Volksgemeinschaft*) wrath by dying themselves. It is truly not an art to drive fast and to endanger the lives of others. Rather it is a great art to drive safely, i.e., carefully. Lack of caution coupled with high speed is the most common cause of automobile crashes. And it is discouraging to realize that the majority of those driving could easily spare the extra ten, twenty, or even thirty minutes that, at best, they can hope to save by their insane reckless driving (*Wahnsinnsraserei*), even on long stretches.

This constitutes a call for all those involved in the training of our drivers. One should point out that the new roads in Germany, especially the Autobahn, distinguish themselves in allowing for a high average speed, although peak speeds may well be relatively low. The *Reichsautobahnen* were not built, as many mistakenly believe, for a speed of 120 to 140 kilometers per hour, but rather for an average, let us say, of 80 kilometers. This is easily obtained by driving at a near-constant speed. In the end, this speed over long distances far exceeds that of even our most rapid trains.

Speaking on a matter of principle, it is indeed un-National-Socialist behavior to be inconsiderate towards other *Volksge-nossen*. At this point, I would like to say today that I expect, in particular of representatives of National Socialist institutions, that, in this realm as well, what otherwise would be mere lip service to the *Volksgemeinschaft* will become a matter of course for them. Besides, in the context of our national supply of raw materials, it is absolutely senseless to drive at speeds that increase the rate at which tires need replacement twice or even three or four times. Naturally, these speeds also cause an uneconomical fuel consumption. In general, our race cars and their drivers set speeds and records for performance, as do others who promote motorization. They do not need the support of more or less talented amateur drivers. Consideration for one's fellow man should have priority for all those on our streets; otherwise they cannot expect the *Volksgemeinschaft* or the state to show consideration to them. All of us should unite to make our country, not only the one with the greatest traffic density, but also the one where traffic is the safest. In the interest of maintaining this traffic safety, the state stands determined to mercilessly destroy and exterminate those criminal elements that set up road traps and rob taxi drivers and commit murder.

I wish to take advantage of today's occasion to thank all those who have not only contributed to the domestic significance of the German automobile and motorcycle industry, but also to its renown worldwide: the businessmen for their enterprising spirit; inventors, engineers, and technicians for their ingenuity; and masters of their trade and laborers for their astounding achievements. The German Volk today can justly be proud of the marvels of an industry that once took its first, gingerly steps toward practical application in this country.

In this spirit, I hereby declare the 1939 International Automobile and Motorcycle Exhibition in Berlin open to the public.

▶ October 2, 1940 *German economic problems were to be solved by exploiting conquered areas. This material is from the notes of Hitler's chief of staff, Martin Bormann.*

Hitler exhaustively expounded on the future treatment of Poland in a conference with Bormann, Frank, and Schirach. The meeting took place in Hitler's suite at the Reich Chancellery. First Hitler rendered a detailed account, replete with long citations of numbers, of the productivity of the German laborer in comparison to that of the Pole who was "born for lowly labor." Toward the end of the conversation, Hitler summed up his convictions in the following revealing manner:

> It must absolutely be taken into account that there must be no Polish "masters;" where such masters do exist, they should, as harsh as it may sound, be killed.
>
> Naturally, we must not mix ourselves by blood with the Poles; hence it would be right only if next to the male Polish harvesters, female Polish harvesters came to the Reich. Whatever the Poles then do with one another in the camps is none of our business. No Protestant zealot is to interfere in these things.
>
> Once more the Führer underlined that there must be but one master for the Poles, and this is the German:

Two masters could not and must not exist next to each other; hence all representatives of the Polish intelligentsia are to be killed. This may sound harsh, but it is the law of life.

The General-Government is a reservation for the Poles, one vast Polish labor camp. The Poles also profit for we keep them in good health, take care that they do not starve, and so on. Never must we elevate them to greater heights, or they will simply become anarchists and Communists. It is most appropriate therefore if the Poles retain their Catholicism; Polish priests will be fed by us, and in turn they will direct their herd in the direction we desire. The priests will be paid by us, and in turn they will preach what we desire. If a priest goes against the grain, then he will be dealt with mercilessly. The priests are to keep the Poles mute and stupid; this is essentially in our interest.

Once the Poles are elevated to greater heights, then they will no longer serve as the labor source we need. Besides, it will suffice if every Pole in the General-Government possesses a small garden. Extensive farming is not necessary; the money the Pole needs for his livelihood he must earn by working in Germany. After all, we need these cheap laborers: their low costs will benefit every German, even every German worker. In the General-Government, strict German administration is necessary to maintain order in the labor reservation. This labor reservation means for us the maintenance of agricultural enterprises, in particular of our vast estates; moreover it means a reservoir of laborers.

In summary, the Führer wished to underline the following:

1. Even the poorest German worker and the poorest German peasant has to be at least ten percent better off economically than any Pole.

2. A method has to be searched for and found so that a Pole living in Germany does not directly receive his earnings but instead part of these earnings are sent to the families back in the General-Government.

3. I do not want a German worker to work more than eight hours in general once the situation has normalized again; even if the Pole works fourteen hours, he must still earn less than the German worker.

4. The ideal picture is: The Pole may possess only small plots in the General-Government to secure to some degree his own sustenance and that of his family. Whatever additional money he needs for clothes, additional foodstuffs, and so on, he has to earn through work in Germany. The General-Government is a central issuing department for unskilled workers, in particular for agricultural workers. The existence of these workers will be secured, as cheap laborers will always be needed.

▸ November 14, 1940 *Even during the war, Hitler maintained interest in public works.*

On November 15, Hitler's attention turned to the post-war period once again. He named Ley "*Reichskommissar* for social housing construction." This move reflected his weakness for buildings, for one thing. Beyond this, it was intended to raise the general mood and draw attention to the magnificent post-war period that was coming. The first and most important part of the decree read:

A successful outcome of the war will give the German Reich tasks it shall be able to fulfill only through an increase in its population. It is therefore necessary to close the gaps that the war inflicted on the population (*Volkskörper*) with an increase in the birthrate. Therefore, in the future, the construction of new housing in Germany must satisfy the demands of a healthy life for large families. In order to guarantee the immediate start of a building project in compliance with these principles after the war, preparatory measures are to be taken now. I order:

Article I
Fulfillment of the tasks I set is the mission of the Reich. To carry out this mission, I appoint a Reich commissar for social housing construction who shall be directly responsible to me.

Article II
(1) Construction of housing shall be conducted in accordance with an annual housing construction plan.
(2) The amount of total units of housing to be constructed in a given year shall be determined by me. [Technical details follow.]

► March 21, 1942 *Labor duties were the code words for slave labor.*

On March 21, Hitler signed a decree on a plenipotentiary for labor duties that would initiate measures in violation of international law and would send Sauckel to the gallows. The decree read as follows:

The securing of the manpower required by the entire war economy, especially by armament, necessitates a uniform management, reflecting the needs of the war economy, of the deployment of all available manpower, including foreign recruits and prisoners of war, as well as the mobilization of the yet unused manpower in the Greater German Reich, including the Protectorate, the General-Government, and the occupied territories.

This mission will be carried out by Reich Governor and Gauleiter Fritz Sauckel as plenipotentiary for labor duties within the framework of the Four-Year Plan. In this capacity, he is directly subordinate to the commissioner for the Four-Year Plan.

On the same day, Hitler issued an ordinance on the protection of the war economy. It dealt with the distribution of raw materials.

► May 23, 1942 *Darre, proponent of "blood and soil," was too soft for Hitler.*

On May 23, Hitler dismissed Reich Minister Walter Darre. The following official announcement was published on this topic:

Reich Minister Darre has taken an extended leave of absence
for reasons of health. For this period, the Führer has entrusted
the conduct of the affairs of the Reich minister and Prussian
minister of food and agriculture to Herbert Backe, who is state
secretary in the Reich Ministry of Food and Agriculture.

That was how another old National Socialist and high Nazi Party leader
(*Obergruppenführer*) disappeared. The "theoretician" Darre, who had made
propaganda for the idea of "blood and soil," was replaced by the servile
Backe, who obediently carried out Hitler's order to exploit the occupied
territories with ruthlessness. In spite of starving these areas, the food situation in Germany too began slowly but surely to deteriorate.

► July 24, 1944 *Finally, Hitler's economy became the "total war" economy.*

On July 24 and 25, Goebbels was Hitler's guest at the *Wolfsschanze* headquarters. The result of the talks, which were attended at times by Göring,
was a renewed emphasis on deployment for a total war, even though a "total
war" had already existed since 1942–1943, at the very latest since 1943.
Hitler named Goebbels his "Reich plenipotentiary for total-war deployment." He signed the following decree:

Führer Headquarters, July 25, 1944

The military situation forces us to see to a full utilization of
all forces for the *Wehrmacht* and armament industry. I therefore order:

I.

    1. The president of the ministerial council for the defense
of the Reich, Reichsmarschall Hermann Göring, has
to adapt public life to the necessities of waging a total
war in every respect. For the implementation of this
task, he will suggest to me a "Reich plenipotentiary for
total-war deployment." He will make sure that all public events correspond to the objective of total war and
do not deny forces to the *Wehrmacht* and armament

industry. He will review the entire state apparatus, including the railroads (*Reichsbahn*), Reich postal service, and all public institutions, organizations, and firms, with the goal of freeing a maximum of forces for the *Wehrmacht* and armament industry by a completely rational deployment of men and means, by suspension or restriction of tasks less important to the war, and by a simplification of organization and procedure. For these purposes, he will be entitled to request information from the high Reich offices and issue directives to them.

2. The legal regulations and administrative directives in principle, that will be decreed by the appropriate supreme Reich offices, will be issued in concurrence with the Reich minister and chief of the Reich chancellery, the head of the party chancellery, and the plenipotentiary for the administration of the Reich.

II. The head of the party chancellery will actively support the measures ordered by me in the deployment of the party based on the authority vested in him.

III. Objections to the directives of the Reich plenipotentiary for total-war deployment will be directed to him. Should an agreement not be obtained, then a decision by me will be sought through the offices of the Reich minister and chief of the Reich Chancellery.

IV. Insofar as earlier issued powers and missions contradict the spirit of this decree, they are rescinded.

V. This decree applies to the territory of the Greater German Reich and, correspondingly, the annexed and occupied territories.

The Führer, Adolf Hitler

This bombastic decree basically meant only that all theaters, concert halls, and cabarets were to be closed and the artists called up for military service or work in the armament industry.

▶ March 19, 1945 *Speer's memorandum on the end of the war pointed out the failure of everything Hitler did.*

On the evening of March 18, Hitler received Speer, who handed him a memorandum. Speer knew just as well as Hitler and his Unterführers that the war was lost. However, he was not willing to carry out the measures of destruction on Reich territory that Hitler had ordered for all military retreats in enemy country and that had either been carried out or were supposed to have been carried out. Such destruction would mean the "elimination of all possibilities for the future life of the German Volk," Speer declared.

After the war, a document was presented to the International Military Tribunal at Nuremberg that Speer claimed to have sent Hitler on March 29. Excerpts from it read as follows:

> From the explanations you gave me on the evening [of March 18]—if I did not misunderstand you—it was clear and unequivocal: if the war is lost, then the Volk will also be lost. This fate is unavoidable. It is not necessary to take into consideration the bases the Volk needs for the continuation of its most primitive existence. On the contrary, it is better to destroy these things yourself. After all, the Volk would then have proved the weaker nation, and the future would exclusively belong to the strongest nation of the east. What would remain after this fight would in any event be inferior subjects, since all the good ones would have fallen.

Speer is the only source for these statements. As such, they cannot be regarded as completely authentic. First, the reference to Russia as the "strongest nation of the east" appears odd, since Hitler always spoke of the "primitive" Soviets. Second, he seemed eager, during the last months of his life as well as before, to be recognized and treated by the German Volk as a hero.

There is no doubt about his indifference to the fate of the German people. They served only as an instrument for him to satisfy his lust for power and to achieve his political and military goals. In the past, Hitler had spoken disparagingly about the German Volk on several occasions, in particular to threaten them in the case of their potential "failure." However, while he scolded the intellectuals, officers, and other leading personalities, he spared the so-called "Volk" to the end and showered it with praises. Even in his last proclamation, his political testament of April 29, 1945, he prophesied "the shining rebirth of the National Socialist Movement and the realization of the true *Volksgemeinschaft*."

Even the often cited and condemned Destruction Order (*Zerstörungsbefehl*) of March 19 was in keeping with this line of thought. All destructive measures were supposed to harm only the advancing enemy. They were supposed to be necessary to win this "fight for the life of the Volk." It would be the enemy who, forced to retreat, would "leave behind only scorched earth and abandon all consideration for the population." Hitler's order of March 19 read as follows:

High Command of the Armed Forces (Operations Staff)

Subject: Demolitions on Reich territory

The Führer issued the following order on March 19, 1945:

The struggle for the existence of our people compels us, even within the territory of the Reich, to exploit every means of weakening the fighting strength of our enemy and impeding his further advance.

Every opportunity must be taken of inflicting, directly or indirectly, the utmost lasting damage on the striking power of the enemy. It is a mistake to think that transport and communication facilities, industrial establishments and supply depots that have not been destroyed or have only been temporarily put out of action can be used again for our own ends when the lost territory has been recovered. The enemy will leave us nothing but scorched earth when he withdraws, without paying the lightest regard to the population. I therefore order:

1. All military transport communication facilities, industrial establishments, and supply depots, as well as anything else of value within Reich territory that could in any way be used by the enemy immediately or within the foreseeable future for the continuation of the war be destroyed.

2. The following are responsible for carrying out these demolitions:

    The military commanders for all military establishments, including the transport and communications networks, the Gauleiters and Reichskommissars for defense for all industrial establishments and supply depots and anything else of value. The troops are to give to Gauleiters and Reichskommissars for defense such help as they require to carry out their tasks.

3. This order will be made known to all officers commanding troops as quickly as possible. Directives to the contrary are invalid.

Adolf Hitler

Hitler was always afraid: his fears revolved around his obsession that a vast
secret conspiracy of all Jews was in control of most governments.

VII
The Jewish Question

At the core of Hitler's beliefs was the "Jewish question," code words for Hitler's conviction that there existed an extraordinary organization of Jewish people that was very pervasive and intent on world domination and whose victory would mark the end of human survival.

▸ March 26, 1933 *The boycott of Jewish businesses in 1933 was an effort to influence the Western European and American press, which Hitler believed was Jewish controlled.*

Abroad, the consequences of the new Enabling Act had been perceived more clearly than in the ranks of the non-National Socialist parties in Germany. The commentaries of the foreign press were less than friendly and aroused Hitler's anger. According to his preconception, so-called world Jewry (*Weltjudentum*) was to blame.

As is generally known, Hitler believed in the existence of a secret Jewish world government that influenced all of the governments around the globe to act in its interests; above all, this entity was determined not to allow the German Volk to come to the fore. On the other hand, he believed the solidarity of Jewry throughout the world was so strong that it would be willing to make concessions in order to alleviate any hardships the Jews in Germany might be made to bear. Therefore Hitler was convinced that he need only harass and threaten the German Jews, and foreign governments would be persuaded to yield in their attitude towards Germany and Hitler: world Jewry would instruct these governments to act accordingly.

Without delay he went to work on setting a warning example. As Reich chancellor, he had until now been extremely reserved on this point, rarely exhibiting his anti-Semitic attitude. Since January 30, even the party and the National Socialist press had, on Hitler's orders, refrained from treating the Jewish problem in their customary fashion. This policy was to undergo a radical change.

From March 26 to March 28, Hitler conferred with his Unterführers in Berchtesgaden and Munich in order to outline an operation against German Jews to commence on April 1, with the expressly announced aim of thus putting pressure on world Jewry and foreign governments. On March 28, Hitler issued the following appeal to all party organizations of the Nazi Party to boycott the Jews:

National Socialists! Party Comrades!

After fourteen years of inner conflict, the German Volk—politically overcoming its ranks, classes, professions, and religious divisions—has effected an uprising (*Erhebung*) that put a lightning end to the Marxist-Jewish nightmare. In the weeks following January 30, a unique national revolution took place in Germany. In spite of long years of exceedingly severe suppression and persecution, the masses of millions who support the government of the national revolution have, in a very calm and disciplined matter, given the new Reich leadership legal sanction for the implementation of its reform of the German nation from top to bottom. On March 5 the overwhelming majority of Germans eligible to vote declared its confidence in the new regime.

The completion of the national revolution has thus become the demand of the Volk. The Jewish-Marxist bosses (*Bonzen*) deserted their position of power with deplorable cowardice. Despite all the fuss, not a single one dared to raise any serious resistance. For the most part, they have left the masses they had seduced in the lurch and fled abroad, taking with them their stuffed strongboxes. The authors and beneficiaries of our misfortune owe the fact that they were spared—almost without exception—solely to the incomparable discipline and order with which this act of overthrow was conducted. Hardly a hair of their heads was harmed.

Compare this act of self-discipline on the part of the national uprising in Germany with, for instance, the Bolshevist revolution in Russia, which claimed the lives of over three million people, and you will begin to appreciate what a debt of gratitude the criminals guilty of the disintegration in Germany would owe the powers of the national uprising. Compare the terrible battles and destruction of the revolution of these very November-Men themselves: their shooting of hostages in the years 1918–19; the slaughtering of defenseless opponents—and you will once again perceive how enormous the difference is between them and the national uprising.

The men presently in power solemnly proclaimed to the world that they wanted to live in international peace. In this, the German Volk constitutes a loyal following (*Gefolgschaft*). Germany wants neither worldwide confusion nor international intrigues. National revolutionary Germany is firmly resolved to put an end to internal mismanagement! Now that the domestic enemies of the nation have been eliminated by the Volk itself, what we have long been waiting for will now come to pass. The Communist and Marxist criminals and their Jewish-intellectual instigators, who, having made off with their capital stocks across the border in the nick of time, are now unfolding an unscrupulous, treasonous campaign of agitation against the German Volk as a whole from there. Because it became impossible for them to continue lying in Germany, they have begun, in the capitals of our former enemies, to continue the same agitation against the young national uprising that they had already pursued at the outbreak of the war against the Germany in 1914.

Lies and slander of positively hair-raising perversity are being launched about Germany. Horror stories of dismembered Jewish corpses, gouged-out eyes, and hacked-off hands are circulated for the purpose of defaming the German Volk in the world for a second time, just as they had succeeded in doing once before in 1914. The animosity of millions of innocent human beings, peoples with whom the German Volk wishes only to live in peace, is being stirred up by these unscrupulous criminals. They want German goods and German labor to fall victim to the international boycott. It seems they think the misery in Germany is not bad enough as it is; they have to make it worse!

They lie about Jewish females who have supposedly been killed; about Jewish girls allegedly being raped before the eyes of their parents; about cemeteries being ravaged! The whole thing is one big lie invented for the sole purpose of provoking a new world-war agitation!

Standing by and watching this lunatic crime any longer would mean being implicated.

The National Socialist party will therefore now take defensive action against this universal crime with means that are capable of striking a blow to the guilty parties.

For the guilty ones are among us, they live in our midst day after day and misuse the right to hospitality that the German Volk has granted them.

At a time when millions of our people have nothing to live on and nothing to eat, while hundreds of thousands of German brain-workers degenerate on the streets, these intellectual Jewish men of letters are sitting in our midst and have no qualms about claiming the right to our hospitality.

What would America do were the Germans in America to commit a sin against America like the one these Jews have committed against Germany? The national revolution did not harm a hair of their heads. They were allowed to go about their business as before; but mind you, corruption will be exterminated, regardless of who commits it. Just as belonging to a Christian confession or our own Volk does not constitute a license for criminals, neither does belonging to the Jewish race or the religion of Moses.

For decades, Germany indiscriminately allowed all aliens to enter the country. There are 135 people to one square kilometer of land in this country. In America there are less than 15. In spite of this fact, America saw it fit to set quotas for immigration and even exclude certain peoples from immigrating.

Without any regard to its own distress, Germany refrained for decades from instituting these measures. As our reward, we now have a clique of Jewish men of letters, professors and profiteers inciting the world against us while millions of our own *Volksgenossen* are unemployed and degenerating.

This will be put to a stop now!

The Germany of the national revolution is not the Germany of a cowardly bourgeois mentality.

We see the misery and wretchedness of our own *Volksgenossen* and feel obliged to leave nothing undone that can prevent further damage to this, our Volk.

For the parties responsible for these lies and slander are the Jews in our midst. It is they who are the source of this campaign of hate and lies against Germany. It would be in their power to call the liars in the rest of the world into line.

Because they choose not to do so, we will make sure that this crusade of hatred and lies against Germany is no longer directed against the innocent German Volk, but against the responsible agitators themselves.

This smear campaign of boycotting and atrocities must not and shall not injure the German Volk but rather the Jews themselves—a thousand times more severely.

Thus the following order is issued to all party sections and party organizations:

Item 1: Action committees for a boycott against the Jews:

Action committees are to be formed in each local chapter (*Ortsgruppe*) and organizational body of the Nazi Party for conducting a practical, organized boycott of Jewish businesses, Jewish goods, Jewish doctors, and Jewish lawyers. The action committees shall be responsible for ensuring that the boycott does not do any harm to innocent parties but instead does all the more harm to the guilty parties.

Item 2: Utmost protection for all foreigners:

The action committees shall be responsible for providing the utmost protection for all foreigners, without regard to their religion and origins or race. The boycott is a purely defensive action that is aimed exclusively at the Jewish people (*Judentum*) in Germany.

Item 3: Boycott propaganda:

The action committees shall immediately popularize the boycott by means of propaganda and enlightenment. Basic

principle: no good German is still buying from a Jew or allowing the Jew or his henchmen to offer him goods. The boycott
must be a universal one. It will be borne by the entire Volk
and must hit Jewry where it is most vulnerable.

Item 4: The central management: party leader Streicher:
    In cases of doubt, one is to refrain from boycotting busi-
nesses until informed otherwise by the central committee
in Munich. The chairman of the central committee is party
leader Streicher.

Item 5: Surveillance of newspapers:
    The action committees shall keep the newspapers under
sharp surveillance in order to ascertain the extent to which
they are participating in the enlightenment crusade of the
German Volk against the Jewish smear campaign of atrocities abroad. If newspapers are not doing so or doing so only
within a limited scope, it is to be seen to that they are instantly removed from every building inhabited by Germans. No
German man and no German business is to continue adver-
tising in such newspapers. These papers must become victims
of public contempt, written for fellow members of the Jewish
race but not for the German Volk.

Item 6: Boycott as a means of protecting German labor:
    In conjunction with the factory-cell organizations of the
party, the action committees must carry the propaganda of
the enlightenment concerning the effects of the Jewish smear
campaign of atrocities for German labor and thus for the
German worker into the factories, enlightening the workers
in particular as to the necessity of a national boycott as a defensive measure for the protection of German labor.

Item 7: Action committees down to the last village!
    The action committees must drive into the smallest villages
in order to hit especially the Jewish merchants in rural areas.
As a basic principle, it should be stressed that the boycott is a
defensive measure that was forced upon us.

Item 8: The boycott is to commence on April 1!

The boycott shall not begin in a desultory fashion but abruptly. For this reason all preparations are to be made instantly. The Nazi Party storm troopers and security squads (SA and SS) will be given orders to set up guards to warn the population not to set foot in Jewish shops from the moment the boycott begins. The beginning of the boycott is to be publicized on posters and in the press, in handbills, etc. The boycott shall commence abruptly at 10:00 in the morning on Saturday, April 1. It will be maintained until an order from the party leadership commands that it be discontinued.

Item 9: Demand of the masses for restricted admission:

In tens of thousands of mass assemblies that are to reach as far as the smallest village, the action committees shall organize the demand for the introduction of a restriction to the number of Jews employed in all professions which should be relative to their proportion in the German population. In order to increase the impact of the action, this demand is initially to be confined to three areas:

a) admission to the German secondary schools and universities;

b) the medical profession;

c) the legal profession.

Item 10: Enlightenment abroad:

A further task of the action committees is to ensure that every German who holds any connection whatsoever abroad shall make use of this to circulate in letters, telegrams, and telephone calls in an enlightening manner, the truth that law and order reigns in Germany; that it is the single most ardent wish of the German Volk to be able to pursue its work in peace and live in peace with the rest of the world; and that it is fighting the battle against the Jewish smear campaign regarding atrocities purely as a defensive battle.

Item 11: Calm, discipline, and no acts of violence!

The action committees are responsible for ensuring that this entire battle is conducted with the utmost calm and the greatest discipline. Refrain from harming a single hair of a Jew's head in the future as well! We will come to terms with this smear campaign simply by the drastic force of these measures cited. More than ever before it is necessary that the entire party stand behind the leadership in blind obedience as one man.

National Socialists, you have wrought the miracle of knocking the November state to pieces in a single offensive; you will accomplish this second task the same way. International Judaism (*Weltjudentum*) should know one thing:

The government of the national revolution does not exist in a vacuum. It is the representation of the working German Volk. Whoever attacks it is attacking Germany! Whoever slanders it is slandering the nation! Whoever fights it has declared war on 65 million people! We were able to come to terms with the Marxist agitators in Germany; they will not force us to our knees, even if they are now proceeding with their renegade crimes against the people from abroad.

National Socialists! Saturday, at the stroke of ten, *Judentum* will know upon whom it has declared war.

National Socialist German
Workers' Party / Party Leadership

Contrary to his accustomed practice, Hitler was reluctant to sign his name to this proclamation, opting instead to use the more anonymous "Party Leadership." But his style and attitude are evident in every line; only the eleven individual items seem in part to be the work of Goebbels. Hitler appointed the well-known, violently anti-Semitic Julius Streicher, local Nazi Party leader (*Gauleiter*) in Nuremberg, to head the action, and made all the necessary arrangements on March 28 in Munich.

▶ March 29, 1933 *Hitler pressured Jews in Germany to influence foreign governments.*

The *Völkischer Beobachter* printed the following report of Hitler's address to the cabinet:

Berlin, March 29

Today's Reich cabinet meeting, the first that is to pass far-reaching resolutions on the basis of the Enabling Act, was opened by Reich Chancellor Adolf Hitler with a declaration on the present political situation. The Führer commented on the defensive measures against the Jewish atrocity propaganda abroad. It had been necessary to organize the defense, the Führer stated, because otherwise it would have come from the Volk itself and perhaps taken on undesirable forms. By means of this organization, the defense measure itself would stay under control and molestation motivated by personal grievances as well as acts of violence would be prevented. However, *Judentum* must, according to the Führer, realize that a Jewish war against Germany would hit *Judentum* in Germany itself with full force.

On April 1, the storm troopers and other party forces set up guards in front of Jewish businesses, doctors' practices, law offices, etc. and prevented customers—to the extent that any even dared to make an appearance—from entering. The reaction abroad seemed to lend support to Hitler's theories. The foreign press took great pains to demonstrate reserve in commenting on the new situation in Germany, albeit not because "world Jewry" had instructed them to do so, but rather because they sympathized with the German Jews and did not wish to aggravate their situation.

On April 4, Goebbels was able to draw the following balance: "Atrocity propaganda abroad has abated quite appreciably. Therefore the cabinet has resolved to refrain for the time being from renewing the boycott but will keep it in readiness as a standing threat."

Thus the German Jews remained a means with which Hitler could exert pressure abroad. They were to be exploited as such until their extermination in the Second World War.

▸ September 10, 1935 *At the root of National Socialism rested the concept of race. Many subsequent commentators disagree with Domarus' assertion that Hitler would have thought that the acceptance of his party flag as national standard was more important than the passing of the laws regarding race.*

On September 10, the "Reich Party Congress of Freedom" commenced. Hitler had coined this epithet as well, which was to emphasize Germany's having regained the freedom to rearm and defend itself. The 1935 party congress in Nuremberg achieved a certain sorry significance by the passage of a number of so-called "Nuremberg Laws": namely the "Reich Flag Act," the "Reich Law of Citizenship," and the "Law for the Protection of German Blood and German Honor," all of which were passed by the Reichstag on September 15, 1935. To Hitler, the most important of these was doubtless the "Reich Flag Act," that provided as follows:

Article 1: The Reich colors are black-white-red.

Article 2: The swastika flag is the Reich flag and the national flag. It is, at the same time, the merchant flag.

By virtue of this law, the swastika was finally granted the status of sole official flag of the Reich. The black-white-red banner of imperial Germany, which the National Socialists had disdained as reactionary, now disappeared altogether. Thus the step the dictator had wanted to take in 1933 but had postponed out of consideration for Hindenburg and the German Nationalists now became reality. The black-white-red imperial flag had been a constant thorn in his side during the preceding two-and-a-half years, particularly on the vessels of the merchant marine, where large imperial banners prominently decorated each ship's stern, dwarfing the small swastika flag flying at the bow. Now one Volk had one flag. Hitler did, however, hesitate until November to declare the swastika the new Reich battle flag (*Reichskriegsflagge*).

Although they marked another climax in German racial policy, the two other Nuremberg laws were merely stepping-stones in Hitler's scheme of things: laws and treaties signified for him not the establishment of a lasting legal status but a mere means to an end, born of the moment, which could be overturned any time they grew to constitute a hindrance and lost their calculated effect. Though Hitler did make frequent use of legislative measures in both his foreign and domestic policies, he never regarded them as binding upon himself or "his" state.

As a consequence, he flew into constant fits over his own party comrades who, schooled in the principles of law, would or could not accept the complete arbitrariness with which their despotic leader treated these time-honored precepts. The German people had been accustomed for centuries to an authoritarian state and wanted only clear-cut legal guidelines by which to abide, regardless of whether these complied with prior legislation or past concepts of what was right.

The Nazi Party leaders went along with Hitler's view that the system of Roman law, civil or public, was to be discarded; but in lieu of this they desired new, binding norms, and they pressed for compliance with the legal regulations passed by their own National Socialist state.

Some National Socialist judges at the time still claimed that they were able to remain independent of the will of the state. Of course Hitler had a natural antipathy to this type of view, and there were times when he favored the even more pliant bourgeois members of the judiciary as, for instance, Reich Minister of Justice Dr. Gürtner and State Secretary Dr. Franz Schlegelberger, over the National Socialist legal protectors (*Rechtswahrer*) with Dr. Frank at their head. Hitler's quarrel with the party jurists lasted until April 26, 1942, when he had his appointment to supreme judge explicitly approved by means of a "Resolution of the Greater German Reichstag." From that point on, he was empowered to dismiss any civil servant or judge without regard to that person's duly acquired rights, as they were called, by virtue of office, rank or position.

The so-called "Reich Law of Citizenship" (*Reichsbürgergesetz*) deprived Jews of German citizenship, designating them as "subjects of the state." The third law made public in Nuremberg, the "Law for the Protection of German Blood and German Honor" (*Gesetz zum Schutz des deutschen Blutes und der deutschen Ehre*), put militant National Socialist anti-Semitism into practice: it forbade marriage (*Rassenverrat*) and sexual relations (*Rassenschande*) between Jews and citizens of "German or cognate blood." Furthermore, Jews were prohibited from raising the Reich flag but "allowed to show the Jewish colors," which was meant to be derisive.

The Nuremberg laws clearly constituted a further escalation of the boycott in force since March 1933, leading to even more open demonstrations of violence. On the other hand, it would be wrong to assume that Hitler viewed the 1935 laws as any more than a momentary measure prompted by the flag act, which was his main concern. It was by no means his goal to "solve" the "Jewish question" by legislation or emigration.

He intended to exploit German Jews as a bird in the hand in his foreign policy dealings; later he brutally sent them to the slaughter in the hope that his inhuman actions would persuade the Western powers to comply with his demands.

In 1935, there were still Nazi Party leaders who believed the answer to the "Jewish Question" lay in legislative measures. Even many German Jews held the opinion that a clarification of their legal status, even if it constituted a temporary change for the worse, was better than no clear status at all. Throughout the centuries in which anti-Semitism had existed in Germany, Jews had often been given a different and lesser status. The times had doubtless been difficult, but they had survived, and they hoped to survive the Third Reich—or at least Hitler—and to afterward regain their former equal status.

▶ September 13, 1937 *Hitler was convinced that eastern Jewish Bolshevism and western Jewish democracy were united in the Jewish effort to gain world domination. In his concluding speech at the "Reich Party Congress of Labor" Hitler reiterates his basic themes.*

The main topic of the final address revolved around the threat Bolshevism posed to the entire international community. This indeed amounted to a grandiose attempt by Hitler to flood the "Western Europeans" with rhetoric to persuade them—particularly the English—to entrust Hitler with the defense of Europe against Bolshevism. Once assigned this mission, he hoped to obtain *carte blanche* to proceed in the east at his own discretion. Thus Hitler liberally applied his anti-Communist rhetoric on a scale equaled only in 1932 and 1933. In these years, this tactic had worked miracles for him in winning the favor of the German Nationalists and their adherents. Hitler declared Bolshevism a brain-child of the Jews, a symptom of "an all-encompassing, general attack against modern societal order." Since the "birth of Christianity, the triumphant advance of Mohammedanism or the Reformation," the world had not seen a similar process.

> One would have to be incredibly naive to dispute the fact that Bolshevism does indeed have that international character, i.e., a revolutionary character, in an age when Bolshevism hardly allows a day to pass without stressing its mission of world revolution as the be-all and end-all of its program, and hence the basis for its very existence! Only a bourgeois-democratic politician would refuse to believe what the programmatic foundation of this Red world movement actually is and what, in reality, is revealed in fact to be the most significant feature of this world movement. National Socialism was

not the first to claim that Bolshevism was international; it was Bolshevism itself—the strictest rendering of Marxism—that solemnly proclaimed its international character.

Now, if one of our western Europeans still insists on denying that Bolshevism is international, i.e., that it uses internationally uniform means and methods to pursue the same goal internationally, one is left to fear that, in the near future, we will be hearing from the lips of one such worldly-wise person that by the same token National Socialism, contrary to its program, does not intend to stand up for Germany, and neither does Fascism for Italy! I would nonetheless find it regrettable if we were not to be believed. And it pains me just as much that no one even believes Bolshevism when it itself asserts its intentions and proclaims what it is.

Moreover, he who has no concept of the magnitude of this world menace and above all holds, for reasons of domestic and foreign policy, that he is not allowed to take this menace seriously, will all too easily willfully overlook everything that might perchance be seen to constitute proof of the existence of this world menace.

As National Socialists, we are fully conscious of the origins and conditions of the fight that is today causing unrest in the world. Above all, we comprehend the extent and dimensions of this struggle. It is a gigantic event in terms of world history! The greatest menace with which the culture and civilization of the human race have been threatened since the collapse of the nations in antiquity!

This crisis cannot be compared to any of the otherwise habitual wars or any of the revolutions that take place so often. No, this is an all-encompassing, general attack against modern societal order, against our spiritual and cultural world. This attack is being launched both against the essential character of the peoples per se, against their inner organization, and against the race's own leadership of these bodies politic, as well as against their spiritual life, their traditions, their economies, and all the other institutions that determine the overall essence, character, and life of these peoples or states. This attack is so extensive that it draws nearly all the functions of life into the sphere of its actions. The duration of this battle is unforeseeable. One thing that is certain is that since the birth of Christianity, the triumphant advance of Mohammedanism, or the Reformation, nothing of this type has ever before taken place in this world.

What others profess not to see because they simply do not want to see it is something we must unfortunately state as a bitter truth: the world is presently in the midst of an increasing upheaval, whose spiritual and material preparation and whose leadership undoubtedly proceed from the rulers of Jewish Bolshevism in Moscow.

When I quite intentionally present this problem as Jewish, then you, my party comrades, know that this is not an unverified assumption, but a fact proven by irrefutable evidence.

Hitler then presented a racial interpretation of the states within Europe and portrayed Russia in a manner that corresponded but little to the historic reality.

All our European states originated in what were initially small racial cores but that are to be regarded as the truly powerful and hence determining factors in this constellation. This fact is most pointedly demonstrated in those states in which, as late as our modern times, the formed and guided masses and the forming and guiding powers were not brought into a balance—or perhaps they could not be, but probably this was not even intended. One of these states was Russia. A very thin—not Russian-*Volklich*, i.e., not Slavic—layer of leadership pieced this state together from an assortment of small and even smaller communities to form a virtual colossus of a state, which was seemingly impregnable, but whose greatest weakness always lay in the discrepancy between the number and merit of its ruling class—non-Russian in terms of blood—and the number and merit of its national Russian elements.

Therefore it was particularly easy for a new racial core to successfully penetrate and attack; it intentionally manifested itself as a *Volklich* leader in disguise in contrast to the old, official leadership of state. Here the Jewish minority, which was in no way proportionate to the Russian Volk itself in terms of

numbers, took the devious course of appropriating the leadership of the national-Russian proletariat to succeed, not only
in ousting the former social and state leadership from its position, but in exterminating it without further ado.

Yet for this reason in particular, the Russia of today is basically no different from the Russia of two hundred or three
hundred years ago. A brutal dictatorship by a foreign race that
has seized utter control of the genuine Russian civilization and
is exercising that control commensurately. To the extent that
this process of forming a new state came to its conclusion in
Russia, one might be able to simply take cognizance of the fact
as a historic reality, just as with any other similar situation,
and leave it at that.

Yet now that this Jewish racial core is seeking to bring about
the same effects in other peoples and thereby views modern
Russia as its already-conquered base and bridgehead for further expansion, this problem has exceeded the dimensions of
a Russian problem and become a world problem that will be
decided one way or another, because it must be decided.

After this digression into his version of Russian history, Hitler returned
to the present and delivered an attack upon the Jews, who aimed at plunging democracy into the chaos of Bolshevism.

While one part of the "Jewish fellow citizens" demobilizes
democracy via the influence of the press or even infects it with
their poison by linking up with revolutionary manifestations
in the form of peoples' fronts, the other part of Jewry has already carried the torch of the Bolshevist revolution into the
midst of the bourgeois-democratic world without even having
to fear any substantial resistance. The final goal is then the ultimate Bolshevist revolution, i.e., not, for example, consisting
of the establishment of a leadership of the proletariat by the
proletariat, but of the subjugation of the proletariat under the
leadership of its new and alien master.

Once the incited, insane masses—gone wild and supported by the asocial elements released from the prisons and
penitentiaries—have exterminated the natural, indigenous
intelligence of the peoples and brought them to the scaffolds

to bleed to death, what will remain as the last bearer of—albeit miserable—intellectual knowledge is the Jew. For one thing should be made clear here: this race is neither spiritually nor morally superior, but in both cases inferior through and through. For unscrupulousness and irresponsibility can never be equated with a truly brilliant nature. In terms of creativity, it is an untalented race through and through. For this reason, if it seeks to rule anywhere for any length of time, it is forced to undertake the extermination of the former intellectual upper classes of other peoples.

Otherwise it would naturally be defeated by their superior intelligence within a very short time. That is because, in everything that has to do with true accomplishment, they have always been bunglers, and bunglers they will remain. In the past year, we have shown in a series of alarming statistical proofs that, in the present Soviet Russia of the proletariat, more than eighty percent of the leading positions are held by Jews. This means that not the proletariat is the dictator but that very race whose Star of David has finally also become the symbol of the so-called proletarian state.

And incidentally, we have all experienced the same thing in Germany, too, of course. Who were the leaders of our Bavarian soviet republic? Who were the leaders of Spartakus? Who were the real financial backers and leaders of our Communist Party? Now that is something even the most well-meaning Mister World-Democrat can neither do away with nor change: it was none other than the Jews! That is the case in Hungary, too, and in that part of Spain that the truly Spanish people has not yet recaptured.

Finally arriving at the topic of Spain, Hitler, unrestrained by any consideration of good taste, declared that not Franco, but the "usurpers" in Valencia bore the responsibility for the bloodiness of the revolution.

As you know, in Spain this Jewish Bolshevism proceeded in a similar fashion, starting with the detour of democracy up to open revolution. It is a crass misrepresentation of the facts to claim, as is being done, that the Bolshevist oppressors of the Volk there were invested with legal power, while the fighters of national Spain were illegal revolutionaries.

No! We regard General Franco's men as the genuine and, above all, lasting Spain, and the usurpers of Valencia as the international revolutionary troop hired by Moscow, a troop that today is ravaging Spain and tomorrow may be ravaging a different state.

Hitler then responded to the accusations of the British and the French in connection with Germany's intervention in the Spanish Civil War. Britain and France feared that this imperiled the balance of power within Europe.

While in England and France one professes to be worried about the idea that Spain might even be occupied by Italy or Germany; we are just as appalled in the face of the possibility that it might be conquered by Soviet Russia! By no means would this conquest have to be effected in the form of an occupation by Soviet Russian troops; rather, it will become a *fait accompli* at that moment when a Bolshevized Spain has become a section, i.e., an integral component, of the Central Bolshevist Office in Moscow—a branch that receives both its political directives and its material subsidies from there. In any case, we principally regard every attempt to further expand Bolshevism in Europe as a shift in the European balance of power.

I am merely stating a fact! Therefore we have a serious interest in preventing this Bolshevist plague from spreading even further in Europe. In other respects, in the course of history we have naturally had a number of confrontations with, for instance, national France. However, somehow or other, we still belong together in the great European family of peoples, most of all when we all look deep into our innermost selves.

It is then I believe that, in essence, we do not really want to lose any of the truly European civilized nations. We have each other to thank not only for a certain amount of aggravation and suffering, but also for an incredible cross-fertilization. We have given each other models, examples, and lessons—just as, on the other hand, we have also given each other a certain amount of pleasure and many things of beauty.

If we are just, we have every reason to harbor mutual admiration instead of hate! In this community of the civilized European nations, international Jewish Bolshevism is a totally alien element that has not the slightest contribution to make to our economy or to our culture but instead wreaks only havoc; that has not a single positive accomplishment to show for itself in an international perspective on European and world life but merely propagandistic tables of forged figures and rabble-rousing posters.

▸ February 24, 1938 *Hitler believed that the Jews were the cause of most problems.*

On February 24, the traditional festivities in Munich celebrated the anniversary of the foundation of the party. Hitler's address on this year's occasion was quite a skimpy one. He had exhausted himself in the speech before the Reichstag four days earlier. Only the "international," i.e., the British, "smear campaign"—with regard to the Austrian legion in this case—had to bear the brunt of his wrath that day. The *Völkischer Beobachter* reproduced the following excerpt from Hitler's speech:

In the course of his exposition, the Führer once again spoke of the smear campaign in the international press. The latter had not even had the decency to let eight days pass after his speech of February 20 to renew its campaign of lies and slander against Germany. For instance, the *News Chronicle* was not ashamed to report that, in spite of the Berchtesgaden agreement, Germany was concentrating 40,000 men of the Austrian legion along the border to Austria.

Supposedly exhibited at the legion's headquarters, as the *News Chronicle* maintains, certain maps revealed that an advance upon Austria was to be launched from three different sides. The columns were to converge outside Vienna and then to march on the Austrian capital together. An additional unit of 10,000 men stood ready to invade Czechoslovakia. All these military formations had supposedly been put together recently, after February 4.

Against a background of thunderous applause, the Führer branded these renewed brazen accusations by the *News Chronicle* as filthy lies from beginning to end. They once again revealed how the Jewish international poisoners fabricated and spread their lies.

"We can learn a lesson from this. We shall move against the Jewish agitators in Germany unrelentingly. We know that they are representatives of an international anti-German movement and we shall treat them all accordingly. They can but lie, defame, and slander, while we know very well that not one of these Jewish agitators would ever join the fight in a war, even though they are the only ones to profit from these wars!"

▶ September 27, 1938 *During the Munich crisis, Hitler found the positive reception given Chamberlain and the lack of enthusiasm shown when troops marched on the Wilhelmstrasse in Berlin very irritating.*

It was characteristic of Hitler not to reflect for very long upon his own conduct as a possible source of his failures. Rather, he would quickly redirect the blame upon the Jews. In his mind, the secret world conspiracy of Jews, Freemasons, Illuminati, etc. must have employed some mysterious means to exert a pernicious influence upon the German Volk.

Hitler also believed that they had, through their hideous influence on the Western governments, in particular the British government and Crown, affected their stance. He felt himself reconfirmed in this suspicion by the latest news from abroad: contrary to his predictions, the Western powers had indeed mobilized and renounced neutrality.

A great number of Jews in Germany had blatantly displayed their satisfaction over Hitler's difficulties. To Hitler, this imprudence was sufficient cause to seek revenge. In reaction to the "shameful" display on the Wilhelmstrasse that day, Hitler swore that he would take new repressive action at the earliest possible date, action that would tighten the thumbscrews on the Jews.

▶ November 9, 1938 *Crystal Night*

Already Hitler had plans at hand for an appropriate measure. On November 7, Herschel Grynszpan, a German Jewish emigré, had shot the legation counsellor Ernst Eduard vom Rath at the German Embassy in

Paris. Vom Rath was seriously wounded in the attack. Through his act, Grynszpan had wanted to protest and draw attention to the denial of rights to Jewish people in Germany. In any event, this was how his deed was assessed worldwide.

Even though one might have expected otherwise, Hitler had not mentioned the incident at all in his speech at the Bürgerbräukeller. He had come up with a far better idea. Since vom Rath had been critically wounded in Paris, Hitler was sure that he would eventually die. As soon as news of his death reached Germany, Hitler would stage a "spontaneous" pogrom in all of Germany.

The customary march to the Feldherrnhalle, and from there to the Königsplatz, took place on November 9. For the first time, the Führer's new military sycophants, Keitel and von Brauchitsch, occupied the places of the dismissed generals von Blomberg and von Fritsch. Raeder and Milch also participated in the march.

In a French hospital, the legation counsellor vom Rath died at 4:30 p.m. on November 9 of the various wounds he had sustained in the attack. What had happened in Paris was a nearly perfect replay of the events of February 1936, surrounding the death of Wilhelm Gustloff in Davos. In both cases, a fanatical Jew had assassinated a representative of National Socialist Germany to protest against the treatment of his fellow Jews there. Regrettable as the deaths of innocent people in these events were, it is extremely unlikely that they could have provoked a "spontaneous" outburst of a thirst for revenge among the German people. The latter had no reason to hold the innocent German Jews responsible for the murders. Under normal circumstances, as in the time of the Wilhelm Gustloff case, an assassination such as that of vom Rath would not have led the German population to seek vengeance in a pogrom.

However, and this was the crucial point, Hitler reacted completely differently to the more recent incident. Gustloff had been killed immediately prior to the occupation of the Rhineland. Hitler did not wish to attract international attention; thus, he had to content himself with a relatively moderate speech at Gustloff's funeral.

But the assassination of vom Rath came at a most opportune moment for Hitler to use it as a pretext for staging a Jewish pogrom throughout the Reich. Hitler sought revenge for the smugness of the German Jews during the Sudeten crisis and believed that this measure would be most effective in pressuring the secret Jewish world government. If this organization, and its members among the English inner circle in the City of London, did not react swiftly to induce a more subservient demeanor in the Western powers facing him, he wanted to make it clear that the Jews in Germany would suffer severely in consequence. Their cries of anguish would cause Jews worldwide to shudder. For the rescue of those "hostages" of the same creed and race in Germany, "world Jewry" would influence the British government to espouse a more moderate stance toward Germany. It was the same attempt at blackmail that Hitler would use again and again during the war.

Of course, this was a completely illusory undertaking, given the fact that the secret Jewish world government existed only in Hitler's mind. Nonetheless, even harsh realities could not succeed in convincing Hitler to abandon his preconceived notions of 1919. From early 1942 onward, when it became obvious that the conquest of Russia was not going as planned, he found himself forced to face the consequences of his previous policy and to demonstrate to the West that even his cruelest threats were deadly serious. Hundreds of thousands, finally millions of Jewish people were slaughtered. However, this did not in the least force the Western powers to consider Hitler's terms of peace.

Nevertheless, in 1938, Hitler still believed that a "simple pogrom" would suffice to serve his interests. He himself did not wish to be implicated in the upcoming incidents. In contrast to the Gustloff case in 1936, he remained silent on the Paris murder and avoided making any specific comments in connection with vom Rath's death. He sent only condolences to the parents of the assassinated legation counsellor in the following telegram, dated November 9:

> To Herr and Frau vom Rath, Paris
>
> Please accept my sincere sympathies on the grievous loss with which you have been afflicted as a result of the cowardly assassination of your son.
>
> Adolf Hitler

This was the only public stance Hitler took with regard to the vom Rath case. Goebbels was to execute the pogrom according to his instructions. Hitler not only desired to keep himself aloof from the affair, but he also wanted to keep his favorite branches of the party organization, such as the political leaders and the SS, from being compromised before the German public. Speaking to SS recruits taking their loyalty oath in front of the Feldherrnhalle at midnight on November 9, Hitler made no mention of the Paris affair either. He presented them only with the customary admonishment to devote their lives to his defense:

> Above all, I expect of you to uphold the motto that you have the honor to bear. Your honor must always and under any circumstances be loyalty.

Hitler passed the infamy generated by the persecution of the Jews on November 9 and November 10 on to the branch of the party he had disliked for a long time already: the SA. Up to January 30, 1933, he had taken advantage of their services in his rise to power. But since that date, Hitler had built his political base upon the military. He loathed the SA's ideas on the establishment of an independent militia. The sight of their hats alone sufficed to pique his anger.

In addition, the majority of these hundreds of thousands of SA men were financially independent of the Führer. They neither entertained ambitious designs nor were their professional careers linked to the success of the Movement. Hence, their situation was completely different from that of political leaders and the SS. The SA men patriotically wished only to serve the cause of the fatherland. Because the SA was a thorn in Hitler's side, he saw it as the ideal scapegoat for the excesses of the upcoming pogrom.

The pogrom aimed to destroy Jewish synagogues, wreck Jewish apartments, and seal the fate of the remaining Jewish businesses. The resulting outcry that was certain to be voiced by the German population against such atrocities could then be blamed on the SA—after all, the SA had long proven to be unreliable.

After the war, an inquiry into the participation of the SA men in the so-called "Crystal Night" was undertaken by the International Military Tribunal in Nuremberg. The fact that only a small percentage of the SA membership took to the streets that night (along with other party members and political leaders) matters less than the revelation at the Nuremberg trials that the orders to act that night had not come from the leaders of the SA.

Indeed, the majority of the SA leadership had not yet returned from the festivities in Munich. Instead, the ministry of propaganda and the designated political leaders had issued the directions on how to proceed that night. Those among the SA men who heeded the call to action on that evening of November 9, 1938, had been deceived by Hitler.

The riots and campaigns directed against the Jews that month included dozens of murders that were later investigated at the Nuremberg trials as well. Taken altogether, however, the Pogrom of 1938 would prove to be relatively mild compared to the later abominations during World War II—the annihilation, by the millions, of Jewish men and women, young and old alike. That night nearly all synagogues went up in flames. Jewish families awoke in terror as their furniture was hacked to pieces. There were incidents of theft of Jewish private property, though these were not very frequent. The goal was destruction, a show of force.

Anyone on the streets of the Jewish quarters of German cities that night would have heard the crashes of breaking furniture and china, a sound they heard again during the Second World War bombings of German cities, when the air shocks from the exploding bombs shook houses and destroyed their furnishings.

The party and state feigned complete surprise on the morning of November 10, when the smoldering ruins of the synagogues were exposed to daylight. With glass of broken windows from Jewish homes scattered about the streets, the government decided that only a "spontaneous outburst of popular fury" could explain such odd behavior, and immediately endeavored to direct this "public outrage" into more orderly channels by staging official marches to protest the assassination in Paris. Göring imposed a "penalty," in the amount of one billion marks, upon the Jewish community in Germany, for its "sin."

Hitler refrained from commenting on the pogrom. Even his "secret speech" in Munich before the German press on the evening of November 10 contained no reference to the events that had taken place less than twenty-four hours earlier.

▶ January 30, 1939 *In his speech to the Reichstag on this date, Hitler set forth numerous policy points. Among them was the very significant "warning to Jews" to which Hitler often referred (incorrectly stating the warning was given in his September 1, 1939 speech to the Reichstag). As Hitler moved toward armed confrontation with the Western powers, he blamed the Jews for thwarting the aspirations of the German Volk and promised "financial Jewry"* (Finanzjudentum) *with annihilation* (Vernichtung) *should war come, as indeed, he certainly planned.*

It is evident that Hitler's firm belief in the identical nature of domestic and foreign policy extended to the Jewish issue as well. National Socialism would "wrestle the Jewish world enemy to the ground" on the international stage, just as it had been vanquished in "Germany's interior." Hence, Hitler believed it appropriate once again to rage on furiously against international Jewry and the supposed secret Jewish world government. He proclaimed:

> The peoples of the world will realize within a short time that National Socialist Germany does not desire to elicit the enmity of other peoples. Allegations of the aggressive designs entertained by our Volk on other peoples are the products of a deranged, hysterical mind or blatant lies by certain politicians struggling for survival. In certain states, businessmen devoid of any conscience try to save their financial interests by propagating these lies. Above all, it is international Jewry that seeks thereby to gratify its thirst for vengeance and its insatiable hunger for profit. And this constitutes the greatest libelous claim ever levied against a great and peace-loving Volk.
>
> After all, German soldiers have never fought on American soil other than for the cause of America's independence and freedom. Yet American soldiers were shipped to Europe and contributed to the suppression of a great nation struggling to preserve its liberty. It was not Germany that attacked America; it was America that attacked Germany. And it did so, according to the findings of an investigative committee in the American House of Representatives, without any compelling reason other than perhaps capitalist considerations.
>
> Nevertheless, let there be no doubt as to one point: all these attempts will not in the least sway Germany from its reckoning with Jewry. I would like to say the following on the Jewish question: it is truly a shameful display when we see today the entire democratic world filled with tears of pity at the plight of the poor, tortured Jewish people, while remaining hardhearted and obstinate in view of what is therefore its obvious duty: to help. All the arguments with which they seek to justify their non-intervention lend only further support to the stance of Germans and Italians in this matter.

For this is what they say: "We"—that is the democracies—"cannot possibly admit the Jews!" And this those world powers claim who can boast no more than ten persons per square kilometer while we must accommodate and feed 135 persons per square kilometer.

Then follow assurances: "We cannot take them unless they receive a certain monetary contribution from Germany to facilitate immigration." Small matter that Germany has already been good enough to provide for centuries for these elements, who possessed little more than infectious political and sanitary diseases. What this people possesses today, it obtained at the cost of the not-so-cunning German Volk by means of the most base manipulation. What we do today is no more than to set right the wrongs these people committed. In the days when the German Volk lost its savings, accumulated throughout decades of hard work, thanks to the inflation incited and nurtured by the Jews; when the rest of the world took the German Volk's assets abroad; when it expropriated our colonial possessions; at that time such philanthropic considerations did not yet play such an influential role in these democratic statesmen's considerations. I wish to assure these gentlemen that, owing to a fifteen-year-long crash course in democracy, we are today steeled against any sentimentality.

We had to live to see how, at the end of the war, after hunger and destitution had killed more than 800,000 children of our Volk, because of the gruesome articles of a *Diktat* that the democratic, humane world apostles had forced on us in the guise of a peace treaty, nearly a million dairy cows were driven from our barns. We had to live to see, one year after the end of the war, over one million German prisoners of war still held captive without any perceptible cause. We had to suffer the sight of how, along our frontiers, far more than one-and-a-half-million Germans bereft of their possessions were driven from their homes with no more than their shirts on their backs. We had to bear the sight of millions of our *Volksgenossen* torn from us, without anyone according them a hearing, and were left without any means of sustaining themselves in the future.

Once he had securely placed the blame on the Jews for the bad fortune Germans had suffered throughout the twentieth century, Hitler set out to steel the audience before him "against any sentimentality" and humanitarian concerns. And—in the context of his previously mentioned strategy of blackmail,—he threatened the "annihilation (*Vernichtung*) of the Jewish race in Europe" in the event that foreign powers should again declare war on Germany.

> I could supplement these examples by dozens of yet more gruesome ones. Do not reproach me on the grounds of your humanitarian concerns. The German Volk does not wish to be governed by another people; it does not wish others to determine its affairs in its place. France for the French; England for the English; America for the Americans, and Germany for the Germans!
>
> We are determined to undermine the efforts of a certain foreign people to nest here; a people whose members know how to capture all leading positions. We will banish this people. We are willing to educate our own Volk to assume these leadership functions. We have hundreds of thousands of the most intelligent children of peasants and workers. We will have them educated, and we are already educating them. We are hoping that one day we can place them all in the leading positions within the state along with others from our educated classes. No longer shall these be occupied by members of a people alien to us.
>
> Above all, as the literal meaning of the term already indicates, German culture is exclusively German; it is not Jewish. Hence we shall place the administration and the care for our culture in the hands of our Volk. Should the rest of the world be outraged and protest hypocritically against Germany's barbarous expulsion of such an extraordinary, culturally valuable, irreplaceable element, then we can only be astonished at the consequences such a stance would imply.
>
> Should not the outside world be most grateful to us for setting free these glorious bearers of culture and placing them at its disposal? In accordance with its own statements, how is the outside world to justify its refusal to grant refuge in its various countries to these most valuable members of the human race?

For how will it rationalize imposing the members of this race on the Germans of all people? How will the states so infatuated with these "splendid people" explain why they are suddenly taking refuge in all sorts of pretenses just in order to deny asylum to these people?

I believe the earlier this problem is resolved, the better. For Europe cannot find peace before it has dealt properly with the Jewish question.

It is possible that the necessity of resolving this problem sooner or later should bring about agreement in Europe, even between nations that otherwise might not have reconciled themselves as readily with one another. There is more than enough room for settlement on this earth. All we need to do is put an end to the prevailing assumption that the dear Lord chose the Jewish people to be the beneficiaries of a certain percentage of the productive capacities of other peoples' bodies and their labors. Either the Jews will have to adjust to constructive, respectable activities, such as other people are already engaged in, or, sooner or later, they will succumb to a crisis of yet inconceivable proportions.

And there is yet one more topic on which I would like to speak on this day, perhaps not only memorable for us Germans: I have been a prophet very often in my lifetime, and this earned me mostly ridicule. In the time of my struggle for power, it was primarily the Jewish people who mocked my prophecy that one day I would assume leadership of this Germany, of this state, and of the entire Volk, and that I would press for a resolution of the Jewish question, among many other problems. The resounding laughter of the Jews in Germany then may well stick in their throats today, I suspect.

Once again I will be a prophet: should the international Jewry of finance (*Finanzjudentum*) succeed, both within and beyond Europe, in plunging mankind into yet another world war, then the result will not be a Bolshevization of the earth and the victory of Jewry, but the annihilation (*Vernichtung*) of the Jewish race in Europe.

Thus, the days of propagandist impotence of the non-Jewish peoples are over. National Socialist Germany and Fascist Italy possess institutions that, if necessary, permit opening the eyes of the world to the true nature of this problem. Many a people is instinctively aware of this, albeit not scientifically versed in it. At this moment, the Jews are still propagating their campaign of hatred in certain states under the cover of press, film, radio, theater, and literature, which are all in their hands. Should indeed this one Volk attain its goal of prodding masses of millions from other peoples to enter into a war devoid of all sense for them, and serving the interests of the Jews exclusively, then the effectiveness of enlightenment will once more display its might. Within Germany, this enlightenment conquered Jewry utterly in the span of a few years.

Peoples desire not to perish on the battlefield just so that this rootless, internationalist race can profit financially from this war and thereby gratify its lust for vengeance derived from the Old Testament. The Jewish watchword "Proletarians of the world, unite!" will be conquered by a far more lofty realization, namely: "Creative men of all nations, recognize your common foe!"

▸ January 30, 1942 *Hitler often referred to his "prophecy" of January 30, 1939, although he fell into the habit of ascribing the statement to his declaration of war speech on September 1, 1939, which was incorrect. Here, in his speech to a mass rally of armament workers, nurses from military hospitals, and wounded soldiers in the Berlin Sportplast, he again referred to the "prophecy."*

Now Hitler voiced his anger and frustration with the Jews. He announced their extermination in Europe, because "all attempts to reach an understanding with the English had proved futile." If England and international Jewry wished to prevent this annihilation, then they would have to make peace with him at last. Otherwise, Jewry, as "the most evil enemy of the world of all time will at least be finished with for the next millennium." Hitler declared as follows:

> We are fully aware that this war can end either in the extermination of the Aryan peoples or in the disappearance of Jewry from Europe. I said as much before the German

Reichstag on September 1, 1939. I wish to avoid making hasty prophecies, but this war will not end as the Jews imagine, namely, in the extermination of the European-Aryan peoples; instead, the result of this war will be the annihilation of Jewry. For the first time, the old, truly Jewish rule of "an eye for an eye, a tooth for a tooth" will obtain.

And the more the fighting expands, the more anti-Semitism will spread—let that be said to world Jewry. Anti-Semitism will be fed in every prisoner-of-war camp, in every family enlightened to the reason why, in the end, it has to make this sacrifice. And the hour will come when the most evil enemy of the world of all time will at least be finished with for the next millennium.

▸ February 14, 1942 *The Holocaust intensified. Subsequent research demonstrates that the Nazi government had already decided to kill the Jews in its control by this time. So Domarus' connection of the Holocaust with the failure to recieve a peace offer from the British is not correct.*

Two weeks had passed since Hitler had threatened a massacre of the Jews, and the English had still not put out a feeler for peace to Germany! His hope that the fall of Singapore would cost Churchill his job had not come true either. Now the Führer had no choice but to go ahead with the massacre of the Jews. By this undertaking he would, so he said, "render mankind an invaluable service." He once again took Goebbels to task, telling him of his resolve to do away ruthlessly with the Jews in Europe. [Hitler said to Goebbels:]

> One should not get sentimental here. The Jews deserve the catastrophe that they are experiencing today. With the annihilation of our enemies, they will experience their own annihilation. We must speed up this process with cold brutality. With this, we render mankind an invaluable service, since it has suffered under and has been tortured by Jewry for millennia. We must enforce this clear anti-Semitic attitude in our own Volk, too, despite the resistance of some circles.

Hitler claimed that he would make this clear to the "group of officers" to whom he would shortly speak. However, this was just big talk intended to impress and encourage Goebbels. Hitler was not about to inform the 9,883 officer candidates he would speak to at the Sportpalast in Berlin on February 15 of the planned annihilation of the Jews.

▶ March 1, 1942 *The Holocaust was Hitler's main objective.*

On the same day, he signed a decree on the "systematic spiritual struggle against Jews, Freemasons, and their allies, the . . . opponents of National Socialism." He called this a "necessary war mission." The decree read as follows:

> Jews, Freemasons, and their allies, the ideological opponents of National Socialism, are the authors of the war presently directed against the Reich. The systematic spiritual struggle against these powers is a necessary war mission.
>
> I have therefore instructed *Reichsleiter* Alfred Rosenberg to carry out this mission in conjunction with the chief of the high command of the *Wehrmacht*. His operational staff for the occupied territories is authorized to search for relevant materials in libraries, archives, lodges, and other ideological or cultural institutions of all types, and to have this material confiscated for the ideological work of the Nazi Party and subsequent research work at the National Socialist Academy.
>
> The same regulations apply to cultural goods in Jewish possession or ownership, or that are derelict, or whose origin is not incontestably established. Implementing regulations on cooperation with the *Wehrmacht* will be decreed by the chief of the high command of the *Wehrmacht* in agreement with *Reichsleiter* Rosenberg. In his capacity as the Reich minister for the occupied eastern territories, *Reichsleiter* Rosenberg will take the necessary measures in the eastern territories under German administration.
>
> Adolf Hitler

This decree on the "spiritual struggle against" the Jews obviously was intended to mask the simultaneous beginning of the "physical struggle," that is, the extermination of the Jews. Even though anti-Semitism had been elevated to a political philosophy in the Third Reich and the torment and harassment of Jews had become a feature of everyday life, never before had there been talk of literally exterminating them and killing them off without exception. It was only recently that Hitler had threatened this, for example, in his speeches of January 30, 1941 and January 30, 1942, and in his message of February 24, 1942. Initially, he had done so by making "prophecies." Now, however, after the failure of the eastern campaign had become evident, he turned to the practical implementation of his plan. And here some resistance had to be overcome first. It took some time to get Goebbels used to the idea of the total, physical annihilation of the Jews in Europe, that is, those in German hands. His diary entries show this. It was a different matter, of course, with Heinrich Himmler and his men. Hitler had long habituated them not only to accept all his ideas—no matter how crazy or criminal—as absolutely correct, but also to carry them out to the letter.

Still on March 7, 1942, Goebbels wrote in his diary: "There are still over eleven million Jews in Europe. Sometime later on, they will have to be concentrated in the east; it is possible that after the war we will be able to assign them an island, perhaps Madagascar." On March 20, 1942, he wrote: "In this matter [the question of the Jews], the Führer is as inexorable as ever: the Jews are to be thrown out of Europe, if necessary with use of the most brutal means."

For Goebbels, the situation then underwent a complete change. On March 27, 1942, he wrote: "Jews are now being deported to the east from the territory ruled by the General-Government, starting with Lublin. Here will be used a fairly barbarous method that one can't come close to describing; not much will remain of the Jews themselves. On the whole, it can be determined that sixty percent of them will have to be liquidated, only forty percent being usable for the purposes of labor. The former district leader of Vienna, who is in charge of the action, is showing a good deal of circumspection in following a method that does not attract a lot of attention. Justice is being meted out to the Jews; although it is barbarous, they fully deserve it. The prophecy that the Führer uttered against them for having brought about a new world war now begins to be realized in the most frightful way. In these matters, sentimentality must not be permitted to hold sway. If we did not defend ourselves against the Jews, they would destroy us. It is a struggle of life and death between the Aryan race and the Jewish bacillus. No other government and no other regime had the strength to resolve this question in its generality. In this respect too the Führer is the constant champion and spokesman of a radical solution.

"The ghettos being vacated in the cities of the General-Government may now be filled with Jews deported from the Reich, and here, after a certain time, the process will start again. It's no laughing matter for Judaism; the fact that its representatives in Europe must pay dearly for the organizing and propagandizing of war against Germany by its representatives in England and America is no doubt justified."

As mentioned before and illustrated by example, the doglike subservience of the SS men to Hitler's will formed a parallel case to the subservience of Napoleon's old guard. Had Napoleon proclaimed the idea of killing the Jews in his hands, his guardsmen would undoubtedly have done this, just as they had killed, on the retreat from Moscow, all Russian prisoners by shooting them through the base of the skull.

Hitler's manservant Linge reported on secret conferences between the Führer and Himmler. Nobody else was allowed to be present at these talks, which in all likelihood concerned the annihilation of the Jews. In practice, the procedure was to be the following: first, Jews in the east, in Poland and Russia, would be exterminated, along with their wives and children, and then, under the pretext of a "resettlement" (*Aussiedlung*), the Jews in Germany and Western Europe would be deported to the east so that the whole process of annihilation could begin anew.

Hitler's argument for this monstrous crime was quite simple: Jews, like Russians, were not human. They were "animals and beasts." If valuable men had to die each day at the front, then it was really of no consequence if such vermin like the Jews were killed. They were no different from "tuberculosis bacilli." If such "innocent natural creatures as rabbits and deer" had to die, then why should "the beasts, who want to bring us Bolshevism, be spared?" Hitler was known to be very fond of animals. He shared this fondness with a number of mass murderers.

In spite of all of Hitler's reasons for the annihilation of the Jews, it was not easy for Himmler to find SS men willing to implement the cowardly annihilation of millions of defenseless human beings: men, women, children. They not only had to be encouraged by extra bottles of brandy; in addition, ethical arguments had to be employed: as difficult and unpleasant as this task might be, those chosen to carry it out had to realize the "exalted nature of their mission," by means of which they were rendering a service to the fatherland, Europe, and mankind.

This confusion of concepts was carried to an extreme reminiscent of the persecution of the Christians in ancient Rome that had prompted Christ to make the following prophecy: "I have said all this to you to keep you from giving up your faith. They will expel you from the synagogues; indeed, the time will come when anyone who kills you will think he is offering service to God." And had not Adolf Hitler written in *Mein Kampf*: "By defending myself against the Jew, I am fighting for the work of the Lord"?

Besides the extermination of the Jews, Hitler also envisioned and carried out the annihilation of the Gypsies. In his eyes, they were vermin, beasts, tuberculosis bacilli, too. In this respect, an ordinance by the then Reich minister of labor is of interest, an ordinance that decreed the "equality of Gypsies and Jews under the labor laws."

As monstrous as Hitler's massacre of the Jews was, as much as it shamed Germany, it nevertheless formed only one part of his rule; and it was not the cause of the fall of the Führer and the Third Reich. Their fate was sealed at eleven o'clock on September 3, 1939. And the reason for it was the same as for the collapse of the Kaiser's empire, namely, the attempt to expand Germany's borders by the use of force. This is a clear, historical fact, and it would be dangerous to try to diminish it by pointing to the Holocaust.

▸ September 30, 1942 *Hitler again returned to his "prophecy", again misdated in this speech at a "Volk rally" opening the Winter Relief Fund effort at the Berlin Sportpalast.*

> At the Reichstag session of September 1, 1939, I said two things: First, since this war was forced on us, neither the power of arms nor time will defeat us. Second, should Jewry instigate an international world war in order to exterminate the Aryan people of Europe, then not the Aryan people will be exterminated, but the Jews. The wire-pullers of this insane man in the White House have managed to pull one nation after another into this war. Correspondingly, however, a wave of anti-Semitism swept over one nation after another. And it

will continue to do so, taking hold of one state after another. Every state that enters this war will one day emerge from it as an anti-Semitic state. The Jews once laughed about my prophecies in Germany. I do not know whether they are still laughing today or whether they no longer feel like laughing. Today, too, I can assure you of one thing: they will soon not feel like laughing anymore anywhere. My prophecies will prove correct here, too.

These prophecies were to prove correct, at least as far as the Jews living within the German sphere of influence were concerned. His extermination machinery was running at top capacity. In the extermination camps at Auschwitz, Belcec, Chelmno, Sibibor, Treblinka, Wolcek, and so on, millions of Jews from Russia, Poland, Germany, France, Holland, Belgium, Norway, and the Balkans were herded together, including women, children, and the elderly. There they were shot, massacred, or gassed with Zyklon B.

These atrocities perpetrated by Hitler's henchmen were unprecedented in history, with regard both to their systematic nature and their technical detail. The persecution of Christians in antiquity, the slaughter of the Saxons by Charlemagne, the Jewish pogroms of the Middle Ages and modern times, the guillotinings of the French Revolution, the murders committed by the Cheka in Bolshevik Russia, the extermination of the Armenians by the Turks—all these pale in comparison with the insane, completely senseless massacre of the Jews by Adolf Hitler and his accomplices.

▸ February 24, 1943 *Hitler did not attend the 1943 commemoration of the Nazi Party's founding just as he avoided the ceremony in 1942. Instead, he wrote his speech and had it read to the assembled party faithful. In this speech, Hitler continued to demonstrate his obsession regarding Jewish control of his enemies.*

Party comrades!

Party comrade Adolf Wagner, who conveyed my greetings to you in the past year, has been seriously ill for many months and is unable to attend the present rally. I have therefore asked party comrade Esser, who as one of my first comrades in arms attended the foundation assembly of the movement, to tell you in my name what I, because of the circumstances, am unable to tell you for the second time now. The German armed forces, who fought excellently this winter, as they have done since the beginning of this war, are involved in a bitter struggle against the danger to the world instigated by the banking houses of New York and London together with the Bolshevik Jews in Moscow.

I myself am in the east and therefore unable to join you on this day. Nevertheless, my thoughts are with you, more so this year than ever before. After all, what fate would have awaited our Volk and all of Europe, had not those ideals of the National Socialist revolution been proclaimed in this hall on February 24, 1920, ideas which took hold of the German Volk and gave it the necessary force not only to restrain the Jewish danger to the world today, but also to crush it in the end!

The thunderous shout (*Sturmlied*) of our unforgettable, dear old Dietrich Eckart is again proving to be a trumpet-call in these months. It can wake up people, open their eyes to the fate that would await all of us in the present and our children in the future—and beyond this, all European peoples—if we do not succeed in bringing about the failure of the devilish plan of the Jewish international criminals. You are all aware of the circumstances, which allowed the enemy in the east, similar to the forces of nature last winter, to reverse in the course of this winter a part of those successes secured by the heroism of our soldiers in the summer. However, you also know that the path along which our party has traveled has likewise not been a secure or comfortable way to success. Indeed, we suffered countless difficulties and setbacks, which the same enemies dealt to us and against whom we must fight today—against the whole world.

As I proclaimed the party program in this hall in the year 1920 and my resolution to destroy with zealousness the enemies of our Volk, I was a lonely and unknown man. Germany had suffered its most profound humiliation. The number of those who believed in its restoration was negligible, and there were even fewer who still hoped for this to happen in our generation. The few followers who joined me at the time were opposed by the almost crushing superiority of the enemy. For every hundred National Socialists, there were millions of

opponents, partly blinded, partly seething with hatred. And
that is not to count those men of little faith who always wait
first for success in order to march on the victorious side with
a brave heart.

What a difference compared with the struggle of today!
No matter how great the coalition of our enemies is, as a power it is less than the strength of the alliance of those peoples
who oppose the Bolshevik-plutocratic destruction. The struggle of the National Socialist movement was often in a position
in which only the most fanatical of its faithful could still believe in a victory, while its otherwise shrewd opponents were
already firmly convinced that they had killed the idea and the
party. Nevertheless, our movement was born again each time;
it overcame every setback and emerged stronger than before
from every crisis. The party was always upheld by the unbend-
ing decision not to capitulate under any circumstances and
not to give up the fight in any case, until the conspiracy of our
enemies at home was crushed and eliminated.

My party comrades!

I taught you this fanaticism. Please rest assured that I am today inspired by the same fanaticism, which will never leave me
as long as I live. You also received this faith from me, and rest
assured that this faith is stronger in me today than ever before. We will break and crush the power of the Jewish international coalition. Mankind in its struggle for its freedom, life,
and daily bread, will gain the final victory in this struggle.
Just as in the time of our struggle for power, every attack by
our enemies and every one of their apparent successes made
me more dogged in my determination not to stray from the
path that sooner or later had to lead to victory, so too I am
today suffused by the same will to persevere to the bitter end
in the task which destiny has given me.

I have a right to believe that Providence has chosen me to
fulfill this task. For without its blessings, I, as an unknown
man, would never have been able to set out on the path leading
from this hall across so many hurdles and through so many

attacks to the takeover of power and, finally, to this struggle which has been crowned by victories the like of which have never been seen in world history, but who has also been weighed down by many worries which would have broken many weaker characters. However, I was blessed by Providence in having a sworn community around me in such hours, a community which in devoted faithfulness always regarded the common fate as its own and which always stood loyally by me, as its Führer in this struggle, and will always stand by me.

As I address this message to you, I do so out of the same profound gratitude as in the past year. In you, my dear party comrades, I have found not only the first representatives of the National Socialist ideology but also of the National Socialist mind-set, a mind-set which has proved its worth in such an unheard-of manner in particular in times of great trial. The bourgeois opportunists failed to understand this, as did the masses of our old parties, indoctrinated by Jewry. Why should this be different today?

There is only one difference: today, the gigantic throng of the German Volk stands behind the new Reich. The Volk is unconditionally determined to accept the new Reich idea, which is inspired by the National Socialist world-view. The party has become the unshakable incarnation of this power. Today it is the internal guarantor not only of victory, but also of the preservation of our Volk in the future. It must fulfill its second great historic task—especially during these months and perhaps in the coming years, too—which is to shake up the German nation constantly, make it aware of the magnitude of the danger, reinforce the sacred faith that will overcome, give strength to weaklings and mercilessly destroy saboteurs. It will work to enlighten in those cases where enlightenment is desired, break terror with ten-times-greater terror, exterminate traitors no matter who they might be and what disguise they are using to realize their intentions against the people.

Even if the elite of the National Socialist movement's men confronts the enemy today and fulfills its duty as soldiers in an exemplary fashion, the old fighters remain the strongest zealots in the assertion of the German will to life. Year after year,

they are joined by a new cohort from Germany's youth, totally educated in accordance with National Socialist principles, forged together by the ideas of our people's community
(*Volksgemeinschaft*), and willing to move against anyone who
should dare to sin against our fight for freedom. In addition,
just as in the time of the party's struggle for power, our female
party comrades, our German women and girls, were the most
reliable supports of the movement, so now again the multitude of our women and girls form the strongest element in the
struggle for the preservation of our Volk.

After all, thank God, not only the Jews in London and
New York but also those in Moscow made clear what fate
might be in store for the German Volk. We are determined
to be no less clear in our answer. This fight will not end with
the planned annihilation of the Aryan but with the extermination of the Jew in Europe. Beyond this, thanks to this
fight, our movement's world-view will become the common
heritage of all peoples, even of our enemies. State after state
will be forced, in the course of its fight against us, to apply
National Socialist theories in waging this war that was provoked by them. And in so doing, it will become aware of the
curse that the criminal work of Jewry has laid over all peoples,
especially through this war.

As our enemies thought in 1923 that the National Socialist Party was defeated for good and that I was finished with in
the eyes of the German Volk because of my trial, so they actually helped National Socialist ideology to spread like wildfire
through the entire German Volk and convey the essence of
Jewry to so many million men, as we ourselves would never
have been able to do under normal circumstances. In the same
manner international Jewry, which instigated this new war,
will find out that nation after nation engrosses itself more
and more in this question to become finally aware of the great
danger presented by this international problem.

Above all, this war proves the irrefutable identity of plutoc-
racy and Bolshevism, and the common ambition of all Jews to
exploit nations and make them the slaves of their international guild of criminals. The same alliance we once faced as our

common enemies in Germany, an alliance between the stock exchange in Frankfurt and the "Red Flag" in Berlin, now again exists between the Jewish banking houses in New York, the Jewish-plutocratic class of leaders in London, and the Jews in the Kremlin in Moscow. Just as the German Volk successfully fought the Jewish enemy at home as a consequence of this realization and is now about to finish it off for good, the other nations will increasingly come to their senses in the course of this war. Together, they will make a stand against the race that is seeking to destroy all of them.

Just as the Jews rejoiced about each supposed setback that we suffered during our struggle within the Reich, and just as they confused their feverish hopes with the hard facts, so they believe today, just as they did last winter, that they will shortly reach their thousand-year-old goal. However, just as they did last year, they will also suffer a terrible disappointment this time. On the contrary, the German Volk will now even more summon and deploy its forces to a degree never before seen for a war in the history of mankind. We will not hesitate one second to seek retribution in this fateful struggle from those countries responsible for the outbreak of this war. We regard it as a matter of course that foreign lives cannot be spared at a time that demands so many difficult sacrifices of our own lives. In indissoluble, loyal association with our allies, we will carry out a mobilization of the spiritual and material values of Europe, the like of which our continent has never seen before in its millennia-old history. This is necessary in order to secure an independent ethnic life for all of Europe, a life that has been the basis not only for our shared culture but also for the material existence of this continent.

My old party comrades,

I greet you as always with an overflowing heart. I thank you for having made it possible for me at the time to start out successfully on the path that was a prerequisite for the salvation of the German Reich and for all of Europe. My thoughts are with you at this hour, just as they always are. During these months, weeks, and days, my duty forces me constantly to think and work, and prepare the coming turn of events for those who as the fighters of our Volk, together with our allies, are fashioning the fate of the world: our brothers and comrades, the German soldiers especially at the front in the east, where the future of Germany and Europe will be decided. The outcome must and will be our victory!

▶ April 17, 1943 *As the war ground on, Hitler believed that killing Jews was more important than winning the war. Admiral of the former Austro-Hungarian Navy, Miklos Horthy had ruled Hungary as Regent (since the throne was vacant) since 1920.*

On April 16 and 17, Horthy was Hitler's guest at Klessheim Castle. In addition to political and military matters, the talks mostly concerned the round-up of Hungarian Jews and their transport to concentration camps, that is, extermination camps. Horthy did not want to deal with this problem, and so Hitler felt forced to explain to him the necessity of the extermination of the Jews in the following manner:

> If the Jews do not want to work there, then they will be shot. If they cannot work, they will go to seed. They must be treated like the tuberculosis bacillus that can infect a healthy body. This is not cruel if you consider that even innocent creatures of nature, like the rabbit and the deer, are shot so that they cannot do harm. Why should you be more kind to these beasts, who want to bring us Bolshevism? Nations that do not fight off the Jews go to seed. The decline of the once-so-proud Persian people is one of the most famous examples of this. Today, they lead as pitiful an existence as the Armenians.

Goebbels noted the following on Hitler's talks with Horthy:

> Horthy did not hear many kind words from the Führer. . . . The Hungarian state is completely infiltrated by Jews. In his talks with Horthy, the Führer did not succeed in convincing him of the necessity of stronger measures. Horthy himself and his family are very much tangled up with the Jews and he will continue to put up a fierce resistance against actively

attacking the Jewish problem in the future. He lists quite valid humanitarian arguments that do not, however, apply in this context. There can be no talk of humanitarianism regarding the Jews. Jewry must be thrown to the ground. The Führer made an all-out effort to convince Horthy of his views; however, he succeeded only partially in this.

▸ November 8, 1943 *In this selection from his speech given in Munich at the Löwenbräukeller, Hitler again demonstrated his paranoid obsession with his fear of the Jews controlling everything beyond his command.*

My party comrades! German *Volksgenossen!*

Almost one-third of a human being's lifetime has passed since the day that we commemorate today and in celebration of which I have returned for a few hours to your midst. And still, hardly an epoch in the history of mankind covers twenty years of such mighty, world-shaking, and decisive events fashioning the destinies of nations. It is appropriate to review the past events in broad outlines.

The obligatory "party narrative" followed. Hitler again recalled the statement falsely attributed to Clemenceau about the "twenty million Germans too many."

The prognosis Clemenceau made on Germany having twenty million men too many was just as candidly brutal as the present undisguised threat by English politicians that there are one hundred or two hundred million men too many moving about in India.

The "party narrative" culminated in the following assertion:

If historiography in coming centuries will one day critically review the years of the National Socialist rebirth, uninfluenced by the pros and cons of an era of warfare, then it will not be able to avoid the conclusion that it was a question of the most wonderful victory of faith over the supposed elements of the materially possible.

Hitler again told his horror stories in the service of anti-Bolshevik propaganda. He meant to prove to the English that only Germany could stem the tide of the "Bolshevik-Asian colossus." He declared the following:

> The second thought which takes hold of us today can be only this one: What would have become of Germany and Europe had there not been a November 8 and 9, 1923, and had the National Socialist world-view not conquered Germany?
>
> After all, the seizure of power in the year 1933 is indivisibly bound up with November 8, 1923. On this day, the young movement underwent its first process of selection; the weak were removed, and those who remained were filled with an even greater fanaticism. Then a period followed in which National Socialist thought took hold of people far more easily than before. The party became the nucleus for the realization of our world-view. Long before 1933, the National Socialist state possessed millions of followers in the collective community of our party. Alas, what would have become of Europe and, above all, our German Reich and our beloved homeland, had there not been the faith and the willingness of the individual to risk everything for the movement? Germany would still be what it was at the time: the democratic and impotent Weimar Republic. To ask this question makes every thinking man today shudder. After all, it makes no difference what Germany would have ended up looking like; the Eastern European, Central Asian, Bolshevik colossus would have completed his armament program and would never have let his goal of destroying Europe out of sight. The German Volk, however, with its completely insufficient armed force of a hundred thousand men and its lack of internal political strength and material weapons, would have faced this world power with the power of only a few weeks of military resistance.
>
> There is no need to substantiate today just how bankrupt an idea it was to have Europe defended by the Poles against Bolshevik Russia. Just as foolish was the widespread belief that it might have been possible to appease the Bolshevik colossus by renouncing all ideas of power; or that its plans of world conquest could have been eliminated by a peaceful Europe that increasingly disarmed.

My party comrades!

This appears to me as though chicken and geese will one day make a solemn declaration to the foxes that they no longer intend to attack them, in the hope that the foxes will then become vegetarians. The Bolshevik-Asian colossus will assail Europe until it is finally broken and defeated. Or does anybody want to claim that Finland threatened world peace? It was attacked nonetheless. Without Germany's intervention, its existence would already have been exposed to a terrible new trial in the year 1941. We need not say a word about the outcome of this new Bolshevik action.

Nobody will seriously believe that the Estonians, Latvians, or Lithuanians really wished to conquer the Ural Mountains. Nevertheless, the Soviet Union decided to chase these people out of their countries and cart them off to Siberia. And Romania surely did not intend to take the Caucasus or the oil wells of Baku. But Russia obstinately pursued the goal of occupying not only the mouth of the Danube, but also the Romanian oil fields, and, beyond that, the entire Balkans, in order to use them as a steppingstone for further expansion. There is only one state capable of successfully opposing this attack that has threatened Europe time and again from the east for the last two thousand years, and that is Germany.

Even if this struggle is also an infinitely difficult one for our Volk, this just proves that no state is capable of withstanding this misery without Germany—and certainly not against it. It proves that the hope of the European peoples to obtain leniency from the Muscovites through good behavior or mental caresses is at best childish stupidity or pitiful cowardice. Above all, the idea that some other power, perhaps from outside Europe, could take over the defense of the continent, is not only harebrained, but also reveals an actual moral weakness. It is due above all to bourgeois politicians not having the foggiest idea about things, when in so many countries people act as though they believed that the Jewish-plutocratic west would defeat the Jewish-Bolshevik east. On the contrary, the Jewish-Bolshevik east will one day relieve Jewry in the west of the necessity of continuing to be hypocritical. With complete candor, it can then announce its actual objectives. The Jewish democracy of the west will eventually lead to Bolshevism. The same naive men who today believe that they have found in Stalin the genius who will pull their chestnuts out of the fire for them, will live to see, perhaps sooner than they anticipate, how the spirits summoned from the underworld will strangle them, and that in their own countries.

▶ *January 1, 1945 In his last New Year's Proclamation, Hitler beat the same drum: the international Jewish conspiracy was set on the destruction of Germany and himself. Not mentioned is the fact that millions of Jews along with tens of millions of combatants and non-combatants had died at the hands of his forces. Nor, indeed was mentioned the fact that the war was lost no matter what happened—and, nothing was going to change that.*

Hitler's last New Year's Proclamation in its entirety read as follows:

German Volk! National Socialists! My *Volksgenossen*!

Only the turn of the year causes me to speak to you today, my German *Volksgenossen*. The times had demanded more than speeches from me. The events of the past twelve months, in particular the incident on July 20, forced me to devote my attention and my capacity for work to a single task, for which I had lived for many years: the fateful struggle of my Volk. Although our enemies had proclaimed our collapse every New Year, they placed particular hopes on the year 1944. Never before did victory seem so close to them, as in those days of August of last year when one catastrophe had followed another. Now that we have managed, as so many times before, to bring about a turn of events, credit is due to not only the struggle and work of all my Volksgenossen in the homeland and at the front, but also to my own work and my own commitment. By so doing, I have only acted in the spirit of a statement that I made at the memorable Reichstag session of September 1, 1939, declaring that Germany would never be defeated by the force of arms or time, and that a day like November 9 would never repeat itself in the German Reich.

Whoever knew Germany only from this time of decline could perhaps hope that this state would not be granted a resurrection or the strength to hold its own against a world of enemies.

That is how the Jewish-international conspiracy has lived on hopes from the first day. Every time when the nations began to become suspicious, these hopes were transformed into prophecies. With a certain rabble-rousing audacity, they were portrayed to the masses as certainties, as matters of course. This propaganda used two methods, even though it has short wings as all lies do. On the one hand, it set dates by which the German collapse was certainly to be expected, in order to calm the impatient masses. On the other hand, it dealt with questions whose solution would become necessary for the Allies following this collapse. Before the war ever started, the first English statement was already published, declaring that the joint Anglo-French declaration of war would lead within seven to eight days, at the latest, to an internal revolution and thereby to the collapse of the German Reich. With nearly astronomical regularity, this was followed by ever-new assurances every winter, spring, autumn, and sometimes even between the seasons, that the unconditional German collapse and surrender—both would mean the same thing—was imminent.

Already in the autumn of 1939, one such assurance followed hot on the heels of the other. One minute it was "General Mud," the next "General Hunger," and then again "General Winter" who were supposed to defeat us. Particularly the beginning of 1940 witnessed such Allied declarations galore. After the campaign in France, new prophecies were made, namely that if Germany was not be able to end the war in two months, by September at the latest, then the German collapse would inevitably come in the spring of 1941. Spring had barely passed when new goals were set for the summer, and new deadlines for our certain destruction were finally set for the winter of 1941. Since this time, the game has repeated itself every year. At one time, it was said that the war would be over before the leaves fall; another time that Germany would be ready to capitulate before the next winter. With the assuredness of a sleepwalker, they called August 1944 the deadline for the unconditional surrender and, shortly afterwards, they planned to arrange a joint meeting of the leading Allied statesmen in Berlin just before Christmas. Not long ago, it was rescheduled for January and then March 1945. Right now, they are cautiously declaring that, in view of the rapidly approaching two months, it would be August. In July, they will surely talk about the winter of 1946, if the war does not actually end in the meantime, not with a German capitulation, which will never come, but with a German victory!

Parallel to these prophecies—in order to stress the correctness of these assumptions psychologically—followed the theoretical appointment of ever new commissions for the treatment of European questions after the war, the foundation of societies for the regulation of food supplies after the German collapse, in other words the resurrection of those profiteer institutions (*Schieberinstitutionen*) that we know from the World War, the proclamation of economic agreements, the setting up of traffic networks and air bases, as well as the drafting and promulgation of sometimes truly idiotic laws on the treatment of the German Volk.

They always acted as though they had already won the war, as though they could now already consider at their leisure all the measures necessary for ruling Europe for those who have themselves set a sorry example of how not to rule peoples. Of course, you can practice this propagandistic maneuver with the unenlightened masses in the democratic states for a surprisingly long time, but even there, it will one day become obvious that this is nothing other than the usual swindle in these countries. Should one or the other of the leading men in these western democratic states nevertheless truly believe all that is told the peoples, and then there are only three possible explanations for this:

1. They do not know the German Volk at all. Above all, they do not realize that the past three hundred years of German history did not give an accurate picture of the essence of the German Volk, but reflected only the consequences

of its inner conflicts at home. Since this German Volk made its appearance in history, it has not only been one of the decisive factors in European and world history but even the most decisive one. It remains so today and will continue to be so even more in the future.

2. They are ignorant about the National Socialist state. They do not have an inkling of the essence of this Volk ideal. The accomplishments that the National Socialist regime secured under the most difficult conditions have remained concealed from most of the people in the countries surrounding us. Perhaps they had to be concealed from them because the Jews inform public life and opinion there, that is, everything is distorted and reported wrongly. They are apparently not yet aware that neither Bolshevism nor the democratic-plutocratic world-view—insofar as you can speak of one—can replace the National Socialist state, since both have proved themselves to be unfit for Germany in terms of their achievements, and the results of their activities in their own countries serve only as the most deterrent example.

3. In these countries they have known something that the masses of the healthy German Volk are not aware of, namely a small coterie of drawing-room politicians and drawing-room generals who, in complete ignorance of their own mental, political, and military insignificance, have tried to convince the world that they will one day seize power in a coup and will then be in a position to offer capitulation without further notice, much as in Italy, Finland, Hungary, Romania, and Bulgaria. The less our enemies were familiar with the German Volk, the less they were aware of the essence of the National Socialist state, the more readily they placed their hopes in the assurances of these spineless characters, believed their fantastic chains of reasoning and outpourings to be true, and rewarded them not only with a strong faith but also with ready cash.

In opposition to that, at the turn of a year which has given us ample opportunity to prove that this Volk, this state, and its leading men are unshakable in their will and staunch in their fanatical determination to fight this war out under any circumstances, even putting up with setbacks imposed on us by the fickleness of fate, I would like to state again what arises for us from the past and present, and what is necessary for the world to know in the future.

1. We know the objectives of our enemies from the past and the present. We are aware of what the Anglo-American statesmen plan to do with the German Reich, what measures the Bolshevik rulers and the international Jews, who in the end are behind them, plan to take against the German Volk. Their successful implementation would not only lead to the German Reich's being torn to pieces, the transport of fifteen to twenty million Germans to foreign countries, the enslavement of the remnants of our Volk, the corruption of our German youth, but it would also and above all bring with it the starvation of millions. Aside from this, you either live in freedom or die in slavery.

In opposition to that, we are determined to do anything necessary. The world should realize that this state would therefore never capitulate. The present German Reich, like all great states of the past, may meet with setbacks on its path, but it will never stray from this path. The world should realize that the present leadership of the state shares the worries and sufferings of its people, but it will never capitulate under these worries and sufferings. On the contrary, it is determined to make the utmost effort to face every crisis, make up for what was lost through carelessness with reinforced eagerness to work, so that it will be able not only to express its great appreciation to every individual German who does his duty, but also to assure him that his contribution to the existence of our Volk will one day be rewarded. On the other hand, it will destroy anybody who tries to escape making his contribution or lowers himself to becoming a tool of foreign powers. Since we know the objectives of our enemies—because they themselves offer the necessary enlightenment thanks to their propagandistic garrulousness from the mouths of their statesmen and journalists—the entire German Volk knows what its fate would be if it lost this war. It will therefore not lose this war. It must and will win it. After all, what our enemies are fighting for, they do not know themselves, aside from their Jews. Yet, what we are fighting for is clear to all of us. It is the preservation of the German human being, it is our homeland, it is our two-thousand-year-old culture, and it is the children and grandchildren of our Volk. It is, in short, everything that makes life worth living for us. For this reason, the Volk has developed the spirit and attitude that justify its belief in its own future and its request for a merciful appreciation of its struggle by Providence.

That this struggle is so endlessly difficult is the result of the essence of the abovementioned objectives of our enemies. After all, since they intend to exterminate our Volk, they are already applying this method in the war by means that civilized mankind has not known hitherto. By wrecking our cities, they hope not only to kill German women and children but also and above all to eliminate the documents of our thousand-year-old culture, to which they have nothing to compare of equal quality. That was also the idea behind the war of annihilation against the cultural sites in Italy, the actual intention behind the continuation of the present fight in France, Belgium, and the Netherlands. Alas, like a phoenix from the ashes, so the strong German will all the more rise up anew from the ruins of our cities. The struggle has taken hold not only of millions of our soldiers, but also of millions of male and female workers, of women, even of children. The suffering inflicted on them individually is immeasurable, but equally immeasurable is the greatness of their belief. Once this time of suffering is over, every German will be incredibly proud of being allowed to be a member of such a Volk. Likewise, the day will come when our enemies will regard the defilement of culture, which they are presently undertaking and which will continue to burn in our memories, as shameful.

I know, my dear *Volksgenossen,* the demands this war makes on you. There may be no man in any large country of the world that knows his people and their homeland better than I know Germany. Not only did I become infinitely close to all the German cities that are now being wrecked in whatever concerns their life and their history but also in whatever concerns my personal life. For decades, I was tied to them not only by the love of their history and culture and of their human feelings, but I was also the most strongly involved in the fate of their future development. This alone makes this suffering somewhat easier for me to bear, because I know better than anybody else that, with its will, the German Volk as such not only always rose up from the most profound misery, but also that this time will end with the German cities again rising up from the debris as new sites attesting to the magnificence of our German cities.

Within a few years, the National Socialist state with its energy and initiative will rebuild all that is being destroyed today. The outward appearance of our cities will be mightier and more beautiful than ever before. Healthier homes for the German human beings will take the place of the destroyed tenement barracks. Our social and cultural demands will then receive greater consideration than was possible before.

However, we will neither possess many of the unfading documents of art and culture nor be able to restore them. More importantly, we cannot replace the sacrifice of countless precious human beings and the loss of their collected belongings that became dear to them in the course of a long life. All these great treasures and small remembrances will in the end be compensated for—even if they cannot be replaced— by our Volk's shared memory of a time of the hardest fateful struggle that a nation ever had to bear and one that it bore with so much heroism.

The year 1944 was the year of the greatest burdens in this mighty struggle. It was a year that again proved conclusively that the bourgeois social order is no longer capable of braving the storms of the present or of the coming age. State after state that does not find its way to a truly social reorganization will go down the path to chaos. The liberal age is a thing of the past. The belief that you can counter this storm of the Volk by parliamentary-democratic half-measures is childish and just as naive as Metternich's methods when the national drives for unification were making their way through the nineteenth century. The lack of a truly social, new form of life results in the lack of the mental will to resist not only in the nations but also in the lack of the moral power of resistance of their leaders. In all countries, we see that the attempted renaissance of a democracy has proved fruitless. The confused tangle of political dilettantes and military politicians of a bygone bourgeois world who order each other around is, with deadly certainty, preparing for a plunge into chaos and, insofar as Europe is concerned, into an economic and ethnic catastrophe. And, after all, one thing has already been proved: this most densely populated continent in the world will either have to live with an order that gives the greatest consideration to individual abilities, guarantees the greatest accomplishments, and, by taming all egotistical drives, prevents their excesses, or states such as we have in central and western Europe will prove unfit for life, which means that their nations are thereby doomed to perish!

In this manner—following the example of royal Italy—Finland, Romania, Bulgaria, and Hungary collapsed during this year. This collapse is primarily the result of the cowardice and lack of resolve of their leaders. They and their actions can be understood only in light of the corrupt and socially amoral atmosphere of the bourgeois world. The hatred which many statesmen, especially in these countries, express for the present German Reich is nothing other than the voice of a guilty conscience, an expression of an inferiority complex in view of our organization of a human community that is suspicious to them because we successfully pursue goals that again do not correspond to their own narrow economic egotism and their resulting political shortsightedness.

For us, my German *Volksgenossen,* this, however, represents a new obligation to recognize ever more clearly that the existence or nonexistence of a German future depends on the uncompromising organization of our peoples' state (*Volksstaat*), that all the sacrifices which our Volk must make are conceivable only under the condition of a social order which clears away all privileges and thereby makes the entire Volk not only bear the same duties but also possess the same vital rights. Above all, it must mercilessly destroy the social phantoms of a bygone era. In their stead, it must place the most valuable reality there is, namely the Volk, the masses which, tied together by the same blood, essence, and experiences of a long history, owe their origin as an individual existence not to an earthly arbitrariness but to the inscrutable will of the Almighty. The insight into the moral value of our conviction and the resulting objectives of our struggle for life give us and, above all, give me the strength to continue to wage this fight in the most difficult hours with the strongest faith and with an unshakable confidence. In such hours, this conviction also ties the Volk to its leadership. It assured the unanimous approval of the appeal that I was forced to direct to the German Volk in a particularly urgent way this year.

Millions of Germans of all professions and ranks, men and women, boys and girls, even children, took up the spade and the shovel. Thousands of militia (*Volkssturm*) battalions were created or are in the process of being created. Divisions were newly formed; Volk artillery corps, mortar brigades, self-propelled assault-gun brigades, as well as fighter groups were conjured up out of nothing and provided with new equipment. Above all, our German factories showed singular achievements with the help of both male and female German workers. They, I may say so today, are being joined by increasingly thoughtful people from other nations who, as workers in Germany, understand the essence of our social community. Therefore, what our enemies shattered was rebuilt with superhuman diligence and unequaled heroism. This rebuilding will continue until what our enemies began will end one day. The German spirit and the German will shall bring this about by force!

This, my *Volksgenossen*, will one day go down in history as the miracle of the twentieth century! A Volk that accomplishes, suffers, and endures so many incredible things at the front and in the homeland can therefore never perish. On the contrary: it will emerge from this furnace of trials stronger and firmer than ever before in its history. However, the power to which we owe all this—the Jewish-international enemy of the world—will not only fail in this attempt to destroy Europe and exterminate its nations but will also end by annihilating itself.

At the end of this year, as the spokesman of the nation and, at this moment, also as the Führer of its fate, I would like to thank the countless millions of my *Volksgenossen* with an overflowing heart for all they have suffered, endured, done, and accomplished, men and women, down to the level of our children in the Hitler Youth, in the cities and small market towns, in the villages and in the countryside. I would like to ask them not to let up in the future either, to trust the leadership of the movement, and to fight this most difficult struggle for the future of our Volk with the greatest fanaticism. What I can do to promote this success, I will do in the future as I did in the past. I am speaking less these days, not because I do not wish to or cannot speak, but because my work leaves me little time for speaking, and because I believe that I am now obliged every hour to think about and seek to increase the power of resistance of our armies, introduce better weapons, form new units, and assemble whatever forces can be mobilized from among my Volk. My enemies are perhaps now seeing the light already and are realizing that I have not been asleep all this time!

For the rest, I wish to assure you, my *Volksgenossen,* again today, as in the many years of the struggle for power, that my faith in the future of our Volk is unshakable. Whomever Providence subjects to so many trials, it has destined for the greatest things! It is therefore my only concern to do my utmost to lead the German Volk through this time of misery and open the gate for it to that future in which we all believe, for which we fight and work.

I cannot close this appeal without thanking the Lord for the help that He always allowed the leadership and the Volk to find, as well as for the power He gave us to be stronger than misery and danger. If I also thank Him for my rescue, then I do so only because through it I am happy to be able to continue dedicating my life to the service of the Volk. In this hour, as the spokesman of Greater Germany, I therefore wish to make the solemn avowal before the Almighty that we will loyally and unshakably fulfill our duty also in the new year, in the firm belief that the hour will come when the victory will favor for good the one who is most worthy of it, the Greater German Reich!

Hitler willingly appeared to be religious at times but he saw organized religion as a threat to his power.

VIII
The Churches and Hitler

Hitler did not believe in any organized religion. He certainly was not a Christian in any accepted meaning of that word. His comments over the years indicate that he saw early Christianity as a corrupting force in the ancient world: the German churches of his time were "Germanized" enough to be "acceptable" to National Socialism. Nevertheless, Hitler understood the turmoil possible from religious disagreement and so tried to avoid confrontations with any large organized church in Germany

▸ July 6, 1933 *While Hitler consolidated power, eliminating political parties and unions, he began to deal with the German churches.*

In no way did Hitler regard himself as a religious reformer, a fact he had clearly stated in *Mein Kampf.* His sole aim was earthly omnipotence. As long as the Christian churches in Germany relinquished all claim to power in a political and social sense and refrained from exerting any influence on schools and youth organizations, they were free to conduct as many religious ceremonies in their churches as they wished. He was even willing to grant them substantial funding, while hoping in exchange for active support in the national "expansion," i.e., future wars, in particular the crusade against the heathen Bolshevist Russia. Primarily, it appeared that the Protestant church in Germany would be most willing to reach the internal consensus Hitler wanted. However, unexpected resistance soon arose that led to the establishment of a "confessional church" (in addition to the "church of German Christians" that Hitler promoted).

Ultimately, Hitler scored higher with the Catholic Church. With few exceptions, the German Catholic bishops and clergy had rejected Hitler from the very beginning. They were relatively immune to nationalistic slogans and justifiably concerned about the future of their youth groups and other organizations. Turning a deaf ear to Hitler's promises, they simply refused to partake of his seeming generosity. The Vatican followed a different policy, for it had gathered experience in dealing with a nationalistic dictatorship, and the Italian Church had not fared badly under Mussolini in spite of the loss of its youth organizations.

Hitler's offer to conclude a concordat thus fell on fertile ground in Rome; it was something that had come to pass neither in imperial Germany nor during the Weimar Republic. The Vatican felt it was wiser to secure the continued existence of the Catholic Church than to be forced to deal with open persecution and suppression.

On July 8, the concordat between the German Reich and the Holy See was signed. German clergy showed little enthusiasm upon hearing the news. Hitler, however, was all the more elated, particularly since the act was bound to make a positive impression on neighboring countries, above all, Poland. He issued the following order on the same day:

> By virtue of the conclusion of the concordat between the Holy See and the German Reich government, there is, in my view, sufficient guarantee that from now on the members of the Roman Catholic confession in the Reich will place their services unreservedly at the disposal of the new National Socialist State. Thus I hereby decree:
>
> 1. The dissolution of those Catholic organizations recognized in the present agreement whose dissolution was effected in the absence of an order of the Reich government shall be repealed immediately.
>
> 2. All sanctions imposed upon priests and other leaders of these Catholic organizations shall be discontinued. Any repetition of such sanctions in future is inadmissible and will be punished in accordance with the laws in force.
>
> It is my strong hope that the settlement of the questions that concern the Protestant confession will very soon comprise a happy close to this act of pacification.
>
> Adolf Hitler

► July 11, 1933 *Hitler wanted to organize the separate German denominations into a German Protestant Reich church. His efforts failed.*

As mentioned above, Hitler experienced some difficulties in attempting to steer the Protestant Church onto the course of the new national politics. On July 11, however, it appeared that the conflicts within the individual Protestant faiths had been settled by a new constitution. Hitler thus addressed the following congratulatory telegram to Ludwig Müller, military pastor and future Reich bishop:

> Berlin, July 12
>
> I was happy to hear that the constitution has now been completed. May this serve to provide the foundation for the unity and freedom of the Protestant Church.
>
> Reich Chancellor Adolf Hitler

Hitler also made use of this occasion to send the following telegram to Hindenburg:

> Esteemed *Herr Reichspräsident,*
>
> After the constitution of the German Protestant Church was completed yesterday, the negotiations to settle the conflict in the Prussian church were similarly brought to a close in a manner satisfactory to both the state and the church. The internal freedom of the church, which is one of my particular concerns, will be placed beyond doubt by removing the state's commissars and deputy commissars. The internal reconstruction of the regional churches will be brought to a speedy close by free choice of the Protestant parishioners in accordance with church law. I am happy, Your Excellency, to be able to report that it is now guaranteed that the wish that you, I, and all those involved have cherished for the pacification of Protestant church life, will be fulfilled within the very near future. In respectful devotion,
>
> Reich Chancellor Adolf Hitler

▶ July 16, 1933 *Hitler stated his position regarding the churches clearly at a mass meeting in Leipzig.*

> The religions and the churches will maintain their freedom. But we are in charge of politics.

▶ July 22, 1933 *Hitler tried to influence the administration of the Protestant churches by supporting some candidates he favored.*

On July 22, Hitler decided to deliver his own remarks on the Protestant elections that were to follow the next day. He spoke in a radio broadcast from Bayreuth, where he was attending the annual festival.

> When I take a stand on the elections in the Protestant Church, I am doing so exclusively from the standpoint of a political leader, i.e., my concern lies not with questions of faith, dogma, or doctrine. Neither the Catholic nor the Protestant nor the Russian Orthodox Church has ever or will ever be able to halt the advance of Bolshevism.

Hitler then proceeded to the subject of the concordat with the Vatican:

> As a National Socialist, it is my most cherished desire to be able to reach an agreement with the Protestant Church that is no less equivocal. However, this presupposes that, if at all possible, a single Reich church take the place of the multiple Protestant churches.

Although the church elections on July 23 did bring positive results for the German Christians, resistance against Nationalist Socialist church leadership remained strong in the Protestant Churches in the local states (*Länder*), particularly in those under Bishops Meiser (Bavaria), Wurm (Württemberg), and Marahrens (Hanover).

Ultimately, Hitler gave up the fight and left them to their own ways, although he did have a number of Protestant pastors imprisoned or sent to concentration camps, among them Niemöller and Lilje, for having, in his view, put up too much resistance.

▶ January 30, 1934 *In his speech to the Reichstag marking the first anniversary of his gaining power, Hitler made clear his intentions of reforming the Protestant churches.*

After having meted out a few blows to the churches, above all to the Protestant Church, he stated:

> The state has dealt no less radically with the two Christian confessions. Filled by the desire to secure for the German Volk the great religious, moral, and ethical values anchored in the two Christian confessions, we have eliminated the political organizations while, at the same time, reinforced the religious institutions. For an agreement with the powerful National Socialist state is more valuable to a Church than the conflict between denominational political associations that, in view of the policy of compromise necessitated by their coalition, are forced to spiritually abandon a truly inward, religious education and stabilization of the Volk in order to pay for personal advantages to party members.
>
> However, we all harbor the expectation that the merger of the Protestant regional churches and confessions to form a German Protestant Reich church might truly satisfy the yearning of those who believe that, in the muddled dividedness of Protestant life, they must fear a weakening in the power of the Protestant faith.
>
> This year the National Socialist state has clearly demonstrated its high regard for the strength of the Christian faiths, and hence it expects the same high regard on the part of the confessions for the strength of the National Socialist state!

▶ May 25, 1937 *The affair of Cardinal Mundelein demonstrated Hitler's efforts to use the Holy See to quiet his critics within the Catholic Church.*

On May 29, Hitler had the German chargé d'affaires in Rome present an extraordinarily pointed note to the Vatican. Already at the May 1 rally, Hitler had spoken against various encyclicals in an uncharacteristic manner. After a speech by the American Cardinal Mundelein, Hitler seized upon the opportunity to declare "the further conduct of normal diplomatic relations between the German government and the Curia as being impossible."

Nevertheless, Hitler's note did not elicit any reproof nor did it carry with it any consequences. Its text read verbatim:

> The German ambassador has recently had to bring before the Holy See remonstrances concerning Cardinal Mundelein, who, in front of a congregation of five hundred priests in the Chicago Archdiocese, has referred to the German head of state, members of the Reich government, and to certain church-and-state affairs in Germany, in a most insulting manner. In particular, the German ambassador expressed his great displeasure that a prelate of such standing as Cardinal Mundelein would debase himself to decrying the German head of state in such unqualified a manner. Hereupon the German ambassador to the Holy See was presented with an oral reply, which was later verified by a written response, to which I replied in the following manner in the name of my government:
>
> The German Reich government based its approach to the dispatch issued to its ambassador in Rome, who completed his task in this spirit, on the premise that, in the interest of the relations between Germany and the Vatican, no one should have a greater interest than the Holy See in discouraging injury, such as has been inflicted upon the relations between Germany and the Curia by the base assaults launched by the cardinal upon the German head of state.
>
> The German Reich government had held it to be self-evident that the Holy See would wish to distance itself from the unfortunate remarks of the cardinal, correct these, and express its regret over the incident. This has at all times been the custom in the conduct of international relations. To the great consternation and displeasure of the German government, the Holy See has evidently deemed it appropriate to reply with the completely unsubstantiated and incorrect remark—which is all the more conspicuous—that the cardinal had at most returned like with like.

Obviously, this was a pretext in order not to have to reply to the note presented by the German ambassador. The German Reich government has hence reached the conclusion that the Holy See has done nothing to amend the unqualified and public defamation by one of its Curia's most distinguished members, of the person of the German head of state, that in the eyes of the world must appear as though it approved of it.

The Holy See must realize that, as long as there is no remedy of the situation, its unexpected and incomprehensible demeanor in this issue has made the further conduct of normal diplomatic relations between the German government and the Curia impossible. The Curia bears sole responsibility for this development.

▶ June 6, 1937 *While Hitler held to no Christian church, he did believe that he had been sent by God to rescue the German people as he stated in this speech to a mass rally in Regensburg.*

For the first time, Hitler himself employed the term "belief in God" (*Gottgläubigkeit*), evidently in order to indicate that in the future he, too, could be counted among the adherents of this confession.

I will never allow anyone to ever again tear this Volk asunder, to reduce it to a heap of warring religious camps. We have gone through enough in German history and need not undergo any more such experiences. They have been the sorriest experiences ever. Once our Volk numbered 18.5 million people; after a Thirty Years' War, a mere 3.6 million were left. It is my belief that some of those who are dissatisfied with the fact that we have finally created one Volk will attempt to reestablish that situation in Germany, but this attempt, too, will fail: they will never, ever destroy the German Volk and the German Reich.

Generation after generation of our Volk will march on thus in our history, with this banner always in mind, this banner that places us under an obligation to our Volk, its honor,

its freedom, and our community—to our truly National Socialist fraternity. They will then consider it only natural that
this German Volk takes but the one path Providence has bade
it take by giving these people a common language. We, therefore, go our way into the future with the deepest belief in God
(*Gottgläubigkeit*).

Would all we have achieved been possible had Providence
not helped us? I know that the fruits of human labor are hard-
won and transitory if they are not blessed by the Omnipotent
(*Allmacht*). Work such as ours that has received the blessings
of the Omnipotent can never again be undone by mere mortals. As long as the pillars of the Movement hold this banner
fast in their grip, there is not an enemy alive, no matter how
powerful, who will ever be able to wrest it from our grasp.

Obviously, Hitler already had arrived at a belief in the divine origin of the
Reich he had created. Hence, it could not be destroyed by mere mortals.

▶ January 30, 1939 *In this significant speech to the Reichstag, Hitler made it
clear that he found church-based opposition irritating and he had decided to
teach the churches a lesson.*

Since Hitler was already in the process of threatening international
Jewry, he determined to go on the offensive against members of the clergy
opposed to his rule. Should they persist in their defiance of the state, he
would see to implementing the appropriate measures for severely restricting church activities. In vivid colors, he depicted an effective separation
of church and state, i.e., the end of state subsidies and tax revenues for
the Church.

Among the reproaches that the so-called democracies have
heaped on Germany has been the claim that National Socialist Germany is a state hostile to religion. On this topic, I wish
to make the following solemn declaration before the entire
German Volk:

1. To date, no one has been persecuted because of his religious affiliation in Germany, nor will anyone be persecuted for this reason in the future either.

2. Since January 30, 1933, the official institutions within the National Socialist state have transferred the following tax earnings to the two churches:

> 130 million Reichsmarks for the fiscal year 1933; 170 million Reichsmarks for the fiscal year 1934; 250 million Reichsmarks for the fiscal year 1935; 320 million Reichsmarks for the fiscal year 1936; 400 million Reichsmarks for the fiscal year 1937; 500 million Reichsmarks for the fiscal year 1938. In addition to this, the Church receives approximately 85 million Reichsmarks annually in the form of *Länder* subsidies, and approximately another seven million Reichsmarks in the form of subsidies by the local communities and associations.
>
> Next to the state, the church constitutes the greatest proprietor of land. It possesses holdings in real estate and forestry in excess of 10 billion Reichsmarks. From these, it derives annual earnings of about 300 million.
>
> Moreover, the church benefits from countless gifts, bequests, and, above all, from donations. Further, the National Socialist state accords the church concessions in a variety of realms: donations and inheritance are tax-exempt, for instance. To make an understatement, therefore, it is with insolent impertinence that foreign politicians accuse the Third Reich of hostility to religion.
>
> Should the churches within Germany regard the situation as unbearable, then please bear in mind that the National Socialist state is willing, and prepared at any time, to undertake a clear separation of church and state, as is the case in France, America, and other countries. In this context, I permit myself to pose the following question: Within this period, how much did official state appropriations to the church amount to in France, England, and the USA?

3. The National Socialist state has not closed even one single church, neither prevented church services nor infringed on the conduct of mass. It has not imposed its views on any confession's church doctrine and faith. In the National Socialist state, man is free to seek absolution in the fashion desired.

However, the National Socialist state will relentlessly deal with those priests who, instead of serving the Lord, see their mission in propagating derisive comments on our present Reich, its institutions, or its leading men. It will bring to their attention the fact that the destruction of this state will not be tolerated. The law will prosecute a priest who implicates himself in illegal activities and he will be held accountable for these in the same manner as any other, ordinary German citizen.

It must, however, be stated at this point that there are thousands upon thousands of priests of all Christian beliefs who attend to their clerical duties in a manner infinitely superior to these clerical warmongers and without entering into conflict with established law and order. To protect these is the mission of the state. To destroy the enemies of the state is the duty of the state.

4. The National Socialist state is neither prudish nor hypocritical. Still there are certain fundamental mores that must be upheld in the interest of preserving the biological health of the Volk. And we shall not allow these to be altered. This state prosecutes pederasty and child abuse as crimes to be punished by the law, irrespective of who perpetrates them.

Five years ago, when leading members of the National Socialist Party were guilty of these crimes, they were shot. Should other men perpetrate similar transgressions, whether in public, privately, or as members of the clergy, the law will duly prosecute them and sentence them to imprisonment. Should men of the cloth perpetrate other transgressions, in violation of their vow of chastity etc., then it is of no interest to us. There has been no mention of this in our press ever.

And besides this, this state has interfered only once in the inner organization of the churches, namely on the occasion when, in 1933, I myself attempted to reunite the impotent, fragmented Protestant regional churches of Germany in the form of a great and mighty Protestant Reich Church. This attempt ran aground on the opposition of individual *Länder* bishops. And therefore I abandoned my efforts since, in the final instance, it is not our task to strengthen or to defend by force the Protestant Church against its own leaders.

The motivation behind certain statesmen in the democracies abroad taking such a vigorous interest in a few German priests is obviously political. For these very same democratic statesmen remained silent when in Russia hundreds of thousands of priests were hacked to pieces and their bodies burnt. These democratic statesmen remained equally silent at the brutal slaughter of priests and nuns in Spain, numbering in the tens of thousands, some of whom were even burnt alive.

These democratic statesmen could not deny these facts, but they remained silent and nothing broke this silence. In the meantime, upon news of these massacres—and of this I must indeed remind these democratic statesmen—countless National Socialists and Fascist volunteers placed themselves at General Franco's disposal. They did so with the aim of precluding an escalation of the conflict, to prevent this Bolshevist bloodbath from enveloping all of Europe and hence the greater part of the civilized world.

Now it was clear why National Socialists and Fascists had volunteered for the fighting in Spain: they had simply not been able to stand the sight of slaughtered priests and nuns any longer! In 1936, however, as the conflict had raged to the south, Hitler had oddly enough published an ordinance in the *Reich Law Gazette* detailing that any German participating in the Spanish Civil War would be jailed, even if he had only instigated others to take part.

▶ March 11, 1940 *Hitler tried to reach agreement with the Catholic Church.*

Ribbentrop requested an audience with Pope Pius XII to convey the Führer's greetings and to discuss Hitler's proposals for a "basic settlement between National Socialism and the Catholic Church."

This advance on the part of Hitler may well have appeared astonishing in consideration of his slight of the Holy Father during his visit to Rome in 1938 when Pius XI had occupied the Holy See. The pope became increasingly unpopular with the National Socialists over time. His successor, Pius XII, was known to be more inclined towards the German government than Pius XI had been from about 1937 on. In view of the pending confrontation in the west, Hitler sought the support of the Vatican or at least assurances of its neutral stance should a conflict erupt. Naturally, this was a question of power politics and not of such peripheral concerns as religious conviction.

On March 11, the pope granted Ribbentrop the audience requested. The German Foreign Ministry kept the following record of the foreign minister's statements to the pope:

> The Führer was of the opinion that a basic settlement between National Socialism and the Catholic Church was quite possible. There was, however, no point in wanting to settle the relations between these two by raising separate questions of this or that kind or by provisional agreements. Rather, they must come at some time to a comprehensive and, so to speak, secular settlement of their relations; this would then form a really lasting basis for a harmonious cooperation between them. However, the time had not yet arrived for such a settlement. Germany was engaged in a struggle for existence that she would fight, in all circumstances, to a victorious end; naturally, this occupied all her efforts and did not permit the Führer to get interested in other problems. Moreover, it ought to be borne in mind, that an understanding between National Socialism and the Catholic Church depended on one principal preliminary condition, namely, that the Catholic clergy in Germany abandon any kind of political activity and limit itself solely to the care of souls, the only activity that was within the clergy's province.

The recognition of the necessity of such a radical separation, however, could not yet be considered to be the dominant view of Catholic clergymen in Germany. Similar to the manner in which England, in international politics, had claimed the role of a kind of guardian of the continent and the right of intervening in every possible problem of third countries, the Catholic Church had also become accustomed, in the course of events, to intervention in politics. The Catholic Church in Germany had come into the possession of positions and rights of the most various kind that it considered, to be sure, duly acquired, but that were not compatible with the absolutely necessary limitation to its spiritual functions.

The Catholic clergy must be imbued with the realization that, with National Socialism, an entirely new form of political and national life had appeared in the world. Only after this had happened could a fundamental settlement and understanding be approached with any chance for a lasting success. One must not repeat the mistake made with the prematurely concluded concordats (*Länder* concordats and Reich concordat), that already had to be considered out of date, if only on account of the formal constitutional development in Germany that had taken place since they were concluded.

In the opinion of the Führer, what mattered for the time being was to maintain the existing truce and, if possible, to expand it. In this respect, Germany had made very considerable preliminary concessions. The Führer had quashed no less than seven thousand indictments of Catholic clergymen. Also, it should not be forgotten that the National Socialist state was spending one billion Reichsmarks annually for the Catholic Church; no other state could boast of such an achievement.

The pope showed complete understanding toward the Reich Foreign Minister's statements and admitted without qualifications that the concrete facts were as mentioned. True, he attempted to turn the conversation toward certain special problems and complaints of the Curia but did not insist on going on when the Reich Foreign Minister once more emphasized the necessity of a fundamental and comprehensive settlement of the whole relationship between church and state that would be possible only at some later date.

In conclusion, the foreign minister pointed to the historic fact that never before in history had a revolution as radical as that carried out in the total life of the German people by National Socialism done so little injury to the existence of the church. On the contrary, it was due, in the last analysis, only to National Socialism that Bolshevist chaos did not break out in Europe and thus destroy church life altogether.

Hitler's favorite references to the threats of "Bolshevism" and to his role as the "savior of Europe," which was now enlarged upon to read "savior of Christianity and of the church," concluded his wordy message to Rome. Ribbentrop could not let the opportunity pass him by without pointing to the imminent collapse of the western powers: "We believe that France and England will sue for peace yet this year. This is the conviction of the entire German Volk."

Having been heard by the Holy Father, Ribbentrop faced a conference with Papal Secretary of State Maglione, who was not content with hearing only platitudes. Insistently, Maglione pointed to the desperate situation of the confessional schools and especially to the dire straits in which the Catholic Church in Poland found itself during these days. But he could not induce Ribbentrop to veer from the letter of Hitler's instructions not to discuss any concrete matter. All he got were vague promises that the German government would investigate the issue of anticlerical writings by the late Ludendorff.

IX

Hitler Becomes Supreme Commander

The center of gravity of Hitler's powers in Germany became his command over the army. As not only head of government and head of state but as actual commander in chief of the armed forces, Hitler received the personal oath of loyalty of each officer and soldier in the armed forces. Domarus saw this as very important and his appendix on the subject is significant in giving his views of how this happened.

It is no doubt impressive how Hitler improved his lot from that of an unskilled laborer, living in a hostel for the homeless in Vienna, to his later position as head of the German Reich. Far more astonishing is his military career. The former corporal assumed supreme command of all three branches of Germany's armed forces under the Third Reich (*Wehrmacht*). Admirals and generals promptly complied with his orders and, for the most part, did so without voicing any objections. And all this took place within a military that jealously guarded its strict rules of conduct and proudly looked back on a three-hundred-year history.

Hitler was never a career military man. He had not even volunteered in peace time. Indeed, in Austria, prior to the First World War, he had done his utmost to avoid making "this most noble sacrifice a man can be asked to make," as he would later call it. His participation in the First World War was his sole qualification for his later position as commander in chief of the armed forces. As a common front-line soldier, he had been a member of an infantry regiment of the Bavarian reserve troops. In recognition of his military service, Hitler had been awarded the Iron Cross, Second and First Class, in addition to the Bronze Badge for wounds sustained in battle. Once he became Reich chancellor, Hitler managed to instill in the admirals and generals a conviction that fate had preordained him to realize the military's domestic and foreign policy ambitions. Moreover, he persuaded them that he possessed expertise in military affairs, supplemented by great intuitive knowledge. Hitler achieved a remarkable feat of rhetorical prowess in claiming that he had "come from the ranks of the armed forces of the German Empire and would always remain one of them," a version that was indeed accepted.

Any investigation of Hitler's phenomenal success with the military has to address the objectives pursued by the military and Hitler's method of subjugating its leaders to his will. Hitler's military ambitions were primarily directed toward the realm of foreign policy. He believed that the realization of his goals hinged upon the establishment of an army based upon a two-year compulsory conscription program. This conscription was crucial to his envisioned conquest of the East, an area he termed the "new lands for the expansion of the German people (*Lebensraum*)." He abhorred militia units (*Wehrverbände*) and similar paramilitary organizations. These military groupings did not know the "blind" obedience ingrained in regular military units, an obedience he deemed crucial to the implementation of his ambitious designs. Hence he placed little faith even in his own Nazi Party storm troopers (SA) and, in 1934, he did not draw back from the cold-blooded murder of its most prominent leaders, among them his closest friends.

On the other hand, Hitler regarded the generals, and in particular the members of the general staff, as his natural allies in the pursuit of his future conquests. To him, these men were mere "blood-hounds," straining at the leash, eagerly waiting for him to unleash them upon an opponent.

In Hitler's opinion, domestic policy served only one end: to create the prerequisites for a "policy of strength toward the outside world." As he would freely admit at a later date, the Party and its various subdivisions were but "a means to an end" to him. At times, he would strive to please the generals far more ardently than he ever sought to accommodate his fellow party members. There is little doubt that, had he succeeded in the conquest of the coveted new *Lebensraum*, he would eventually have rid himself of the *Wehrmacht*'s generals in order to build up an army with officers more to his liking.

In direct opposition to Hitler's ambitions, the armed forces of the Weimar Republic's (*Reichswehr*) leaders concerned themselves largely with issues of a more domestic nature. In compliance with the constitution of the Weimar Republic, the *Reichswehr* was an institution devoid of any political function. However, this neutral role applied primarily to enlisted men and officers of lesser standing. The leading figures within the *Reichswehr* sought to transform it into a potent instrument of political power.

The entire body of the *Reichswehr* generals regarded the existence of the Weimar Republic as a national disgrace, a most embarrassing institution they would have to eliminate at the first opportunity that arose. The leading members of the *Reichswehr* openly supported the "stab-in-the-back" legend, a myth purporting that the German army had been on the brink of victory in the autumn of 1918. As victory appeared to be within reach, traitors without conscience—aided by mysterious dark forces—robbed the army of the fruits of its victory, thus stabbing Germany in the back.

These "November criminals," as Hitler called them, supposedly were none other than the founding fathers of the "confounded" Republic of Weimar. The *Reichswehr* generals blamed them for the outcome of the Versailles Treaty, in particular with regard to its provisions concerning Germany's military. And moreover, in the eyes of the generals, these men supposedly guilty of high treason were responsible as well for the replacement of the cherished black-white-red banner and cockade with the despised black-red-gold flag. While being allowed to retain the black-white-red "Reich naval ensign," the military men were coerced into accepting a black-red-gold canton that had to be placed on the flag. This antagonism typified the bitter enmity between the leaders of the *Reichswehr* and the Weimar Republic.

Nevertheless, the *Reichswehr* generals had no intention of directly involving themselves in any coup attempt. Neither were they willing to resort to revolution or other illegal measures in pursuit of such an end. Needless to say, the generals were not opposed to taking action themselves in the event of "chaos" or the erosion of the legal authority of the government.

It is not entirely clear precisely what type of state the generals envisioned to replace the "interim government" of the Weimar Republic. There is no doubt that most of the generals would have welcomed the restitution of the monarchy and feudal privileges that had been lost to them in the aftermath of the military defeat of 1918.

A small, radical group among the generals toyed with the idea of establishing a military dictatorship. This group was composed of men and associations as disparate as General von Schleicher and the veterans' organization (*Soldatenbund*). Members of the *Soldatenbund* had been particularly active in the early years of Hitler's rule. Even as late as 1938, they openly advocated the transformation of the Third Reich into a military state.

Another less radical formation within the army sought to achieve its goals through limited cooperation with the men in power in the Weimar Republic. The majority of this group's members had belonged to the last army high command (*Oberste Heeresleitung*), and they had worked side by side with the Social Democrats in 1918. It was a relatively small grouping within the German army composed of men such as Groener, Heye, von Stülpnagel, and von dem Busche. In his function as Reich minister of defense in 1932, Groener bore the brunt of the fervent and passionate opposition of the remainder of the *Reichswehr*—and of Hindenburg as well.

As is evident from the above, the goals pursued by the military were of a predominantly domestic nature and aimed at destroying the Republic of Weimar so despised by the generals, as well as the reintroduction of general conscription to Germany, which would bring sweeping sociopolitical consequences and restore their status. In matters of foreign policy, the *Reichswehr* endeavored to render null and void the provisions of the Treaty of Versailles. To the generals, this meant at the very least the restitution of the 1914 eastern boundaries. For this, the generals saw the maintenance of good relations with the Soviet Union and the Red army as crucial to their effort to circumvent the provisions regarding Germany's military as established in the Versailles Treaty. For instance, German officers could be trained in the Soviet Union and instructed by members of the Red Army in the handling of weaponry prohibited in Germany.

In 1920, Poland had appropriated for itself territories along its eastern frontier by the use of brute force and in defiance of the recommendations put forth by the Western powers. The land at stake was located east of the so-called Curzon Line in White Russia and the Ukraine, and hence a concerted action by Germany and the Soviet Union directed against the Polish state was within the realm of the possible. Within the *Reichswehr*, an assault upon Poland was at the center of debate and strategic planning. Naturally, the fact that East Prussia had been severed from the Reich played an important role in these considerations as well.

The manner in which the German-Polish border had been redrawn in accordance with the Versailles Treaty entailed further complications. Its course was a most unfortunate one that contained all the necessary ingredients to torch Europe once more. In the days of the Weimar Republic, East Prussia had consistently been administered by special military law apart from the main body of the republic. The Versailles Treaty reinforced its special status. East Prussian fortifications were the only military installations within Germany that were permitted to maintain heavy artillery units for their defense. It came as no surprise that Hitler took advantage of the extraordinary status of the territory in an effort to gain the favor of the *Reichswehr*.

Contrary to Hitler, the generals of the *Reichswehr* had no intention of realizing their foreign policy aims through a general war. Rather, they hoped for the development of a more favorable situation abroad such as a possible armed conflict between either the Soviet Union and the Western powers or between the Soviet Union and Poland. The generals considered the latter scenario a distinct possibility. Like Hitler, they were taken in by the deceptive belief that the Anglo-Saxon powers would stand aside in the event of an outbreak of open hostilities between Germany and Poland— particularly if Germany had obtained the implicit consent of the Soviet Union prior to such action.

The aims pursued by the *Reichswehr* and Hitler had various aspects in common. Both strove to put an end to the Weimar Republic, to reintroduce general conscription to Germany, to reunite East Prussia with the Reich, and to rid Germany of the black-red-gold flag. The ambitions of Hitler and the generals in the question of power politics were closely related as well. Both parties sought to secure for themselves a central position within the power structure of a future German state. However, these shared ambitions bore within themselves the seeds of future conflict.

Prior to 1932, the *Reichswehr* generals had been willing to accept Hitler as the national "drummer." They had consented to integrate Hitler's SA men into the *Reichswehr* under the pretext of establishing new militia units. Nevertheless, the generals' disdain for the former Austrian corporal—who by no means fit into their social circles—was such that it never occurred to them to accord him any position of power, either in the military or in the political realm. They had no room for him in the new German state they coveted. In their minds, Hitler was to set the stage for a "national revival" within Germany. He was to clear the streets of Communists, rid the parliament of democratic majorities and popularize the idea of defense. After he had accomplished this, he was expected to step down and leave center stage to the generals themselves or to the royal family, so that either of these could assume power as guarantors of the "new national" law and order within Germany.

Needless to say, the generals had failed to account for the man Adolf Hitler in their calculations. They had underestimated his tactical abilities. Hitler, on the other hand, knew only too well the strength and weaknesses of the generals opposing him, and he was determined to take full and relentless advantage of their faults. Nevertheless, he had pledged himself to pursuing the legal path to attaining this goal. To this end, he relied completely upon his "national" oratory prowess instead of revolutionary overthrow:

for the one time that he had employed revolutionary tactics, the venture had failed miserably. The debacle of the 1923 Putsch had taught Hitler a valuable lesson he took to heart. He realized that, as a rule, Germany's generals would always bow to the authority of a legitimate government, even if they despised it. As long as the state maintained its power in a legal fashion, the generals could never be moved to support a revolutionary movement, no matter how sympathetic they might be to its cause.

Hence, in this instance, Hitler trod the legal path to power, thereby assuring himself of the generals' approval. He knew well that the use of force was simply not an option for the realization of his goals. He also realized that any armed units that might march on the capital would succumb to the bullets of police and *Reichswehr* long before they ever reached Berlin. While he had drawn together armed militia units in Mecklenburg in 1932, he had merely been bluffing at that point. In fact, Hitler had never seriously contemplated instigating an armed rebellion on a national scale.

In the course of the year 1932, Hitler had repeatedly tried to take hold of power by means of various plebiscites. None of these attempts bore any fruit, and thus Hitler resorted to the last device left at his disposal in order to gain power in a legal fashion: he would attempt to convince Reich President von Hindenburg to personally appoint him Reich chancellor.

The main obstacle to be overcome in this undertaking was the heavy reliance of Hindenburg upon his old advisers, the majority of whom came from the ranks of the *Reichswehr* generals and the East Prussian Junkers. Hence, Hitler deduced that it would be most advantageous to secure for himself the support of the East Prussian officers prior to any further action. Hitler began his campaign by rallying numerous generals to his cause. For the most part, these military men had retired from active duty during the times of the German Kaiser, and their discontent with the present regime made them easy prey for Hitler's national slogans. The connections his principal negotiators, Röhm and Göring, had formed with the *Reichswehr* were of crucial importance to this undertaking.

Unrelated to these circumstances, Hitler enjoyed strong support in the Reich navy in 1932. The enthusiasm of the "Christian officers at sea" was such that the "landlubber" Hitler was hailed whenever he came aboard to inspect a warship, even if he did so merely as a civilian. On May 26, 1932, prior to a tour of the cruiser *Köln*, Hitler entered the following memorable dedication into its visitors' book: "With the hope of being able to help in rebuilding a fleet worthy of the Reich. Adolf Hitler."

Nonetheless, in the months prior to the take-over, the navy did not rally to Hitler with such enthusiasm and unity simply because of his national persuasion and his solemn pledges to blow the dust off the "violated black-white-red cockade of the old army and navy." The motives behind the navy's enthusiasm for Hitler were of a psychological nature as well. The sailors had suffered greatly from a sense of national shame that had been attached to them ever since the events in November 1918. In the eyes of nationalists both within the *Reichswehr* and outside of it, the navy had been the pivotal cause of collapse since it was the first branch of the armed forces to succumb to signs of demoralization that fateful month. Pointing accusingly to the mutiny on ships of the navy at the time, the conviction spread that the German navy as a whole had failed its country at the end of the war. The navy officers had supposedly confined their high-seas fleet to harbor when they should have been leading their men to battle. The ensuing inactivity—the most disgraceful condition for any soldier—had led the "blue boys" astray and caused them to commit such deplorable acts as the 1918 revolts in Kiel and Wilhelmshaven.

Although unsubstantiated, this story's popularity rivaled that of the myth that Germany was defeated in the Great War because of intentional internal disruption, the "stab-in-the-back" myth, so popular in nationalist circles. As a result, the navy's men felt a vague feeling of guilt. Army officers and other dignitaries of national renown, who felt they had no share in this disgrace, looked upon the navy with condescending pity.

Given this background, the navy's men felt Hitler to be the awaited Messiah who would deliver them of their guilt and restore the honor of the navy. While Hitler was fond of speaking out against the "November criminals," not once did he reproach the seamen for their actions. To the contrary, whenever appearing before an audience composed of naval officers, Hitler made certain to pay the navy his respects. Indeed, Hitler appears to have been completely earnest on this subject, for he greatly admired the navy's moral code of conduct. Hitler was enormously impressed by the navy's pledge to "fight unto one's last breath," even in a hopeless situation. He also doted on the seamen's maxim to go down with their ship rather than ever to surrender to the enemy. This fascination with the navy's unwritten code of conduct stayed with Hitler to the last. In his political testament of April 29, 1945, he expressed great disappointment with the officers of the army but lauded the navy, sparing it from his wrath.

Before his rise to power, Hitler feared the majority of the *Reichswehr* generals less than he did those officers who wished to pursue paths different from his own. The majority of generals were traditionalist in outlook and monarchist at heart. A small number of officers, however, were not categorically opposed to cooperation with the parties of the Weimar Republic. Others continued to dream of the establishment of a military dictatorship.

In 1932, Hitler found himself faced by two proponents of these divergent points of view: General Groener, Reich minister of defense and of the interior and member of the Brüning cabinet; and General von Schleicher, chief of the ministerial office. Hitler was determined to oust Groener and, if at all possible, to remove Schleicher from office in the wake of Groener's dismissal. In the case of Groener, a pretext for action presented itself rather quickly. As mentioned earlier, Hitler greatly valued the maintenance of good relations with the East Prussian *Reichswehr*. As early as 1931, he had placed local SA units at the disposal of the army there. After the April 13, 1932, election reinstating Hindenburg in office one last time, Brüning and Groener forced a measure through the cabinet that banned both the SA and SS. However, neither of these two officials were prepared for the strong reaction of the *Reichswehr* to this move.

General Groener proved remarkably short-sighted in his assessment of the situation. His own state secretary, General von Schleicher, conspired to remove him from office. Within a few days after the measure had passed the cabinet, Hindenburg had been persuaded that a decree banning the SA was detrimental to the *Reichswehr* and would considerably weaken it. Groener was forced to resign as minister of defense on May 13, 1932. His fall signaled the impending fate of Brüning who resigned on May 30. Schleicher took over Groener's post as Reich minister of defense in the von Papen cabinet, and the decree banning the SA was rescinded. Nevertheless, despite frequent consultations with each other, Schleicher remained Hitler's declared enemy.

Once the returns of the July 31 election revealed that Hitler could not secure more than 37 percent of the popular vote, Schleicher determined to summarily deal with Hitler by assigning him the post of vice chancellor, a position of hardly any significance. When Hitler rebuffed this offer, Reich President Hindenburg summoned him on August 13 and accused him of being incapable of forming a government on his own.

Hitler pledged to himself to seek bloody revenge on Schleicher for having trapped him in so embarrassing a situation. Prior to any further action, however, Hitler knew he had to come to terms with the "cabinet of barons."

For this purpose, he required a strong and effective "nationalist" slogan. He came upon one quickly in the form of five death warrants. Dated August 22, 1932, these warrants were the outcome of an extraordinary trial at Beuthen conducted by the von Papen government. The verdict was a death sentence for five SA men guilty of having murdered a Polish guerilla in Potempa. Swiftly Hitler seized the opportunity and branded the von Papen cabinet as the "hangman of national freedom fighters for the German Volk." Unrelated to this, Hitler shocked Germany once more by announcing National Socialist cooperation with the Communists in the Berlin transportation workers' strike. This move sought to terrify right-wing circles bringing to mind the possibility of a Red-Brown alliance.

Although Hitler had lost two million votes in the Reichstag election of November 6, the Nazi Party still remained the strongest party. Von Papen's cabinet stood no chance of being tolerated by such a parliament, and thus it was forced to step down. Now Hindenburg had to intervene in person. He summoned Hitler to his office several times. As early as November 1932, Hindenburg indicated willingness to entrust a cabinet to Hitler as long as the latter respected the parliamentary principles it was based upon.

At this point, however, Hitler had little desire of assuming such a responsibility. Rather, he intended to deal with his most dangerous opponent, General von Schleicher, prior to any further move. Hitler assumed that Schleicher would lose greatly in popularity as the "winter chancellor" and that he would isolate himself within the *Reichswehr* in the process. Although undoubtedly unintentionally, Schleicher indeed presented Hitler with the first opportunity to strike. He had commissioned the head of his department, Lieutenant Colonel Eugen Ott, to call on Hitler. For three hours, Hitler prevailed upon the officer, persuasively arguing that the appointment of Schleicher to the post of chancellor brought with it far more dangers than the *Reichswehr* had realized.

On December 4, Hitler planted the next land-mine in Schleicher's path. This time the conspiracy against Schleicher was to take place within the inner circles of the East Prussian *Reichswehr*. This body was headed by General Werner von Blomberg in his capacity as military commander of the area and by Colonel Walter von Reichenau who served as chief of staff. The latter received a voluminous, carefully composed letter in which Hitler pointed out that he held "General von Schleicher's present cabinet to be particularly unfortunate because it cannot solve this problem of the inner, spiritual rearmament of the nation."

Hitler desired to "overcome Marxism, to establish a new unity of spirit and will in the Volk and a universal spiritual, moral and ethical armament of the nation." He expressed the aim of bringing about "technical rearmament, the organizational mobilization of the power of the people (*Volkskraft*) for the purpose of national defense, and the attainment of a legal recognition by the rest of the world of the new situation that has already been brought about." As Hitler put it: "East Prussia can be saved only if Germany is saved. It is clear that Schleicher's cabinet will once more delay and impede this one and only possible deliverance" [Hitler's accession to power]. On December 6, the newly elected Reichstag met for its first session. Hitler had seen to having one of his party members appointed chairman by seniority, the eighty-two-year-old General Karl von Litzmann, popularly known as the "lion of Brzeziny," an ardent admirer of the Führer. Litzmann's opening address contained a long list of accusations aimed at Hindenburg, whom he accused of having vested his trust in a certain Hermann Müller, a Brüning, or a von Papen as Reich chancellors, but had to this date declined to call upon Hitler.

Subsequently, Göring, who had distinguished himself as a recipient of Germany's highest military award, the *pour-le-mérite*, and as Hitler's "best man," was elected president of the Reichstag with the help of the votes cast by the Center Party and the Bavarian People's Party. In his address, Göring declared that the National Socialists profoundly regretted that "the appointment of the Reich minister of defense as chancellor had made the *Reichswehr* into a bone of political contention."

The stage was set. Hitler had only to stand by and observe the further development of the situation up to the certain downfall of Schleicher. Moreover, he could prepare the setting for his presidential cabinet by either directly influencing the advisers of Hindenburg himself or by indirectly proceeding through the offices of his military experts Göring and Röhm. Two conferences with von Papen, held on January 4 and 18, were crucial to this drive, as were the later meetings with Colonel Oskar von Hindenburg, the Reich president's nephew, and State Secretary Otto Meissner on January 22. By January 28, Schleicher was forced to resign, since Hindenburg had not accorded him the right to dissolve the Reichstag. The next day, Göring assured Meissner in a most innocent manner that the National Socialists would not oppose the reinstitution of the monarchy, provided that two thirds of the people expressed this desire.

Rumors that Schleicher intended to stage a Putsch and that the Potsdam garrison would march on Wilhelmstrasse hastened the formation of
a new government. Because of the tense and unstable situation, the new
Reich minister of defense was sworn into office as a precautionary measure. It is revealing to note that the position was to be occupied by the
former commander of the army corps (*Wehrkreis*) of East Prussia, General
Werner von Blomberg. The aforementioned Colonel von Reichenau, previously chief of staff of the division deployed in East Prussia, was assigned
the post of chief of the ministerial office.

The East Prussian landowner and Reich president, Field Marshal von
Hindenburg, gave his blessings to the new Presidential Chancellor Adolf
Hitler on January 30, 1933. In doing so, he accorded Hitler his complete
trust from that day onward. The Reich president yielded to all the chancellor's demands and even granted the dissolution of the Reichstag, a measure
he had earlier denied Schleicher. Having become chancellor, Hitler immediately seized the opportunity to gain the favor of the military. He strove to
win over to his cause those generals who had not yet joined the ranks and
files of his more ardent admirers.

Already on February 3, Hitler spoke before the men in command of the
army and navy and expounded his principles to them. As he would do repeatedly throughout the years to come, Hitler expressed his desire that the
army remain the sole armed force within Germany. He insisted that there
would not be any absorption of party formations into the military, as in the
prototype Fascist militia units. He promoted the idea of instilling a military spirit in the general populace by all possible means while the twin evils
of Marxism and pacifism were eradicated. Hitler explained the motivation
behind his struggle to be that of reversing the Treaty of Versailles and the
restrictions it had imposed upon Germany's military. He claimed that he
would invest in the military all and everything he could manage to save.
Since 1918, no head of government had proposed such an enticing program
to the generals. Not surprisingly, the generals rejoiced at the prospect of additional funding and suppressed any and all doubts they might still have
entertained. In the course of the following years, Hitler liberally distributed
promotions, awards, and remuneration among the generals. They became
some of his most faithful and loyal followers. Ignoring vulgar insults, unjustified accusations, and headmaster-like admonitions, the generals bore the
reign of the former corporal with patience and without much resistance.

On March 12, 1933, the customary commemoration of the dead of the First World War took place, at the time still termed the Day of National Mourning (*Volkstrauertag*). Hitler had decided not only to rename the holiday, calling it the Heroes' Memorial Day (*Heldengedenktag*) from 1934 on, but also customarily took advantage of the occasion to announce additional measures to strengthen the armed forces. He did this nearly every year prior to the Second World War, staging impressive military parades to give his announcements the proper setting. March 12, 1933, was the first in a series of similar annual celebrations. Hitler marked the day by proclaiming that both the black-white-red banner and the swastika flag would serve as the official standards of the Reich. In spite of the fact that this measure was in blatant defiance of the Weimar Constitution, both Hitler and Hindenburg signed their names to it, and the *Wehrmacht* rejoiced at the return of its beloved black-white-red ensign.

March 21, 1933, "Potsdam Day," was to signify the union of old imperial Germany and its young "nationalist" counterpart, personified by Hindenburg and Hitler respectively. The multitude of generals of the old army and members of the German high nobility assembled on this occasion created a grandiose backdrop for the *Reichswehr* units, SS and SA men, members of the nationalist veterans' group (*Stahlhelm*), and various other national military associations as they marched past the rostrum. Judging by outward appearances alone, an unwitting member of the audience that day might have thought that the restoration of monarchy and the feudal state was imminent.

Regardless of all princes, barons, and generals present at Potsdam, the future of Germany would be determined by one man alone—Adolf Hitler. To him, these remnants of the feudal system were no more than pawns in a game, pawns he knew how to handle and how to make into willful instruments for his designs.

As a first step toward this end, it was imperative for Hitler to sever all of Germany's international ties and, above all, to prepare for Germany's withdrawal from the League of Nations. He knew that he would have to bring about such a measure prior to the implementation of equality of rights in military affairs that the League of Nations had determined to grant Germany in its December 11, 1932, session.

With these considerations in mind, Hitler delivered his first "peace speech" on May 17, 1933—one of the many such addresses that were to follow. It was the primary purpose of this speech to preclude any contractual settlement of these matters by placing exorbitant demands upon the League of Nations, demands it could not possibly meet.

In the meantime, the number of *Reichswehr* generals who admired Hitler without reservation had grown steadily, but there still were several important members of the military who were ill at ease with the Führer. General Freiherr von Fritsch, the new commander in chief of the army, figured most prominently among these. For Hitler, it had become increasingly clear that he needed to place a more reliable man, a party member, amongst the top-ranking army men—and he chose Göring for the task.

In order to transform this former air force captain into a general of the *Reichswehr*, Hitler required Hindenburg's connivance. He arranged for Göring to present Hindenburg with a tax-exempt country estate, renamed "Hindenburg Neudeck," at a celebration in Tannenberg on August 27, 1933. In addition, Hindenburg received the Prussian estate Langenau and the Preussenwald forest. He demonstrated his appreciation for these gifts by promoting Göring, the former captain, to the rank of general of infantry—a process without doubt unparalleled in the history of the Prussian-German army. Later, at the September "Reich Party Congress of Victory," Hitler accompanied the new *Reichswehr* general at the maneuvers of the Fifth *Reichswehr* division stationed in Ulm instead of his usual routine of conducting "*Wehrmacht* Day."

Hitler announced Germany's withdrawal from the League of Nations on October 14, 1933. To his great astonishment, neither Great Britain nor France undertook any steps militarily to counter his move. In his eyes, this lack of resolution on their part provided ample proof of their internal weakness and inferiority.

At the same time, he secured Hindenburg's approval for new elections to the Reichstag. This meant that the legislature would be composed exclusively of National Socialists in the future. Hindenburg had expressed concern with regard to this topic, fearing for the preservation of his rights as Reich president within the framework of such a newly constituted Reichstag.

In order to dispel Hindenburg's reservations, Hitler assured him that he did not intend to infringe upon the Reich president's privileges. In an October 14 press release, Hitler instructed the *Reichswehr* not to assign guards of honor to him on official occasions, "for he desires that this high military honor be reserved for the Reich president and the high military officers."

On November 8 and 9, 1933, the festivities in commemoration of the 1923 Putsch afforded Hitler the opportunity to regain the favor of the armed forces. Hitler proclaimed his commitment to both *Reichswehr* and regional police. He also took it upon himself to swear in recruits for both his personal body guard (*Leibstandarte Adolf Hitler*), members of which were allowed to carry arms from March 17 onward, and the recruits for Göring's and Röhm's equally armed staff guards (*Stabswachen*).

Clearly, Hitler's insistence that the *Wehrmacht* constituted "the sole bearer of arms" in Germany was not entirely true. What he neglected to mention, furthermore, was the fact that the number of recruits for Göring's police units had constantly been on the rise.

In his January 30, 1934, address before the Reichstag, Hitler made clear his opposition to the restoration of monarchy in Germany. Shortly thereafter, on February 3, he dissolved all monarchist clubs and associations. On the occasion of the War Remembrance Day (*Heldengedenktag*), following a proposal by Blomberg, Hindenburg bestowed the chief emblem of the party, the eagle and swastika, upon all members of the *Reichswehr*, despite the fact that it was not yet accepted as the national emblem. Members of the armed forces would henceforth bear Hitler's sign on tunic, cap, and steel helmet. Warships suffered a similar fate. Apparently, Hindenburg, Blomberg, and the entire *Reichswehr* had entered into a competition with party organizations to see which of them could implement the National Socialist revolution the fastest.

Nonetheless, Hitler was far from satisfied. It was the question of Hindenburg's succession that was foremost in his mind during those days. Undoubtedly, Hitler himself intended to ultimately assume the post of Reich president. Unlike the late Reich President Ebert, Hitler had little desire to function as the commander of the military in name only. He coveted both titular and actual control over the Reichswehr generals, much like the control Hindenburg had enjoyed.

Still Hitler doubted whether the generals would truly accept him as their superior: he decided to improve his image by proving his "manly" courage in a rather peculiar manner. He attempted to gain the generals' favor by having a number of top-ranking SA men, some of whom had been personal friends for years, murdered in cold blood. In the course of time, irreconcilable differences between *Reichswehr* and the SA had become apparent. These differences in opinion threatened to overshadow the earlier successful cooperation between both groups, as in East Prussia.

It is highly probable that the true issue at stake was the coordination (*Gleichschaltung*) of party and state, which strongly affected all realms of public life at the time and particularly the party storm troopers (SA). The SA units (*Standarten*) had, with Hitler's full approval, appropriated for themselves the numbers of old imperial garrison regiments. The *Reichswehr* generals most feared the application of the *Gleichschaltung* process to the top echelons of *Reichswehr* and SA. Röhm, the SA chief of staff, sought to promote this development in the hope of personal advancement. After all, if Göring, a former captain, could rise to the rank of *Reichswehr* General of Infantry, then Röhm, a retired captain and lieutenant colonel in Bolivia, could be promoted to general with equal justice.

Although Hitler actively pursued the process of *Gleichschaltung* of party and state, he stood firmly opposed to it insofar as the SA was concerned. He strongly believed that the establishment of an army based upon two years of compulsory military service was crucial to his plans for conquest in the East. Hence, he was willing to defer to the generals. While neither Röhm nor any of the other SA leaders so much as contemplated mutiny, Hitler nonetheless had the most prominent among them arrested for "attempted treason" on June 30, 1934. For this, he chose those SA men whose past had been tainted by their involvement in the 1919–1920 *Freikorps* movement. These men were then summarily shot without the benefit of a public trial.

The *Reichswehr* aided and abetted Hitler in the preparation for these assassinations both in a material and in a spiritual sense. As early as June 28, the Reich minister of defense, General von Blomberg, put the armed forces on alert. At the same time, Blomberg published an article in the *Völkischer Beobachter*, applauding the Führer and claiming that "the *Wehrmacht* stands by the leadership of the state in discipline and loyalty" and by "the Führer of the Reich, Adolf Hitler, who once came from our ranks and will always remain one of us."

On June 28 as well, the chief of the ministerial office, General von Reichenau, whose recent promotion had advanced him to the rank of major general, had Röhm expelled from the German Officers' League. This action was tantamount to declaring Röhm an outlaw to be hunted down at will. On July 1, the Berlin garrison goosestepped by the chancellery, hailing Hitler for the murder of the SA leaders. The *Reichswehr* stood by silently, tolerating the events in return for the convenient elimination of two of its most unpopular generals—former minister of defense, General von Schleicher, and his state secretary, Major General von Bredow. In the aftermath of these events, Hitler no longer needed to fear that control of the military might slip from his hands following the imminent death of Hindenburg. Indeed, he eagerly assumed control and charged on with his plans for the military even prior to Hindenburg's demise. In clear defiance of the constitution, Hitler arranged for the cabinet to appoint him successor to the Reich president the day before Hindenburg finally passed away. On August 2, the very day Hindenburg died, Hitler hurriedly altered the loyalty oath to be taken by all incumbent soldiers to read, "to render unconditional obedience to Adolf Hitler."

On August 6, the Reichstag met to mourn Hindenburg. Immediately after its session, the *Reichswehr* paraded by its new commander in chief (*Oberbefehlshaber*) for the first time. The parade provided a curious illustration of precisely what Hitler had neglected to mention when he had earlier promised the generals that the army would remain "the sole bearer of arms in the nation." Armed contingents of the regional police, the SS *Leibstandarte*, and the *Feldjägerkorps* strode in step behind the *Reichswehr* units.

Naturally, such displays were not in the least to the taste of the generals. At times, it appeared as though a sharp controversy would arise between *Reichswehr* and SS. However, an emotional appeal by Hitler at the "Rally of German Leadership" in Berlin on January 3, 1935, dispelled such notions. Moreover, as mediator between the front lines, Göring read a declaration of loyalty to the Führer, emphasizing that he spoke in his capacity as "a high-ranking National Socialist leader and at the same time as a *Reichswehr* general and a member of the Reich cabinet."

Hitler announced the reintroduction of general conscription to Germany on the 1935 *Heldengedenktag*. While the generals were exceedingly well pleased by this measure, the general public in Germany was shocked and deeply disturbed by the possible consequences of this action. Perhaps sensing this disquiet, Hitler made ample use of the services of old Field Marshal von Mackensen, who made several token appearances at military ceremonies. Hitler used Mackensen's presence to cover his back so that he could proceed with his plans in spite of Hindenburg's demise. While Hitler displayed great skill in dealing with military men in general, the extent to which Mackensen came under his spell was truly astonishing. On July 31, 1935, Mackensen even terminated his honorary membership in the *Stahlhelm*, thereby facilitating Hitler's dissolution of the front-line veterans' association. As a sign of appreciation for the services rendered by Mackensen, Hitler presented the marshal with the estate of Prüssow on October 22. Shortly thereafter, on November 7, 1935, the *Stahlhelm* ceased to exist.

At the September 16 "Reich Party Congress of Honor," the elite of Germany's generals, men such as Blomberg, Fritsch, Raeder, and Göring, marched up in front of Hitler as though they were mere recruits. At the same party congress, Hitler declared the swastika flag the exclusive official

Reich banner. On November 7, 1935, he introduced the flag with the swastika emblem as the Reich battle flag to the *Wehrmacht* and abolished the old black-white-red flag.

Parallel to these developments, General von Reichenau was assigned to head the Seventh Army Corps in Munich. In his capacity as chief of the ministerial office in the renamed Ministry of War, Reichenau was replaced by Major General Keitel, who assumed his post on October 1, 1935.

On March 7, the 1936 *Heldengedenktag*, Hitler sent troops to occupy the demilitarized zone in the Rhineland, thereby extending the military sovereignty of the Reich to encompass this area as well. On March 16, he introduced unit flags (*Truppenfahnen*) to the *Wehrmacht*. On April 20, Hitler created the first field marshal of his career, his Reich minister of war, General von Blomberg. In the course of the following years, Hitler accorded this title to twenty-eight members of his staff.

In July of 1936, Hitler secretly instigated the Third Reich's entanglement in the Spanish Civil War. On August 24, he decreed the extension of the compulsory conscription from one year to two years of military service. At the Reich party congress that year, Hitler had the audacity to claim that this two-year compulsory service would prove so beneficial to the young recruits that it would add ten years to their life expectancy.

The year 1937 passed much like the quiet before the storm. Not even the customary celebration of the *Heldengedenktag* was accompanied by any spectacular event connected to the military—as was usually the case. The bombing of the Spanish harbor Almería on May 31 was the only event worthy of note that year. Hitler had ordered the expeditionary force's venture as a reprisal for the shelling of the pocket battleship *Deutschland* while in Spanish coastal waters.

Behind the scenes, Hitler was busily preparing for his conquest of the East. On November 5, 1937, Hitler astonished his generals by revealing to them his intention of launching attacks upon Czechoslovakia and Austria in the near future. To Hitler's great displeasure, Blomberg and Fritsch did not in the least rejoice at such prospects. Instead, they ventured to voice misgivings over the Führer's military analysis of the situation and, in particular, they disputed his a priori assumption that the western powers would remain neutral and indifferent to a German move of such importance.

Hitler realized that, given their views on this topic, both Blomberg and Fritsch might become costly liabilities in the event of a war. Hence, he decided to rid himself of the two generals as soon as possible. This did not prove particularly difficult. Hitler succeeded in luring Blomberg into a marriage that provoked the minister's downfall, and Fritsch was discredited on account of alleged homosexuality. On February 4, 1938, Hitler made official the removal of both military men from office. He himself took over the Reich Ministry of War and thereby secured for himself an unchallenged position as supreme commander (*Oberster Befehlshaber*) of the *Wehrmacht*.

General of Artillery Keitel assumed Hitler's earlier responsibilities in presiding over the high command. Hitler appointed General of Artillery von Brauchitsch the new Commander in Chief of the Army. By promoting Göring to the rank of field marshal, Hitler made him the highest-ranking officer on active duty with the *Wehrmacht*. Furthermore, Hitler reassigned forty-six leading military men to various new command posts, while retiring fourteen others.

On March 10, Hitler issued the first mobilization order of his career. He called up several Bavarian military districts, judging their manpower sufficient for the invasion of Austria. On the same day, Hitler effected the dissolution of the *Soldatenbund*, the last bastion of the reactionary generals. Two days later, Hitler slipped into his new role as warlord. As an outward sign of this change, Hitler wore the *Wehrmacht's* cockade in the center of a wreath of the oakleaf cluster on his cap. After the Austrian venture had proven a complete success, Hitler had himself celebrated as a "victorious warlord" on the front pages of the *Völkischer Beobachter*. On March 13, the day of the *Heldengedenktag* festivities, Austria was officially incorporated into the German Reich.

On May 28, Hitler gave orders pertaining to "Case Green" in preparation for the invasion of Czechoslovakia. The date was set for October 2, 1938. At the same time, Hitler issued instructions for the construction of a new line of fortification along the Reich's western border, the West Wall. By August, it had become increasingly clear that Hitler intended to proceed as planned with the assault upon Czechoslovakia, in spite of strong opposition by the generals. Hitler was greatly annoyed, however, by the fact that the Munich Conference had ruined his plans for a forced entry into Czechoslovakia. An agreement was signed at the September 29 conference which provided for the ceding of the Sudeten German territories to the Reich and thus robbed him of his pretext for invasion.

General von Brauchitsch expressed his disappointment in the following terms: "Our weapons were not allowed to speak." Hitler vowed to make up shortly for the defeat he deemed himself to have suffered at

Munich. On October 9, he made public his plans for the construction of further fortifications in the vicinity of Aachen and Saarbrücken. And on October 21, despite solemn pledges to the contrary, Hitler instructed his generals to proceed with preparations for "the elimination of the remainder of Czechoslovakia."

In light of the remarkably short time period in which Hitler rose to his position as the unchallenged supreme commander of the *Wehrmacht*, one has to grant him considerable political cunning. Hitler followed the path of legality to power, an approach greatly appreciated by the *Wehrmacht* generals. As he fought them with their own weapons, he secured victory for himself in the end. The military's leaders bowed to his command even if his orders blatantly violated the constitution or obviously defied international law. No general ever refused to obey the Führer in public.

Among the three thousand generals—of whom a good number were opposed to Hitler's handling of military matters—only one, Colonel General Beck, had the courage of his convictions. Because his conscience did not allow him to further support Hitler's policies, Beck voluntarily handed in his resignation as chief of the general staff, and he was allowed to do so without suffering any retribution from Hitler.

Wehrmacht Day 1935
Hitler salutes the Wehrmacht Commanders in Chief. Included are Field Marshal
von Blomberg, Colonel General Göring, General von Fritsch, and Admiral Raeder.

X

Life in Hitler's Germany

Life changed for almost everyone when Hitler's Germany emerged. New technology gave to the new masters immense powers of which absolute rulers and despots in the past had never even dreamed. The radio, telephone, and automobile meant that the National Socialist writ ran from corner to corner of Germany. Some few people ignored the existence of the New Order, but it was very hard to do so. The Nazi Party intended to "coordinate all aspects of life (Gleichschaltung)" in Germany and many people agreed with both the objectives and methods of the Nazis. For those who did not agree, there was always a trip to a concentration camp, even if only for a few weeks. As Hitler saw them, there existed four areas of concern: youth and education, the position of women, the use of sports in Germany, and the arts.

YOUTH

▸ June 18, 1933 *Youth was always a focus for the Nazis. In many ways, National Socialism was a "youth" movement, tapping the energies and idealism of the young. While Hitler abolished all political parties, he took their youth groups and merged them with the National Socialist youth organization, the Hitler Youth.*

The same day, Hitler announced the nomination of Baldur von Schirach, the youth leader of the Nazi Party (*Reichsjugendführer*), to the position of youth leader of the German Reich. By virtue of this appointment, Schirach became head of a public office that presided over all of the youth associations and similar organizations in the entire Reich. This facilitated the speedy establishment of the Hitler Youth (HJ) as the one and only youth organization in Germany.

The military associations (*Wehrverbände*) were naturally to be subsumed under a single organization in like fashion. For this purpose the Young Steel Helmets (*Jungstahlhelm*) and the German Nationalist *Scharnhorstbund* were both integrated into the Hitler Youth (HJ) and the Nazi Party storm troopers (SA). Hitler had succeeded in convincing their leaders, in particular Franz Seldte, of the national necessity of such a measure, and he rewarded this cooperation with the following proclamation of June 26:

> National Socialists! Men of the SA and SS! Men of the *Jung-stahlhelm*!
>
> An aim that has been pursued steadily for fourteen years has now been accomplished. With the subordination of the *Jung-stahlhelm* to my command as supreme commander of the SA and the integration of the *Scharnhorstbund* in the Hitler Youth, the unification of the political fighting movement of the German nation has been carried out and completed. The SA, the SS, the *Stahlhelm* and the HJ will now and for all time comprise the sole organizations that the National Socialist state recognizes as responsible for the political education of our youth and our men.
>
> It was understandable that, in the years following the revolution, resistance against the November traitors and their disastrous regime was attempted in the most diverse corners of our German fatherland. Independently and without any knowledge of each other, the men rose up and organized parties and associations to fight the Marxist state. Doubtless they all wanted only the best. However, if Germany was to be saved, this could be done only by one single movement and not by thirty different ones.
>
> The future of our Volk does not depend upon how many associations stand up for this future, but whether or not one is successful in subordinating the desires of many to a single will and thus effectively uniting them in one movement. Just as the German armed forces (*Reichswehr*) were once forced to eliminate the independent armed units (*Freikorps*), in spite of the many merits of individual units, in order to once again give the German Volk a single army, the National Socialist Movement was no less forced to eliminate the countless federations, organizations and associations, regardless of their merits or lack of merits, in order to finally construct for the

German Volk a single uniform organization built upon its political will. A great number of the best of Germans failed to comprehend this task, and many others did not wish to understand it.

Today the meaning and hence the necessity of this tremendous fight is clear to anyone who loves our Volk and believes in its future.

Thus in past years, we have been forced to suppress numerous associations purely out of these considerations. Similarly, we will also prevent the emergence of any new association that would serve only to perpetuate the old fragmentation. The inalterability of this decision imposes upon us the obligation to be just.

Therefore it is our desire as Germans and National Socialists to acknowledge honestly the difference that existed between the other associations and the *Stahlhelm*. We are willing to admit that the hundreds of thousands of German men who had served as soldiers at the front were drawn into this organization and thus withdrawn from the system. However, in the hour in which the fate of Germany turned, the foremost leader of this association (*Bundesführer*) declared his support for the National Socialist revolution.

Now this man has drawn the final conclusions from the historical developments and decreed that, with the exception of the traditional association of the old front-line soldiers, the entire younger generation of the *Stahlhelm* is to be subordinated to the SA, and the *Scharnhorstbund* is to be integrated into the Hitler Youth and placed under my command.

My SA leaders and SA comrades!

This decision will one day be judged in German history to have been an extremely rare proof of a truly magnanimous, national outlook. What might otherwise have only been achieved after years of disagreements and drawn-out struggles—that in turn would have used up German power—has been resolved by the insightful deed of a man who has been sitting next to me in loyal solidarity in the cabinet since January 30.

Our further order, that in the future the remaining traditional association of the old front-line fighters would recognize no other party membership than that of the National Socialist Movement, finally provides me with the opportunity to lift the membership ban on our part.

In view of this great development, I feel moved to first of all thank you, my old comrades in the party, the SA and the SS, from a heart that is overflowing, for the boundless loyalty with which you have stood by me in good times and in bad through so many years. This is attributable primarily to your steadfastness. You were once fanatic fighters against the old system, and today you are the unshakable guards of the National Socialist revolution.

Second, I would also like to now thank those who voluntarily took what was certainly no easy decision to relinquish their proud independence for the sake of a greater community. And thus for the first time I may welcome the comrades of the *Jungstahlhelm* who are now marching in our ranks.

From this day onward, I order all leaders and SA and SS men to accept the men of the *Stahlhelm* who have entered our community as comrades and to include them in the eternal bond that binds us and that shall never be broken. No matter what memories the past holds, for you and me, nothing counts but the great future to which we have committed ourselves.

If we have succeeded, in the course of many years, in converting millions of former Marxists, in leading them to us, in admitting them into our ranks, then certainly we must and will be able to take on national men who come out of another camp to enter into a bond of amity with us as friends and as comrades. I thus expect of every National Socialist that he recognize the magnitude of this historic development and contribute, by his own behavior, to bringing about the most profound fusion between ourselves and the newcomers as quickly as possible.

Men of the SA, SS and *Stahlhelm*, to our wonderful National Socialist Movement and our German Volk:

Sieg Heil!

► September 14, 1935 *Hitler congratulated the "new German youth."*

On the morning of September 14, Hitler spoke before 54,000 members of the Hitler Youth in the Nuremberg stadium, where he used the later much-quoted phrase describing the ideal German man of the future that he had coined in *Mein Kampf* "Swift as greyhounds, tough as leather, and hard as Krupp steel."

German youth!

You are now lining up for this roll call for the third time, more than 54,000 representatives of a community that grows from year to year. The importance of those you personify here each year has become consistently greater. We can see it not only in terms of quantity, but in terms of quality as well. If I think back on the first roll call and on the second and compare them to this one today, I can see the same development we see evidenced throughout the rest of German *Volksleben*: our Volk is becoming increasingly disciplined, sturdier, more taut—and youth is beginning to as well.

The ideal of the man has been subjected to different views in our Volk as well. There were times—they seem to be long ago and are almost incomprehensible to us—when the ideal of the young German man was, to use the jargon, a beer-drinking, hard-living fellow. Today we are happy to note that the ideal is no longer the beer-drinking and hard-living young man, but the tough young man, impervious to wind and weather. For the main thing is not how many glasses of beer he can drink, but how many blows he can withstand; not how long he can make the rounds night after night, but how many kilometers he can march.

Today the beer-happy bourgeois (*Bierspiesser*) of those times is no longer regarded as the ideal of the German Volk, but men and girls who are fit as a fiddle, who are string taut. What we want from our German youth is different from what the past wanted of it. In our eyes, the German youth of the future must be slender and supple, swift as greyhounds, tough as leather, and hard as Krupp steel. We must cultivate a new man in order to prevent the ruin of our Volk by the degeneration manifested in our age.

▸ December 1, 1936 *All youth were to be members of the Hitler Youth and subject to its discipline.*

On December 1, Hitler gave a short talk before the Reich cabinet, detailing foreign policy. A dozen laws were enacted that day, of which the most remarkable was the "Law Regarding the Hitler Youth:"

§1 Within the boundaries of the Reich, the entire German youth is integrated in the Hitler Youth.

§2 Outside of home and school, the entire German youth is to be educated in the Hitler Youth with regard to physical exercise, mental functioning and ethical requirements, in the spirit of National Socialism, for service to the Volk and the national community (*Volksgemeinschaft*).

▸ April 30, 1938 *Hitler always put German youth at the front of his programs.*

On April 30, Hitler issued an appeal for donations to the Youth Hostel Association. On May 1, Hitler himself established a "medal in commemoration of March 13, 1938," the day he designated as marking the Austrian union with Germany. At 9:00 a.m. on May Day, Hitler addressed the German youth in the Olympic Stadium. His speech that day is reproduced below verbatim:

My youth! My German boys and girls!

You have the great fortune to live in an age of which the German nation shall never have to be ashamed. In your youth you have witnessed the rise of our Volk. Your young hearts were set aglow and became impassioned by the historic events of these last weeks and months that stood under the spell of the reunion of the German Volk. This outward development was, my boys and girls, only the outcome of an inward development in our German Volk reflecting its union. And today we celebrate the day of this union of our Volk!

For centuries, our Volk was torn and at odds with itself, and hence it was incapacitated in its outside dealings; it was unhappy, lacking means of defense and a sense of honor. Ever since the victory of the Movement, under the banner of which you stand today, the unification of the German people has been accomplished. And now Providence allows us to reap the fruits of our labor: Greater Germany! This union did not come about as a matter of coincidence, but rather as the result of the National Socialist Movement's systematic education of our Volk.

The Movement has rescued this Volk from its division into a wild agglomeration of parties, classes, confessions, and ranks and has made an entity of it. And this educational process begins at an age where the individual's views are not yet encumbered by prejudice. Our youth is the building block of our Reich! You are Greater Germany! It is for you that the German *Volksgemeinschaft* restructured itself.

At the fore of the Reich there stands a Führer; at the fore of the Reich there stands a Volk; and at the fore of this one Volk stands our German youth!

Seeing you here, my belief in Germany's future becomes boundless and unshakable! For I know that you will fulfill all our expectations!

So on this May Day, I greet you in our new great Germany! For you are our springtime! Through you shall and must be accomplished what has been fought for by generations throughout the centuries:

Deutschland!

▸ March 25, 1939 *The Hitler Youth were to include all German boys.*

On March 25, Hitler signed into law two "Ordinances on the Implementation of the Law on the Hitler Youth." The first of these provided for the creation of a *Stamm-Hitlerjugend* (core Hitler Youth), privileged as a subdivision of the Nazi Party. Hitler Youth members of good standing were to be granted admission to this "core" unit after a one-year membership in the Hitler Youth movement.

The second ordinance decreed that all German boys between the ages of ten and eighteen years were to partake in the activities of the Hitler Youth and were obliged to accept compulsory membership in general Hitler Youth sections. This decree contained a slogan to inspire German youngsters to take part in the labor service and to participate in defense exercises: "Service with the Hitler Youth is an honorable service to the German Volk."

▸ May 1, 1939 *Hitler gave a charge to German youth.*

On May 1, the celebration of the "German Volk's National Holiday" afforded Hitler the opportunity to deliver two major speeches. He was painfully aware that the tide of public favor had turned against him after the events in Prague. Despite his speech before the Reichstag with its staged applause and paid claquers, the dictator felt the lack of enthusiasm throughout the country.

After all, the public was well aware that Hitler's reckless undertakings could spell ruin, not only for himself, but for all of Germany. While Hitler indulged in rhetoric, his words revealed that friendly relations with Britain and Poland were no longer possible. The German public's appraisal of the situation was decidedly more realistic than Hitler's. The man in the street understood perfectly well that, if the German government insisted on continuing its present course, Germany was headed for collision with numerous other states, primarily with the Western powers and Poland, and would soon find itself entangled in another world war, unless a miracle occurred at the last minute.

It was hardly surprising that the prevailing opinion in the country greatly infuriated Hitler. Who did these ungrateful people think they were? Had not the incredible, indeed miraculous, story of his life demonstrated over and over again that he was always right? Had not his domestic struggle lent credence to the fact that he always reigned supreme in the end and that it would be no different in his dealings abroad? Why did they no longer trust him?

Hitler finally arrived at the conclusion that it would be best for all concerned if he simply ignored the opinions of this "stubborn German Volk," and these "old troublemakers," who constantly indulged in undue criticism of their leaders. And it was thus that Hitler came to address Germany's youth, which he hoped to prevent from following along the same path as their fathers before them. Hitler was still confident that, provided there was sufficient and systematic indoctrination, he could instill in the next generation the unshakable belief in their Führer, to whom they owed blind obedience.

Germany's youth was to be "steeled" against any foreign interference. If he were ever forced to call on them, so he contemplated, Germany's youth would stand united behind him and head off to do battle unto death in the name of their beloved Führer.

In the morning hours of May 1, Hitler addressed a crowd of 100,000 Hitler Youth members gathered at the Olympic Stadium in Berlin. In the course of the past six years, this annual address to Germany's youth had become a national institution. Launched in 1933, in the days when Hindenburg was still alive, this forum served Hitler exceedingly well in his effort to rally Germany's youth around their leader. Without fail, every year he found it necessary to remind them of how fortunate they were to live in "such great times as these." Since the tide was to turn against National Socialist Germany soon, this speech, held on May 1, 1939, constituted the last in the series of Hitler's addresses to the youth.

In the future, he would restrict his efforts to inspire proper young Germans to a select group of officer cadets joining the *Wehrmacht*.

On May 1, 1939, Hitler would no longer speak of the "great times" in store for the German youth. At this point, appropriately, he placed many a demand on the unsuspecting young people whom he forewarned to stand ready "should the hour come." He challenged them to "steel" themselves to become "tough men" who "know from the start that nothing in life is free." Hitler's May 1 address had the following content:

My German youth!

In 1933 I was able to greet you for the first time, standing alongside the venerable Field Marshal von Hindenburg, in the Berlin Lustgarten. In greeting you then, my youth of Berlin, I greeted the youth of the Germany of that time! Six years have passed by since, years in which our Volk underwent a tremendous, historic transformation. The Germany then trodden upon, an impotent empire, has become today's Greater Germany. A nation then not worthy of respect has become a Volk greatly respected. A people without arms has become one of the best-armed nations in the world. What was then at the mercy of its surroundings has become something secure today, secure thanks to our own force and to the friends we possess today.

That you, the youth of today, should belong to a respected and strong Volk is exclusively the result of the work we wrought domestically. When, twenty years ago, the Nazi Party was created, it already raised a new banner to be borne by the new Germany. After barely fifteen years of struggle, this symbol has become the official flag of the German state. Ever since, the resurrection of Germany has been inexorably tied to this new symbol.

You German boys and girls will one day be called on to assume the protection of this flag. But you shall be able to carry it forth and protect it successfully with dignity only if you stand by this flag with the same unity as does the National Socialist Movement and, through it, the German Volk of today. And for you, it will be decidedly easier. We had to laboriously fight for this flag. It is yours already today; you have been raised beneath this flag. In your youth already, you bear this symbol on your sleeves, you march on its orders. I count on you! You shall never forget what has made Germany great. In your youth, you have witnessed the most profound and rare of historic transformations. Many of you cannot quite grasp this yet.

Those among you who are more mature have experienced, and reflected on, its glowing essence. I know that your young hearts already beat strongly and sensitively when, in this year, I strode forth to fashion the Greater German Reich and to reassert its rights derived from a history one thousand years old. You shall be called on, in light of the greatness of this time, to fulfill tasks as they confront you, and assuredly they will confront you above all. The German nation will one day in the future represent a power that has its point of departure in youth. We shall never be more than what we are essentially ourselves. And we shall never be more than what our youth is today.

And I expect of you that you shall become straightforward, tough German men and reliable German women. You shall be men who know from the start that nothing in life is free. You must struggle for everything in this world; you can keep only that for which you are willing, at all times, to stand up and defend, if necessary. The deceptive slogans of the outside world shall not penetrate your hearts; it tries to poison an upright Volk and thereby to introduce divisions and to destroy it. In your youth, you must already attend to both body and spirit. You must be healthy. You must resist everything that might conceivably poison your body. For the future will assess the individual German in accordance with the works of his spirit and the strength of his health. Above all, we want to see in you a youth that crosses its arms and forms a solid, impenetrable communion.

Germany has witnessed many years of profound inner divisions and impotence. These days are over now thanks to the inner resurrection of our Volk. It shall find its ultimate embodiment in you. And thus it is of supreme importance that you should be aware of this in your youth.

We are surrounded by peoples who do not desire this realization on our part. They wish to deny our Volk the plain necessities of life, the right to life so accepted as a matter of course for so many other peoples. We and the other young peoples must laboriously seek to regain this right to life that our forefathers so thoughtlessly forfeited. Perhaps one day we shall even need to stand up for it. And in this, too, I count on you primarily, my German boys!

Above all, I expect that, should the hour come in which an outside world believes it can seize the freedom of Germany, a cry of millions will shatter the air. It will be a cry in unison and hence so forceful that all will have to acknowledge that the times of inner divisions in Germany are finally over. The hard school of National Socialist education will then have successfully fashioned the German Volk. And thereby we shall obey the commandment of the Almighty who has imparted to us a common blood and a common language. In the acknowledgment of this commandment within the past six years, Germany has once more become great and respected, albeit perhaps too little beloved. Alas, we Germans shall have to be content with the love of our fellow countrymen (*Volksgenossen*).

And I am content to know that you, my *Volksgenossen* and my German youth, above all, stand behind me. I know I am in your hearts just as you know my heart belongs to you without reservation! And should the outside world threaten us and thunder against us—they shall not succeed for the very reason they have never yet succeeded: German unity!

That it will prevail in the future, for this you are the guarantors just as the great men of today guarantee this at present. Just as you have every right to look back to those who created Germany with great pride, so we wish to rest at ease looking to you in the future! The days in which our youth had to be ashamed of the generation then alive are over. You can truly be proud of the men who lead Germany today. And I am equally proud that you constitute the German youth of today.

In this spirit, we come together on this day that once marked Germany's inner divisions. Today it is the day of the unity of the German *Volksgemeinschaft*. It is the day of our faithful avowal, our avowal of our Volk and of our thousand-year-old Greater German Reich.

To our Volk and to our Greater Germany:

Sieg Heil!

SPORT

Sports in National Socialist Germany were to form a strong and healthy people.

▶ December 12, 1933 *The Olympic Games represented both a showcase for Hitler's Germany and a means to demonstrate German superiority.*

On December 14, Hitler took initial steps toward organizing the Olympic games to be held in Berlin in 1936 and issued the following proclamation:

Today I have granted my final approval for the commencement and completion of the structures on the stadium grounds. With this, Germany is being given a sports arena the likes of which is to be found nowhere in the world. The fact that the completion of the planned large-scale construction work is creating many thousands of days of work is something that fills me with particular joy.

However, buildings alone are not sufficient to guarantee that German sports are accorded a position in the international competitions that correspond to the world prestige of our nation. Much more significant is the unified, committed will of the nation to choose the best competitors out of all Germans and to train and steel them so that we may pass the forthcoming competition with honors.

A no less important task is the sustained and lasting attention to physical exercise in the entire German Volk as one of the most important cultural assets of the National Socialist state. We will make of this a permanent basis for the spirit of the New Germany in the physical strength of its Volk. The Reich sports leader (*Reichssportführer*) is solely responsible to myself and the competent Reich Minister of the Interior for the successful accomplishment of these two tasks. I ask all organizations, official bodies, etc. to grant him every possible support and encouragement.

Berlin, December 14, 1933
Adolf Hitler

▶ March 14, 1935 *For Hitler, sport was simply military training.*

On March 14, as a prelude to the announcement of the resumption of conscription, Hitler outlined the future military sports function of the SA in the following decree:

The new state requires a robust, hardy race. Our superior training of the spirit must be accompanied and reinforced by an aggressive training of the body by means of simple, useful, and natural physical exercises.

In order to give added impetus and direction to the efforts of our youth, I am establishing the award of the SA sports badge for the entire SA and all of its former sections; it is to be awarded upon completion of a conscientiously discharged period of training when an achievement test has been passed.

In order to lend a more conscious expression to the cultivation of military spirit (*wehrhafter Geist*) in every area of the German Volk, I further direct that this SA sports badge may also be acquired and worn by non-members of the Movement insofar as they fulfill, within a racial and superior sense, the National Socialist requirements.

The implementation provisions will be issued by the chief of staff.

The Supreme Commander of the SA: Adolf Hitler

▶ March 15, 1937 *Hitler was also interested in keeping older men fit. This policy turned out to be quite useful in the later days of the Second World War.*

On March 18, Hitler ordered renewed exercises for the holders of the SA sports badge in an effort to preserve the men's fitness for military service "up to an advanced age." The ordinance stated:

> In my February 15, 1935 decree, I defined the SA Sports Badge as a means for combat training of the body and for keeping alive the spirit of defense in the Volk in all walks of life.
>
> In order to assure the fitness for military service among the recipients of the SA sports badge up to old age, I authorize the chief of staff of the SA to make the further possession of the SA sports badge contingent upon successful participation in certain training exercises. I further upgrade the *Leistungsbuch* (record booklet) of the SA sports badge to a document that shall afford information on the physical condition and the political attitude of its bearer.
>
> Berlin, March 18, 1937
> Adolf Hitler

WOMEN

In general the Nazi Party took a very traditional view of the role of women. Still, many women voted for Hitler and National Socialist candidates.

▶ September 8, 1934 *Hitler always made much of women in the party and movement.*

On the morning of September 8, Hitler addressed the Hitler Youth in the Nuremberg Stadium and, at noon, spoke at a convention of the *NS Frauenschaft*, where he stated:

For the first time in years, I am once again taking part in a convention of National Socialist women and thus of National Socialist women's work. I know that the prerequisites for this have been established by the work of innumerable individual women and, in particular, by the work of their female leaders. The National Socialist Movement has not only seen but also found in woman its most loyal assistant from the time of its conception onward.

I remember the difficult years of the Movement's fight and especially those times in which good fortune seemed to have turned away from us, those times when many of us were in prisons, others had once more become fugitives, still others were in foreign parts; many of us were lying wounded in hospitals or had been killed. I remember the time when there were those among us who turned back, believing that we would never make it in the end, a time in that the spirit pervading Germany arrogantly believed that it could approach the problems only from the angle of reason, and when many lost faith in us as a result. I know that back then there were innumerable women who remained unshakably loyal to the Movement and to me.

At that time, the power of emotion truly proved itself to be stronger and better. We have seen that the clever mind can be misled only all too easily, that ostensibly intellectual arguments can cause men of weak intellect to falter, and that it is particularly in these times that the most profound inner instinct of preservation of the self and of the Volk awakens in a woman. Woman has proven to us that she knows what is right! In those times when the great Movement seemed, to many, to falter and all were united against us, the stability and sureness of emotion prevailed as stable factors when confronted with brooding intellect and supposed knowledge.

For only very few are endowed with the talent of penetrating superficial knowledge to the most profound inner meaning. But this most profound insight is ultimately the root of the world of emotion. That which perhaps only few philosophically gifted intellects are capable of analyzing scientifically can be sensed by the nature of an unspoiled human being with instinctive certainty. The feeling and, above all, the nature of woman has always acted throughout the ages as a supplement to the intellect of man.

And if at times in the course of human life the working spheres of men and women have shifted to become unnaturally aligned, this happened not because woman aspired to rule over man; rather, the reason lies in the fact that man was no longer capable of completely fulfilling his task. That, of course, is the miraculous thing about nature and Providence: no conflict is possible in the relations between the two sexes as long as each fulfills the task assigned to it by nature.

The catchword "women's liberation" is merely a phrase invented by the Jewish intellect, and its contents are marked by the same spirit. The German woman will never need to emancipate herself in an age supportive of German life. She possessed what nature gave her automatically as an asset to maintain and preserve; just as the man, in such an age, never had to fear that he would be ousted from his position in respect to woman.

Woman has been the last to contest man's right to his position. Only when he was no longer sure of himself in recognizing his duty did the immortal instinct of survival and preservation begin to revolt in woman. After this revolt, a shift took place that was not in accordance with Nature's design, and it prevailed until both sexes returned to what an eternally wise Providence assigned to them.

If it is said that a man's world is the state, that the man's world is his struggle, his willingness to devote himself to the community, one might perhaps say that a woman's world is a smaller one. For her world is her husband, her family, her children, and her home. But where would the larger world be if no one wanted to care for the small world? How could the larger world survive if there was no one who would make the cares of the smaller world the content of his life? No, the large world is built upon this small world! This greater world cannot survive if the small world is not firm. Providence assigned to woman the care of this, her very own world, and it is only on this foundation that the man's world can be formed and can grow.

However, these two worlds are never opposed to one another. They mutually complement each other, they belong together, just as man and wife belong together.

We do not feel that it is right when a woman forces her way into a man's world, in territory belonging to him; instead, we feel it is natural when both of these worlds remain divorced from one another. One of the worlds is home to the power of feelings, the power of the soul! The other is home to the power of recognition, the power of toughness, of resolution, and of fighting morale! In one case, this power requires the full willingness of the woman to devote her life to maintaining and nurturing this important sphere, and in the other case it requires the willingness of the man to safeguard life.

What a man sacrifices in struggling for his Volk, a woman sacrifices in struggling to preserve this Volk in individual cases. What a man gives in heroic courage on the battlefield, woman gives in eternally patient devotion, in eternally patient suffering and endurance. Every child to which she gives birth is a battle that she wages in her Volk's fateful question of to be or not to be. And hence both must mutually value and respect each other by recognizing that each part is accomplishing the task assigned to it by Nature and Providence. The performance of these two tasks will necessarily result in mutual respect. What the Jewish intellect maintains is not true—that respect is determined by the overlapping of the spheres of activity of the two sexes—but rather this respect requires that neither of the sexes endeavors to do what belongs to the other. This respect ultimately lies in the knowledge of each half that the other is doing everything necessary to maintain the whole!

Therefore, woman throughout the ages has always been the helpmate of man and thus his most loyal friend, and man, too, has been the protector of his wife throughout the ages and thus her best friend. And both perceived in this manner of living the common foundation for the existence of what they loved, and of its continued subsistence in the future. Woman is an egoist in maintaining her small world, putting man in a position to preserve the greater world, and man is an egoist in maintaining this greater world, for the one is indissolubly bound up with the other. We will stand up against an intellectualism of the most depraved sort that would tear asunder what God hath joined together.

Because woman originates in the most basic of roots, she is also the most stable element in the preservation of a people.

Ultimately, she has the most infallible sense for whatever is necessary to prevent a race from ceasing to be, for her children would bear the major brunt of all the suffering.

Man is often far too mentally unstable to find the right path by means of these basic insights. However, given favorable times and a good education, man will know just as well what his task is. We National Socialists have therefore protested for many years against deploying woman in political life, for in our view this would be unworthy.

A woman once said to me: you must see to it that women join parliament, for woman alone is capable of ennobling it. I do not believe, I replied to her, that human beings were meant to ennoble what is bad by its very nature, and a woman who became caught in the gears of this parliamentary system would not ennoble parliament; rather, this system would dishonor such a woman. I do not want to leave something to women that I intend to take away from men. Our opponents claimed that we would then never gain women for the Movement. But we have gained more than all of the other parties put together, and I know that we would have won over every last German woman had she been given just one opportunity to study parliament and the degrading role women play there.

For this reason we have integrated woman in the fight of the national community in accordance with the decrees of nature and Providence. To us, our women's movement is thus not something that inscribes on its banner the fight against man as its program, but rather something that takes up in its program the mutual fight together with man. It is thus that we have strengthened the new National Socialist coordination (*Volksgemeinschaft*), thus that we have gained, in millions of women, the most loyal and zealous fellow fighters. Female fighters for a life together in the service of together preserving our life. Fighters who fix their gaze not upon the rights that a Jewish intellectualism pretends to offer them, but upon the obligations that nature has imposed upon us all.

Whereas in the past, the liberal and intellectualistic women's movements included many, many items in their programs that originated in so-called intellect, the program of our National Socialist women's movement actually contains only a single item, and this item is: the child, this tiny creature who must come into being and flourish, who constitutes the sole purpose of the entire struggle for existence. For what would be the point of our fighting and struggling if there were not something to come after us that could make use of and pass on what we achieve today for its own benefit and reward?

What else could be the purpose of humanity's entire struggle? Why else the worry and the suffering? For the mere sake of an idea? Only for an idea? Only for a theory? No, that would not be worth traversing this earthly vale of tears. The only thing that allows us to overcome all of that would be to shift our gaze from the present to the future, away from ourselves to that which is growing up to follow us.

A few moments ago, I spoke before the youth rally. It is a glorious thing to look out over this golden youth in the knowledge that it will one day be Germany when we no longer exist! It will preserve the sum of what we are creating and building up. It is for this youth that we are working. That is the real purpose of the entire struggle! And in recognizing this, the most elementary and basic goal of nature, the labors of the two sexes will logically and rightfully fall into place for us, not in conflict, but in a common fight for the real life.

You, my female party comrades, are waging this battle as leaders, organizers, and helpers. You have joined in taking on a glorious task. That which we wish to shape within our Volk on a large scale is that for which you must internally form a firm support and a solid foundation. You must impart spiritual and emotional reinforcement and stability from within! In this battle that we are waging today for the freedom, equality of rights, honor, and peace of our Volk, you must be a complement to man, so that we can prevail as real fighters before our Volk and for our Volk with our sights set on the future.

Then strife and discontent will never be able to flare up between the two sexes, but they will instead traverse this life fighting together, hand in hand, fulfilling the wishes of a Providence that created both of them for this purpose. And then the blessings of these mutual endeavors will not be withheld. Then no mad fight over theories will flare up, then man and woman will not turn against one another because of false notions, for then the blessing of the Almighty will rest upon their joint struggle for life!

▸ September 13, 1935 *Hitler pointed out that women have certain tasks and so do men.*

The same day, Hitler gave a speech before the Nazi woman's organization (*NS Frauenschaft*). He had glowing words of praise for the female party members, who had actually demonstrated an unparalleled devotion to their Führer in the early years following the failure of the 1923 Putsch. Hitler also assured his audience that he would never send "a single woman to the front" in the event of war and that he would be ashamed to be German, were such a thing ever to come to pass. His statements, published partly in indirect speech, read as follows:

> Today women's battalions were being formed in Marxist countries, and to that one could only reply, "That will never happen here! There are things a man does, and he alone is responsible for them. I would be ashamed to be a German man if ever, in the event of war, a single woman were made to go to the front."
>
> The woman had her own battlefield. With every child to which she gave birth for the nation, she was waging her battle for the nation. The man stands up for the Volk just as woman stands up for the family. A woman's equal rights lie in the fact that she is treated with the high regard she deserves in those areas of life assigned to her by nature.

Women still respected brave, daring and determined men, and men have always admired and been attracted to feminine women. These were the two opposites that attracted each other in life. And if good fortune would have it that these two people find each other, then the question of equal rights became superfluous, for it had already been answered by nature: it was no longer equal rights, but a single unity! Man and woman represented two intrinsically separate natures. In men, reason was dominant. But more stable than this was the emotion evidenced in women.

When I returned after thirteen months of imprisonment, when the party had been shattered, it was above all female party comrades who had held the Movement together. They did not succumb to clever or reason-oriented deliberation but acted according to their hearts, and they have stood by me emotionally until today.

If our opponents were to allege, "You want to degrade women by assigning to them no other task beyond providing children," he would reply that it is not a degradation to a woman to become a mother, but the contrary—it is her utmost elevation.

There was, the Führer continued, no greater nobility for a woman than to be the mother of sons and daughters of a Volk. All the members of our youth lining the streets, so strong and beautiful, these beaming faces, these shining eyes—where would they be had not woman after woman been willing to give them the gift of life? The last immortality here on earth lay in preserving our Volk and our national way of life.

People should not be able to accuse us that we have no understanding of the dignity of women. Quite the opposite! We have been in power now for three years, but I believe that when we have had a National Socialist government for thirty, forty, or fifty years, women's position will have become quite different from what it was in the past—a position which cannot be gauged politically but appreciated only in human terms. We are happy knowing that the German woman, with her instinctive insight, will understand this.

There was a time when liberalism was fighting for "equal rights" for women, but the faces of German women and German girls were devoid of hope, bleak and sad. And today?

Today we see countless beaming, laughing faces. And here again it is woman's instinct that tells her for good reason: we can laugh once again, for the future of the Volk is guaranteed.

The compensation that National Socialism gives woman in exchange for her work lies in that it is once again training men, real men, men who are decent, who stand erect, who are brave, who love honor. I believe that when, in the past few days, our healthy, unspoiled women have watched the marching columns, these sturdy and faultless young men of the labor service, they must have been saying to themselves: what a healthy, marvelous race is growing up here! That is also an achievement that National Socialism has wrought for the German woman in the scope of its attitude toward women in general. We have now reintroduced general conscription, because it is a wonderful education we wish to confer upon the upcoming young German generation, a wonderful breed that we are rearing in the Hitler Youth, the SA, and the labor service. I believe that the German Volk will not grow older during the next few years but will create the impression that it remains forever young.

This all applies to our girls, too. They too are growing up in a different world, with different ideas, and they, too, will become healthier than before. Thus the two columns march along their respective paths and in that way will assuredly discover their true natures.

► September 11, 1936 *According to Hitler, children were the gift of women.*

On September 11, in an address to the Nazi women's organization (*NS Frauenschaft*), Hitler thanked all German women for bearing "him" hundreds of thousands of children each year, as their special "gift" to the Führer. At several points in his speech, Hitler indeed sounded as though he were claiming all these children as his own.

When I drive through Germany like this, I see in all the millions of children exactly what allows all this work to make any sense at all. I see in them the children who belong to their mothers just as, at the same time, they do to me.

Hitler then concluded:

> I am of the conviction that no one understands the Movement better than the German woman.

This verbose laudation of the German woman meant little in relative terms, for Hitler was constantly honoring one group or another, most generous with regard to the praise he distributed. Frequently, he would maintain that the German peasant, worker, youth, or old guard was the sole person or group that truly understood him.

▶ September 10, 1937 *At the Reich Party Congress of Labor, Hitler addressed the* N.S. Frauenschaft *and spoke on marriage.*

Despite initially declaring that he merely wanted to express his "gratitude for the great work accomplished," he launched into a lengthy address to the Nazi woman's organization (*NS Frauenschaft*) the same day. Soon he found himself "philosophizing" upon the relationship between man and woman, purporting the following insights:

> The more masculine a man is, the more he is undisputed in his sphere of influence from the very start; and the more feminine a woman is, the more her own work and thus her own position is conversely uncontested and undisputed. And the mutual respect of the sexes for each other will ultimately not be achieved by the rules set up by two different communities, i.e., the community of men and the community of women: instead, it must be acquired day by day in real life. The more a man is faced with a woman who is truly female, the more his arrogance will be disarmed from the very beginning—indeed at times too much so; and conversely, the more a man is a whole man and carries out his work and his life-task in the highest sense of the word, the more the woman will find her natural and self-evident place beside him. In this constellation, the two can never cross each other on their life-paths; they will instead join one another in a wholly shared, great mission; and ultimately this mission is none other than preserving the community of mankind as it exists today, and ensuring that, in the future, it will be the way we desire it to be.

Thus the individual alliance of man and woman will always stand out from this joint alliance of the two sexes. We know that here, too, this alliance—if it is to be really lasting—must equally rest upon the awareness of this great comradeship for life. Yet because this is so, we must also understand that seeking and finding this comradeship for life cannot simply be brought about by commands or orders either, but that it is moreover ultimately a problem not only of reason, but here an affair of the heart as well. And, therefore, it is also understandable if there are many—particularly women—who do not succeed in solving this problem for the simple reason that the heart cannot always bow to reason. We wish to have a maximum of understanding for this. For there is yet another great task ahead, the work in our community itself.

In the course of such rhetoric, he naturally could not refrain from such exclamations as, "everything we do we are ultimately doing for the child!" In his peroration, Hitler extolled the virtues of the leader of the NS women's organization, Frau Gertrud Scholtz-Klink:

The way you have begun here—and this I can say to you, Party Comrade Scholtz-Klink—is right, and it will help us to more easily achieve this goal [of building a community of the German Volk]. For you have demonstrated a truly remarkable talent for avoiding the danger that the organization of women might create, for instance, antagonism to men, but on the contrary have ensured that the German women's organization has become a complement to the male fighting organization.

ART

Hitler saw himself as an artist. He was always ready to comment on a work of art. For the most part, Hitler's tastes were conventional, although his own designs demonstrate an interesting mixture of various styles.

▸ August 30, 1933 *Hitler did not appreciate abstract art.*

At the "Convention of Culture" on September 1, Hitler took the podium himself and held forth at length on the character and aims of art as he had done in *Mein Kampf.* This time he also voiced his own antipathy to modern art:

> The fact that something has never existed before is no proof of the quality of an accomplishment; it can just as easily be evidence for an inferiority that has never existed prior thereto. Thus if a so-called artist perceives his sole purpose in life as presenting the most confusing and incomprehensible portrayals of the accomplishments of the past or the present, the actual accomplishments of the past will nevertheless remain accomplishments, while the artistic stammerings of the painting, music, sculpture, and architecture produced by these types of charlatans will one day be nothing but proof of the magnitude of a nation's downfall.

▸ September 11, 1935 *Hitler claimed that great states constructed great buildings. He would make sure that National Socialist Germany would have the greatest buildings.*

On that September 11, Hitler laid the cornerstone for a new gigantic Congress Hall that was to bespeak the glory of the Third Reich for millennia to come. He stated:

> National Socialists! Party comrades!

> Sixteen years ago the spiritual cornerstone was laid for one of the greatest and most significant manifestations of German life. The resolution of but a few men at that time to extricate Germany from the fetters of its internal corrupters and to liberate it from the yoke of external bondage constituted one of the boldest decisions in world history. Now, after sixteen years of hard struggle, this scheme has evolved to become a decisive historic achievement. A world of internal adversaries and obstacles was overcome, and a new world is on the verge of being born. On this day, we hereby lay for this new world of the German Volk the cornerstone of its first great monument.

A hall shall rise that is to serve the purpose of annually housing within its walls a gathering of the elite of the National Socialist Reich for centuries to come.

Should the Movement ever be silent, even after millennia, this witness shall speak. In the midst of a hallowed grove of ancient oak trees will the people then marvel in reverent awe at this first colossus among the buildings of the German Reich. With this premonition I hereby lay the cornerstone of the Congress Hall of the Reich party congresses in Nuremberg in the year 1935, the year of the freedom of the German nation hard won by the National Socialist Movement.

The same day, Hitler also delivered his obligatory speech on the arts, in which he expounded upon the cultural past of the human species and declared ex cathedra, "No Volk lives longer than the evidence of its culture!" Referring to modern art, he pointed out:

But if such a so-called "artist" feels himself called upon to portray human life under any circumstances from the viewpoint and perspective of what is inferior and diseased, then he should do so in an age in which there is a widespread appreciation for just this type of viewpoint. Today this age is over, and hence it is also over for this type of "would-be creative artists." And though we are becoming ever firmer and more strict in our rejection of this, we hold that we are not making a mistake. For he who is chosen by Providence to lend external, graphically visible expression to the innermost and thus eternally healthy substance of a Volk will never find himself on the path to such aberrations.

Thus we are not talking about a "threat to the freedom of art." Just as a murderer is not granted the right to kill his fellow men in body simply because this would mean interfering with his own freedom, a person similarly cannot be granted the right to kill the soul of the Volk merely so as to avoid placing any restrictions on his dirty fantasy and his total lack of restraint.

Hitler finally came to the more pertinent point of his treatise, namely the construction of edifices that should be as great and overwhelming as the "age of Hitler" itself:

In the case of really great tasks, as a general rule, both those men who have commissioned the task and those who accomplish it should bear in mind that, although the assignment was given within a certain age, its accomplishment shall, by being performed to the utmost, become ageless. To this end it is necessary that the really great tasks of an age must be accomplished with greatness too—that is, public commissions must, if their accomplishment is to generate eternal value, be in proportion to the rest of life.

It is impossible to place the monumental architecture of the state or the Movement on a scale corresponding to that of one or two centuries ago, while the products of bourgeois creation in the sphere of private or even purely capitalistic architecture have expanded and increased many times over. What lent the cities of antiquity and the middle ages their characteristic and hence admirable and endearing features was not the size of the private bourgeois structures but the manifestations of community life towering above them.

In the bourgeois epoch, the architectural expression of public life was unfortunately repressed in favor of buildings documenting private-capitalistic business life. But the great historical-cultural task of the National Socialist lies above all in departing from this trend.

We must, however, be guided not only by artistic but also by political considerations in endowing upon the new Reich, with a view to the great precedents of the past, a worthy cultural personification. Nothing is better suited to silence the little grumblers than the eternal language of great art. Millennia bow to its utterances in reverent silence. May God grant us the stature to formulate these tasks in a manner equal to the stature of the nation. This is doubtless a difficult undertaking.

The heroic feats of greatness that our Volk accomplished in history over 2,000 years number among the most tremendous experiences of mankind. There were centuries in which works of art corresponded to a spiritual human greatness in Germany—and in the rest of Europe. The unique eminence of our cathedrals represents an incomparable standard for the truly—in a cultural sense—monumental attitude of these ages. They demand from us more than admiration for the work itself; they demand reverence for the races that were capable of planning and carrying out such great ideas.

Since then, our Volk has risen and fallen with the changing tides of fate. We ourselves were witnesses of a world-defying heroism, of the deepest despair and shocked bewilderment. Through us and in us, the nation has risen once again. When today we call upon German art to take on new and great tasks, we are assigning these, not only in order to fulfill the wishes and hopes of the present, but in the sense of a thousand-year legacy. By paying homage to this eternal national genius, we summon the great spirit of the creative power of the past to come dwell in the present.

But such elevated tasks will make people grow, and we do not have a right to doubt that, if the Almighty gives us the courage to demand what is immortal, He will give our Volk the power to accomplish what is immortal. Our cathedrals are witnesses to the glory of the past! The glory of the present will one day be gauged by the eternal values it leaves behind. Only then will Germany undergo a revival of its art and our Volk become conscious of a higher destiny.

▸ July 19, 1937 *Hitler believed that art was a significant part of national existence and intended to enforce his views about what was good and what was bad on German society.*

On July 13, Hitler honored his old Munich party comrade, Frau Carola Hoffmann, with a visit on her eightieth birthday. The next day, talks took place in preparation for the "Day of German Art," that was to be held in Munich on July 18. Numerous activities were scheduled for that day, such as a procession through town depicting "2,000 years of German culture." In the presence of the Führer, a performance of *Tristan und Isolde* in the Munich National Theater opened the festivities. The dedication of the *Haus der Deutschen Kunst* in the Prinzregentenstrasse took place on July 19. Hitler had laid the cornerstone there in 1933. The new building was to serve as a replacement for the old "Glass Palace," that had been an art gallery located at the old Botanical Garden. In former times, art collections had been exhibited in the building until it had been completely destroyed by a fire in 1931. The opening of an art exhibition complemented the dedication of the new building. Another exhibition, entitled "Degenerate Art" (*Entartete Kunst*), was on display at the same time.

On this occasion, Hitler gave a "culture speech" that was markedly more interesting than his annual lectures on the subject, which he delivered at the party congresses. Speaking in a building, the construction of which he himself had directed and architecturally influenced, Hitler found inspiration for an unprecedented succinct articulation of his ideas on art. The concepts he expressed in his speech revealed that Hitler's understanding of art was steeped in the bourgeois mentality of the nineteenth century. His speech also demonstrated more clearly than ever his determination to see his opinions on the subject prevail—even if coercion was necessary to that end. The "party narrative" on this occasion included a lengthy description of the "decadence of civilization," that had emerged in the times of the Weimar Republic:

> Thus at this time I would like to make the following observation: Before National Socialism acceded to power, there was a so-called "modern art" in Germany, i.e., just as the word itself indicates, a new art every year. National Socialist Germany, in contrast, wishes to re-establish a "German art," and this art shall and will be eternal, just as is every other creative merit of a people. If it lacks such eternal merit for our Volk, then it is today without significant merit as well.
>
> When the cornerstone was laid for this building, it marked the beginning of construction of a temple not for a so-called modern, but for a genuine and eternal German art—or better: a building for the art of the German Volk and not for some international art of 1937, '40, '50, or '60. For art is not established in terms of a time, but only in terms of peoples. Thus the artist does not so much erect a memorial to a time, but rather to his people. For time is something changeable: the years come and go. Whatever would exist only within a certain time would have to be as transient as time itself. And not only what was accomplished before our time would fall prey to this transience; it would also encompass what is being accomplished today or will be shaped at some future time.

We National Socialists acknowledge only one type of transience, and that is the transience of the Volk itself. We know the reasons. As long as a Volk prevails, it constitutes the calming influence in the world of fleeting phenomena. It is that which is abiding and permanent! And hence art, too, as the characteristic feature of this abiding, constitutes an immortal monument, itself abiding and permanent, and thus there is no such criterion as yesterday and today, or modern and out of date; instead, there is but the single criterion of "worthless" or "valuable," and hence "immortal" or "transient." And this immortality lies anchored in the life of the peoples as long as these themselves are immortal, i.e., prevail.

The question has often been asked what it really means "to be German." Among all the definitions that have been put forth by so many men throughout the centuries, there is one I find most fitting; one that makes no attempt whatsoever to provide any basic explanation, but instead simply states a law. The most marvelous law I can imagine as the lifelong task for my Volk in this world is one a great German once expressed as: "To be German means to be clear!" Yet that would signify that to be German means to be logical and above all to be true.

A splendid law—yet also one that puts every individual under an obligation to subordinate himself to it and thus abide by it. Taking this law as a starting-point, we will arrive at a universally applicable criterion for the correct character of our art, because it will correspond to the life-governing law of our Volk.

A deep-felt, inner yearning for such a true German art bearing the marks of this law of clarity has always been alive in our Volk. It inspired our great painters, our sculptors, those who have designed our architecture, our thinkers and poets, and perhaps above all our musicians. On that fateful sixth of June, 1931, when the old Glass Palace went up in flames, an immortal treasure of truly German art perished with it in the fire. They were called "Romantics" and yet were the most splendid representatives of that German search for the real and true character of our Volk and for a sincere and decent expression of this inwardly sensed law of life.

What was significantly different in characterizing the German essence was, not only the choice of subject matter they portrayed, but also their clear and simple way of rendering these feelings.

And thus it is no coincidence that these masters were closest to the most German—and hence most natural—part of our Volk. These masters were and remain immortal, even today when many of their works no longer exist in the original but have been preserved only as copies or reproductions. Yet how far removed were the deeds and works of these men from that pitiful marketing of so many of our so-called modern "creative artists," from their unnatural smearing and dabbling that could only be cultivated, sponsored and approved of by the doings of characterless and unscrupulous men of letters and that were always completely alien—and in fact detestable—to the German Volk with its sound instincts? Our German Romantics of yore had not the slightest intention of being or wanting to be ancient or even modern. Feeling and sensing as Germans, they naturally assumed their works would correspondingly be valued permanently—corresponding to the lifetime of the German Volk.

After further statements on the topic, Hitler expressed his great satisfaction that he, and not his political opponents, had erected the building:

In 1931, the National Socialist takeover was still so far off in the distant future that there was no way of foreseeing the construction of a new exhibition palace for the Third Reich. In fact, for a while it did seem as though the "men of November" (founders and supporters of the 1919 republic) would provide an edifice for the exhibition of art in Munich that would have had as little to do with German art as it, conversely, reflected the Bolshevist affairs and circumstances of their time. Many of you perhaps still recall the plans for that building that was intended for the old Botanical Garden that has now been given such a beautiful design. A building quite difficult to define. An edifice that could just as easily have been a Saxon thread factory as the market hall of a mid-sized city—or perhaps a train station, or then again even an indoor swimming pool. I need not press upon you how I suffered at the thought back then that the first misfortune would be followed by yet another. And that therefore, in this case in particular, I was truly glad, really happy about the fainthearted lack of determination on the part of my political opponents at the time. In it lay the only chance of ultimately saving the erection of a palace for art exhibitions in Munich to become the first great undertaking of the Third Reich.

Thereafter, Hitler eulogized the late architect Professor Troost:

Now, you will all understand that I am presently filled with truly painful concern that Providence has not allowed us to witness this day with that man who, as one of the greatest German architects, drew up the plans for this work immediately after the takeover.

When I approached Professor Ludwig Troost, who was already working on the party buildings at that time, with the request to erect an edifice for exhibiting art on this square, that exceptional man had already produced a number of grandly conceived sketches for such an edifice—corresponding to the specifications given at the time—on the site of the old Botanical Garden. And these plans, too, revealed his masterful skill!

He nonetheless did not even send these plans to the jury as part of the competition—for the sole reason, as he bitterly confessed to me, that he was convinced it would have been a completely futile endeavor to submit such work to a forum that regarded all sublime and decent art as detestable, and whose sole aim and ultimate purpose was the Bolshevization—in other words, the chaotic infiltration—of our entire German and hence cultural life. Thus the public never became aware of these plans at all. Later it did come to know the new draft that now stands consummated before you.

And this new concept of building—you will all have to concede this today—is a truly great and artistic success. This edifice is so unique and so original that it cannot be compared to anything else.

There is no such thing as a building of which one could say that it is the original, and here is the copy. As all truly great creative works of architecture, this building is unique and memorable; not only will it remain, in its originality, in everyone's memory—moreover, it is in itself a symbol; yes, I might even say it is a true monument to this city and above and beyond that to German art.

At the same time, this masterpiece is great in beauty and practical in its design and features, without allowing any utilitarian technical requirements to dominate the work as a whole. It is a temple of art, not a factory, not a district heating plant, not a train station, and not a power house!

This great and unique artistic structure matches the specifications and the site itself; moreover, the precious materials used and the painstakingly exact execution do so as well. I am talking about the careful execution that is part of the great school of that departed master who wanted this building not to be a market place for artistic goods but rather a temple of art. And it has been in accordance with his wishes that his successor, Professor Gall, has loyally adhered to this legacy and brilliantly continued the construction, advised and accompanied by a woman who has a proud right not only to bear the name but also the title of her husband.

Master builder Heiger later became the third to join the group. Its plans have now been carried out and completed by the industriousness and artistry of German workers and craftsmen. Hence an edifice has been built that is worthy of providing the highest accomplishments of art the opportunity to show themselves to the German Volk. And therefore the construction of this building shall also mark a turning point, putting an end to the chaotic architectural bungling of the past. This is one of the first new buildings to take its fitting place among the immortal achievements in the history of German art-life.

Next Hitler's attention turned to the first art exhibition in the new building. He called the event a change that marked the end of art's deterioration and the beginning of its heyday.

You will, however, understand that it cannot suffice to donate this building to the German fine arts, this building that is so decent, clear-cut and genuine that we can rightly call it the House of German Art (*Haus der deutschen Kunst*); the exhibition itself must now work toward bringing about a change from the deterioration we have witnessed in art, sculpture and painting.

When I presume at this time to pass judgment, to voice my views and to take action corresponding to these insights, I am claiming the right to do so not only because of my attitude toward German art as such, but above all because of the contribution I myself have made to the restoration of German art. For it was this modern state—that I won over and organized with my fellow fighters in a long and difficult struggle against a world of adversaries— that has provided the great basis upon which German art can blossom new and strong.

It has not been Bolshevist art collectors and their literary henchmen who have laid the foundations for the establishment of a new art or even ensured that art can survive in Germany; we have been the ones, we who breathed life into this state and have been allocating immense sums to German art ever since, funds it needs to ensure its survival and its work, and above all: we are the ones because we ourselves have assigned to art new and great tasks.

Had I accomplished nothing else in my life but this one building here, I would already have done more for German art than all the ludicrous scribblers in our former Jewish newspapers or the petty art-dabblers (*Kunstkleckser*) who, anticipating their own transience, have nothing to recommend themselves but their own praise of the modernity of their creations.

Yet I know that, quite independent of this new work, the new German Reich will bring about a tremendous blossoming in German art, for never before has it been assigned more gigantic tasks than is the case in this Reich today and will be the case in the future. And never before have the funds thus required been appropriated more generously than in National Socialist Germany.

Yet when I speak before you here today, I am also speaking as the representative of this Reich, and just as I believe in the eternity of this Reich— that is to be nothing other than the living organism comprised of our Volk—I am likewise capable only of believing in and hence working on and for an eternal German art.

The art of this new Reich therefore cannot be gauged by the standards of ancient or modern; rather, as German art, it will have to secure its immortality in our history.

The fact is, art is not a fashion. Just as the essence and blood of our Volk does not change, so must art, too, dispose of its transient character in order to embody instead in its constantly improving creations a graphic and worthy expression of our Volk's course of life. Cubism, Dadaism, Futurism, Impressionism, etc. have nothing to do with our German Volk. For all these terms are neither ancient nor are they modern: they are merely the affected stuttering of people from whom God has withheld the grace of a truly artistic talent and instead whom He endowed with an ability to talk rubbish and to deceive.

After Hitler had asserted his expertise and expounded his opinions in this matter, he proclaimed his "inalterable decision" to wipe out the so-called modern art.

Therefore I wish to pledge a vow in this hour that it is my inalterable decision to now purge—just as I have the field of political confusion—the life of German art of modern jargon. "Works of art" that cannot be understood in and of themselves but require, as justification for their existence, a bombastic set of instructions as to how to finally discover that shy creature who would patiently accept such stupid or insulting nonsense will from now on no longer find their way to the German Volk!

All these catchwords such as, "inner experience," "strong cast of mind," "powerful intention," "promising sensation," "heroic attitude," "sympathetic significance," "time experienced as order," "primal crudeness," etc.—all these stupid, false excuses, phrases and prattles will no longer be able to absolve or even recommend themselves for products that show no talent and are hence merely worthless. If a person has a powerful intention or an inner experience, let him prove it in his work and not in driveling phrases.

Basically, we are all much less interested in so-called intention than in ability. Hence an artist who anticipates exhibiting his work in this building or playing any public role whatsoever in tomorrow's Germany must have ability. The intention goes without saying from the very onset!

It would be absolutely unthinkable for a person to pester his fellow citizens with works in which he ultimately pursues no aim at all. When these drivellers attempt to make their works attractive by presenting them as the expression of a new age, they must be told that it is not art that creates new times; rather the people's life in general takes on a new shape and therefore frequently attempts to find a new form of expression. Yet those who have been talking about a new art in Germany in the past decades have not understood the new German age. For a new epoch is not shaped by litterateurs but by the fighters, i.e., by those contemporaries who truly shape and lead peoples and hence make history. Furthermore, it is either an insolent affront or a nearly inconceivable stupidity to present works, above all in an age such as ours, that could have been done ten or twenty thousand years ago by a Stone-Age man.

They talk about the primitive nature of art—and completely ignore the fact that it is not the task of art to detach itself backwards from the evolution of a Volk; instead, its task can be only to symbolize the living evolution. These pitiful, muddled artists and scribblers can hardly be deemed as belonging to this group.

After other sarcastic remarks, Hitler declared:

The opening of this exhibition marks the beginning of the end of German artistic folly (*Kunstvernarrung*) and with it the destruction of our Volk's culture. From now on we will wage a ruthless war to eradicate the last few elements that are subverting our culture.

After directing a few cordial phrases to the established and the coming generation of artists, whose works were on display, Hitler concluded his speech:

> And when one day in this field as well, sacred conscientiousness has been restored to its rightful position, I have no doubt that the Almighty will once more choose those few from among the masses of decent artists and elevate them to the heights of the eternal starry skies where the immortal, divinely gifted artists of great ages dwell.
>
> For we do not believe that the age of the creative power of gifted individuals has ended with the great men of past centuries, and will, in the future, be replaced by a respective power of the collective masses!
>
> No, we believe that today above all, at a time when superlative individual achievements are being accomplished in so many areas, the most highly valued power of the individual will once more become triumphantly manifest in the field of art. Therefore, the sole desire I wish to express at this moment is that this new building may be fortunate enough to be able to house within its walls many more works of great artists in coming centuries and to show them to the German Volk, thereby making a contribution, not only to the fame of this truly artistic city, but also to the honor and standing of the entire German nation.
>
> With that I hereby declare the 1937 Great German Art Exhibition in Munich open to the public!

▶ July 31, 1937 *Hitler enjoyed German song and traditional music.*

Later that day, he journeyed to Breslau and spoke at a one-hour commemoration at the German Sängerbund Festival before a crowd allegedly numbering more than 500,000. Numerous German chapters of the Sängerbund had come from abroad to participate in the festival. Hitler's particular gift no doubt was his facility for arousing nationalistic instincts in his audience. He reminded his listeners that of the ninety-five million Germans, only two thirds enjoyed the privilege of living within the borders of the German Reich. Then he emphasized the importance of an "ideal" substitute for "the lack of actual political unity." In his view, this national oneness expressed itself through the common use of the German language and through German song (*Lied*).

As an expression of this view, he assigned the anthem *Deutschland, Deutschland über Alles* to a prominent place in the middle of his speech, as if his primary concern were to unite all Germans present through song. His speech is reproduced below.

> Germans! German *Volksgenossen!* My German singers!
>
> It has not always been the case that the German nation could welcome you at these festivals in the German Reich through the words of one man. Today I have the right to both welcome you to this city for your great festival of German song and to congratulate you in the name of these sixty-eight million people who live within the boundaries of the Reich.
>
> You who have come here from all the lands of the Reich and from those territories lying outside its boundaries in which you nonetheless live as members of our German nation! It has nearly always been the misfortune of our particular Volk to lack political unification. Even today, millions of Germans live outside the Reich, nearly half the number of those who have their homes and residences within Germany itself.
>
> Yet especially a Volk that has not been able to form a political unit for so many centuries must possess other attributes that allow it to compensate, at least in an ideal sense, for the lack of actual political unity. The first of these is our German language, for it is spoken not by sixty-eight million, but by ninety-five million people.
>
> A second factor is German song (*Lied*), sung not only within the boundaries of the Reich but sounding beyond them, everywhere Germans live throughout the world. This song accompanies us all the way from the cradle to the grave. It lives in us and with us and, no matter where we are, it conjures up in our mind's eye the image of our ancient homeland, namely of Germany and the German Reich. A bird that has lost its sight tends to sing and express its sorrow and its feelings even more fervently in its song. And perhaps it is no coincidence either, that the German—so often forced to endure a sorely

tormented existence on this earth—has sought refuge in singing in times like those; there he was able to express everything harsh reality denied him.

Today we are perhaps more conscious than ever of that bitter truth. Particularly in these world-shattering and troubled times, the German nation as a whole—including its members beyond the Reich's boundaries—is looking to that ancient homeland, to Germany, and in the absence of any other way of establishing a bond, it is seeking a connection in German song! And thus the songs of our Volk are resounding today not only within the Reich, but far beyond its borders, too. They are sung with faithful ardor, for in them resides the hope and yearning of all Germans.

Thus it follows that the song that we Germans perceive as most sacred is a great song about this yearning. There are many, in other countries, who do not understand this: in this song above all they choose to see something as imperialistic which is as far removed from their idea of imperialism as can be. What hymn for a Volk can be more splendid than that which constitutes a vow to seek one's fortune and well-being within one's Volk and to place one's Volk above everything else on earth?

And when today you sing this song of the Germans that was born in an age of torment, you are singing it with the joyful feeling that this Germany has now once again become worthy of being our Germany; that in our eyes it once again truly deserves to stand above everything else the world has been able to offer us. Whoever loves his Volk this much, whoever loves his homeland thus cannot be bad! Whoever stands behind his Volk and stands behind his homeland thus will continuously reap new strength from both! This is why German song has always been a source of strength in the past and why it has today again taken on this role. Today *Deutschland Über Alles* is a pledge that fills millions with great strength, with the faith that is stronger than any other power on earth can be.

Hence this song also constitutes a pledge to the Almighty, to His will and to His work: for man has not created this Volk, but God, that God who stands above us all. He formed this Volk, and it has become what it should according to God's will, and according to our will, it shall remain, nevermore to fade!

Once again we have before us a proud Volk and a strong Reich, and all those who must leave this city at the close of these days of festivities and cross the boundaries of the Reich will reflect with pride, with joy, and with confidence on what they were able to witness here and what was revealed to them. They will all leave with the feeling: a Volk has arisen once more, a Reich has been born anew! The German being has come unto himself. And in doing so, he has acted in accordance with the will of his Creator. What power would have the right and the strength to block the course of life of a Volk that seeks, in its song, none other than itself: a strong Reich, a proud Volk, so great and so sublime that now every German can once more gladly proclaim: I am a German, and I am proud of it!

And this recognition must come upon us in such a solemn hour! We who are gathered here today from all the German lands, from many territories outside the Reich, we all perceive ourselves here as one community. You are singers and thus the spokesmen of the German nation!

It is such a pleasure for us to be able to overlook all that divides us in this hour and to perceive ourselves as indissolubly united and belonging together, one for all, and all for one. And I myself am infinitely pleased and proud to welcome you here in this hour on behalf of the Reich and the German nation residing within the Reich, and to be able to thank you not only for cultivating German song, but also for devoting yourselves with this song to your German homeland and allying yourselves with it.

To you who were not deterred by the lengthy journey, to you who have come to this city from all the corners of Europe and beyond, I may extend a special welcome! May you leave this place with the firm belief: Germany stands strong, and nevermore will this Reich fade!

▶ September 7, 1937 *In his "culture speech" to the Reich Congress of Labor, Hitler asserted that abstract art and its supporters were corrupters of genuine artistic traditions.*

In his "culture speech" of that same day, Hitler sharply attacked the art critics and authors concerned with cultural issues within Germany, whom he derided as "bourgeois ballad singers of freedom."

> The weapons of those bourgeois ballad singers of freedom (*Freiheitssänger*) were, at worst, pen and ink. Yet the National Socialists were expected to bear a thousand privations. But their struggle gradually brought about genuine freedom. A freedom that is not the product of poetic contemplation but the result of hard political battles compounded, not of essays or leading articles, but of historically established events and hence accomplishments. Of course it was more difficult to arrive at a March 16, 1935 (introduction of military conscription), or to occupy the Rhineland than to concern oneself in newspapers or literary pamphlets with theoretical discussions on the true nature of genuine freedom.
>
> In history, however, surely only the factual counts; that means that in history, neither political desire nor theoretical contemplation will be material, but political achievement, and that means the deed itself. It is the task of cultural policy—just as in the area of politics in general—to lead onwards to new and, in this case, cultural achievements!
>
> Therefore, the civilized nations have always been poles apart from nations without culture, just as within them the artist is, in turn, the solitary figure, in contrast to the masses of the artistically indifferent or to people even lacking any understanding whatsoever. This, however, is due to the following: the genius consistently stands out from the masses in that he unconsciously anticipates truths of which the population as a whole only later becomes conscious!
>
> Of all the questionable concoctions of our so-called "modern art," not even five percent would have been able to gain a place in the art collection of the German Volk had it not been that, by means of propaganda having nothing at all to do with art but oriented along political and philosophical lines (*politisch-weltanschaulich*), public opinion had been talked into them—indeed, even forced into them—by like-minded

political factors. The Volk's deep-seated aversion to the enrichment of its art by virtue of such products is something obvious to anyone from the impressions made upon the viewers of the Degenerate Art (*Entartete Kunst*) exhibition in Munich.

However, clever and indeed cunning Jewish cultural propaganda has nonetheless succeeded in talking at least his so-called "appointed art experts"—but not healthy individuals—into smuggling these supremely pitiful concoctions into our galleries and thus ultimately forcing them upon the German Volk after all.

The path from the sacred and serious work of our good old German masters to the great painters of the seventeenth, eighteenth, and nineteenth centuries was certainly more difficult than the path from the average decent art of the nineteenth century to the primitive scrawlings of our so-called "Moderns," whose products basically attract attention only because they are behind modern times by a few thousand years. We have our litterateurs to thank for this ignominious retrogression. They have succeeded, by perpetually using the word *"Kitsch"* to describe a well-meant, decent, average accomplishment, in breeding those exalted aberrations that, to a blasé literary attitude, might perhaps seem to present an interesting and even phenomenal innovation, but in fact are nothing but a disgraceful reversion, a deterioration of culture that has never before taken place at any time in the past—and never could take place, either, because never before had litterateurs been accorded such an outrageous influence on the performing and visual arts. In this context, it is now amusing to note that it is least of all the products of these so-called "moderns" that can be judged as being, for example, "original" or possessing "originality." On the contrary, all of these so-called modern artists are the most pathetic and inept copyists of all time. Naturally, not copyists of what is decent, but of nonsense!

Above all, Hitler cherished his building projects. While expanding on the topic, he betrayed the true incentives that had prompted him to insist on their construction. In his eyes, they served as pillars and tangible expressions of his authority.

Never before in German history were greater and more noble edifices planned, commenced, and completed than in our time.

The authority that is saving the German Volk from collapse in the twentieth century, that has snatched it away from the chaos of Bolshevism, is not the authority of an economic association, but that of the National Socialist Movement, of the National Socialist Party and thus of the National Socialist State! The opponents will sense it, but the adherents above all must know it: it is to fortify this authority that these structures are being built!

Therefore these edifices are neither designed for the year 1940 nor for the year 2000; instead, they are to tower, like the cathedrals of our past, for millennia of the future. And if today God perhaps allows the poets and singers to be fighters, He has, in any case, given the fighters the architects who will ensure that the success of this fight finds an immortal substantiation in the documents of a unique and great art! That is something small minds perhaps cannot comprehend, but then again they have not understood our fight on the whole. It may embitter our opponents, but then again their hatred has never yet been capable of thwarting our success either. One day, however, it will be understood with utmost clarity how very great the blessing is which shines forth throughout the centuries from the tremendous edifices of this history-making age.

For they above all will help, in a political sense, to unify and fortify our Volk more than ever before; in a collective sense, they will—for Germans—become part of a proud feeling of belonging together; in a social sense, they will prove the ridiculousness of any other differences of this world in comparison to these tremendous, gigantic witnesses of our sense of community.

This state shall neither be a power without culture nor a force without beauty. For the armament of a Volk is morally justified only when it is the sword and shield of a higher mission. Therefore we are not striving for the brute strength of someone like Genghis Khan but instead for an empire of strength that is instrumental in shaping a strong social and protected community as the support and guard of a higher culture!

It was because of this "higher mission" that Hitler believed his assault upon Poland, the Soviet Union and other countries to be ethically justified.

▸ May 31, 1938 *Hitler intended to eliminate corrupting art.*

The next day in Berlin, as a suitable preliminary to his culture speeches and the "Day of German Art," Hitler enacted a law regarding the "confiscation of works of degenerate art." This measure had already been enacted in 1937, but not yet applied to Austria. The decree is reproduced verbatim below:

> The Reich government has enacted the following law, which hereby is officially made public:
>
> §1 Products of degenerate art, that prior to this law taking effect have been secured in museums or other collections accessible to the general public, and objects that have been designated as products of degenerate art by the appropriate administrative office determined by the Führer and Reich chancellor may be confiscated by the Reich without compensation. This shall apply to such pieces of art that were in the possession of Reich citizens or local entities at the time of confiscation.
>
> §2 (1) The Führer and Reich chancellor shall give orders for confiscation. He shall determine the future disposition of the items transferred to the possession of the Reich. He may delegate the authority granted in the above two sentences to others.
>
> (2) Under exceptional circumstances, steps may be taken to alleviate undue financial hardship.
>
> §3 In agreement with the respective Reich ministers, the Reich Minister of Public Enlightenment and Propaganda shall decree the legal and administrative measures necessary for the implementation of this law.

The Führer and Reich Chancellor, Adolf Hitler
The Reich Minister of Public Enlightenment and
Propaganda, Dr. Goebbels

▶ June 14, 1938 *Hitler was very interested in city planning and urban renewal.*

On June 14, Hitler attended the laying of the cornerstone for the House of German Tourism on Potsdamer Strasse in Berlin and delivered a lengthy address at this location. He called the building the first structure along what would become "the widest street in the Reich capital." In his address, Hitler paid great attention to details of the traffic problems that the future would entail, declaring:

> Once more we National Socialists cannot leave the resolution of such important issues, which we today can already anticipate, to posterity. It has always been our principle to approach such problems ourselves and to resolve them ourselves! It is for this reason that the newly constructed roads were not built for the years 1938, 1939, or even 1940. Rather they were constructed to account for the gigantic increase in flow of traffic certain for the coming decades, indeed for the coming centuries.
>
> Yes, it is at this time—now that we can more easily deal with these issues—that we aim to avoid in Berlin the traffic problems we are witnessing today in many another metropolis. One day posterity will judge what many perhaps cannot comprehend today as a beneficial decision and its implementation as a most fortunate occurrence.
>
> And so we are building not only great traffic circles in this city, but also we are constructing two great arteries of traffic flowing through Berlin: one in an east-west direction and one in a north-south direction.
>
> Parts of the east-west axis are already under construction and, in all likelihood, they will be opened for traffic within a few months' time. Completing the corresponding connection to the east will be a task for the coming years. And today, in a sense, we find ourselves placing the cornerstone for the north-south axis at this location as well. These great sections will

later be connected to the great *Reichsautobahn* ring. In the future, they will lead the motorist from outlying areas directly into the heart of the city of Berlin. Again both stretches are not planned for the year 1940 but for centuries to come.

For I believe in an eternal Germany, and hence I believe in its capital! I believe that just as we today are grateful to those men who three hundred years ago planned and brought to life the Unter den Linden Avenue, posterity will be grateful to us three hundred years from now! With this road system, we will find a generous solution for the rapid transit traffic that no doubt will remain the primary means of transportation for the masses. Millions of people already utilize these trains to go to work each day and people will use them increasingly in the future. Thus this problem, too, has found a comprehensive solution for the immediate future.

There is yet another consideration that compels us to carry through this project: we want to introduce orderly planning into cultural development. My fellow German citizens (*Volksgenossen*), all that will be built here within the next ten, fifteen or twenty years, would be built in any event. However, as experience has shown, everyone would build exactly as he wished and where he wished to build. With this plan, all these construction projects will be synchronized, planned, and completed more efficiently. Furthermore, buildings and construction designed to bring benefit to the inner city, but that were continually postponed, will be built.

Just imagine where it would lead if everyone—the Reich, the land, the Movement, the community, economy, trade, industry, etc.—built as he pleased in such a city, choosing a spot somewhere and putting up his house there. That could only lead to complete chaos. It is here that I intervened and led construction in this city into more orderly channels! And on this foundation the new Berlin will be built!

In addition, there is the necessity to create new residential areas and to link these up to the rapid transit system that leads into the city. For the first time in over one-hundred-and-fifty years, methodical order will be restored to the appearance of the city of Berlin.

And thus it is a day of great pride for me as I lay the cornerstone to the first building in this city, a building that owes its existence to the new planned order. The *Haus des deutschen Fremdenverkehrs* justly deserves to be the first in a series of new buildings in the inner city of Berlin. After all, everything we are building here today will one day lead to an immense increase in foreigners visiting Germany. The mighty structures we are erecting in the Reich today will pay off in the end as Germany increasingly becomes the center for tourism we imagine. The world will come to see us and will above all want to ascertain that this Germany is indeed a stronghold of European culture and human civilization.

I am placing this cornerstone for the remodeling of the *Haus des deutschen Fremdenverkehrs* in Berlin, and hence I order commencement of the redevelopment work for greater Berlin!

It appeared to have completely slipped Hitler's mind that he had already claimed that the day of the laying the cornerstone to the Faculty of Defense Technology of the Technical University in Berlin had marked the beginning of the "period of developmental redesign" of Berlin.

▶ January 9, 1939 *Hitler saw himself as an architectural artist and often worked on design features of important buildings himself. The person who was just about his only friend, Albert Speer, compensated for whatever technical expertise he may have lacked. Hitler's favorite project was the new Reich Chancellery building, which he saw as a backdrop for his major governmental functions. His article shows his personal enthusiasm for the structure.*

In the context of the dedication ceremony at the new Reich Chancellery building, it is appropriate to reproduce an article at this point that Hitler would publish in July 1939 in a magazine called *Art in the Third Reich*. The essay was entitled "*The Reich Chancellery*" by Adolf Hitler, and it dealt with the construction and significance of the old Reich Chancellery, but most of all, with the history of the new one. In the article, Hitler's scorn for the old structure was shown in sarcastic comments on his predecessors' obviously mediocre frame of reference and their stilted lack of taste in general. In contrast, he showered praise on his own initiative and grandeur, on the intricate and expert planning, and on the "truly magnificent effect" of the building. At this point, Hitler added the words: "this edifice that, by the way, will serve a different purpose from the year 1950 on." Hitler obviously entertained plans for the construction of a yet more magnificent and representative building to reflect the ever-increasing importance that the Reich would undoubtedly have achieved by that year.

Hitler's essay, which was to be his last effort as an author, read:

The Reich Chancellery

by Adolf Hitler

When, after the re-establishment of the Reich, Bismarck determined to purchase the Radziwill Palace, later to become the Reich Chancellery, he himself retained his office in the foreign office building. The proximity of this building to the foreign ministry was, in all likelihood, the reason for the purchase of this particular structure. It afforded virtually no actual work space. Dating from the first half of the eighteenth century, it had initially served as a town house for the nobility. Its façade was well preserved. Inside, repeated attempts at modernization had disfigured the building. The end of the nineteenth century witnessed further such embellishments and degraded the palace by bestowing on it a heavy-handed elegance. Bombastic plasterwork was intended to hide the faults of the actual material and thereby, unfortunately, obscured its well-balanced proportions. Even the hall in which the Congress of Berlin had once been convened was not spared like "improvements." Apparently, weak lighting along the walls and gigantic chandeliers of tin were then regarded as especially attractive. As regards the paintings in the house, these were mainly amateur copies of originals on loan from Prussian collectors. With the single exception of a portrait of Bismarck by Lenbach, the portraits of former chancellors were devoid of any artistic merit.

The chancellery gardens were ill-tended and had begun to be overgrown by weeds. A superstitious fear of replacing old and dying trees led first to covering increasing numbers of their moldy trunks with shingles and then to filling them with cement. Had this process been allowed to continue, the park would undoubtedly have begun to resemble the *Houthulster Wald* after three years of bombardment by the English.

While chancellors before 1918 strove to make more or less tasteful improvements, the condition of the house began to deteriorate steadily after the revolution of 1918. When I determined to move into the chancellery nonetheless in 1934, the roof was leaky, for the most part, while the floors beneath us were thoroughly rotten. The police restricted access to the hall in which congresses and diplomatic receptions were held to a total of sixty persons at one time, for fear the floor might give way. A few months before this, on the occasion of a reception held by Reich President von Hindenburg, approximately 100 guests and servants had crowded one hall. As we began to tear out the floors, we came across beams that had become little more than brittle sticks that disintegrated as we rubbed them between our palms.

During rainstorms, water penetrated the building, not only from above, but from below as well. From the Wilhelmstrasse, a veritable flood spilt over into the ground floor rooms. Its flow was augmented by a back-up in the plumbing throughout the house, including the toilets. As my predecessors could rarely count on remaining in office for more than three, four, or five months, they had neither the motivation to clear away the dirt of those before them nor to improve conditions for those to succeed them. As the world took little notice of them in the first place, they were not generally troubled with appearances before foreign representatives.

By 1934, the entire structure exuded decay: ceilings and floors were giving way while wall and floor paneling was rotted out. An unbearable stench pervaded the house. Meanwhile, the new office space created for the chancellery along the Wilhelmsplatz took on the appearance of a storage house or a station for the municipal firefighters. Its interior suggested a sanatorium for those with lung disease, although this was not primarily the disease that those laboring inside were in fact suffering from. In an effort to restore the structure as much

as possible, I decided to undertake a general renovation project in 1934. The expenses incurred were not to be assumed by
the state, as I myself provided the financial means necessary.

Professor Troost himself was still able to draw up the blue-
prints for this project. His goals were:

1. to reassign living space as well as space for receptions to
    the lower floors of the building, and
2. to furnish the second floor for the practical exigencies of
    running a Reich Chancellery.

My office as Reich chancellor up to this point had been
located in a room facing the Wilhelmsplatz. Its size and interior decoration made it more appropriate for housing a general
salesman for cigarettes and tobacco in the office of a medium-
sized enterprise. It was virtually impossible to work in this
office: with the windows closed, the heat suffocated anyone
inside; with the windows open, there was the noise rising up
from the streets.

The upper floors had customarily been reserved for official
receptions by the chancellor. In the days of the renovation of
the Reich president's palace, the old Reich president had held
various receptions there, too. This, however, meant that these
rooms were not in use for most of the year and stood empty.
This was the reason behind my relocating the reception rooms
to the lower floors and remodeling the upper floors vacated
thereby, to accommodate offices. The hall for congresses, also
vacant for most of the year and without any practical application, became the meeting room for cabinet sessions.

Since there was no room of sufficient size to accommodate
the large-scale receptions I had to give for diplomatic purposes
as head of government, I instructed the architect, Professor
Gall, to build a large hall to hold approximately 200 persons.
At this point, it appeared as though the remodeling of the
lower floor would suffice for this purpose. In the course of
1934, however, the merging of the offices of Reich Chancellor and Reich president necessitated the adding of rooms to

house the presidential office and staff and provide space for the *Wehrmacht* secretariat within the building. Also, official receptions required an appropriate setting. The realization of these necessities led to the purchase of the Borsig Palace. Admittedly built in a style not looked on favorably in our age, its interior surpassed that of the miserable chancellery building by far. Professor Speer was entrusted with the first remodeling of the chancellery. Within a markedly short time and without altering the facade, the structure built by the architect Lucae was connected to that factory building on the Wilhelmstrasse, and its interior design splendidly renovated. At least for the time being, it provided the presidential office, the *Wehrmacht* staff, and the SA leaders with office space. Under the guidance of Party Comrade Bouhler, the council of the party was accorded a few rooms, too. The former office building of the Reich Chancellery was adorned with a balcony facing the Wilhelmstrasse. This was the first decent architectural element in the structure. Further expansion of the existing structures, while providing temporary relief, did not represent a solution to the housing problem. Two further considerations were instrumental in bringing about my decision of January 1938 to seek an immediate solution.

1. In an effort to facilitate traffic flow through the city from east to west, a lengthening of the Jägerstrasse had been determined on, to lead it through the ministerial gardens and the zoo and thereby connect it to the Tiergartenstrasse. The Municipal Berlin Building Inspectorate of that time had drawn up these plans, which in my eyes did not represent a solution to the problem. Therefore I asked Professor Speer to come up with a more sensible plan to relieve traffic flow along the Leipziger Strasse and the avenue Unter den Linden by securing a direct passage to the west of the Wilhelmsplatz. To this end it was necessary to transform the narrow passage along the Vossstrasse into a wide transit route. Since obviously this could not be realized at the expense of the Wertheim Department Store and would have been attended by construction difficulties in the first place,

an attempt had to be undertaken on the opposite side of
the street. Consequently, it was necessary to tear down the
entire block and build from scratch.

2. Moreover, in the days of late December 1937 and early
   January 1938, I had determined to resolve the Austrian
   question and to erect a Greater German Reich. Hence
   the old chancellery building could not possibly accommodate the additional administrative, as well as representative duties, necessitated thereby.

On January 11, 1938, I therefore instructed General
Building Inspector Professor Speer to undertake the construction of a new chancellery building located in the
Vossstrasse. The structure was to be completed by a January 10, 1939 deadline. On that day, it would be turned over.
Once we devoted ourselves to the project in numerous meetings, its colossal scope became apparent, as well as the incon-
ceivably short deadline.

For on January 11, 1938, the construction of the new
building could not even begin as the old houses along the
Vossstrasse had to be torn down first. Therefore, actual construction work could not be started before late March at the
earliest. This left a term of nine months at our disposal to
carry out the project. That this was indeed feasible we owe
to this genius of an architect, his artistic inspiration, and his
enormous organizational talents, as well as to the enterprise
of those assisting him. The Berlin worker has outdone himself
in his performance at this site. I do not think that a similar
task, purely with regard to the labor involved, could have been
carried out anywhere else in the world. I need not expand on
the fact that naturally everything possible was undertaken to
insure the social welfare of those involved in this construction
project. In light of the winter temperatures, the severe frosts,
the completion of this building was conceivable only—as emphasized earlier—in consideration of the enormous ability to
perform demonstrated by the Berlin worker.

The plan of this project is magnificent, and can be easily understood if one considers the structure's purpose and the space at the architect's disposal. The solution found in the gigantic, long structure along the Vossstrasse was dictated by the circumstances as well as artistic ingenuity. The sequence of rooms inside not only satisfies practical exigencies but also makes a truly striking impression on the observer. The interior decoration is truly excellent, thanks to the combined talents of interior decorators, sculptors, painters, etc., involved in the project. This applies also to the achievements of German craftsmanship here. The landscaping in the park is complete with the exception of one section that still serves as a construction site. The short period of construction has not yet allowed the banquet room at the end of the great hall to project its full size and layout. This room, therefore, is makeshift, so that the structure can be used. The banquet room will be completed in two years.

This Reich Chancellery building—this edifice which, by the way, will serve a different purpose from the year 1950 on—represents a practical but no less artistic achievement of the highest order. It speaks for its ingenious designer and architect: Albert Speer.

Hitler's charge that the old chancellery building left much to be desired was not unfounded. To a far greater extent this was true also of the Reich foreign ministry building, located at Wilhelmstrasse Nos. 74–76. However, one wonders whether splendor, or its absence, in a state's seat of government is truly a criterion of its might, as Hitler apparently assumed. London's Downing Street No. 10 and the White House in Washington suggest differently. While there was assuredly no causal relationship between the two, it was in fact rather curious how, once Hitler had set up house in the fabled new chancellery building, things started to go decidedly downhill for him.

A peculiar trait of the Third Reich, its excessive preoccupation with questions of etiquette, taste, and representation, became particularly prominent in 1939. While Hitler purposely fostered these outward displays of power, such efforts found little resonance among the German populace. The man on the street stood by on the sidelines and observed the goings-on with apprehension, distrustful of all the superficial glory. It was almost as if the ordinary citizen had a presentiment that in proportion to the increased demonstrations of might and self-confidence, the power needed to justify such pretense was getting less and less. Even the political leaders within the party appeared ill at ease in the gold-bespangled uniforms and rank insignia which Hitler so liberally distributed amongst them in April 1939.

The length to which Hitler went to show off the newly built chancellery appeared excessive and unnatural. The first months after its opening, torrents of guests were ushered through its ostentatious hallways. Every imaginable sort of guest from party, state, and *Wehrmacht* was instructed duly to admire the product of Hitler's vanity.

Hitler explains a project.

Hitler always paid close attention to what the press said.

XI
How the Press Viewed Hitler

Hitler and his party understood the importance of publicity and positive "spin." During the 1920s and 1930s, the primary source of mass-news information was through the daily newspapers. From early in the 1920s, Hitler had bought control of his own newspaper, Racial Observer (Völkischer Beobachter), *complete with press chief and reporting staff. Editorial decisions were not independent. Moreover, occasionally, Hitler would "grant" interviews to certain journalists, allowing them an interesting "scoop." Hitler worked well in a one-to-one interview. He was charming, moderate, and always reasonable. He never told the truth. Germany was the victim; others, led by the despicable Jewish Bolshevik conspiracy, were leading the world to destruction. Germany wanted only equal rights. Hitler and Germany were so misunderstood.*

▸ January 8, 1933 *In his struggle to gain power, Hitler used his own newspaper to get his message across. Essentially, in these selections, Hitler is interviewing himself.*

In an interview on January 8 with his press chief, Otto Dietrich, Hitler emphasized that any new government would have to include him as chancellor. At the same time, he once more confirmed his discussion with von Papen:

> Question: The crux of the public attacks and propaganda of your opponents aimed at the very fact of your political leadership appears to center on the recurring claim that your consistent opposition to even the present government—which is in fact endeavoring to gain your support—is rooted in an attempt by you and your movement to avoid assuming responsibility in the state. Does this argument have any basis in fact?

Answer: No! The fact that our opponents can still afford to make claims of that type is conceivable only as a result of the lack of political education on the one hand and the unfathomable forgetfulness of our intellectual classes in particular on the other. In point of fact, my demand was none other than the transfer of responsibility to the Nazi Party. However, this naturally requires that the party then be given the leadership it deserves. To expect me to assume responsibility for what others do is simply ridiculous. The present powers-that-be would never have dared to set a trap like this for the Social Democrats, for instance, and we will show and educate these gentlemen that we too are to be treated decently. Incidentally, I made a simple but straightforward proposal to the Reich president in November for solving the German crisis. If, at that time, the Reich president believed—thanks to the advice of those around him—that he could not answer for giving me the responsibility, then today these men are also responsible for the sad consequences and all the misery that must be suffered by the German Volk due to this refusal.

Question: Is the opposition press correct in claiming that you, Herr Hitler, have sought contact with Herr von Papen? What is your position particularly in response to the claim that you had attempted to establish a connection via Herr von Papen to the powers in heavy industry allegedly backing him?

Answer: It is obvious that I have not attempted to establish contact with Herr von Papen. But it is equally obvious that I do not allow anyone to dictate with whom I may speak or not speak. I am a politician and shall, if I regard it as expedient, have any talks I choose. I have no intention of letting newspapers beholden to the Reich chancellor who happens to be in office tell me what to do. Germany's heavy industry is a part of the German economy. For that reason I do not need to make "contact" with it any more than with any other economic group. And when a politician like myself has to reckon with all existing factors, he cannot simply charm them away. However, if ever I feel the need in the future to take up special contact with any economic group, I certainly do not require a special advocate. National Socialism is also a factor whose existence cannot be ignored. All that gossip and overblown fuss in the press because of the Cologne talks is merely the product of a guilty conscience and the fear resulting from it.

Question: How do you rate the chances for success of the program for providing work for the unemployed (*Arbeitsbeschaffungsprogramm*) developed by Schleicher's government, the implementation provisions of which have now been disclosed?

Answer: Such programs do not exist for their own sake. Thus I refrain from any judgments on those types of problems and will rather judge only their effects on the German economic crisis in general. But the measures taken by Schleicher's cabinet will not eliminate this crisis.

On January 9, Hitler delivered a campaign speech at Lage in the state of Lippe and then drove to Berlin. The official reason was, cited as a visit to the new office buildings of the *Völkischer Beobachter*; the paper had been appearing in Berlin as well since January 1 (Berlin and northern Germany editions). In reality, however, Hitler's presence in Berlin was designed to demonstrate once more that he was at the very threshold of power, and it did in fact provoke a great deal of gossip. Schleicher's position became increasingly shaky.

On the return trip from Berlin to the Lippe election campaign, Hitler gave another interview to Otto Dietrich:

Question: The gutter press in Berlin has been circulating new rumors by the hour regarding your temporary stay in Berlin. Now that your alleged visit to the Reich Chancellor as the reason for your visit has been proven a mere invention of this same press, the papers are now fabricating stories about money problems of the Nazi Party, about a Swedish loan for the party negotiated in Berlin, and more of the same. What was the real reason for your trip to Berlin?

Answer: My visit to Berlin had been planned for more than two weeks to make use of my one-day break in the Lippe election campaign. Aside from the talks with Reichstag President Göring and other leading party comrades, its main purpose was a tour of the office buildings and a visit to the editors of the *Völkischer Beobachter*. Since newspapers friendly to the present government have already told their readers—yesterday, to be exact—about important clandestine talks that supposedly took place in the evening, I will disclose the location of this "conference." At the time in question, I was at the opera, once more enjoying a marvelous performance of Verdi's *La Traviata*. I might also note that the positively hysterical preoccupation with my personal doings exhibited by a certain Berlin newspaper is the best indication of the real position that the Nazi Party has, contrary to the claims made by this very press.

Question: Who, in your opinion, are the men behind this press campaign?

Answer: I believe that the government press office in Berlin is the source of this political drivel.

Question: People with sharp ears have been writing and saying lately that you, Herr Hitler, are willing to drop your well-known basic demands for taking over the government due to "fear of a dissolution of the Reichstag and new elections." The reason for this is cited as the claim that the Nazi Party is presently in a difficult and tactically unfavorable position. Do you intend to make a statement regarding this question?

Answer: Yes, indeed! Those allegations are equally stupid and ridiculous inventions. I have so often explained my basic attitudes with regard to the formation of government in depth that the Berlin papers seem to be the only ones with memories short enough to have forgotten them. But it does serve to shed a revealing light on the position of the government.

It is not the National Socialist Party that is in trouble but rather Schleicher's cabinet. What I prophesied in November has finally come to pass. Thus there is no need for me to fear new elections—the political elite (*Herrschaften*) will see for themselves on January 15—the government is the one who should be anxious. At any rate, the present cabinet will not accomplish its goal, but I will accomplish mine.

▸ January 13, 1933 *Hitler was a master of propaganda. Here he takes a mixed collection of different rumors, some of which the Nazis may have started themselves, and builds them up into a publicity announcement, which was used to smear his enemies.*

On January 13, Hitler published a statement against the "flood of lies" disseminated by the press:

In the last few days, the press, well disposed toward the government of the Reich, has systematically publicized a flood of untrue allegations about the Nazi Party and myself. Among other things, it is alleged that current Nazi Party revenues do not cover current expenditures; that, for this reason, west German industrialists had also made an "attempt at negotiating" between the former Reich Chancellor Herr von Papen and myself; that I was willing to accept the political demands of the industrialists in exchange for money; that I was attempting to take money from the government in exchange for pledging to tolerate Schleicher's cabinet; and that I had taken out a loan from a Swedish banker by the Jewish name of Markus Wallenberg of four million Reichsmark for myself or the Nazi Party in exchange for corresponding securities and political promises.

All of these allegations are completely fictitious and fabricated from beginning to end.

Adolf Hitler

▶ February 3, 1933 *Hitler had assumed office but his power was circumscribed. The Nazis were moderate and reasonable as they talked to the press about their policies. But, at the same time, they plotted to take absolute control.*

The subject matter of a press conference held with representatives of the English and American press was summarized in an interview with the Associated Press.

> First of all, the chancellor pointed out that the leftist parties had had a completely unrestricted hand for fourteen years.
>
> "Just look at the outcome today," he exclaimed to us. "Give us four years, the constitutional term for a Reichstag, and then let the country pass judgment on us."
>
> In reply to a request for an explanation of the government's Four-Year Plan, Reich Chancellor Hitler stated: "I am glad that you have asked this question. Had I wanted to deliver a propaganda speech for my party, I would have been able to guarantee that unemployment will disappear by March 15 and that agriculture will be restored to its former position by May 1. However, I am more honest than most of my opponents are and have therefore made no such promises. It is impossible to set the ship of state on the right course so quickly. That requires time. Four years is all I ask."
>
> The chancellor added with a smile: "Don't forget that I am persistent, I have strong nerves. Were I not filled with determination, I would not be standing here before you today."

Following this short conference, a number of correspondents from the English and American press were received, to whom the chancellor declared:

> I hope that the world is aware of what is happening in Germany. There can be no compromise here. Either the red flag of Bolshevism will be planted before long, or Germany will find the way back to its true self. I appeal to the world press not to pass premature judgment on the events happening now. I ask that you judge the new government on the basis of its accomplishments and regard these accomplishments as a whole and not pick them apart into isolated fragments.

The chancellor added special emphasis to these remarks and continued in a louder voice:

> I have been described as a man who makes bloodthirsty, inflammatory speeches against foreign states, and the world is now astounded at my moderation. Gentlemen, I have never made an inflammatory speech. On the contrary, my speeches, even those I made ten or twelve years ago, testify to this. Anyone who, like myself, knows war also knows how much energy war consumes. One can only surmise what a future war might bring. Thus no one wants peace more than I do, more than the German Volk does. However, we must insist that we are given rights equal to those of the other nations and are allowed to take our fitting place in the world, just as any American would demand the same for his own country. I cannot imagine that any other patriot would think differently regarding his country than we do regarding ours. Naturally my own interest lies with Germany.

► February 5, 1933 *Hitler's stated position was that the enemies of moderation and reason just keep twisting his word and deeds.*

One interview that Hitler gave to the reporter from the *Daily Mail*, Colonel Etherton, met with disapproval upon its publication; Hitler thereupon had the following "authentic text" published in the *Völkischer Beobachter.*

Berlin, February 13

> On February 6, the Reich chancellor granted an interview to the English Colonel Etherton, who was acting as a representative of the *Daily Mail* and other associated organs of the press. However, the interview that had been given to Colonel Etherton in writing after the conference was not published in the *Daily Mail* on February 12 but in the *Sunday Express*, in a completely distorted version containing arbitrary changes and additions, which had neither been brought to the attention nor received the approval of the competent German authorities. Evidently, the writer used fragments from a former interview and falsely attributed other remarks to the Reich chancellor.

We hereby publish the text of the interview, that began with Colonel Etherton's question to the Reich chancellor as to his views on disarmament.

The Reich chancellor:
"Every German government is naturally of the opinion that disarmament is worth striving for with all our might—not some kind of disarmament bogged down in restrictive clauses, but rather an honest and forthright one.

"The solution of this difficult problem depends mainly upon how the Anglo-Saxon peoples, i.e., the British and the Americans, view this question and how much they really plan to work to make disarmament a reality.

"For Germany's part, it has made its contribution to the solution of this problem not only in theoretical terms: it has actually disarmed a gigantic army to such an extent that only a disproportionately small force remains."

In reply to the question of what the Reich chancellor thinks of the Treaty of Versailles, he stated:

"The Treaty of Versailles is a misfortune, not only as regards Germany, but also as regards other peoples. It is an unfortunate mistake to want to divide the world into victors and vanquished; the attempt to make such a division undermines mutual trust among peoples, and extends to the economy as well, an area that has been done the greatest injustice by virtue of this treaty; with regard to the chances for improving this miscalculated treaty, we are combating all damaging differences of opinion between the nations that it has brought about.

"Certainly one can differentiate, shortly after a war, between the victors and the vanquished, but this can never, ever serve as a basis for a world order.

"I believe that we are not alone in crying out for a revision of the Treaty of Versailles, that one day the whole world will join in this cry. In any case, every German government will demand that the injustice provided for in this treaty is righted."

In answer to the question as to how the Reich chancellor believes France will react to these endeavors, the chancellor replied that at present he is still hoping that Paris will also recognize how untenable the treaties of 1919 are.

Asked to comment on the continual French armament, Hitler stated:

"I believe not only we, but the other states as well, are surprised at the amount of money the French have at their disposal for which they seem to have no purpose. We demand that the existence of every nation be secured to the extent required by its environment. For our part, we also have the right to demand this as laid down in the proceedings of the League of Nations, and we will demand it.

"The situation as it is today has never before existed in history. Even in 1814, when the allies united against the imperious attempt to force Europe to subject itself to French domination, although they crushed Napoleon's rule, no one insisted that France be branded as forever vanquished and stripped bare of all its rights."

Asked about the so-called "Polish Corridor," the Reich chancellor noted that, in his opinion, this constituted a particularly grave injustice to the German nation.

In regard to the problems of Communism, he added in closing that this was not a question involving a foreign state but rather the manifestation of an infiltration that presented a domestic problem. He was of the opinion that Communism must be overcome and exterminated in Germany in order to facilitate peaceful development and allow the German nation to flourish once more.

► April 6, 1933 *In a talk to German national reporters, Hitler described the purpose of the press.*

For this very reason we recognize the significance of the press much more clearly than our predecessors did. However, may the press also recognize the significance of a regime that, by righting general conditions in Germany, is bringing about the moral and political, and hence also the economic, ascent without which the press cannot exist for long.

Thus I for my part would also like to warmly welcome you, gentlemen, as representatives of the non-local German press and thank you for what you have already accomplished in terms of giving our Volk a good education, and I warmly invite you to take part in a work that is sure to one day nobly prevail in German history.

For, even though ages of greatness always alternate with ages of disintegration in our Volk, the final judgment of history on the actions of humanity will nonetheless be passed by the spirit of *Lebensbejahung* (affirmation of life).

One day it will be our judge, and it will one day be forced to realize that day and night, in sleep and in waking, one single idea dominated our thoughts: *Deutschland*.

▶ October 18, 1933 *In this interview, Hitler affirmed that all his actions had the purpose of making peace more secure. Charming, candid, open, the interview went well. He lied very well.*

Neither France nor Great Britain was willing to take military action against Germany for its withdrawal from the League of Nations. The decision to let Germany join in 1926 had marked a break with the past. If Germany was now no longer interested in belonging to the League of Nations, that was its own concern—but not enough reason to justify armed intervention.

Hitler took this lack of action on the part of the West to be evidence in support of his new theory, i.e., that the French and the British had ceased being heroic peoples and would thus keep silent or make only feeble protests on paper when he launched his expansionist offensives in the east. The extent of Hitler's misjudgment of the British mentality is reflected in an October 18 interview with the well-known correspondent of the *Daily Mail*, Ward Price.

Hitler repeated his claim that Great Britain and Germany were "related nations," "both great Germanic peoples." Hitler's answers to the journalist's precise questions were evasive and trivializing, and his circumlocution served only to reinforce the distrust of the British.

Hitler nonetheless naively regarded Ward Price as friendly to—and even sympathizing with—his cause, until the journalist published *I Know These Dictators* in 1937 (German edition in 1939) and Hitler was taught the error of his ways.

The interview of October 18 read as follows:

> Question: It might interest Your Excellency to know that there are indications in London that your personal popularity with the British public has increased enormously since last Saturday. Lord Rothermere, with whom I spoke on the telephone yesterday evening, told me that when your picture was shown in the news in London cinemas on Monday evening animated applause broke out. It is, however, a fact that within certain circles in the British public and press, Germany's sudden withdrawal from the Disarmament Conference has given rise to distrust and concern. It would greatly contribute toward assuaging these fears were the Reich chancellor to allow me to ask him genuinely objective questions in this connection. First of all, I would like to cite the speech of the undersecretary in the Ministry of War, Duff Cooper, who said that "no people in the history of the world has ever prepared for war with the enthusiasm with which the German Volk is now doing." It would be futile to deny that this view is widespread in England. What answer can be given to this?

> Answer: At one time, on August 4, 1914, I was deeply unhappy that both great Germanic peoples who had lived in peace side by side for so many hundreds of years, through all the aberrations of human history, were now thrown into war. I would be happy were this lamentable psychosis to come to an end and the two related nations were to find their way back to their old friendship.
> The allegation that the German Volk is enthusiastically preparing for war is, for us, a simply inconceivable misjudgment of the meaning of the German revolution.

We leaders of the National Socialist Movement were soldiers at the front, almost without exception. I would like to see a former front-line soldier who enthusiastically prepares for a new war! We are devoted to our Volk with a fanatic love, just as every decent Englishman is also devoted to his people. We are educating German youth to combat our domestic-foes, and primarily to fight the Communist threat, the extent of which had not, and probably still has not, been grasped in England. Our revolutionary songs are not songs aimed against the other peoples, but songs promoting fraternity at home and combating class conflict and self-conceit; songs for work and bread and for the national honor.

The best evidence of this is the fact that, prior to our accession to government, our exclusively political storm trooper organization (SA) was most terribly persecuted by the state; it even happened that our followers were not only not allowed to enter the army but not even allowed to work as laborers in military factories.

Question: The suspicion that Germany's ultimate objectives are warlike rests on the following considerations. People believe that the National Socialist government is educating the German Volk in the view that it has a serious and real quarrel with France that can be mended only by a German victory.

Answer: The National Socialist Movement is not educating the Volk in the view that it has a real or serious quarrel with France but rather to love its own people and to believe in the concepts of honor and decency. Do you think that we are only educating our youth, which is our entire future and to which we are all devoted, to let it be shot to bits on the battlefield? I have already stressed so often that we have no reason to be ashamed of the military accomplishments of our Volk at war.

Question: There is another widespread opinion to the effect that Germany's armaments have already progressed much further than is publicly admitted. For instance, there are claims that the German government has acquired munitions factories in Sweden, Holland, and other countries in which large supplies of war materials are kept in stock to be brought over the German border immediately on the threat of war.

Answer: These opinions are ridiculous. Where are these factories in Sweden, Holland, and other countries that we have supposedly acquired as munitions factories? Our enemies abroad always have the most detailed news about what, in their belief, has happened in Germany. It surely would be mere child's play for them to finally come out and say that we have acquired factories in Holland and in Sweden. As far as I know, there are no National Socialists in power in Sweden, and none in Holland. It would not be difficult for intelligence agencies to find out that a Dutch or Swedish factory is manufacturing and storing munitions for Germany.

At any rate, they would have to be relatively large warehouses. Every normal soldier knows from the war how large a normal munitions store is even for a single army corps. And all of this is supposed to be kept hidden from the eyes in an inquiring environment?

And what is more, presumably we are going to get these munitions to Germany by air in case of war, or would France issue passes to our ships? No. The whole thing is too ridiculous, but unfortunately it is sufficient to blacken the reputation of a Volk that wants nothing but what it is entitled to in a world that is, in reality, nothing but a gigantic arms factory.

Question: Although the use of heavy field artillery was prohibited in the peace treaty, there are claims in France that artillerymen of the armed forces (*Reichswehr*) are being trained in the use of heavy artillery at the German coastal fortifications. It may be that these accusations will be made official within the next few weeks. Would it not be advantageous for the Reich chancellor to publicly take a stand on this in advance?

Answer: Do you really believe that we allow ourselves the luxury of training the artillerymen of our army of 100,000 to use the heavy artillery in the coastal fortifications so that they can then fire field guns? At our Königsberg fortress, we have received permission for only a ridiculously limited number of heavy guns, and naturally men are being trained to use them. In other respects, however, the army unfortunately does not have sufficient field artillery, and we would rather train men on artillery with which they would have to fight than on artillery we do not even have!

Question: A further cause for concern is the view that Germany's admitted intention of one day repossessing the Polish Corridor is not compatible with preserving the peace. Under what conditions does the Reich chancellor believe it possible to undertake negotiations toward this aim?

Answer: No one in his right mind could describe the solution to the problem of the Corridor as one of the particularly spectacular accomplishments of the peace conference. The only purpose this solution could serve is that of making Germany and Poland enemies for all time.

None of us is even considering starting a war with Poland because of the Corridor. We would all like to hope that both nations will one day dispassionately discuss and negotiate the problems they have. It can then be left for the future to decide whether the two nations can find a practical approach to a solution acceptable for both sides.

Question: The expression, "people without space" (*Volk ohne Raum*) has given rise to some uncertainty. By what means does the Reich chancellor envision an opportunity for Germany's territorial expansion? Does the recovery of Germany's former colonies form one of the government's goals? If so, which colonies would come under consideration, and would Germany be satisfied with a system of mandates, or would Germany demand full sovereignty?

Answer: Germany has too many people for its area. It is in the world's interest not to deny a great nation the vital necessities of life. For us, the question of allocating colonial territories, no matter where, would never be a question involving war. We are of the conviction that we are just as capable of administering and organizing a colony as other peoples are. However, we do not perceive these questions as containing any problems at all that might concern world peace in any way, for they can be solved only by means of negotiations.

Question: In certain circles in Britain, it is expected that the present government will reveal itself to be a prelude to the restoration of the imperial family. Would it be possible for the Reich chancellor to define his standpoint on this question?

Answer: The government that is in power in Germany today is working neither for the monarchy nor for the republic but rather exclusively for the German Volk. Everywhere we look we see want, misery, unemployment, disintegration, and destruction at every turn. To eliminate this is the mission we have set ourselves.

Question: Since Your Excellency's government took power, the Weimar Constitution has been amended de facto in particular cases without ever having been formally invalidated. Does the Reich chancellor contemplate effecting a constitutional amendment on a different basis?

Answer: I once stated that I intended to fight only with legal means. I have also adhered to this statement. The entire reorganization of Germany took place in a "constitutionally admissible manner." Naturally it is possible and also probable that we will submit the overall results of the reorganization presently taking place as a new constitution for the German Volk in a plebiscite. As I must, in any case, stress that there is no government in existence at present that has more right than we do to claim that it is a true representative of its people!

Thus we have nothing to make good in this respect, either. The only thing we were ashamed of is the men who left the fatherland out on a limb in the time of our worst crisis. These persons have been eliminated without exception. The fact that German youth once again possess a feeling of honor fills me with joy. But I do not see why that should mean a threat to another nation. And I refuse to see why a nation that usually thinks as fairly as England does could inwardly blame us for this. I am convinced that, had England met with the same misfortune as Germany, even more English would be National Socialists than is the case with us. We do not want a "quarrel" with France, but rather an honest willingness to negotiate—on a basis, however, that can be accepted by a Volk with a feeling of honor. And besides, we want to be able to live!

Question: A large part of the German youth is presently being trained in military discipline in labor camps (*Arbeitslager*) or as members of the SA and other formations. Even if the German government is not planning to effect this training for the eventuality of a war, there is fear in France and, in part, in England that the development of a military spirit in young Germans could lead to the consequence that they will one day demand that the military knowledge they are now acquiring be put to practical use.

Answer: Neither in the labor camps, nor in the SA, nor in the subordinate formations is the German youth being equipped with military knowledge that could act as an incentive for them one day to exploit this knowledge. In view of this, how much more reason would Germany have to complain that, year after year, millions of recruits in the other countries are given genuine military training? Our labor service is a tremendous social institution that, at the same time, also serves to reconcile the classes. We have taken an army of young people who were going to waste in the countryside and made of it a productive work force. We are educating hundreds of thousands of others, who had already been corrupted in the big cities.

Question: Does the Reich chancellor look upon the League of Nations as an institution that has outlived its purpose, or can he imagine certain conditions under which Germany would be inclined to consider returning to the League of Nations?

Answer: If the League of Nations continues on its present course and grows more and more to become a syndicate promoting the interests of certain states against the interests of others, I do not believe it has a future. In any case, Germany will never again join or take part in an international organization if it is not recognized as a completely equal power. We know that we lost a war. But we also know that we defended ourselves courageously and bravely as long as we possibly could. We are men enough to realize that, after having lost a war, whether or not one was to blame, one naturally has to bear the consequences. We have borne them!

But that now, as a Volk of 65 million people, we are to be permanently and repeatedly disgraced and humiliated is something we cannot bear. We cannot bear this perpetual discrimination, and as long as I live, I shall never, as a statesman, put my signature on a treaty that I would never sign as a man of honor in private life either, even if it were to mean my ruin! For I would also never want to put my signature on a document knowing in the back of my mind that I would never abide by it! I abide by what I sign. What I cannot abide by, I will never sign.

Question: Does Germany thus regard itself as released from the existing international obligations on the grounds that it has not been accorded equal treatment?

Answer: Whatever we have signed we will fulfill to the best of our ability.

Question: Could the Reich chancellor give the British public some indication of his plans for relieving the economic misery in Germany in the coming winter?

Answer: We are approaching a very hard winter. Of a total of more than six million unemployed, we have brought more than two-and-a-quarter million back to productivity within eight months. It is our task, if in any way possible, to prevent a drop-off from occurring in winter. In spring we want to launch a new general offensive against unemployment.

For this purpose, we have been instituting a number of measures from which we expect a favorable outcome. Parallel to relieving the economy of unbearable taxes, generally restoring trust, eliminating a great number of laws hampering the economy that were inspired to a greater or lesser degree by Marxism, there is a large amount of work being created. Since our roads are, to some extent, insufficient and to some extent in disrepair, a network of approximately six-and-a-half thousand kilometers of roads for motorized traffic is being built and work has already been started this winter with tremendous energy. The financing is to be accomplished by means of our taxes on motor vehicles and fuel and by charging tolls. There is a whole series of further major projects—the building of canals, dams and bridges—which are also in progress.

We have expended an extraordinary amount of effort on promoting the fertility of our soil and the housing connected to it.

For the winter period, the sum of approximately two-and-a-half billion, which has been raised in a combination of public and private funds, will be utilized for the repair of our buildings, some of which urgently require renovation work. The idea is that the state makes a financial contribution corresponding to the amount that it would otherwise have to bear as the costs of unemployment.

In order to help young people, we will bring them together in labor camps and assign them to meaningful tasks, admittedly for very little pay but sufficient for upkeep. They do not yet have families of their own and thus can easily be accommodated in barracks and similar lodgings at their worksites.

By means of special measures, we are making it possible, by establishing families, for young girls to be taken out of the production process and for men to gradually take their places. However, since distress will nonetheless still be very great, we have organized the gigantic winter relief effort (*Winterhilfswerk*) that asks our rural population in particular to help the poor and needy industrial and urban population by supplying foodstuffs. It is a huge exchange organization and hence, at the same time, a tie between the city and the country.

By means of this organization, we will provide at least the absolute minimum amounts of fuel and foodstuffs and, in part, clothing to approximately six million people. In any case, we are doing our utmost to ensure that at least the worst effects of hunger are brought to a halt.

Until now, thanks to the Peace Treaty of Versailles, an average of approximately twenty thousand people per year in Germany have been forced by need and despair to take their own lives.

You will understand that a government and a Volk facing such tasks can desire nothing other than rest and peace. And with it, finally, equality of rights.

► November 15, 1933 *Just as he did with his rivals in Germany before he gained power, Hitler spoke soothing words expressing how reasonable were his ideas of how to make Europe better.*

Germany's courting of Poland in November 1933 naturally caused suspicion in France. To allay these fears, Hitler granted an interview on his future "peace policy" to Fernand de Brinon, the foreign correspondent of the French business periodical *L'Information.*

"It is an insult to me when people continue to say that I want war," Hitler claimed indignantly. "I alone decide Germany's politics, and when I give my word, it is my practice to keep it." *Le Matin* published the following report on Hitler's remarks to de Brinon:

> The Reich chancellor had declared, the special reporter stated, that he had consistently upheld the same attitude. He desired dialogue and mutual agreement, because he perceived them to constitute the guarantee for peace.
>
> It was his desire that a true peace be concluded between law-abiding opponents. He had stated this repeatedly but received only words of distrust in reply. However, his will had not altered. "I believe," the Reich chancellor said, "that the result of the plebiscite gives fresh strength to my desire. When Stresemann or Brüning negotiated, they could not claim that the German Volk was behind them. But I have the whole of Germany behind me! I have not concealed from the Volk what I wanted. The Volk approved of my policy."

The talk then turned to the Franco-German problem. Reich Chancellor Hitler, Brinon writes, believes in the necessity of a Franco-German dialogue. "I am of the opinion," the chancellor is reported as having said, "that, once the question of the Saar—which is German land—has been resolved, there is nothing that can bring Germany and France into conflict with each other. Alsace-Lorraine is not in dispute. But how often do we have to repeat that we neither want to absorb what does not belong to us, nor do we want to be loved by anyone who does not love us! In Europe there is not a single matter of dispute that could justify a war.

"Everything can be settled by the governments of the nations if they possess a feeling for their honor and responsibility. There is a Poland imbued with patriotic sentiment and a Germany no less devoted to its traditions. There are differences of opinion and matters of friction between them, arising from a bad treaty, but nothing that would make it worth sacrificing precious blood, for it is always the best who are killed in battle. That is why a friendly, neighborly agreement is possible between Germany and Poland. It is an insult to me when people continue to say that I want war.

"Am I supposed to be insane (*wahnwitzig*)?

" War?

"It would not settle anything, but only make the world situation worse. It would mean the end of our elite races, and in the course of time one would witness how Asia would take root on our continent and how Bolshevism would triumph. How could I want a war when we are still bearing the burdensome consequences of the last war and will continue to be made to feel them for another thirty or forty years to come?

"I do not think of the present, I think for the future. I have a long domestic task ahead of me. I have restored the concept of honor to the Volk. I also want to give it back its joy of living.

"We are combating misery. We have already succeeded in driving down unemployment. But I want to accomplish better things! I will need years to get there. Do you think that I want to destroy my work by a new war?"

In this context, the reporter pointed out what was on display throughout Germany: the joy and the glorification of strength. The Reich chancellor replied that Germany must be capable of defending itself. His program could be summarized as follows:

No Germans for a new war, but the entire Volk for the defense of its fatherland. The youth in Germany were marching in rank and file, and in uniform, because they personified the new order and its guarantee.

The talk then turned to the means by which the Franco-German problem could be solved.

According to de Brinon, the Reich chancellor said: "How can two neighboring countries enjoying equal rights reach an agreement? My fatherland is not a second-class nation but a great nation that was subjected to unbearable treatment. If France is contemplating basing its own security on Germany's inability to defend itself, then there is nothing it can do, for the times when this was possible have come to an end.

"However, if France wishes to conclude an agreement as a basis for its security, I am willing to listen to anything, understand anything, and do anything. There is little doubt as to which equal rights Germany is asking for. The practical implementation can be effected in steps, and the details can be negotiated. But they say to me: certainly, equality, but no equality without something in return. What in return? It should finally be made known what the French mean by the word 'security'!"

In response to de Brinon's remark that France would like to be certain that no new difficulties will arise once the problems are settled once and for all, the chancellor stated: "I alone decide Germany's politics, and when I give my word, it is my practice to keep it.

"What more is required? I did not inherit a throne, but I have a doctrine to uphold. I am a person who acts and assumes his share of the responsibility. I pledge myself as security for the Volk that I lead and that gives me strength. But let us talk about French security! If someone would tell me what I can do for it, I would gladly do it if it does not mean dishonor or a threat to my country.

"An English journalist wrote that, in order to quiet things down in Europe, an agreement would have to be reached by Germany and France, and France would have to be given the additional security of a defensive alliance with England. If it is an alliance of this sort, I will gladly sign it: for by no means do I intend to attack my neighbors. Poland has realized this by now, but because Poland lies further east than France, it knows us better!"

In response to the question of whether Germany would return to Geneva, the Reich chancellor, Brinon reported, replied: "In leaving Geneva, I performed an act of necessity, and I believe that, in doing so, I contributed toward clarifying the situation.

"We will not return to Geneva. The League of Nations is an international parliament in which the power groups are at odds against one another. The misunderstandings were only heightened there instead of being resolved.

"I am willing at any time—and I have proven this—to enter into negotiations with governments that want to talk to me."

▶ February 18, 1934 *Hitler presented himself as the representative of the will of the peace-loving German people.*

Hitler made his views on the events in Austria public in an interview with Ward Price, the special reporter of the *Daily Mail*. In his remarks, Hitler indulged in juggling figures as he was wont to do, this time with the aim of stressing the lack of bloodshed and relative innocence of the National Socialist revolution in contrast to other uprisings.

The interview granted to Ward Price, which also touched upon the topics of Russia and Poland, was published in London on February 18 and cited in the February 19 edition of the *Völkischer Beobachter* as follows:

Hitler had replied that some people believed the German National Socialists had something to do with the unrest in Austria. This, he stated, was absolutely false.

"We sympathize neither with Herr Dollfuss nor with his opponents. Both sides are using the wrong methods. Nothing of permanence can be achieved by the violent methods to which they have resorted."

It had been impossible for the Austrian Socialists to achieve power by proceeding as they had, the chancellor stated. It had been equally impossible for Dollfuss to draw the opponents over to his side by using the means he had.

Everyone knew that it was possible to raze buildings using shell fire, but these methods would never convince an opponent; they would serve only to embitter him. The only way to make a revolution successful lay in gaining a hold on one's opponent by persuasion.

"That is what we have achieved in Germany. Herr Dollfuss, on the other hand, attempted to carry out a *coup d'etat*. He violated the constitution and his methods were doomed to fail from the beginning."

Assuming one had proceeded in like fashion in Germany, what would have been the result? In Austria, Hitler noted, 1,600 persons had been killed and four to five thousand wounded. Germany's population was eleven times that of Austria's, which meant that Germany would have had 18,000 dead and 50,000 wounded.

"What are the facts? The total number of our adversaries killed in the disturbances amounted to twenty-seven, while the number of wounded was 150. Among them was not a single woman nor a single child. Not one building was destroyed, not one shop raided.

"Germany's critics will say, 'That may well be, but the Austrian Socialists were heavily armed!' "

So were the German Communists, Hitler continued. All kinds of weapons imaginable had been found in their possession. The reason that the German Communists had not made use of these weapons was that they had been won over to the cause of the National Socialists by persuasion, he said.

The proof for this lay in the election of this past November, in which a mere two million people had voted against the new regime, although previously the German Communists had numbered six million and the Social Democrats seven million. The remaining eleven million former opponents of National Socialism had not been suppressed, but converted.

The correspondent asked the chancellor whether the developments in Austria would influence Germany's attitude toward that country. Hitler replied: "By no means; the policies I uphold are determined solely by German interests."

Naturally the incidents of this week would serve to strengthen the position of the present Austrian government, but on the other hand the number of Austrian National Socialists would increase. He was expressing only his private and personal view, Hitler stated, but it was his conviction that particularly the workers of Austria would side with the National Socialist cause as a natural reaction against the violent methods the Austrian government had used against them.

The correspondent then remarked to the chancellor that the German peace pact with Poland had come as a great surprise to the world and that several people were interpreting it as his intention to establish a basis for a joint attack on Russia by Germany and Poland with the aim of territorial expansion.

Hitler had laughed incredulously and stated:

"... What? We take territory from Russia? Ridiculous!"

The correspondent interjected that, ten years before in his book, *Mein Kampf* Hitler had recommended acquiring new territory in Russia as a home for future German settlers but that the decrease in the birth rate that had taken place since then had halted the growth of the German population, so that the necessity of a larger area was now of lesser importance.

Later in the interview, Hitler had said that all prior attempts to lay the groundwork for a lasting peace in Europe had failed because public opinion had held that Poland and Germany were irreconcilable enemies. He had never held this view. The first thing he had done after achieving power had been to take steps to initiate negotiations with Poland.

He had found that the Polish statesmen were very magnanimous and just as peacefully minded as he himself. The gulf that had been regarded as unbridgeable had now been crossed. The two nations had come closer together, and it was his sincere hope that this new understanding would signify that Germany and Poland had permanently abandoned the idea of resorting to arms, not only for ten years, but for all time. With respect to the situation within Germany, the chancellor had stated that many thousands who had been in the concentration camps had already been released, and he hoped that even more would be freed. They had been interned not as an act of revenge—as had been the case in Austria—but rather because these opponents were not to be allowed to disrupt the process of restoring Germany's political health. They had been given time to change their views. As soon as they were willing to take a pledge to relinquish their hostile attitude, they would be released.

The reporter countered with the question, "Do you intend to free Dimitrov, Popov and Tanev?" and Hitler replied, "The court has pronounced its judgment; the sentence will be carried out." The correspondent stressed that these had been the exact words of Hitler's response.

"Do you believe," the correspondent continued, "that these people will be released and allowed beyond the German border?"

Hitler had replied, "They certainly will." He had added that he nevertheless believed that their release did not reflect the will of the German Volk, but the court's judgment would be carried out.

▶ April 4, 1934 *As usual, Hitler made the point that he and Germany were the victims of an unscrupulous and evil plot concocted by those who would destroy civilization.*

Hitler's next public statement was made in an interview with Louis P. Lochner, an Associated Press correspondent, published on April 4. He presented himself as an opponent of what was termed "secret diplomacy" and claimed that one could have unreserved faith in what he said. His sole aim was to eliminate unemployment, and he was extremely concerned with the question of how he could protect Germany from enemy attacks. The interview was quoted as follows:

> Reich Chancellor Adolf Hitler pointed out at the beginning of the interview that he was a staunch advocate of personal interchange, of "man-to-man diplomacy." He would most prefer, he said, being able to speak privately with the responsible leaders of the most important nations, including America.

The antiquated diplomatic method of exchanging notes defeated its own purpose; that was evidenced in the fact that, despite the endeavors of the diplomats, in 1914 the nations had slid into the biggest war in history, although—in his own personal opinion—the diplomats had been most astonished of all when the Great War had, in fact, broken out.

The Führer continued: "Any representative of a foreign power will find, when he confers with me, that I am absolutely frank in stating what Germany is willing to do and that I do not make my demands any higher than is necessary. For instance, if I say that we need a *Wehrmacht* of 300,000 men, I will not condescend to reduce the number to 250,000 afterwards.

"I want to make Germany's word and signature respected once more.

"Under no circumstances will I subject to a *Diktat*. If I have once become convinced that a certain course is the only right course for my Volk, I will adhere to it, come what may. And what I do, I do openly. For instance, I will never be capable of outwardly accepting 150,000 men as a sufficient force for our *Reichswehr* and then secretly train and equip another 150,000 men."

Speaking of the armament problems resulting from France's refusal to adopt the English, Italian and German position, the Reich chancellor stated:

"No one would be happier than I were the world to disarm. We want to devote all of our energies toward productive ends. We want to lead our unemployed back to work.

"Then we intend to raise each individual's standard of living. We want to drain our swamps, reclaim and improve unproductive land, if possible put our Volk in a position to provide for its own needs, enable the peasant to reap the maximum from his soil, put the manufacturer and industrial worker in a position to work as productively as possible, supply our country as far as possible with man-made substitutes for the raw materials it lacks. By building roads, digging canals, draining swampland, and installing dams and sluices, we are accomplishing constructive work that has a right to claim our energies.

"As a statesman who is responsible for the welfare of his country, I cannot allow Germany to be exposed to the danger that one of its neighbors might attack it or drop bombs on our industrial plants or wage a so-called preventive war only in order to distract from its own internal difficulties. For this reason only—and for none other—do we demand an armed force (*Wehrmacht*) that fulfills the requirements of a genuine defense."

In response to the question whether "work for all" meant that a proletarian leveling would take place, in other words whether the Reich chancellor would be satisfied if, by stretching the available work, each person would in fact be assured of a certain minimum income, but that larger incomes would then disappear, the Reich chancellor replied: "Just the opposite! Naturally the first step must be to eliminate the scourge of unemployment. However, as soon as our Volk has work again, buying power will also increase, and then the logical next step is an increase in the standard of living. We do not want to become a primitive Volk but one with the highest possible standard of living. In my opinion, the Americans are right in not wanting to make everyone the same but rather in upholding the principle of the ladder. However, every single person must be granted the opportunity to climb up the ladder. I also believe that it is absolutely right that an invention should first be the property of the inventor; however, his endeavors must be aimed toward having his invention benefit the general public.

"The first windowpane was a luxury article, but today everyone wants glass. It has become an article of daily use. The first light bulb was a luxury article, but its inventor aimed at making it available to everyone. The aim and the purpose of all progress must be to make a Volk as a whole, and humanity as a whole, happier than before."

Subsequently, in the words of the *Völkischer Beobachter*, Lochner "was allowed" to pose "a number of questions for the purpose of making Adolf Hitler's personality more comprehensible to the American people."

A notable feature is the extent to which Hitler boasted of the "blind" devotion of his staff (including, of course, the Reich ministers), who had subordinated themselves to his wishes "in an admirable way." "The world has never witnessed a more wonderful example of blind empathy than that which my staff provides," he declared.

Lochner's initial question was: "Mr. Chancellor, what is your attitude toward criticism, both personal and that in the press?"

The chancellor replied: "Do you know something else? That I have surrounding me an entire staff of experts thoroughly versed in economic, social, and political life whose sole purpose is to criticize? Before we pass a law, I show these men the draft and ask them, 'Would you tell me what is wrong with this, please?' I do not want them to simply say amen to everything. They are of no value to me if they are not critical and do not tell me what defects might, under certain circumstances, detract from our measures. I am similarly not in support of the press simply printing only what it has been instructed to print.

"It is no pleasure to read newspapers that all have almost exactly the same text. In the course of time, our editors will be so trained that they will be able to make their own valuable contributions to building the nation. However, there is one thing of which I can assure you: I will never tolerate a press whose exclusive aim is to destroy what we have undertaken to build up.

"If an editor's policy is to hold up his own fascinating world-view (*Weltanschauung*) in contrast to ours, let him take note that I will then equally make use of the modern opportunities afforded by the press in order to combat him. I will allow the agents of foreign powers no opportunity whatsoever. People like these agents are infringing upon their privilege of hospitality. I warmly welcome foreign correspondents who report what they see and hear in Germany objectively and without bias. However, each and every correspondent should make it a matter of his own concern, for his own sake and for the sake of his reputation as a journalist, not to expose himself to the risk of having to deny his own reports because he has failed to correctly assess the effectiveness of our regime. Bear in mind that the press was forced to change its opinion of Richard Wagner."

"Whereas on the one hand I want criticism," the chancellor continued, "on the other I insist that those who work for the welfare of the entire Volk must have the security of knowing that they can go about their work in peace. The mistake of the systems that preceded our own lay in the fact that none of the ministers nor anyone in public office responsible to the state knew how long they would be at the helm. This had as a consequence that they were able to neither do away with the deplorable state of affairs their predecessors had left behind nor dare to concern themselves with questions involving the future. I assured the gentlemen when I took over the government—even those who were not members of my party—that they could be certain of the stability of their offices. As a result, they were all enthusiastic and wholeheartedly devoted to what they were doing, and their sights were set solely on a constructive future."

Lochner then asked, "Mr. Chancellor, it has occasionally been said that, among the gentlemen in your immediate vicinity, there are those who would like to take your place. It is claimed, for instance, with respect to one of your most prominent staff members that he attempts to thwart your measures."

Describing his own impressions after having posed this question, Lochner wrote: "The chancellor's features became illuminated. It was as though the faces of the various men who had been closest to him in the struggle were passing by his mind's eye, and what he saw there pleased him."

The Führer replied: "Of course I know that you are asking this question in order to clarify my relationship to my staff and not because you are personally questioning their loyalty. It would really be slanderous to insinuate that any one of the men who have stood by me year after year had any desire to get me out of the way.

"The world has never witnessed a more wonderful example of total allegiance than that which my staff provides. Perhaps the reason that this type of story comes into being lies in the fact that I have not surrounded myself, so to speak, with wash-outs, but with real men. Washouts have no backbone. They are the first to collapse when things are going badly. The men around me are strong and upstanding men. Each of them is a person of stature; each has his own will and is filled with ambition. If these men were not ambitious, they would not be where they are today. I welcome their ambition.

"When such a group of powerful personalities comes to-gether, it is inevitable that some friction may ensue. But never has a single one of the men who have given me his allegiance at-tempted to force his will upon me. On the contrary: they have subordinated themselves to my wishes in an admirable way."

Lochner's final question was: "Mr. Chancellor, in the days before you came to power, you were always among the people and had constant personal contact with them. When you go anywhere today, the streets are decorated, you are given wel-coming addresses, and you are greeted by the chief authori-ties. How do you nevertheless manage to keep your finger on the pulse of the nation? How do you maintain contact with the man on the street?"

With an almost boyish laugh, the Führer replied: "First of all, you should see what my lunch hour is like upstairs in this building. You would see how new faces appear there ev-ery day. My home is like a central station. My home is always open to my fellow fighters, regardless of how plain and simple their circumstances may be. Our organization reaches all the way down to the smallest village, and the men of my retinue come from all over to visit me in Berlin.

"We sit at the table and, with time, they tell me their cares and problems. Then again, there are naturally many other op-portunities to come into contact with the Volk. I have men-tioned this only as a typical example. However, I would like to stress one thing: although I listen to all of these minor cares and put together a composite picture of the whole from a wealth of details, I never allow my overall view to become clouded. I must constantly keep my sights focused on our pri-mary aim and pursue this goal with unwavering tenacity. I am not equally satisfied with every single detail. Admittedly, I am forced to leave it to my staff to settle the minor matters.

"We are pursuing great aims. Our primary task consists of adhering to this method. I need four years to translate the first segment of our program into reality. Then I will require another four years for the next segment, and so on. We are striving for an important, a better, and a happier Germany."

▸ January 16, 1935 *Hitler was ecstatic that the Saar voted to return to Germany. He vowed that he would win over his opponents in the Saar by his efforts and time—and, although unsaid, if need be—by a trip to the camps.*

On January 16, Hitler granted an interview at the Obersalzberg to the American journalist Pierre Huss, a correspondent for the Hearst Press:

Question: *Herr Reichskanzler,* what is your opinion of the outcome of the Saar plebiscite?

Answer: The results of the plebiscite fill me—and every single one of my staff—with infinite pride in the German Volk. At the same time, this is a subsequent condemnation of the Peace Treaty of Versailles of truly historic dimensions. For in this treaty, this region was torn from Germany on the grounds that 150,000 French lived there. After a fifteen-year rule of the League of Nations and thus ultimately of France, it has now been ascertained that not 150,000, but a scant 2,000 French reside in this region, i.e., not even four French per 1,000 inhabitants of the Saar. How can anyone be surprised no good can come of a treaty based upon such incorrect assumptions?

Question: Will the Social Democrats or Communists in the Saar and other non-National Socialist inhabitants of this territory who have cast their ballots for Germany have anything to fear in the future due to their former political leanings?

Answer: Sixteen years ago, I began my struggle for Germany with six men; that means my struggle for the German Volk. The number of my followers, to wit, the followers of the National Socialist Movement of the new state, has risen to nearly thirty-nine million since then. Do you think that all these people did not belong to some other party before? No, at one time they were all part of some movement or another.

They have been won over to the National Socialist idea with effort and with time. And we will not give up this struggle for the soul of our Volk now. Therefore, we never ask what an individual was in the past but what he wants to be today. This is how we have succeeded in dissolving the feuding German parties and formed a true national community (*Volksgemeinschaft*) in which former Communists and adherents of the Center coexist, joined in their mutual struggle for the National Socialist state, the new Reich. But a part of this Reich is the Saar, and its inhabitants comprise a part of our Volk.

Question: *Herr Reichskanzler,* you have frequently stated that the last obstacle to amicable relations with France would be removed when the Saar question was settled. In view of your untiring, further pursuit of this goal in the interest of world peace, do you have a specific plan in mind?

Answer: I have frequently stated that, after the return of the Saar to Germany, I would make no further territorial demands on France. I have repeated this statement definitively today before the whole world. In historical terms, it is a very difficult thing to renounce this as I am doing in the name of the German Volk. But I am making this most difficult sacrifice in order to contribute to the pacification of Europe. One cannot expect more from Germany. It is now up to the rest of the world to draw the consequences of such a decision. Never shall I—and never shall the new German Reich—consent to any limitations to the rights of our people. We wish to be a peaceful Volk, but under no circumstances without honor.

We are willing to make a very big sacrifice, but never to renounce our freedom. We reject any differentiation between moral equality and factual equality: there is but one equality of rights, and that is the right of a sovereign state and a sovereign nation. If the world recognizes this, there is no need for grandiose plans to fortify peace in Europe.

Question: *Herr Reichskanzler*, do you now, after your great success in the Saar plebiscite, have anything to say that might be of particular interest to the American people?

Answer: I have but one request to address to the American people. For years now and in the past months, millions of American citizens will have been hearing and reading the opposite of what has now been affirmed in this free and open ballot on the Saar. I would be happy if this were to be taken cognizance of, so that in the future no one will any longer believe a word of what the professional international well-poisoners and rabble-rousers among our emigrants say. Just as they lied about the Saar, they are lying about Germany and, in doing so, practically lying to the whole world.

The American people should hear only eyewitness reports on Germany and, if possible, personally come to Germany in order to see for themselves a state whose regime is today supported by the overwhelming majority of the nation.

An interview with Ward Price followed on January 17. Noteworthy is the fact that, although Ward Price emphasized the "*fait accompli* of the restoration of German arms," Hitler did not deign to utter a single word on the subject.

Question I. Under which conditions could Germany return to the League of Nations?

Answer: Neither I nor anyone else in Germany would even consider placing any "conditions" on our possible return to the League of Nations. Whether or not we return to this body depends exclusively upon whether we can belong to it as a completely equal nation. This is not a "condition," but a matter of course. Either we are a sovereign state, or we are not! As long as we are not, we have no business in a community of sovereign states. As long as the National Socialist Movement is leading Germany—and that will be the case for the next few centuries, no matter how often our émigrés conjure up the opposite view—this opinion will not change. Incidentally, I stated this explicitly in my May speech in 1933.

I would like to stress that the German Volk feels that the differentiation between "moral" and "factual" equality is an insult. Whether or not 68 million people are morally equal in this world or not is ultimately something that can be decided by no one save the relevant people itself. Either one is factually equal, and consequently morally equal as well; on the other hand, if one is morally equal, there is no reason why one should contest factual equality of rights or simply refuse to grant them.

Question II. Will it be necessary to separate the general provisions of the League of Nations from those of the Treaty of Versailles?

Answer: As long as the League of Nations constitutes only a treaty of guarantee for the victorious nations, it is by no means worthy of its name. The fact that, with time, this league—that was presumably designed by its founders to exist for all eternity—cannot be coupled with a treaty, the short term of which is inherent in its own weaknesses and impracticabilities, is a point that can perhaps be contested by today's interested parties, but that history will judge on its intrinsic merits.

Question III. Should the recognition of equality of rights be a precondition, or could granting equality of rights and rejoining the league take place simultaneously?

Answer: German equality of rights is the prerequisite for any participation on Germany's part in international conventions and agreements. I certainly am not alone in the world with this demand; I am in the best of company. Let it be said that no self-respecting people and no responsible government would be able to think or much less act differently in such a case. The world has already seen a great many wars lost in the past.

If in the past, after every lost war, the unlucky vanquished were divested forever of their honor and their equality of rights, the League of Nations would even now have to be satisfied with a group of non-equal and thus ultimately dishonorable and inferior nations. For there is hardly a state or nation in existence that has not once had the misfortune, even if it was in the right a thousand times over, to be defeated by a stronger opponent or a stronger coalition.

Until now, this abominable absurdity has not yet been able to gain a foothold in the world, and we are determined to ensure that Germany will not be the first to set an example for the introduction of such an absurdity.

Question IV. Does Your Excellency not find that a reform of the League of Nations is called for? What practical steps would this entail? Which arguments could be used to obtain public support?

Answer: Since we are not in the League of Nations in any case, we do not devote our attention to reflecting on its internal reforms.

Question V. Recently I spoke with a high-ranking political personage in France. I asked him the following: Why does France choose not to recognize the *fait accompli* of the restoration of German arms? We English always hold that it is more sensible not to ignore such facts. The politician replied: "Yes, we believe that Germany will uphold a policy of reconciliation only until the *Reichswehr* judges itself capable of successfully waging a war. In France, there is fear that the overtures to the French associations of front-line soldiers are only a camouflage to conceal aggressive future intentions." What is Your Excellency's reply to this fear?

Answer: That politician has never led a people. Otherwise, how could he believe that one can talk about peace for a decade and then suddenly, with the same people, simply start a war without further ado? When I talk about peace, I am expressing none other than the innermost desire of the German Volk. I know the horrors of war: no gains can compensate for the losses it brings. The disastrous consequences of widespread European butchery in the future would be even worse.

I believe that the madness of Communism would be the sole victor. But I have not fought this for fifteen years to elevate it finally to the throne by way of a detour. What I want is the well-being of my Volk! I have seen that war is not the highest form of bliss, but the contrary: I have witnessed only the deepest suffering. Hence I can quite frankly state two of my beliefs:

1. Germany will never break the peace of its own accord, and

2. He who would lay hands upon us will encounter thorns and barbs! For we love liberty just as we love peace.

And if, without being compelled to do so, I submit to France on behalf of the entire German Volk the pledge that we will place no further territorial demands upon it and thus of our own accord eliminate any grounds for revenge, at the same time I pledge an equally sacred vow that no measure of need, pressure, or violence will ever move us to relinquish our honor or our equality of rights.

I hold that this must be said, for treaties make sense only when concluded by honor-loving peoples and honor-conscious governments. Germany wishes to establish honest relations with the peoples of neighboring countries. We have done this in the east, and I believe that not only Berlin but Warsaw as well will rejoice in the clearing of the atmosphere brought about through our joint efforts. I hold to my conviction that, once this path of mutual understanding and consideration has been taken, more will come of it in the end than through ever-so-extensive pacts inherently lacking in clarity.

In any case, I will reflect a thousand times over before I allow the German Volk to become entangled in agreements whose consequences are not readily evident. If, on our own account, we do not intend to wage war, we are much less willing to do so for interests that do not concern Germany and are alien to it. I may add that we have more than once stated our willingness to conclude non-aggression pacts with the states neighboring our own!

▸ March 17, 1935 *After he announced the introduction of military conscription, Hitler sought to make clear that his objective in developing a new armed force was not war, just equal rights for Germany. But, of course, Germany was at war within five years.*

On March 17, Hitler granted an interview to Ward Price in Munich, in which he took pains to paint the reaction of the German public to the announcement of general conscription in positive colors.

1. In response to the question whether Germany was still as willing to negotiate with England and France as had been stated in his note of February 15, the chancellor replied:

> Establishing German military sovereignty is an act that restores the sovereignty of a great state that had been violated. It would be absurd to assume that a state that has become sovereign would be less inclined to negotiate than one that is not sovereign. It is for the very reason that we are a sovereign state that we are also willing to negotiate with other sovereign states.

2. Ward Price then asked the chancellor whether Germany continued to feel bound by the territorial provisions of the Treaty of Versailles, to which the Chancellor responded:

> The act of restoring German military sovereignty touches only upon those points in the Treaty of Versailles that have in any case long since lost their legal validity by virtue of the refusal of the other states to perform their respective obligations to reduce arms. The German government is conscious of the fact that unilateral measures can never prompt a revision of the territorial provisions of international treaties.

3. In conclusion, Ward Price asked the Führer what impression the proclamation of March had made on the German Volk. The Führer's reply was:

> You yourself, Mr. Ward Price, saw the mood of the German Volk in Berlin, and you have now seen it in the south of the Reich, in Munich. It is no different in any other place

in Germany. And this may make something clear to you: the German Volk perceives the German government's action taken yesterday, not so much as a military, but as a moral step.

It has suffered for fifteen years from provisions by which it felt that a self-evident, intrinsic right of each and every people was violated. Had the world disarmed on an international scale, the German Volk would have been more than satisfied. But the fact that the rest of the world was arming itself while denying Germany any right to self-defense was perceived as a monstrous and degrading desecration and that this defenseless position provoked an incessant stream of humiliations over and above that, begins to explain the proud satisfaction which the nation feels now that its honor has been restored.

If you were to now ask one of these millions whether he is thinking of peace or war, he would gaze at you in total incomprehension. For all these rejoicing people are moved, not by some kind of animosity towards any one other nation, but solely by the satisfaction of knowing that their own Volk has regained its freedom.

They are moved by only a single idea: that they may once again, without having to be ashamed, count themselves as part of a great people. You do not understand this and are not able to understand it. Yet had you gone through anything similar to what the German Volk has gone through, you would perhaps comprehend the emotions that overcome a person who has been kept for years in a dishonorable position and who has now, of his own accord, regained his honor.

And thus I am able, in the same proclamation with which I have reestablished the military sovereignty of the German Reich, to plead loudly and clearly for peace and to offer our cooperation in securing that peace. The German Volk does not want war; it wants only the same rights as all others. That is all.

▶ November 28, 1935 *Hitler often stated his basic objective: to protect Germany and the world from the Jewish–Bolshevik threat.*

To both Great Britain and the United States, Hitler presented himself as a bulwark against the bogy of Bolshevism. He believed himself capable of bluffing these countries just as he had the German Nationalists: because of their fear of Communism, the Anglo-Saxons would not interfere but instead allow him free rein in the east. The interview the German dictator granted in late November to the American journalist and president of the United Press, Baillie, bore witness to this tactic. There Hitler stated:

> "Germany is the bulwark of the West against Bolshevism and will fight propaganda with propaganda, terror with terror, and violence with violence to combat it."
>
> In response to a question as to the reasons behind the Jewish legislation in Nuremberg, he replied:
>
> "The necessity for combating Bolshevism is one of the main reasons for Jewish legislation in Germany. This legislation is not anti-Jewish, but rather pro-German. It is designed to protect the rights of Germans against destructive Jewish influences."
>
> Hitler then pointed out that nearly all the Bolshevist agitators in Germany had been Jews and further that Germany was separated from Soviet Russia by only a few miles, which meant that effective defense measures were called for at all times to protect Germany from the machinations of the mostly Jewish agents of Bolshevism.
>
> In the further course of the discussion, Hitler noted that the tens of thousands of officers who had been dismissed after the Great War had evolved into an intellectual proletariat of sorts, and that many of them, although they were academically educated, had had to take work as street sweepers, drivers, and in other similar occupations in order to eke out an existence. On the other hand, the Jews—who made up less than one percent of the population—had attempted to seize for themselves the cultural leadership and swarmed into the intellectual professions such as jurisprudence, medicine, etc. The influence of this intellectual *Judentum* in Germany had left its subversive mark at every turn.
>
> "For this reason it was necessary to take steps to put a halt to this subversion and bring about a distinct and pure division between the two races."

The basic principle governing the handling of this question in Germany was that Germans were to be given that to which Germans were entitled and Jews that to which they were entitled. He stressed that this also served to protect the Jews, citing as evidence the fact that since the restrictions had been established, anti-Jewish feeling in the country had lessened.

In reply to Mr. Baillie's question whether further legislative measures were to be expected on this point, Hitler answered that it was the main endeavor of the Reich government to prevent by means of legislative measures the Volk taking the matter into its own hands—for that could give way to dangerous explosions—and, by means of such measures, to maintain peace and order in Germany as hitherto. On the Kurfürstendamm in Berlin there were just as many Jewish shops as in New York and other major cities, and, as a close look would show, these shops were operating without any disruption whatsoever. He believed that new tensions had likely been averted by means of the Nuremberg Laws.

However, should new tensions arise, among other things, further legislative measures would become necessary.

Turning to the question of Bolshevism, he declared that Germany was the bulwark that protected the West from Bolshevist expansion spreading from Soviet Russia.

In the United States, a country geographically far distant from Soviet Russia, this would probably not meet with understanding on every front! However, the context would be readily understandable for anyone who viewed the situation from Germany's perspective, i.e., from that of a country that was only very few hours' distance from Russia by airplane or fast train. "Germany will continue to fight Communism with the weapons that Communism itself uses."

Asked to comment on the buildup of the German army, Hitler stated: "The purpose of restoring the German *Wehrmacht* is to protect Germany from attacks by alien powers. Germany is a major power of the first rank and has a right to have a first-class army."

In response to a question as to the size of today's German *Wehrmacht* compared to its military strength in 1914, Hitler stated that an army of millions such as the one Germany had raised in 1914 could only come about because of the demands of a new war—a new war from which God, as he confidently hoped, would preserve Germany and the coming generations. Furthermore, he drew attention to his earlier proposals for stabilizing the size of European armies at 200,000 to 300,000 men. These proposals had been categorically rejected at the time.

When discussing German military strength, one was also to take into consideration Germany's geographical position. If a strip of land 100 kilometers wide were occupied by an enemy in America, this would be a mere scratch that America could easily put up with. By way of contrast, in the event of an invasion that would perhaps be but minor for the United States, Germany would be crippled.

Finally, Mr. Baillie asked the Führer and Reich chancellor whether Germany was endeavoring to recapture its colonies. Hitler answered that Germany would never relinquish its colonial claims.

▸ January 19, 1936 *Hitler was always able, during this time, to get a "fair hearing" from reporters. His charm and affable manner appeared to demonstrate his sincere desire for understanding and peace. Nothing could be further from the truth—and the reporters should have known this.*

The interview Hitler had granted to Madame Titayna, the correspondent of the French newspaper *Paris Soir*, was published on January 26. In view of his plans to reoccupy the Rhineland, Hitler was very anxious to get good publicity in France during the months of January and February 1936. His intent is mirrored in the January conversation with Titayna.

Titayna's description of her meeting with Hitler began with the following observation:

> No matter which political ideals we espouse, it will always be the personality of the man who, like Adolf Hitler in this case, enters into the history of his people and therefore of the world, that captivates us most. No one can escape this enchantment. As soon as I was informed that the German chancellor was willing to receive me and that he would grant an interview

to the readers of *Paris Soir*, my elation, resulting from my professional interest in the matter, was superseded by the thrilling sensation that now finally I would know who "he" is and how "he" speaks. Maybe then I would come to understand the power he exercises over the crowds rallying to him.

The palace in the Wilhelmstrasse, in which the Führer lives and works, is characterized by an austerity of architectural and interior design reflecting the straight-forward nature of the new Germany: a wide and well-lit staircase leads to a gallery through unassuming rooms to the office of the Führer.

I did not have to wait long. Five minutes to eleven I arrived; the interview was set for eleven o'clock. State Secretary Funk led me out of the anteroom, which was equipped with numerous modern and comfortable easy chairs. The minute I had sat down in one of them, I was reminded of the reception I had received a few months earlier from Mussolini. At the time I had been made to wait for the Duce in a room filled with uncomfortable, wooden Gothic chairs. Once I had entered the Italian dictator's office, I saw him standing about 30 meters away from me, where he had posed himself between window and desk, seeming all the more remote since we were separated by a parquet floor that seemed to be endless.

Today my experience at the Führer's is quite to the contrary; everything is marked by modesty and great simplicity. The Führer comes up to me with his hand extended in greeting. I am surprised and astonished by the vivid blue of his eyes, which on photographs had always appeared to be brown. I remark that indeed he does look very different from any pictures I have seen of him. I much prefer the real-life Hitler, that face that radiates intelligence and energy, and emits a special glow when he speaks. At this very moment, I understand his magical appeal to the masses and the power he wields over them.

When I was called to Berlin by wire, I had prepared a good dozen of questions at night on the train, that no matter under what circumstances, I intended to pose. In any case, only the answers to these questions could be indiscreet. Within the first few words he utters, I can tell that the Führer has no intention of hiding out behind diplomatic phrases but rather that he wishes to speak openly and honestly to the French people.

In the room, I hear my voice sound uncertain while speaking German. I try to explain my own and thereby the fears of all of us:

"The French are afraid of and despise war more than anything else, and because constantly preoccupied with this fear; we are prone to see war lurking just around the corner. I would like to hear from you that Germany's foreign policy is solidly based on pacifist principles. "

The man sitting across from me reflects for just a moment and then responds:

"The word 'pacifism' has two meanings, and does not have the same meaning for France as for us. We cannot accept a pacifism that means forfeiting one's vital rights. For us, pacifism can only become a reality if it is built on the basic human premise that each and every people has a right to live. I said 'to live,' and not 'to vegetate.' Whoever truly wants peace must first acknowledge this right of the nations. In other words, there is not a single German who wants war. The last one cost us two million dead and seven-and-a-half million wounded. Even if we had been victorious, no victory would have been worth paying that price."

To my question whether it would be possible to revise the Treaty of Versailles without endangering the interests of other nations, Hitler replies: "The Treaty of Versailles had two consequences. It confirms the fact of a territorial conquest, and it establishes a moral conquest. Every territorial solution has its weak points. In all territorial questions, the voice of the Volk and its economic needs should alone decide. But seen from the moral point of view, it is outrageous and inadmissible to humiliate and discriminate against a Volk. In the case of the Treaty of Versailles, the human conscience should give justice priority over interests and parties.

"Each Volk has the right to live on its own soil with its own faith, history, customs, and economic potential. To favor some to the detriment of the others is absurd, for this destroys the balance of human society. In European politics, too, peace can issue only from a balance, in other words, from justice. We have sixty-eight million inhabitants in Germany, sixty-eight million creatures who want food, clothing, shelter, and a place to live. No treaty in the world can change that. The statesman too must give his Volk what it needs."

I respond, "Certainly. We are touching upon a very serious question. The population policy being advocated in Germany by necessity creates a desire to expand the empire in order to accommodate the additional countrymen—that means war. You complain of not having enough bread to go around, and then you want more mouths to feed."

"There are talented and untalented peoples in the world. The European countries belong to the former category. One must become conscious of the fact that, in this sense, they comprise a community of peoples, though they are sometimes a quarrelsome family."

I am silent for a moment, since I myself share his opinion. Through my travels I too have become aware of an inequality among the races, and of the significance of the term European. "Does this mean that because of the more numerous population, Germany will need to subdue colonies?"

"Wouldn't you agree?" Hitler replied.

To the question of how he intends to turn this ambition into a reality, Hitler states:

"If the conscience of the other peoples were receptive to the idea of a balance and of justice, then it would be easy to arrange the material details. What concerns me most at the moment is the world's awakening to the insight that the good will of the peoples must combine in a cooperative effort, without ulterior motives, to make possible a better life for each separate people."

I interject, "I will be traveling to China within a few days, because the far east . . ."

"How lucky you are," Hitler interrupted me. "Unfortunately, I myself am unable to travel. You will see Japan where, under completely different working conditions, goods are manufactured that are flooding the world market. One day, that will apply to Russia, too. If necessary, Moscow's rulers will allow a part of the population to die to secure an export trade. Communism can survive in Russia because it has established itself at the head of a population lacking the bare necessities in an enormous, undeveloped territory. But if Communism had come to Germany, there would have been a catastrophe of unforeseeable proportions, because in Germany only 25 percent of the population live in the country and 75 percent inhabit the cities, whereas in Russia 92 percent live in the country and eight percent in the cities. And because a much more complicated apparatus would have fallen prey to the destruction."

"What is your opinion with regard to the union of Austria with Germany (*Anschluss*)?

"That is a question no one here is excited about. In Vienna, they need this bogey for reasons of domestic politics. In Berlin, the Anschluss question is not acute."

The hands on my watch keep moving relentlessly forward; I fear I am running out of time and that I will not be able to pose all the questions I had intended to, nor hear the responses to them. Quickly I ask:

"What about the role of the women? Do you honestly believe they are only there to bear the children of men?"

This time the Führer laughs: "Who told you that?"

"The press!", I said.

"I accord women the same right as men, but I do not believe they are alike. Woman is man's life companion. She should not be burdened with work for which men are made. I am not envisioning women's battalions; I believe they are better fit for work in the social sector. But in any event, a woman who does not marry—and we have many in Germany, because we do not have enough men—has the right to earn her living just as a man does. Incidentally, I might remind you that it was a woman who made the great party congress film, and a woman will shoot the Olympic film.

"Just one word on the Olympic Games. We are quite happy; we are looking forward to welcoming the French here—we hope a great many of them. We will do everything to show them they are welcome here and that they are encountering a supremely hospitable German Volk. I sincerely hope that your travelers will come, not only for the sporting events, but will also visit our country, the whole country. They will not find prearranged propaganda trips that would steer them away from the truth. We will not tell them that Germany is a paradise, for there is no such thing in this world. And they can roam about freely here and see for themselves that Germany lives in peace and order and in work. They will see our upswing, our efforts, our will for peace. That is all I want."

The Führer rises. I have been able to ascertain that he is in the best of health and that rumors of an illness are unfounded. I retreat, happy to be in a position to communicate his ideas to the French people. The entire conversation took no longer than fifty minutes.

Hitler had proven himself to be a charming conversationalist in this interview and had demonstrated an agility in avoiding compromising issues. The openness he displayed obviously did not fail to impress his French guest.

However, Hitler's rhetoric failed him miserably when he had to face representatives of the great powers, be they British, American, or Russian. Yet to a certain extent, his oratory impressed people from small countries or neighboring states, who shared an affinity with German culture. This was, above all, the case with regard to representatives from the Balkans, Poland, Czechoslovakia, and Italy. Sometimes, his rhetorical versatility even left its mark on some people from the Netherlands, and he also managed to impress Frenchmen sympathetic to the German cause with his eloquence such as Laval, de Brinon, and others. At times the French ambassador to National Socialist Germany, André François Poncet, could not help falling under the influence of Hitler's powerful oratory as well.

▸ March 9, 1936 *Hitler never changed his line: he was only Hitler fighting for peace.*

For two hours on March 9, Hitler granted an interview to Ward Price. Here once again, Hitler detailed his various "peace plans" and gave a rather lame explanation of his forced entry into the Rhineland. Ward Price presented Hitler with five specific questions.

First question: Does the Führer's offer of a non-aggression pact to every eastern neighbor of Germany also apply to Austria? Does be consider Czechoslovakia as a state neighboring Germany in the east, too?

Answer: My proposal for the conclusion of non-aggression pacts both to the east and west of Germany was of a general nature, i.e., there were no exclusions. Hence, this applies to both Czechoslovakia and Austria.

Second question: Does the Führer intend to return Germany to the League of Nations so that his proposals might be placed before that body for consideration, with Germany a full member of the league's council? Or would he prefer to call for an international conference to deal with the matter?

Answer: Speaking for Germany, I declared it willing to immediately join the League of Nations. I do so in the expectation that, in due time, both the question of colonial claims and the question of a divorce of the Covenant of the League of Nations from the so-called peace treaty would be resolved.

I believe it would be most practical if the governments in question would directly take responsibility for the conclusion of the non-aggression pacts proposed by the German government. This means that in the case of pacts securing the borders between Germany, France, and Belgium (and perhaps, given the circumstances, even Holland) the powers invited to participate would consist of the governments involved and England and Italy—the signatory powers and guarantors of the agreement. It might be a good idea if those countries that will be secured by these pacts approach their future guarantors. The non-aggression pacts with the other states could then be negotiated in the manner in which the German-Polish pact was concluded, in other words, directly between the governments involved. In addition to that, Germany would certainly be content if another power—for instance England—assumed the role of an impartial mediator in the practical resolution of these questions.

Third question: It is highly unlikely that, given the upcoming elections in France in April, any French government will be in a position to discuss your suggestions, even if it wanted to. Is Germany willing to keep its offer in force until after that date? Will Germany be undertaking any steps in the meantime that again might alter the present situation?

Answer: There need not be any change of the current situation, at least not on the part of the German government. We have restored its sovereign rights to the German Reich and have brought ancient Reich territory back under the protection of the entire nation. Hence, for us, there is no need to set deadlines. I would like to make one thing clear, however. Should these proposals fail, or simply be ignored, like so many before them have been, then the German government will not impose upon Europe any further suggestions.

Fourth question: Now that the Führer has reclaimed complete sovereignty over the entire German territory, is he willing to restrict the forces deployed in the Rhineland to a number that would preclude any offensive actions directed against France on the part of Germany?

Answer: It was not our intention to commit an act of aggression against France as we occupied the so-called "demilitarized" zone. Rather, we consider that such an enormous sacrifice by a nation is only conceivable and hence supportable if it is met with objectivity and political understanding on the part of the other party to the contract.

It is not Germany that is in breach of contract! Ever since the signing of the armistice agreement based on President Wilson's Fourteen Points, the following customs have been observed in Europe. Whenever victor and vanquished draw up a treaty between each other, the vanquished becomes obliged to observe its conventions while the victor may proceed as he sees fit and as suits his purposes.

You cannot deny the fact that the provisions of Wilson's Fourteen Points and the three additional codicils supplementing it were not upheld. Further, you cannot deny the fact that their general disarmament provisions were not upheld on the part of the victorious powers. Moreover, the Locarno Pact has a political significance over and above its literal meaning.

Had the Franco-Russian agreement of May 2, 1935 been on the books already upon the signature of the Locarno Pact, then naturally there would have been no signing of the Rhine Pact. It is unacceptable that, retroactively, a treaty should take on a different meaning or should be interpreted in a manner not intended. In the case before us not only the spirit but also the letter of the Locarno Pact was violated. The conclusion of a military alliance between the Soviet Union and France brings Germany into a position in which it is forced to draw certain conclusions. It is nothing but these conclusions that I have drawn!

After all, it is clearly impossible that, with France concluding such a military alliance, a densely populated and economically vital border region of the German Reich should be left defenseless and without protection. This is the most natural and instinctive reaction to such a move.

Perhaps in England, I fear, there may be many persons who do not realize that the so-called "demilitarized" zone has about as many inhabitants as does, for instance, the Czechoslovakian state or Yugoslavia. The area is merely being furnished with garrisons to protect its freedom precisely as in the other parts of the Reich—no more and no less! There cannot be any talk of massing troops along the border for offensive purposes because:

a) Germany no longer has anything to demand of France and it will not demand anything anymore;

b) Germany itself has called for the establishment of non-aggression pacts, expressing the desire that England and Italy might become signatory powers and guarantors of these agreements;

c) massing troops along the border would be unnecessary from a military point of view and, as a matter of fact, it would be senseless!

Moreover, we want to create a future in which these two countries no longer feel threatened by one another. When M. Sarraut declares that he cannot tolerate the sight of German cannons threatening the Strasbourg fortress, it ought to be quite obvious that we too cannot tolerate the sight of French fortress cannons threatening our open cities Frankfurt, Freiburg, Karlsruhe, etc. Such a perceived threat could be prevented by finding a mutual solution to the question of the "demilitarized" zone.

Fifth question: Will the Führer tell the world why he has chosen this particular path to attain his goal? Why did he not first present his suggestions to the public and then demand the remilitarization of the Rhineland in return? I am certain that the entire world would have agreed enthusiastically. Does he have any particular motive necessitating such a speedy action on his part?

Answer: I have already dealt with this topic at great length in my speech before the Reichstag. However, let me touch upon your remark that any solutions proposed by me, divorced from a military occupation of the Rhineland, would have assuredly been greeted with great enthusiasm. That is very possible. Yet this regrettably is not the crucial point.

It was I, for instance, who proposed the 300,000-man army. I still think that was a most reasonable proposal. It certainly was a concrete proposal and it would greatly have contributed to a lessening of tensions in Europe. No doubt, many people welcomed it. Indeed, the French and British governments have even adopted this proposal.

Nonetheless, it was rejected. Thus, for better or for worse, I had to proceed as sole bearer of responsibility. After all, I sought to secure equal rights for Germany in questions of armament, thereby resolving one of the most burning issues in Europe today. No one can deny Germany's moral claim to these rights. And this time as well, the outcome would have been no different. It is well possible that if I had first made my proposal public, demanding the restitution of full sovereignty to the Reich in the demilitarized zone as well, it would have been welcomed and understood by the world public.

However, based on my experiences in the past, I did not believe that we ever would have come together at the conference table. Yet if one party to an agreement moves against the spirit and letter of a treaty, then it is only natural that the other party withdraw from its obligations as well. And that is precisely what I did! Moreover, if ever a French or British statesman found his people in distress similar to that in which I found my own Volk, then I have no doubts that he would have proceeded in precisely the same manner, given the same circumstances. He will do so in the future as well, I am certain.

Rarely does the present realize the full import of an event of historic proportion. No doubt, posterity will see that it was morally more decent and appropriate to eliminate the cause of these insupportable tensions in order to arrive finally at a reasonable approach to the "open-door" policy which we all desired. It was far better to proceed in this manner than to try to maintain such a position, a position that ran contrary to any considerations of common sense and reason.

Once the proposals of the German Reich government have been accepted, it is my firm conviction that posterity will deem these proposals to have rendered a great service to Europe and to the cause of peace.

▶ May 20, 1937 *Hitler could always fool reporters.*

Hitler agreed to a discussion of social problems with Abel Bonnard, a member of the Académie Française. The interview was printed in the French newspaper *Le Journal* on May 22. Bonnard reported:

Everything the Führer told me corresponded exactly to what I had seen in Germany during the past few days. Every word of our conversation pertained to the subject of the social reforms in the country of which he is head of state—with the exception of a remark about former front-line soldiers. To him, these men represented the most trustworthy group in any country because of their great experience and good judgment.

Our talk began with a comparison of the pre-World War society to its present state. Because I consider it a self-evident truth, I had maintained that even if the world had been a more comfortable and agreeable place in former times, granted that the well-being of the individual had been rendered greater justice, the present has its advantages, too. Precisely because it is not an easy life we live, the world today offers us splendid and numerous opportunities to prove our manliness. Today's reality is a harsher and more dramatic one, but it may also be more poetic, as our struggle with reality leads us to greater depths of understanding life and all it entails.

With a wave of his hand, the Führer signals his assent to this, but I still can tell that he is not quite in agreement with my opinion.

"Without doubt," says he, "the world today may provide some men of energy with a thrilling sensation in view of these challenges. I for my part would never have been happy living in the period from 1860 to 1914. However, these feelings apply to very few individuals, and the mass of the people simply is not interested in these problems.

"Certainly one can raise the crowd's awareness so that the people appreciate the vital interests of their fatherland. However, this in itself does not satisfy the masses. Many people work eight hours a day, subjected to a working environment that may be most unpleasant, and in a profession they themselves did not choose. They need to have an inner drive, a feeling of happiness that makes life bearable for them. To really improve their lot, it does not suffice merely to change the material conditions of their existence!"

Then the Führer turns to speak of the organization Strength Through Joy (*Kraft durch Freude*), the purpose of which is "to spread joy among the people and teach them to enjoy themselves."

"All in all, I say, a human being ought to be understood in his soul, as in his profession, so that he can arrive at a better understanding of his essence as reflected in his work and in his personality. It is not merely a question of building each citizen a house; one also needs a light to shine inside of it."

The chancellor continues: "The majority of people abroad seem to believe that we in Germany live under a dictatorship, without realizing that prior to 1933 there was a much greater dictatorship we suffered under. A government like ours could never remain in power without the will of the people to support it. The German Volk stands behind me because it knows that I truly care about its spiritual problems and advocate its concerns."

The chancellor proceeds to explain what he has done for his Volk already and what he still intends to do. Returning to his comparison of past and present, he maintains that it is an extraordinarily difficult and unprecedented struggle for Germany to attain autarky. Germany is trying to extract sufficient natural resources from its own soil since it cannot obtain sufficient thereof on the world market to meet its current needs. Foreign countries do not buy enough German products to allow for this.

Next he mentions the general distinction that was commonly made to differentiate between mental and manual labor. He correctly appraised this distinction as one that is not as easy as it may seem at first. There is mental work that is involved in physical tasks; certain mechanics and production line workers do indeed perform mental calculations as well. On the other hand, there is the bookkeeper, who thinks that he is performing a mentally demanding task while actually most of his work consists of automatic or mechanical routines.

Nevertheless, the chancellor's train of thought keeps returning to that one key problem, i.e., how to go about instilling the largest social class of the Volk with a different mental approach to its daily life.

Nearly up to the present, he says, there has always been a most striking contrast between the way passengers and the way the men of the crew were accommodated on the luxury liners of the great shipping lines. On the one side, there was everything that could be desired and all sorts of refinement imaginable; on the other, neither comfort nor amenities found their way into the crews' quarters, but rather there were plenty of difficulties engendered in the daily exigencies of life and survival, not to mention those posed by the unsanitary and unhealthy surroundings.

All our efforts to change this had been for naught. When we demanded that the crew members be given better quarters, the ship owners simply replied that space on a liner was too expensive to accomodate our wishes. When we demanded that there ought to be a deck reserved for the crewmen, where they might catch a breath of fresh air, we received the reply that this posed construction problems that had not yet been resolved by the engineers.

"Today the cabins of the crew members are decent ones. There is a deck at their disposal, equipped with good lounge chairs, with radios for entertainment. Further, there is a saloon where they can dine with the petty officers—and all these improvements were not that expensive—one just had to will them."

The Führer then turns his attention to the motor vehicle. As he states, the number of cars on German roads is persistently on the rise. He spoke of voyages that workers today can undertake to Madeira or the Canary Islands, or to the island of Rügen, where a beach with a yearly capacity of between 800,000 and 900,000 visitors is being constructed. In this manner, amenities that previously had been reserved for a small and exclusive group are now accessible to the general public.

This way the fuel for jealousy is cut back significantly. In Berlin, an enormous luxury hotel is under construction. But at the same time and on the same street, a house for the Strength Through Joy (*Kraft durch Freude*) organization will be built, designed to bring light into the lives of the common people.

According to the Führer, it is not a question of taking much from a few but rather of giving a little to the many. The chancellor speaks in a calm and composed manner, with few pauses. His face is drawn, perhaps because of the gravity of the concerns of which he speaks.

▸ February 20, 1938 *Hitler never let negative press stories go without a strong response. And it did not matter if the stories were accurate or not. Hitler always claimed to be right.*

In the following sarcastic remarks, Hitler revealed how annoyed he was with the manner in which the British press had reported on the *Wehrmacht* crisis:

> Therefore, I am also no longer prepared to sit idle and tolerate that unrestrained method of constantly denigrating and insulting our country and our Volk. From now on we will respond, and respond with National Socialist thoroughness. What has been strewn about only these past few weeks in the way of altogether crazy, stupid, and reckless allegations about Germany is simply outrageous.
>
> What can one possibly say when Reuters invents attacks on my life, and English newspapers talk about huge waves of arrests in Germany, about the closing of the German borders to Switzerland, Belgium, France, etc.; when yet other newspapers report that the crown prince has fled Germany, or that a military Putsch has taken place in Germany; that German generals have been taken prisoner, and on the other hand that German generals have stationed themselves with their regiments in front of the Reich Chancellery; that a quarrel has broken out between Himmler and Göring on the Jewish question, and as a result I am in a difficult predicament; that a German general has established contact with Daladier via intermediaries; that a regiment has mutinied in Stolp; that 2,000 officers have been dismissed from the army; that the entire German industrial sector has just received orders to mobilize for war; that there are extremely strong differences between the government and private industry; that twenty German officers and three generals have fled to Salzburg; that fourteen generals have fled to Prague with Ludendorff's corpse; and that I have completely lost my voice, and the resourceful Dr. Goebbels is presently on the lookout for a man capable of imitating my voice to allow me to speak from gramophone records from now on. I take it that tomorrow this journalistic zealot of truth will either contest that I am really here today or claim that I had only made gestures, while behind me the Reich minister of propaganda ran the gramophone.

In a recent speech, Mr. Eden waxed eloquent on the various liberties in his country. However, one particular liberty was left out: the liberty of journalists to insult and slander other peoples, their institutions, men, and governments without reprimand or restriction! One thing that increased—if this is even possible—our liking for Italy is the fact that there, the leadership of state and the policies of the press go hand in hand, instead of letting the leadership of state talk about understanding while the press is launching a smear campaign in the other direction!

This chapter on the disruption of international relations should also include the audacity to write letters to a foreign head of state with the request for information on court judgments. I recommend that the members of the British House of Commons concern themselves with the verdicts of British courts-martial in Jerusalem instead of with the judgments of German people's courts. While we might be able to understand an interest in German traitors, it does not help to improve the relations between England and Germany.

Furthermore, let no one delude himself that he might be able to influence German courts or the German penal system by such tactless meddling. In any case, I will not allow deputies of the German Reichstag to worry themselves with the affairs of British justice.

The interests of the British world empire are certainly quite extensive, and we recognize them as such. But as regards the concerns of the German Volk and Reich, the German Reichstag and I myself as the delegate of the Reichstag decide, and not a delegation of English letter-writers. I think it would be a commendable deed were one able to outlaw internationally, not only the dropping of toxic, incendiary, and explosive bombs on the civilian population, but above all to ban the distribution of newspapers that have a worse effect on the relations between the states than toxic or incendiary bombs could ever have.

Since this international smear campaign of the press must naturally be interpreted, not as a reconciling element, but as one presenting a threat to international peace, I have resolved to undertake the reinforcements of the German *Wehrmacht* which will lend us the certainty that this wild threat of war against Germany will not one day be transformed into a bloody reality. These measures have been in progress since February 4 of this year and will he continued with speed and determination.

Hitler blamed the responsibility for the military measures and preparations for war that he had been forced to take, on the "international smear campaign of the press." On the one hand, these accusations could be disregarded as just one of the numerous attempts on the part of Hitler to find a scapegoat for his actions. On the other hand, it does appear as though Hitler indeed greatly overestimated the importance of the press, as he did propaganda in general. Hitler's interpreter Schmidt recalled that whenever Hitler received an Englishman, the Führer complained of the stance espoused by the British press. Hitler would be particularly piqued when his guest replied by referring him to the principle of the freedom of the press. Later, as Hitler moved against Czechoslovakia and Poland, he accorded the German press a significance far beyond its capabilities.

▸ August 31, 1938 *Hitler worked for understanding among all people–as long as the understanding was his.*

As August gave way to September, the French author Alphonse de Chateaubriant visited Hitler at the Obersalzberg, where he was granted an interview. In the wake of the occupation of the Rhineland on March 7, 1936, Hitler had claimed that one of the considerations that had prompted such speedy action on his part had been the signing of the Franco-Russian Pact. At the time, he had maintained that the pact proved beyond all doubt that France was definitely on its way to becoming a Bolshevist state.

Such a bold argument seemed inopportune to him now, in light of his upcoming venture against Czechoslovakia. Thus he proclaimed that the French had successfully warded off this danger. Indeed, France and Germany would do better to look at each other with admiration than to insist upon fighting each other over petty disagreements. In this elegant play with words, Hitler cloaked his attempt to pull the moral foundation for French assistance to Czechoslovakia from under the feet of the French statesmen. He explained the matter to Chateaubriant:

The greatest threat to Europe is that of a Bolshevist infiltration, a threat similar to that in Germany at the time. I
no longer think that such an infiltration is possible in countries such as Holland, Belgium, and France. These countries
have vanquished Russo-Asiatic Communism. While internal
crises may and will take place there yet, France will not, for
instance, fall prey to this philosophy of destruction. As long
as each European state is concerned exclusively with the conduct of its affairs to its own advantage, the economic situation
in Europe will continue to breed discontent and discord.

The nations of Europe were created to work together in
the interest of the welfare of their peoples. We must regard
those wars, such as the last one in particular, that split Europe up in an arbitrary assignment of territory and peoples—
these wars we must regard as baneful errors committed by
those nations. In the realm of economic policy, as well as in
all other realms, peoples should think primarily of productive cooperation.

Germany is being accused of severing its ties to the world
and of becoming a recluse in the pursuit of its economic interests. Apparently no one considers that Germany was far more
severely affected by the collapse of the international economy
than others because of its restricted economic space and its
overpopulation. Moreover, it was not until we had realized
that comprehensive trade agreements with other nations were
not possible that we resolved to fashion Germany's economic
system to be independent of foreign economies. New ways
had to be found.

It is because of this that our Four-Year Plan endeavors to
attain self-sufficiency for Germany. It is not our goal to isolate
ourselves. In the course of our history we fought many a battle
with France: nonetheless, we remain peoples of one family. I
turn to all of Germany to say: bonds exist between us, bonds
we cannot simply erase from our memory.

We have exchanged ideas, set examples for one another,
and learned lessons from each other. Let us be honest: we have
little reason to hate each other and all the more reason to admire one another.

▶ September 16, 1938 *Hitler wanted to appear as a peacemaker.*

Two days after Chamberlain's visit to the Obersalzberg, Hitler granted an interview to Ward Price for the *Daily Mail*. Hitler declared that no one in Germany was even considering a war with the Western powers. It would be insane for such a war to break out on account of Czechoslovakia. To facilitate the Western powers visualizing the full extent of such "insanity," Hitler maintained that "half a million workers are building a gigantic fortification line in record time." At the same time, he drew attention to Polish and Hungarian claims to Czechoslovakian territory. The interview was reproduced in the following manner:

> "The Czechs say they cannot conduct a plebiscite, since there are no provisions for such a measure in their constitution. But to me it seems as though their constitution provides for one thing only, that seven million Czechs shall oppress eight million members of minority peoples. This Czech illness must be dealt with once and for all, immediately. It is like a cancer in the entire organism of Europe: if allowed to grow, it will infect international relations until they finally break down.
>
> "This situation has lasted for twenty years. No one can estimate how much it has cost the peoples of Europe in this time. As an ally of the Soviet Union, Czechoslovakia points like a dagger at the heart of Germany. It has reinforced my determination to create a mighty German *Luftwaffe*. This in turn drove Great Britain and France to build up their own air forces. Recently, I have doubled the *Luftwaffe* forces because of the present situation in Czechoslovakia. If we do not succeed in resolving the crisis now, Field Marshal Göring would soon be asking me to double the German *Luftwaffe's* forces once again, and then, in turn, Great Britain and France would double theirs as well, and so the insane race would go on.
>
> "Do you believe that I enjoy having to halt my great building and job creation plans throughout the country to send half a million workers to the western front to build a gigantic fortification line in record time? I would prefer to deploy them in the construction of workers' quarters, super-highways, new schools, and social institutions, instead of in

the construction of unproductive fortifications. However, as long as Czechoslovakia is responsible for the European fever caused by the oppression of a German minority, I must be prepared for all eventualities.

"I have studied the Maginot Line, and I have learned much in the process. Nonetheless, we have built something according to our own ideas that is even better and that will resist any power in the world should we, when attacked, actually choose to remain on the defensive.

"However, all of this is insanity since no one in Germany thinks of attacking France. We do not harbor any resentments against France; to the contrary, there is a strong feeling of sympathy for the French people in Germany. Neither does Germany want a war with Great Britain.

"Good Lord, all the things I could do in Germany and for Germany, if it were not for this Czech oppression of millions of Germans that must end. And it will end!"

The promise that French ministers have made to stand by Czechoslovakia up to this point, Herr Hitler continued, starkly contradicts their own deeds in the past. France has allowed the Saar to disassociate itself from French control, and this in spite of the fact that the Saar was of great economical, political and strategical importance to France.

"However, now some people in France are talking about unleashing the dogs of war for a country in which they have neither economic nor any other direct interests at stake.

"And they are doing this simply to allow the Czechs to refuse the Sudeten Germans the right they themselves have accorded the Saarlanders. In the same manner, Great Britain granted complete autonomy to Southern Ireland, and guaranteed the full independence of Holland and Belgium a hundred years earlier.

"The Czechs have never been an autonomous people: it was not until peace treaties raised them to an unmerited and artificial supremacy over minorities that are more numerous than they themselves. Bohemia was a German electorate in the Middle Ages. The first German university was founded in

Prague two hundred years before the days of Queen Elizabeth. The modern German language itself was derived from the language of the diplomats who served in the governmental offices of that city, the site that the German emperor had made his capital for a time. Only in the course of the Hussite wars were the Czechs independent for any period of time. They made use of their independence in the same manner the Bolshevists do, plundering and pillaging until the Germans roused themselves and fought back.

"The creation of this heterogeneous Czechoslovakian republic after the war was complete insanity. It does not have any characteristics of a nation, either from an ethnological or linguistic point of view, or from an economic or strategic one.

"It was a deed of insanity and ignorance to have a handful of obviously inferior Czechs rule over minorities that belong to the German, the Polish, and the Hungarian peoples, peoples who can look back upon a culture one thousand years old. The Sudeten Germans have absolutely no respect for the Czechs and will not submit to their rule.

"Following the war, the Allies declared the Germans not worthy to rule over blacks, while at the same time placing a second-rate people like the Czechs in control of three-and-a-half million Germans, people of a most noble character and culture.

"Had there been a strong Germany at that time, this would never have been possible, and as soon as Germany regained its strength, the Sudeten Germans began to speak out. The Czechoslovakian government is making a desperate attempt to pit the European superpowers against one another—else the Czech state would no longer exist. But it is impossible to maintain such an unnatural configuration through political and diplomatic trickery!"

Herr Hitler spoke bitterly and indignantly of the hatred the Czech government had for Herr Henlein.

"If Henlein is imprisoned, I will be the leader of the Sudeten Germans, and then let us see for how long Dr. Benes will manage to issue his decrees. Hopefully, he will not have me jailed as well! Had the Czechs a great statesman, he would long have permitted the Sudeten Germans to link up with the Reich and would have been glad to have secured continued autonomy for the Czechs themselves. But Dr. Benes is a politician, not a statesman."

In reply to the question of whether the visit of the prime minister had succeeded in rendering a peaceful resolution of the Sudeten German problem more likely, Hitler stated: "I am convinced of the honesty and good will of Mr. Chamberlain."

▶ January 30, 1939 *In his significant speech to the Reichstag on this day, Hitler turned his attention to the press.*

Hitler then turned his attention to the press campaign in Great Britain that had infuriated him especially. He threatened retaliation through a similar campaign in the German media.

We have no right to presume that, should Germany suffer yet another attack of weakness, its destiny would take on a different appearance. On the contrary, they are in part the very same men who once kindled the fire to scorch the entire world who today strive to prepare the grounds for another, renewed struggle as the paid henchmen at the service of those promoting hatred among peoples, to augment existing animosities.

Deputies, men of the Reichstag!

I implore you in particular not to forget one thing: It is apparently one of the exquisite privileges of democratic, political livelihood, enjoyed in certain democracies, to indulge in artificially feeding the flame of hatred against so-called totalitarian states. By a flood of partially distorted, partially fictitious reports, these arouse public opinion against certain peoples who have done nothing to harm others nor wish to undertake anything of this nature but have only suffered from the great injustice done to them throughout the decades.

And when we venture to defend ourselves in view of the injurious attacks of such apostles of war as the gentlemen Duff Cooper, Eden, Churchill, or Ickes, then this is portrayed as though we were infringing on the most sacred of rights in these democracies. According to the understanding of these gentlemen, they apparently have the unchallenged right to attack other peoples and their leadership, but no one in turn has the right to defend himself against these attacks. I need not assure you that, as long as the German Reich shall exist as a sovereign state, its leadership will not allow one or another English or American politician to forbid it to reply in kind to such attacks. In the future, the weapons we forged shall insure that we remain such a sovereign state, as shall a great number of our friends.

Actually we could simply laugh off the libelous claim that Germany intended to attack America. And, indeed, we would much prefer to remain silent on the topic of the campaign of hatred pursued by certain British apostles of war and to simply ignore them. Yet we may not forget the following:

1. The democracies in question are states in which the political structures make it possible that, within a few months' time, the most notorious of these warmongers may actually have emerged as the leaders of their governments.

2. We hence owe it to the security of the Reich to enlighten the German Volk about the true nature of these men in a timely manner. The German Volk harbors no hatred for England, America, or France, and desires nothing other than to live calmly and peacefully, while the Jewish and non-Jewish agitators persist in arousing the animosity of these peoples against Germany and the German Volk. In the event that these warmongers should succeed in their undertakings, our own Volk would be confronted with a situation incomprehensible to it, as it was not psychologically prepared for anything of this nature.

Therefore, I believe it necessary that from now on our propaganda and press shall answer immediately to any such attacks and inform the German Volk of them. It must know who these men are who so desperately seek to provoke a war, no matter what the circumstances. I am convinced that the calculations of these elements will prove faulty as soon as National Socialist propaganda begins to reply in kind to these provocations. We shall deal with them as successfully as we did in Germany when we wrestled the Jewish world enemy to the ground through the forceful use of our own propaganda.

▸ May 1, 1939 *In his May Day speech of 1939, Hitler referred to "unknown international scribblers," including, of course, all his critics.*

There is no need for me to name names in this context. They are unknown international scribblers. They are ever so clever! They are truly omniscient. There is only one thing that they failed to foresee, namely, my rise to power. Even in January 1933, they could simply not believe it. They also failed to foresee that I was going to remain in power. Even in February 1934, they could simply not believe it. They failed to foresee that I was going to liberate Germany. Even in 1935 and 1936, they could simply not believe it.

They failed to foresee that I was going to liberate our German *Volksgenossen* and to return them home. Even in 1937 and 1938, they could simply not believe it. They failed to foresee that I was determined to liberate and return home the rest of them, too. Even in February of this year, they could simply not believe it. They failed to foresee that I was going to eliminate the unemployment afflicting seven million. Even two, three years ago, they could simply not believe it. They failed to foresee that I was going to implement the Four-Year Plan in Germany with success. This they simply could not believe either. They foresaw nothing! And they know nothing even today!

These people have always been parasites. Lately I do not know, but I have the feeling sometimes that they are a kind of cerebral parasite. They know only too well what is happening in my brain, for instance. Whatever I say today, as I stand before you, they knew of it yesterday already. And even if I myself did not know of it yesterday—they did, these most excellent receptacles of wisdom!

Actually, these creatures know everything. And, even if facts prove their pronouncements blatant lies, they have the nerve to come up with new pronouncements immediately. This is an old Jewish trick. It keeps the people from having time for reflection. Should people truly reflect on all these various prophecies, compare them to reality, then these scribblers would not get a penny for their false reports. Therefore their tactic is, once one prophecy has been disproved, to come up with three new ones in its stead. And so they keep on lying, according to a type of snowball tactics, from today until tomorrow, from tomorrow until the next day.

► March 19, 1944 *In this last interview, Hitler continued his usual tactic of ignoring the truth.*

It was clear that Finland would accept the Soviet terms sooner or later. The question of the internment of the German troops, however, remained an unresolved issue. Hitler was not in a position to force a resolution in Finland, as he had done with Hungary. He could not prevent the conclusion of a peace settlement. In spite of this, he made several attempts to keep the Finns from taking this step. For instance, he granted an interview to the Berlin correspondents of the Swedish newspaper *Stockholm Tidningen,* which was published on March 19. The last interview of Hitler's life read as follows:

Question: Foreign news items claim that the Führer has attempted to approach King Gustav of Sweden because the Swedish king offered to mediate with Finland. Is this correct?

Answer: No, this is not correct. I do not know why I should have undertaken such a step. I am not aware whether or not King Gustav has tried to bring his influence to bear on Finland in this matter and, above all, when this supposedly took place. Should this be true, however, then it is a question of a purely Swedish affair.

Question: In this context, may I ask you how you assess the situation based on the terms of the armistice?

Answer: I assess the armistice terms announced by the Soviets exactly as they were meant. Of course, their objective is to bring about a situation in Finland in which further resistance would be impossible so that they can carry out with the Finnish people what Molotov demanded in Berlin at the time. It makes absolutely no difference whatever slogans or pretexts accompany the announcement of the Soviet terms. It is a question of placing the noose around the victim's neck in order to be able to tighten it at the right time. That the Soviet Union feels compelled to undertake such a step proves how skeptically it assesses its own military potential. Nobody can doubt the final goal of Bolshevism: the extermination of the non-Russian, non-Bolshevik nations of Europe. In this case, it is the extermination of the Finns. In order to reach this goal, they unleashed a war of nerves against Finland, as our enemies openly admit.

Question: Repeatedly the question of a guarantee for Finland on the part of England and the United States of America has been raised. What do you think of such guarantees for Finland?

Answer: The question of guarantees for Finland on the part of England and the United States of America served only the end of making submission more palatable to the Finns. In practical terms, any guarantee by the English or the Americans would be utopian. Neither England nor the United States of America would be in a position to dictate final objectives to a victorious Soviet Union, even if they should want to do this. In reality, however, neither England nor America is in the least willing to intervene honestly in this manner. In both countries, the same powers rule—even though from behind the bourgeois mask—that openly abuse power through violence. As regards American guarantees, Germany already had its own experiences with them following the end of the World War. The solemn Fourteen Points promised by Wilson were forgotten after Germany laid down its arms. In reality, every individual point led to the opposite of what the German Volk had been solemnly promised. The case of Poland is a striking illustration of the value of British guarantees. Moreover, England and America themselves face grave internal crises. The question is not whether they will be in a position to dictate to Bolshevism, but how long they will be able to avoid a Bolshevik revolution in their own countries. As always in the life of nations, a country's own strength is the only guarantee for continued existence.

The Great Reviewing Stand in the Year 2000

Hitler's painting illustrates his interest in form, structure, and order.

XII
Expanding the Reich

Hitler based his foreign policy on two objectives: reversing the decision of the Great War and uniting all the German Volk in one state that, by its size, would exercise hegemony over Europe. Hitler used the same methods he found so successful in dealing with internal German politics: duplicity, threats of violence, backed by a readiness to use violence, pragmatic alliances made for specific purposes, and a singleness of purpose that often baffled his opponents.

▶ *May 17, 1933 Hitler had spoken against the Treaty of Versailles since its signing. He had always scorned the League of Nations. On gaining power, he worked to free Germany from the restrictions of the Treaty of Versailles and to pull Germany out of the League of Nations. His announced reasons for doing this involved taking the underlying principles upon which both the treaty and the league were based and turning these principles against the document and organization. This kind of maneuver was typical of the way Hitler worked. However, his real complaint was that Germany did not win the Great War. This is clearly stated in Hitler's important speech to the Reichstag that marked his personal assumption of absolute political power.*

From France's perspective, the regular army of 100,000 men that the Treaty of Versailles had accorded Germany represented an imminent threat, for every single officer and man was trained as a cadre leader or sub-leader and thus together this body formed the framework for a future conscription army. This logic lay behind France's proposals for establishing militias and its refusal to disarm. Placards posted throughout France in 1932 proclaimed: "France has been through four invasions in 100 years. France does not need to disarm!"

In the course of 1932 and 1933, the Western powers had come to realize that it was necessary to amend the Treaty of Versailles and hence had initiated negotiations to find an acceptable solution. Were they to reach a consensus, Hitler would be robbed of arguments for his planned use of force, and thus he summoned up all of his powers of oral persuasion in order to prevent any agreement from being reached. True to his belief that domestic and foreign policy were all of a piece, he had acquainted himself with the provisions of the Treaty of Versailles as thoroughly as he had previously gained a complete grasp of the articles of the Weimar Constitution. He intended to justify his military plans by citing the injustice of the Treaty of Versailles, thereby setting himself up as the apostle of peace and branding the other nations as the guilty parties who had been unwilling to accept his well-meant proposals. Hitler deployed this tactical approach for the first time on May 17, 1933.

His speech also marked the beginning of another new phase: on May 17, Hitler spoke to a Reichstag that, although still containing representatives of the Social Democratic Party (SPD), the Center, and the right-wing parties in addition to the Nazi Party, for the first time had to play the new role Hitler had assigned to it: that of acting as forum for the speeches he was delivering not only to the German *Volk*, but to the entire world.

This already became evident in the opening sentences of his speech to the Reichstag, which follows verbatim:

Deputies, ladies and gentlemen of the German Reichstag!

In the name of the Reich government I have asked the Reichstag president to convene the Reichstag so that I may take a stand before this forum on the questions that today affect not only our Volk but the entire world. The problems that you know so well are of such great significance that, not only political pacification, but the economic salvation of all are contingent upon finding a satisfactory solution.

When I express the desire on behalf of the German government that the handling of these problems be totally removed from the sphere of passion, I do this not least of all in the realization dominating us all, namely that the crisis of our time owes its deepest origin alone to those passions that dimmed the insight and intelligence of the nations after the war. For all of the problems causing today's unrest lie anchored in the deficiencies of the peace treaty, which was unable to provide a judicious, clear and reasonable solution for the most important and most decisive questions of the time for all ages to come. Neither the national problems nor the economic—not to mention the legal—problems and demands of the peoples were solved by virtue of this treaty in a manner that would allow them to withstand the criticism of reason for all time.

Thus it is understandable that the idea of a revision is not only an integral part of the lasting side effects of the consequences of this treaty; indeed, the necessity of revision was foreseen by its authors and hence given a legal foundation in the treaty itself. When I deal briefly here with the problems this treaty should have solved, I am doing so because the failure in these areas inevitably led to the subsequent situations under which the political and economic relations between nations have been suffering since then. The political problems are as follows: in the course of many centuries, the European nations and their borders evolved from concepts that were based exclusively upon the idea of a political state as such. With the triumphant assertion of the national idea and the principle of nationalities in the course of the past century, the seeds of numerous conflicts were sown as a result of the failure of states that had arisen under different circumstances to take these new ideas and ideals into account.

At the end of the Great War, there could have been no greater task for a real peace conference than to undertake, in the clear recognition of this fact, a territorial and political reorganization of the European states that would do justice to this principle to the greatest possible degree. The more closely the borders between peoples coincided with the borders between states, the more this would have done away with a whole series of future potential conflicts. In fact, this territorial reorganization of Europe, taking into account the actual borders between peoples, would have constituted the solution in history that, with a view to the future, might have allowed both victors and vanquished to perceive that the blood sacrifices of the Great War were perhaps not completely in vain, for they might have served the world as the foundations for a real peace.

As it was, solutions were chosen—partly due to ignorance, partly to passion and hatred—that contained the perpetual seed of fresh conflicts in their very lack of logic and fairness.

The economic problems the conference was to have solved are as follows: The present economic situation in Europe is characterized by the overpopulation of the European west and, in the land comprising this territory, by the dearth of certain raw materials that are indispensable for the customary standard of living in these very areas with their ancient culture. Had one wished to bring about a certain pacification of Europe for the humanly foreseeable future, it would have been necessary—instead of relying upon the unproductive and dangerous concepts of penance, punishment, reparations, etc.—to rely upon and take into account the deep realization that lack of means of existence has always been a source of conflict between peoples. Instead of preaching the precepts of destruction, one would have had to initiate a reorganization of the international, political, and economic relations that would have done justice to the vital needs of each individual people to the fullest possible extent.

It is unwise to deprive a people of the economic resources necessary for its existence without taking the fact into consideration that the population dependent upon them must of necessity continue to live in this territory. It is absurd to believe that one is performing a useful service to other peoples by economically destroying a people numbering 65 million. Peoples who would proceed in such a manner would very soon, under the laws of nature linking cause and effect, come to experience that they would be subjected to the same catastrophe that they intended to impose upon another people. One day the concept of reparations and their enforcement will become a classic example in the history of nations of the extent to which disregard for international welfare can be damaging to all.

As it was, reparation politics could be financed only by German exports. The export industry of the creditor states was made to suffer to the same extent to which Germany, because of the reparations, was regarded as a sort of international export company. Hence the economic advantages of the reparation payments could bear no relation to the damage caused to the individual economies by these reparations. The attempt to avoid this development by compensating for the limits placed on German exports by means of granting loans to make the payments possible was imprudent and ultimately failed. For the conversion of political debts to private obligations led to an interest requirement, the fulfillment of which unavoidably produced the same results. However, the worst of the matter was that the development of domestic economic life was artificially checked and destroyed. Competition in the world markets by a constant undercutting of prices led to an over-intensification of rationalizing measures in the economy. The millions of our unemployed constitute the final consequence of this development. Were one inclined to limit the reparation obligations to deliveries of goods, this would result in no less substantial damage to the domestic production of the peoples profiting from them. This is because deliveries of goods in the magnitude in question are not conceivable without acute danger to the continued existence of the peoples' own production.

The Treaty of Versailles is to blame for having inaugurated a period in which the mathematical genius of finance is bringing about the demise of economic reason.

Germany has fulfilled these obligations imposed upon it, in spite of their inherent lack of reason and the foreseeable consequences, so faithfully as to be virtually suicidal.

The international economic crisis is the indisputable proof of the correctness of this statement. The plan of restoring a general international sense of justice was no less destroyed by the treaty. In order to justify all of the measures of this edict, Germany had to be branded as the guilty party. This is a procedure that is, however, just as simple as it is impossible. This would mean that in the future, the vanquished will always bear the blame for conflicts, for the victor will always be in a position to simply establish this as a fact.

This procedure therefore assumed a terrible significance because, at the same time, it served as a reason for transforming the relative strength existing at the end of this war to a lasting legal status. The concepts of victor and vanquished were hence made to constitute the foundations of a new international legal and social order.

The degradation of a great people to a second-rate, second-class nation was proclaimed in the same breath with which a League of Nations was called into being.

This treatment of Germany could not lead to a pacification of the world. The disarmament and defenselessness of the vanquished that was considered necessary—an unheard of procedure in the history of the European nations—was even less suited to diminish the general dangers and conflicts; rather, it led to a state of affairs consisting of those perpetual threats, demands, and sanctions that threaten to become, by virtue of the continual unrest and insecurity they cause, the death of the entire economy. If, in the lives of peoples, every consideration of the risks involved in certain actions is ignored, unreason will all too easily triumph over reason.

At any rate, until now the League of Nations has been incapable of providing appreciable assistance to the weak and unarmed on such occasions. Treaties that are concluded for the pacification of the lives of peoples in relation to one another have any real meaning only when they are based upon a genuine and honest equality of rights for all. And this is the main reason for the turmoil that has dominated the world for years.

Finding a reasonable and lasting solution to the problems existing today lies in the interests of all. No new European war would be capable of bringing about anything better in place of the unsatisfactory conditions of the present.

On the contrary, the use of any type of violence in Europe could not serve to create a more favorable political and economic situation than exists today. Even if a fresh violent European solution were a decisive factor in solving the problems, the final result would be an increase in the disturbance to the balance of power in Europe, and therefore, one way or another, the seed of further conflicts and complications would be sown.

New wars, new uncertainty, and a new economic crisis would be the consequences. The outbreak of such madness without end would, however, lead to the collapse of today's social and political order. A Europe sinking into Communist chaos would give rise to a crisis of unforeseeable proportions and unforeseeable length.

It is the earnest desire of the national government of the German Reich to prevent such an unpeaceful development by means of its honest and active cooperation.

This is also the real meaning behind the radical change that has taken place in Germany. The three factors that dominate our revolution do not contradict the interests of the rest of the world in any way.

First: preventing the impending Communist subversion and constructing a people's state (*Volksstaat*) uniting the various interests of the classes and ranks, and maintaining the concept of personal property as the foundation of our culture.

Second: solving the most pressing social problems by leading the army of millions of our pitiful unemployed back to production.

Third: restoring a stable and authoritarian leadership of the state, supported by the confidence and will of the nation that will finally again make of this great Volk a legitimate partner to the rest of the world.

Speaking now, conscious of being a German National Socialist, I would like to proclaim, on behalf of the national government and the entire national uprising, that, above all, we in this young Germany are filled with the deepest understanding of the same feelings and convictions and the justified demands of the other nations to live. The generation of this young Germany, that until now has come in its lifetime to know only the want, misery, and distress of its own Volk, has suffered too dearly from this madness to be capable of contemplating subjecting others to more of the same.

In that we are devoted to our own identity as a Volk in boundless love and faith, we also respect the national rights of other peoples on the basis of a common conviction and desire from the very bottom of our hearts to live with them in peace and friendship.

Thus the concept of Germanization is alien to us. The mentality of the past century, on the basis of which it was believed possible to make Germans of Poles and Frenchmen, is foreign to us, just as we passionately reject any attempt in the opposite direction. We view the European nations as a given fact. The French, the Poles, etc. are our neighbors, and we know that no historically conceivable event can change this reality.

It would have been fortunate for the world had these realities been given due consideration with respect to Germany in the Treaty of Versailles. For the object of a genuinely lasting treaty should not be to cut open fresh wounds or keep existing ones open, but rather to close and heal the wounds. A judicious handling of the problems could easily have arrived at a solution in the east that would have accommodated both the understandable claims of Poland as well as the natural rights of Germany. The Treaty of Versailles failed to provide this solution. In spite of this, no German government will of its own accord violate an agreement that cannot be eliminated without being replaced by a better one.

Yet this recognition of the legal character of such a treaty can be merely a general one. Not only the victor, but the vanquished as well has claim to the rights accorded it therein. But the right to demand a revision of the treaty lies anchored in the treaty itself. The German government wishes to base the reasons for and the extent of its claims on nothing other than the present results of past experiences and the incontestable consequences of critical and logical reasoning. The experiences of the last fourteen years are both politically and economically unequivocal.

The misery of the peoples was not alleviated; instead, it increased. The deepest root of this misery lies, however, in the division of the world into victor and vanquished as the intended permanent basis for all treaties and any future order. The worst effects of this order are expressed in the forced defenselessness of one nation in the face of an exaggerated armament on the part of the others. The reasons that Germany has been staunchly demanding universal disarmament for years are as follows:

First of all, the demand for equality of rights expressed in actual facts is a demand of morality, right, and reason; a demand that was acknowledged in the treaty itself and the fulfillment of which was indissolubly tied to the demand for German disarmament as a starting point for world disarmament.

Secondly, because conversely the degradation of a great Volk cannot be maintained in history forever but must of necessity one day come to an end. How long is it believed to be possible to impose such an injustice upon a great nation? What is the advantage of the moment worth in comparison to the ongoing developments of centuries? The German Volk will continue to exist, just as the French and, as we have learned from historical evolution, the Polish have done. What significance and what value can the successful short-term oppression of a people of 65 million have in comparison to the force of these incontrovertible facts? No state can have a greater understanding of the newly established young European national states than the Germany of the national revolution that has arisen from the same will. It wants nothing for itself that it is not prepared to accord to others.

When Germany today lodges its demand for genuine equality of rights with respect to the disarmament of the other nations, it has a moral right to do so given its own fulfillment of the treaties. For Germany did disarm, and Germany performed this disarmament under the strictest international control. Six million rifles and carbines were handed over or destroyed; the German Volk was forced to destroy or surrender 130,000 machine guns, huge numbers of machine gun barrels, 91,000 pieces of artillery, 38.75 million shells, and an enormous supply of other weapons and munitions.

The Rhineland was demilitarized, the German fortresses were pulled down, our ships surrendered, our aircraft destroyed, our military system was abandoned, and thus the training of reserves prevented. Even the most needed weapons of defense were denied us.

If, in the face of these indisputable facts, anyone should come forward today, citing truly pitiful excuses and pretexts and claiming that Germany did not comply with the treaty and had even rearmed, I must reject this view at this time for being as untrue as it is unfair.

It is equally incorrect to claim that Germany has not complied with the provisions of the treaty in respect to personnel. The allegation that the Nazi Party storm troopers (SA) and the Nazi Party security squads (SS) are connected in any way with the *Reichswehr* in the sense that they represent formations with military training or army reserves is untrue!

A single example serves to illustrate the irresponsible thoughtlessness with which such allegations are made: last year in Brünn, members of the National Socialist Party in Czechoslovakia were put to trial. Sworn experts of the Czech army claimed that the defendants maintained connections to the National Socialist Party in Germany, were dependent upon it and thus, as members of a popular sports club (*Volkssportverein*), were to be equated with members of the SA and SS in Germany that constituted a reserve army trained and organized by the *Reichswehr*.

At the same time, however, the SA and SS—just as the National Socialist party itself—not only had no connection with the *Reichswehr* whatsoever: on the contrary, they were regarded as organizations hostile to the state and persecuted, banned, and finally dissolved. And even beyond that: members of the National Socialist Party and those belonging to the SA and SS were not only excluded from all public offices—they were not even allowed to take on employment as simple workers in a weapons plant. Nonetheless, the National Socialists in Czechoslovakia were given long prison sentences on the basis of this false view.

In reality, the SA and the SS of the National Socialist Party have evolved totally without aid, totally without financial support from the state, the Reich, or even less the *Reichswehr*; without any sort of military training and without any sort of military equipment, out of pure party political needs and in accordance with party political considerations. Their purpose was and is exclusively confined to the elimination of the Communist threat, and their training, which bears no connection to the army, was designed solely for the purposes of propaganda and enlightenment, mass psychological effect, and the crushing of Communist terror. They are institutions for instilling a true community spirit, overcoming former class differences, and alleviating economic want.

The *Stahlhelm* came into being in memory of the great age of the common experiences at the front, to nurture established traditions, maintain comradeship, and finally also to protect the German Volk from the Communist revolution that has been threatening the Volk since November 1918, a threat that admittedly cannot be fathomed by countries who have never had millions of organized Communists as we have and have not suffered at the hands of terror as Germany has. For the real objective of these national organizations is best characterized by the type of struggle in which they are actually engaged and the toll this has taken.

As a consequence of Communist slayings and acts of terror in the space of only a few years, the SA and SS suffered over 350 dead and about 40,000 injured. If today the attempt is being made in Geneva to add organizations that exclusively serve domestic purposes to the armed forces figure, then one might as well count the fire brigades, the gymnastics clubs, the security corps, the rowing clubs, and other sports organizations as members of the armed forces, too.

However, when at the same time the trained short-term contingents of the other armies of the world are not included, in contrast to these men totally lacking in military training; when one deliberately overlooks the armed reserves of the others while commencing to count the unarmed members of our political associations, we have before us a procedure against which I must lodge the sharpest protest!

If the world wishes to destroy confidence in what is right and just, these are the best means of doing so.

On behalf of the German Volk and the German government, I must make the following clear: Germany has disarmed. It has fulfilled the obligations imposed upon it in the peace treaty to an extent far beyond the limits of what can be deemed fair or even reasonable. Its army consists of 100,000 men. The strength and character of its police is internationally regulated.

The auxiliary police instituted in the days of the revolution is exclusively political in character. In those critical days, it replaced the other part of the police that, at the time, the new regime suspected of being unstable. Now that the revolution has been successfully carried through, this force is already being reduced and will be completely dissolved even before the year is over. Germany thus has a fully justified moral right to insist that the other powers also fulfill their obligations pursuant to the Treaty of Versailles. The equality of rights accorded to Germany in December has not yet become reality. Since France has repeatedly asserted that the safety of France must be given the same consideration as Germany's equality of rights, I would like to pose two questions in this regard:

1. So far, Germany has accepted all of the obligations with respect to security arising from the signing of the Treaty of Versailles, the Kellogg Pact, the Treaties of Arbitration, the Pact of Non-Aggression, etc. What other concrete assurances are there that Germany could assume?

2. On the other hand, what security does Germany have? According to the information of the League of Nations, France alone has 3,046 aircraft in service while Belgium has 350, Poland 700, and Czechoslovakia 670. In addition, there are innumerable quantities of reserve aircraft, thousands of armored vehicles, thousands of pieces of heavy artillery, and all of the technical means required to conduct warfare with poison gas. Doesn't Germany have more reason, in view of its lack of defenses and weapons, to demand security than the armed states united by alliances?

Germany is nonetheless prepared at any time to assume further obligations to ensure international security if all other nations are willing to do so as well and Germany also benefits from this step. Germany would also be more than willing to disband its entire military establishment and destroy those few weapons still remaining at its disposal, were the bordering nations to do the same without exception. However, if the other states are not willing to comply with the disarmament provisions imposed upon them by the Peace Treaty of Versailles, then Germany must, at the very least, insist upon its demand for equal treatment.

The German government sees in the British plan a possible basis for the answer to these questions. However, it must demand that it not be forced to destroy its existing military establishment without being granted at least qualitatively equal rights. Germany must demand that change in the military situation in Germany—a situation we do not want, but one that was forced upon us from abroad—is performed only to the extent of the actual disarmament performed concurrently by the other states.

In this connection, Germany is essentially willing to agree to a transitional period of five years to bring about its national security in the expectation that, subsequent thereto, Germany will be accorded genuine equality with the other states. Germany is also perfectly prepared to completely abandon offensive weapons if, within a certain period, the armed nations destroy their own offensive weapons in turn and the use of such weapons is banned by international convention. It is Germany's sole desire to maintain its independence and be in a position to protect its borders.

According to a statement made in February 1932 by the French minister of war, a large portion of the colored French troops are available for immediate use on the French mainland. He therefore has explicitly included them in the home forces.

Thus it is only fair to take the colored forces into account as an integral part of the French army in the disarmament conference as well. Although one refuses to do this, one nevertheless proposes counting associations and organizations as part of the German army that serve purely educational and sporting purposes and are given no military training whatsoever. In the other countries, there is no question of these types of associations being counted as part of military strength. This is obviously a completely impossible situation. Germany would also be willing at any time, in the event that an objective international arms control board is created, to subject the associations in question to such control—given the same willingness on the part of the other states—in order to demonstrate to the whole world its wholly unmilitary character. Furthermore, the German government will reject no ban on arms as being too drastic if it is likewise applied to the other states.

These demands do not mean rearmament but rather a desire for the disarmament of the other states. On behalf of the German government, I may once again welcome the farsighted and just plan of the Italian head of state to create, by means of a special pact, close relations of confidence and cooperation between the four major European powers, Great Britain, France, Italy, and Germany. Mussolini's view that this would serve as a bridge to facilitate an understanding is a view with which the German government agrees out of its most deeply seated convictions. It desires to oblige to the fullest possible extent, if the other nations as well are inclined to genuinely overcome any difficulties that may stand in the way.

Thus the proposal made by the American President Roosevelt, of which I learned last night, deserves the warmest thanks of the German government. The government is prepared to consent to this method for solving the international crisis, for it is of the opinion that, if the question of disarmament is not solved, permanent economic reconstruction is inconceivable. It is willing to make a selfless contribution to this task of restoring the political and economic state of the world to order. It is also, as I have stressed in the beginning, of the conviction that there can only be one great task in our time: securing peace in the world.

I feel obliged to state that the reason for today's armaments in France or Poland can under no circumstances be the fear of these nations of a German invasion. For such a fear would be justified only by the existence of modern offensive weapons. But these modern offensive weapons are exactly the ones that Germany does not have: it has neither heavy artillery nor tanks nor bombers nor poison gas. The only nation that has reason to fear an invasion is the German nation, which is not only barred from having offensive weapons, but even restricted in its right to possess defensive weapons and prohibited from erecting fortifications on its borders. Germany is prepared to renounce offensive weapons at any time if the rest of the world does the same. Germany is willing to join any solemn pact of non-aggression, for Germany's concern is not offensive warfare, but its own security.

Germany would welcome the opportunity suggested in President Roosevelt's proposal of incorporating the United States in European relations in the role of guarantor of peace. This proposal very much encourages all those who wish to seriously cooperate toward maintaining peace. Our one most fervent desire is to contribute toward permanently healing the wounds inflicted by the war and the Treaty of Versailles. And Germany will take no path other than that which is recognized by the treaties themselves as just. The German government wishes to engage in peaceful discussions with the other nations on all difficult questions. It knows that, given any military action in Europe, even if it be completely successful, the losses thus incurred would bear no relation to the gains.

Under no circumstances, however, will the German government and the German Volk allow themselves to be coerced into signing anything that would constitute a perpetuation of Germany's degradation. Any attempt to influence the government and the Volk with threats will be to no avail. It is conceivable that, contrary to everything that is right and moral, Germany could be raped; it is, however, inconceivable and out of the question that such an act could be accorded legitimacy by means of our own signature.

The attempt has been made in newspaper articles and regrettable speeches to threaten Germany with sanctions, but a method as monstrous as this can only be the punishment for the fact that, by demanding disarmament, we are asking that the treaties be fulfilled. Such a measure could lead only to the

ultimate moral and defacto invalidation of the treaties themselves. But even in that case, Germany would never give up its
peaceful demands. The political and economic consequences—
the chaos that such an attempt would cause in Europe—would
be the responsibility of those who resorted to such measures to
fight a people that is doing no harm to the world.

At this point Hitler revealed the ulterior purpose of his entire speech:
laying the groundwork for Germany's withdrawal from the League of Nations and the Disarmament Conference.

Any such attempt, any attempt at doing violence to Germany by means of forming a simple majority against the
unequivocal spirit of the treaties could be dictated only by
the intention of excluding us from the conferences. But today the German Volk possesses enough character to refrain,
in such an event, from imposing its cooperation upon other
nations; it would rather, albeit with a heavy heart, draw the
only possible conclusions.

It would be difficult for us to remain a member of the
League of Nations as a Volk subjected to constant degradation. The German government and the German Volk are
aware of the present crisis. For years, warnings have come
from Germany to desist from the methods that have inevitably produced this political and economic state of affairs. If
the present course is maintained and the present methods are
continued, there can be no doubt as to the final result. Seeming political successes on the part of individual nations will be
followed by all the more severe economic and hence political
catastrophes affecting all. We regard it as our first and foremost task to prevent this.

These words were motivated by Hitler's apprehension that the Western powers might take military action against Germany should it withdraw from the League of Nations. Hence he judged it expedient to close
his speech with a flourish of pathos, deploring the bitter hardships of the
German people and citing the number of suicides committed since 1919.
He continued:

No effective action has been undertaken to date. The rest of the world tells us that people did, in fact, harbor a certain amount of sympathy for the former Germany; now at least we have become acquainted with the consequences and effects of this "sympathy" in Germany and for Germany!

Millions of lives destroyed, entire trades ruined, and an enormous army of unemployed—an inconsolable wretchedness, the extent and depth of which I would like to convey to the rest of the world today in a single figure:

Since the day when this treaty was signed, that was, as a work of peace, to be the foundation for a new and better age for all peoples, there have been 224,000 people in our German Volk who, moved almost exclusively by want and misery, have chosen to take their own lives—men and women, young, and old alike!

These incorruptible witnesses are an indictment against the spirit and fulfillment of a treaty, from the effects of which, not only the rest of the world, but also millions of people in Germany once expected salvation and good fortune (*Heil and Segen*).

May this also serve to make the other nations understand Germany's unshakable will and determination to finally put an end to an era of human aberration in order to find the way to an ultimate consensus of all on the basis of equal rights.

After the speech, the Reichstag gave its unanimous approval to Hitler's statement of policy. Even the Social Democrats consented with one voice— then again, they had already stood behind Hitler's foreign policy as early as March 23. This vote of approval on May 17 was to be their last appearance before being swept off the political stage.

To increase the impact of his "peace speech," Hitler attended a naval maneuver in Kiel on May 22. There he appealed to the onshore marine troops to "do everything in their power for the fatherland" and paid visits to the battleship *Schleswig-Holstein* and the cruiser *Leipzig*.

On May 27, Hitler delivered a radio speech from Munich on the upcoming *Volkstag* elections in the Free State of Danzig that also dealt mainly with foreign policy. The address was designed to whet Poland's appetite to enter into an alliance with Germany. Hitler apparently felt no scruples about stating that he would "never attempt to subjugate foreign peoples."

This was a prelude to his speech of September 26, 1938, in which he exclaimed: "We do not want any Czechs at all."

▸ **November 5, 1937** *In the mid-thirties, Hitler talked a great deal about peace. Clearly the peace he envisioned was that of the new Germany's dominance in Europe and so being a great world power. As he talked peace, he built arms in great numbers and was ready to use them. The "Hossbach Minutes" are a record of an important conference Hitler had with the army high command and Foreign Minister Neurath. There have been commentators who question the authenticity of this document, but their doubts do not seem well-founded.*

Hitler had taken all the precautions he believed vital to his Czechoslovakian enterprise. With Italian membership in the Anti-Comintern Pact assured and the German-Polish Declaration on the Minorities Question signed, Hitler finally felt ready to ask the highest-ranking military officers of the *Wehrmacht* (Blomberg, Fritsch, Göring, Raeder) and Foreign Minister Neurath to a meeting at the chancellery. On November 5, Hitler delivered an address to the generals in a closed session. It lasted from 4:15 p.m. to 8:30 p.m. The only surviving record of the discussion are the notes taken at the meeting by Hitler's adjutant Friedrich Hossbach, who transcribed them on November 10, 1937. The "Hossbach Minutes," discovered by the Allies at the end of the war, played a key role in the proceedings before the international military tribunal in Nuremberg.

Of course, these notes only give a rough sketch of the thoughts the Führer entertained at the time. Naturally, at a conference of such length, Hitler preceded his actual talk with a "party narrative." This time it lasted nearly an hour, its duration serving the purpose of lowering the psychological resistance of the audience. As usual, Hitler gave a detailed account of his achievements prior and subsequent to his accession to power.

He then discussed at great length Germany's economic and demographic policies. The exigencies of the situation led Hitler to speak of the necessity of conquering new colonies to serve as living space (*Lebensraum*) for the German people. Here he drifted into a description of the weakness of Great Britain, asserting that the country was no longer capable of defending the far reaches of its empire.

Finally Hitler approached the heart of the matter and declared that the "German question" could be resolved only by the use of force. The only questions remaining were "where" and "when" this was to happen.

He declared that it was his "inalterable decision" to resolve the matter of territorial acquisition at the very latest in the period 1943 through 1945. Hitler explained that he had cited this date because the present, modern German armament would then start to become obsolete (case 1). However, he stated that, should an opportune moment arise, it might become necessary to act at an earlier date. Such an opportunity might come about as a result of a civil war in France (case 2). Or war between an Anglo-French alliance and Italy could develop as an outgrowth of the tensions in the Mediterranean (case 3).

Hitler thought the latter scenario to be the most likely and predicted that, if this were the case, such a war would break out by the summer of 1938. For Germany, this would signal a magnificent opportunity to assault both Czechoslovakia and Austria.

In any event, Hitler maintained that the attack on Czechoslovakia would have to proceed "with lightning speed" (*blitzartig schnell*). Military intervention need not be feared since Great Britain could not risk entanglement in armed conflict, and undoubtedly, the French would follow suit.

Hossbach's Minutes are reproduced verbatim below:

MEMORANDUM

Berlin, November 10, 1937
    Minutes of the conference in the Reich Chancellery,
    Berlin, November 5, 1937, from 4:15 p.m. to 8:30 p.m.

Present:
    The Führer and Reich Chancellor,
    Field Marshal von Blomberg, Minister of War,
    Colonel General Freiherr von Fritsch, Army Commander in Chief,
    Admiral Dr. h.c. Raeder, Navy Commander in Chief,
    Colonel General Göring, *Luftwaffe* Commander in Chief,
    Foreign Minister Freiherr von Neurath.

                                        Colonel Hossbach.

The Führer began by stating that the subject of the present conference was of such importance that its discussion would, in other countries, certainly be a matter for a full cabinet meeting, but he—the Führer—had rejected the idea of making it a subject of discussion before the wider circle of the Reich cabinet just because of the importance of the matter.

His exposition to follow was the fruit of thorough deliberation and the experiences of his four and a half years of power. He wished to explain to the gentlemen present his basic ideas concerning the opportunities for the development of our position in the field of foreign affairs and its requirements, and he asked, in the interests of a long-term German policy, that his exposition be regarded, in the event of his death, as his last will and testament.

The Führer then continued:

The aim of German policy was to make secure and to preserve the racial community (*Volksmasse*) and to enlarge it. It was therefore a question of space.

The German racial community comprised over 85 million people and, because of their number and the narrow limits of habitable space in Europe, constituted a tightly packed racial core such as was not to be met in any other country and such as implied the right to a greater living space than in the case of other peoples. If, territorially speaking, there existed no political result corresponding to this German racial core, that was a consequence of centuries of historical development, and in the continuance of these political conditions lay the greatest danger to the preservation of the German race at its present peak. To arrest the decline of Germanness (*Deutschtum*) in Austria and Czechoslovakia was as little possible as to maintain the present level in Germany itself. Instead of increase, sterility was setting in, and in its train disorders of a social character must arise in the course of time, since political and ideological ideas remain effective only so long as they furnish the basis for the realization of the essential vital demands of a people.

Germany's future was therefore wholly conditional upon meeting the need for space, and such a solution could be sought, of course, only for a foreseeable future of about one to three generations.

Before turning to the question of the need for space, it had to be considered whether a solution holding promise for the future was to be reached by means of autarky or by means of an increased participation in world economy.

Autarky:

Achievement only possible under strict National Socialist leadership of the state, which is assumed; accepting its achievement as possible, the following could be stated as results:

A. In the field of raw materials only limited, not total, autarky.

    1) In regard to coal, so far as it could be considered as a source of raw materials, autarky was possible.

    2) But even as regards ores, the position was much more difficult. Iron requirements can be met from home resources and similarly with light metals, but with other raw materials—copper, tin—this was not the case.

    3) Synthetic textile requirements can be met from home resources within the limit of timber supplies. A permanent solution impossible.

    4) Edible fats—possible.

B. In the field of food the question of autarky was to be answered by a flat "no."

    With the general rise in the standard of living as compared with that of thirty to forty years ago, there has gone hand-in-hand an increased demand and an increased home consumption even on the part of the producers, the farmers.

The fruits of the increased agricultural production had all gone to meet the increased demand and so did not represent an absolute production increase. A further increase in production by making greater demands on the soil, that already, in consequence of the use of artificial fertilizers, was showing signs of exhaustion, was hardly possible, and it was therefore certain that even with the maximum increase in production, participation in world trade was unavoidable. The not inconsiderable expenditure of foreign exchange to insure food supplies by imports, even when harvests were good, grew to catastrophic proportions with bad harvests. The possibility of a disaster grew in proportion to the increase in population, in which, too, the excess of births of 560,000 annually produced, as a consequence, an even further increase in bread consumption, since a child was a greater bread consumer than an adult.

It was not possible over the long run, in a continent enjoying a practically common standard of living, to meet the food supply difficulties by lowering that standard and by rationalization. Since, with the solution of the unemployment problem, the maximum consumption level had been reached, some minor modifications in our home agricultural production might still, no doubt, be possible, but no fundamental alteration was possible in our basic food position. Thus autarky was untenable with regard both to food and to the economy as a whole.

Participation in world economy.

To this there were limitations that we were unable to remove. The establishment of Germany's position on a secure and sound foundation was obstructed by market fluctuations, and commercial treaties afforded no guarantee of actual execution. In particular it had to be remembered that since the World War, those very countries that had formerly been food exporters had become industrialized. We were living in an age of economic empires in which the primitive urge to colonization was again manifesting itself; in the cases of Japan and Italy, economic motives underlay the urge for expansion, and with Germany, too, economic need would supply the stimulus.

For countries outside the great economic empires, opportunities for economic expansion were severely impeded.

The boom in world economy caused by the economic effects of rearmament could never form the basis of a sound economy over a long period, and the latter was obstructed above all also by the economic disturbances resulting from Bolshevism. There was a pronounced military weakness in those states that depended for their existence on foreign trade. As our foreign trade was carried on over the sea routes dominated by Britain, it was more a question of security of transport, than one of foreign exchange, that revealed, in time of war, the full weakness of our food situation.

The only remedy, and one that might appear to us as visionary, lay in the acquisition of greater living space—a quest that has at all times been the origin of the formation of states and of the migration of peoples. That this quest met with no interest at Geneva or among the developed nations was understandable. If, then, we accept the security of our food situation as the principal question, the space necessary to insure it can be sought only in Europe, not, as in the liberal-capitalist view, in the exploitation of colonies. It is not a matter of acquiring population but of gaining space for agricultural use.

Moreover, areas producing raw materials can be more usefully sought in Europe in immediate proximity to the Reich than overseas; the solution thus obtained must suffice for one or two generations. Whatever else might prove necessary later must be left to succeeding generations to deal with. The development of great world political constellations progressed but slowly after all, and the German people with its strong racial core would find the most favorable prerequisites for such achievement in the heart of the continent of Europe.

The history of all ages—the Roman Empire and the British Empire—had proved that expansion could be carried out only by breaking down resistance and taking risks; setbacks were inevitable. There had never in former times been spaces without a master, and there were none today; the attacker always comes up against a possessor.

The question for Germany was simple: where could she achieve the greatest gain at the lowest cost?

German policy had to reckon with two hate-inspired antagonists, Britain and France, to whom a German colossus in the center of Europe was a thorn in the flesh, and both countries were opposed to any further strengthening of Germany's position either in Europe or overseas; in support of this opposition they were able to count on the agreement of all their political parties. Both countries saw in the establishment of German military bases overseas a threat to their own communications, a safeguarding of German commerce, and, as a consequence, a strengthening of Germany's position in Europe.

Because of opposition of the Dominions, Britain could not cede any of her colonial possessions to us. After England's loss of prestige through the passing of Abyssinia into Italian possession, the return of East Africa was not to be expected. British concessions could at best be expressed in an offer to satisfy our colonial demands by the appropriation of colonies that were not British possessions—e.g., Angola. French concessions would probably take a similar line.

Serious discussion of the question of the return of colonies to us could be considered only at a moment when Britain was in difficulties and the German Reich armed and strong. The Führer did not share the view that the empire was unshakable. Opposition to the empire was to be found less in the countries conquered than among her competitors. The British Empire and the Roman Empire could not be compared in respect of permanence; the latter was not confronted by any powerful political rival of significance after the Punic Wars. It was only the disintegrating effect of Christianity, and the symptoms of age that appear in every country, that caused ancient Rome to succumb to the onslaught of the Germans.

Besides the British Empire, there exists today a number of states stronger than it. The British motherland was able to protect her colonial possessions, not by her own power, but only in alliance with other states. How, for instance, could Britain alone defend Canada against attack by America, or her Far Eastern interests against attack by Japan!

The emphasis on the British Crown as the symbol of the unity of the empire was already an admission that, in the long run, the empire could not maintain its position by power politics. Significant indications of this were:

(a) The struggle of Ireland for independence.

(b) The constitutional struggles in India, where Britain's half-measures had given to the Indians the opportunity of using later on as a weapon against Britain the non-fulfillment of her promises regarding a constitution.

(c) The weakening by Japan of Britain's position in the Far East.

(d) The rivalry in the Mediterranean with Italy who—under the spell of her history, driven by necessity and led by a genius—was expanding her power position and thus was inevitably coming more and more into conflict with British interests. The outcome of the Abyssinian War was a loss of prestige for Britain that Italy was trying to accelerate by stirring up trouble in the Mohammedan world.

To sum up, it could be stated that, with 45 million Britons, in spite of its theoretical soundness, the position of the Empire could not in the long run be maintained by power politics. The 9:1 ratio of the population of the Empire to that of the motherland was a warning to us not, in our territorial expansion, to allow the foundation constituted by the numerical strength of our own people to become too weak.

France's position was more favorable than that of Britain. The French Empire was better placed territorially; the inhabitants of her colonial possessions represented a supplement to her military strength. But France was going to be confronted with internal political difficulties. In a nation's life about ten percent of its span is taken up by parliamentary forms of government and about 90 percent by authoritarian forms. Today, nonetheless, Britain, France, Russia, and the smaller states adjoining them, must be included as power-factors (*Machtfaktoren*) in our political calculations.

Germany's problem could be solved only by means of force and this was never without attendant risk. The campaigns of Frederick the Great for Silesia and Bismarck's wars against Austria and France had involved unheard-of risks, and the swiftness of the Prussian action in 1870 kept Austria from entering the war. If one accepts as the basis of the following exposition the resort to force with its attendant risks, then there remain still to be answered the questions "when" and "how." In this matter there were three cases (*Fälle*) to be dealt with:

Case 1: Period 1943–1945 After this date only a change for the worse, from our point of view, could be expected.

The equipment of the army, navy and *Luftwaffe*, as well as the formation of the officer corps, would be nearly completed. Equipment and armament were modern; with further delay there lay the danger of their obsolescence. In particular, the secrecy of "special weapons" (*Sonderwaffen*) could not be preserved forever. The recruiting of reserves was limited to current age groups; further drafts from older, untrained age groups were no longer available.

Our relative strength would decrease in relation to the rearmament that would by then have been carried out by the rest of the world. If we did not act by 1943–45, any year could, in consequence of a lack of reserves, produce the food crisis, to cope with which the necessary foreign exchange was not available, and this must be regarded as the "turning point of the regime." Besides, the world would be expecting our attack and would be increasing its counter-measures from year to year. It would be while the rest of the world was still preparing its defenses that we would be obliged to take the offensive.

Nobody knows today what the situation would be in the years 1943–45. One thing only was certain, that we could not wait any longer.

On the one hand, there was the great *Wehrmacht* and the necessity of maintaining it at its present level, and the aging of the movement and its leaders; and on the other hand, the prospect of a lowering of the standard of living and of a limitation of the birth rate, that would leave no choice but to act. If the

Führer were still living, it was his unalterable resolve to solve
Germany's problem of space at the latest by 1943–45. The necessity for action before 1943–45 would arise in cases 2 and 3.

Case 2: If internal strife in France should develop into such a
domestic crisis as to absorb the French army completely and
render it incapable of use for war against Germany, then the
time for action against the Czechs would have come.

Case 3: If France is so embroiled by a war with another state
that she cannot proceed against Germany.

For the improvement of our politico-military position,
our first objective, in the event of our being embroiled in war,
must be to overthrow Czechoslovakia and Austria simultaneously in order to remove the threat to our flank in any possible
operation against the West. In a conflict with France it was
hardly to be regarded as likely that the Czechs would declare
war on us on the very same day as France. The desire to join in
the war would, however, increase among the Czechs in proportion to any weakening on our part and then her participation could clearly take the form of an attack toward Silesia,
toward the north or toward the west.

If the Czechs were overthrown and a common German-
Hungarian frontier achieved, a neutral attitude on the part of
Poland could be the more certainly counted on in the event
of a Franco-German conflict. Our agreements with Poland
retained their only force as long as Germany's strength remained unshaken. In the event of German setbacks a Polish
action against East Prussia, and possibly against Pomerania
and Silesia as well, would have to be reckoned with.

On the assumption of a development of the situation leading to action on our part as planned, in the years 1943–45,
the attitude of France, Britain, Italy, Poland, and Russia could
probably be estimated as follows.

Actually, the Führer believed that almost certainly Britain, and probably France as well, would have already tacitly
written off the Czechs and be reconciled to the fact that this
question would be cleared up in due course by Germany. Difficulties connected with the empire, and the prospect of being

once more entangled in a protracted European war, would be decisive considerations for Britain against participation in a war against Germany. Britain's attitude would certainly not be without influence on that of France. An attack by France without British support, and with the prospect of the offensive being brought to a standstill on our western fortifications, was hardly probable. Nor was a French march through Belgium and Holland without British support to be expected; this also was a course not to be contemplated by us in the event of a conflict with France, because it would certainly entail the hostility of Britain.

It would of course be necessary to maintain a strong defense (*eine Abriegelung*) on our western frontier during the prosecution of our attack on the Czechs and Austria. And in this connection it had to be remembered that the defense measures of the Czechs were growing in strength from year to year, and that the actual worth of the Austrian army also was increasing in the course of time. Even though the populations concerned, especially of Czechoslovakia, were not sparse, the annexation of Czechoslovakia and Austria would mean an acquisition of foodstuffs for five to six million people, on the assumption that the compulsory emigration of two million people from Czechoslovakia and one million people from Austria was practicable.

The incorporation of these two states with Germany meant, from the politico-military point of view, a substantial advantage because it would mean shorter and better frontiers, the freeing of forces for other purposes, and the possibility of creating new units up to a level of about twelve divisions, that is, one new division per million inhabitants.

Italy was not expected to object to the elimination of the Czechs, but it was impossible at the moment to estimate what her attitude on the Austrian question would be; that depended essentially upon whether the Duce were still alive.

The degree of surprise and the swiftness of our action would be decisive factors for Poland's attitude. Poland—with Russia at her rear—will have little inclination to engage in war against a victorious Germany.

Military intervention by Russia must be countered by the swiftness of our operations; however, whether such an intervention was a practical contingency at all was, in view of Japan's attitude, more than doubtful.

Should case 2 arise—the crippling of France by civil war—the situation thus created by the elimination of the most dangerous opponent must be seized upon whenever it occurs, for the blow against the Czechs.

The Führer saw case 3 coming definitely nearer; it might emerge from the present tensions in the Mediterranean, and he was resolved to take advantage of it whenever it happened, even as early as 1938.

In the light of past experiences, the Führer did not see any early end to the hostilities in Spain. If one considered the length of time that Franco's offensives had taken up till now, it was fully possible that the war would continue another three years. On the other hand, a 100% victory for Franco was not desirable either, from the German point of view; rather we were interested in a continuance of the war and in the keeping up of the tension in the Mediterranean. Franco in undisputed possession of the Spanish Peninsula precluded the possibility of any further intervention on the part of the Italians or of their continued occupation of the Balearic Islands. As our interest lay more in the prolongation of the war in Spain, it must be the immediate aim of our policy to strengthen Italy's rear with a view to her remaining in the Balearics. But the permanent establishment of the Italians on the Balearics would be intolerable both to France and Britain and might lead to a war of France and England against Italy—a war in which Spain, unless she is entirely in the hands of the Falangists, might fight on the side of Italy's enemies. The probability of Italy's defeat in such a war was slight, for the road from Germany was open for supplementing her raw materials. The Führer pictured the military strategy for Italy thus: on her western frontier with France she would remain on the defensive and carry on the war against France from Libya against the French North African colonial possessions.

As a landing by Franco-British troops on the coast of Italy could be discounted, and a French offensive over the Alps against northern Italy would be very difficult and would probably come to a halt before the strong Italian fortifications, the crucial point (*Schwerpunkt*) of the operations lay in North Africa. The threat to French lines of communication by the Italian fleet would to a great extent cripple the transportation of forces from North Africa to France so that France would have only home forces at her disposal on the frontiers with Italy and Germany.

If Germany made use of this war to settle the Czech and Austrian questions, it was to be assumed that Britain—herself at war with Italy—would decide not to act against Germany. Without British support, offensive action by France against Germany was not to be expected.

The time for our attack on the Czechs and Austria must be made dependent on the course of the Anglo-French-Italian war and would not necessarily coincide with the commencement of military operations by these three states. Nor had the Führer in mind military agreements with Italy but wanted, while retaining his own independence of action, to exploit this favorable situation, which would not occur again, to begin and carry through the campaign against the Czechs. This descent upon the Czechs would have to be carried out with "lightning speed."

Evidently, Hitler was convinced that his disclosure of these revelations meant that he was doing the German generals present a favor. Politically, he had suffered numerous disappointments at their hands in the past. The events of 1923 had forced upon him the realization that the generals would much rather bow to the despised legal government in place than cast their lot in with a nationalist revolutionary. Moreover, Hitler greatly disliked the elitist attitude displayed by the officers' corps. Nevertheless, throughout, Hitler had retained his firm belief that the generals shared his convictions in their areas of expertise—at the least in military affairs. He could not fathom that historic, ethical and religious factors played a role in their considerations. Rather, he saw them as "bloodhounds" just waiting to be unleashed to pounce upon the perceived or actual adversary.

Up to this point, this understanding had been central to Hitler's military policy formation. He had conspired in the 1934 murder of some of his closest friends within the storm troopers (SA), sacrificing them in an attempt to appease the generals. And what happened now? The generals failed to welcome his plan for the rape of Czechoslovakia with the proper enthusiasm! The Führer had not anticipated such a reaction. Moreover, he found himself faced by Blomberg and Fritsch, who rose to voice doubts concerning the military analysis presented by their supreme commander. Evidently, hours of exposition had not dulled their sense of perception. Neither of the two officers was persuaded by Hitler's argument that France would remain neutral in the event of a German offensive against Czechoslovakia. Both military men voiced concern about a strategy based upon such a notion. Fritsch was so upset by Hitler's exposition that he offered to delay his November 10 vacation. Hitler even had to reassure him by insisting that the entire issue was not so immediate!

Subsequently, Hitler continued to insist that neither France nor Great Britain would intervene in the event of a German move against Czechoslovakia. For his part, Neurath doubted the possibility of a war between Italy and a coalition of French-British forces at any time in the immediate future. Raeder made no contribution to the debate. Ever since 1932, Raeder had been a staunch National Socialist and thus knew only too well that he was expected to offer no opposition to Hitler's position. On the other hand, Göring immediately carried Hitler's thoughts further and suggested that Germany curtail its involvement in Spain. Hossbach described the discussion as follows:

> In appraising the situation Field Marshal von Blomberg and Colonel General von Fritsch repeatedly emphasized the necessity that Britain and France must not become our enemies and stated that the French army would not be so committed by the war with Italy that France could not at the same time enter the field with forces superior to ours on our western frontier. General von Fritsch estimated the probable French forces available for use on the Alpine frontier at approximately twenty divisions, so that a strong French superiority would still remain on the western frontier, with the role, according to the German view, of invading the Rhineland. In this matter, moreover, the advanced state of French defense

preparations (*Mobilmachung*) must be taken into particular account, and it must be remembered apart from the insignificant value of our present fortifications—on which Field Marshal von Blomberg laid special emphasis—that the four motorized divisions intended for the west were still more or less incapable of movement. With regard to our offensive toward the southeast, Field Marshal von Blomberg drew particular attention to the strength of the Czech fortifications, which had acquired by now a structure like a Maginot Line and that would gravely hamper our attack.

General von Fritsch mentioned that this was the very purpose of a study, which he had ordered made this winter, namely, to examine the possibility of conducting operations against the Czechs with special reference to overcoming the Czech fortification system; the general further expressed his opinion that under existing circumstances he must give up his plan to go abroad on his leave that was due to begin on November 10. The Führer dismissed this idea on the ground that the possibility of a conflict need not yet be regarded as so imminent. To the foreign minister's objection that an Anglo-French conflict with Italy was not yet within such a measurable distance as the Führer seemed to assume, the Führer set the summer of 1938 as the date that seemed to him possible for this. In reply to considerations offered by Field Marshal von Blomberg and General von Fritsch regarding the attitude of Britain and France, the Führer repeated his previous statements that he was convinced of Britain's non-participation, and therefore he did not believe in the probability of belligerent action by France against Germany. Should the Mediterranean conflict under discussion lead to a general mobilization in Europe, then we must immediately begin action against the Czechs. On the other hand, should the powers not engaged in the war declare themselves disinterested, then Germany would have to adopt a similar attitude to this for the time being.

Colonel General Göring thought that, in view of the Führer's statement, we should consider liquidating our military undertakings in Spain. The Führer agrees to this with the limitation that he thinks he should reserve a decision for a proper moment.

The second part of the meeting was concerned with concrete questions of armament.

Certified correct: Hossbach, Colonel (General Staff)

Hitler was deeply disappointed in Blomberg and Fritsch for advocating such contrary views. No longer did he refer to them as "my dear field marshal" and "my dear colonel general." He realized that, given their apprehensions, he could not rely on them for the implementation of his plans. He decided to rid himself of them at the first opportunity. Neurath also incurred Hitler's displeasure for his attitude and the Führer decided to remove him from office as well. The ministers in Hitler's government could voice objections to his policies, but only if they were willing to resign from their positions as a consequence. If they did not comply voluntarily, as had Hugenberg and Eltz von Rübenach, then obviously they required a little assistance in the process.

There have been attempts to discredit the "Hossbach minutes." These attempts are based on two facts. First, Hossbach did not write down his recollections of the meeting and the ensuing discussion until five days later. Furthermore, the minutes bear no signature by Hitler attesting to the validity of their content. However, the second criticism is weakened by the fact that Hitler's signature on such documents was neither required nor part of any standard bureaucratic procedure.

Those who question the authenticity of the Hossbach minutes aim to undermine the evidence which implies that, as early as November 5, Hitler had already determined to use force in both Czechoslovakia and Austria. However, the further course of events lends credibility to Hossbach's recollections. First of all, those members of Hitler's military staff who had, as Hossbach detailed, opposed his radical approach at the conference were shortly thereafter dismissed from office. Secondly, the credibility of the Hossbach minutes is further reinforced by the fact that the later military build-up along Germany's southeastern border reflects the policy aims expressed in the meeting. Finally, in the months immediately preceding the annexation of Austria, Hitler repeatedly articulated in public the aims listed in Hossbach's notes.

According to public statements by the *Gauleiter* of Mainfranken, Otto Hellmuth, in Würzburg on March 4, 1938 (i.e., even prior to Schuschnigg's Innsbruck appeal) Hitler had contemplated the following:

He [Hellmuth] had just returned from a conference with Hitler in Berlin. The Führer had explained to him that for the time being the goals of the Reich Colonial League (*Reichskolonialbund*)—namely the conquest of colonies in Africa—were a dead issue. The resolution of the difficult situation faced in both Austria and Czechoslovakia had complete priority. Hitler was determined to resolve the matter "one way or another."

Hellmuth added that he naturally could not expand upon these comments by Hitler. Nonetheless, with a sweeping gesture, he reassured his audience that the problems would be resolved in either "one way" (by peaceful means) or "another." It was obvious to every one of Hellmuth's listeners that the second option meant war. The general public, however, was left in the dark regarding the Führer's aspirations during the last two months of 1937. With the exception of an increase in the number of references to the question of *Lebensraum* in his speeches, there were no signs that Hitler had resolved on war.

▸ September 26, 1938 *Having seized Austria, Hitler set his sights on Czechoslovakia. His method was the usual mixture of threats of violence and claims of monumental injury.*

After the British diplomats had left, Hitler began to get ready for his speech. In it, he would announce to the German people that events were coming to a head, and then make the most momentous statement of the day: "Now I march before my Volk as the first of its soldiers!"

Hitler already felt himself to be a soldier. In all likelihood, he had the field-gray uniform tunic already at hand in his closet, the one that he had always claimed to be the "holiest and dearest" to him. Naturally, the tunic was not the same he had worn as a corporal up to the years 1918 and 1920. For one, the cut was different, and further, he was to wear it as the supreme commander of the *Wehrmacht*. One of the most significant distinctions of this tunic was the national emblem on the left sleeve that adorned the otherwise plain uniform. By wearing it the same way as did the Nazi Party security squad police (*SS Verfügungstruppe*), Hitler wanted the generals to take note that there was no doubt on whose side he stood in the event of any domestic trouble between the army and the Nazi Party security squads (SS).

In any case, Hitler was planning to wear the new field-gray uniform tunic on the first day of the war, completely dedicating himself to his role as warlord. For the speech at the Sportpalast, he still wore his brown double-breasted uniform tunic and black pants, an ensemble he always wore at social occasions. He did not want to appear before his audience in the same knee breeches, straps and belts, an attire he always sported at reviews and demonstrations at party congresses. Rather he would clad himself in a modest fashion in order to emphasize in his outward appearance the most "moderate" stance he espoused. Everyone should clearly see how peace-loving he actually was and how much he regretted having to resort to the sword.

Once he had arrived at the Sportpalast around 8:00 p.m., he was greeted by Goebbels in an address. The latter knew this to be the last occasion on which Hitler would speak publicly prior to the invasion of Czechoslovakia. He put much effort into assuring Hitler that the German Volk was prepared for war and proclaimed:

> You can rely upon your Volk, just as it relies upon you. It stands behind you as one man. We are aware that no threat and no pressure, from whatever source, can keep you from pursuing your and our inalienable rights. The entire German Volk shares this spirit and firm conviction. Many times we have stated and pledged ourselves to this in the historic hours of our nation. Now in this hour of difficult decisions, we repeat it before you with all our heart, full and strong:
> *Führer befiehl! Wir folgen.*
> We greet you, *mein Führer*, with our old battle cry:
> Adolf Hitler, *Sieg Heil!*—The Führer speaks.

That evening, Hitler was fully aware of the importance of this particular appearance. He knew that numerous foreigners, diplomats and journalists were present in the hall. He summoned all of his rhetorical talent and acting ability to convincingly play the part of a man who was filled with holy zeal and determination to be prepared for anything, while nonetheless radiating a firm belief in the justice of his cause. He began his speech with the following words:

German *Volksgenossen!*

Speaking before the German Reichstag delegates on February 20, I made, for the first time, a demand based on an irrevocable principle. Back then the entire nation heard me and understood me! One statesman did not understand. He has been removed, and I have made true my promise given at the time! At the Reich Party Congress, I spoke on the topic of this demand for the second time. And once more the nation heard this demand. Today I step before you to speak directly to the Volk for the first time just as in the days of our great struggles, and you know well what that means!

The world may no longer have any doubts: it is not one Führer or one man who speaks at this point, rather it is the German Volk that speaks! As I now speak for this German Volk, I know that this Volk of millions joins in the chorus of my words, reaffirms them, and makes them a holy oath in its own right. Some of the other statesmen might do well to consider if this is the case with their peoples as well. The question that has moved us so profoundly within the last few months and weeks is an old one.

It reads not so much "Czechoslovakia," but rather "Herr Benes." This name unites all that moves millions of people today and that lets them either despair or instills in them a zealous determination. How could such a question rise to such supreme importance? I wish to reiterate before you, my *Volksgenossen,* a short summary on the essence and goals of Germany's foreign policy.

As one can tell, not even on the eve of war, on a most crucial occasion, was Hitler willing to do without his "party narrative." It began with the Treaty of Versailles and ended with Hitler's numerous "peace proposals." When he spoke of the armament he had undertaken, he claimed that none like it had yet been seen on the face of the earth.

After two years of having made offer upon offer to the world and receiving rejection upon rejection, I gave orders to rearm the German *Wehrmacht* and to bring it to the highest level possible. Today I can openly admit: we rearmed to an extent the like of which the world had not yet seen. I offered to disarm as long as this was possible. After yet another rejection, I decided to go all the way. I am a National Socialist and an old German front-line soldier!

If the world does not want disarmament, so be it: now you Germans wield weapons of your own. Germany can be proud of its *Wehrmacht*!

Indeed, I did rearm within the past five years. I spent billions on it. That the German Volk has a right to know. I took care that the new army carried the newest, most modern weapons that exist. I ordered my friend Göring: now build up a *Luftwaffe* for me capable of protecting Germany against any onslaught conceivable.

And so we built up a *Wehrmacht* of which the German Volk can be proud today and that the world will respect whenever it shall be introduced. We have created for ourselves the best anti-aircraft defense and the best anti-tank defense ever seen on the face of this earth!

Once Hitler believed he had done justice to the task of frightening the Western powers by describing the military might of Germany, he praised his friendship pact with Poland. He claimed that it was worth more than "all the idle talk in the League of Nations' palace in Geneva." He continued:

We worked night and day during these five years. On one topic only did I succeed in bringing about an understanding. I shall speak of this later. Nevertheless, I continued to pursue the ideas of limiting armament and of a disarmament policy. In these years, I truly pursued a pragmatic policy for peace. I approached any and all topics, firmly determined to resolve them peacefully—even if this should involve great sacrifices on the part of Germany. I myself am a front-line soldier and know the hardships of war. I wished to spare the German Volk this experience. I approached each and every problem firmly determined to attempt anything to bring about its peaceful resolution.

The most pressing problem I was faced with was the relationship between Germany and Poland. The danger was present that the idea of a "hereditary enmity" would take hold of our Volk as well as of the Polish people. I wanted to avoid this.

I know only too well that I should not have succeeded had Poland had a democratic constitution at that point in time. For these democracies, dripping all over with their peace rhetoric, are the most blood-thirsty of all warmongers. Democracy did not reign in Poland; one man did! With him we reached an accord within one year's time, an accord that, for the time being, eliminates a clash between both countries in principle for the duration of ten years. All of us are convinced that, in time, this accord will prove to be one of substance. All of us realize that these are two peoples that need to exist side by side and that neither can eliminate the other.

A state of thirty-three million will always strive for an outlet to the sea. Hence, we had to arrive at some sort of settlement. And we did arrive at a settlement that is constantly being improved upon. What is decisive in this instance is that both governments and all reasoned and rational people in both countries have the firm will to increasingly improve relations. This deed was truly in the service of peace, worth substantially more than the idle talk in the League of Nations' palace in Geneva.

Then Hitler addressed the topic of Great Britain. After a few friendly remarks upon the naval agreement, Hitler expressed his displeasure at the British threat of war should Germany employ force. He wished never again to hear the like of what Great Britain had told him through the offices of Wilson that afternoon. Hence he proclaimed:

> In this time period, I attempted to improve relations to other nations also and to make these durable. We gave guarantees to all western states and have assured all countries bordering on us that Germany will respect their territorial integrity. This is not just empty talk. This is our holy will. It is not in our interest to disturb their peace. These offers on the part of Germany encountered increasing good will.
>
> Gradually, more and more states divorce themselves from the insanity produced in Geneva, that, if I may say so, does not serve the interests of peace, but rather entails an obligation to war. These states divorce themselves from it and begin to reflect upon problems in a more rational manner. They are willing to negotiate, and they desire peace.

I went even further and offered my hand to England! In order to afford the British Empire a feeling of security, I voluntarily renounced entering into a naval armament race with Great Britain. I did so not because I would not have been capable of producing additional ships—let no one be deceived. Rather, I did so for the sole reason of wishing to secure peace between the two peoples, a peace of permanence.

Of course, certain conditions have to be met. It is simply not possible for one side to say: "I will never again lead a war, and to this end I offer you the voluntary reduction of my weapons to 35 percent," while the other side declares: "Whenever I feel like it I may lead a war on occasion." Impossible! Such an agreement is morally tenable then only if both peoples pledge never to make war on each other again. Germany has that will!

We all hope that among the British people, those will prevail who share that will!

Having dealt with Great Britain, Hitler now spoke of France and Italy:

Again I went further. Immediately subsequent to the return of the Saar to Germany by way of the plebiscite, I approached France and informed it that there were no longer any differences between us. The question of Alsace-Lorraine no longer existed as far as we were concerned. It is a border area. The people there have never really been asked their opinion during the past decades. It is our impression that the inhabitants of the area would be the most happy if all the fighting about them ended. We do not wish for war with France. We want nothing of France! Nothing at all! And once the Saar had returned to the Reich, thanks to the integrity of France in interpreting the treaties that I must give it credit for, I solemnly declared: now all differences on territorial matters between France and Germany have been resolved. I do no longer see any differences between us today. All that is there are two great peoples both wishing to work and live. And they will live best once they work together.

After this unprecedented and irrevocable renouncement 1 turned to yet another problem, one easier to resolve than others because a shared ideological belief facilitates mutual understanding: the relationship between Germany and Italy. Of course, the resolution of this problem is only in part my own achievement because the other part is the achievement of a great man whom the Italian people have the great fortune to call their leader.

This relationship long ago transcended the boundaries of economics and politics as such, and, after countless contracts and alliances had been concluded, it has developed into a friendship from the heart. Two peoples with shared ideals, world view (*Weltanschauung*), and politics have formed a friendship and an axis, the strength of which defies separation. In consideration of my responsibility to my *Volksgenossen* here, too, I have carried through a unique and final measure. I have solved a problem that henceforth no longer exists. No matter how bitter this might be for the individual: the common interest of the Volk ranks above all of us. And this interest means: to be able to work in peace. This work in the service of peace, my Volksgenossen, it is not an empty phrase, rather this work is supported by facts that no liar can deny.

Now that Hitler felt he had proven his policy to be one of pure restraint, he turned to more contemporary subjects, declaring that he must now once and for all end his eternal "moderation."

Two problems remained to be solved. Here I had some reservations, however. Ten million Germans found themselves outside of the boundaries of the Reich in two principal areas of settlement; Germans who wished to return to their homeland! Ten million is not a negligible figure. In France, ten million make up a quarter of its total population.

Given that for over forty years, France never relinquished its claim to the few million Frenchmen in the Alsace-Lorraine region then, before the eyes of God and of the world, we also had a right to maintain our claim on these ten million Germans.

My *Volksgenossen!*

Moderation had reached its limits; any further moderation would have been construed as a most fatal weakness. I would not have had the right to appear in the annals of German history, had I nonchalantly abandoned these ten million to their fate. I would not have had the moral legitimacy to be the Führer of this Volk. I had made sacrifices, and I had shown great restraint. Now I had reached the point beyond which I could not have gone. The plebiscite in Austria proved me right. A most fervent avowal was made then, an avowal that the rest of the world had most certainly not anticipated. Have we not witnessed it time and time again how in the eyes of democracies a plebiscite becomes irrelevant and even detrimental to their cause the moment it does not produce the desired results? Despite all this, the problem was resolved to the benefit of the entire great German Volk.

Hitler followed this introduction with the vow that the Sudeten German question was the last that required an immediate solution. He was brazen enough to make the unguarded statement that "it is the last territorial demand that I shall make in Europe." He continued with a spiteful tirade against Benes, the "father of the lie." He accused the Czechoslovakian of having "slaughtered thousands of Germans" and lambasted his partial mobilization of May 20 and 21. Neither could Hitler resist taking side-swipes at Great Britain and the United States. On the other hand, he had much praise for Mussolini:

> And now we face the last great problem that must be resolved and that will be resolved! It is the last territorial demand I shall make in Europe. It is a demand that I shall insist upon and a demand that I will satisfy, God willing!
>
> A short history of this problem: Waving the banner of the right to self-determination of the peoples, central Europe was torn apart in 1918 as certain crazed statesmen set to redraw the political landscape. Atomized and divided, new states were arbitrarily created in central Europe in complete

disregard of the origins of their peoples, their national desires, and of economic necessities. It is to this process that Czechoslovakia owes its existence.

The Czech state was born a lie. The name of the father of the lie was Benes. He made his great appearance in Versailles, claiming that there was such a thing as a Czechoslovakian nation. He resorted to this lie to make his own people sound, despite their meager numbers, more important and to lend credence to its demand for greater influence. At the time, the Anglo-Saxon powers, renowned for their great lack of knowledge in geographical and *völkisch* matters, did not deem it necessary to investigate Benes' claim. Otherwise they most certainly would have realized that there is no such thing as a Czechoslovakian nation. All there is are Czechs and Slovaks, and the Slovaks have little desire of being with the Czechs, rather the opposite.

In the end, thanks to the efforts of Herr Benes, the Czechs annexed Slovakia. Since this state did not appear to be a viable structure, they simply took three-and-a-half million Germans in clear defiance of the rights and desires of the Germans for self-determination. Since that evidently did not suffice, the Czechs took another million Magyars, adding a number of Carpatho-Russians and several hundreds of thousands of Poles.

That is the state that would later call itself Czechoslovakia. It exists contrary to the clear desire and will of the nations thus raped and in clear defiance of their right to self-determination. As I speak to you today, I naturally have pity on the fate of these oppressed peoples. I am touched by the fate of these Slovaks, Poles, Hungarians, and Ukrainians. Yet I can only be the voice of the fate of my Germans.

As Herr Benes was busily cementing this state on a foundation of lies, naturally he promised to construct a state on the Swiss canton model, for after all, there were a few among the democratic statesmen who were plagued by a guilty conscience. All of us know how Herr Benes resolved the matter of cantons. He built up a regime of terror! Back then already, a number of Germans attempted to protest against this arbitrary rape of their people. They were summarily executed. Ever since, a war has been waged to exterminate the Germans there. Nearly 600,000 Germans were driven from their homes during these years of "peaceful development" in Czechoslovakia. The reason for this is a fairly simple one—they would have starved otherwise!

The entire development since 1918 is proof of one thing only: Herr Benes is determined to exterminate the German community in Czechoslovakia slowly but surely. He has been successful to a certain degree. He has plunged countless numbers into unspeakable despair. He managed to make millions timid and fearful. Thanks to his unceasing terror campaign, he has managed to silence these millions while at the same time leaving no doubt as to the "international" mission of his state. There was little effort to conceal the fact that, if necessary, it was to be used against Germany. One man who expressed this in a rather frank manner was the French minister of aviation, Pierre Cot, who said: "We need this state as a base from which to launch bombs with greater ease to destroy Germany's economy and its industry." And now Bolshevism resorts to this state as a means of entry. It was not us who sought contact with Bolshevism; rather it was Bolshevism that used this state to open avenues into central Europe.

And it is at this point that we bear witness to the greatest brazenness imaginable. This state, resting upon a minority as support for its regime, forces its various nationalities to partake in a policy that one day will force them to shoot at their own brothers. Herr Benes demands of the German man: "If I go to war with Germany, then you will have to shoot at Germans. If you should not be willing to do this, then you become a traitor, and I will have you shot." He demands the same of the Hungarian and of the Polish man. He demands of the Slovaks to defend policies that are completely irrelevant to Slovakia's situation. The Slovak people wish to live in peace; they have no wish to become involved in adventures. Herr Benes, however, manages to portray these people either as traitors to their state or as traitors of their people's cause. Either they agree to shoot at their compatriots and to betray their people, or Herr Benes tells them: "You are traitors to your country, and because of that I will shoot you."

Can you imagine greater brazenness than to demand of other people to shoot their own compatriots if the circumstances warrant this? And all this simply because a rotten, disgusting, and criminal regime demands that of them? Let me assure you that as we occupied Austria, the first order I issued was that no Czech need to, that no Czech be allowed to serve in the German army. I did not want to place him in that predicament.

Whoever opposes Herr Benes will always be silenced by the application of economic pressure. This is a fact those democrats and apostles of a better world cannot lie about. In this state of Herr Benes the consequences for the various nationalities have been dreadful ones. I speak for the Germans only. Amongst them, infant mortality is the highest, and the lack of progeny is the greatest among all of Germany's Volk tribes. The unemployment rate affects them terribly. How long is this to go like this? For twenty years, the Germans in Czechoslovakia as well as the German Volk in the Reich have had to stand by and watch. They did not do so because they accepted this state of affairs. No, they did so because they were powerless and helpless faced with their torturers, abandoned in this world of democracies.

Yes, if there is a traitor locked up here or someone is placed under surveillance for slanders delivered from his pulpit, then the English are outraged, and the Americans are incensed. These are the same prototype world democrats (*Patentweltdemokraten*) who utter not a word when hundreds of thousands are driven from their homes, when tens of thousands are thrown into prison or when thousands are slaughtered. We learned a great lesson in the course of these past years. We have only disdain for them now.

We see merely one great power in Europe headed by one man who understands the despair of the German Volk. It is my great friend—I believe I may call him this—Benito Mussolini. What he has done for us in these difficult times and how the Italian people stands in relation to us, we shall never forget! And if there is ever an hour of equal need in Italy, then

I will stand up before the German Volk and demand that it do the same. And then, too, it will not be two states defending themselves, but one single block defending itself.

In my speech before the Reichstag on February 20 of this year, I declared that there had to be a change in the lives of the Germans living outside of the borders of the Reich. Indeed, Herr Benes has changed their lives in the meantime. He launched an even more repressive campaign against them, terrorizing the German minority to an even greater extent. He heralded a time of dissolution, prohibition, confiscation, and the like. And things went on like this until May 21 came along. My *Volksgenossen*, you cannot deny that we displayed exemplary patience. But this May 21 was insupportable. At great length, I reiterated its history at the Reich Party congress. At long last, there was to be a plebiscite in Czechoslovakia, a plebiscite that could not be put off any more.

Undaunted, Herr Benes, came up with a way of intimidating the Germans there: the military occupation of the territories in question. And he plans to persevere with this military occupation in the hope that no one can be found to stand up to him as long as his henchmen are around. It was that unbelievably brazen lie of May 21, which claimed that Germany had mobilized on that day, that now had to serve as an excuse, to gloss over and to serve as a disguise for the Czech mobilization.

You all know what came then: a virulent international campaign. Germany had not called up one man. It was not even contemplating resolving this matter militarily. I still entertained hopes that, at the last minute, the Czechs would realize that this tyranny could not go on any longer. Herr Benes was still convinced that, supported by France and Great Britain, he could do whatever he wished with Germany. What could happen to him? And after all, he could still turn to the Soviet Union should all else fail. Thus he was encouraged in his reaction to all those he did not fancy: shoot them, jail them, lock them up. It was then that I made my demand in Nuremberg. For the first time, I demanded clearly that now, twenty years after President Wilson's pledges, the right to self-determination must become reality for these three and a half million as well. And once more Herr Benes responded in his customary manner: more dead, more imprisoned, more incarcerated. Germans were forced to flee.

And along came England. I was perfectly open with Mr. Chamberlain as to what we considered the sole solution possible. It is the most natural there is. I know that none of the various nationalities wish to remain with Herr Benes. Yet, I am but the speaker of the Germans. For them I spoke, as I asserted that I was no longer willing to stand by silently without intervening as this crazed man continues to believe that he can maltreat three and a half million people as he sits there in Prague.

I left no doubts as to the fact that Germany's patience had reached its limit. I left no doubt that while it may be a characteristic trait of us Germans to bear up under something for a long time and with great patience, once our patience has reached an end, that is the end!

And it is now that England and France have finally demanded of Czechoslovakia what is the sole solution possible to this situation, to release the German areas and to cede them to the Reich.

Today we have intelligence of what Herr Benes discussed during this time. Faced with England's and France's declared intent to divorce themselves from the fate of Czechoslovakia, should not the fate of these peoples be changed and these areas be ceded, Herr Benes found yet another loophole. He ordered the cession of these territories. That he declared! Yet what did he do? He is not ceding the territories; rather he is driving the Germans from them. This is the point at which his game is up!

Barely had Herr Benes finished his declarations when yet another campaign of oppression by the military was launched, the only difference being that its nature was intensified this time around. We see the gruesome figures: one day there might be 10,000 refugees; the next day 20,000; yet another day later 37,000; and yet another two days later 41,000; then

62,000; and then 78,000; and now 90,000, 107,000, 137,000; and today we count 214,000. Entire regions are depopulated, villages burnt to the ground, and with grenades and gas the Germans are driven out. Benes, however, sits in Prague and is comfortable believing: "Nothing can happen to me. England and France will always back me."

And now, my *Volksgenossen,* I believe the time has come to tell him what's what. You simply cannot deny that someone truly loves peace when he has borne up under such shame, such disgrace, and so pitiful a fate for twenty long years, as we have done. When someone displays such unending patience as we have demonstrated, then truly you cannot accuse him of being a warmonger. After all, Herr Benes may have seven million Czechs, but here there is a Volk of 75 million.

Hitler's arguments betrayed his conception of "heroism" and revealed the true basis of his "credentials as a warlord" as he pitted 75 million Germans against seven million Czechoslovakians. In this misconceived spirit of fairness, he challenged Benes to a "duel" and divulged that the "secret" of his military success consisted of nothing other than brute numerical superiority. When dealing with the greater powers, he would proceed with moderation until he felt he had attained numerical superiority over them as well.

In his speech, Hitler then turned to the topic of his September 23 memorandum. He endeavored to prove to his audience what enormous restraint he had exercised in making one last proposal for the maintenance of peace, the same tactic he would employ eleven months later in Poland. However, Benes had insisted that he could not withdraw from the territory in question. "That's over now," cried Hitler. The time had come for the duel between Herr Benes and Hitler:

> I have placed a memorandum at the disposal of the British government, a memorandum representing the last and the final proposal on the part of Germany. This memorandum demands nothing other than the implementation of what Herr Benes already promised. The contents of this memorandum are quite simple: any territory that is German according to its populace and that wants to come to Germany belongs to Germany. And we shall not wait until after Herr Benes has

had a chance to drive one or two million Germans from it;
it shall come to Germany now and immediately! The border
I have redrawn does justice to the realities of the decade-old
distribution of ethnic and linguistic groups in Czechoslovakia. Yet, I am a man more just than Herr Benes, and I do not
wish to abuse the power at present in our hands. That is why,
from the very beginning, I made it clear that a territory will
come under the sovereignty of the Reich only if the majority of its inhabitants are German. The final demarcation of
the border I leave to the vote of our *Volksgenossen* there! I
have, therefore, decided to conduct a plebiscite in the area in
question. And just so no one can come and claim that this
is not fair, this plebiscite will be held in accordance with the
ground-rules of the Saar plebiscite.

I have always been willing, and I am still willing, to conduct plebiscites in the entire region if need be. However,
Herr Benes and his friends were opposed to this. They desired that plebiscites were to be held in certain regions only.
All right, here too I gave in. I even agreed to having an international commission survey the conduct of the plebiscites.
I went even further and agreed to having a Czech-German
commission draw the border. Mr. Chamberlain asked if this
could not be done by an international commission instead. I
agreed to that as well.

I was even willing to withdraw our troops from the region
for the duration of the plebiscite. Today I even agreed to invite the British Legion (*a World War I veterans' association*) to
these territories as it had offered to ensure law and order there
in the interim period. I was willing to go further and to have
the final course of the border determined by an international
commission and to have the details negotiated by a commission made up of Germans and Czechs alike.

This memorandum is nothing other than the implementation of what Herr Benes promised, calling upon the most for-
midable of international guarantees. Now Herr Benes claims
that this memorandum places him in a completely "new situation." And of what does this "new situation" consist in reality? The only thing new about this situation is what Herr

Benes has promised is to be kept for a change. That is, indeed, a completely "new situation" for Herr Benes. The promises that man has made in his life—none of which he kept! Now for the first time, he will have to keep a promise.

Herr Benes says: "We cannot withdraw from the area." Evidently, Herr Benes understood the cession of the area to imply that the Reich assumed the legal title of the land while it continued to be raped by the Czechs.

That's over now! Now I demand that Herr Benes be forced to honesty after twenty years. He will have to give over the territories on October 1.

Herr Benes now places his last hopes in the world, and he and his diplomats do little to disguise this. They declare: "It is our only hope that Chamberlain be overthrown, that Daladier be done away with, that there are revolutions all over." They place their hope with the Soviet Union. He still believes he can escape fulfillment of his obligations.

All I can say to this: "There are two men facing each other down. Over there stands Herr Benes. And here I stand!" We are two entirely different men. While Herr Benes danced on the world stage and hid himself there from his responsibilities, I was fulfilling my duties as a decent German soldier. And as I face this man today, I am but a soldier of my Volk.

After Hitler had introduced himself in his capacity as a soldier, he added a few polite words of thanks to Chamberlain. He solemnly assured that he had no intention of laying hold of the remainder of the Czechoslovakian state in the process of resolving the Sudeten German issue. "We do not want any Czechs at all," he exclaimed.

I have little more to add. I am grateful to Mr. Chamberlain for his efforts. 1 have assured him that the German Volk desires nothing but peace. Yet, I have also told him that I cannot retreat behind the lines drawn by our patience.

I have assured him further that, and this I repeat here before you, once this issue has been resolved, there will no longer be any further territorial problems for Germany in Europe!

I have assured him further that I will take no more interest in the Czechoslovakian state once that country has resolved its internal problems, that is, once the Czechs have dealt with the other minorities there in a peaceful manner and not by means of oppression. And I will guarantee this for him! We do not want any Czechs at all. Yet I do declare before the German Volk that my patience is at an end with regard to the Sudeten German problem! I have put forth an offer to Herr Benes, an offer that is nothing other than the realization of his promises. The decision is his now! Be it war or peace!

He can either accept my offer and give the Germans their freedom, or we Germans will go get it for ourselves. The world must avow that in my four-and-a-half years in the Great War, and in the long years of my political life, no one could ever have accused me of one thing: I have never been a coward!

Without a doubt, Hitler's remark that he had "never been a coward" aimed to impress both the German people and international public opinion. He reassured his listeners that he would lead their march as Germany's "first soldier."

Now I march before my Volk as the first of its soldiers. And behind me, let it be known to the world, marches a Volk, a Volk that is a different one than that of 1918! Even though, at the time, a visiting professor succeeded in poisoning the Volk with democratic jargon, let it be known that the Volk of today is not the Volk of that time! Such phraseology touches us no more than stings of bees; we have become immune to them. At this hour, the entire German Volk unites itself with me.

It will regard my will as its will, just as I regard the Volk's future and fate as the mandate of my actions. And we now want to strengthen this common will so that it might stand as strong as in the fighting times, a period in which I strode forth as a simple, unknown soldier and set out to conquer a Reich, a time in which I did not doubt the certain success and the final victory. Then a group of brave men and women congregated around me. And they marched with me. And to-day I implore you, my German Volk: stand behind me man by man, woman by woman.

At this hour, let all of us resolve a common will. It shall be stronger than any despair and danger imaginable. And once this will has become stronger than any despair and danger, then one day it will vanquish despair and danger.

We stand determined! May Herr Benes now make his choice.

Towards the end of his speech, Hitler's words left him in a veritable state of ecstasy. He repeatedly gazed to the heavens, overwhelmed by the historic greatness of the moment and his own words. Nearly every one of his sentences was followed by roars of applause. When he stopped speaking, the frenzied crowds burst out in prolonged storms of thunderous applause. The crowd reverberated Goebbels' introductory chant: "Leader command! We follow." (*Führer befiehl! Wir folgen.*)

Hitler then returned to his seat and left the floor to Goebbels, who declared:

Mein Führer!
In this historic hour I shall speak in the name of the entire German Volk, as I solemnly declare: the German nation is solidly behind you to carry out your orders loyally, obediently, and enthusiastically. The German Volk has once again a feeling of national honor and duty. It will know how to act accordingly. Never again will a November 1918 be repeated. Whoever in the world counts on this has miscalculated. Once you call upon it, our Volk will move strongly and unrelentingly into battle in order to defend the life and the honor of the nation to its very last breath.
This we swear to you, so help us God!

Actually, what Goebbels repeated was nothing other than Hitler's own words in the guise of a loyalty oath. Nonetheless, Hitler believed that he would have to once again prove his theatrical abilities. William L. Shirer, who was in Berlin as a radio journalist at the time, gives the following description of Hitler's acts:

Goebbels . . . shouted: "One thing is sure: 1918 will never be repeated!" Hitler looked up to him, a wild, eager expression in his eyes, as if those were the words that he had been searching for all evening and hadn't quite found. He leaped to his feet and with a fanatical fire in his eyes that I shall never forget brought his right hand, after a grand sweep, pounding down on the table, and yelled with all the power in his mighty lungs: "*Ja*." Then he slumped into his chair exhausted.

When Hitler finally left the Sportpalast, the crowd began to chant the nearly forgotten patriotic song from the wars of liberation against Napoleon: "The God who made iron grow did not want any slaves!" (*Der Gott, der Eisen wachsen liess, der wollte keine Knechte.*) Those who had staged this "spontaneous" outburst wanted to recreate the war enthusiasm of 1914. However, the 20,000 ecstatic listeners from Berlin whom Goebbels had called together in no way represented the entire German Volk. The majority of Germans were of a completely different attitude, which Hitler would discover the very next day.

▶ April 28, 1939 *The German occupation of Bohemia and the destruction of the Czecho-Slovak state set off alarm bells in Europe and the United States. Hitler reacted as if nothing significant had happened and announced that he would reply to his critics in a speech to the Reichstag on April 28, 1939. In that lengthy speech he replied to President Roosevelt's telegram and also made the following comments.*

I believe that it was fortunate for millions and millions of people that I was able to prevent this explosion, thanks to the insight that the responsible men on the other side had at the last minute. It is my conviction that we found a solution that has settled this dispute and has eliminated it as a source of danger for Central Europe.

The claim that this solution contradicts the Munich Agreement cannot be justified any more than it can be substantiated. Under no circumstances can the Munich settlement be regarded as a final one. After all, it makes concessions for the solution of additional questions and the need to resolve them. Truly, and this is decisive, it cannot be held against us that the concerned parties appealed to Italy and Germany, and not to the four powers. Nor can it be held against us that Czechoslovakia disintegrated on its own and, hence, ceased to exist. It is only natural that, once these ethnographic principles no longer applied, Germany again took charge of its thousand-year-old interests, which are not only of a political, but also of an economic nature. Time will tell whether the solution Germany found was the right one.

One thing is sure, however: this solution should not be subject to English control or criticism. For the lands of Bohemia and Moravia have nothing at all to do with the Munich Agreement since they constituted the final remnants of the former Czechoslovakian state.

With the brazen remark that the remainder of Czechoslovakia had "nothing at all to do with the Munich Agreement," Hitler opened his verbal assault on the British. He maintained that his personal understanding with Chamberlain, which had been arrived at on September 30, 1938, and which had provided for mutual consultations, was not applicable to his move against the remainder of Czechoslovakia. Hitler argued that if it were applicable, this would oblige him to monitor British actions in Northern Ireland and Palestine. Should Great Britain be "incapable of understanding this, our attitude" and should the prime minister believe that Britain could not possibly "place any trust in assurances by Germany," this meant that the "foundations" for the Anglo-German Naval Agreement had been destroyed. Thus he had resolved "to inform the British government of this today."

These arguments were textbook examples of the "slap in the face" tactics Hitler employed in his dealings with the British. Their forceful nature would frighten them and induce them to search for ways of obtaining his favor. In order not to prevent the British from showing themselves to be conciliatory, Hitler yielded and expressed his hope that "an arms race with England" could still be avoided. He detailed:

> As little right as we have to subject English measures, whether just or unjust, to German control and criticism, for instance in Northern Ireland, as little right does England possess to do this in the case of the old German electorates. I completely fail to understand how the personal understanding

reached by Mr. Chamberlain and myself at Munich can be applied to this case. After all, the case of Czechoslovakia was dealt with in the Munich Agreement insofar as it was possible to deal with it at that point. Beyond this, it was only planned that, should the concerned parties be unable to arrive at a agreement themselves, they could appeal to the four powers. After a period of three months, the four powers would meet again for further consultations.

Now the concerned parties have not appealed to the four powers, but to Germany and Italy. Evidence for the legitimacy of this step lies in the fact that neither England nor France voiced any objections. Moreover, they have accepted without any further ado the award arbitrated by Germany and Italy.

No, the agreement Mr. Chamberlain and I entered into has nothing to do with the problem at hand. It applies exclusively to questions concerning the coexistence of England and Germany. This is equally evident in the statement that such questions, in the future, ought to be dealt with in the spirit of the Munich Agreement and the Anglo-German Naval Agreement, which advocate friendly relations by means of mutual consultations. Should this agreement apply to any and all future German political activities, then England could not take any further steps, for instance, in Palestine or anywhere else for that matter, without consulting Germany before taking action. We certainly expect nothing of the kind and, in turn, we protest that this is expected of us. When Mr. Chamberlain now concludes that the Munich Agreement is null and void because we abrogated it, I shall take note of his disposition as of today and I shall draw the proper conclusions.

Throughout my years of political activities, I have always advocated the idea of establishing close Anglo-German friendship and cooperation. I found countless congenial people in my Movement. Perhaps they even joined my Movement because of this conviction of mine. The desire for Anglo-German friendship and cooperation not only reflects my own proper sentiments on the topic, derived from the common heritage of our two peoples, but also my opinion that the existence of the British Empire is of importance to mankind and in its best interest. Never have I left any doubt about my conviction that the maintaining of this empire is an object of inestimable value to mankind's culture and economy.

By whatever means Great Britain may have gained its colonial possessions—and I know this entailed the use of force, the use of most brutal force in many instances—I nevertheless realize that no other empire has ever been created by different means. In the end, world history values not the method so much as the success; and this not in terms of the success of the method employed, but of the general utility derived from the method.

Undoubtedly, the Anglo-Saxon people have accomplished a great colonizing work on this earth. I sincerely admire this achievement. From a higher humanitarian point of view, the thought of its destruction has always seemed to me, and seems to me today, the product of a wanton thirst for fame (*Herostratentum*). However, my sincere respect for their achievement does not mean I will refrain from assuring the life of my own Volk. I believe it is not possible to bring about a lasting friendship between the German and the Anglo-Saxon peoples if the other side fails to realize that next to British interests there are German ones also. As for the men of Britain, the sustenance of the British Empire lends meaning and purpose to life, so the sustenance and liberty of the German Reich do for the men of Germany! A lasting friendship between these two nations is conceivable only in the framework of mutual respect.

The English rule a mighty empire. They built this empire in the days of the German Volk's slackening. In former times, the German Reich also was a mighty empire. It once ruled the West. In bloody battles and religious confrontations, as well as because this state split up internally, this Reich lost its might and greatness and finally fell into a deep sleep. Still, as the old Reich was nearing its end, the seed for its ultimate rebirth began to germinate. A new Germany grew out of Brandenburg and Prussia: the Second Reich. And, in the final instance, this became the German *Volksreich* of today.

Perhaps now the English will understand that we have no reason to feel in the least inferior to them. For this, truly, our historic past is too colossal! England has given the world many a great man; Germany has done no less. The difficult struggle for the survival of our Volk has demanded of us, in the course of three centuries, a blood sacrifice in the defense of the Reich far outstripping the sacrifices other peoples had to make to secure their existence. That, perpetually the victim of aggression, Germany was not able to retain its wealth, but had to sacrifice many provinces, has been the result of the state's failure, and resulting impotence.

We have now overcome this condition. We, as Germans, therefore do not feel inferior to the British. Our respect for our country is just as great as that of every Englishman for England. The history of our Volk throughout the past two thousand years affords us grounds enough and deeds to fill us with sincere pride.

Should England declare itself incapable of understanding this, our attitude, and should it instead perhaps regard Germany as a vassal state, then our offer of love and friendship for England will have been for naught. We shall neither despair nor lose heart because of this. Instead, we shall then set out on a path—conscious of our own strength and that of our friends—that shall secure our independence and not prejudice our dignity.

I am aware of the British prime minister's declaration in which he maintains he cannot place any trust in assurances by Germany. Under the circumstances, I felt that we should no longer burden him or the English people with conditions, unthinkable without mutual trust. When Germany became National Socialist and thus initiated its resurrection, I made a proposal, for my part, in pursuit of my stalwart policy of friendship for England, to impose voluntary limits on German armament at sea. This implied the will and conviction that war should never again be possible between England and Germany. And this remains my will and my conviction even today.

However, I am now forced to concede that England's official and unofficial policies leave no doubt that London no longer shares this conviction. Quite the contrary, it is my conviction that, irrespective of what type of conflict Germany might be drawn into, Britain will always oppose Germany. War with Germany is regarded as a matter of course.

I deeply regret this since my only demand of England today is, and will continue to be, the return of our colonies. However, I have always made it perfectly clear that this does not constitute grounds for a war. I remain true to my conviction that England, for whom the colonies have no value, would come to understand Germany's position one day. Then it would undoubtedly realize that Germany's friendship far outweighed these objects, that, while they are of no real use to England, are of vital importance to Germany.

Beyond this, I have never made any demands that affected British interests, posed a real danger to its world empire, or were detrimental to England in some other manner. I have restricted myself to demands in the framework of Germany's *Lebensraum*, questions closely tied to the German nation's eternal possessions. Now that journalists and officials in England publicly advocate opposition to Germany in any case, and this is confirmed by the well-known policy of encirclement, then the foundations on which the Anglo-German Naval Agreement rested have been destroyed.

Thus, I have resolved to inform the British government of this today. This is not a question of naval armaments—since I continue to cherish the hope that an arms race with England can be avoided—but a question of self-respect. Should the British government reconsider and wish to negotiate this matter with Germany in order to reach a clear and definite understanding, then no one would be happier than I.

Beyond this, I know my Volk—I rely on it. We desire nothing that was not ours before. Never will we rob another state of its rightful possessions. Alas, he who believes he can attack Germany will encounter such a power and such a resistance that those of the year 1914 will have been negligible in comparison.

▸ April 28, 1939 *Having attended with little difficulty to the destruction of Czecho-Slovakia, Hitler now turned to the problem of Poland. His comments come from his Reichstag speech of this date.*

Now finally the time had come for Hitler to vent his anger at the impudent Poles' refusal to let him have Danzig and the extraterritorial motorway. He openly admitted to the demands he had made on Poland, the territorial nature of which could not be denied. They stood in contrast to his earlier assurances that the return of the Sudetenland had been "his last territorial demand in Europe."

Notwithstanding this openness, Hitler remained silent on his explicit insistence to the Poles that any treaty to be entered into by Poland and Germany would have to contain a decidedly anti-Soviet element. Instead, Hitler claimed that Poland had rejected his proposals although they represented a "truly unique compromise." To add insult to injury, Poland had concluded a mutual assistance pact with Great Britain that forced him, so Hitler lamented, to "regard the agreement reached at the time with Marshal Pilsudski as unilaterally abrogated by Poland and therefore null and void." Hitler declared:

> There is little to be said on the topic of Polish-German relations. In this instance as well, the Peace Treaty of Versailles has grievously and intentionally wounded the German Volk. Above all, the strange delimitation of the corridor, granting Poland access to the sea, served to preclude a reconciliation between Poland and Germany for all time. And, as emphasized earlier, this problem is perhaps the most painful one for Germany to bear.
>
> This notwithstanding, I remained steadfast in my conviction that the necessity of granting the Polish state free access to the sea cannot be ignored. Moreover, in principle, I have always maintained that it would be expedient that people whom Providence has destined—or damned, for all I care—to live next to one another, did not needlessly and artificially poison their relations. The late Marshal Pilsudski, who adhered to this view also, was willing to reexamine Polish-German relations and finally to arrive at an agreement, in which Germany and Poland pledged themselves to renounce war as a means of settling conflicts between them.
>
> Poland was granted one exception from this agreement: the provision that pacts of assistance previously entered into by Poland would not be affected by this regulation. Reference here was solely to the Mutual Assistance Pact with France. It

was accepted as a matter of course that this provision applied only to the pact already concluded and was not to be extended to pacts to be concluded in the future. It is a fact that this German-Polish Pact considerably contributed to a relaxation of tensions in Europe.

Nevertheless, one question remained open, one issue that would naturally have to be resolved sooner or later: the question of the German city of Danzig. Danzig is a German city and it wishes to return to Germany. On the other hand, this city does have treaty obligations to Poland, although they were forced on it by the dictators of peace at Versailles. Now that the League of Nations—previously a great contributor to the unrest—has commissioned an untypically tactful high commissioner to represent its interest, the question of Danzig was destined to land on the conference table once more, at the very time when this moribund institution itself began to disappear from the scene.

I regard the peaceful resolution of this question as a further contribution to a final relaxation of tensions in Europe. This relaxation of tensions is assuredly, not promoted by the smear campaign of warmongers gone crazy, but rather by the elimination of real sources of danger. Since the problem of Danzig was discussed several times a few months ago, I forwarded to the Polish government a concrete proposal. I will now inform you, my deputies, of the contents of this proposal. You shall be able to judge for yourselves whether this proposal was not the most positive concession imaginable in the service of peace in Europe.

As emphasized previously, I have always recognized the necessity for this state to have access to the sea and I have taken account of this. I am not a democratic statesman; I am a realistic National Socialist. However, I held it equally necessary to point out to the government in Warsaw that, just as it desires access to the sea, Germany desires access to its province in the east. These are indeed difficult problems. Germany bears no responsibility for this. The ones to be blamed are the magicians of Versailles who either out of malice or thoughtlessness set up a hundred powder kegs all around Europe, each equipped with a fuse virtually impossible to put out.

You cannot solve these problems in the same old way. I hold it to be absolutely essential that new ways be found. After all, Poland's access to the sea and Germany's access to the corridor are devoid of any military significance. Their significance is of a psychological and economic nature exclusively. To assign military significance to this traffic route would mean succumbing to military naivety to an exceptional degree.

I have therefore made the following proposal to the Polish government:

1. Danzig is reintegrated into the framework of the German Reich as a free state.

2. A highway and a railroad line through the corridor are placed at Germany's disposal. They are accorded the same extraterritorial status that the corridor now enjoys.

In return, Germany is willing:

1. to recognize all the economic rights of Poland in Danzig;

2. to secure for Poland a free port of whatever size it desires in Danzig and to guarantee free access thereto;

3. to regard and accept the borders between Germany and Poland as final;

4. to enter into a twenty-five-year pact of non-aggression with Poland, a pact that would far outlive me; and

5. to secure the independence of the Slovak state through cooperation between Germany, Poland, and Hungary, which is tantamount to a virtual renunciation of a one-sided German hegemony in this area.

The Polish government has refused this proposal of mine and has declared itself willing:

1. to discuss only the question of a potential replacement of the present League of Nations' high commissioner and

2. to consider facilitating transit traffic through the corridor.

I sincerely regret the attitude of the Polish government, which I fail to understand. This alone is not decisive, however. What is far worse is that Poland, like Czechoslovakia a year ago, now apparently believes it has to call up troops, under pressure from a mendacious worldwide campaign of rabble-rousing. And this though Germany has conscripted not one man nor in any way intended to take action against Poland.

As stated earlier, all this is regrettable in itself. It will be up to posterity to decide whether it was wise to refuse the new proposal that I had made. As stated earlier, this was an attempt to resolve a question that moves the entire German nation emotionally through a truly unique compromise and to solve it to the advantage of both countries.

It is my conviction that Poland was not interested in the give and take of this solution—it sought exclusively to take. That Danzig could never again become Polish was completely beyond doubt. And the plans for an attack, falsely attributed to Germany by the international press, now led to the so-called offers of a guarantee. It also led to a commitment by the Polish government to a pact of mutual assistance that would force Poland to oppose Germany militarily in the event of war between Germany and another power—in which England would appear on the scene again.

This commitment violates the agreement that, at the time, I had entered into with Marshal Pilsudski. For this agreement bore solely on commitments then already in existence, i.e., on Poland's commitment to France, of which we knew. To expand on these commitments retroactively is inconsistent with the German-Polish Non-Aggression Pact. Under the circumstances, I would never have concluded this pact. For what is the meaning of a non-aggression pact, when one party leaves open countless exceptions to its provisions!

Either collective security exists, that is, collective insecurity and the perpetual threat of imminent war, or there are clear agreements, that, in principle, prevent the contracting parties from resorting to arms. Thus, I regard the agreement reached at the time with Marshal Pilsudski as unilaterally abrogated by Poland and therefore null and void. I have informed the Polish government of this. I can only repeat once again that this does not signify a fundamental change in principle in my views of the stated problems.

Should the Polish government consider it worth its while to renegotiate a treaty defining its relations to Germany, then I shall naturally welcome this with the one proviso that such a regulation must contain clear commitments that must be mutually binding for both parties. Germany is gladly willing to undertake such obligations and to fulfill them as well.

Hitler's words clearly indicated that, at this point, he had not given up hope that his abrogation of the treaty would frighten the Poles into submission to his demands. Hence, he did not hesitate to use Spain as an example of the gruesome fate international Bolshevism held in store for countries such as Great Britain and Poland should they fail to comply with his requests and speedily place themselves under his protection.

There have been repeated claims that Hitler, in order not to alienate a potential ally, refrained from verbally assaulting the Soviet Union and Bolshevism in his April 28 speech. This is incorrect. Given the focus of his talk on Great Britain, Poland, and the United States, it is true that Bolshevism and the Soviet Union did not play a major role, as they had in earlier speeches. Nonetheless, token references to the dangers of world Bolshevism, intended to frighten the bourgeois Western powers, were contained in the Reichstag address also.

For example, Hitler spoke of the threat of "Bolshevism's annihilation of European culture"; of the dangers posed by "Bolshevist murderers and incendiaries"; not to mention "the Bolshevist subhumans in Spain." He maintained that "Soviet Russia has been involved in ten wars and military actions since 1918 carried out by use of force and bloodshed."

▸ August 13, 1939 *Having decided to move against Poland, Hitler was confronted by British opposition. He decided to look east. Dahlerus, a Swedish businessman, was Göring's personal representative to the British government and unofficially represented German interests with Hitler's approval.*

If the move against Poland was to be launched in "late August," as Hitler had insisted in his meeting with Ciano on August 13, then time was beginning to run out. Barely two weeks remained to get either the British or the Soviets to commit themselves. While Hitler felt confident that Dahlerus' secret negotiations with the British would ultimately bear fruit, the question was when. Quick results were far from certain. To force England to its knees in time, as the circumstances demanded, Hitler resolved to pull the one ace he still held out of his sleeve: the "Devil's brew."

The prospects for an agreement with the Soviets were good. Hastening its conclusion seemed, not only possible, but attainable within a short time. There were many reasons for this. For centuries, Russians had cherished a certain weakness for Germans, irrespective of whatever regime ruled their vast lands. Time and time again, negotiated settlements between the two countries had been arrived at with surprising swiftness.

This was particularly true of all matters concerning Poland. The three partitions of that unfortunate country provided ample proof. Why should Germany and Russia fail to arrive at an understanding in this respect at this particular point in time? Why not seek a fourth partition of Poland? The Russians were still hurting from the loss of the Tsarist provinces in the Ukraine and in Belorussia that they had been forced to cede as a result of the war against Poland in 1920–21. Given the general propensity for revising the peace settlements of 1919–20 and restoring national borders to what they had been in 1914, why should the Soviets not share in the spoils of such a revisionary movement? Why should they not demand or force a restitution of the territories lost to Poland, in the Baltic States, in Finland, and in the Balkans, in the course of the past two decades?

And ever since the Munich Agreement, the Russians could not help but feel that the Western powers had resigned themselves to allowing Hitler to proceed as he desired and to conquer the *Lebensraum* he coveted in the east at the expense of the Soviet Union. The slow pace of the negotiations led by the British to integrate Russia into a unitary front in opposition to National Socialist Germany may well have reinforced them in this mistaken conviction, and the fact that only second-level diplomatic personnel had been sent to Moscow to debate the potential role of the Soviets in the coming conflict lent further credence to this false notion.

In the meantime, not much progress had been made in the secret German talks with Moscow either, although they had led to Litvinov's dismissal as commissar for Foreign Affairs, due to the German hesitancy to get involved too deeply. Up to this point, Hitler had been confident he could bring about a change of heart in the British attitude by continuing to pronounce exaggerated threats. As he was becoming increasingly pressed for time, he now began to take up the Russian matter once more. On August 14, Ribbentrop relayed an offer for an agreement to Moscow and proposed to travel there in person to conclude it. Based on what Hitler had experienced domestically in the Berlin transportation workers' strike in 1932, he firmly believed he could quickly reach an understanding with the "primitive" Bolshevists, if this proved necessary.

In anticipation of what he considered the certain success of Ribbentrop's mission, Hitler made the following statements, according to Halder's notes, in a speech before the commanders of the *Wehrmacht* on August 14.

> England's position must be viewed in the light of internal politics. Decision in 1914. England would not have stepped in if she had foreseen the consequences. England stands only to lose. Even when a war is won, the victor emerges with diminished strength. This is the key to an understanding of the actions of men of less than heroic cast. In view of their experiences in the World War, there is little chance that opponents will deliberately run the risk of a major war.

> Russia is not in the least disposed to pull other's chestnuts out of the fire. Nothing to gain, but much to fear. War at the periphery a possibility, perhaps even welcome. Not so in the center. A war lost as much a threat as a victorious army. Interested in disruption of the Western states, access to Baltic. Norway, Sweden, Denmark. Will be genuinely neutral, from inner convictions. Britain's overtures to Russia have caused intense irritation. Switzerland will certainly remain neutral. Holland: neutral on principle; danger to Far East possessions. Belgium will endeavor to remain neutral.

Hungary requires no mention. Italy is not interested in a major conflict, but would welcome certain adjustments. A victory of the democratic nations would be the end of Italy. Spain will look with disfavor upon any victory of the Western democracies. Democracies would introduce a monarchy and dependence on Western powers. England and France will have to shoulder burden alone. Offensive: Between Basel and Saarbrücken hopeless. No immediate relief could be afforded by any Anglo-French action. There is nothing to force them into a war.

The men of Munich will not take the risk. Were England resolved to help, she would have given money to the Poles. But the English will not put any more money into a bankrupt business. If England had made any positive commitments, the Poles would be much more cocky. Führer concerned lest England hamper showdown by last-minute offers. Under consideration whether a negotiator should go to Moscow, and whether or not this should be a prominent figure.

[The Führer] has hinted to England that he will approach her with a new offer after disposal of the overriding Polish question. It all comes down to London. Paris, too, is informed about his determination. So the great drama is now approaching its climax. The British commotion happened because of some careless German boast that the Führer's calculations had always proved correct.

The other nations must be given proof that there will be a shooting war no matter what. (Poland will be polished off in six to eight weeks, even if England should step in.) Central problem is Poland. Must be carried through at all costs. Attack possible with violation of Belgian-Dutch neutrality.

Success, political or military, cannot be had without taking risks. The Führer regards the foreign policy risks involved in a German attack on Poland in the light of the risks that he had to take in all his decisions to date, and that, to his mind, were great at first and then steadily decreased.

As opponents, only a matter of England—apart from Poland herself—with France towed in her wake. England, unlike in 1914, will not allow herself to blunder into a war lasting for years. Talk of England wanting a long war discounted. No government will make a long war its primary aim. England, knowing war, is well aware that she stands to lose in a war, and that even a victorious war would not make up for the cost of such a war.

Such is the fate of rich countries. England is overburdened with responsibilities because of the excessive size of her empire. She has no leaders of real caliber. ("The men I got to know in Munich are not the kind that start a new world war.")

Further evidence that no determined action is to be expected on the part of England may above all be inferred from Poland's attitude. Poland would be even more cocky if she knew she could depend on England. Even now England is putting out feelers to find out how the Führer envisages developments after Poland has been disposed of.

All this supports the conviction that while England may talk big, even recall her ambassador, perhaps put a complete embargo on trade, she is sure not to resort to armed intervention in the conflict.

In the eyes of the generals present at the talk, many of whom cherished fond memories of the *Reichswehr*'s very profitable cooperation with the Red Army, the chances for Britain remaining uninterested seemed good at this point.

▶ August 19, 1939 *Hoping his "Devil's brew" would deter Britain, Hitler pushed for agreement with his "worst enemy," the dreaded Bolshevik.*

On August 19, the Soviet-German Commercial Agreement was concluded. The German News Bureau reported the following on the matter:

> The negotiations between Germany and the USSR concerning an expansion of bilateral trade, underway for a considerable time already, came to a successful conclusion on August 19, 1939. The outcome of the negotiations has been a trade and credit agreement signed by the deputy Legation Counselor Schnurre on behalf of Germany and the deputy head of the Soviet Russian trade legation in Germany, E. Barbarin. The trade agreement provides for Germany extending a credit

to the amount of 200 million Reichsmarks to the USSR, the money being earmarked for the purchase of German goods. The agreement further stipulates that the USSR shall see to the delivery of goods to Germany, within the subsequent two years, to the amount of 180 million Reichsmarks.

This text from the German News Bureau made perfectly clear that a rapprochement between Germany and the Soviet Union was being actively pursued. At least, by establishing ties with the Russians, the Germans hoped to thwart the effectiveness of potential economic sanctions by the Western powers. These now appeared certain if there were an attack on Poland. Meanwhile, in spite of repeated intervention by the German ambassador in Moscow, Graf von der Schulenburg, the Russians proved insufficiently receptive to the urgency of the matter for Germany. Apparently, they could not, or were unwilling to, understand why such haste was suddenly needed for the conclusion of a nonaggression pact between the Soviet Union and Germany. Further, a division of Eastern Europe between Soviet and German spheres of interest was not a matter to be settled in the shortest possible time in the eyes of the Soviets.

Hitler, by contrast, grew increasingly nervous as the date he had named for the attack, "late August" and "September 1," drew ever closer. Time was running out and the English appeared no less intransigent. They seemed not about to allow a German military intervention in Poland. Hitler urgently needed the Russians to cover for him in the east, unless he wished to scrap the plans for the war in view of the rapidly advancing cold season.

On August 20, given the pressure for a timely conclusion of the affair, Hitler once more resorted to his persuasive powers and penned the following personal note:

Herr Stalin, Moscow

1) I sincerely welcome the signing of the new German-Soviet Commercial Agreement as the first step in the restructuring of German-Soviet relations.

2) The conclusion of a non-aggression pact with the Soviet Union means to me the establishment of German policy for a long time. Germany thereby resumes a political

course that was beneficial to both states during bygone centuries. The government of the Reich is therefore resolved in such a case to accept all the consequences of such a far-reaching change.

3) I accept the draft of the non-aggression pact that your foreign minister, Herr Molotov, handed over but consider it urgently necessary to clarify the questions connected with it as soon as possible.

4) The substance of the supplementary protocol desired by the Soviet Union can, I am convinced, be clarified in the shortest possible time if a responsible German statesman can come to Moscow himself to negotiate. Otherwise the government of the Reich is not clear as to how the supplementary protocol could be cleared up or settled in a short time.

5) The tension between Germany and Poland has become intolerable. Polish behavior toward a great power is such that a crisis may arise any day. Germany is at any rate determined, in the face of this presumption, from now on to look after the interests of the Reich with all the means at her disposal.

6) In my opinion, it is desirable, in view of the intentions of the two states to enter into a new relationship to each other, not to lose any time. I therefore again propose that you receive my foreign minister on Tuesday, August 22, but at the latest on Wednesday, August 23. The Reich foreign minister has full powers to draw up and sign the non-aggression pact as well as the protocol. A stay in Moscow longer than one or two days at most would be impossible for the foreign minister in view of the international situation. I should be glad to receive your early answer.

Adolf Hitler

Hitler was pressed for time indeed. The Reich foreign minister was to travel to Moscow on August 22, "at the latest on Wednesday, August 23." Ribbentrop was to spend no more "than one or two days at most" in the Soviet capital. By August 25, Hitler wished the matter to be settled. Ribbentrop was to receive "full powers," i.e., the permission to sign anything the Russians desired so long as things moved along in a speedy fashion. To lure Stalin into cooperation with National Socialist Germany, Hitler insisted the agreement signified the "establishment of German policy for a long time." Close cooperation had always proven "beneficial to both states during bygone centuries."

▶ August 22, 1939 *The deadline for attacking Poland was very close; Hitler expected the agreement with the USSR to deter Britain.*

In the meanwhile, Ribbentrop had set out for Moscow, traveling from Berlin to Königsberg. Hitler had provided him the following sweeping authority:

Full Powers
Obersalzberg, August 22, 1939

I hereby grant to the Reich Foreign Minister, Herr Joachim von Ribbentrop, full power to negotiate in the name of the German Reich with authorized representatives of the government of the Union of Soviet Socialist Republics regarding a non-aggression treaty, as well as all related questions, and to sign both the non-aggression treaty and other agreements resulting from the negotiations, with the provision, if need be, that this treaty and these agreements shall come into force immediately on signature.

Adolf Hitler

Nevertheless, Ribbentrop was not left solely to his own devices. Instead, in addition to the usual foreign ministry entourage, Ribbentrop found Heinrich Hoffmann at his side. This odd procedure greatly upset Soviet protocol. Notwithstanding the strangeness of the situation, Hitler had appointed his friend and personal photographer Hoffmann his official representative on the occasion of the diplomatic visit. Needless to add, the public was not informed of this measure.

Hitler apparently placed greater stock in a frank report by Hoffmann than on the official and tedious account Ribbentrop was bound to render. Hoffmann would assuredly recount the impressions Stalin made on him more colorfully and truthfully. While Hitler publicly placed great emphasis on "blind obedience," he personally felt only contempt for those who obeyed him so unquestioningly. Ribbentrop's fawning annoyed him at times despite the foreign minister's undeniable dedication and professed desire to serve his Führer well. Undoubtedly this all contributed to Hoffmann's singular commission. Stalin, however, accepted the presence of the German head of state's peculiar "special emissary" at the talks. He even toasted the well-being of "Herr Hitler and his friend, Herr Heinrich Hoffmann."

Speaking before the generals, Hitler had maintained that the "announcement of the non-aggression pact with Russia came as a bombshell." This was doubtless true but especially for Hitler's friends, Japan and Italy, whom he had obviously not apprised in any way of his secret negotiations. They felt they had been lied to and betrayed, and rightly so. The Japanese ambassador to Berlin, Hiroshi Oshima, went white as a sheet when the German State Secretary von Weizsäcker called on him to present him with the news. The completely unexpected turn of events ultimately forced the Japanese prime minister to step down.

Mussolini was also nettled by this latest in a series of "surprise" moves Hitler had presented him with. This contributed to Mussolini's decision of August 25 to remain neutral in the upcoming conflict.

Hitler's alliance with Bolshevist Russia did not meet with approval in Germany either. Though there were voices that applauded this diplomatic feat as a "masterpiece of the Führer," most Germans were appalled. They were outraged less at the thought of Germany becoming the ally of a Communist state than at the lack of character this implied on the part of Hitler, the self-proclaimed enemy of all Bolshevists. As once before domestically, after the Röhm Purge, this complete turn about in foreign policy revealed Hitler as a hazardous desperado, an opportunist of whom only the worst was to be expected in the future. To secure an advantage for himself, this man was ever ready to abandon the best and most worthy of his friends to the knife. Many Germans remembered only too well Hitler's resounding proclamations, his ranting against the dangers of Bolshevism just three years earlier (March 7, 1936):

And I believe that this ruin would come at that point at which the leadership decides to stoop to become an ally at the service of such a destructive doctrine. I would see no possibility of conveying in clear terms to the German worker the threatening misfortune of Bolshevist chaos that so deeply troubles me were I myself, as Führer of the nation, to enter into close dealings with this very menace. As a statesman and the Führer of the Volk, I wish to also do myself all those things I expect and demand from each of my *Volksgenossen*. I do not believe that statesmen can profit from closer contact with a world view (*Weltanschauung*) that is the ruin of any people.

I broke off these relations and thus jerked Germany back from the verge of destruction. Nothing can persuade me to go any other way than that dictated by experience, insight, and foresight.

More pertinently, in a speech a year after these remarks, Hitler had insisted (January 1, 1937):

I hold the Bolshevist doctrine to be the worst poison that can be administered to a people. I therefore do not want my own people to come into contact with this doctrine in any way. And as a citizen of this Volk myself, I will not do anything I would be forced to condemn in my fellow citizens. I demand from every German worker that he refrain from having any relations or dealings with these international pests, and for his part he will never see me drinking or carousing with them. In other respects, every additional German diplomatic link with the present Bolshevist Russia would be completely useless to us. It would be equally inconceivable for National Socialist German soldiers to help protect Bolshevism; nor would we on our side accept any aid from the Bolshevist state. For I fear that every Volk that reaches out for such aid will find it to be its own ruin.

In 1939, nevertheless, the question remained of how this "Devil's brew" now would truly affect those it had been brewed for. How would England and France react to news of the German-Soviet agreement?

Papers in Paris carried one particularly revealing headline commenting on the new alignment of powers: "Brest-Litovsk 1939." This was a succinct summation of the situation as it appeared to the perceptive French in 1939: Just as the conclusion of the separate peace between Germany and Russia at Brest-Litovsk had failed to prevent an Allied victory in 1918, the agreement binding the Soviet Union to Germany in 1939 would not prove successful. As unpleasant a reality as this may well have been for Germany's leadership, "Brest-Litovsk 1939" simply meant that, while a German-Soviet collaboration might delay victory for the West, the Western powers would, nevertheless, be victorious in the end.

Reactions in London were more pronounced still. At 2:40 p.m., Lord Halifax informed Warsaw by telephone that the pact "does not modify the attitude or the policy of His Majesty's government or the relations between His Majesty's government and Poland." The cabinet convened at 3:00 p.m. on August 22 and declared that "they had no hesitation in deciding that such an event [the German-Soviet Pact] would in no way affect their obligations to Poland."

▸ August 23, 1939 *The Greater German Reich reached agreement with the Union of Soviet Socialist Republics.*

As ratification of the German-Soviet Pact was scheduled for August 23, Hitler issued orders for the attack on Poland to be launched on August 26. Halder recorded in his diary: "Day Y definitely set for the 26th (Saturday)." Simultaneously, a rationing of foodstuffs, fossil fuels, textiles, and certain raw materials was to go into force.

Already on August 23, the Danzig senate passed a resolution elevating local Nazi chief (*Gauleiter*) Albert Forster to the post of head of state. This move was unconstitutional, as the statutes of the Free City of Danzig provided for no such office. However, Hitler had long resolved to arrange a virtual coup d'état there and, for this purpose, he needed a reliable man in this key position. Forster, who apparently had been summoned to Hitler on August 21 once again, was to take over the city. As soon as Hitler so desired, Forster would then be in a position to remove the troublesome city senate and institute a "basic law." This in fact meant nothing less than presenting the world with the *fait accompli* of an annexation of the free city by the Greater German Reich.

This curious undertaking reflected the excessive precautions Hitler always took in cases related to power politics. Undoubtedly, Danzig's senate could well have passed a "basic law" without outside prodding. Its president,

SS Gruppenführer and Deputy *Gauleiter* Arthur Greiser, might well have seen to this on his own. Nevertheless, Hitler was not taking any risks. He feared that, if he left the senate to its own devices, legal bickering could delay timely action at a crucial moment. So he needed an absolutely reliable man, i.e., a stooge, to wield uncontested power in Danzig.

In the evening hours of August 23, the Berghof established yet another telephone connection with Moscow. Ribbentrop was confronted with a minor difficulty in his negotiations with Stalin, as the Soviets insisted on having the Latvian ports Libau and Windau. And despite the sweeping power of attorney provided by Hitler, Ribbentrop did not want to give in on this point on the Russians' agenda, unless he had Hitler's written approval in hand, on which he must insist, as he informed Hitler. By 11:00 p.m., a telegram lay on the foreign minister's desk reading: "Answer is: Yes, agreed."

The swiftness of Hitler's decision in favor of the Soviets came as no surprise. He was understandably eager to have the treaty with the Russians signed and was largely indifferent to the precise terms of the articles that lay the ground-work for such a collaboration, as he never really intended to uphold the provisions of the treaty in any event. At this point, he would willingly have made even greater concessions to the Russians in the east: Belorussia, the Polish section of the Ukraine, Latvia, and Estonia could have belonged to the Soviet Union. Moscow could even have demanded Finland, half the Balkans, and perhaps Turkey. Hitler, however, stood always prepared to launch a surprise attack tomorrow on the ally of today. Whatever he had to cede to Russia voluntarily during those days, he would surely try to take from it again by force at a later time.

On August 23, the Non-Aggression Pact between Germany and the Soviet Union was signed shortly before midnight. At 1:00 a.m. on August 24, Ribbentrop reported its successful conclusion to Hitler on the phone.

The agreement read as follows:

> Treaty of Non-Aggression between Germany and the Union of Soviet Socialist Republics
>
> The government of the German Reich and the government of the Union of Soviet Socialist Republics, desirous of strengthening the cause of peace between Germany and the USSR, and proceeding from the fundamental provisions of the Treaty of Neutrality, which was concluded between Germany and the USSR in April 1926, have reached the following agreement:

Article I
The two contracting parties undertake to refrain from any act of violence, any aggressive action and any attack on each other either severally or jointly with other powers.

Article II
Should one of the contracting parties become the object of belligerent action by a third power, the other contracting party shall in no manner lend its support to the third power.

Article III
The governments of the two contracting parties will in future maintain continual contact with one another for the purpose of consultation in order to exchange information on problems affecting their common interests.

Article IV
Neither of the two contracting parties will join any grouping of powers whatsoever that is aimed directly or indirectly at the other party.

Article V
Should disputes or conflicts arise between the contracting parties over questions of one kind or another, both parties will settle these disputes or conflicts exclusively by means of a friendly exchange of views or, if necessary by the appointment of arbitration commissions.

Article VI
The present treaty shall be in force for a period of ten years with the proviso that, in so far as one of the contracting parties does not denounce it one year before the expiration of this period, the validity of this treaty shall be deemed to be automatically extended for another five years.

Article VII
The present treaty shall be ratified within the shortest possible time. The instruments of ratification will be exchanged in Berlin. The treaty shall go into force immediately upon signature.

Done in duplicate in the German and Russian languages.

Moscow, August 23, 1939

For the government of the German Reich: v. Ribbentrop
With the full power of the government of the USSR: V. Molotov

A secret additional protocol that was not published at the time was added to this:

> Secret additional protocol on the occasion of the signature of the non-aggression treaty between the German Reich and the Union of Soviet Socialist Republics. The undersigned plenipotentiaries of the two parties discussed in strictly confidential terms the question of the delimitation of their respective spheres of interest in Eastern Europe. These conversations led to the following result:

> 1. In the event of a territorial and political transformation in the territories belonging to the Baltic states (Finland, Estonia, Latvia, Lithuania), the northern frontier of Lithuania shall represent the frontier of the spheres of interest both of Germany and the USSR In this connection the interest of Lithuania in the Vilna territory is recognized by both parties.

> 2. In the event of a territorial and political transformation of the territories belonging to the Polish state, the spheres of interest of both Germany and the USSR shall be bounded approximately by the line of the rivers Narev, Vistula, and San.

>> The question whether the interests of both parties make the maintenance of an independent Polish state desirable and how the frontiers of this state should be drawn can be definitely determined only on the course of further political developments.

In any case, both governments will resolve this question by means of a friendly understanding.

3. With regard to south-eastern Europe, the Soviet side emphasizes its interest in Bessarabia. The German side declares complete political *désintéressement* in these territories.

4. This protocol will be treated by both parties as strictly secret.

Moscow, August 23, 1939

For the government of the German Reich: v. Ribbentrop

With the full power of the government of the USSR: V. Molotov

On the morning of August 24, Hitler summoned State Secretary von Weizsäcker for a discussion. The Führer was exuberant and certain of the future. He was fully confident that, after the scene he had made with Henderson, the British would finally yield. And once a change of heart was evident on the part of England, Poland had no choice but to retreat. A solution could then be reached "step by step and peacefully." In fact, England would shortly drop Poland just as it had abandoned Czechoslovakia earlier when the danger of war was imminent.

Nonetheless, to Hitler's astonishment, none of the news from London carried any reports of the fall of Chamberlain's cabinet. Flying back to Berlin and landing at the Tempelhof airport at 6:35 p.m., he was baffled and visibly disappointed not to find any such news on his desk at the Reich Chancellery.

During the next hours, however, Hitler was far too busy to concern himself with the "confused" statesmen across the channel. Ribbentrop had also just arrived in Berlin, at 6:40 p.m., together with his entourage—including the "special emissary" Heinrich Hoffmann. At 7:00 p.m., the Führer told Germany's diplomatic delegation to the Soviet Union to report on its experiences. The stories Hoffmann and Ribbentrop told of their days in Moscow left Hitler wide-eyed with the same utter disbelief Marco Polo once encountered when summoned to speak before the doge of Venice of his journeys to the Far East. Napoleon had reacted in a similar manner to the tales Caulaincourt told of St. Petersburg. Ribbentrop said that he felt in Moscow "as though amongst old party comrades, so to speak." Hoffmann praised Stalin's acumen, the authority he exuded, the sincerity and warmth of his speech.

The persistent ridicule of the Russians in the German press was beginning to exact its toll. German propaganda had described the Bolshevists as subhumans (*Untermenschen*), wild, raving animals, assuredly going about clad in nothing but furs and hides, gnashing their teeth. And now the representatives of National Socialist Germany had traveled to Moscow only to report back that the city looked like any other European metropolis. And people even drove cars in its streets—astounding, truly! Apparently, Russians were completely normal human beings. One could negotiate with them in a civilized manner, provided one treated them with friendship. Such a striking contrast to the official black-and-white propaganda naturally had to elicit a corresponding reaction, especially with many Germans of the time, who loved to rush from one extreme to the other.

Hitler did not truly desire to cultivate friendly relations with the Soviet Union in the future. The present alliance served as a means to an end in his drive to eliminate Poland and later spring a surprise attack on Russia. He must have been no more pleased than Napoleon at the sudden pro-Russian sentiments of his closest colleagues. If a two-day stay in Moscow was enough to turn convinced National Socialists into friends of Russia, then how much more detrimental to his cause might it be to allow further contacts with Russians? Under no circumstances, thought Hitler, could he allow himself now to stray from the path assigned to him by his notions dating back to 1919. After all, the Russians were a notoriously primitive nation. Their lot was subservient to the German master race. They were to be subdued and their soil converted into "*Lebensraum* for Germany." Germany's true friends were England and Italy, even if the English failed to perceive this at this time. Surely England and Italy would allow their enthusiasm to surface once presented with the *fait accompli* of German territorial conquests in the east. It might well prove disastrous to cede ground now. He simply had to persevere. The Italians and the British needed perhaps little more than yet another thorough working-over to come to see his point of view, which was inherently theirs as well.

The final agreement was settled on September 28, 1939.

Signing of the "German-Soviet Boundary and Friendship Treaty" was scheduled for September 28 in Moscow. Negotiations had not gone as well as anticipated. This was due largely to Stalin's demand that the spheres of interest, as delineated in late August, be revised: the Soviet Union wanted Lithuania within its sphere of influence. In return, while previously the Vistula and San rivers had constituted the border of Germany's sphere stretching into Poland, the Reich was to be accorded all lands up to the Bug river. The Russians valued the Baltic states as a buffer in the event of a German aggression against their territory. For reasons of both foreign and domestic policy, the Soviet government apparently thought it opportune to restrict themselves to the Belorussian and Ukrainian areas in Poland. Ribbentrop would have liked to see the German side claim the oil-rich territories of Drohobycz and Boryslav. Yet, the only additional terrain yielded was Suvalki, between East Prussia and Lithuania.

Having obtained Hitler's consent by phone, Ribbentrop and his Soviet counterparts proceeded with the signing of the treaty. It read:

> German-Soviet Boundary and Friendship Treaty, Moscow, September 28, 1939
>
> The government of the German Reich and the government of the USSR consider it as exclusively their task, after the disintegration of the former Polish state, to re-establish peace and order in these territories and to assure to the peoples living there a peaceful life in keeping with their national character. To this end, they have agreed upon the following:
>
> Article I
> The government of the German Reich and the government of the USSR determine as the boundary of their respective national interests in the territory of the former Polish state the line marked on the attached map that shall be described in more detail in a supplementary protocol.

Article II
Both parties recognize the boundary of the respective national interests established in article I as definitive and shall reject any interference of third powers in this settlement.

Article III
The necessary reorganization of public administration will be effected in the areas west of the line specified in article I by the government of the German Reich, in the areas east of this line by the government of the USSR.

Article IV
The government of the German Reich and the government of the USSR regard this settlement as a firm foundation for a progressive development of friendly relations between their peoples.

Article V
This treaty shall be ratified and the ratification shall occur in Berlin as soon as possible. The treaty becomes effective upon signing.

Done in duplicate, in the German and Russian languages.

For the government of the German Reich: v. Ribbentrop

By authority of the government of the USSR: V. Molotov

In addition to the treaty, three secret protocols were also signed in Moscow that day, none of which was published:

Confidential Protocol

The government of the USSR shall place no obstacles in the way of Reich nationals and other persons of German descent residing in its sphere of influence if they desire to migrate to Germany or to the German sphere of influence. It agrees that such removals shall be carried out by agents of the Government of the Reich in cooperation with competent local authorities and that the property rights of the emigrants shall be protected.

A corresponding obligation is assumed by the government of the German Reich in respect to the persons of Ukrainian or White Russian descent residing in its sphere of influence.

For the government of the German Reich: v. Ribbentrop

By authority of the government of the USSR: V. Molotov

Secret Additional Protocol

The undersigned plenipotentiaries declare the agreement of the government of the German Reich and the government of the USSR upon the following:

The Secret Additional Protocol signed on August 23, 1939, shall be amended in item 1 to the effect that the territory of the Lithuanian state falls to the sphere of influence of the USSR, while, on the other hand, the province of Lublin and parts of the province of Warsaw fall to the sphere of influence of Germany (cf. the map attached to the Boundary and Friendship Treaty signed today). As soon as the government of the USSR shall take special measures on Lithuanian territory to protect its interests, the present German-Lithuanian border, for the purpose of a natural and simple boundary delineation, shall be rectified in such a way that the Lithuanian territory situation to the southwest of the line marked on the attached map falls to Germany.

Further it is declared that the economic agreements now in force between Germany and Lithuania shall not be affected by the measures of the Soviet Union referred to above.

For the government of the German Reich: v. Ribbentrop

By authority of the government of the USSR: V. Molotov

Secret Additional Protocol

The undersigned plenipotentiaries, on concluding the German-Russian Boundary and Friendship Treaty, have declared their agreement upon the following:

> Both parties will tolerate in their territories no Polish agitation that affects the territories of the other party. They will suppress in their territories all beginnings of such agitation and inform each other concerning suitable measures for this purpose.

For the government of the German Reich: v. Ribbentrop

By authority of the government of the USSR: V. Molotov

The talks in Moscow also opened prospects for the conclusion of a large-scale economic agreement. The German press carried an exchange of correspondence by Ribbentrop and Molotov on this subject. A joint statement of the Reich government and the Soviet government received explicit mention in the German press as Hitler accorded it paramount importance. He hoped this statement would greatly impress peace activists in England.

Banner headlines announced the publication of this declaration, which read:

> After the government of the German Reich and the government of the USSR have, by means of the treaty signed today, definitely settled the problems arising from the disintegration of the Polish state and have thereby created a firm foundation for a lasting peace in eastern Europe, they mutually express their conviction that it would serve the true interest of all peoples to put an end to the state of war existing at present between Germany on the one side and England and France on the other. Both governments will therefore direct their common efforts, jointly with other friendly powers if occasion arises, toward attaining this goal as soon as possible.

Should, however, the efforts of the two governments remain fruitless, this would demonstrate the fact that England and France are responsible for the continuation of the war, whereupon, in case of the continuation of the war, the governments of Germany and of the USSR shall engage in mutual consultations with regard to necessary measures.

For the government of the German Reich: v. Ribbentrop

By authority of the government of the USSR: V. Molotov

The author of this "joint declaration" undoubtedly was Hitler. It singularly served his aims, namely, to exert pressure on the British to conclude an early peace.

Should they prove recalcitrant once again, they would have to face joint German-Soviet action "with regard to necessary measures." This in particular was to create the impression that the Russians would declare war on England should it fail to comply with Hitler's persistent demands.

▶ August 31, 1939 *Hitler believed his usual methods of threats of violence, pretended response to grave injury, and unexpected alliances would give him a free hand in Poland. He was mistaken, but the sorry truth is that Hitler did not care: he would just as soon go to war.*

At 12:30 p.m. on August 31, Hitler issued definite orders for the attack on Poland, placing his signature beneath the following directive for wartime operations:

Directive No. 1 for the Conduct of the War

1. Now that every political possibility has been exhausted for ending by peaceful means the intolerable situation on Germany's eastern frontier I have determined on a solution by force.

2. The attack on Poland is to be carried out in accordance with the preparations made for "Case White" (*Fall Weiss*), with the alterations, with respect to the army, resulting

from the fact that strategic deployment has by now been almost completed.

Assignment of tasks and the operational objective remain unchanged.

Day of attack . . . September 1, 1939.

Time of attack . . . 4:45 a.m.

This timing also applies for the Gdynia-Gulf of Danzig, and Dirschau Bridge operations.

3. In the west, it is important that the responsibility for the opening of hostilities should be made to rest squarely on Britain and France. Insignificant frontier violations should, for the time being, be opposed by purely local action. The neutrality about which we have given assurances to Holland, Belgium, Luxembourg, and Switzerland must be scrupulously respected.

On land, the German western frontier is not to be crossed at any point without my express permission. At sea, the same applies for all warlike actions or actions that could be regarded as such.

The defensive measures of the *Luftwaffe* are, for the time being, to be restricted to those necessary to counter enemy air attacks at the Reich frontier, whereby the frontiers of neutral States are to be respected as long as possible in countering single aircraft and smaller units. Only if large French and British formations are employed over the neutral states in attacks against German territory and the air defense in the West is no longer assured, are counter measures to be allowed over these neutral territories.

The speediest reporting to *Wehrmacht* high command (*OKW*) of any violation of the neutrality of any third state by our Western opponents is particularly important. (*This refers to a Franco-British move into Belgium.*)

4. If Britain and France open hostilities against Germany, it is the task of the *Wehrmacht* formations operating in the west to conserve their forces as much as possible and thus

maintain the conditions for a victorious conclusion of the operations against Poland. Within these limits, our forces are to inflict the maximum losses possible on enemy forces and their materiel. Orders to go over to the attack are reserved to me in every case.

The army will hold the West Wall and make preparations to prevent its being outflanked in the north through violation of Belgian or Netherlands territory by the Western powers. If French forces enter Luxembourg, the demolition of frontier bridges is authorized.

The navy will carry on warfare against merchant shipping, directed mainly at Britain. To intensify the effects, a declaration of danger zones may be expected. Navy high command (*OKM*) will report in which sea areas, and to what extent, danger zones are appropriate. The wording of a public announcement is to be prepared in consultation with the foreign ministry and submitted to me through *OKW* for approval. The Baltic Sea is to be protected from enemy raids. The commander in chief of the Navy will decide whether the approaches to the Baltic Sea should be blocked by mines for this purpose.

The *Luftwaffe* is, in the first place, to prevent the French and British air forces from attacking the German Army and German *Lebensraum*. In conducting the war against Britain, preparations are to be made for the use of the *Luftwaffe* in disrupting British supplies by sea, the armaments industry, and the transport of troops to France. A favorable opportunity is to be taken for an effective attack on massed British naval units, especially against battleships and aircraft carriers. Attacks against London are reserved for my decision. Preparations are to be made for attacks against the British mainland, bearing in mind that partial success with insufficient forces is in all circumstances to be avoided.

Adolf Hitler

In retrospect, this decision to schedule the opening of hostilities against Poland for Friday, September 1, was the last one Hitler was to make of his own free will. All other ventures he was yet to embark on, until his dying day, were mere reactions to events and developments connected to the fateful decision of August 31, 1939.

As Churchill had aptly put it in a radio broadcast, the decision to begin the war had been Hitler's, but the decision to end the war would not be his. Hitler had thrown the first stone. The resulting avalanche that would ultimately crush him could no longer be stopped.

It was Hitler alone who took this fateful, final step towards the opening of hostilities against Poland. Neither Goebbels or Himmler, Göring or Ribbentrop, Keitel or Brauchitsch, Raeder or Halder, civil servant or party leader, military commander or admiral, had assisted him in making this decision or influenced him in any manner.

The decision to go to war was fully in keeping with the ideas Hitler had conceived in 1919: the conquest of new *Lebensraum* in the east, with the "sacrifice" that "blood is shed"; and the British and Italians would provide friendly help. No well-meant advice, resolute warning, or outside development could induce Hitler to veer from his "preconceived" path. And it was hence that Germany's "train of government" with Hitler at the helm set out on its journey towards destruction.

In retrospect, was the attack on Poland Hitler's only recourse at this point in the negotiations? Could he no longer restrain his generals, these "bloodhounds" who were supposedly "waiting to be unleashed"? Was it they who forced him to fire the first shot of this world war? Would rescinding the order to attack Poland have placed in question his authority within the Third Reich? Could he not have declared the military preparations simply a bluff? Would his party comrades perhaps have staged a mutiny, or would the state apparatus have denied him its support by resorting to a vote of no confidence? Nothing of the sort. The entire German Volk—party members, politicians, leaders of the economy—they all would have greatly rejoiced had this bitter cup passed them by once more.

What weighed so heavily on Hitler in autumn, 1939 was the force of his ego compelling him onward at all costs. He had rationalized his actions in the following manner in the 1936 campaign: "Because I am living *now,* that's why it has to be now!" There had to be war because he was alive on this day in 1939. As he had explained his idiosyncratic stance to Henderson on

August 23, "he was now 50, and therefore if war had to come, it was better that it should come now than when he was 55 or even 60 years old." On July 4, 1944, Hitler maintained in speaking before the German leaders of the military and the economy: "I am of the conviction that no other man could have done what I have done. Another would not have had the nerve."

Chamberlain hit the nail on the head when, in a speech to the House of Commons on September 1, 1939, he blamed "one man, the German chancellor," for the outbreak of the Second World War.

On the other hand, Hitler's decision to go to war was made long before August 31, 1939. It represented the culmination of a long process of decision-making. The story of his life led up to this one development, though he had undoubtedly envisioned the outcome of the war differently. The chain of reasoning that brought it about was evident already, also to experts abroad, in *Mein Kampf.* This edifice of ideas had remained unchanged.

Admittedly, it would be an over-simplification to place the fault for the war exclusively with Hitler and the Third Reich. However, it was undeniably Hitler who exploited the weaknesses of Germany's politicians and military, of other prominent members of society at the time, of the "stab-in-the-back" legend, of the Versailles Treaty, only to unleash a war on a scale hitherto unknown. He summoned those evil spirits that had inflicted so much woe and suffering on the German people on so many previous occasions.

One man who knew Hitler extraordinarily well, and whom the Führer mistakenly held to be a sympathizer for the National Socialist cause, was the British journalist Ward Price. Already in October 1937, he had observed the ongoing preparations in Germany with great concern and had pointed out the strategic consequences to be drawn by Britain.

Like any other compulsive gambler, Hitler soon found it impossible to stop even once he realized he might have gone too far. His early successes clouded his view of the seriousness of the setbacks he later suffered. Neither reason nor common sense were at hand to restrain him. He was incapable of reviewing past actions or rescinding orders once he had given them. By 1939, he had become the prisoner of his own ideas.

To the British, Hitler seemed nothing other than a new Napoleon, or a new Wilhelm II, who strove to subjugate Europe, behind each a country that had become mighty enough to disturb the balance of power on the continent and thereby to threaten Britain's hegemony. Their behavior towards Hitler reflected this assessment, which the later course of events proved to have been correct.

British statesmen stood determined to declare war on the German dictator the minute he breached international peace and law. Hitler, whose knowledge of history was insufficient at best, and nonexistent when it came to Britain. was also ignorant of the limitations on his freedom of action. This ignorance doomed his efforts.

Hitler discounted US war-making potential but his error is evident in this picture of the buildup on Normandy a few days after the landings.

XIII
Hitler Confronts America

Hitler had nothing but contempt for the United States of America. He ignored the fact that U.S. forces in 1918 were a major reason for the defeat of Imperial Germany; as far as he was concerned, it was the lack of internal unity that led to the German defeat. Hitler also held that President Wilson's Fourteen Points were a fraud that allowed Germany's enemies to create internal conflict. Of course, in Hitler's view, self-determination for Germany meant control of most of Europe. The greater number of U.S. citizens found Nazism and Hitler unacceptable but felt what went on in Europe did not affect the security of the U.S. President Roosevelt tried to moderate the most egregious Nazi actions but feared that the U.S. would eventually have to go to war with Germany.

▶ September 26, 1938 *As the Czechoslovak crisis came to a head, President Roosevelt sent a plea for peaceful methods of solving disputes.*

The President of the United States had sent an identical telegram to the heads of state of Germany, Czechoslovakia, Great Britain, and France and called for peaceful negotiations to resolve the crisis. At the same time he indicated that, should open hostilities ensue, the United States could not guarantee remaining neutral in the long run.

Roosevelt's telegram read verbatim:

Washington, September 26, 1938

To His Excellency Adolf Hitler,
Führer and Chancellor of the German Reich, Berlin.

The fabric of peace on the continent of Europe, if not throughout the rest of the world, is in immediate danger. The consequences of its rupture are incalculable. Should hostilities break out, the lives of millions of men, women, and children in every country involved will most certainly be lost under circumstances of unspeakable horror. The economic system of every country involved is certain to be shattered. The social structure of every country involved may well be completely wrecked.

The United States has no political entanglements. It is caught in no mesh of hatred. Elements of all Europe have formed its civilization. The supreme desire of the American people is to live in peace. But in the event of a general war they face the fact that no nation can escape some measure of the consequences of such a world catastrophe.

The traditional policy of the United States has been the furtherance of the settlement of international disputes by pacific means. It is my conviction that all people under the threat of war today pray that peace may be made before, rather than after, war.

It is imperative that peoples everywhere recall that every civilized nation of the world voluntarily assumed the solemn obligations of the Kellog-Briand Pact of 1928 to solve controversies only by peaceful methods. In addition, most nations are parties to other binding treaties obligating them to preserve peace. Furthermore, all countries have today available for such peaceful solution of difficulties that may arise treaties of arbitration and conciliation to which they are parties.

Whatever may be the differences in the controversies at issue, and however difficult of pacific settlement they may be, I am persuaded that there is no problem so difficult or so pressing for solution that it cannot be justly solved by reason rather than by the resort to force.

During the present crisis the people of the United States and their Government have earnestly hoped that the negotiations for the adjustment of the controversy that has now arisen in Europe might reach a successful conclusion. So long as these negotiations continue, so long will there remain the hope that reason and the spirit of equity may prevail and that the world may thereby escape the madness of a new resort to war.

On behalf of the 130 millions of people of the United States of America and for the sake of humanity everywhere, I most earnestly appeal to you not to break off negotiations looking to a peaceful, fair, and constructive settlement of the questions at issue.

I earnestly repeat that so long as negotiations continue, differences may be reconciled. Once they are broken off, reason is banished and force asserts itself. And force produces no solution for the future good of humanity.

Franklin D. Roosevelt

Such appeals and warnings meant little to Hitler, and he replied with a verbose telegram twice as long as Roosevelt's initial telegram:

Berlin, September 27, 1938
To His Excellency, the President of the United States of America,

Mr. Franklin Roosevelt, Washington.

In your telegram received on September 26, Your Excellency addressed an appeal to me in the name of the American people, in the interest of the maintenance of peace, not to break off negotiations in the dispute that has arisen in Europe, and to strive for a peaceful, honorable, and constructive settlement of this question. Be assured that I can fully appreciate the lofty intention on which your remarks are based, and that I share in every respect your opinion regarding the unforeseeable consequences of a European war. Precisely for this reason, however, I can and must decline all responsibility of the German people and their leaders, if the further development, contrary to all my efforts up to the present, should actually lead to the outbreak of hostilities.

In order to arrive at a fair judgment regarding the Sudeten German problem under discussion, it is indispensable to
consider the incidents in which, in the last analysis, the origin
of this problem and its dangers had its cause. In 1918 the German people laid down their arms in the firm conviction that,
by making peace with their enemies at that time, those principles and ideals would be realized that had been solemnly announced by President Wilson, and just as solemnly accepted as
binding by all the belligerent powers. Never in history has the
confidence of a people been more shamefully betrayed than it
was then. The peace conditions imposed on the conquered nations by the treaties concluded in the suburbs of Paris have fulfilled none of the promises given. Rather they have created in
Europe a political regime that made of the conquered nations
world pariahs without rights, and that must have been recognized in advance by every discerning person as untenable.

One of the points in which the character of the dictates
of 1919 was most clearly revealed was the founding of the
Czechoslovak state and the establishment of its frontiers
without any consideration for history or nationality. The Sudetenland was also included therein, although this area had
always been German and although its inhabitants, after the
destruction of the Habsburg monarchy, had unanimously
declared their desire for union (*Anschluss*) with the German
Reich. Thus the right of self-determination, that had been
proclaimed by President Wilson as the most important basis
of national life, was simply denied to the Sudeten Germans.

But that was not enough. In the treaties of 1919, certain
obligations with regard to the German people, which according to the text were far-reaching, were imposed on the Czechoslovak State. These obligations too were disregarded from the
first. The League of Nations has completely failed in the task
assigned to it of guaranteeing the fulfillment of these obligations. Since then the Sudetenland has been engaged in the severest struggle for the maintenance of its German character.

It was a natural and inevitable development that, after the
recovery of strength of the German Reich and after the reunion of Austria with it, the desire of the Sudeten Germans
for preservation of their culture and for closer union with

Germany increased. Despite the loyal attitude of the Sudeten German Party and its leaders, differences with the Czechs became ever stronger. From day to day it became more evident that the government in Prague was not disposed to consider seriously the most elementary rights of the Sudeten Germans. On the contrary, they attempted by increasingly violent methods to enforce the "Czechization" of the Sudetenland. It was inevitable that this procedure should lead to ever greater and more serious tension.

The German government at first did not intervene in any way in this development and maintained its calm restraint even when, in May of this year, the Czechoslovak government proceeded to a mobilization of their army, under the purely fictitious pretext of German troop concentrations. The renunciation of military counter-measures in Germany at that time, however, served only to strengthen the uncompromising attitude of the Prague government. This was clearly shown by the course of the negotiations for a peaceful settlement of the Sudeten German Party with the government. These negotiations produced the conclusive proof that the Czechoslovak government was far from treating the Sudeten German problem in a fundamental manner and bringing about an equitable solution. Consequently, conditions in the Czechoslovak State, as is generally known, have in the last few weeks become completely intolerable. Political persecution and economic oppression have plunged the Sudeten Germans into untold misery.

To characterize these circumstances it will suffice to refer to the following:

We reckon at present 214,000 Sudeten German refugees who had to leave house and home in their ancestral country and flee across the German frontier, because they saw in this, the last and only possibility of escaping from a disgraceful Czech regime of force and bloodiest terror. Countless dead, thousands of wounded, tens of thousands of people detained and imprisoned, and deserted villages are the accusing witnesses before world opinion of hostilities, as you in your telegram rightly fear, carried out for a long time by the Prague government, to say nothing of German economic life in the

Sudeten German territory being systematically destroyed by the Czech Government for twenty years, and which already shows all the signs of ruin that you anticipate as the consequence of an outbreak of war.

These are the facts that compelled me in my Nuremberg speech of September 13 to state before the whole world that the deprivation of the rights of three-and-a-half million Germans in Czechoslovakia must cease, and that these people, if they cannot find justice and help by themselves, must receive both from the German Reich. However, to make a last attempt to reach the goal by peaceful means, I made concrete proposals for the solution of the problem in a memorandum delivered to the British prime minister on September 23, which in the meantime has been made public. Since the Czechoslovak government had previously declared to the British and French governments that it was already agreed that the Sudeten German settlement area should be separated from the Czechoslovak state and joined to the German Reich, the proposals of the German memorandum aim at nothing else than to bring about a prompt, sure, and equitable fulfillment of that Czechoslovak promise.

It is my conviction that you, Mr. President, when you consider the entire evolution of the Sudeten German problem from its inception to the present day, will recognize that the German government has truly not been lacking either in patience or in a sincere desire for a peaceful understanding. It is not Germany that is to blame for the fact that there is a Sudeten German problem at all and that the present untenable conditions have arisen from it.

The terrible fate of the people affected by the problem no longer allows for a further postponement of its solution. The possibilities of arriving at a just settlement by agreement are therefore exhausted with the proposals of the German memorandum. It now rests, not with the German government, but with the Czechoslovak government alone, to decide if it wants peace or war.

Adolf Hitler

After receiving this message, Roosevelt sent another telegram, now directed to Hitler alone, at 10:00 p.m. of September 27, 1938. He reinforced his appeal for a settlement by negotiation, stressing that "the question before the world today is not the question of errors of judgment or of injustices committed in the past; it is the question of the fate of the world today and tomorrow."

▸ November 17, 1938 *The United States found the actions in Germany during "Crystal Night" unacceptable.*

In Düsseldorf on November 17, Hitler attended the funeral services for the assassinated legation counsellor vom Rath. The Führer himself did not speak on the occasion and his demeanor was quite the opposite of the behavior he had displayed two-and-a-half years earlier at the funeral of Wilhelm Gustloff, where he had delivered a lengthy address.

This time he was concerned about appearances and wished in no way to be connected to the pogrom that had followed the death of vom Rath. He may have found credulous listeners in his German audience, but his tactic failed him with regard to the international public. To protest the atrocities committed, the United States recalled its ambassador in Berlin, Hugh R. Wilson. An American ambassador would never return to National Socialist Germany. Hitler was forced to react by recalling the German ambassador, Dieckhoff, from Washington on November 18. Only a chargé d'affaires remained in the American capital.

▸ April 15, 1939 *President Roosevelt, viewing the German occupation of Bohemia as an explicit violation of the Munich Agreement and noting the development of the Polish crisis, sent an explicit warning to Hitler. Hitler responded with scorn.*

The President of the United States addressed this message to Hitler on April 15:

> Washington, April 15, 1939
> His Excellency Adolf Hitler, Chancellor of the German Reich, Berlin

You realize, I am sure, that throughout the world hundreds of millions of human beings are living today in constant fear of a new war or even a series of wars. The existence of this fear and the possibility of such a conflict is of definite concern to the people of the United States, for whom I speak, as it must also be to the peoples of the other nations of the entire western hemisphere. All of them know that any major war, even if it were to be confined to other continents, must bear heavily on them during its continuance and also for generations to come. Because of the fact that after the acute tension in which the world has been living during the past few weeks, there now seems to be at least a momentary relaxation because no troops are at this moment on the march, this may be an opportune moment for me to send you this message.

On a previous occasion I addressed you on behalf of the settlement of political, economic, and social problems by peaceful methods and without resort to war; but the tide of events seems to have reverted to the threat of arms. If such threats continue, it seems inevitable that much of the world must become involved in common ruin. All the world, victor nations, vanquished nations, and neutral nations will suffer. I refuse to believe that the world is of necessity such a prisoner of destiny. On the contrary it is clear that the leaders of great nations have it in their power to liberate their peoples from the disaster that impends. It is equally clear that in their own minds and in their own hearts, the peoples themselves desire that their fears be ended. It is, however, unfortunately necessary to take cognizance of recent facts. Three nations in Europe and one in Africa have seen their independent existence terminated. A vast territory in another independent nation of the Far East has been occupied by a neighboring state. Reports, which we trust are not true, insist that further acts of aggression are contemplated against still other independent nations. Plainly the world is moving towards the moment when this situation must end in catastrophe unless a more rational way of guiding events is found. You have repeatedly asserted that you and the German people have no desire for war. If this is true there need be no war. Nothing can persuade the peoples of the earth that any governing power has any right or need to inflict the consequences of war on its own or any other people save in the cause of self-evident home defense.

In making this statement we, as Americans, speak not through selfishness or fear or weakness. If we speak now it is with the voice of strength and with friendship for mankind. It is still clear to me that international problems can be solved at the Council table. It is therefore no answer to the plea for peaceful discussions for one side to plead that unless they receive assurances beforehand that the verdict will be theirs they will not lay aside their arms. In Conference rooms as in Courts it is necessary that both sides enter upon the discussion in good faith assuming that substantial justice will accrue to both and it is customary and necessary that they leave their arms outside the room where they confer.

I am convinced that the cause of world peace would be greatly advanced if the nations of the world were to obtain a frank statement relating to the present and future policy of governments. Because the United States, as one of the nations of the western hemisphere, is not involved in the immediate controversies that have arisen in Europe, I trust that you may be willing to make such a statement of policy to me as the head of a nation far removed from Europe in order that I, acting only with the responsibility and obligation of a friendly intermediary, may communicate such declaration to other nations now apprehensive as to the course that the policy of your Government may take.

Are you willing to give assurances that your armed forces will not attack or invade the territory or possessions of the following independent nations: Finland, Estonia, Latvia, Lithuania, Sweden, Norway, Denmark, the Netherlands, Belgium, Great Britain and Ireland, France, Portugal, Spain, Switzerland, Liechtenstein, Luxembourg, Poland, Hungary, Romania, Yugoslavia, Russia, Bulgaria, Greece, Turkey, Iraq, the Arabias, Syria, Palestine, Egypt, and Iran? Such an assurance clearly must apply not only to the present day but also to a future sufficiently long to give every opportunity to work by peaceful methods for a more permanent peace.

I therefore suggest that you construe the word "future" to apply to a minimum period of assured non-aggression, ten years at the least, a quarter of a century if we are to look that far ahead. If such assurance is given by your Government I will immediately transmit it to the Governments of the nations I have named and I will simultaneously inquire whether, as I am reasonably sure, each of the nations enumerated above will in turn give like assurance, for transmission to you.

Reciprocal assurances such as I have outlined will bring to the world an immediate measure of relief. I propose that, if it is given, two essential problems shall promptly be discussed in the resulting peaceful surroundings and in those discussions the Government of the United States will gladly take part. The discussions which I have in mind relate to the most effective and immediate manner through which the peoples of the world can obtain progressive relief from the crushing burden of armament that is each day bringing them more closely to the brink of economic disaster.

Simultaneously the Government of the United States would be prepared to take part in discussions looking towards the most practical manner of opening up avenues of international trade to the end that every nation of the earth may be enabled to buy and sell on equal terms in the world market as well as to possess assurance of obtaining the materials and products of peaceful economic life.

At the same time those Governments other than the United States which are directly interested could undertake such political discussion as they may consider necessary or desirable. We recognize complex world problems which affect all humanity but we know that study and discussion of them must be held in an atmosphere of peace. Such an atmosphere of peace cannot exist if negotiations are overshadowed by the threat of force or by the fear of war.

I think you will not misunderstand the spirit of frankness in which I send you this message. Heads of great Governments in this hour are literally responsible for the fate of humanity in the coming years. They cannot fail to hear the prayers of their peoples to be protected from the foreseeable chaos of war. History will hold them accountable for the lives and the happiness of all even unto the last.

I hope that your answer will make it possible for humanity to lose fear and regain security for many years to come.

A similar message is being addressed to the chief of the Italian Government.

Franklin D. Roosevelt

This letter represented Roosevelt's reaction to the preceding weeks' events in Czechoslovakia and the Balkans. Moreover, it was also a reply to Hitler's speech in Wilhelmshaven, where he had attempted to justify his advances to the east by reference to "ancient German right," the history of the thousand-year Reich, and the role played by German kings and architects in the building of Prague. This speech had provoked Roosevelt's list, which encompassed nearly all European states, as well as those that had established themselves on the ruins of the Ottoman Empire. These had a long history of relations with Germany, which they had maintained even during the First World War.

Roosevelt's telegram was tantamount to an unmistakable warning that should Great Britain be drawn into a war with Germany, the United States might well engage in the fighting also. While remonstrating with Hitler, Roosevelt expressed the uncompromising solidarity of the English-speaking nations, and this was reinforced by a note published three days later in London. In concert with Roosevelt's telegram, Buckingham Palace announced on April 18 that the king and queen of Great Britain would pay an official visit to the White House from June 7 to June 11.

Hitler failed to comprehend the true import of Roosevelt's telegram. He was convinced that it was merely a diplomatic bluff, designed to rouse public opinion in Germany against him. This was precisely how he had assessed Wilson's Fourteen Points many years earlier. Most revealing, too, was the headline of the *Völkischer Beobachter* on the pending publication of the telegram: "The 'message' of the US President—an infamous attempt at deception of the public à la Wilson."

Hitler resolved to parry such an impudent maneuver by replying in a rhetorical masterpiece of even greater length than the original. Wilson had once preached Fourteen Points; Hitler would now catapult twenty-one points at Roosevelt.

At once, he had the following official note published on the matter:

> The American President has addressed a telegram to the Führer
> with the request that he indicate his stance on certain issues.
> The Führer has deemed this matter of paramount importance
> and has therefore resolved to respond to the American President
> on behalf of the German Volk, before the forum of the Reich-
> stag. He has thus called on the German Reichstag to convene
> on April 28 to bear witness to the delivery of this declaration.

Before the announced speech, Germany's diplomatic missions abroad
received instructions to counter Roosevelt's "infamous" propaganda campaign. Immediately, Hitler extended diplomatic feelers to the smaller nations listed to investigate whether these states had granted Roosevelt license
to speak in their name. Despite negative replies hastily issued in most of the
capital cities enumerated, he remained insistent on the conclusion of several
bilateral non-aggression pacts. He was less than satisfied with the results:
only Denmark, Latvia, and Estonia were willing to enter into such agreements with Germany. Norway, Sweden, and Finland declined Hitler's offer
to his great displeasure.

▶ April 28, 1939 *Hitler responded to Roosevelt in his Reichstag speech of April
28, 1939.*
    *Domarus used published texts of documents in his collection. This speech
comes from the Nazi Party paper* Völkischer Beobachter *for April 29, 1939.
There are noticeable differences between this published text and films of parts
of the speech particularly concerning Hitler response to President Roosevelt's
letter. As he read the list of independent countries that President Roosevelt
had included in his letter, Hitler emphasized the word "independent" repeatedly, implying that he did not consider the countries independent. As Hitler
mentioned each country, the Reichstag deputies laughed boisterously. As Hitler continued, the laughter became louder and louder. The published text did
not indicate these actions.*

After a digression of one-and-a-half hours, he finally addressed the issue of the day: Roosevelt's telegram. Hitler again resorted to a sarcastic
and presumptuous tone that, so he believed, had proven its value in the
long years of domestic struggle. As mentioned before, Hitler greatly overestimated the importance of propaganda. The speech before the Reichstag

on April 28, 1939 also proved that he failed to realize that even the most skilled arguments and oratorical masterpieces were ineffective against an external adversary of superior strength.

Hitler sought to discredit Wilson and Roosevelt as "magicians" whose sole ambition was to deceive and seduce both German and international public opinion with their rhetoric. He failed to realize that the military and political might of the United States or, as the case might be, the Anglo-Saxon world, gave powerful and decisive weight to the statements of American presidents. Hitler obviously had resolved to outdo Roosevelt by presenting him with an even longer and more detailed reply. Whereas Wilson had restricted himself to his famous "Fourteen Points," Hitler listed twenty-one points of contention with the Anglo-Saxon powers.

Many of Hitler's remonstrances were well-founded. After all, the history of the United States is full of military interventions in Latin American states. In his attempt, however, to use these historic facts as precedents for his own actions in Eastern Europe, his arguments lost their persuasiveness. Neither Austria nor Germany had the military potential to successfully carry out such military ventures without suffering retribution; and neither of the Anglo-Saxon powers was willing to allow the territorial expansion of Germany or Austria by force, irrespective of what particular direction this might lead them. The Anglo-Saxon powers and their allies stood prepared to thwart any such aggression by force of arms. And in this context, Hitler's feeble attempts at belatedly rationalizing his actions were simply grotesque. His reply to Roosevelt's telegram comprised twenty-one separate answers to each of the questions posed:

> As I mentioned in my introduction earlier, the world was informed of the contents of a certain telegram on April 15, 1939. I did eventually see this telegram myself, though not until somewhat later. It is difficult to classify this document. It simply fits into no known category. Therefore, my Deputies of the German Reichstag, standing before you and hence before the German Volk, I will try to analyze the contents of this curious document. From there I will go on to give the necessary answers in your name and in the name of the German Volk.
>
> 1. Mr. Roosevelt is of the opinion that I also ought to be aware that "throughout the world hundreds of millions of human beings are living today in constant fear of a new war or even

a series of wars." This was of definite concern to the United States, for whom he spoke, "as it must also be to the peoples of the other nations of the entire western hemisphere."

Answer:

To this I would like to say that the fear of war has undoubtedly haunted mankind throughout the ages, and rightly so. For example, from the conclusion of the Peace Treaty of Versailles in 1919 until 1938, fourteen wars have been waged, in none of which Germany has been involved. However, the same cannot be said of states of the "western hemisphere" in the name of which Mr. President Roosevelt claims to be speaking. To these wars one must add, within the same time period, twenty-six armed interventions and sanctions imposed by brute force, and resulting in bloodshed. And in this, too, Germany has not been involved in the least.

The United States has participated in six cases of armed intervention since the year 1918; Soviet Russia has been involved in ten wars and military actions since 1918 carried out by use of force and bloodshed. And in these cases, too, Germany has not been involved. Nor has it caused any of these incidents. Hence, in my eyes, it would be a mistake to attribute the fear of war of the peoples of Europe and beyond right now to precisely those wars for which Germany could be held responsible.

Instead, the cause for this fear lies in an unbridled smear campaign in the press, as mendacious as it is vile, in the dissemination of nasty pamphlets to foreign heads of state, in the artificial scaremongering that has even made interventions from other planets seem possible, that, in turn, has led to dreadful scenes of utter confusion.

I believe that the minute the responsible governments exercise the necessary restraint themselves and demonstrate greater love of truth, and impose this criterion on their journalistic organs, with regard to international relations and the internal affairs of other people, then assuredly this constant fear of war will vanish immediately. And then, the peace we all desire will be forthcoming.

2. Mr. Roosevelt professes the belief in his telegram that "any major war even if it were to be confined to other continents must bear heavily on everyone during its continuance and also for generations to come."

Answer:
No one knows this better than the German Volk. The Peace Treaty of Versailles placed so heavy a burden of debt on its shoulders that even a hundred years would not have sufficed to pay it off. And all this despite the fact that it was American specialists in constitutional law, historians, and professors of history who proved conclusively that Germany could not be blamed for the outbreak of the World War any more than any other nation.

Still, I do not believe that every struggle has catastrophic consequences for the environment, i.e. the entire earth, especially if it is not artificially drawn into this conflict by a system of impenetrable alliances. Since the world has experienced wars not only in the past centuries, but also frequently in more recent decades, as I have demonstrated in my earlier comments, then this would mean that, if Mr. Roosevelt's views are correct, the sum of the consequences of these wars would bear heavily on mankind for millions of years to come.

3. Mr. Roosevelt declared that already "on a previous occasion" he had addressed me "on behalf of the settlement of political, economic, and social problems by peaceful methods and without resort to war."

Answer:
This is precisely the same opinion I have always advocated myself. Also as history proves, I have settled the necessary political, economic, and social problems without resort to arms, without resort to war. Regrettably, a peaceful settlement has been rendered more difficult through the agitation by politicians, statesmen, and news reporters, who were neither concerned nor in the least affected by the issues in question.

4. Mr. Roosevelt believes that "the tide of events seems to have reverted to the threat of arms. If such threats continue, it seems inevitable that much of the world must become involved in common ruin."

Answer:
As far as Germany is concerned, I am not aware of such threats to other nations. Nevertheless, each day in democratic newspapers I read lies concerning such threats. Daily I read about the mobilization of German troops, troop-landings, and threats. And all this is supposedly directed against states with whom we live in peace and enjoy the most friendly of relations.

5. Mr. Roosevelt further believes that, in the event of war, "all the world, victor nations, vanquished nations, and neutral nations will suffer."

Answer:
This is a conviction I have expressed as a politician during twenty years in which, regrettably, the responsible statesmen in America could not bring themselves to see their involvement in the World War and the nature of its outcome in this light.

6. Mr. Roosevelt believes that "it is clear that the leaders of great nations have it in their power to liberate their peoples from the disaster that impends."

Answer:
If this is indeed clear, then it must be truly criminal negligence—not to employ a less refined expression—by the leaders of these peoples if they prove incapable of curtailing, in view of the powers at their command, the excesses of their warmongering press and thereby of sparing the world the disaster that threatens in the case of armed confrontation.

Moreover, I fail to comprehend how the responsible leaders, instead of cultivating diplomatic relations internationally, can recall their ambassadors or take like actions to disrupt and render these relations more difficult without a good reason.

7. Mr. Roosevelt declares that "three nations in Europe and one in Africa have seen their independent existence terminated."

My answer:
I do not understand which three nations in Europe are being referred to. Should reference be made to the provinces that have been reintegrated in the German Reich, then I must bring a mistaken notion of history to the attention of the President. These nations have by no means lost their independence within Europe. Rather it was in the year 1918 when, through the breach of a solemn promise, they were torn from the communities they belonged to. The stamp of nationhood was imprinted on their brow, one they neither desired nor deserved. Independence was likewise forced on those who gained no independence thereby, but who instead were forced into a dependency on foreign powers whom they despised.

As far as the nation in Africa is concerned, which supposedly lost its freedom too, this is evidently yet another case of mistaken identity. Not one nation in Africa has lost its freedom. Rather nearly all former inhabitants of this continent have been subjected by brute force to the sovereignty of other peoples. This is how they lost their freedom. The people of Morocco, the Berbers, the Arabs, the Negroes, and so on, all of them became the victims of foreign powers, whose swords assuredly did not bear the inscription *"Made in Germany,"* but instead *"Made by democracies."*

8. Mr. Roosevelt then says that reports that he trusts are not true "insist that further acts of aggression are contemplated against still other independent nations."

Answer:
I hold such rumors, devoid of any basis in reality, to constitute a violation of peace and quiet in the world. I perceive therein an attempt to frighten small nations or at least an attempt to make them increasingly nervous. Should Mr. Roosevelt have concrete cases in mind, then I would request that he name the states threatened by an attack and the potential aggressors in question. Then it will be possible to eliminate from the face of this earth these outrageous and general accusations by a simple statement.

9. Mr. Roosevelt declares that "plainly the world is moving toward the moment when this situation must end in catastrophe unless a more rational way of guiding events is found." He then goes on to declare that I have repeatedly asserted that I and the German people "have no desire for war. If this is true there need be no war."

My answer:
Once again, I would like to state that, first of all, I have not waged war. And, second, I have lent expression to my distaste for war as well as for warmongering for many years. Third, I do not know why I should wage war. I would be greatly indebted to Mr. Roosevelt if he could explain all this to me.

10. Mr. Roosevelt finally espouses the opinion that "nothing can persuade the peoples of the earth that any governing power has the right or need to inflict the consequences of war on its own or any other people save in the case of self-evident home defense."

My answer:
I hold this to be the attitude embraced by all reasonable men. Only it seems to me that in almost every war both parties tend to claim to be acting in self-evident home defense. Regrettably, the world does not possess any institution, including the person of Roosevelt, able to resolve this problem unequivocally.

For example, there is no doubt that America did not enter into the World War in "self-evident home defense." A commission appointed by Mr. Roosevelt himself to investigate the reasons for America's entry into the World War arrived at the conclusion that this entry had been essentially for the furthering of capitalist interests. Now, all there is left for us to do is to hope that the United States itself shall adhere to this noble principle in the future and will not make war on another people "save in the case of self-evident home defense."

11. Mr. Roosevelt further argues that he speaks "not through selfishness or fear of weakness, but with the voice of strength and with friendship for mankind."

My answer:
Had America raised its voice of strength and friendship for mankind in a more timely fashion and, above all, had this voice carried with it practical applications, then at least the treaty could have been prevented, which has become the source of the greatest disruption for mankind of all time, namely, the *Diktat* of Versailles.

12. Mr. Roosevelt further declares that it is clear to him that "all international problems can be solved at the council table."

My answer:
Theoretically that may well be possible, since one ought to think that, in many instances, reason would prevail in pointing to the justness of the demands on the one side,

and to the necessity of making concessions on the other. For example, according to all laws of reason, logic, and the principles of an all-encompassing higher justice, even according to the commandments of a divine will, all nations should partake equally in the goods of this world. It is not right that one nation should occupy so large a *Lebensraum* that not even fifteen inhabitants live on one square kilometer, while other nations are forced to sustain themselves with 140, 150, or even 200 inhabitants per square kilometer. And, under no circumstances, could these fortunate nations then seek to restrict the existing *Lebensraum* of those already impoverished, for example, by taking away their colonies. Thus, I would be happy if these problems could actually be solved at the council table.

My skepticism is based on the fact that it was America that lent expression itself to pronounced reservations regarding the effectiveness of conferences. Without doubt, the greatest council of all time was the League of Nations. It was the will of an American president that created this body. All nations of this world together were to solve the problems of mankind at its council table. However, the first state to withdraw from this endeavor was the United States. And this was the case because President Wilson himself already had voiced severe misgivings about the possibility of solving truly decisive international problems at the council table.

With all due respect to your opinion, Mr. Roosevelt, it is contradicted by the actual fact that, in the nearly twenty years of the League of Nations' existence—this greatest permanent conference of the world—it did not manage to solve even one truly decisive international problem.

Throughout many years, the Treaty of Versailles had selectively excluded Germany from active participation in this great international conference in breach of the promise given by President Wilson. In spite of the bitter experiences of the past, the German government nevertheless did not believe it ought to follow the example of the United States, but instead chose to occupy its seat at the council table at a later date. It was not until after many years of futile participation that I finally resolved to imitate the Americans and withdraw from this greatest conference in the world. And since then I have set out to solve the problems concerning my Volk, that regrettably were not solved at the council table of the League of Nations like all the others, and, without exception, I solved them without resort to war!

Beyond this, many problems were brought to the attention of international conferences in the past years, as emphasized earlier, without a solution of any kind being found. And, Mr. Roosevelt, if your view is correct that all problems can be solved at the council table, then all nations, including the United States, must have been led either by blind men or criminals in the last seven or eight thousand years. For all of them, including some of the greatest statesmen in the United States, have made history, not by sitting at council tables, but by making use of the strength of their nation. America did not gain its independence at the council table any more than the conflict between its northern and southern states was solved at the council table.

I am leaving out of consideration here that the same holds true for the countless wars in the course of the gradual conquest of the North American continent. I mention all this only to observe that, with all due respect to the assuredly noble nature of your views, Mr. President Roosevelt, they are not in the least confirmed by either the history of your own country or the history of the rest of the world.

13. Mr. Roosevelt further asserts that "it is therefore no answer to the plea for peaceful discussion for one side to plead that unless they receive assurances beforehand that the verdict will be theirs they will not lay aside their arms."

My answer:
Truly, Mr. Roosevelt, you cannot believe that when the fate of the nation is at stake any government or leadership of the nation will lay down its weapons before a conference, or surrender them, simply in the blind hope

that the intelligence or insight, or whatever, of the other participants in the conference will make the right decision in the end. Mr. Roosevelt, there has been only one people and one government in all of world history that has adhered to the formula that you recommend: that of Germany. Acting on solemn promises by the American President Wilson and the endorsement of these assurances by the Allies, the German nation once trustingly laid down its arms. It approached the council table unarmed.

However, once it had laid down its arms, the German nation no longer was even invited to the conference. Instead, contrary to all assurances, the greatest breach of promise of all time was affected. And then, one fine day, instead of resolving the greatest disorder of all time at the council table, the most inhuman *Diktat* in the world brought about even more terrible disorder. The representatives of the German Volk, having laid down their arms and trusting in the solemn assurances of the American President, appeared unarmed to accept the *Diktat* of Versailles. They were received not as the representatives of a nation that throughout four years had withstood the whole world with immense heroism in its struggle for its freedom and independence, but instead were treated in a more degrading manner than could have been the case with Sioux chiefs.

The German delegates were called names by the mob, stoned. They were dragged to the greatest council table in the world no differently than prisoners to the tribunal of a victor. There, at gunpoint, they were forced to accept the most shameful subjugation and pillage of all time.

Let me assure you, Mr. Roosevelt, that it is my own unshakable will to see to it that not only now, but in the future as well, no German ever again shall step into a conference room defenseless. Instead, every representative of Germany shall perceive behind him the united force of the German nation, today and in the future, so help me God.

14. Mr. Roosevelt believes that "in conference rooms as in courts it is necessary that both sides enter upon the discussion in good faith assuming that substantial justice will accrue to both."

Answer:

The representatives of Germany shall never again enter into a conference that means nothing other than a tribunal for them. For who is to judge them? In a conference, there is neither a prosecution nor a judge; there are only two warring parties. And if the common sense of the concerned parties cannot find a solution or a settlement, then surely they will not submit themselves to a judgment by disinterested foreign powers. Besides, it was the United States that declined to step before the League of Nations for fear of becoming the unwitting victim of a court that could decide against the interest of individual parties, provided the necessary majority vote was attained.

Nevertheless, I would be greatly indebted to Mr. Roosevelt if he could explain to me how precisely this new world court is to be set up. Who are to be the judges? How shall they be selected? To whom shall they be held responsible? And, above all, for what shall they be held responsible?

15. Mr. Roosevelt believes that "the cause of world peace would be greatly advanced if the nations of the world were to obtain a frank statement relating to the present and future policy of governments."

Answer:

In countless public addresses, Mr. Roosevelt, I have already done this. And in today's session, I have made such a frank statement before the forum of the Reichstag—insofar as this is possible within the span of two hours. I must decline, however, to make such statements to anyone but the Volk for whose existence and life I am responsible. It alone has the right to demand this of me. I render an account of

German policy objectives in so public a manner that the whole world can hear it anyway. Alas, these clarifications are of no consequence to the rest of the world, as long as there is a press capable of distorting any explanation, making it suspect, placing it in question, and concealing it beneath fresh lies in response.

16. Mr. Roosevelt believes that "the United States, as one of the nations of the western hemisphere, is not involved in the immediate controversies that have arisen in Europe." Hence, he trusts that I should "be willing to make such a statement of policy to him as the head of a nation far removed from Europe."

Answer:
Apparently Mr. Roosevelt seriously believes it would render a service to the cause of peace worldwide if the nations of the world would make such frank statements relating to the present policy of governments.

Why does President Roosevelt burden the German head of state in particular with the request to make such a statement without inviting other governments to make similar statements relating to their policies?

I do not believe that it is permissible at all to demand that such statements be made to a foreign head of state. Instead, in accordance with President Wilson's demand at the time for the abolition of secret negotiations, such statements should best be made to the entire world. I have not only consistently been willing to do this, but—as mentioned before—I have also done so all too frequently. Regrettably, it was precisely the most important statements on the goals and intentions of the German policies that the press in many of the so-called democratic states either withheld from the people or misrepresented.

When, however, the American President Roosevelt feels called on to address such a request to Germany or Italy of all states simply because America is far removed from Europe, then, since the distance between Europe and America is equally great, our side also would have

the right to question the President of the United States
on the foreign policy goals pursued by America and the
intentions on which this policy is based, for instance with
regard to the states of Central and South America. In this
case, Mr. Roosevelt surely would refer us to the Monroe
Doctrine and decline this request as an uncalled-for interference in the internal affairs of the American continent.
Now, we Germans advocate exactly the same doctrine
with regard to Europe and, in any event, we insist on it
insofar as this regards the domain and the interests of the
Greater German Reich.

Besides this, of course, I would never allow myself to
direct a similar request to the President of the United
States of America, as I assume he would justly regard this
as tactless.

17. Mr. Roosevelt now declares further that he is willing to
"communicate such a declaration to other nations now
apprehensive as to the course that the policy of your government may take."

Answer:
By what means does Mr. Roosevelt determine which nations are apprehensive as to the course of the policy of Germany and which are not? Or is Mr. Roosevelt in a position,
in spite of the surely enormously heavy load of work on
his shoulders in his own country, to assess by himself the
inner state and frame of mind of foreign peoples and their
governments?

18. Mr. Roosevelt demands finally that we "give assurance
that your armed forces will not attack or invade the territory or possessions of the following independent nations:
Finland, Estonia, Latvia, Lithuania, Sweden, Norway,
Denmark, the Netherlands, Belgium, Great Britain, Ireland, France, Portugal, Spain, Switzerland, Liechtenstein,
Luxembourg, Poland, Hungary, Romania, Yugoslavia,
Russia, Bulgaria, Greece, Turkey, Iraq, Arabia, Syria, Palestine, Egypt, and Iran.

Answer:

As a first step, I took pains to inquire from the cited states whether, first, they are apprehensive.

Second, I asked whether Mr. Roosevelt's inquiry on their behalf was initiated by them or whether, at least, he had secured their consent in this. The responses obtained were negative throughout, in part even marked by outright indignation. However, a number of the cited states could not forward their response to us because, like Syria for example, they are presently not in the possession of their liberty since their territories are occupied by the military forces of the democratic states that have robbed them of all their rights.

Third, far beyond this, the states bordering Germany have all received many binding assurances, and many more binding proposals, than Mr. Roosevelt requested of me in his peculiar telegram.

Fourth, should there be a question as to the weight of these general and specific statements that I have repeatedly made, then would not any additional statement of this nature, even if it were made to Mr. Roosevelt, be equally worthless? After all, what is decisive is not Mr. Roosevelt's opinion of such statements but the weight given to them by the states in question.

Fifth, I must yet point out to Mr. Roosevelt a few additional mistaken notions of history. For instance, he mentions Ireland and requests a statement that Germany not attack Ireland. Now, I have just read a speech by the Irish Prime Minister De Valera, in which, contrary to the opinion of Mr. Roosevelt, he oddly enough does not accuse Germany of oppressing Ireland and instead reproaches England for the persistent aggression under which his state suffers. And, despite Roosevelt's great insight into the needs and concerns of other states, it can safely be assumed that the Irish prime minister knows better what threatens his country than the President of the United States does.

Equally, it appears to have slipped Mr. Roosevelt's mind that Palestine is not being occupied by German troops but by English ones. By brute force, England is curtailing Palestinian freedom and is robbing the Palestinians of their independence to the advantage of Jewish intruders for whose cause the Palestinians suffer the cruelest of abuses. The Arabs living in this territory assuredly have not complained to Roosevelt of German aggression. Rather, in persistent appeals to international public opinion, the Arabs lament the barbaric methods by means of which England seeks to overpower a people who love their freedom and fight only to defend it.

This may well be one of the problems Mr. Roosevelt would like to see solved at the council table. It ought to be decided by an impartial judge and not by brute force, military means, mass executions, the torching of villages, the dynamiting of houses, and so on. One thing is certain: in this case, England cannot claim to be repelling the threat of an Arab attack on England. Instead, England is the invader, whom no one bade come, and who seeks to establish her rule by force in a country not belonging to her. A number of similarly mistaken historic notions of Mr. Roosevelt are to be noted, not to mention how difficult it would be for Germany to conduct military operations in states and countries some of which are at a distance of two to five thousand and more kilometers.

I wish to state the following in conclusion: the German government nonetheless is willing to extend an assurance of the type desired by Roosevelt to each and every one of the cited states, if this state desires it and approaches Germany with such a reasoned request. However, there is one prerequisite: this assurance must be absolutely mutual in nature. This will be superfluous in a number of the cases of the states cited by Roosevelt since we are either already allied to them or, at the very least, enjoy close and friendly relations with them. And, beyond the duration of such an arrangement, Germany will gladly enter into agreements with each of these states, agreements of the nature desired by this state.

I would not like to let this opportunity pass without extending assurances to the President of the United States on the issues of territories of most immediate concern to

him, namely, the United States itself and the other states
of the American continent. And herewith, I solemnly
declare that any and all allegations of a planned German
attack on American territories or an intervention to be
pure swindle and crude fabrication. Not to mention that,
assessed from a military standpoint, such allegations can
only be the products of an overwrought imagination.

19. Mr. Roosevelt declares in this context that he considers
of crucial importance the discussions that are to "relate to
the most effective and immediate manner through which
the peoples of the world can obtain progressive relief from
the crushing burden of armament."

Answer:
Mr. Roosevelt apparently is not aware that this problem
already was completely resolved as far as Germany was
concerned. In the years 1919 to 1923, the German Reich
completely disarmed, as explicitly confirmed by the allied
commissions, to the extent enumerated below.

And here once again followed Hitler's favorite listing in which he detailed the tens of thousands, hundreds of thousands, yes millions of guns,
machine guns, trench mortars, and the like that Germany had been forced
either to surrender or to destroy after its defeat in the First World War.
Hitler had used exactly the same listing on many previous occasions. He
could not well let this opportunity pass him by without demonstrating his
detailed knowledge of military affairs.

The following were destroyed in the Army:

59,000 field artillery and gunbarrels; 130,000 machine guns; 31,000 trench mortars and mortar barrels;
6,007,000 rifles and carbines; 243,000 machine gun barrels; 28,000 gun carriages; 4,390 trench mortar carriages;
38,750,000 shells; 16,550,000 hand grenades and rifle grenades; 60,400,000 live fuses; 491,000,000 rounds of small

arms ammunition; 335,000 tons of shell cases; 23,515 tons of cartridge cases; 37,600 tons of gunpowder; 79,000 ammunition gauges; 212,000 telephone sets; 1,072 flamethrowers, and so on.

Further destroyed were: sledges, mobile workshops, anti-aircraft batteries, limbers, steel helmets, gas masks, the machine tools of the war industry, and rifle barrels.

Further destroyed were: 15,714 fighter planes and bombers; 27,757 aircraft engines.

At sea, the following were destroyed: 26 battleships; 4 coastal defense ships; 4 battlecruisers; 19 light cruisers, 21 training ships and special ships; 83 torpedo boats; 315 U-boats.

Also destroyed were motor vehicles of all types, gas bombs, and, in part, anti-gas defense equipment, propellants, explosives, searchlights, sighting devices, range finders and sound rangers, optical instruments of all kinds, harnesses, and so on; all airplane and airship hangars, and so on.

In accordance with the solemn assurances that were given to Germany and repeated in the Peace Treaty of Versailles, this was to constitute merely an advance payment to enable the outside world for its part to disarm without danger. As in all the other cases, having placed its faith in the promises given, Germany was to be shamefully deceived once more. As you are aware, all subsequent attempts sadly failed, in spite of years of negotiation at the council table, to bring about a disarmament of other states which would have constituted at the very least an element of prudence and justice, and the fulfillment of commitments made.

I myself have contributed to these discussions a series of practical suggestions, Mr. Roosevelt, and I sought to initiate debate to at least reduce armament as much as possible. I suggested a 200,000-man ceiling for standing armies, an abolition of all offensive weapons, bombers, gas warfare, and so on.

20. Mr. Roosevelt finally asserts his preparedness to "take part in discussions looking towards the most practical manner of opening up avenues of international trade to the end that every nation of the earth may be enabled to buy and sell on equal terms in the world market as well as to possess assurance of obtaining the materials and products of peaceful economic life."

Answer:

I believe, Mr. Roosevelt, that it is not a matter of discussing these problems in theory. Instead, it is imperative to take concrete actions to remove actual impediments to the international economy. The greatest impediments lie within the respective states themselves. Previous experiences have shown that all great international conferences on trade failed simply because the respective states were not capable of keeping their domestic economies in order. Currency manipulation carried this insecurity to the international capital market.

Above all, this resulted in constant fluctuations in the exchange rates. It likewise places an intolerable burden on world trade relations if, because of ideological considerations, it is possible for certain countries to unleash a campaign of wild boycotts of other peoples and their goods, and thereby to practically exclude them from participation in the market. I believe you would render us a great service, Mr. Roosevelt, if you took advantage of your strong influence in the United States to eliminate these particular impediments to the conduct of truly free trade.

However, it did not prove possible to implement these proposals in the rest of the world, in spite of Germany's complete disarmament. I therefore advanced proposals for a ceiling of 300,000 men to be put up for discussion. The result was equally negative. I thereupon continued to place a series of other detailed disarmament proposals before the forum of the German Reichstag and hence before the international public.

Nobody even thought of joining in these discussions. Instead, the rest of the world began to reinforce its existing vast armament. It was not until the year 1934 that I ordered a thorough German rearmament, after the last of my comprehensive proposals on behalf of Germany, regarding the 300,000-man ceiling, had been rejected for good.

Still, Mr. Roosevelt, I should not like to stand in the way of the discussion of armament questions in which you intend to participate. I would only like to request that, before you turn to me and Germany, you contact the others. I can still see in my mind's eye all my actual experiences, and I am inclined to remain skeptical until reality sets me right. For I simply cannot believe that, if the leaders of other peoples are not even capable of putting production in their own states in order and of eliminating the campaign of wild boycotts for ideological reasons that so detrimentally affect international economic relations, there can be much hope of international accords bearing fruit in the improvement of economic relations. Only in this manner can we secure the right for all to buy and sell on equal terms in the world market.

Besides this, the German Volk has made concrete demands in this context. I would be delighted if you, Mr. President, as one of the successors to the late President Wilson, would speak up for finally redeeming the promise that once led Germany to lay down its arms and to surrender to the so-called victors. I am speaking in this context, not so much of the countless billions of so-called reparation payments extorted from Germany, as of the return of the areas stolen from Germany. The German Volk has lost three million square kilometers of land both in Europe and overseas.

Moreover, unlike the colonies of other nations, the colonial possessions of the German Reich were not acquired by conquest but instead by treaties and purchase. President Wilson solemnly pledged his word that Germany's claims to its territorial possessions, as well as all others, would undergo just scrutiny. Instead, those nations that have already secured for themselves the mightiest colonial empires of all time have been awarded the German possessions. This causes our Volk great concern, especially today, and will increasingly in the future as well. It would be a noble deed if President Franklin Roosevelt fulfilled the promise made by President Woodrow Wilson. This would constitute a practical contribution to the moral consolidation of the world and the improvement of its economy.

21. Mr. Roosevelt declared in conclusion that "Heads of great governments in this hour are literally responsible for the fate of humanity in the coming years. They cannot fail to hear the prayers of their peoples to be protected from the foreseeable chaos of war." I, too, would be held "accountable."

Mr. President Roosevelt!

I certainly can see how the greatness of your country and its immense riches allow you to feel responsible for the fate of the entire world and for the fate of all peoples. However, Mr. Roosevelt, my situation is much more modest and limited. You have 135 million inhabitants living on nine and a half million square kilometers. Your land is one of untold riches and vast natural resources. It is fertile enough to sustain half a billion human beings and to provide them with all the necessities.

I once took over a state on the brink of ruin thanks to its ready trust in the assurances of the outside world and the feeble leadership of a democratic regime. Unlike America, where not even 15 persons live on one square kilometer, this state has 140 persons per square kilometer. The fertility of our soil does not equal yours. We lack the numerous natural resources that nature places at the disposal of your people. The billions of German savings, accumulated in the form of gold and currency during the years of peace, were extorted from us and taken away. We lost our colonies. In the year 1933, there were seven million unemployed in my country.

Millions worked part-time only, millions of peasants were reduced to misery, commerce was nearly destroyed, trade was ruined; in short, chaos reigned.

I have been able to accomplish only one task in the years since, Mr. President Roosevelt. I could not possibly feel myself responsible for the fate of a world that showed no sympathy for the woeful plight of my own Volk. I saw myself as a man called on by Providence to serve this Volk and to deliver it from its terrible hardships. Within the six and a half years now lying behind us, I lived day and night for the one thought: to awaken the inner forces dormant in this Volk forsaken by the outside world, to increase them to the utmost, and, finally, to use them in the salvation of our community.

I overcame chaos in Germany. I restored order, enormously raised production in all spheres of our national economy, labored to create substitutes for a number of the raw materials we lack, smoothed the way for new inventions, developed transportation, ordered the construction of superhighways. I had canals dug, colossal new factories brought to life. In all this, I strove to serve the development of the social community of my Volk, its education, and its culture. I succeeded in bringing those seven million unemployed, whose plight truly went to heart, back into a useful production process. Despite the difficulties faced, I managed to preserve his plot of soil for the German farmer, to rescue this for him. I brought about a rebirth of German trade and fostered commerce.

To preclude threats from the outside world, I have not only united the German Volk politically, I have rearmed it militarily. Further, I have sought to tear to shreds page upon page of this treaty, whose 448 articles represent the most dastardly outrage ever committed against a people and mankind. I have restored those provinces to the Reich that were stolen from it in 1919. I have led home to the Reich millions of despondent Germans torn from us. I have restored the one thousand year old, historic unity of the German *Lebensraum*. And I have labored to do so, Mr. President, without bloodshed and without bringing either upon my own Volk or other peoples the hardships of war.

I have done this all by myself, Mr. President, although a mere twenty-one years ago, I was but an unknown laborer and soldier of my Volk. And, hence, before history, I can truly claim the right to be counted among those men who, as individuals, do the best that can reasonably and in all fairness be expected of them.

Your task is infinitely easier, Mr. President. In 1933, when I became Reich chancellor, you became the President of the United States. From the start, you thereby placed yourself at the head of the largest and richest state in the world. It is your good fortune to have to nourish barely 15 human beings per square kilometer in your country. You have virtually never-ending natural resources at your disposal, more than anyone else in the world. The vastness of the terrain and the fertility of the soil are capable of providing each individual American with ten times the foodstuffs possible in Germany. Nature permits you to do this. While the inhabitants of your country number barely a third more than those of Greater Germany, they have 15 times its *Lebensraum* at their disposal.

Thus, the vastness of your country allows you to have the time and leisure to attend to problems of a universal nature. You hence conceive of the world as so small a place that you can intervene beneficially and effectively wherever this might be required. In this sense, your concerns and suggestions can be far more sweeping than mine. For my world is the one in which Providence has put me, Mr. President Roosevelt, and for which I am responsible. It is a much smaller one. It contains only my Volk. But I do believe I am thereby in a better position to serve those ends closer to the hearts of all of us: justice, welfare, progress, and peace for the entire community of man!

Hitler had instructed the German chargés d'affaires both in London and Warsaw to present to their host country's governments memoranda containing a formal abrogation of the Anglo-German Naval Agreement of 1935 and the 1934 Pact at the same time as he was giving the speech before the Reichstag. The American chargé d'affaires in Berlin received a transcript of the Reichstag speech as Germany's official response to Roosevelt's message. Hitler assuredly thought he had achieved a great deal in the two and a half hours he spoke before the Reichstag. He had relied both on tirades and sarcasm to give the English and the Poles a salutary shock by tearing up the two treaties.

Undoubtedly, they would now be reduced to subservience. The American President would be so embarrassed and disgraced by this forceful and cunning response to his ludicrous telegram that he would assuredly never again expose himself in a like manner. Instead, he would keep silent in the future, desist from speaking out against Hitler, and cautiously follow in the footsteps of a Brüning, von Papen, or Wels.

In spite of the great effort Hitler invested in his masterly speech, which represented beyond doubt an impressive rhetorical and mnemonic achievement, its effect abroad was negligible at best. The situation would not have been any different had he not said anything. What counted in the end were not so much words as deeds, and the Führer's actions spoke against him. Anyone who employed phrases as grandiose as Hitler did needed real power to back them up. In spite of impressive military displays, Germany's armed forces were obviously inferior to the united might of theAnglo-Saxon powers—not to forget their potential ally, Russia.

▶ September 1, 1939 *At the outbreak of the Polish war, President Roosevelt requested that the German armed forces target only military targets.*

At noon on September 1, the American chargé d'affaires in Berlin, Alexander Kirk, called at the foreign ministry to deliver a message from his President. Roosevelt had this note transmitted to all parties involved in the conflict. He urged bombardment to be restricted to purely military objectives:

> The ruthless bombing from the air of civilians in unforti-
> fied centers of population during the course of the hostilities
> that have raged in various quarters of the earth during the
> past few years, which has resulted in the maiming and in the
> death of thousands of defenseless men, women, and children
> has sickened the hearts of every civilized man and woman and
> has profoundly shocked the conscience of humanity. If resort
> is had to this form of inhuman barbarism during the period
> of the tragic conflagration with which the world is now con-
> fronted, hundreds of thousands of innocent human beings

who have no responsibility for and who are not even remotely participating in the hostilities that have now broken out will lose their lives. I am therefore addressing this urgent appeal to every government that may be engaged in hostilities publicly to affirm its determination that its armed forces shall in no event and under no circumstances undertake the bombardment from the air of civilian populations or of unfortified cities upon the understanding that these same rules of warfare will be scrupulously observed by all of their opponents. I request an immediate reply.

Franklin D. Roosevelt

While Hitler had ignored Roosevelt's two messages of August 24 and August 25, he now decided to answer in the following manner:

The opinion expressed in President Roosevelt's message, that it is a law of humanity to refrain in all circumstances during military operations from dropping bombs on non-military objectives, entirely coincides with my own view, which I have always held. I therefore agree without reservation to the proposal that the governments taking part in the present hostilities make a public declaration to that effect.

For my part, I have already stated publicly in my speech in the Reichstag today that the German air forces have received the order to confine their operations to military objectives. It is of course a condition for the maintenance of this order that the air forces of the enemy observe the same rule.

Adolf Hitler

▶ September 3, 1939 *President Roosevelt warned Hitler that the U.S. sympathized with Britain.*

The United States was still hesitant officially—because public opinion was not yet prepared—but unquestionably it was determined to side with Britain. For the time being, in a radio address on September 3, 1939, the American President expressed his hope that "the United States will keep out of this war" and concluded: "As long as it remains within my power to prevent, there will be no blackout of peace in the United States." Roosevelt stated:

> Tonight my single duty is to speak to the whole of America. Until 4:30 this morning, I had hoped against hope that some miracle would prevent a devastating war in Europe and bring to an end the invasion of Poland by Germany. For four long years, a succession of actual wars and constant crises have shaken the entire world and have threatened in each case to bring on the gigantic conflict that is today unhappily a fact.
>
> It is right that I should recall to your minds the consistent and at times successful efforts of your government in these crises to throw the full power of the United States into the cause of peace. In spite of spreading wars I think that we have every right and every reason to maintain as a national policy the fundamental moralities, the teachings of religion, and the continuation of efforts to restore peace—for some day, though the time may be distant, we can be of even greater help to a crippled humanity.
>
> It is right, too, to point out that the unfortunate events of these recent years have been based on the use of force or the threat of force. And it seems to me clear, even at the outbreak of this great war, that the influence of America should be consistent in seeking for humanity a final peace that will eliminate, as far as it is possible to do so, the continued use of force between nations.
>
> When peace has been broken anywhere, the peace of all countries everywhere is in danger.
>
> It is easy for you and me to shrug our shoulders and say that conflicts taking place thousands of miles from the continental United States, and, indeed, the whole American hemisphere, do not seriously affect the Americas—and that all the United States has to do is to ignore them and go about our own business. Passionately though we may desire detachment, we are forced to realize that every word that comes through the air, every ship that sails the sea, every battle that is fought does affect the American future.

Roosevelt's address left no doubt about the country's moral and political stance. Should England's position be seriously threatened, it was clear that America would enter the war on its behalf.

▸ February 29, 1940 *In the winter of 1940, President Roosevelt sent Sumner Welles to press the Italians and the Germans for peace.*

From late February to early March 1940, President Roosevelt's Under-Secretary of State, Sumner Welles, had announced to the Axis powers his intent to visit first Rome and then Berlin. Thereafter he planned to go to London and Paris, before returning to Rome.

On February 29, the Führer himself dictated guidelines for the "conversations with Mr. Sumner Welles." This extraordinary step notwithstanding, those German officials scheduled to meet with the American representative were in no need of special instructions. Göring, Hitler's fabled "best man," was surely intelligent enough not only to reiterate his master's arguments but to do so with zeal in an attempt to convince his caller that these ideas were indeed his own. However, Ribbentrop repeated Hitler's slogans with such monotony that Göring dubbed him "Germany's No. 1 parrot."

The reason Hitler troubled himself with penning the secret directive for the talks to be conducted with Sumner Welles was undoubtedly so that he could transmit these to the Italians and thereby influence their behavior towards the American emissary as well.

The guidelines to be observed read as follows:

1. In general I request that on the German side, reserve be exercised in the conversations, and that as far as possible, Mr. Sumner Welles be allowed to do the talking.

2. With regard to Germany's relations with the United States, it may be stressed that the present situation is unsatisfactory to both nations. The government of the Reich has done nothing for its part to bring about this development in the relations between the two countries; if by sending Mr. Sumner Welles to Berlin the American government is seeking to bring about a change in this regard, that would doubtless be in the interest of both countries.

3. Germany's viewpoint with regard to the international situation and the war has been made known to the world through my speeches. In particular, the following points are to be stressed: Germany did not declare war on the Western powers, but, on the contrary, they declared war on Germany.

England and France had no just reason at all for a war against Germany. Just as on the basis of the Monroe Doctrine the United States would firmly reject any interference by European governments in Mexican affairs, for example, Germany regards the eastern European area as her sphere of interest, and believes that she must come to an understanding with Russia alone, not along with England and France. After the end of the Polish campaign, Germany came to terms with Russia on eastern questions and thus conclusively safeguarded her European position by this restructuring in the East, which had become unavoidable. Then at the beginning of October, I again made one last offer of peace to England and France. Thereupon both these countries committed the biggest blunder they could possibly have made: they considered this offer a sign of weakness and rejected it with scorn.

Germany drew the only possible conclusion from this: she accepted the challenge of England and France. Since then, the war aim of England and France has been revealed more and more clearly. It consists, as it now openly stated, in the destruction of the German state and the dismemberment of the German people under a Versailles system even worse than before. Considering this development, Germany, as a state under attack, has nothing to say on the subject of peace. She is unshakable in her determination once and for all to break the will to annihilate [Germany] that now dominates British and French policy and to use the power of her 80 million people to this end. Not until the Anglo-French will to annihilate [Germany] has been broken can a new, really peaceful Europe be built. While in their unprecedented delusion England and France are more and more openly proclaiming as their war aim the annihilation of Germany and a new division of Europe into nations with rights and others without rights, even today Germany does not demand the annihilation of the British Empire and France; rather she regards the satisfaction of the vital interests of the great nations in their natural *Lebensraum* as a guarantee for the consolidation of Europe, in which there is room for small states that have proved their viability in the course of history as well as for the large ones. Germany is convinced that this goal can be attained only by a German victory.

4. As regards economic matters, it can be stated that the British blockade is not of decisive importance to Germany. In both food and raw materials Germany can defeat any blockade by her self-sufficient economy and her trade with European countries, with Russia, and by way of Russia with Japan and a large part of the world. National Socialist Germany is not at all opposed to a world economy. The trade policy of the world forced upon her the development of her own self-contained economy. Only with its attainment, which is coming ever closer to realization, will Germany be in a position to participate in the world economy again as a sound partner.

5. A discussion of single concrete political questions, such as the question of a future Polish state, is to be avoided as much as possible. In case the other side brings up subjects of this kind, the reply should be that such questions are decided by me. It is self-evident that it is entirely out of the question for Germany to discuss the subject of Austria and the Protectorate of Bohemia and Moravia, which has constantly been brought up by England and France.

6. Attention may be called to Germany's completely changed international position as compared to 1914. All statements are to be avoided that could be interpreted by the other side to mean that Germany is in any way interested at present in discussing the possibility of peace. I request rather

that Mr. Sumner Welles not be given the slightest reason
to doubt that Germany is determined to end this war victoriously and that the German people—united today as
never before in their thousand-year history—and their
leadership are unshakable in their confidence in victory.

Adolf Hitler

Hitler's intent in pursuing the strategy indicated above was an obvious one: he wished to convince Sumner Welles of his "unshakable"
determination to fight and his certainty he would win. This, the American would duly relate to London. The unity and determination of the
German people he portrayed were to dissuade the English from further
opposing Germany.

The English did not take fright as desired, since the supposed "unity" of
the one belligerent rarely outweighs the numerical superiority of the arsenal
commanded by the other in a real conflict. The old myth still dominated
Hitler's thinking: the idea that the divisiveness of Germany had prevented
its rise to world power and had precipitated its fall. In the Second World
War, the German people were "united," i.e., they resigned themselves to
Hitler's rule, and yet the outcome was no different. Germany was not in
a position in either of the world wars to succeed in an aggressive policy of
expansion opposed by the remainder of the world.

► March 2, 1940 *The Welles mission continued.*

On March 2, Hitler received the American Under-Secretary of State,
Sumner Welles, at the Reich Chancellery in the presence of the American chargé d'affaires in Berlin, Kirk, and of von Ribbentrop and Meissner.
Although he himself had ordered that "Mr. Sumner Welles be allowed to
do the talking," Hitler could not restrain himself for long. Barely had the
American made a few introductory statements, when Hitler found himself dominating the conversation. In long monologues, he lamented how
England and France were bent on destruction, how America was incom-
prehensibly blockading the transport of goods to Germany. He reiterated
details of German-American financial relations and of his own ever so "generous" proposals for disarmament. Having exhausted these topics, Hitler
proceeded to lecture Sumner Welles on the formation of "public opinion."

He dwelt on "historical memories," spoke of political interests and various theories of international trade. Afterwards, he sought to document his familiarity with the American scene by referring to the Monroe Doctrine and the 1932 Ottawa Conference. These examples led him right up to the outstanding issue of the return of Germany's former colonies.

Sumner Welles responded to Hitler's lecture. He also briefly philosophized on politics and economics, and then came to the point, asking what precisely Hitler's intentions were regarding disarmament and economic distress in the event of a peaceful settlement. Hitler naturally immediately retorted by proposing international conferences that, given certain prerequisites, might serve as a means for solving such problems:

> The Führer repeated that the decisive thing was that it was not a matter of the German war aims but the war aims of the others who were seeking the annihilation of Germany. He could assure Mr. Sumner Welles that Germany would never be annihilated. He had been a soldier on the Western front for four years, and was of the opinion that Germany would not have been defeated then either if there had been another regime at the helm. It was not a question of whether Germany would be annihilated; Germany would know how to defend herself from annihilation, and in the very worst case everyone would be annihilated.
>
> Today Germany was in a totally different situation from the last war and he, the Führer, had made all preparations, and made them thoroughly, in order to be able to break the determination of others to annihilate Germany. The German war aim—"peace"—stood opposed to the war aim of the others—"annihilation." The German people, who had learned from the terrible experience of 1918, stood behind him to a man. Anybody who wanted to establish peace had to induce Germany's opponents to abandon their war aims of annihilation. Germany was of the view that America, even with the best will in the world—which was recognized by the Germans without question—would find it difficult to attain this goal.

Sumner Welles thereupon thanked Hitler for the "open and candid way in which he had made his statements" and assured him he would relay the thoughts expressed to President Roosevelt. The American government nevertheless hoped that "all" parties to the present conflict were spared destruction rather than only Germany. Hitler's rhetoric had apparently failed to impress the American. On a side note, Sumner Welles was the last Anglo-Saxon statesman Hitler was to speak to in person before his death with the exception of the American chargé d'affaires, who remained in Berlin until December 1941.

▶ June 15, 1940 *Hitler, who usually did well in one-to-one press interviews, explained his views of German-U.S. relations. Hitler's description of the Monroe Doctrine and, indeed most of U.S. governmental structures, was hardly accurate.*

On June 15, Hitler granted the American journalist Karl von Wiegand an interview. This was destined to be the last occasion on which Hitler had the opportunity to explain himself to a representative of the Anglo-Saxon press. In Germany, the *Völkischer Beobachter* published the following account of the meeting with Wiegand:

> On Germany's attitude toward America, the Führer declared that Germany is one of the few states that has to the present time refrained from interfering in America's affairs. "Germany has pursued no territorial or political interests on the American continent in the past, nor does it at present. Whoever maintains the contrary is deliberately lying, for whatever reasons. Therefore, however the American continent chooses to fashion its life," the Führer emphasized, "it is of no interest to us. This applies not only to North America but to South America also."
>
> On the Monroe Doctrine, the Führer remarked: "I do not believe that a doctrine such as Monroe proclaimed could or can be interpreted as a unilateral statement of non-intervention. For the aim of the Monroe Doctrine was not to prevent the interference of European states in American affairs—Britain, by the way, continues to involve itself there, as it possesses

enormous territorial and political interests in America—but rather that, in turn, America should not involve itself in European matters. The fact that George Washington himself issued a similar warning to the American people affirms the logic and the reasonableness of this interpretation. Therefore I say: America to the Americans, Europe to the Europeans!"

Questioned as to Germany's stance on the armament program announced by President Roosevelt, the Führer replied: "I look to the Monroe Doctrine in answering this question as well. I do not pass judgment on the U.S.A.'s armament program—I am not interested in it. I have been forced to work on the greatest armament program in the world for years now, and thus I can well differentiate fantastic talk from the real opportunities of practical life. There appear to be many fantastic opinions currently in circulation on this point."

To the question of an American intervention by supplying planes and war materials, the Führer replied: "An American intervention by mass deliveries of planes and war materials will not change the outcome of the war. There is no need to enumerate reasons. Reality will be the ultimate judge." The Führer summarized his opinion on the supposed existence of a German fifth column, widely propagated in the news and in various reports in America, in the following manner: "I cannot imagine what precisely this so-called fifth column is supposed to be, for it appears not to exist other than in the imagination of lunatics, or as a bogeyman invented for transparent purposes by unscrupulous propaganda.

When incapable governments first drive their peoples into war and then witness a pitiful collapse, it is only understandable that they should prefer to lay the blame on someone else. The main goal of this slogan is to create nothing other than a catch-all term for the domestic opposition that naturally exists in all countries. Such an opposition has nothing at all to do with Germany. Quite to the contrary! They tend to be radical nationalists, or Communists of an internationalist orientation, or pacifists and other opponents of war. Alas, because these politicians seem incapable of dealing with their own opposition in a decent manner, they accuse these elements of high treason. Thus they attempt to hide illegal methods beneath a cloak of patriotic rhetoric and to justify this before the eyes of the world by coining the blood-curdling term "fifth column."

Our enemies will lose this war not because of some fifth column, but because they have corrupt, unscrupulous politicians with no vision. They will lose it because their military organization is bad; their leadership in this war is truly a miserable one. Germany will win this war because the German Volk knows it is fighting for a just cause, because the German military organization and leadership are the better ones, and because we have the best army and the best equipment.

It was never my intention or my goal," so the Führer further explained, "to destroy the British Empire. On the contrary, even before the outbreak of the war that Britain and France have unleashed, I presented proposals to the British government in which I went so far as to offer Great Britain the Reich's assistance for [the protection of] the existence of the Empire. I asked nothing more of Britain than to regard and treat Germany as an equal, that Britain protect Germany's coast should we become involved in a war, and that the German colonies be returned. And I will get them back! In London, they declared and wrote publicly that National Socialism must be destroyed, that Germany must be divided and completely disarmed and rendered powerless. Never have I expressed similar goals or intentions with regard to Britain.

Once Britain began to lose battle upon battle, the rulers in Britain pleaded with America, tears in their eyes. They declared that Germany was threatening the British Empire, that it was trying to destroy it. There is one thing that will be destroyed in this war, namely, the capitalist clique that has been ready and is ready, motivated by base personal interests, to destroy millions of human beings. But it will be done—of this I am convinced—not by us, but by their own peoples."

The fashion in which Hitler chose to interpret the Monroe Doctrine on this occasion was a shrewd one. His mistake was only in believing that such *bons mots* would make an impression on the Anglo-Saxon world. His claim to be working on the "greatest armament program in the world" may have aroused considerable mirth.

Hitler apparently aimed to dissuade America from actively assisting the British in the future. The latter were to be made aware that they stood alone in the world. Should they persist in refusing to submit and fail to arrive at a peace settlement with Germany, they would be left to the mercy of the dreadful German war machine. Moreover, so Hitler argued, the British statesmen faced the distinct possibility that the populace might well rise up against its leadership to protest involvement in a senseless debacle.

In spite of the great number of interviews Hitler granted Anglo-Saxon journalists in the years 1932 to 1940, he never gained any insight into the English mentality, so engrossed was he in his own ideas during these talks.

▶ August 29, 1941 *Hitler had nothing but scorn for the Atlantic Charter.*

On August 29, the Führer headquarters published a communiqué on the talks that was obviously intended to counteract the Atlantic declaration of August 14 by Roosevelt and Churchill. It read as follows:

> The Führer and the Duce met at the Führer's headquarters in the period between August 25 and 29.
>
> During the talks, which took place at the Führer's headquarters, all military and political questions concerning the development and the duration of the war were discussed in great detail. These questions were examined in the spirit of the close comradeship and the feeling of being united by a common fate that are characteristic of the relations of the two Axis powers. The talks were suffused by the unchangeable will of the two peoples and their leaders to bring the war to a victorious end.
>
> The new European order that will result from this victory should, as far as possible, eliminate the causes that in the past have led to the European wars.
>
> The destruction of the Bolshevik danger and of plutocratic exploitation will create the possibility of a peaceful, harmonious, and fruitful cooperation between all peoples of the European continent in the political, as well as in the economic and cultural spheres.

In the course of this visit, the Führer and the Duce went to significant points on the eastern front. An Italian division deployed in the struggle against Bolshevism was inspected. Field Marshal von Rundstedt greeted the Führer and the Duce on their visit to the southern front. In addition, visits to the headquarters of the *Reichsmarschall* and the commander in chief of Army Group South took place.

The Italian ambassador to Berlin, Dino Alfieri, the chief of the Italian armed forces general staff, General Cavallero, the cabinet chief envoy Anfuso, who substituted for Foreign Minister Count Ciano (who was unable to come because of an illness), Generals Marras and Gandin, as well as a series of other high-ranking general staff officers, accompanied the Duce. The German ambassador von Mackensen and the German military attaché to Rome, Lieutenant General von Tintelen, likewise accompanied the Duce on his tour. On the German side, Reich Foreign Minister von Ribbentrop and the chief of the high command of the *Wehrmacht*, Field Marshal Keitel, participated in the political and military discussions.

▸ December 7, 1941 *Hitler was very pleased with the Japanese attack on Pearl Harbor.*

On the night of December 7, he sat pensive at the Wolfsschanze headquarters and stared ahead. Then news of the Japanese bombing of the American naval base at Pearl Harbor on Hawaii arrived. Without an official declaration of war, Japanese bomber formations had attacked on a Sunday—just as Hitler would have done. Now, that was news to his liking! He slapped his thighs, jumped up as if electrified, and cried: "Finally!"

Hitler had neither foreseen nor anticipated this Japanese action. Just as *he* usually did with *his* allies, the Japanese had left him in the dark regarding their intentions. Hitler had never encouraged them to attack the United States; instead, he had advocated proceeding against England, for example, by attacking Singapore. Moreover, the Tripartite Pact of September 27, 1940, between Germany, Italy, and Japan had been intended to prevent involving the United States in the war.

In the past months, Hitler had attempted to induce the Japanese to move against Russia. He had hoped that this would provide relief for the German troops, but the Japanese had declined. Instead, they had now opened hostilities against the United States; unlike Hitler, the Japanese knew that England and the United States formed one entity.

Formally, the Japanese-American conflict did not oblige Hitler to declare war on the United States according to the stipulations of the Tripartite Pact, since the United States was not yet involved in the European theater of war as a belligerent power. However, as Hitler told the worried von Ribbentrop, in the long run things could "not continue without a German-American war." This was true, of course, but it was still odd that the Tripartite Pact would result in Germany itself declaring war on America first!

On the other hand, the American declaration of war on Germany would probably have been a question of days anyway, now that the attack on Pearl Harbor finally motivated the American people to take part in a conflict that was far away from their minds previously. The declaration of war on Germany by Chiang Kai-shek's China, which was transmitted on December 9, also made this clear.

For Hitler, the Japanese attack came just at the right time. It diverted attention from his own failures and from the catastrophic situation in the east. He regarded it as a turning point, as if Providence were beckoning him with her finger, and resolved to press on with full force and deliver a formal victory speech before the Reichstag.

Later, he would frequently stress that Japan's entry into the war could not have come at a more "opportune time." The mood of the Germans, who had felt "at a real low point because of the Russian winter," had been greatly improved by the Japanese intervention. Hitler worried that Roosevelt might possibly beat him to a declaration of war. He wanted to be the one to open hostilities.

► February 14, 1942 *Hitler expressed his view of the United States of America.*

Hitler also spoke of the American "lack of culture" and the "colonization of England by Germans."

When Mr. President Roosevelt stutters about culture, then I can only say: what Mr. President Roosevelt calls culture, we call lack of culture. To us, it is a stupid joke. I have already declared a few times that just one of Beethoven's symphonies contains more culture than all of America has managed to produce up to now!

Strictly speaking, we colonized England and not the other way around.

War on the Eastern Front, Winter 1941–42
The German army was not ready for the Russian winter.

XIV

Hitler Fights His War

After the end of the Polish operations, Hitler began to consider how to achieve his often-stated goals for his Germany. He smashed the Western allies in 1940 but did not succeed in ending the war. He attacked the Soviet Union thinking it would collapse easily. The Soviet Union did not collapse and the Western powers revived. Hitler had lost the war but refused to admit it.

▸ October 9, 1939 *As soon as Hitler's armies had secured Poland, he began looking west. Hitler had made what he considered an honorable peace offer to the British and waited for a response. If there was no positive answer, he intended to attack and destroy the armies of Britain and France.*

On October 9, Hitler lost patience since he had still not received word from the British. If they did not promptly make it "apparent" that they were prepared to refrain from war, he would be exceedingly sorry to drive them "back to the Thames." In his anger, Hitler swiftly wrote his sixth war directive:

Directive No. 6 for the Conduct of the War

1. If it should become apparent in the near future that England, and, under England's leadership, also France, are not willing to bring the war to an end, I am determined to act vigorously and aggressively without delay.

2. If we wait much longer, not only will Belgian and perhaps also Dutch neutrality be lost to the advantage of the Western powers, but the military strength of our enemies will grow on an increasing scale, the neutrals' confidence in a final German victory will dwindle, and Italy will not be encouraged to join us as a military ally.

3. Therefore I give the following orders for further military operations:

   a. Preparations are to be made for an attack on the northern wing of the western front through the territoy of Luxembourg, Belgium, and Holland. This attack must be carried out with as much strength and at as early a date as possible.

   b. The purpose of this attack will be to defeat as strong a part of the French field army as possible as well as the allies fighting by its side, and at the same time to gain as large an area as possible in Holland, Belgium, and northern France as a base for conducting a promising air and sea war against England and as a protective zone for the vital Ruhr area.

   c. The timing of the attack depends on the readiness of tanks and motorized units for use—this must be speeded up by every possible effort, especially considering the weather conditions then prevailing and the weather prospects ahead.

4. The *Luftwaffe* is to prevent the Anglo-French air force from attacking our own army, and, if necessary, to give direct support to the army's advance. In this connection, it will also be essential to prevent the establishment of the Anglo-French air force in Belgium and Holland, as well as British troop landings there.

5. The naval command must concentrate for the duration of this attack entirely in giving direct and indirect support to the operations of the army and *Luftwaffe*.

6. Apart from these preparations for starting the attack in the west according to plan, army and *Luftwaffe* must be ready at any time and, with increasing strength, to meet

an Anglo-French invasion of Belgium as far forward on Belgian territory as possible, and to occupy as much of Holland as possible in the direction of the west coast.

7. The cover explanation for these preparations must be that they are merely precautionary measures in view of the threatening concentration of French and English forces on the French-Luxembourg and French-Belgian borders.

8. I request the commanders in chief to give me, as soon as possible, detailed reports of their plans on the basis of this directive and to keep me currently informed, via the *Wehrmacht* high command (*OKW*), of the state of the preparations.

Adolf Hitler

In addition to this directive, Hitler also drafted a lengthy memorandum on October 9. He sought to justify the offensive in the West by referring to the 1648 Peace of Westphalia. Ever since then, a confrontation had been certain and had merely been postponed. Developments had come to a head in 1939, and any further delay would doubtless be to Germany's detriment. Hence, the upcoming conflict had to be viewed as a matter of course.

The German objective in this war must include the final military destruction of the West, i.e., the destruction of the power and capability of the West to oppose yet again the consolidation of German statehood and the further development of the German Volk within Europe.

No treaty and no agreement can permanently assure the continued neutrality of Soviet Russia. At this time, indications are against their abandonment of this neutrality. Things might well look different eight months, or one or more years, hence.

On October 10 at 11:00 a.m., Hitler read this memorandum to Göring, Raeder, Brauchitsch, Keitel, and Halder. Thereafter, he handed them the information and insisted on the immediate start of the offensive in the West, i.e., before the beginning of winter. The generals were shocked at Hitler's proposals, not only because a winter campaign went contrary to all previous military tradition, not to mention common sense. They were also haunted by memories of a similar, and ill-fated, move in the First World War and greatly feared a second Verdun. The experts' misgivings failed to dissuade Hitler. He had other things on his mind than arguing with disgruntled generals.

▸ March 1, 1940 *Hitler did not attack the West in the winter of 1939–1940 because of bad weather. However, he planned an attack in the spring and, in order to protect his flank, intended to attack Denmark and Norway.*

On March 1, Hitler signed the directive for the "Weser Exercise" (*Fall Weserübung*), which detailed the following:

1. The development of the situation in Scandinavia requires the making of all preparations for the occupation of Denmark and Norway by a part of the *Wehrmacht*. This operation Weser Exercise should prevent British encroachment on Scandinavia and the Baltic. Further it should guarantee our ore base in Sweden and give our navy and *Luftwaffe* a wider starting line against Britain. The part that the navy and the *Luftwaffe* will have to play, within the limits of their capabilities, is to protect the operation against the interference of British naval and air striking forces. In view of our military and political force in comparison with that of the Scandinavian states, the force to be employed in Weser Exercise will be kept as small as possible. The numerical weakness will be balanced by daring actions and surprise execution. On principle, we will do our utmost to make the operation appear as a peaceful occupation, the object of which is the military protection of the neutrality of the Scandinavian states. Corresponding demands will be transmitted to the governments at the beginning of the occupation. If necessary, naval and air demonstrations will provide the necessary emphasis. If, in spite of this, we meet resistance, all military means will be used to crush it.

2. I put in charge of the preparations and the conduct of the operation against Denmark and Norway the commanding general of the XXI Army Corps, General of Infantry von Falkenhorst. In questions of the conduct of operations, the above-named is directly under my orders. The staff is to be completed from all three branches of the *Wehrmacht*. The forces that will be selected for the purpose of the Weser Exercise will be under separate command. They will not be allocated for other operational theaters. The part of the *Luftwaffe* detailed for the purpose of the Weser Exercise will be tactically under the orders of Group XXI. After the completion of their task, they will revert to the command of the commander in chief, *Luftwaffe*. The employment of the forces that are under direct naval and *Luftwaffe* command will take place in agreement with the commander of Group XXI. The administration and supply of the forces posted to Group XXI will be ensured by the *Wehrmacht* branches themselves at the direction of the commander.

The crossing of the Danish border and the landings in Norway must take place simultaneously. I emphasize that the operations must be prepared as quickly as possible. In case the enemy seizes the initiative against Norway, we must be able to apply immediately our own countermeasures. It is most important that the Scandinavian states as well as the Western opponents should be taken by surprise by our measures. All preparations, particularly those of transport and of readiness, drafting and embarkation of the troops, must be made with this factor in mind. In case the preparations for embarkation can no longer be kept secret, the leaders and the troops will be given fictitious objectives. The troops may be acquainted with the actual objectives only after putting to sea.

► May 10, 1940 *On this day, Hitler launched his armies in a massive assault in the west.*

On the same day, Hitler composed a "Proclamation to the Soldiers of the Western Front." It read:

Berlin, May 10, 1940

The hour of the most decisive battle for the future of the German nation has come. For over 300 years it has been the ambition of British and French rulers to prevent a real consolidation of Europe and, in particular, to keep Germany weak and impotent. To this end, France alone has declared war on Germany thirty-one times in the course of two centuries. For decades it has also been the ambition of the British rulers of the world to prevent Germany, under any circumstances, from attaining unity while denying the Reich those vital goods necessary to sustain a people of eighty million. England and France have pursued this policy regardless of which regime ruled in Germany at any point in time. Their target was always the German Volk.

Men of responsibility in those countries proclaimed this ambition openly. Germany was to be shattered and dissolved into many small states. Then the Reich would lose its political power and hence its means of securing for the German Volk its vital rights upon this earth. For this reason, all my offers of peace were rejected and war was declared on us on September 3 of last year. The German Volk harbors neither hatred nor animosity toward either the English or the French people.

Today, however, it faces the question whether it desires to live or rather to perish. Within a few weeks, the valiant troops of our armies have defeated the Polish enemy sent up to the front by Britain and France. Thereby they have eliminated the danger in the east. Consequently, Britain and France determined to assault Germany in the north. Ever since April 9, the *Wehrmacht* has quelled this attempt from its very beginnings.

Now what we have envisioned as a threatening danger throughout the past months has come to pass. Britain and France aim to push for the Ruhr territory through Holland and Belgium while undertaking a gigantic effort at diversion in southeast Europe.

Soldiers of the Western Front!
Your hour has come.
The battle beginning on this day will determine the fate of
the German nation for the next one thousand years.
Now do your duty.
The German Volk is with you in its desire for victory.

Adolf Hitler

The hour had struck for the launching of the offensive in the west. If one believed Hitler's words, this campaign was to determine Germany's fate for the "next one thousand years." According to his estimates, one million German soldiers would lay down their lives in the attack. In his mind, this was not a matter of great concern! The enemy stood to lose at least an equivalent number of its men. And since Greater Germany boasted a population of 80 million, a sacrifice of one million seemed of little consequence to the Führer.

▸ May 14, 1940 *The great attack ground on, achieving a spectacular break-through.*

On May 14, German tank units broke through the French lines in the Sedan-Charleville section of the front and turned to the west. Motorized divisions followed in their wake. Infantry units were to secure the breakthrough in the south and to constitute a southern front along the line Aisne-Somme.

On this day, Hitler issued his eleventh directive for the conduct of the war:

1) The course of the offensive thus far shows that the enemy has failed to recognize in time the basic idea of our operation. He is still bringing up strong forces to the Namur-Antwerp line and seems to be neglecting the sector in front of Army Group A.

2) This situation and the rapid forcing of the Meuse crossings in the Army Group A sector have produced the first prerequisite for achieving a great success on the lines of Directive No. 10 by a thrust executed in a north-westerly

direction north of the Aisne with a concentration of the strongest forces. The troops fighting north of the Liège-Namur line will then have the mission of tying down and diverting as strong an enemy force as possible by an attack with their own forces.

3) On the north flank the power of resistance of the Netherlands army has proven to be stronger than was anticipated. Political as well as military considerations require that this resistance be broken speedily. It will be the mission of the army to bring about rapidly the collapse of Fortress Holland by means of adequate forces from the south in conjunction with the attack against the eastern front.

4) All available motorized divisions are to be brought into the operational area of Army Group A as quickly as possible. The armored and motorized divisions of Army Group B must also be released as soon as operational actions are no longer possible there and the situation permits and be brought up to the left attacking wing.

5) The mission of the *Luftwaffe* will be to concentrate strong offensive and defensive forces for employment in the sector of Army Group A as the point of main effort, in order to prevent the bringing up of additional enemy forces to the offensive front and to support this front directly. In addition, the rapid conquest of Fortress Holland is to be facilitated through a deliberate weakening of the forces hitherto operating before the Sixth Army.

6) The navy will operate within the framework of the possibilities open to it against sea communications in the Hoofden and in the channel.

Adolf Hitler

It was evident that Hitler intended to conduct the war in the manner he felt it ought to have been led from 1914 on. This conviction had already been apparent from his words to the generals on May 23, 1939: "Had the navy been stronger at the beginning of the World War, or had the army attacked the harbors along the English Channel, the outcome of the war would have been a different one." The Second World War afforded Hitler the opportunity to prove his theory. The battles for Flanders and France demonstrated that, although the *Wehrmacht* prevailed in the taking of the harbors, this changed neither the course of events nor the outcome of the war. Hitler's appeal to the *Luftwaffe* to facilitate "the rapid conquest of fortress Holland" was realized that same day. German pilots made terror attacks on the center of Rotterdam, with the result that the Dutch army offered to surrender on the evening of May 14. By 11:30 the next morning, the capitulation was signed.

On May 15 as well, Hitler issued the following proclamation to the soldiers fighting in Holland:

> Soldiers of the Dutch Theater of War!
>
> In five days you have attacked a strong, well-prepared army that doggedly defended itself behind apparently invincible barriers and military fortifications. You have eliminated its air force and finally you have forced its surrender. Yours is an accomplishment of a truly unique nature. The future will demonstrate its military significance. This success has been rendered possible only through your exemplary cooperation, through the determination of your leadership, as well as through the valor of the individual soldier.
>
> This is true especially of the men of the death-defying parachutist and airborne troops and their heroic mission.
>
> In the name of the German Volk, I convey to you my gratitude and my admiration.
>
> Adolf Hitler

On May 16, Hitler conferred with Göring and Jeschonnek, the chief of staff of the *Luftwaffe*. One of the topics discussed in the talk, lasting from 4:00 p.m. to 6:30 p.m., was the possible reinforcement of the *Luftwaffe* at Narvik after the swift success encountered in Holland.

On May 17, Halder noted in his diary: "Führer terribly nervous. Surprised by his own success, he fears going too far; would like to put us on a leash."

By May 18, Halder was forced to concede that it was actually not the general staff, but Hitler himself who determined how to proceed. As Jodl remarked in his notes, it was "a day of tension." Hitler had found out that, contrary to his express orders, infantry divisions were continuing to march westward, instead of "speedily building up a flank to the south." This latter measure aimed to preclude a re-establishment of links by the French with the divisions cut off earlier. Brauchitsch and Halder were summoned immediately, so Jodl recorded, "and were brusquely told to take the necessary steps immediately." Halder saw the matter differently and confided to his diary: "He [Hitler] rages and cries we are ruining the entire campaign for him."

▶ May 20, 1940 *Having outflanked the Allied armies, Hitler's forces drove to victory.*

On May 20, German tank units reached the channel coast at Abbéville, thus cutting off the Allied troops fighting in Flanders and Artois. The "greatest offensive operation of all time," as the *Wehrmacht* high command (*OKW*) report had entitled it, was beginning to bear fruit. Hitler was "beside himself with joy" and had "words of the greatest appreciation for the German armed forces and their leadership. Now concerns himself with peace treaty that shall read: return of the territories robbed from Germany for over 400 years and other assets. First, negotiations in the Forest of Compiègne as in 1918. English can have a separate peace at any time after a return of the colonies."

This was precisely how Hitler envisioned the further course of events. In all earnestness he was convinced that, after "attacking the harbors along the channel," England and France would accept that the war had been decided and would come to see that a peace settlement with Germany was in their own best interest.

At any rate, Hitler took care to pursue the campaign in France. It was still May 20 when he issued the following instructions to the army on how to proceed:

> 1st act: Destruction of the enemy north of the Somme and winning of the coast.

> 2nd act: Advance between Oise and the sea up to the Seine.

3rd act: Main attack on both sides of Reims in a south-
westerly direction, the right flank east of Paris accompanied
by light forces.

In the intermission of this three-act play, Hitler hoped to receive an
Allied offer of capitulation. He quickly abandoned his earlier plan to allow twenty Italian divisions to take part in the action at the section of
the Maginot Line running approximately along the upper course of the
Rhine. As he had made known before, he had no intention of sharing the
glory with anyone.

On May 21, news reached Berlin that measures were being taken to evacuate the British Expeditionary Force from various ports along the channel.
Naturally this item caught Hitler's eye. If the English chose to evacuate the
continent voluntarily, then this would eliminate the necessity of driving
them "back to the Thames," as he had promised. This in turn convinced
Hitler that nothing stood in the way of a friendly settlement with England
any longer. To hurry matters along, he determined to allow the English to
escape, instead of seeing to their destruction in Flanders. This gesture would
surely persuade them of his good intentions. In eternal gratitude, England
would finally accept Germany's hand extended in friendship.

On May 24, Hitler flew to a meeting at the headquarters of Army Group
A, then located at Charleville, in the company of Jodl and Schmundt. Once
there, he issued the necessary instructions and ordered the tank divisions
to halt at the channel coast. Hitler was in high spirits; a peace settlement
appeared to be within grasp. Speaking to the generals gathered at Charleville, he claimed the war would be over in six weeks. Now it was imperative
to conclude a "reasonable peace with France." This would open the way
towards "an understanding with England." According to the recollections
of General Blumentritt, Hitler's ill-concealed admiration for the British
Empire came as a complete surprise to his audience, since the generals were
not familiar with this pro-British orientation of their Führer. To their astonishment, they heard him speak with reverence of "the necessity for its
existence and the civilization that England had brought this world."

All he wanted from England, so Hitler continued, was that it should
respect Germany's position on the continent. It was desirable, though not
essential, that Germany's colonies be restored. It was his goal to conclude
a peace with England on this basis, which he could reconcile with his
concept of honor.

This idea was not by any means new. Napoleon I and Wilhelm II, ignorant both of Great Britain's position and the real power structures in the world, had already propagated the notion that the British Empire, in view of its mastery of the lands overseas, ought to leave the continent to mainland powers.

Despite their differences, Hitler's and Napoleon's shared admiration for the empire was undermined by the perpetual affronts and provocation of Britain. Hitler carried matters a step further yet than the French emperor by allowing, in a "magnanimous" gesture, for the escape of the British Expeditionary Force, which would otherwise have faced virtually certain destruction. This move greatly perplexed and angered Hitler's generals. Von Brauchitsch, for example, had already ordered several divisions to join Army Group B in the north, naturally without requesting express permission. Hitler was outraged and made a scene, demanding that Brauchitsch immediately rescind the order.

That evening, Hitler ordered the fast forward units moving towards the channel to halt on reaching the coast. They were not to venture beyond a line running from Sandez to St. Omer and Gravelines. This was in keeping with Hitler's firm resolve to spare the British as much as possible.

On May 24 as well, Hitler issued "Directive No. 13 for the Conduct of the War."

1. The next aim of the operations is the destruction of the French, English and Belgian forces that have been encircled in Artois and in Flanders through a concentric attack by our northern wing and the speedy occupation and securing of the channel coast there. It will be the mission of the *Luftwaffe* to break all resistance by the encircled forces of the enemy, prevent the escape of the English forces across the channel, and secure the south flank of Army Group A. The fight against enemy air forces is to be continued at every favorable opportunity.

2. The operation of the army to destroy the enemy forces in France, which is to follow as quickly as possible, is to be prepared in three phases.

1st Phase: A thrust between the sea and the Oise to the Lower Seine below Paris with the object of accompanying and protecting the later main operation with weak forces on the right flank. If the situation and the available reserves allow, efforts are to be made even before the conclusion of the battle in Artois and in Flanders to take possession of the territory between the Somme and the Oise by a concentric attack in the direction of Montdidier and thereby prepare and facilitate the later thrust to the lower Seine.

2nd Phase: An attack with the bulk of the army, including strong armored and motorized forces in a southeasterly direction past Rheims on both sides with the object of defeating the bulk of the French army in the triangle Paris-Metz-Belfort and of bringing about the collapse of the Maginot Line.

3rd Phase: A supplementing of this main operation at the appropriate time, by a secondary operation with weaker forces that will breakthrough at the Maginot Line at its weakest point between St. Avold and Sarreguemines in the direction of Nancy Lunéville. In addition, depending on the development of the situation, an attack across the upper Rhine may be planned provided that not more than 8 to 10 divisions are to be committed to it.

3. The mission of the *Luftwaffe*

   (a) Independent of the operations in France, the *Luftwaffe*—as soon as sufficient forces are at its disposal—will be given complete freedom to carry on the fight against the English homeland. It is to be opened with a devastating attack in reprisal for the English attacks against the Ruhr area.

   Targets for attacks will be determined by the commander in chief of the *Luftwaffe* according to principles contained in Directive No. 9 and the supplements thereto which will be issued by *Wehrmacht* high command (*OKW*). The date and the proposed plan of operations are to be reported to me.

(b) With the beginning of the main operation of the army in the direction of Rheims, it will be the task of the *Luftwaffe*, in addition to maintaining air superiority, to give direct support to the attack, to destroy newly arriving enemy formations, to prevent regrouping, and in particular to secure the west flank of the offensive front. As far as necessary, cooperation is to be given in the breakthrough at the Maginot Line.

(c) Further, the high command of the *Luftwaffe* will consider by what means the air defense can be strengthened in areas that at present are being most heavily attacked by the enemy, through the use of additional forces from areas that previously have been less endangered. In so far as the interests of the navy are affected hereby, the commander in chief of the navy will participate.

4. Missions of the Navy: previously restricting regulations are rescinded, and the navy will be given complete operational freedom in the waters around England and off the French coast. The commander in chief of the navy will submit a proposal for delimiting the sea areas in which the combat measures permitted for the blockade may be applied.

I reserve for myself the decision as to whether and in what form a public announcement of the blockade shall be made.

5. I request the commanders in chief to submit to me orally or in writing their plans based upon this directive.

Adolf Hitler

The further course of events proved that only the section of the directive dealing with the subjugation of France was meant seriously. Obviously, the "annihilation of the forces encircled" applied to all enemy forces other than the British, as was manifest in the recent order to arrest tank movement along the coast. Months would pass before Hitler finally launched a determined strike against the British mainland in September, 1940. Despite his newly found resolve, the "Battle of Britain" turned out to be a complete failure.

May 25 was a day of repose. Apparently, the German tanks were to have a "good rest." Hitler used the momentary quiet to pen yet another letter to Mussolini.

On May 26, Halder described the situation as follows in his diary: "By highest orders, tanks and motorized units stand as though frozen in their tracks." In the evening of this day, Hitler finally allowed "the tank units and infantry divisions to advance from the west in the direction of Tournai, Cassel, and Dunkirk." By this time, the two-day lull in the fighting had permitted the Allied units to organize and to mount their defenses properly.

▸ June 5, 1940 *Hitler announced his great victory.*

In celebrating what he termed the "greatest battle of all time," Hitler issued the following two appeals, one to the German people, another to the soldiers of the army in the west:

> Führer Headquarters, June 5, 1940
>
> To the German Volk!
>
> Our soldiers have emerged victorious from this greatest battle of all time.
>
> In a few weeks, we have taken over 1.2 million enemies as prisoners of war. Holland and Belgium have capitulated. The British Expeditionary Force has been largely destroyed, the remainder either taken prisoner or driven from the continent. Three French armies no longer exist. The danger of enemy penetration into the Ruhr territory has been eliminated for good.

German Volk!

Your soldiers have fought bloodily for this most glorious deed in history, at the risk of life and limb and with therefore the greatest of exertions.

I order that flags fly from every roof throughout Germany for eight days. This is to do honor to our soldiers. I further order, for eight days, the ringing of bells. May their sound be accompanied by the prayers of the German Volk, that shall accompany its sons once more. For on this morning, German divisions and fighter squadrons have once again embarked upon the continuation of the fight for the liberty and future of our Volk.

Adolf Hitler

Führer Headquarters, June 5, 1940

Soldiers of the Western Front!

Dunkirk has fallen! 40,000 Frenchmen and Englishmen have been taken prisoner as the remainder of once-great armies. Immeasurable amounts of material have been taken. Thus the greatest battle in world history has ended.

Soldiers!

My trust in you was a boundless one. You have not disappointed me. The most daring plan in the history of war was realized, thanks to your unequaled valor, your ability to endure the greatest pains, exertions, and efforts.

In a few weeks, you have forced two states to capitulate in a most difficult battle against, in many instances, an enemy of great valor. You have destroyed France's best divisions. You have defeated the British Expeditionary Force, either taking its men prisoner or driving them from the continent. All units of the *Wehrmacht*, on land and sea, outdid one another in the most noble competition in the mission for our Volk and the Greater German Reich. The valiant men of our navy shared in these deeds.

Soldiers!

Many soldiers have sealed their loyalty by giving their lives; others are wounded. The heart of our Volk is filled with profound gratitude, and it is with them and with you.

But the plutocratic rulers of Britain and France, who have conspired to prevent the blossoming of a new, better world with all means at their disposal, want to continue the war. Their wish shall be fulfilled.

Soldiers!

As of this day, the Western front comes to the fore again. Countless new divisions shall join you that will meet the enemy for the first time and that will defeat him. The battle for the liberty of our people, for its present and its future, shall be continued until we have destroyed those hostile rulers in London and Paris who still believe they have found in war the best means to realize their plans against other nations.

Our victory shall teach them a historic lesson!

All of Germany is with you once more in spirit!

Adolf Hitler

▸ July 31, 1940 *Hitler saw Great Britain as his chief enemy. Included in his ideas for dealing with Britain was the thought that the occupation of the Soviet Union would force Britain's acquiescence to German hegemony.*

On July 31, another conference was scheduled at the Berghof with the Third Reich's military leaders. Once more, Halder's notes on the meeting reveal the confusion reigning in Hitler's mind at the time. He grasped at every straw to induce the English to yield. He was still hoping for the submarine and aerial warfare to bear fruit sooner or later, only to return once again to the idea of attacking Russia. According to his calculations, the British had already felt completely "down" before the idea of turning to Russia had served to lift their spirits once more.

If only Russia were eliminated, the English would go "down" once again and for good. Moreover, Hitler speculated that eliminating the Soviet Union would improve Japan's position in Asia immensely, a fact that would serve to preoccupy and tie down the United States. Halder's notes on the discussion of a possible landing in England read:

Führer: Consider for crossing:

a) natural weather conditions, no force possible against (admits to possible storm and tide difficulties);

b) enemy action. If enemy action, army need count only on poor British forces. No advantage has been taken of their combat experience. New formations not possible to date. In eight to ten months new formations possible: equipment for 30 to 35 div [divisions] by spring. On location that means a lot. Perhaps destroy production sites in the war in the air to hinder new formations. Possibilities for propaganda. This is opposed by possible hopes on Russia and America. Questionable staying power of Italians, namely, East Africa. What can be done in the meantime, besides war in the air? If attack on England not possible at present, then in May only. How can we bridge gap until May (draw Spain in)?

Proposal Army: Support Italians in North Africa. 2 Pz. Div. [Panzer divisions].

Führer: Must investigate these diversions. Repercussions for France? Truly decisive action only through attack on England. [Here follow details on Raeder's comparison of the German and British fleets]

Führer: Hindrance, if things continue. War in the air starts now. It will determine comparative strengths we will get. If result of war in the air unsatisfactory, then halt preparations. If impression that the English are being thrown down and, after some time, effects set in, then attack. Put up with economic difficulties for another ten days. In case of postponement until next year, refurbishing of coastal vessels can continue throughout the winter. Diplomatic actions: Spain. Question of north Africa being discussed. Führer considering action against enemy harbors. Action against fleet? Stukas against armored decks.

Order: Continue preparations; decision in eight to ten days on actual attack; prepare for date September 15, broad base.

Führer: asks about U-boat action.
[Following Raeder's presentation and departure, Hitler continues:]

Führer: a) Emphasizes skepticism techn. [technical] possibilities. Even content with accomplishments of the navy. b) Stresses weather. c) Discusses possibility of enemy action. Our small Navy 15% of enemy; 8% of enemy destroyers; E-boats equal to 10–12% of enemy. Defenses at sea = 0. Remains: mines [not completely reliable]. Coast art. [artillery]—good! *Luftwaffe.* Decision will take in consideration that we are not risking anything in vain. d) Exception: England steps down; elimination of hopes that might cause England to anticipate a turn [of events] still.
  War actually won. France eliminated for British convoy duty; Italy ties down British forces. Submarine warfare and war in the air decisive but will last one to two years.
  England's hopes are Russia and America. If hope in Russia is eliminated, then America is eliminated because elimination of Russia will lead to enormous increase in importance of Japan in East Asia. Russia is England's and America's east Asian sword against Japan. Here no smooth sailing for England. Japanese have their own agenda, like the Russians, which is to be carried out before the end of the war.
  Russian victory film on Russian war! Russia is factor England counts on the most. Something has happened in London! The English were quite "down" already, now they stand tall again. Overheard conversations. Russia uneasy about swift development of situation in Western Europe.

Russia need not say more to English than that it never again wants to see Germany great, and already the Englishman, like a man drowning, hopes that things will look different in six to eight months. Once Russia is defeated, then England will be robbed of its last hope. The master of Europe and the Balkans will then be Germany.

Resolve: An end must be put to Russia in the course of this confrontation. Spring 1941. The quicker we defeat Russia the better. Operation makes sense only if we destroy this state in one strike. A certain amount of territorial gains insufficient as such. Standstill in winter dangerous. Hence better to wait though resolve certain to destroy Russia. Necessary also because of situation in Baltic Sea. Second great power on Baltic Sea troublesome. May '41. Five months time for completion. Preferably this year still. Not possible to ensure synchronized conduct of operation.

Goal: Destruction of vital power of Russia. Subdivide into:

1. Push through Kiev. Follow Dnieper. *Luftwaffe* destroys crossings Odessa.

2. Push through border states in the direction of Moscow.

   Subsequent concentration to the north and south. Later partial operations oil field Baku. Insofar as Finland and Turkey might take interest remains to be seen. Later: Ukraine, Belorussia, Baltic States, for us. Finland up to the White Sea.
   7 Div. [divisions] Norway
   50 Div. France
   3 Div. Holland, Belgium
   60 Div.
   120 Div. for east
   180 Div.
   The more contingents we come with, the better. We have 120 plus 20 div. on leave.

Formation by pulling out one battalion from every div.
After a few months, pull out another div. in three sections
from divisions 1/3.
Cover operations: Spain, North Africa, England, new formations in areas with air cover.
New formations: In the east: 40 div. with combat-tested
troops. Details on intended settlement Balkans: Intended
settlement Hungary/Romania. Then guarantee Romania.

▶ August 2, 1940 *Hitler decided to use the* Luftwaffe *to attack England. The
Battle of Britain began.*

On August 1, another disillusionment awaited Hitler. A project he had
earlier launched to sow discord in England and to force London to its knees
proved to be wishful thinking when the duke of Windsor set sail for the
Bahamas. The German envoy in Lisbon, Baron von Hoyningen-Huene, was
forced to report that the duke had not reacted as hoped for to clandestine
German overtures. Instead, the duke of Windsor had accepted the post of
governor in Nassau. Ludicrously, Hitler had truly believed he could, given
the duke's cooperation, oust the British government from office.

In view of these repeated failures, Hitler turned his attention to the *Luftwaffe* in order "to overcome the English air force . . . in the shortest possible
time" and "to establish the conditions necessary for the final conquest of
England." On this August 1, Hitler issued Directive No. 17 for the Conduct
of Air and Naval Warfare against England:

> In order to establish the conditions necessary for the final
> conquest of England, I intend to continue the air and naval war
> against the English homeland more intensively than heretofore.
> To this end I issue the following orders:

> 1. The German air arm is to overcome the English air force
> with all means at its disposal and in the shortest possible
> time. The attacks are to be directed primarily against the
> planes themselves, their ground organization, and their sup-
> ply installations, also against the aircraft industry, including
> plants producing anti-aircraft material.

2. After gaining temporary or local air superiority, the air war is to be carried on against harbors, especially against establishments connected with food supply, and also against similar establishment in the interior of the country. Attacks on the harbors of the south coast are to be undertaken on the smallest scale possible, in view of our own intended operations.

3. On the other hand, air attacks on warships and merchantmen of the enemy may be diminished, unless particularly advantageous targets of opportunity offer themselves, unless additional effect would be achieved in connection with actions described in paragraph 2, and unless such attacks are necessary to train crews for future operations.

4. The intensified air war is to be carried out in such a manner that the *Luftwaffe* can be called upon at any time to support naval operations against advantageous targets of opportunity in sufficient strength. Also, it is to stand by in force for operation Sea Lion (*Seelöwe*).

5. I reserve for myself the decision on terror attacks as a means of reprisal.

6. The intensified air war may commence on or after August 5. The exact time is to be selected by the *Luftwaffe* itself according to the weather, after preparations have been completed.

The navy is authorized to begin the projected intensified naval warfare at the same time.

Adolf Hitler

The "intensified air war" (*verschärfter Luftkrieg*) that Hitler desired was scheduled to begin on August 5, or a few days later. Special instructions for "terror attacks" he reserved for another time. These measures would find their application only if the Royal Air Force obstinately held on, and no change in the situation became apparent within a few days or weeks.

▶ December 18, 1940 *Hitler delivered an address to young officer candidates at the Berlin Sportpalast. He continued with a tirade about his ideas.*

Finally Hitler did speak of the present war:

> The rise of the German Volk began to have its repercussions politically abroad in the year 1938. The Greater German Reich was born. In the autumn of that year, the Sudetenland returned home. As of this moment, it was clear that England had decided to step up against Germany once again at any rate. And now, my young comrades, you must understand one thing: in the year 1919, I took up a struggle that appeared nearly hopeless at the time. An unknown man who undertook to rid a world of resistance, to tear down walls of prejudice. Prejudice at times is worse than divine force.
>
> A man took a stand against all the figures in public life back then, against the parties, against their press, against the whole system of capitalist fabrication of public opinion. I led this struggle until the final seizure of power.
>
> You must understand one thing: that at this moment I could have only one wish, namely, that if this war is indeed inevitable, that it still be fought during my lifetime, because I am the man who possesses the greatest authority with the German Volk. And moreover, because I believe that, based on the experiences of my life, I am the most able to strengthen the nation in this battle and to lead it into this battle. Thus, once I became aware that England was determined to fight this battle, I did not capitulate but in an instant determined to do everything to prepare Germany to hold its own in this most difficult struggle for its existence. And my appeal to the German nation was not in vain. I labored in these years to build up armament for the German Volk.
>
> I subordinated everything to the one thought: how can Germany be made strong? How can its armament be made powerful? I was determined to do nothing by half-measures but to stake everything on one throw. I knew that this struggle would determine whether Germany will be or will not be. It is not a question of a system. It is a question of whether these 85

million people, in their national unity, can carry through on their right to life or not. If yes, then the future of Europe belongs to this Volk. If no, then this Volk shall perish, shall sink back, and it will no longer be worthwhile to live in this Volk.

Faced with this alternative, I was determined to employ all means—down to the last—in this struggle. The nation understood this. Millions of men never spoke of it. Still all thought the same. And throughout this period, nobody ever reproached me for this enormous mobilization of public means for one goal: national armament.

I also wished that, if the hour were to come and come it would, the German soldier should not set out against the enemy as, regrettably, has been the case far too often in Germany's past. This phrase, "the best weapons for the best soldier in the world," has profound meaning. The best soldier must and will despair once it dawns on him that, in spite of his valor, the effectiveness of his arms does not suffice to gain the victory. Therefore, I was determined to do my utmost to secure for us the best arms. And, before German history, I may be faulted on many a thing, but on one topic assuredly not: that I had not done my utmost, what was humanly possible, to prepare the German Volk better for this struggle than, regrettably, it was prepared in the year 1914.

In this, I found the support of countless people, men of the state, the party, and in particular the *Wehrmacht*. They walked by my side. And thus we were able, in barely seven years, to make the German *Wehrmacht* once more the world's best. And, for my person, I have always been convinced that for us Germans there are only two possibilities: either we are no soldiers or we are the world's best. There is no in-between.

In fighting, politics employ, not only changing means, but also changing methods. It is the task of the political leadership to constantly and carefully reevaluate the situation and make its decisions in accordance with the changing circumstances. And it is the task of the soldier to implement these decisions with lightning speed. It is therefore necessary that the individual be profoundly suffused by the realization and the conviction that the fight in which he is involved is a fight that will determine the fate of the nation for centuries—perhaps forever.

I know that there are hours when it is necessary to hold on to this harsh realization, hours in which the individual is threatened by death, when fear and worry clutch at his heart. Then duty alone must serve as his guide. Then the individual must fight his way through to this realization: "Here I stand so that later generations will be spared this fate. Here I stand so that the regrettable sins of earlier generations will be atoned for. Here I stand so that my Volk can live."

As difficult as my struggle might be, it cannot be any more difficult than the struggle of the generations before us.

▶ January 8, 1941 *Since the air campaign against Britain had failed, Hitler was unsure of his ability to successfully invade England and saw an attack on the Soviet Union as the best way to win the war. Using his usual tactics of duplicity and violence, Hitler continued with his plans.*

On January 8 and 9, there were conferences at the Berghof that Raeder, Keitel, Jodl, and other officers attended. Once again, Hitler tried to whet their appetite for the campaign in Russia. Among other things, he declared the following:

> Russia's position in the event of Germany's forthcoming entry into Bulgaria is not yet clear. Russia needs Bulgaria as access to the Bosporus. England is supported by hope in the United States and Russia.
>
> If the United States and Russia enter the war, [it will create] a very great burden for our military. So, any possibility of such a threat must be precluded from the start. Having eliminated the threat from Russia, we will be able to continue the war against England under quite acceptable conditions. The break-up of Russia would be a great relief for the United States.

Hitler appeared extraordinarily optimistic, as Raeder noted the following:

> The Führer is absolutely convinced that the situation in Europe can no longer take an unfavorable turn for Germany, even if we should lose the whole of North Africa.
>
> The English can win the war only if they strike us on the continent. The Fürher considers that absolutely impossible.

This was also the tenor of the talks on January 9. In the course of an afternoon meeting, Hitler gave the following assessment of the situation:

> [He says that] a landing in England would be possible only if we have achieved full supremacy in the air, and in England a certain paralysis would set in. The purpose of the English war is, in the long run, to crush Germany on the continent. But their own forces are insufficient. The British navy is weaker than ever as a result of engaging in battles in two theaters of war operations located at a great distance from each other; its strengthening to the extent needed is impossible. For the British air force, the existing shortage of its supply of raw materials, especially aluminum, owing to canceled imports, and the effect of the German air and naval war on English industry have become painfully obvious; the aircraft industry itself has been so damaged that the number of airplanes produced has not been increased but reduced.
>
> This damage must be continued by the German air force even more regularly than up to now. As far as the British troops are concerned, it is absolutely out of the question to consider them as an invading army. The only thing that supports England is her hope in the United States and Soviet Russia, because in time the extermination of the English motherland is inevitable. However, England hopes to hang on until a great continental bloc is brought down upon Germany. The diplomatic preparations for this are clearly recognizable.
>
> [He says that] Stalin, the master of Russia, has a shrewd head. He doesn't take an open stand against Germany; however, one should expect that he would increasingly create troubles in a difficult situation for Germany. He is willing to inherit an impoverished Europe; he has all the necessary prerequisites for that, and he is full of enthusiasm to push to the west. He is well aware of the fact that after Germany's absolute victory, the Soviet Union's position will become extremely difficult.
>
> [He says that] the possibility of Russian intervention in the war bolsters the English. They will give up this contest only when their last continental hope dies out.

He doesn't believe that the English will be "recklessly brave"; if they see that there is no possibility of victory, they will stop. So, if they lose the war, they will have no power left to keep their empire together. Should they persist, and succeed in deploying 40 to 50 divisions, and if the United States and Russia help them, then a very serious situation would arise for Germany. It must not happen. So far, he would always act on the principle of smashing the most important positions of the enemy in order to take the next step.

Therefore, Russia must be crushed. Then either the English would surrender, or Germany would continue the struggle on favorable conditions for Germany. Besides, the smashing of Russia would enable Japan to turn itself with all its strength against the United States. This would prevent the latter from joining in the war.

On January 10, a further German-Russian economic agreement was signed. The Russians did their utmost to satisfy the German demands for the delivery of goods.

▶ March 30, 1941 *The purpose of Hitler's war against the Soviet Union was not only to remove Britain's "last chance" but was really to gain the* Lebensraum *he had talked about since 1919. This meant a war not only against the Soviet state but a war against the Russian people whom he would enslave and, in good part, remove from the lands that he saw as becoming a part of the Great German Empire.*

By March 30, the pending campaign in the Balkans had ceased to be foremost in Hitler's mind. He dedicated himself completely to Operation Barbarossa. At 11:00 a.m., he assembled his generals and commanders in chief at the Reich Chancellery to give a two and a half hour talk on the development of the situation from June 1940 on. He first spoke of England's mistake in rejecting the German peace proposals. In this context, he spoke of Russia and once again played the man who knew everything, whose awareness of the military potential of Russia was complete, and who knew about every single Russian tank!

At this time, he hinted that the rules of engagement in Russia would be different: current ideas of severity would become "mild" compared to what will happen to the Russians. It was simply a question of annihilating the Bolshevik commissars and the Communist intelligentsia.

The record of Hitler's speech in Halder's diary read as follows:

> 11:00 a.m. meeting at the Führer's; almost a two and a half hour address:

> Situation after June 30 (1940). English mistake to reject possibility of peace. Description of further events. Sharp criticism of Italian conduct of the war and policy. England's situation benefits because of Italy's failures.

> England places its hopes on America and Russia. Maximum effectiveness only in four years; Russian problems with transportation. Role and possibilities. Reasons for the necessity of clearing up Russian situation. We will only be able to master, within two years, our missions in the air and on the ocean in terms of materiel and personnel if we resolve the questions on land for good and thoroughly. Our mission against Russia: smash the armed forces, dissolve state.

> Comments on Russian tanks (respectable): 4.7 cm—good, heavy model, mass old. In terms of the number of tanks, the Russians are the strongest in the world. But they have only a small number of the new giant models *(Riesentypen)*.

> Air force has large numbers, but very many old models, only a small number of modern models.

> Problem of Russian terrain: the infinite vastness of the terrain makes concentration on decisive points necessary. Massive deployment of *Luftwaffe* and tanks at decisive location. *Luftwaffe* cannot cover this gigantic terrain at one time. At the start of the war, it can control only parts of this gigantic front. Its deployment must therefore be closely linked to land operations. The Russians will break down when confronted with a massive deployment of tanks and planes.

> No illusions about allies: Finns will fight bravely, but they are weak in number and have not recovered. Romanians are completely hopeless. Perhaps, they will do all right in providing

security behind a strong barrier (river), as long as they are not attacked. Antonescu (dictator of Romania) expanded his army, instead of making it smaller and improving it. The fate of large German units should not depend on the steadfastness of the Romanian units.

The Pripet Marshes: security, defense, mines.

Question of Russian evasive movements: Not likely, because tied to Baltic Sea and Ukraine. If the Russians want to avoid contact with the enemy, they would have to do this very early on; otherwise they will not escape unscathed. After solving the problems in the east, fifty to sixty (tank) divisions will suffice. It will be possible to release a part of the infantry forces in order to produce armaments for the *Luftwaffe* or the navy; another part will be needed for other tasks, for example, in Spain. (Halder's marginal note: colonial tasks).

Struggle of two ideologies. Scathing condemnation of Bolshevism: equals social criminality; Communism immense danger to the future. We must distance ourselves from the idea of soldierly good fellowship. A Communist is not a comrade, neither before nor afterwards. It is a matter of a struggle of annihilation. If we do not see it this way, then we will still defeat the enemy, but the Communist enemy will confront us again in thirty years. We are not waging war in order to preserve the enemy.

Future states: northern Russia will belong to Finland. Protectorates: Baltic countries, Ukraine, and Belorussia.

Fighting against Russia: annihilation of Bolshevik commissars and Communist intelligentsia. The new states must be Socialist states, but without their own intelligentsia. The formation of a new intelligentsia must be prevented. A primitive Socialist intelligentsia will suffice here. The poison of demoralization must be fought. This is not a case for court-martial. The commanders of the troops must know what it is all about. They must exercise leadership in combat.

The troops must defend themselves by all means if they are attacked. Commissars and Soviet secret police (*GPU*) people are criminals and must be treated accordingly. Still, the reins of leadership must not slip out of the commander's hands. The commander must issue his orders in consideration of the troops' sentiments. Fighting will be very different from fighting in the west. In the east, what is now severity will be mildness in the future. The commanders must demand of themselves the sacrifice of overcoming their scruples.

In order to rationalize the brutality of his actions against the Russians, Hitler argued that the Soviet Union was not a "party" to the Hague Convention. This was an obvious lie, since Russia acknowledged as binding the regulations of the Geneva Convention and the stipulations of the Hague Convention on war on land and at sea.

And even if Russia had not signed the Geneva Convention and the international agreement at The Hague, this would still not have justified the Germans in declaring the Russians outlaws on the outbreak of war or shooting them at random while taking them prisoner or at a later time. After all, the signatories to these agreements, Germany included, had pledged themselves to respect the rules that were agreed upon in any circumstance, even if they were waging war against a power not party to the conventions. On questions of international law, the German generals were not well informed in any event, as the Geneva Convention and treatment of the wounded were not subjects taught at military academies.

Even if they had been better informed, the situation on March 30, 1941, would have been no different. Ever since 1934, whatever Adolf Hitler said, did, or ordered served as the norm in Germany, even if it violated constitutional, penal, or international law. As president of the Reichstag, Göring had once solemnly proclaimed: "We will always approve of everything our Führer does." And even the Reich minister of justice, the bourgeois jurist Gürtner, had declared on July 3, 1934, in connection with the Röhm purge, that all measures taken by Hitler, including the shooting of defenseless prisoners without prior trial, were not only "justified," but a "statesmanlike duty."

These statements were made in the year 1934, in the midst of peace, at a time when there could be no talk of a total dictatorship. Given this set of mind, it is not surprising that, in the war year 1941, the generals had no qualms about executing Hitler's orders to liquidate defenseless Russian prisoners of war without prior trial and thought such measures justified. Still, they were glad that this macabre task was left to the Nazi Party security squads (SS) and not to the *Wehrmacht*.

The Commissar Order *(Kommissarbefehl)* was put into writing on March 31. Twice amended, it finally read on May 12 as follows:

Memorandum. Subject: Treatment of captured Russian political and military funtionaries.

I. The *Wehrmacht* high command *(OKW)* presented draft "guidelines" concerning the treatment of political officials, etc., for the concerted accomplishment of the assignment that had already been given on March 31, 1941 and that is enclosed as enclosure no. 1. This draft provides for:

1. The elimination of political officials and leaders (commissars).

2. If they are captured by the troops, an officer with disciplinary powers must decide whether the person in question is to be eliminated. In this context, the establishment of this person's identity as a political official suffices.

3. Political leaders captured among the enemy troops will not be recognized as prisoners of war and will be dealt with at the transit camps for Russian POWs at the latest. No sending them off to the rear.

4. Expert leaders of economic and technical enterprises are to be arrested only if they rebel against the German *Wehrmacht*.

5. The carrying out of operations may not be disturbed by these measures. Planned search and mopping-up operations will not take place.

6. In rear operational areas of the army, officials and commissars, with the exception of political leaders captured among the enemy troops, will be handed over to the special squad of the security police.

II. By contrast, memorandum no. 3 by *Reichsleiter* Rosenberg provides that only officials of the highest ranks be eliminated, since functionaries in the governments, communes, and the economy are irreplaceable in the administration of the occupied territories.

III. Therefore, a decision by the Führer is necessary concerning what principles should apply here. Proposal for case II:

1. Functionaries who operate outside their units, as is to be expected from the radical element, fall under the "decree on the exercise of trial by court-martial in the Barbarossa area." They will be dealt with as volunteer irregulars. The same treatment is provided for by the "guidelines on the conduct of the troops in Russia."

2. Functionaries who are innocent of hostile actions will at first not be molested. However, the troops cannot be expected to be able to differentiate between the various functionaries of the individual sectors. Only further penetration into the country will enable us to decide whether the remaining functionaries can be left in these locations or whether they are to be handed over to special commandos, if they are in a position to carry out the investigation.

3. Functionaries captured with their troops will be treated in accordance with the proposal by the *Wehrmacht* high command (*OKW*). They will not be recognized as prisoners of war; they will be dealt with at the transit camps at the latest, and under no circumstance will they be sent to the rear.

Everything Hitler did in the spring of 1941 was in some way connected to the assault on Russia. The war in Africa played a role of lesser importance. That was only natural, as Hitler was convinced that he could obtain the desired friendship with England by attacking the Soviet Union. Why should he engage in major operations in North Africa? Under no circumstances was he willing to attack Egypt at this point. This would only needlessly provoke the English and lessen their readiness for peace.

▶ June 22, 1941 *Hitler's statement to the German people and the world about his reasons for starting another war while the war in the west continued contained his usual mixture of fabrications and accusations.*

Undoubtedly June 22, 1941, was an important day in the life of Adolf Hitler. It was on this day that he launched the undertaking that, in addition to the concept of friendship with England and Italy, had been central to all his ideas and plans after 1919: the war against Russia, the conquest of new *Lebensraum*. It was true that he had planned things differently; he had thought he could go to war with the explicit approval of England and Italy and their help and friendship.

While he could be sure of Italy's support, its assistance did not count for much. Things had not worked out as well with England: Germany was in the midst of a war with England!

But did that matter to Hitler? After all, in his opinion, it made little difference in which sequence he realized the concepts of 1919: friendship with England and Italy, war with Russia. He had Italy's friendship, he was ready to attack Russia, and so friendship with England simply had to follow! It would do so all the more since he was now employing the same old trick abroad—the menace of Bolshevism—that he had used so successfully in his fight against the senile German Nationalists at home.

Hitler did not worry too much about the war against Russia at this point. Accustomed to victory, the German *Wehrmacht*, this "most mighty instrument of war of all time," could easily deal with the "primitive" Russians, whom Bolshevism had instilled with a "cowardly, anxious acquiescence."

All Hitler needed now was a plausible pretext for this unheard-of attack on a friendly power, with whom, according to his own words, Germany never again wanted to fight. In his proclamation "to the German Volk" on June 22, Hitler maintained that it was all the fault of the "Jewish-Bolshevik rulers." They had kept him from a "radical ending of the war in the West." They had blackmailed him and threatened "European culture and civilization." They had "organized the Serb Putsch," and "together with England and the help of the expected American deliveries," they wanted "to suffocate and crush the German Reich." Hitler's proclamation read as follows:

Berlin, June 22, 1941

German Volk! National Socialists!

The hour has finally come for me, weighed down by heavy burdens and sentenced to remain silent for months, to speak openly.

When, on September 3, 1939, the German Reich received the English declaration of war, the British attempted again to foil the consolidation and rise of Europe by fighting the strongest power on the continent. This is how England once destroyed Spain in many wars. This is how it waged war against Holland. This is how, with the help of all Europe, it later fought France. And this is how, at the turn of the century, it began the encirclement of the German Reich and then in the year 1914, it began the World War.

It was only because of its inner discord that Germany was defeated in the year 1918. What followed was terrible. First, they claimed hypocritically that they were only fighting the Kaiser and his regime. Then, after the surrender of the German army, the systematic destruction of the German Reich was started. While the prophecies of a French statesman that there were twenty million too many people in Germany, that is, people who had to be eliminated by hunger, disease, or emigration, seemed to become literally true, the National Socialist movement began its work of uniting the German Volk and thereby initiating the rise of the Reich.

This new rising up of our Volk from need, misery, and shameful contempt was a sign of a purely inner rebirth. England, in particular, was neither concerned nor threatened by this. In spite of this, a new policy of encirclement, seething with hatred, immediately set in again against Germany. At home and abroad, there was the well-known conspiracy between Jews and democrats, Bolsheviks and reactionaries, with the single goal of preventing the establishment of a new German people's state and plunging the Reich again into impotence and misery.

Besides us, the hatred of this international, worldwide conspiracy singled out those peoples whom fortune has likewise overlooked and who are also forced to earn their daily bread in a hard struggle for existence. Italy and Japan especially were denied their share of the goods of this earth, like Germany—yes, they were virtually forbidden them. The alliance of these nations therefore was only an act of self-defense in view of the threatening, egotistic international coalition of wealth and power.

In 1936, Churchill declared, according to the statements of the American General Wood before a committee of the American House of Representatives, that Germany was again becoming too powerful and therefore had to be destroyed.

In the summer of 1939, England thought the time had come to realize the new destruction by a repetition of a comprehensive policy of encirclement directed against Germany. The method of the campaign of lies staged for this purpose was to declare other peoples threatened, to trap them with British guarantees and promises of assistance, and then, as in the World War, to let them march against Germany.

And so England, from May to August 1939, succeeded in spreading the idea that Lithuania, Estonia, Latvia, Finland, Bessarabia, as well as the Ukraine, were directly threatened by Germany. Some of these states were thereby seduced into accepting the guarantees connected to these claims, and so joined the new front of encirclement against Germany. Under those circumstances, I believed, before my conscience and the history of the German Volk, that I could, not only assure these states, that is, governments, of the falsehood of the British claims, but also calm the strongest power of the East by making solemn declarations on the limits of our respective interests.

National Socialists!

Probably all of you felt that this step was bitter and difficult for me. Never has the German Volk harbored feelings of animosity against the peoples of Russia. Alas, for over two decades, the Jewish-Bolshevik rulers have labored from Moscow to set afire not only Germany, but also all of Europe. Never has Germany attempted to carry its National Socialist ideology into Russia. However, the Jewish-Bolshevik rulers in Moscow have constantly undertaken to force their rule on our people and others in Europe as well, and not merely ideologically, but especially in terms of military force and power. In all countries, the consequences of the activities of this regime were chaos, misery, and famine.

In contrast to that, I strove in the past two decades to achieve a new socialist order in Germany with a minimum of intervention and without destroying our production, a new socialist order that not only eliminated unemployment, but also increasingly let the profit from the work go to the working man.

The successes of this policy of a new economic and social order for our Volk, the systematic overcoming of social differences and class distinctions, are unequaled in the world.

Therefore, in August 1939, despite great misgivings I sent my foreign minister to Moscow to attempt there to counteract the British policy of encirclement against Germany. I did this only because of a sense of responsibility to the German Volk, and, above all, in the hope of achieving a lasting détente in the end and, perhaps, lessening the sacrifices that might otherwise be demanded of us.

And then, after Germany solemnly declared in Moscow that the aforementioned areas and countries were outside the German sphere of interest—with the exception of Lithuania—a special agreement was made in case England succeeded in driving Poland to war against Germany. Here, too, the German demands were limited and stood in no relation to the accomplishments of the German arms.

National Socialists!

The consequences of this treaty that I desired in the interest of the German Volk were very hard on the Germans living in the countries concerned.

Far more than half a million German *Volksgenossen*—all small farmers, craftsmen, and workers—were forced, practically overnight, to leave their former homeland in order to escape a new regime that at first threatened them with infinite misery and, sooner or later, with complete extermination. In spite of this, thousands of Germans disappeared! It is impossible to know what happened to them or where they are now. Among them, there are a 160 men with German Reich citizenship.

I remained silent about all this, because I had to remain silent! After all, it was my wish to bring about a détente for good and, if possible, a lasting settlement with this state.

However, as soon as we advanced into Poland, the Soviet rulers suddenly claimed Lithuania in violation of the treaty. The German Reich never intended to occupy Lithuania. Not only did it not make any such demand on the Lithuanian government—on the contrary, it also declined a request by the Lithuanian government at the time to send German troops to Lithuania for that purpose, as this did not correspond with the goals of the German policy.

In spite of this, I yielded to this new Russian demand. However, this was only the beginning of constantly new extortions that since then have been repeated time and again. The victory in Poland, exclusively secured by German troops, induced me to direct a new offer of peace to the Western powers.

It was rejected because of the international and Jewish warmongers.

Already at that time, the cause of this rejection was that England was still hoping to mobilize a European coalition against Germany, including the Balkans and Soviet Russia. And so they decided in London to send Ambassador Cripps to Moscow. He received clear instructions to enter again into diplomatic relations with Soviet Russia and to develop them in the interest of England. The English press reported on the progress of this mission for as long as tactical reasons required.

In the autumn of 1939 and the spring of 1940, the first consequences became apparent. While Russia undertook to subjugate, not only Finland militarily, but also the Baltic states, it all of a sudden tried to justify doing so with the mendacious and ridiculous claim that it had to protect these countries from, that is, to prevent, an external threat. No power other than Germany could penetrate these areas along the Baltic Sea or wage war there. In spite of this, I had to remain silent. But the ruling powers in the Kremlin immediately went a step further.

While, in the spring of 1940, Germany withdrew its armed forces far behind the eastern frontier in the spirit of the so-called Friendship Pact, thereby virtually clearing most of these areas of German troops, Russian forces immediately began to deploy to such an extent that this could only be seen as a deliberate threat to Germany.

According to a personal statement made by Molotov at the time, 22 Russian divisions were in the Baltic states alone. Since the Russian government always maintained that it had been called in by the local population, the purpose of its presence there could only be a demonstration against Germany. While— from May 10, 1940, on—our soldiers broke the French-British power in the West, the Russian concentration along our eastern front continued to an increasingly dangerous degree.

From August 1940 on, therefore, I believed that, in the interest of the Reich, I could not any longer leave our eastern provinces, which have so often been devastated in the past, unprotected from this colossal concentration of Bolshevik divisions.

This brought about what the Anglo-Soviet cooperation aimed for, namely to tie down strong German forces in the east, so that, especially in terms of the [war in the] air, a conclusive end of the war in the West would no longer be possible for the German leadership.

This was not only the goal of British but also of Soviet policy. England as well as Soviet Russia intend to let this war last as long as possible in order to weaken Europe and to make it increasingly impotent.

The alarming Russian attack on Romania ultimately served the purpose of getting hold of an important element of the economic life, not only of Germany, but also of all Europe, and, possibly, destroying it. However, it was the German Reich that, from the year 1933 on, strove with infinite patience to win the states of southeastern Europe as trading partners. Therefore, we had the greatest interest in their internal governmental consolidation and order. Russia's invasion of Romania, and Greece's political ties with England, threatened to transform these areas shortly into a theater of war, too.

Contrary to our principles and customs, at that time I directed an urgent appeal to the Romanian government, which itself was responsible for this development, and I advised it to yield to the Soviet extortion for the sake of peace and to cede Bessarabia.

The Romanian government believed that it could tolerate this before its own people only if Germany and Italy gave a guarantee that the continuing existence of the remainder would not be disputed. I did this with a heavy heart. Because, after all, if the German Reich gives a guarantee, this means it will vouch for it. We are neither Englishmen nor Jews.

So I believed myself to have rendered a service to peace in these areas practically at the last minute, even if this meant taking on a heavy responsibility myself. In order to resolve these problems for good and to obtain clarity on the Russian attitude to the Reich, as well as under the pressure of the consistently increasing mobilization along our eastern borders, I invited Mr. Molotov to Berlin.

The Soviet foreign minister now demanded a clarification by Germany, that is, its answer to the following four questions:

Molotov's first question:
In the event of a Soviet attack on Romania, will the German guarantee to Romania be directed against Soviet Russia?

My answer:
The German guarantee is a general one and is absolutely binding for us. Russia has never informed us that, apart from Bessarabia, it has any interests in Romania. The occupation of northern Bukovina has already violated this assurance. Therefore, I do not believe that Russia could suddenly have further intentions against Romania.

Molotov's second question:
Russia again feels threatened by Finland. Russia is determined
not to tolerate this. Is Germany ready not to assist Finland in
any manner and, in particular, immediately to withdraw the
German troops that are marching through it to Kirkenes for
replacement?

My answer:
As before, Germany has no political interests in Finland. A
new war by Russia against the small Finnish people cannot
be regarded as tolerable by the German Reich government, all
the more so as we cannot believe that Finland is threatening
Russia. However, we do not wish the Baltic Sea to become a
theater of war again.

Molotov's third question:
Is Germany willing to agree to Soviet Russia's extending a
guarantee to Bulgaria and sending Soviet troops into Bulgaria
for this purpose? He, Molotov, also wished to declare, for example, that the Soviets did not intend to eliminate the king
on this occasion.

My answer:
Bulgaria is a sovereign state, and I do not know whether, unlike Romania, Bulgaria has even requested such a guarantee
from Soviet Russia. Besides this, I will have to talk with my
allies about this matter.

Molotov's fourth question:
Soviet Russia in any event needs free transit through the
Dardanelles. To protect it, Russia requires the occupation of
strongholds along the Dardanelles, that is, at the Bosporus.
Will Germany agree to this or not?

My answer:
Germany is prepared to give its consent at any time to a change
in the status of Montreux (*the international agreement regarding the Dardanelles*) in favor of the Black Sea states. Germany
is not willing to agree to Russia's taking possession of bases
along the straits.

National Socialists!

I assumed an attitude here that I had to assume not only as the accountable Führer of the German Reich but also as the responsible representative of European culture and civilization. The consequence was a reinforcement of the Soviet activities directed against the Reich, particularly the immediate start of subversive activities inside the new Romanian government and the attempt to remove the Bulgarian government by propaganda.

With the help of the confused, naive heads of the Romanian Legion, a coup d'etat was staged in Romania with the goal of toppling the head of state, General Antonescu, and to create chaos in the country so that the elimination of legitimate authority would remove the preconditions for the German guarantee to take effect.

Despite this, I still believed that it was best to remain silent.

Immediately following the failure of this undertaking, a renewed reinforcement of the Russian troop concentrations along the eastern border of Germany took place. Armored units and parachute troops were moved in increasing numbers alarmingly close to the German border. The German *Wehrmacht* and the German homeland know that, only a few weeks ago, not a single German Panzer or motorized division was on our eastern border.

Had there been need of conclusive proof of the coalition between England and Soviet Russia that had meanwhile come about despite all the diversions and disguises, then the Yugoslav conflict would have served as such.

While I labored to make a last attempt to pacify the Balkans and, with the understanding cooperation of the Duce, I invited Yugoslavia to join the Tripartite Pact. England and Soviet Russia worked together to organize the turmoil that overnight removed the government that was willing to negotiate.

The German Volk can be told today: the Serbian upheaval against Germany took place, not only under the English, but essentially under the Soviet, flag. Since we remained silent on this matter as well, the Soviet leadership went a step further. Not only did it organize the Serb Putsch, but also, only a few days later, it concluded the well-known Friendship Pact with its new subservient creatures. This was intended to encourage the Serbs in their resistance to a pacification of the Balkans and to goad them on against Germany.

And this was not a simple change of administration. Moscow demanded the mobilization of the Serbian army. Since I still believed that it was better not to speak, the ruling powers in the Kremlin went a step further: the German Reich government today possesses documents that prove that Russia, in order to get Serbia finally to fight, promised to deliver weapons, planes, ammunition, and other war materiel via Salonika.

And this occurred almost exactly at the same moment when I gave the Japanese foreign minister, Matsuoka, advice to seek a détente with Russia, always in the hope of rendering peace a service.

Only the rapid breakthrough to Skopje and the taking of Salonika by our peerless divisions have prevented the ambitions of this Soviet-Anglo-Saxon conspiracy. The Serbian air-force officers escaped to Russia and were welcomed there immediately as allies.

The victory of the Axis powers in the Balkans alone prevented the plan to engage Germany in battle in the southeast for months on end this summer, while, in the meantime, the concentration of the Soviet armies would be completed, their readiness for battle reinforced, and then, together with England and supported by the expected American deliveries, Russia would strangle and eventually crush the German Reich and Italy. Through this, Moscow not only violated the provisions of our Friendship Pact, it has also betrayed this pact most wretchedly. And all this, while the ruling powers in the Kremlin, as in the case of Finland and Romania, hypocritically spoke of peace and of friendship abroad.

If, previously, circumstances forced me to be silent time and again, the time has come when continuous sitting back and watching would, not only be a sin of omission, but also a crime against the German Volk, yes, against all of Europe.

Today, approximately a hundred sixty Russian divisions stand at our border. For weeks, there have been persistent violations of this border not only down here, but also far up north, as in Romania. Russian pilots amuse themselves by lightheartedly looking over these borders, perhaps to prove to us that they already feel themselves the masters of these territories.

On the night of June 17 to 18, Russian patrols reconnoitered German Reich territory and could only be driven back after a lengthy exchange of fire.

Therefore, the hour has now come in which it has become necessary to oppose this conspiracy of the Jewish-Anglo-Saxon warmongers and likewise the Jewish ruling powers in the Bolshevik control station at Moscow.

German Volk!

At this moment, the greatest concentration that the world has ever seen in terms of scope and dimensions is taking place. In unison with the Finnish comrades, the victorious warriors of Narvik stand at the Arctic Ocean. German divisions under the command of the conqueror of Norway protect Finnish soil, together with the heroic Finnish freedom fighters under their marshal. The formations of the German front in the east reach from East Prussia to the Carpathian Mountains. On the banks of the Pruth River, the lower reaches of the Danube, up to the shores of the Black Sea, German and Romanian soldiers unite under General Antonescu.

The mission of this front, therefore, is no longer the protection of individual countries but the securing of Europe and, hence, the salvation of all.

Today, I have therefore determined to lay the fate and the future of the German Reich and of our Volk again into the hands of our soldiers.

May the Lord Almighty help us especially in this battle!

Adolf Hitler

In addition to this proclamation, Hitler issued an order of the day for the soldiers of the eastern front on June 22. While the main ideas were those already expressed in the proclamation, it contained the following passage at the end:

German soldiers!

Hereby you enter a very hard battle, laden with responsibility. Because the fate of Europe, the future of the German Reich, the existence of our Volk now lie in your hands alone.

May the Lord Almighty help us all in this!

As turgid and wordy as the proclamations of June 22 were, at their core was the claim of a Russian-English "conspiracy" against the Reich—yes, against Europe—and of Russia's breach of the alliance treaty with the Reich.

▸ February 3, 1943 *After bitter battles lasting over a year and a half, German forces had failed to destroy the Soviet Union. The Red Army surrounded the German Sixth Army in Stalingrad on the Volga and Hitler was not able to save it. Rather than allow the soldiers to surrender, Hitler wanted them to fight to the death. But this did not happen.*

At a noontime discussion of the situation at his military headquarters on February 1, Hitler was no longer able to control his anger:

> They surrendered—a perfectly formal ceremony! Instead, they should have formed a circle and shot themselves dead with their last bullet. When the nerves give out, there is nothing left anyway except "I couldn't take any more" and shoot oneself. One can also say: A real man must be able to shoot himself, just as, in the past, officers used to throw themselves upon a sword, seeing that the matter was lost. This is quite understandable. Even Varus ordered his slave, "Kill me now!"
>
> In this war, no one will become a field marshal any more. This will happen only after the war is over. One mustn't praise the day before the evening has come.
>
> I feel such great pain to think that the heroism of so many soldiers can be wiped out by a deed of one spineless weakling—and now the man is going to do it. He comes to Moscow, and now imagine: a rattrap! He signs everything there. He will make confessions and declarations. You will see that they will take the way of spinelessness and go all the way, to the lowest depth.

What is life? Life is people. Some of them die, but those who survive are the people. But how can one fear the moment that may free him from the sorrows of life, if only he is not held back by his sense of duty in this trouble?

He (*Paulus*) will be speaking on the radio in the near future. You will see for yourselves. Seydlitz and Schmidt will speak on the radio. They will be locked up in the rat cellars and will break down in a day or two and will speak up at once.

In spite of this, Hitler apparently attempted to exert influence on Paulus even in captivity and to silence him. While radio broadcasts in the rest of the world reported on the capture of the German generals at Stalingrad, Hitler decided to conceal this fact from the German public. He preferred the version of their heroic death, "shoulder to shoulder with the officers, noncommissioned officers, and men of the Sixth Army."

These tactics met with little success, however. Like wildfire, news of the capture of Paulus and 24 other generals spread through Germany. Not even party heads or policemen dared to try and stop those spreading the news. Obviously, they also had been listening to foreign radio stations. Hitler's final communiqué of February 3 succeeded only in completely discrediting him. It reads as follows:

Führer Headquarters, February 3, 1943

The High Command of the *Wehrmacht* announces:

Fighting in Stalingrad has ended. True to its oath of allegiance to fight to the last breath, the Sixth Army under the exemplary command of Field Marshal Paulus has succumbed to the superiority of the enemy and unfavorable circumstances. Its fate is shared by an antiaircraft division of the German *Luftwaffe*, two Romanian divisions, and one Croatian regiment, which fulfilled their duty to the utmost in loyal brotherhood in arms with their comrades of the German army.

It is not yet the time to describe the course of the operations that have led to this development. One thing can already be said today, however: the sacrifice of the Sixth Army was not in vain. As the bulwark of the historic European mission, it defied for many weeks the assault by six Soviet armies.

Completely surrounded by the enemy, it tied down strong enemy forces for several more weeks of heavy fighting and great privations. Thereby, it gave the German leaders time and opportunity to take countermeasures on whose success the fate of the entire eastern front depended.

Faced with this task, the Sixth Army held out even after the *Luftwaffe* was no longer capable, in spite of its great efforts and heavy losses, of furnishing sufficient supplies by air due to the duration of the encirclement and the development of the operations. The possibility of relief at that point had become increasingly unlikely and finally completely disappeared.

Surrender demanded twice by the enemy met with proud rejection. Beneath the swastika flag, which flew on top of Stalingrad's tallest ruins and could be seen from afar, the final battle took place. Generals, officers, noncommissioned officers, and men fought shoulder to shoulder down to the last bullet. They died so that Germany might live. Their example will do good far into the future, despite all untruthful Soviet propaganda. The divisions of the Sixth Army are already in the process of being formed anew.

Hitler's behavior in the case of Stalingrad had been unwise from the beginning. At first, he had boasted that the German troops would "rush on Stalingrad and take the city." Only six weeks later, he had said that he did not want a second Verdun and would only deploy "very small assault parties." After that, he had kept silent for months about the encirclement of the Sixth Army by the Russians. This had been followed by his ill-fated attempt to make a heroic epic out of the battle for Stalingrad.

While Stalingrad was no doubt a milestone in Hitler's decline, it was neither the first nor the decisive one. Ever since September 3, 1939, to be precise, Hitler had suffered one great diplomatic and military defeat after another. What was new about the Stalingrad debacle was that Hitler no longer attempted to transform a defeat into a victory, as he had done on earlier occasions.

▸ December 20, 1943 *While the war in the East became more hopeless, the fact that there would soon be a new front in Western Europe became clear.*

It became clear in the course of the discussion of the situation on the evening of December 20, that Hitler was greatly disconcerted by the threat of a landing by the Allies in Western Europe. No more did he vainly propose to "evacuate" the area in question in order to spare the Allies "the difficulties of a landing." Now he declared the following:

> There is no doubt that the attack in the West will come in the spring. You have to count on a landing in Norway, also as well as on a diversionary attack in the Bay of Biscay and perhaps in the Balkans.
>
> It would be highly unpleasant if the swine gains a foothold and lures our *Luftwaffe* out.
>
> If he gains a foothold in Norway, then that would be disastrous for our entire northern army. Then, the transports will not be possible any more. We know what it means in the south, when the swine sits on an island.
>
> There is no doubt about it: they have committed themselves. From mid-February, early March on, the attack will take place in the West. I do not have the feeling that, let us say, the English really have their heart in this attack.
>
> If they attack in the West, then this attack will decide the war. If this attack is parried, then the whole story is over.

The impending Allied landing was an unpleasant prospect for Hitler. But what could he do about it? He had an idea: flame-throwers were all that he needed! Immediately, he began trying to convince himself and his audience that this was the solution. As he explained:

> Can't we arrange for a special allocation of flame-throwers for the West? Flame-throwers are the best thing for the defense; after all, they are terrifying weapons. But also battery flame-throwers. In the worst case, you would have to use force on Speer. He has workers available because of the destroyed factories. You could stick them in somewhere and have them make flame-throwers. Especially in defense, the flame-thrower is the most terrifying thing there is.

That will take the pluck out of the attacking infantry, I should say, before it starts hand-to-hand fighting. It will lose its pluck when it suddenly gets the feeling that there are flame-throwers on all sides.

Also in battery positions, there must be flame-throwers. Everywhere there should be flame-throwers. I also thought about using them against low-level flights, but that cannot be done.

Then Hitler telephoned Saur:

Saur, how many flame-throwers are you making per month now?—I need three times as many as you are making now and that in two months. You have to stick workers in there as quickly as possible. So in all of January/February three times as many as you are doing now! That is the minimum requirement. That makes only 1200? I thought 2400. I want three times as many. You already noticed that the numbers come out. So, fast, more, more! We need it really urgently. Thank you! Heil! Happy Holidays!

He said that he had increased production to 1200. He said that he thinks he can increase it even further. He can increase it, because this is a type of production where you do not need many primary products. And, because of the bomb attacks, he has workers available whom he can stick in there. We can never be taken by surprise, if there are 20 to 30 thousand flamethrowers in the West.

From where on earth was he going to get the thousands of flame-throwers that he needed for an endless front at the coast all the way from Spain to northern Norway, in southern France, and in the Balkans? Who would operate them? And what would the flame-throwers do against the heavy naval artillery of the Allied fleet and the thousand kilogram to five thousand kilogram bombs of the Royal Air Force?

Hitler was getting nervous thinking of where the Allies might land. He had no idea where. Not surprisingly, he declared: "I am convinced that the moment it starts will be a relief."

Invasion: June 1944

Early on June 6, the Anglo-American invasion armies, from bases in England, started to land along the coast of Normandy. Montgomery was in command of the ground troops; Eisenhower was in command of the entire invasion. Since the days of Napoleon, the world had seen nothing like it. Heavy naval-artillery bombardment and attacks by the Royal Air Force had preceded the invasion. While the first decisive fighting on the ground was taking place, Allied naval and air forces pinned down the German bases behind the front and made bringing up reinforcements impossible. Parachutes and transport gliders landed great numbers of Allied airborne troops. Within a few hours, the first beachheads were fortified and secured. The German troops were no longer in a position to score any lasting successes.

Hitler was having breakfast at the Berghof when news of the beginning of the invasion arrived. Keitel and Jodl rushed to him from their quarters to inform the supreme commander of the latest developments. Hitler acted as though they were bringing him news of a great victory. He immediately stepped up to a map of the French coast and had Keitel outline the situation for him.

He then said: "The news could not be any better! As long as they were in England, we could not get hold of them. Now, we finally have them somewhere where we can beat them." When Göring arrived, Hitler immediately took him to the map table and told him: "They are landing here—they are landing there: exactly where we expected them."

It was true that, on December 27, Hitler had called the front of the Fifteenth and Seventh German Armies on the Cotentin Peninsula ". . . especially dangerous."

Later, he also repeatedly mentioned Normandy. However, this was not any "bright idea" by Hitler but reflected a sober assessment of the situation, which had also led the Allies to decide on this operation. Normandy was just across the Channel from southern England, and the crossing was the shortest here, since the area of Dover-Calais was under fire from German long-range artillery.

It is therefore out of place to speak about Hitler's "uncanny intuition" in the context of the Allied invasion of Normandy. It is remarkable, however, that he was unable to put up serious opposition to the invasion at this "expected" location for even a day. After all, Hitler had many times declared in earlier years:

A place taken by a German soldier will never be taken by any other soldier!

We had provided for every eventuality from the start.

Nothing is impossible for the German soldier!

I have read several times now that the English intend to launch a big offensive somewhere. I would like to ask that they tell me beforehand. I then would like to have the area evacuated. I would like to spare them the difficulties of a landing. And then we could introduce ourselves once again and discuss matters—and this in a language they alone understand!

I can assure him: no matter which place he chooses next, he can consider himself lucky if he stays on land for nine hours!

On January 1, 1944, he could still exclaim:

No matter where the plutocratic world will undertake the threatened attempt to land in the west, it will fail!

It is an open question whether Hitler's optimism on June 6 was real or whether he was just trying to impress his "unshakable certainty of victory" on his entourage. In any event, on the afternoon of June 6 he still acted as though the beachheads would be destroyed within a matter of hours.

In order to remind the German troops at the invasion front of their duty in this regard, he ordered the commander in chief of the West, Field Marshal von Rundstedt, to force the Allies back to sea on the same day. This order was relayed to the Seventh Army at the coast, as follows:

The commander in chief of the West, as instructed by the *Wehrmacht* high command *(OKW)*, emphasizes that the enemy beachheads are to be destroyed on the evening of June 6, since there are fears of reinforced airborne landings and further naval landings. The invasion there must be cleared up before day's end.

In spite of Hitler's orders, the "invasion" was not "cleared up" on June 6 nor on any of the following days. No matter how bravely the German troops fought, they were hopelessly inferior to the Anglo-American army, navy, and air force.

Hitler had said that the Allies ought to "consider themselves fortunate" if they managed to stay ashore for nine hours. Indeed, these were the most critical hours. However, once they were over, and the Allies were still on the beaches and continued to advance, it was clear that the landing had been a success, and the most decisive battle of the Second World War had begun. Not only did the German generals realize this but so did the public in Germany. After all, Hitler had said as much himself: "If they attack in the West, then this attack will decide the war."

Hitler's boast that the invasion would be repelled within nine hours had proved an embarrassment. Of course, he did not admit this. He had an idea on how to postpone the final catastrophe: with the help of his new *V-Waffen* (i.e., retaliatory weapons: *Vergeltungswaffen*).

Hitler had ordered the bombardment of England with long-range rockets to begin in mid-June. This proved to be a timely choice insofar as it diverted attention from the invasion front. It would instill new hope in his generals that a miraculous turn of events might still come about in the war, a last-minute rescue. Even though he had ordered this months ago, he acted as though it represented his response to the invasion and would soon make it disappear.

The *Wehrmacht* high command (*OKW*) report of June 16 read as follows:

> Last night and this morning, southern England and the city of London were bombed with a new type of high explosive.

In view of this, Hitler believed that he could risk facing the generals in the west. On June 17, he departed from Berchtesgaden by plane and flew to Metz, then drove to Margival north of Soissons. There he discussed the situation with von Rundstedt, Rommel, and several other generals from 9:00 a.m. to 4:00 p.m. Rommel had taken over command of Army Group B (i.e., northern France, Belgium, Holland), in addition to his role as inspector of the coastal fortifications.

According to Speidel, Hitler looked sallow and as if he had not had enough sleep. He was nervous, playing with his glasses and all sorts of colored pencils that he held in his hand. While the field marshals were standing, he sat hunched over on a stool. His earlier power of suggestion appeared to have vanished. After a brief and cool welcome, the Führer expressed his displeasure, speaking about the successful landing of the Allies with his voice raised and full of bitterness. He tried to put the blame on the local commanders.

In November 1942, after the disaster at El Alamein, Rommel had already told Hitler that, in his opinion, no army would in the long run be able to withstand the Allies. Now, he reasserted that he felt that the struggle was hopeless in view of the enemy's enormous superiority on land, at sea, and in the air. Hitler simply ignored him. He would one day show this defeatist!

Then Hitler took control of the discussion again. He began an enthusiastic lecture on the new rockets. He said that this "V-1 weapon" would have an "effect that would decide the war" and would make the English "ready for peace." The senile English would certainly collapse in face of this.

The generals were impressed with Hitler's exposition. They demanded the deployment of the new weapon against the Allied beachheads. However, the general responsible for the V-weapons, Heinemann, warned them about "unpredictable scattering" of the rockets. He claimed that they could go "15 to 18 kilometers" off course, although up to 200 kilometers would have been a more realistic figure. The generals began to complain about the failure of the *Luftwaffe*. Hitler quickly calmed them by saying that soon "masses of jet fighters" would chase the English and American aircraft from the skies.

The mid-day meal had to be relocated inside a bunker because of the threat of an air raid. Another situation briefing took place. Rommel again repeated his negative assessment of the prospects of the war in the West and alluded to the necessity of drawing the political consequences. Hitler immediately cut him off and said: "Do not concern yourself with the future course of the war but with your own invasion front."

It would certainly have been nice had Hitler also shown a bit more concern for it. The generals invited him to the headquarters of Army Group B at La Roche-Guyon. Hitler pretended to accept this invitation for June 19. However, he did not feel like risking his own precious life. Hurriedly, he left France on the next day.

On that June 18, he went by plane from Metz to Berchtesgaden. The evening discussion of the situation revealed to Hitler that the Americans had broken through to the western part of the Cotentin Peninsula (near Barneville) that morning. The decisive words exchanged during this discussion were laconically brief:

> Hitler: "You reported that the Americans broke through. Now, are they through or are they not?"

> Jodl: "They are through."

The Americans had really broken "through," and this meant that the Allies would shortly take Cherbourg. Additional landings would then be possible on a much larger scale. However, Hitler continued his ostrich-like policy and remained at the Berghof. He sent out diplomatic congratulatory telegrams, like the one to Horthy on his birthday on June 18. For the rest, he staked his hopes on the psychological effect of the new German "wonder weapons," the *V-Waffen*.

As revolutionary as they were, one could not speak of a great military significance of these rocket bombs at the time, given the status of the technology. The V-1 was an unmanned monoplane carrying a bomb, powered by a simple kind of jet engine (i.e., *pulse jet*). Agile British fighters and antiaircraft equipment were largely capable of intercepting the V-1 missiles prior to impact. This was no longer the case with V-2 bombs, which were deployed from September 1944 on. Unlike its predecessor, the V-2 was, not merely an improved bomb with wings, but an advanced model of rocket technology. Designed as a rocket bomb with a preset guidance system, the V-2 was the first long-range ballistic missile in the world. The V-2 was 14 meters (47 feet) long, weighed 12.6 tons, traveled at a maximum speed of 5500 kilometers per hour (3400 miles per hour), carried a one-ton warhead, and had a range of 320 kilometers to 400 kilometers.

In the period up to March 1945, a total of 9000 V-1 rockets hit England, a number augmented by approximately 1100 to 1500 V-2 models fired. While little is known on the precise effects this bombardment had in England, various detailed studies of the period between October 1944 and March 1945 show the magnitude of bomb strikes in Belgium.

Having lost the rocket launching ramps located in northern France and Belgium to the Allied advance, Hitler decided to use the remaining V-rocket capacity to terrorize the Belgian civilian population. Rumors quickly spread that the harbor of Antwerp was the main target of this undertaking, and numerous hits in the surrounding area substantiate this hypothesis. A veritable shower of V bombs came down over nearly two-thirds of Belgium at the same time, a fact indicative of the V weapons' inability to hit a precise target.

From a military point of view, neither of the missile models could be aimed at precise targets: a missile was liable to miss by up to 200 kilometers—too great a risk for military strategists to take. Therefore, the new V weapons could only serve as an instrument of terror. However, Hitler's terrorization of the English civilian population by his rocket-fire brought no success. On the contrary, it merely induced the Allies to speed up their advance and increase their bombardment.

July 7, 1944 *Any perceptive observer could see that Germany had lost the war. Hitler refused to consider such a thought. A plot to remove him was formed.*

On July 7, a few soldiers, especially detailed for this duty, paraded new army uniforms and pieces of field equipment in front of Hitler at the Berghof, in the presence of Speer and Major General Helmut Stieff. Allegedly, there was a plan to hide a bomb in the field pack of one of the soldiers and blow him up along with Hitler.

Regardless of whether this assassination attempt was supposed to be carried out on July 7 or at another opportunity, it underlined the fact that the assassins did not dare to face Hitler themselves. They preferred to kill innocent people along with Hitler, since they wished to stay alive themselves. The excuse that it was not possible to shoot Hitler with a pistol because he was constantly guarded by Nazi Party security squad (SS) is not compelling. Many of Hitler's entourage agreed that it would have been quite possible to shoot him on numerous occasions without his servants or guards being able to prevent this.

Hitler had not been at his headquarters in East Prussia for four months. He preferred the more private and comfortable atmosphere of the Berghof. It was likewise understandable that the men at the Wolfsschanze headquarters thought that it was a good idea to relocate to safer zones, at least insofar as the high command of the army was concerned. After all, the Russians had not only taken Minsk in the course of their great offensive in the central sector, but they had also begun to advance on Vilnius. It was only a question of months or weeks until they would reach the borders of East Prussia.

In early July, Chief of Staff Zeitzler began transferring the army high command from Rastenburg to Zossen. Hitler was outraged when he heard of this. He ordered an immediate return to East Prussia. However, this meant that he also had to return to Rastenburg, whether he liked it or not. He scheduled his arrival for July 15.

Before he left, however, a series of situation briefings took place at the Berghof, like those of July 6 and 11. They dealt mostly with the mobilization of the home army (*Heimatheer*). Colonel Claus Graf Schenk von Stauffenberg among others attended these meetings. Since July 1, he had been serving as chief of staff to Colonel General Fromm, the commander of the replacement army.

The resistance movement felt it had finally found its man in von Stauffenberg. The count would carry through on the attempt on Hitler's life. The leading heads of the resistance movement had great plans on what they would do, whom they would appoint as ministers, what appeals they would issue, and so on, but all these plans presupposed that Hitler was dead. However, not one of these men dared to kill him or obtain his dismissal from office through the Reichstag. They were greatly relieved when Graf von Stauffenberg offered to take care of Hitler.

It was sad that the heads of the resistance movement had to turn to the count in this matter. After all, von Stauffenberg had been seriously injured in the campaign in Africa. He had lost his left eye, his lower right arm, and two fingers of his left hand. Moreover, he still carried shrapnel in his skull, and it had to be removed. In every respect, the count cut a tragic figure; he was physically weakened and nervous, although undoubtedly ambitious. His method was no different from those of the other would-be assassins who had previously tried to kill Hitler. He was also prepared to answer for innocent people being killed along with Hitler. But he wanted to stay alive since he counted on an appointment as state secretary with the war ministry in the planned Goerdeler cabinet.

An assassin who is not prepared to sacrifice his own life in the attempt is ill-suited to such an undertaking. Normally, his life is over after the attack: if the attempt fails, then he will either be shot on the spot or put on trial shortly afterward and executed. If the attack succeeds, then the followers of the victim will try to kill him or, in many cases, his fellow conspirators will seek to eliminate him later. As far as it is humanly possible to tell, Graf von Stauffenberg was destined to die. He deserves to have his memory honored as a man who dared more than the other members of the German resistance movement, and as one of Hitler's victims, like so many million people of all nations, who suffered a horrible death.

At the talks at the Berghof, von Stauffenberg did not activate the bomb that he had brought along. He claimed that he failed to do so because Himmler was not present.

▶ July 20, 1944 *The attempt to kill Hitler failed.*

For the afternoon of July 20, Hitler planned a reception for Mussolini at the Wolfsschanze headquarters. For this reason, he rescheduled the noon discussion of the situation for 12:30 p.m. instead of 1:00 p.m. as was the usual time. The bunker where the briefings normally took place had been closed for some time because of construction work to reinforce the concrete floor. A barracks that usually housed guests now served as a temporary room for the meeting. This change was not favorable for the assassination attempt, because the windows and walls of the barracks—in contrast with the massive concrete of the bunker—naturally diminished the effect of the explosion. Von Stauffenberg was again summoned to attend the meeting; he was to report on the mobilization of the home army.

First, however, General Heusinger made a presentation on the situation at the eastern front. In the meantime, von Stauffenberg put the briefcase with the bomb beneath the table where Hitler was sitting. Saying that he had to make a telephone call, he left the barracks.

Just when Hitler was trying to locate something on a map and leaning over the heavy oak table at 12:40 p.m. or 12:42 p.m., the bomb went off. Hitler was catapulted up along with the tabletop. He suffered bruises on his right arm and back, and some scratches on his left hand. His ear drums were injured, and his hair was singed, but other than that he was fine, even though his pants were in shreds.

Many of the other participants in the conference were so seriously injured that they later died: Reichstag stenographer and senior executive officer Heinrich Berger, who had been detailed along with other Reichstag stenographers to attend the situation briefings and could hardly be blamed for Hitler's politics; Hitler's chief *Wehrmacht* adjutant Lieutenant General Rudolf Schmundt, *Luftwaffe* chief of staff General Günther Korten, and Colonel (G.S.) Heinz Brandt. The following suffered serious injuries: Air Force General Karl Bodenschatz, Rear Admiral Karl-Jesko von Puttkammer, Major General Walter Scherff, Lieutenant Colonel (G.S.) Heinrich Borgmann, and Captain Heinz Assmann.

The following men were only slightly injured: Keitel, Jodl, Infantry General Walter Buhle, Lieutenant General Adolf Heusinger, Rear Admiral Hans-Erich Voss, SS Gruppenführer Hermann Fegelein, Colonel Nicolaus von Below, Lieutenant Colonel Heinz Waizenegger, Major (G.S.) Herbert Büchs, Major von Jahn, and SS Hauptsturmführer Otto Günsche. Undeniably, Hitler was lucky to survive the explosion with barely any injuries. This was due less to a "miraculous rescue" than to a chain of certain coincidences, since most of those present sustained only slight injuries.

Von Stauffenberg had waited at a signal bunker, about 80 meters away, until he saw the explosion, and the barracks collapse. Convinced that Hitler was dead, he headed for the exit. Even though the gate was already closed, he managed to persuade the guards to let him out, after some discussion. It was 12:44 p.m.

The count had a car take him to the airfield as quickly as possible. After all, he intended to play a leading role in the revolution that would now begin in Berlin. On the way, his chauffeur noticed that he threw a small package containing explosives no longer needed out of the window.

In the meantime, Hitler had himself treated by his physician Dr. Morell. His servant Linge brought him a new uniform. Hitler remained admirably calm. He ordered Linge to look for additional explosives, because he initially thought that construction workers had hidden the bomb beneath the floor. All the construction workers at the headquarters were kept in custody for the time being.

Soon, however, it was discovered that the actual assassin had been von Stauffenberg. His departure just before the explosion had attracted notice. And, hastily, he had departed by plane at 1:00 p.m. The package with the remaining explosive that he had thrown away was recovered. Immediately, Hitler ordered von Stauffenberg's arrest in Berlin, in the event that he had not escaped behind the Russian lines, as some suspected.

In the meantime, von Ribbentrop, Göring, and Himmler had arrived at the headquarters in order to prepare for Mussolini's reception. The interpreter Schmidt had also arrived.

The Duce was scheduled to arrive at a nearby station at 2:30 p.m. However, his train ran one hour late. Hitler personally went to the station to pick up his guest. He was in complete control of himself. He was only experiencing some problems in using his right arm so that he had to extend his left hand in greeting. Mussolini had quite a fright when he heard that there had just been an assassination attempt at the headquarters. Since it was beginning to rain a little, Hitler put on his black cape, and the entire company, including Göring, Himmler, von Ribbentrop, Bormann, and so on, returned to the headquarters by foot.

As they reached the site of the explosion, Hitler, Mussolini, and Schmidt entered the heavily damaged barracks. Hitler coolly described the explosion to his friend as follows:

It happened here. I stood here, at this table. I was leaning on the table with my right arm like this in order to look at something on the map, when suddenly the tabletop came flying at me and threw my arm upward. Here, directly at my feet, the bomb exploded.

For some time, none of them said anything. Then Hitler sat down on a box, and Schmidt had to bring up one of the few usable chairs for Mussolini. As they sat face to face in the rubble, Hitler began to speak again in a low voice:

As I let things pass again before my mind, my miraculous rescue proves that, while others present in the room sustained serious injuries, and one was even catapulted out of the window by the air pressure, nothing happened to me—fate spared me—especially since this wasn't the first time that I escaped death in such a miraculous fashion.

After my rescue from certain death today, I am more convinced than ever before that I am destined to bring to a happy conclusion our great common cause!

Hitler's "miraculous rescue" by Providence meant one thing: triumph of the god-man over all earthly challenges and "trials of the Devil, Satan, and Hell." Hitler found the new attitude he would strike, the new slogan he would use. Now, at a time when the opposition of his inner circle was becoming clear, he felt that he could again speak to the public, armed with this new catchword.

Hitler had not spoken to the German *Volksgenossen* since January 30, because he faced a constantly deteriorating situation. Even then, he had addressed them only on the radio. This time, he was not ready to do much more, but he did want to speak. He would personally inform the Germans of his "miraculous rescue" and show his opponents that divine Providence stood by him. It did so because he was steadfast; he refused to capitulate; he was ready to fight on to "the last battalion," even until "five minutes past twelve."

Mussolini was much impressed with Hitler's poise and his remarkable coolness. He declared: "After what I have seen here, I agree with you completely. This was a sign from Heaven!"

The two dictators rose in order to continue their conversation in the bunker. The tone was subdued on this day. Schmidt reported that he felt there was "an aura of farewell" in the air at their relatively inconsequential talks. Indeed, it was the last time that Hitler and Mussolini would meet face to face. In the course of the past decade, they had met 17 times. The circumstances at their last meeting presaged the violent death they would each meet only months later at nearly the same time, though in different locations—the one in Berlin, the other south of the Alps.

The following communiqué was published on the talks:

> The talks between the Führer and the Duce were marked by a spirit of great warmth. The Führer and the Duce examined the situation and, among other things, discussed the question of the Italian prisoners of war. They set guidelines for the resolution of this question in the spirit of the moral and material obligations of the two countries. This solution provides for the prisoners of war to be granted the status of free laborers or deployed as helpers within the German *Wehrmacht*.
>
> The discussions at the Führer headquarters were attended by Reichsmarshal Hermann Göring, Reich Foreign Minister von Ribbentrop, and Field Marshal Keitel. On the Italian side, Marshal Grazini and under state secretary in the foreign ministry, Count Mazzolini, attended.

The talks between Hitler and Mussolini had repeatedly been interrupted as new information arrived from Berlin. Upon the false report of Hitler's death, several generals had gathered at the *Reichswehr* ministry located at Bendlerstrasse. The following men had planned to take power: Field Marshal von Witzleben; the former chief of the general staff, Colonel General Beck; Colonel General Hoeppner, a former Panzer commander who, in front of Moscow, had been demoted by Hitler and dismissed from the *Wehrmacht*; and General of Infantry Olbricht.

Olbricht, together with Colonel Graf von Stauffenberg who in the meantime had arrived in Berlin, undertook to persuade the commander of the replacement army, Colonel General Fromm, to side with the new "government." However, Fromm was a cautious man and wanted to know first whether Hitler was really dead or not. At 4:00 p.m. he telephoned the Führer headquarters. He spoke with Keitel, who told him that, while there had been an assassination attempt, Hitler had sustained only minor injuries.

That was enough for Fromm. He knew what he owed the legal government and recommended that von Stauffenberg shoot himself right away. But neither von Stauffenberg nor Olbricht agreed to this. They were cornered and so they decided to arrest Fromm. They placed him under house arrest at his apartment, which was located in the same building, and requested his "word of honor" that he stay there.

Now the events of November 8, 1923, repeated themselves. At the time, Hitler and his comrades had detained the commander of the *Reichswehr* in Munich, von Lussow, on his "word of honor." Both generals— von Lussow as well as Fromm—were opponents of Hitler but both could think only of proving their loyalty to the legal government authority. In 1923, Hitler had been a Putschist. In 1944, he was the head of state and government, as well as supreme commander of the *Wehrmacht*. Fromm's decision was clear.

Once Witzleben found out that the assassination attempt had failed, he became quite indignant, got into his Mercedes, and drove home. The other generals were not as quickly informed of the true facts, since the Putschists had given the code word *"Walküre"* (Valkyrie) that sounded the alarm for the replacement army in the case of domestic unrest, and had announced "the Führer's death."

The military commander of Paris, General Heinrich von Stülpnagel, had all high-ranking SS officers in the city arrested. They did not put up any resistance and submitted to the arrest in a "collegial" manner, so to speak.

The commandant of Berlin, Lieutenant General Paul von Hase, ordered the guards battalion *Grossdeutschland* to occupy the governmental district. However, at the urging of Lieutenant Hans Hagen, a Nazi Party security officer, the commander of the battalion, Major Otto Remer, first inquired of Goebbels personally whether or not Hitler was really dead. At 5:00 p.m., the major went to the propaganda ministry. Goebbels had just spoken on the telephone with Hitler, who had told him all about the assassination attempt. Immediately, he put another call through and handed the receiver to Remer, who clearly heard Hitler say the following:

> Major Remer, can you hear my voice?
> Major Remer, they tried to kill me, but I am alive.
> Major Remer, I am speaking to you as the supreme commander of the *Wehrmacht*.

Only my orders are to be obeyed. You must secure Berlin for
me. Deploy every means of force that you feel necessary.
Shoot any person who tries to disobey my orders.

This telephone call was the end of the "revolution." There was no need
for Remer to deploy "means of force." The troops returned to their quarters.
Lieutenant General Hase surrendered his pistol to Goebbels. A few Putschists still held out at the Reich War Ministry in the Benderstrasse, but Fromm,
though under arrest, had secretly sent three generals out to get help.

However, Fromm had nevertheless become suspicious in Hitler's eyes.
After all, his chief of staff von Stauffenberg had carried out the assassination attempt. The replacement army in Berlin had been put on alert.
Hitler felt that Fromm had to have been involved in the conspiracy in
some manner.

On the spot, Hitler decided to set an example and put a civilian in
command of the renegade generals. So he appointed Himmler as the new
commander of the replacement army.

In addition, Hitler dismissed Zeitzler, who had dared to relocate the
headquarters from Rastenburg to Zossen without asking his approval. He
considered giving the position to Guderian. At 6:00 p.m., he telephoned
Guderian's chief of staff, General Thomale, in order to ask Guderian to the
headquarters on the following day.

Hitler stated his contempt for the Putschists in a conversation with his
manservant Linge:

They are no revolutionaries, these conspirators; they are
not even rebels.
If Stauffenberg had pulled out a gun and shot me, he would
have been a man. What he did was cowardly.

Göring, Dönitz, von Ribbentrop, and Hitler's Unterführers who gathered at the headquarters were somewhat depressed by the assassination attempt. They were nervous and blamed one another for the bad military and
political situation. Hitler listened to their verbal exchanges for a while and
then struck a pose: if anybody had a right to shout in this case, it was he!
And he began to launch a tirade against the conspirators. He shouted that
he would exterminate them. Their wives and children would be brought to
concentration camps, and nobody would be spared.

▶ July 21, 1944 *The retribution was harsh.*

In Berlin, in the meantime, Fromm had again taken control of the war ministry and arrested the leading conspirators. He was eager to summon a drumhead court-martial so that the persons arrested could be sentenced to death and executed on the spot. Fromm was trying to save his own skin: by taking swift action, he hoped to eliminate those who knew about his ambiguous stand and curry favor with Hitler. However, he was mistaken in this. Whoever issued death sentences without Hitler's approval committed a sacrilege by appropriating a privilege of power that Hitler considered his very own. Whoever dared to do this had to die.

The consequences of the failed assassination attempt were grave. Undoubtedly it resulted in a deterioration of the domestic situation in Germany. A veritable psychosis took hold of the military and political Unterführers of the Third Reich. They competed with one another in proving their devotion to Hitler and sending him telegrams that paid homage to him.

Himmler was compelled to launch a relentless campaign of persecution of all opponents of the regime. Up to this point, he had pretty much let the reins go slack and not done anything about the activities of the resistance circles around Beck, Goerdeler, Canaris, and others, even though he was aware of them.

Although Himmler was devoted to Hitler, he was not so stupid that he had not long ago realized that Hitler's policies were bringing ruin to all Germans. The old fighters around Hitler had had greater opportunity to observe him up close than the military men and the bourgeois. Consequently, they had seen what was coming for some time already, even though not one of them dared to make a move against Hitler.

By 1944, the leading Nazi Party security squad (SS) men would also have been happy to get rid of Hitler and his fateful policies somehow. In the beginning, the SS had attempted to emulate the ideals of the Prussian officer corps and form an elite. They had chosen the uniform that recalled that of the famous Great War cavalry regiments, the Death's Head Hussars under the command of Field Marshal Mackensen and Crown Prince Wilhelm. However, Hitler had used the SS for his own ends. And this had led slowly but surely to the SS being stamped a criminal organization in the eyes of the world and of the German Volk.

The Italians noticed already in 1942 that Himmler was beginning to distance himself from Hitler's politics. Himmler's Finnish physician Kersten made similar observations. Other SS leaders were also becoming increasingly unhappy about Hitler's leadership. Of course, they had no plans to kill him, but they would not have been too unhappy about his death. This became clear in the course of the arrests of the SS leaders in Paris on July 20 after the supposed death of the Führer. The SS leaders did not put up any resistance. Both parties in the arrests were somewhat embarrassed when the order was canceled only hours later.

After the failure of the assassination attempt, it was clear that Himmler had to move without mercy against the resistance movement in order to please Hitler. And the men of the resistance deserved no mercy in his eyes because they had shown themselves incapable of taking successful action. In addition, the manner in which von Stauffenberg had proceeded in his assassination attempt, that is, killing or injuring high-ranking *Wehrmacht* members, was not suited to gaining new friends for the resistance movement within the *Wehrmacht*.

Hitler waited a few days before he issued orders on how to deal with the arrested individuals. He stayed in bed on July 21 but replied to the congratulations he received from the satellite states on his escape. The following sent him telegrams: Laval, Quisling, Tiso, Neditsch, Hácha, and the prime minister of Manchuria, Chang Teng-hai. The Japanese emperor inquired about Hitler's state of health at the German embassy.

Hitler received Guderian around noon to appoint him chief of the general staff. On this occasion, he already called the present commander in chief of the West, von Kluge, "an accessory in the assassination attempt," even though von Kluge had sent him a telegram of loyalty. The arrest of the SS men in Paris had led Hitler to this conclusion. In his eyes, von Kluge was no better than Fromm.

Hitler was determined to eliminate the reactionary spirit in the *Wehrmacht*. Symbolically, the military salute that was used within the *Wehrmacht* was to be replaced at this late date by the Fascist or so-called "German salute." Göring, Keitel, and Dönitz anticipated this wish. The following official announcement was published:

> The *Reichsmarschall* of the Greater German Reich, as the senior officer in the German *Wehrmacht*, has reported to the Führer, in the name of Field Marshal Keitel and Grand Admiral Dönitz as well, that all branches of the *Wehrmacht* have requested on the occasion of his rescue to be allowed to introduce to the *Wehrmacht* the German salute as a sign of

unswerving loyalty to the Führer and of the close solidarity between the *Wehrmacht* and the party. The Führer has granted the *Wehrmacht* this wish and has given his approval.

Effective immediately, the salute that consisted of raising the right hand to the headgear will be replaced by the German salute.

On July 23, Hitler composed this general note of thanks:

On the occasion of the attack directed against me and my coworkers, I have received so many congratulations and demonstrations of loyalty from all parts of the German Volk, especially the party and the *Wehrmacht*, that I would like to express in this manner my heartfelt thanks, also on behalf of my comrades, to all those who thought of me in the course of these days.

Adolf Hitler

► August 2, 1944 *The retribution continued.*

In the meantime, Hitler had decided how he would deal with the participants in the military Putsch of July 20. For years, he had considered how he could best put down attempted rebellions by the generals. Whoever rose against him would suffer an ignominious death. On March 4, 1943, he had already authorized courts-martial to execute death sentences by hanging. On June 21, 1943, he had decreed the establishment of a central special drumhead court-martial for the *Wehrmacht* in order to deal with offenses against the leaders of the state and *Wehrmacht*. However, all these preparations now appeared to him to have been tactically unwise. It would be better not to leave the sentencing of the offenders up to a military court at all!

Hitler knew the caste mentality of the military well. He would certainly run into difficulties if he tried to get a field marshal sentenced to be hanged. He did not wish to repeat Groener's mistake. In 1930, *Reichswehr* Minister Groener had caused a virtual palace revolution by having three *Reichswehr* lieutenants, who were accused of subversive National Socialist activities, arrested by the police, in disregard of the military code of conduct. Hitler wished to proceed as he had in the Röhm case. At the time, the Officers' League had expelled Captain Ernst Röhm from its ranks on his request and, thereby, had made it possible for Hitler to have the Nazi Party storm trooper (SA) chief of staff killed three days later.

Hitler planned to proceed in the same manner with the arrested generals of the German *Wehrmacht*: the *Wehrmacht* should simply expel them from its ranks. For this reason, Hitler summoned an army court of honor, whose members (Keitel, Guderian, and other generals) surrendered their own comrades to the highly questionable Peoples' Court (*Volksgerichtshof*) and to a disgraceful death by strangulation. The members of this court of honor would not have to trouble their consciences any more than the officers who had expelled Röhm from the Officers' League. By virtue of their resolutions, Röhm, Witzleben, and the others no longer belonged to the officer corps, and Hitler could do what he wanted with them!

After Hitler had summoned the court of honor for August 4, he visited the officers injured in the explosion. Hypocritically, he played the role of the devoted supreme commander who had considered all aspects of the assassination attempt and was concerned only for the welfare of the German Volk and the "terribly struggling eastern front." All this weighed naturally more heavily than his own life in his considerations! He told the injured General Bodenschatz the following:

> Well, you know, Bodenschatz, I am being asked a lot these days what I say to the assassination attempt, what I think about political murder. I do not reject it 100 percent! I can also understand that it may be necessary to remove a statesman if the situation of the nation demands it and a people can have a better future after the elimination of a ruler.
>
> I know that von Stauffenberg, Goerdeler, and Witzleben believed that they could save the German Volk through killing me. However, up to now, only one thing has been ascertained: these people had no concrete plan of what they wanted to do afterwards. They had no idea what army supported their Putsch, what defense district command would help them. They had not even managed the obvious, to establish communications with the enemy. Yes, I even found out that the enemy had rejected offers of negotiation.

Think about it, Bodenschatz. There are German soldiers in the midst of a bitter battle at the Eastern front. Nearly nine million. And now imagine the effect! It would have become a war of everybody against everybody, a civil war in the German army. The Russians would have been the real winners and have taken a terrible toll. You see, Bodenschatz, this and only this was the crime of the assassins in my eyes!

On August 3, Hitler received a delegation of leading National Socialist officers at the *Wolfsschanze* headquarters in the presence of Keitel and General Ritter von Hengel. This communiqué was published on the convening of the "Court of Honor of the German army":

Führer Headquarters, August 4

The army has submitted a request to the Führer for the immediate restoration of its honor in the quickest manner through a merciless purge of the last of the criminals involved in the assassination attempt of July 20, 1944. It would like to surrender the guilty persons to civil justice. The Führer has granted this request all the more since the speedy and energetic action of the army itself nipped the assassination attempt in the bud.

The Führer has ordered the following: a court of honor by field marshals and generals will examine who was involved in whatever form in the assassination attempt and hence, should be expelled from the army, and who must be regarded as suspicious and will be temporarily suspended.

The Führer has appointed to this court of honor the following: Field Marshal Keitel, Field Marshal von Rundstedt, Colonel General Guderian, General of Infantry Schroth, Lieutenant General Specht. As substitutes: General of Infantry Kriebel, Lieutenant General Kirchheim. The Führer has reserved for himself the right to decide about the petitions of the court of honor. Soldiers expelled by the Führer no longer have anything in common with the millions of honorable soldiers of the Greater German Reich who wear the army uniform and with the hundreds of thousands who sealed their loyalty with death. They will not be placed before a *Wehrmacht* court but will be sentenced together with other offenders by the Peoples' Court (*Volksgerichtshof*). The same applies to all soldiers who are for the time being suspended from the *Wehrmacht*.

The army court of honor summoned by the Führer convened on August 4 and, based on the results of its investigations, submitted the following recommendations to the Führer: The following are dismissed from the Wehrmacht:

1. Persons in custody:
   Field Marshal von Witzleben, General of the Signal Corps Fellgiebel, Lieutenant General von Hase, Major General Stieff, Major General von Tresckow, Colonel (G.S.) Hansen, Lieutenant Colonel (G.S.) Bernardis, Major (G.S.) Hayessen, Captain Klausing, Lieutenant Colonel (Res.) Graf von der Schulenburg, Lieutenant Colonel (Res.) von Hagen, Lieutenant (Res.) Graf Zorck von Wartenburg.

   Persons shot by sentence of a court-marital on July 20: General of Infantry Olbricht, Colonel (G.S.) Graf von Stauffenberg, Colonel (G.S.) Quirnheim, First Lieutenant (Res.) von Haeften.

2. The traitors who acknowledged their guilt by committing suicide: Colonel General (retired) Beck, General of Artillery Wagner, Colonel (G.S.) Freytag-Loringhoven, Lieutenant Colonel Schrader.

3. The deserters: Artillery General Lindemann, Major (G.S.) Kuhn (defected to the Bolsheviks).

A recommendation for the expulsion of former Colonel General Hoeppner is unnecessary since Hoeppner—already expelled from the *Wehrmacht* in the year 1942—no longer belongs to the army. The Führer has approved of these petitions. Those expelled will be surrendered to the *Volksgerichtshof* for sentencing. The trial of the guilty parties will shortly be held before the *Volksgerichtshof*.

On this day of "triumph," on which the army court of honor fulfilled all his requests, Hitler gathered his Reichsleiters and Gauleiters around him at his military headquarters. The Reichsleiter General von Epp and Major General Hierl paid homage to him on behalf of those assembled. He shook hands with everyone, using his left hand, since he still wanted to spare his right hand.

The following communiqué was published on Hitler's speech before the Reichsleiters and Gauleiters:

> The Führer spoke to his top political leaders. He illuminated the background and context of July 20. In assessing this crime, it should not be forgotten that these traitors have in fact, not only since 1941 but ever since the National Socialist seizure of power, continuously sabotaged the efforts and struggles of the nation.
>
> The clique, the Führer declared, had been limited in numbers but had had significant influence. The Führer described in detail how permanent resistance by these circles was directed against all measures by the leadership. It culminated in open betrayal of the fighting troops and direct sabotage of supplies for the front. The overwhelming majority, hundreds of thousands of brave German officers, had nothing in common with this clique of criminals and turned away from it with outrage and disgust. The Führer himself felt that it was an act of Providence and a relief for him personally that this previously intangible internal resistance had finally been uncovered and the clique of criminals eliminated. Now it was a question of drawing one's conclusions from these events. In the end, it would one day be realized that this presently very painful act may perhaps have been beneficial for the entire future of Germany.
>
> "I do not shy away from the battle against these enemies" the Führer declared, "we will in the end deal with them in spite of everything. I just need to know that absolute security, faithful confidence, and loyal assistance back me up. This is the prerequisite. We could not have undertaken the mobilization

of all forces of our Volk, as is presently taking place, if the criminal activities of the now-eliminated saboteurs had continued. By deploying the complete military and inner strength of the nation, we will overcome all difficulties.

I am grateful to Providence for sparing my life, only because I can now continue this battle. I believe that the nation needs me, that it needs a man who will under no circumstances capitulate, and who instead holds high the banner of faith and confidence, and because I believe that no other could do this better than I am doing it. Whatever blows of fortune may come, I will always stand straight as the bearer of this banner! Through the events of July 20 in particular, I have received a new confidence, the likes of which I have never before experienced in my life. We will, therefore, victoriously survive this war in the end!"

At Nuremberg, Speer expanded on this official excerpt from Hitler's speech. By calling on Schirach as another witness, he recalled the following passage:

> Should the German Volk be overpowered in this struggle, then it will have been too weak; it will not have passed its test before history, and it will therefore be doomed.

▸ December 11, 1944 *Hitler attempted a great counter-attack in the West.*

On December 11 and 12, Hitler summoned the generals in groups of 20 to 30 to the Ziegenberg headquarters in order to discuss the plans for the new operation with them. Most of the shorthand record of Hitler's speech on December 12 has been preserved. His rhetorical techniques and tactics had not changed since the time of his seizure of power. Even on this occasion and despite the desperate situation of the Reich, he went far back in endless "party narratives" and tried to tire his listeners by pseudo-historical and pseudo-philosophical explanations. He finally addressed the current situation and again claimed that Germany had as many men as its opponents.

You should not forget that the total number of the men deployed on our side is, after all, as great as that on the side of our enemies.

Hitler added to this statement that it was time to start the offensive again. Being on the defensive for too long used up too many resources.

In spite of this, you must realize that overly long periods of a merely defensive steadfastness eat you up in the long run. In any event, they must alternate with successful strikes. It was, therefore, my intention from the start to wage this war, if possible, offensively, to wage it strategically, not to let us be maneuvered into a situation as in the World War. Since that still happened, then there was a simple connection with the desertion of our allies, which of course had strategic consequences.

Wars are decided in the end by the realization by one side or the other that the war as such cannot any longer be won. To get this realization across to the enemy is therefore the most important task. This realization is made clear to him in the speediest manner by destroying his vital energy, by occupying his territory. If you are forced to defend yourself, to go on the defensive, then it is all the more your task to make it clear to the enemy from time to time by ruthless blows that he has not won anything in spite of this, and that the war will incessantly continue to be waged. It is likewise important to reinforce these psychological moments by never letting an opportunity pass to make it clear to the enemy that, no matter what he does, he can never count on a capitulation—never, never.

Then Hitler described the situation in the Seven Years' War and the "miracle" Frederick the Great had supposedly experienced.

The steadfastness of the man had made it possible that this war was fought out and, in spite of everything, a miraculous turn of events came about in the end.

Germany would now also witness such a "miracle." It was only a question of "biding one's time" until the enemy coalition fell apart on its own.

> The enemies we have today are the greatest extremes conceivable on earth: ultra-capitalist states on the one hand, and ultra-Marxist states on the other; on the one hand, a dying empire, Great Britain, on the other hand, a colony out for the inheritance, the United States of America. These are states whose objectives today clash more and more by the day. And whoever follows this development—let me say, like a spider sitting in his web—can see how these conflicts develop by the hour. Should a few bad blows ensue here, then it can happen at any minute that this artificially sustained joint front suddenly collapses in a gigantic thunderbolt.

Hitler wanted to land a "few bad blows" on the Allies in the West. He recalled the campaign in France in 1940 and claimed that the chances were as good now as they had been then.

> Now, you could object to me that (in one respect) there is a big difference between 1940 and the present: at the time, we faced an enemy army that had not yet been tried in battle; and today, it is an army we know well that has been in the war for some time. That is correct, gentlemen. But in terms of strength, little has changed, if we leave the *Luftwaffe* aside.
>
> We have many battle-weary troops, and the enemy also has battle-weary troops and has suffered heavy losses in blood. We now have the first official information from the Americans that, within a period of barely three weeks, they lost about 240,000 men. These are figures that are simply gigantic, that are far above what we ourselves believed that they might have lost. So they are battle-weary, too. Technically speaking, both sides are about the same. Regarding the tank weapon, the enemy might have more tanks at his disposal, but we have the better tanks with our latest models.

With such eyewash, Hitler believed he could make the new offensive more palatable to the generals. It is still an open question whether they left the headquarters in better spirits. In any event, Hitler need not have troubled himself. In principle, the generals were always ready to comply with the orders of their supreme commander, if this was technically possible.

The Bunker, Hitler's Last Dominion

XV
Hitler's War Ends

Germany could not win the war by the middle of 1943 and had obviously lost by July 1944. But Hitler refused to believe this plain fact. Having stated so many times since 1919 that it was the November Criminals and internal dissension that lost the Great War, he was trapped in his own lies. So the great German empire fought on hopelessly.

▶ January 27, 1945 *Hitler saw hope for his regime by using the "Bolshevik threat" as a tool to gain British support. The United Nations Alliance against Fascism's policy of unconditional surrender precluded that tactic.*

On January 24, Guderian called on von Ribbentrop in order to discuss the initiation of peace negotiations with him, in view of the catastrophic military situation. Von Ribbentrop was appalled and refused to discuss it. When Guderian arrived at the Reich chancellery for the evening discussion of the situation, Hitler greeted him with these words:

> When the chief of the general staff goes to see the Reich foreign minister and informs him of the situation in the East with the objective of achieving an armistice with the Western powers, then he is committing high treason.

Hitler said this only to frighten Guderian. He never took any concrete steps against him.

Hitler, Guderian, Göring, and Jodl, among others, met again for a discussion of the situation on January 27, which took place at the Reich Chancellery at 4:00 p.m. They engaged in endless talk about what could be done to improve the situation. Hitler, with his head in the clouds, claimed the following:

The Americans lost 85,000 men this month. That amounts
to 50 percent of their total losses in the World War.

At the same time, he announced a "great armament program." More
than 900,000 *Sturmpistolen* (machine pistols) would be produced every
month, he claimed, not to mention the new *Volksgewehr* (gas-operated
militia machine-gun.)

When a suggestion was made to move 6,000 SS men from the Lich-
tenfelde barracks to the eastern front, Hitler quickly returned to reality
and refused this transfer categorically. While he did not state his reasons
for doing so, it was sufficiently clear that he needed those men for his own
personal security in the event of a revolt in Berlin.

In the course of the conversation, Hitler, Göring, and Jodl discussed
Generals Student, Hausser, Blaskowitz, and others. Oddly enough, they
hoped that an offer to accept a surrender would come from the English.
After all, they had to be frightened out of their wits in view of the Russian
advances, the men at Hitler's headquarters believed.

> Hitler: I don't really know. Do you think that the English are
> still following all Russian developments with the same inner
> enthusiasm?

> Jodl: No, certainly not. The plans were entirely different. Per-
> haps the full extent of this will become visible only later.

> Göring: That we hold on over there and let the Russians con-
> quer all of Germany in the meantime is certainly not what they
> want. If things go on like this, we will get a telegram in a few
> days saying that the English want to join the Germans. There is
> nothing to the view that we do not let them in at all and that,
> according to the present view of the enemy, we are holding out
> like crazy in the West while the Russians keep moving into
> Germany and occupying practically all of Germany.

> Hitler: In that respect, the national committee, this organiza-
> tion of traitors, could be of a certain significance. If the Rus-
> sians really proclaim a national government (in Germany),
> then fear will take hold of England.

Jodl: Yes, the English have always regarded the Russians with suspicion.

Hitler: I have arranged for something to fall into their hands, namely, the report that the Russians are deploying 200,000 of our men under the command of German officers completely infected by Communism, and that they want to let them go on the march. I asked that this report be dropped into English hands. I gave it to the foreign minister [von Ribbentrop]. That is something that will have an effect on them, as if you stick them with a needle.

Göring: They entered the war so that we wouldn't get to the East but not so that the East would get all the way to the Atlantic.

Hitler: That is perfectly clear. It would be unnatural. English papers are already asking with bitterness: Does the war make any sense?

This was Hitler's old favorite theory that he would gain England's friendship by preventing a Russian expansion to the Atlantic. In reality, the English had always, at least in the twentieth century, considered German expansionism much more dangerous than Russian expansionism.

▸ April 13, 1945 *By mid-April 1945, the fronts were closing in on Berlin and Hitler, who still struggled to find hope.*

On April 13, the army of Marshal Tolbukhin took Vienna. A major Russian offensive was expected at any moment at the Oder front. Undoubtedly, the goal of this operation was Berlin. Under this impression of an impending attack, Hitler issued an order on April 15 concerning the structure of command in case the Allies from the west and the east should join in central Germany. This Führer order read as follows:

In case communications on land in central Germany are broken, I order as follows:

1. In the separate area in which I am not present myself, a commander in chief appointed by me will conduct all military operations and will, in the area concerned, take command of all forces of the three branches of the *Wehrmacht* on all fronts, of the reserve army, the Waffen SS, the police, and other organizations attached to them.

2. If I myself should be south of the interrupted communications, Admiral Dönitz will be appointed commander in chief in the northern area. An army general staff (commander, Lieutenant General Kinzel), which will be kept as small as possible, will be attached to him as operations staff. The following will come under his command:

   (a) commander in chief of the Army Group Vistula, who will command the eastern front;

   (b) commander in chief northwest, who will command the western front;

   (c) commander of the armed forces Denmark;

   (d) commander of the armed forces Norway;

   (e) commander in chief of the air fleet, Reich, for the air forces engaged.

3. If I myself should be north of the interrupted communications, Field Marshal Kesselring will be appointed commander in chief in the southern area. The following will come under his command:

   (a) commanders in chief of Army Groups South and Center, for the eastern front;

   (b) commander in chief Army Group G, for the whole of the western front;

(c) commander in chief, southeast;

(d) commander in chief, southwest;

(e) commander in chief of the air fleet, for the air forces engaged.

4. The commanders in chief appointed for separate areas in paragraphs 2 and 3 will conduct the overall defense of the Reich in their areas, if necessary independently, should my orders and decisions, even by wireless, not reach them in time in view of the communications situation.

They are personally responsible to me for the entire employment of their entire war potential, in closest cooperation with the *Reichskommissar* for defense of the separated area. Apart from this, as far as communications allow, the unified control of operations by myself personally, as hitherto, will not be altered. In particular, the duty of supplying day-to-day reports is not affected.

The high command of the *Luftwaffe* and the *Reichsführer SS,* as the superior officer responsible for the military duties of the *Waffen SS,* will be kept informed of decisions as quickly as the technical possibilities of communications allow.

5. The commander in chief in an area that is temporarily cut off will also avail himself of the services of the local representatives of the supply, transport, communications, and armaments organizations as laid down in the order issued on April 11, 1945.

6. The headquarters of the proposed commander in chief of a separated area will be identified and prepared forthwith, in agreement with the chief of armed forces communications, General of the Signal Corps Praun, and in accordance with the order by the chief of the high command of the armed forces dated April 11, 1945, "Establishment of subsidiary headquarters."

7. The activity of the commander in chief of a separated area will be initiated only on special orders from me. These will also define the army groups under whose command each army will come.

8. Similarly, I shall appoint a supreme Reich commissar for defense for a separated area under whom all authorities of the party and the state will be coordinated, and who must cooperate closely with the commander in chief of the separated area.

9. The chief of the high command of the armed forces will issue operational orders. The following supplementary order is for the commander in chief of the navy:

I entrust the commander in chief of the navy with immediate preparations for the total utilization of all possible sources of manpower and matériel for defending the northern area, should land communications in central Germany be interrupted. I delegate to him plenipotentiary powers to issue the orders necessary for this purpose to all authorities of the state, the party, and the armed forces in this area.

Hitler's order revealed that, at this time, he had not yet definitely decided to remain in Berlin and that he favored Dönitz and Kesselring among his commanders because of his belief in their determination to hold out to their last breath.

At the time of the order to the commands in the northern and southern areas, Hitler issued a proclamation for the soldiers on the eastern front that was to be given to them once the Russian attack on Berlin had got underway.

Like Napoleon at one time, Hitler tried to portray the fight for the capital as a desirable outcome that would, against all realistic considerations, lead to a decisive defeat of the enemy. "Berlin will remain German. Vienna will again become German, and Europe will never become Russian." At a time when Providence had "removed Roosevelt, the greatest war criminal of all time, from this earth," he felt certain that "the turning point of this war is being decided."

Hitler's proclamation was written in his usual demagogic style as follows:

Soldiers of the German Eastern Front!

For the last time, our deadly Jewish-Bolshevik enemy has lined up his masses for the attack. He is trying to smash Germany and exterminate our Volk. To a great degree, you soldiers of the east know yourselves what fate is threatening all German women, girls, and children. While the old men and children will be murdered, women and girls will be degraded to barrack whores. The rest will be marched off to Siberia.

We have anticipated this hour. Since January, everything possible has been done in order to erect a strong front. Our mighty artillery greets the enemy. Our infantry's losses have been made good by countless new units. Units on the alert, newly-activated units, and the *Volkssturm* reinforce our front. The Bolshevik will this time meet the old fate of Asia, that is, he must and will bleed to death in front of the capital of the German Reich. He who fails to do his duty at this time commits treason against our Volk. Any regiment or division that abandons its position acts so disgracefully that it should be ashamed before the women and children who are enduring the terror bombing against our cities.

Above all, watch out for the few treacherous officers and soldiers who, in order to save their own lives, will fight against us, paid by the Russians, perhaps even wearing German uniforms. Whoever orders you to retreat must be immediately arrested and, if necessary, killed on the spot, no matter what his rank may be.

If, in the coming days and weeks, every soldier does his duty at the eastern front, then the last Asian attack will be broken, just as the invasion of our enemies in the West will be broken in spite of everything.

Berlin will remain German.

Vienna will again become German, and Europe will never become Russian.

Form a sworn community not upon the empty concept of a "fatherland" but for the defense of your homeland, your women, your children, and thereby our future.

In this hour, the entire German Volk looks to you, my fighters in the East, and hopes that, through your steadfastness, zeal, arms, and leadership, the Bolshevik attack will drown in a bloodbath. At this moment, in which Providence has removed the greatest war criminal of all time from this earth, the turning point of this war is being decided.

Adolf Hitler

On April 16, the major Russian offensive began, both on the Oder front and in Silesia. The attack progressed quickly.

▶ *April 29, 1945 The end came. Hitler married Eva Braun shortly before they killed themselves. Hitler left some documents that still attempted to justify his regime.*

At the signing of the marriage license, two of those involved made mistakes because of the great excitement: Eva Braun was about to sign her maiden name and started with a "B," then crossed it out and wrote "Hitler, born Braun;" the civil magistrate signed "Waagner" instead of Wagner.

After the formalities were over, the wedding couple stepped out into the hallway to accept the best wishes of the entourage. A small festive dinner in their private rooms followed. Goebbels, his wife, Bormann, Hitler's secretaries Mrs. Christian and Mrs. Junge, and later Generals Krebs and Burgdorf, and Colonel von Below attended, as well as Adjutant Günsche and Hitler's dietary cook, Miss Manzialy. Champagne was offered, only Hitler had tea. They spoke about the good old times, especially about Goebbels' wedding, at which Hitler had been witness.

After some time, Hitler retired in order to dictate to Mrs. Junge his political and private last will and testament.

Hitler had previously made a political testament, at the end of the second volume of *Mein Kampf.* At the time, he had written the following:

The political testament of the German nation concerning its actions toward others should and must always be as follows: never tolerate the emergence of two continental powers in Europe. Regard every attempt to organize a second military force along German borders, even if it consists merely in the formation of a state with the potential of becoming a military power, as an act of aggression against Germany. Regard it not as your right, but as your duty, to employ all means at your disposal, including force of arms, to hinder the emergence of such a state or, if such a state has already emerged, to destroy it.

Take care that the strength of our Volk is not derived from colonies, but from the soil of the homeland in Europe. Never think the security of the Reich assured, unless it is able, for centuries to come, to give every scion of our Volk his own piece of property. Never forget that the most sacred right in this world is the right to the soil you want to cultivate yourself, and the most sacred sacrifice is the blood you shed for this earth.

This political testament of 1928 was supposed to come into force as soon as Hitler had established the German continental empire that he envisioned and that would encompass all of central and eastern Europe up to the Urals, and as soon as he had destroyed all "military powers" at Germany's borders (hence, France, Poland, Russia, Italy, and so on).

In his political testament of 1945, Hitler used less high-flown phrases. All that counted in 1945 was the incredible chaos he had provoked by his politics. Naturally, he was not about to admit any guilt in this respect. On the contrary, he kept serving up the old sentimental phrases about how he had "used up" his health in the fight for Germany. He spoke of his unsurpassed love for peace, his countless offers of friendship to England. Not surprisingly, he blamed the Jews for the outbreak of the war and its "murderous" consequences for the German people. Not only the Jews were at fault, but so were the officers of the German army who, unlike those in the navy, had no "sense of honor." He also blamed the "former" *Reichsmarschall* Hermann Göring and the "former" *Reichsführer* SS Heinrich Himmler.

Even now, he saw himself at the center of the universe. Just as he had announced at the beginning of the war, on September 1, 1939, that he wished not to "live to see the day" if things went badly, he now said that he did "not wish to fall into the hands of the enemy who, for the amusement of their incited masses, need a new spectacle directed by the Jews."

After his death, the fight should "under no circumstance be given up" and should be continued "no matter where." For this reason, Hitler appointed Grand Admiral Dönitz as his successor in the office of head of state and supreme commander of the *Wehrmacht*. This appointment came as a surprise to many, including Dönitz. However, considering Hitler's mentality, it was not really all that surprising. The reason was quite obvious. He even said it explicitly in this last will: "May it one day form part of the sense of honor of the German officer—it is already the case with our navy—that the surrender of a region or city is impossible and that, above all, the leaders should set a shining example of loyal fulfillment of duty unto death."

Hitler made Dönitz's mission perfectly clear in the above sentence: he should continue to wage the fight mercilessly until the glorious end, even if the entire German Volk would go down with him, like the crew of a ship. Dönitz should follow the example that fleet commander Admiral Lütjens had set on May 26, 1941, when, confronted with a hopeless situation, he scuttled the no longer maneuverable *Bismarck* with its flag flying, a crew of 2,000 men and himself on board. That was the "sense of honor" Hitler was referring to and he believed that the grand admiral was the only officer in his entourage whom he could trust to carry out this mission. But Hitler was mistaken in this, as in so many other regards! Hitler's political last will and testament read as follows:

ADOLF HITLER

My Political Testament

More than 30 years have passed since I deployed my modest forces as a volunteer in the First World War, a war forced on the Reich.

In these three decades, all my thoughts, actions, and life have been guided by my love for and loyalty to the Volk. The Volk gave me the power to make many more difficult decisions than any mortal man before me. I have used up my time, my working power, and my health in these three decades. It is untrue that I or any other person in Germany wanted war in the year 1939. It was desired and instigated exclusively by those international statesmen who are either of Jewish origin or work for Jewish interests. I made too many proposals for the limitation and control of armaments, which posterity will not be able to deny eternally, for the responsibility for this war to be placed on me. Further, I never wanted, after the first accursed World War, a second one against England or even America to come about. Centuries will go by, but from the ruins of our cities and monuments of art, hatred for the people who are ultimately responsible will always renew itself; against those whom we have to thank for all this: international Jewry and its helpers!

Only three days before the outbreak of the German-Polish war, I proposed a solution for the German-Polish problems to the British ambassador in Berlin—similar to the one for the Saarland under international control. That proposal cannot be disavowed. It was rejected only because the influential circles in English politics wanted war, partially for business reasons, partially driven by propaganda directed by international Jewry.

I never left any doubt about it: should the nations of Europe again be regarded only as the portfolio of stocks of these international monetary and financial conspirators, then the race would be held responsible that actually is guilty in this murderous struggle: Jewry! Further, I made it perfectly clear that this time millions of grown men would not die and hundreds of thousands of women and children would not burn in the cities or die under the rain of bombs without a punishment being inflicted on the guilty, although by more humane means.

After a six-year-long fight that, in spite of all the setbacks, will one day go down in history as the most glorious and brave avowal of a Volk's will to live, I cannot leave this city, the capital of the Reich. Since there are not enough forces to withstand the enemy attack at this point and our resistance is slowly being weakened by blinded and spineless characters, I wish to join my fate to that which millions of others have taken upon themselves and remain in this city. In addition, I do not wish to fall into the hands of an enemy who, for the amusement of its incited masses, needs a new spectacle directed by the Jews.

I have, therefore, decided to remain in Berlin and to choose death there voluntarily at the moment when I believe that the seat of the Führer and chancellor cannot be held any longer. I die with a joyous heart in view of the immeasurable deeds and accomplishments of our soldiers at the front, which I am well aware of; of our women at home, of our peasants and workers, and the unparalleled deployment, unique in history, of our youth, which bear my name.

That I express to all of them my profound heartfelt gratitude is as natural as my wish that they may under no circumstance abandon the fight. Instead they will continue to wage it no matter where against the enemies of the fatherland, loyal to the creed of the great Clausewitz. From the sacrifice of our soldiers and my own solidarity with them unto death, a seed will one day germinate in German history, one way or another, and bring about the shining rebirth of the National Socialist movement and the realization of a true *Volksgemeinschaft*.

Many of the bravest men and women decided to bind their lives to mine unto death. I asked them and finally ordered them not to do this but to participate in the continued fight of the nation. I ask the commanders of the armies, the navy, and the *Luftwaffe* to reinforce—with the utmost efforts in the National Socialist spirit—the power of resistance of our soldiers. I especially point to the fact that I myself, as the founder and creator of this movement, preferred death to a cowardly resignation much less a surrender.

May it one day form part of the sense of honor of the German officer—as is the case with our navy already—that the surrender of a region or city is impossible and that, above all, the leaders should set a shining example of loyal fulfillment of duty unto death.

Second Part of the Political Testament

Before my death, I expel the former *Reichsmarschall* Hermann Göring from the party and strip him of all his rights that might be derived from the decree of June 29, 1941, and my Reichstag declaration of September 1, 1939. In his place, I appoint Grand Admiral Dönitz as Reich President and supreme commander of the *Wehrmacht*. Before my death, I expel the former *Reichsführer SS* and Reich Minister of the Interior Heinrich Himmler from the party and all state offices.

In his place, I appoint Gauleiter Karl Hanke as *Reichs-führer* SS and chief of the German police, and Gauleiter Paul Giesler as Reich Minister of the Interior.

Göring and Himmler, by their secret negotiations with the enemy, which took place without my knowledge and contrary to my will, as well as by attempting to usurp power in the state in violation of the law, have done immeasurable damage to the country and the entire Volk, not to mention their disloyalty to my person.

In order to give the German Volk a government made up of men of honor, who fulfill their duty to continuing the war by all means, I appoint, as the Führer of the nation, the following members of the new cabinet: Reich president, Dönitz; Reich chancellor, Goebbels; party minister, Bormann; foreign minister, Seyss-Inquart; minister of the interior, Gauleiter Giesler; minister of war, Dönitz; commander in chief of the army, Schörner; commander in chief of the navy, Dönitz; commander-in-chief of the *Luftwaffe*, Greim; *Reichsführer* SS and chief of the German police, Gauleiter Hanke; economy, Funk; agriculture, Backe; justice, Thierack; culture, Dr. Scheel; propaganda, Dr. Naumann; finance, Schwerin-Krosigk; labor, Dr. Hupfauer; armament, Saur; head of the German labor front and member of the Reich cabinet, Reich minister Dr. Ley.

Although a number of these men, like Martin Bormann, Dr. Goebbels, and others, including their wives, joined me out of their own free will and wished to leave the capital of the Reich under no circumstances, but instead were willing to go down with me, I have to ask them to comply with my request and to place the interest of the nation above their own feelings in this case. Through their work and loyalty, they will be as close to me as companions after death, as I hope to be among them in spirit and will always accompany them. May they be hard, but never unjust, may they never allow fear to become the guide of their actions, and may they place the honor of the nation above all else there is on earth. May they finally realize that our mission in expanding the National Socialist state will be a work for coming centuries, which obliges every individual always to serve the common interest and to put aside his own advantage in its favor. I demand of all Germans, all National Socialists, men and women, and soldiers of the *Wehrmacht* that they will be loyal and obedient to the new government and its president unto death.

Above all, I oblige the leadership of the nation and its followers to a meticulous observance of the racial laws and to a merciless resistance to those world-wide poisoners of all *Völker,* international Jewry.

Given at Berlin, April 29, 1945, four o'clock

Adolf Hitler

As witnesses:
Dr. Joseph Goebbels, Wilhelm Burgdorf,
Martin Bormann, Hans Krebs

Hitler still persevered in the role of the god-man in this "political testament" whose various versions were addressed to Fleet Commander Dönitz, Field Marshal Schörner, and "the public." He did not mention his marriage with Eva Braun. Such a human touch would have been out of place in this last grandiose proclamation. The German public was truly astonished when, following the complete collapse of the Third Reich, it heard about the "last-minute marriage" of Eva Braun and Hitler.

The only place Hitler mentioned this marriage was in his "private testament." It is not entirely clear whether or not he wished this document to be published. He could not resist using the same proclamation style in this last private piece of paper, although it was less heroic in tone than his political testament. He admitted that it was possible that the party "no longer existed," and spoke once again of the "disgrace of a withdrawal" (*Absetzen*) that he wanted to avoid. He probably meant to say "make off" (*sich absetzen*), "escape" in plain English, not "being deposed" (*abgesetzt werden*) by a legal resolution of the Reichstag, as Napoleon had experienced in a similar form. Hitler had always feared such a resolution's removing him from office, especially since 1942.

Hitler's private last will and testament read as follows:

ADOLF HITLER

My Personal Testament

Although I believed in the years of fighting that I could not take the responsibility of entering into a marriage, now, before the end of my life, I decided to take as my wife the lady who, after many years of true friendship, came into this all but besieged city of her own free will in order to share my fate. At her own wish, she will go into death with me as my wife. This will compensate us both for what my work in the service of my Volk took from us.

Insofar as they are of any value, my possessions are the property of the party and, should it no longer exist, of the state. Should the state be destroyed, then any further directives by me would be superfluous. The paintings in the collections that I bought over the years I never intended for private purposes but for the establishment of a gallery in my home town of Linz on the Danube. It is my most heartfelt wish that this bequest be executed.

As the executor of my testament, I appoint my dearest party comrade Martin Bormann. He will be entitled to make all decisions final and legal. He will be allowed to give everything of personal value as a remembrance or as necessary to maintain a modest bourgeois living standard for my siblings, likewise especially for my wife's mother, and my secretaries, whom he knows well, Mrs. Winter, and others who supported me for many years in my work.

My wife and I choose to die in order to escape the disgrace of a deposition or surrender. It is our wish to be cremated immediately at the site where I did the larger part of my daily work in the course of a twelve-year-long service to my Volk.

Given at Berlin, April 29, 1945, four o'clock

Adolf Hitler
As witnesses: Martin Bormann,
Dr. Goebbels, Nicolaus von Below

Both last wills were signed at 4:00 a.m. It was remarkable that the witnesses who countersigned the documents were not exactly the same in both cases.

Following the signature, Hitler went to rest, while Goebbels wrote an "addendum" to Hitler's private testament. He signed it at 5:30 a.m. The "addendum" read as follows:

> The Führer has ordered me to leave Berlin in the event of a failure of the defense of the capital, and to take part in a leading capacity in the formation of a new government, which he will appoint.
>
> For the first time in my life, I must categorically refuse to comply with an order by the Führer. My wife and my children join me in this refusal. First, because of humanitarian considerations, it would break our hearts to abandon the Führer in his hour of greatest need.
>
> Second, for the rest of my life I would feel myself to be a worthless subject devoid of honor. I would lose all self-respect along with the respect of my Volk. I believe I will hereby render the greatest service to the German Volk in the future, for it will need inspiring examples more than actual men in the difficult times to come.
>
> It is for these reasons that, along with my wife, I wish to express the unshakable determination not to leave the Reich capital, and rather to end my life alongside my Führer than to lead a life that will have lost all its meaning unless it can be spent in his service or at his side.

For "the first time in his life," Goebbels said, he refused to comply with an order by the Führer. He preferred to die rather than to go on without him. Bormann added the following postscript to the letter:

> Dear Grand Admiral! As none of the divisions have broken through and our situation appears hopeless, the Führer dictated the enclosed political testament last night.
>
> > *Heil* Hitler!
> > Yours,
> > Bormann

The three official versions of the testament were handed to the following couriers: Bormann's adjutant, SS *Standartenführer* Wilhelm Zander, took the copy for Dönitz; Hitler's army adjutant, Major Willi Johannmeier the one for Schörner; and press chief Heinz Lorenz the one for "the public."

At the noon discussion of the situation, Krebs suggested sending out three officers in order to try to establish contact with Wenck: Major Freiherr Freytag von Loringhoven, Cavalry Captain Boldt, and Lieutenant Colonel Weiss. Hitler had him find an escape route and then gave his approval. He shook hands with each of the officers and said: "My regards to Wenck. He should hurry up or it will be too late!"

In the afternoon, Hitler had had his dog Blondi poisoned by his former surgeon, Professor Haase, head of a military hospital in the big air-raid shelter under the Reich Chancellery, which was open to the public. News of this event, which made it clear that the end was near, caused a number of nurses, wounded men, and other patients of the hospital to ask to see the Führer one last time before he died. Hitler granted this request and, his hands in his coat pockets, walked through the room in silence.

Hitler handed his secretaries poison capsules and said that he regretted not being able to give them a nicer parting gift.

In spite of all this, he had not yet given up completely. Colonel Nicolaus von Below, inspired by the departure of the three army officers, had come to the conclusion that he could try something similar in order to escape a macabre end in the bunker of the Reich Chancellery. Hitler agreed and gave him a dispatch for Keitel at 10:00 p.m. Below reported the following on the content of this message:

> In it, Hitler declared that the battle for Berlin was nearing its end, that he preferred suicide to surrender, that had named Dönitz as his successor, and that two of his earliest followers, Göring and Himmler, had betrayed him in the end.
>
> Then he talked about the accomplishments of the *Wehrmacht*. He praised the navy: its great courage had redeemed the disgrace of 1918; it could not be blamed for the defeat. He excused the *Luftwaffe*, since it had fought bravely.
>
> The Volk and the *Wehrmacht* had given their all and everything in this long and hard fight. It had been a great sacrifice. However, his trust had been abused by many people. Disloyalty and treason had undermined the power of resistance

throughout the war. He was therefore unable to lead his Volk to victory. The general staff of the armed forces could not be compared with the general staff of the First World War. Its achievements were far behind those of the fighting front.

> "The efforts and sacrifices of the German Volk in this war were so great that I cannot believe that they were in vain. It must continue to be its objective to gain space (*Lebensraum*) for the German Volk in the East."

So even in the last hours of his life, Hitler was still preoccupied with the question of *Lebensraum* in the East. He was his old self. No hard facts could move him to abandon his theories of 1919.

"For what would be the point of our struggles if there were not something to come
after us that could use and pass on what we achieve today?" (p. 479)

Eva Braun

XVI
Epilogue

Hitler is undoubtedly the most extraordinary figure in German history. This is not only true because of his rise from unskilled laborer and resident of a homeless shelter in Vienna to become the German head of state and government and supreme commander of the German *Wehrmacht*. It is above all true of the extent of the power that he amassed in the course of only a few years, that he incessantly expanded, and that he jealously defended until he died.

No German king or emperor, no German statesman—head of state or government—no German general ever held and exercised as much power as Hitler did.

Hitler was unwilling to allow any person to exercise power that did not devolve from his person. He wanted to be in complete control, no matter whether it was a question of national or local government functions, judicial or military issues, economic, cultural, or social spheres of influence. Everything was all right as long as prominent persons in influential positions submitted to Hitler and were willing to comply with his orders. Then he let them have their way. However, he moved mercilessly against any person who tried to expand a position that could be significant in terms of political power and threatened him, even if only theoretically. Hitler did not shrink from any intrigue or even murder in order to eliminate such a person.

Hitler was power incarnate, a true demon, obsessed with power, the like of whom the world has rarely seen. In this respect, Hitler was a supranational phenomenon. Since Napoleon, there had been no tyrant on this scale. Of course, the special circumstances of the times played a great role in both cases. Without them, the rise of such men as Napoleon and Hitler would have been inconceivable.

Marshal Foch, who was a great admirer of Napoleon, acknowledged that the circumstances of the times—the chaos of the French Revolution—opened up a range of possibilities for the Corsican: "Assume that Bonaparte had been born under Louis XIV or, as was I, had been sent to the garrison in Tarbes or Montpellier when he was 24 years old, then even his most extraordinary talents would not have allowed him to reach the goal that he did."

Foch was honest enough to concede that Napoleon's downfall was caused by his intoxication with power: "Among the reasons that decided his overthrow, the problem was mainly that Napoleon confused the greatness of his country with his own, that he wanted to found the fate of the nation exclusively on the force of arms, as if a nation could live on glory instead of work, and as if, in a civilized world, there was no room for morals next to a power based on force, no matter how clever this power might be."

Just as Napoleon benefited from the chaotic times during the French Revolution, so Hitler was able to use to his advantage the chaos in Germany that followed on the revolution of 1918, defeat in the First World War, and the international economic crisis of 1931.

To let Hitler's case rest at that, not to go beyond such terse statements and historic parallels, would be a considerable mistake. After all, Hitler's rule was made possible not just by the chaos in Germany after 1918. It should not be overlooked that his demagogic ideas fell on fertile ground because many mischievous falsehoods were in circulation at the time. They represented the fateful legacy of imperial Germany and the Austro-Hungarian monarchy and formed the basis for Hitler's rhetorical creations.

All of the following theses were used by Hitler in his speeches from 1919 to 1945: that the "November criminals" had robbed the German army of the victor's laurels in 1918; that Wilson's Fourteen Points had led to ruin because they had lured the Germans into laying down their arms prematurely; that there existed something like an international solidarity among all Socialists that had worked to the disadvantage of Germany's interests; and that the Germans would be invincible if only they were united. All these ideas can be found almost verbatim in the works of Wilhelm II and other nationalist authors. The idea that "the Jews are to be blamed for everything," especially for Germany's misfortune, was an established slogan, current at least since 1918, and popular with nationalist parties and groups in Germany.

Another essential role in Hitler's rule was played by the supposedly constant threats to Germany that allowed him to operate permanently with martial law and special laws.

Even the most exemplary democracy will immediately be transformed into an authoritarian state if it is threatened by war or if war is declared on it. Any violation of the laws of the state will then automatically become "high treason." The legal regulations and moral rules of conduct that normally apply will be suspended for the most part. Even the ten commandments will largely lose their force.

The so-called "people" (*Volk*) has no say in such developments. What ordinary man on the street can assess whether the war that is being waged is offensive or defensive in character, especially given the fact that the government in question will always claim only to be defending itself? And even if he is in a position to assess the situation, he really has no choice: either he submits to the decisions of the government or he commits high treason at the risk of severe punishment.

When a government claims to be acting in the national interest, it will always be difficult or impossible, even for the influential circles made up of politicians, parliamentarians, military men, leaders of the economy, bishops, and so on, to resist governmental measures.

Of course, such a situation was ideal for Hitler's purposes. For this reason, he declared one state of emergency after another. Germany was always in danger: Communists supposedly threatened a revolt in Germany in 1933, the Nazi Party storm troopers (SA) were allegedly planning a Putsch in 1934, the Bolsheviks and their "101 Soviet divisions" and the introduction of a two-year compulsory conscription in France were supposed to be threatening the country in 1935. By 1936, there was the threat of a "Bolshevization" of Europe, based on a French-Russian mutual-assistance pact. The danger reappeared in 1937 because of the Spanish Civil War. By 1938, Czechoslovakia, "the aircraft carrier in the heart of Europe," was supposedly planning an attack on Germany. Poland meant to attack in 1939. Even though all of these "threats" did not really exist, Hitler's claims were effective.

Who in Germany would have dared to oppose a measure that served to rescue the German Volk and Europe from Bolshevism? Who in Germany would have risked being regarded as a Communist or Bolshevik?

Hitler's use of nationalist arguments was no less successful. Everything he did, planned, and ordered done supposedly served the welfare of the German people and was therefore necessary in the interest of the German Volk!

In Germany, the workers made up the class that was the most susceptible to this nationalist rhetoric. This had already been evident in the First World War. Hitler was least afraid of speaking before uncritical groups of workers. Moreover, he could still impress them with his nationalist slogans and fantastic descriptions of the future, even when hard facts already provided unequivocal evidence of the failure of his politics. The German intellectuals were more or less immune to wild nationalist proclamations. It was not surprising that Hitler poured scorn on them and vented his anger in tirades full of hatred.

Yet, who could tell whether or not a certain move was truly in the best interest of the German Volk? Had there been only Germans on earth, this question would never have arisen. Nor would the Third Reich ever have collapsed and Hitler might still be in power today (*1973*). However, Germany is not alone in the world. To a decisive degree, it is dependent on other powers in the world. While at home the Germans are free to live as they wish, there are limits to their foreign policy. As soon as measures in Germany begin to affect or threaten other countries, they cease to be in "the interest of the German Volk." Other states are not willing to tolerate Germany's highhanded measures, either in the East or in the West. They strike back. Naturally, this is not to the advantage but to the disadvantage of the German people. Their historical experience in this context is clear.

The Second World War and the destruction of Hitler and his Reich undoubtedly taught Germany a lesson. Apparently, the lesson of the First World War did not bear any fruit. Only the future will tell whether the lesson of the Second World War has been of any use.

In any event, it is necessary to draw the proper inferences from Hitler's rise and fall. In summary, they are the following:

1. The world has no desire to be healed by the "German essence." And surely it does not want to be healed by force!

2. Any attempt to use force in changing the borders of the German state will result in the declaration of war by the Western powers. This was true both in 1914 and in 1939. This principle also applies to areas such as Danzig that are inhabited by Germans or that belonged to the German Reich at one time.

3. There was no such thing as a "secret Jewish world government." All claims that the Jews as an international corporation influence the governments of the great powers, or exercise political or military influence in non-Jewish states, are mere fantasy. Perhaps, in certain ages, the Jews may have had the opportunity of exercising influence internationally in

matters of economics or culture, but never have they achieved political influence on the international stage. Hitler's fight against the Jews was nothing other than tilting at windmills.

Regardless of how abominable and horrible Hitler's slaughter of the Jews was, it was not the cause of his fall. It would be a grave mistake to assume that he could have reached his power-political goals had he treated the Jews differently. Like Napoleon I and Wilhelm II, in whose undertakings the Jewish question did not play a role, he would still have failed. His fate was sealed at 11 o'clock on September 3, 1939. And the reason for it was the same as for the collapse of the Kaiser's empire in World War I, namely, the attempt to expand Germany's borders by the use of force. This is a clear, historic fact, and it would be dangerous to try to diminish it by pointing to the Holocaust.

4. Hitler's claim that the Germans had the best soldiers, scientists, leaders of the economy, workers, peasants, and so on, represents a subjective judgment. Nobody can tell the Germans not to believe this, whether or not it corresponds to reality. Even should it be objectively correct, no universally valid conclusions can be drawn from it. Above all, it is not possible to derive from such statements of quality a German right to hegemony in Europe or in the world.

Hitler repeatedly claimed that the German Volk was not only the best, but also the numerically strongest in the whole world, with the exception of China. The figures that he presented were all too transparently false to merit further consideration. Both world wars amply prove that Germany was never in a position, either in terms of strength or power base, to force its beliefs on the rest of the world.

5. Neither the betrayal of military secrets nor the invention of new weapons decisively influence the outcome of a war. While they could temporarily obstruct individual measures or operations, and perhaps postpone the end of the war, they do not result in a different outcome of the war.

6. Propaganda (so-called psychological warfare) is effective only with the aggressor's own people or with inferior nations, whose inevitable collapse may be hastened by them. The weapon of propaganda is ineffective when used against an opponent of equal or superior strength. By no means does it out-perform military weapons. Words cannot change hard facts.

7. Bravery, perseverance, unity, self-sacrifice, and other such national virtues may at best delay an unfortunate end to a war for some time, but
they cannot prevent it. The outcome of a war is determined by the military resources of a country. Neither the Leonidas myth nor the legend
of Frederick the Great can erase the hard facts presented by the military
superiority of a strong country over a weaker one.

In all likelihood, the entrusting of absolute power to one man will lead to
disastrous consequences in most countries. The temptations of power are so
great that even individuals who only want "the best" for their country can be
induced to pursue over-ambitious plans and thus end up the victim of their
lust for power. This must spell ruin, not only for these individuals, but also
for their supporters and their nation. History affords us countless examples
of it. Nevertheless, history also proves that men will make the same mistakes
time and again, and that the warnings of the past go unheeded.

It would be wrong, however, to hold the "people," that is, all those
who have no say in the state, responsible for such development. The appeal should be directed instead to the responsible statesmen and influential
circles, the parliamentarians, the leaders of the economy, the military men,
the bishops, and so on. It is their responsibility to be aware of the lessons of
history and act accordingly.

In extraordinary times, when war, misery and chaos prevail, there is
a great danger that extraordinary men will attempt to seize power—all
power. The fact that Hitler managed to win power and to remain in power
for twelve years without being challenged proves that such a development
could come about time and again, given the same conditions. Laws and
constitutional provisions provide only slight protection against such a development. After all, the born dictator will soon eliminate such limitations,
either legally or illegally.

History teaches us that all the extraordinary figures who made their way
to become dictators and conquerors—Alexander the Great, Caesar, Napoleon, and Hitler among them—did so with the help of the demon of rhetoric, which they used in a manner that befitted their extraordinary times.

The series of great demagogues in world history, who rose to triumph
and pulled their nations down in their fall, reached its barbaric climax in
Adolf Hitler. That this was once again possible in a highly civilized country
and in the twentieth century should be a warning to us all.

Afterword

This work proves Hitler's statements incorrect in many crucial aspects, particularly regarding his military and foreign policies. No matter how masterly his speeches were composed, they could not change the hard facts. Declarations like those below could not stand up against reality:

> "A place taken by a German soldier will never be taken by any other soldier!

> "Germany shall not be overrun, neither from within nor from without!

> "Today's Reich is different from that of yesterday. It is not just a passing fancy."

In addition, it has been the intention of the author to demonstrate that, while Hitler's rhetoric had a certain influence on the masses, they were by no means decisive for his seizure of power and the fashioning of his rule. After Hitler had taken over the government, it was no longer a question of whether the people approved of him or not, since he was determined to see his ideas through—one way or another.

What was important and decisive was Hitler's rhetorical success as a convincing personality speaking with influential figures. Their circles in Germany had theoretically been in a position to keep him from power or to remove him from office once he had seized power. However, he managed to instill the belief in them that only he was capable of saving Germany and that all his actions served this goal.

It is remarkable that in Germany Hitler's foreign policy was the least criticized of his ideas, even though it was foreseeable that it was exactly his foreign policy theory that was to prove the most fateful for Germany and that was responsible for the declaration of war by the English and their allies.

After 1945, Hitler was praised for eliminating unemployment, sponsoring the Volkswagen, generously funding the Autobahn, and so on. He was condemned for his harassment of the Jews, the limitation of the Church's rights, the outlawing of all parties save his own, the dissolution of the unions, the muzzling of the press, the regimentation of cultural life, and the elimination of most of the rights of the individual.

While the above negative aspects of Hitler's rule at home were the characteristic symptoms of a despicable dictatorship, they did not cause his downfall. Had they been practiced within the borders of the Reich, they would never have led to the armed intervention of the Western powers. The English and their allies moved against Hitler only after he attacked Poland in 1939. They had made up their minds to intervene, no matter what country Hitler attacked. Of course, Hitler was also criticized in postwar Germany for his decision to attack Poland. However, it was often overlooked in this context that this decision was only the logical consequence of his ideas on foreign policy.

They were based on a number of claims. For one, the German Volk had been denied its rightful "place in the sun." Second, a trick (i.e., Wilson's Fourteen Points) had led Germany to lay down its arms in 1918, when it was on the brink of gaining the victory. Moreover, the Treaty of Versailles was a great injustice to the German people. The elimination of its provisions—that is, the restoration of the borders to their status in 1914 and the return of the German colonies—was a matter of course. He maintained that Germany was "threatened" by all sorts of enemies in the East and West. As long as the German Volk was united, he claimed, it would be invincible. It had a right to a *Lebensraum* that corresponded to its population.

Hitler believed that domestic and foreign policy were identical. Therefore, his enemies abroad would behave just as those at home had. The Anglo-Americans were "nothing other than a branch of our German Volk." It was Germany that had "colonized England."

Therefore, the English would sooner or later become Germany's friends. The English resembled the German nationalists: they were just as "senile" and would under no circumstances be able to resist a German policy of expansion. On the contrary, they would welcome the German campaign against Russia in order to prevent a Bolshevik invasion of western Europe. The English had done their best to reinforce Hitler in this belief, which had to prove fatal for Hitler's strategy and for Germany. A similar strategy had already proved successful for England in the case of Napoleon, to keep him from invading the British Isles and to bring about his downfall. English experts already knew from detailed studies of Hitler's ideas after the publication of *Mein Kampf* in the mid 1920s that Hitler strikingly resembled Napoleon in his boundless ambition, megalomania, and lust for power, but that he likewise lacked the intellectual background and the historical-political knowledge to recognize the real power structures of the world or to think through superior world-historical contexts and refined strategic considerations.

Hitler likened the Bolsheviks to the Communists in Germany. He felt that "Communism is not a higher evolutionary stage, but the most primitive basic form of shaping peoples and nations." The Soviets were best dealt with by brute force.

These were the guiding principles of Hitler's foreign policy. They did not at all correspond to the actual power structures in the world that had developed during the last centuries. Hitler's attempt to apply his foreign-policy concepts in the real world inevitably ended in the greatest political and military catastrophe that Germany ever suffered.

Since Hitler's foreign policy was intertwined with his dictatorial domestic and racial policies, the danger existed and exists today that the actual cause of the great German catastrophe of 1945—Hitler's foreign policy—is overlooked and ignored. Therefore, this work has also tried to elucidate his foreign policy.

Hitler in the Reich Chancellery

Glossary

Anschluss: the union of the post World War I state of Austria with Germany. The Treaty of Versailles forbade this because of fears Germany would become too strong. Hitler forced the union with Austria in 1938 through threats of violence and demagoguery.

Anti-Comintern Pact: an agreement first reached with Japan in November 1936, directed specifically against the Soviet Union but portrayed as anti-Communist. This pact was subsequently expanded to include Italy in 1937 and became the main diplomatic instrument uniting Germany and her allies. Comintern refers to the Communist International, founded under the Bolsheviks in Russia in 1919 and dedicated to the overthrow of the bourgeoisie.

Autarky: the economic theory of national self-sufficiency in which all-important resources and manufacturing processes are within the boundaries of the state. If necessary, the state may expand to include important resources.

Barbarossa, Operation: the German plan to invade the Soviet Union, named after the crusader emperor Frederick Barbarossa. Hitler formulated the plan in late 1940 and invaded the Soviet Union in June 1941. The plan called for massive strikes trapping and annihilating Soviet forces in the west, then pushing what remained back to a line from Archangel to Astrakhan.

Blut und Rasse: blood and race, an expression used to describe Nazi theories of "Aryan" racial superiority.

Bonzen: important persons, with the idea of self-importance (from the Japanese).

Brüning, Heinrich: Reich Chancellor 1930–1932, led a cabinet of "experts" governing in the national interest. He operated under President von Hindenburg's emergency decrees rather than with Reichstag support. His strict deflationary policies and inability to win popular support led to the strong electoral showings of the extreme parties, especially the Nazis.

Curzon Line: the supposed ethnic frontier between the Poles and other Slavic peoples to their east, drawn by the office of Lord Curzon, British Foreign Secretary, 1919. While ignored during the turmoil of the Polish-Russian War of 1919–1920 and subsequently by the Polish Republic (1920–1939), this line approximates the boundary of the German-Soviet partition of Poland in 1939 and, to a large extent, became the Polish eastern frontier when Stalin redrew her boundaries in 1945.

Dolchstosslegende ("stab-in-the-back" legend): Many Germans believed that in late 1918 they should have fought on and not asked for an armistice from the Allies. That Germany gave up was ascribed to internal disorder and treason for personal gain. This became a major issue in the 1920s when parties of the right accused parties of the left of not supporting the war and saddling Germany with the Treaty of Versailles.

Ebert, Fredrich: (1871–1925), Social Democratic Party leader, last imperial Reich Chancellor, became first Reich President and presided over the first years of the Weimar Republic until his death in 1925.

Enabling Act: Passed by the Reichstag, March 23, 1933, in response to the threat of "Communist insurrection," the Enabling Act allowed the Nazis to ignore the provisions of the Weimar Constitution and formed the basis of Hitler's dictatorship. The Enabling Act was for set periods but was always extended.

Endsieg: ultimate victory, the goal of the Nazi war effort.

Erhebung: uprising, Hitler's term for the Nazi seizure of power.

Fifth column: During the Spanish Civil War (1936–1939), Nationalist General Emilio Mola bragged that he would take Madrid with the four military columns deployed outside the city through the actions of his "fifth column" of secret supporters inside the city. Subsequently, "fifth columnists" was a description of secret supporters of their country's enemies.

Freikorps: voluntary units of soldiers formed after the breakup of the Imperial German army in 1918. Each *Freikorps* formed around a cadre of ex-army officers. Generally, they had a political orientation and pressed for the establishment of "law and order." *Freikorps* became the basis of the Nazi storm troopers and other such organizations.

Gauleiter: The Nazi party divided Germany into so-called "tribal" districts for administrative purposes. These districts were called *Gau* and did not follow political boundaries. Hitler appointed each *Gau* manager (*Leiter*) who was usually one of the "old fighters" from early party days.

General-Government: After the German conquest of Poland, Germany annexed large areas, and organized what remained into a separate administrative district.

Gleichschaltung: "bringing into line" or co-ordination, the Nazi policy of managing all organizations and institutions as part of the National Socialist society. Everything from chess clubs to universities became part of the Nazi social apparatus.

Gottgläubigkeit: Hitler's self-description as one who believes in God without any particular denominational preference. In fact, Hitler used the term to hide his rejection of the Judeo-Christian tradition.

Hugenberg, Alfred: chief executive of Krupp during World War I, owner of a newspaper empire during the twenties. Hugenberg's party, the German Nationalists People's Party (DNVP) allied itself with the Nazi Party in the late twenties, thus giving Hitler a degree of respectability. Hugenberg supported Hitler's appointment as chancellor and then served as Minister of Economics and of Agriculture in Hitler's first cabinet. Hitler soon discredited him, then dissolved his party.

Internationale: the anthem of the Communist International.

Junker: "young noble," referring to aristocratic families with landed estates in East Prussia. Many served in the *Reichswehr* as officers.

Kristallnacht: "Crystal Night," so-called from the shattered glass of Jewish shops, broken by Nazi mobs supposedly in retaliation for the murder of a German embassy attaché in Paris by a Jew, Herschel Grynszpan.

Länder: the old states of the Holy Roman Empire that Bismarck united to form the German Empire of 1871. The largest was Prussia, which dominated the imperial organization. However, Germany, whether imperial or republican, was a federal state and the *Länder* had important local functions.

League of Nations: After World War I, the Allied powers set up an international organization to provide mutual aid and resolve disputes. While the league functioned well for the most part, its operations were based on the assumption that good will existed on all sides. Moreover, the League's enforcement methods were various forms of economic sanctions, which proved ineffective.

Lebensraum: living space, Hitler's assertion, already current in the nineteenth century, that a Volk needs land for producing everything it needs to live. Population determines the amount of land needed.

Levée en masse: an army raised by drafting all able-bodied men. This was the favorite military structure of the left because it eliminated the aristocratic tendencies of a professional army.

Locarno Treaties (1925): They attempted to solve international disputes peacefully. The German Reich Chancellor and Foreign Minister, Gustav Stresemann, worked to achieve international acceptance. Germany accepted her western borders and became a member of the League of Nations. Stresemann was successful, but died in 1929, and the Depression swept away popular support for his approach.

Maginot Line: French fortifications that ran from Switzerland to Belgium, blocking direct German invasion routes, designed in the twenties and built in the thirties. In 1940 the *Wehrmacht* simply made an end-run around it.

Mittelstand: middle class, the "middle" order of society, homeowners, shop-keepers, and anyone with steady work.

Nacht und Nebel Decree: the "Night and Fog" laws, which allowed German forces to kill or secretly deport to Germany anyone endangering German personnel and operations.

National Socialism: a concept that developed before World War I, the basic idea being to apply socialistic ideals to a specific national community, as opposed to worldwide. The Marxist program of abolishing private property is not applied but the capitalist must operate his business in the national interest.

"November Criminals:" the right's name for the statesmen who surrendered in 1918 and established the Weimar Republic in 1919–1920. See SPD.

Putsch, Putschist: a coup d'état, one who attempts a coup.

Reichsbahn: German State Railway.

Reichsleiter: the highest Nazi party officials, responsible for nation-wide projects and institutions, appointed by Hitler. They were often "old fighters."

Reichstag: the lower house of the legislature of the German Empire and Republic. Under the republic, the Reich Chancellor and his cabinet were responsible to the Reichstag, unless they were directly appointed by the president under an emergency decree.

Reichswehr: the army of the German Republic. In 1918 the Social Democrats agreed to support the army, and the army would defend the state against internal enemies, viewed by both sides as far-left revolutionaries. *See* Junker.

Saar and Saar plebiscite: The coal-rich Saar Basin was detached from Germany by the Treaty of Versailles and placed under the League of Nations. Operation of the coal mines was handed over to France as reparations. The treaty provided that the Saarlanders would vote within 15 years whether to join France or Germany. In 1935, they voted to rejoin Germany.

Schutzstaffel (SS): "Security Squad" or echelon in the early days of the Party. Once the Nazis gained power, under *Reichsführer SS* Himler the SS became a "Security Service" or secret police superior to the regular police and judicial system. It was the extralegal "state within a state" that ran the concentration camps and deployed "special mobile units" (*Einsatzgruppen*) for extermination throughout the occupied East.

SPD: The Social Democratic Party was the largest party of the left, with a majority in the Reichstag before the war. Its early support of the Weimar Republic, though, made it seem the party of treason—the "men of November."

Sturmabteilung (SA): "storm troopers." Armed units of the early Nazi party, it guarded Nazi meetings, disrupted other parties' meetings, and staged street demonstrations.

Sudetenland: the mountain region surrounding the Bohemian Plain in Czechoslovakia with a large German-speaking population. In 1918 it had tried to join German Austria but was incorporated into Czechoslovakia by force.

Thirteen-Years Struggle: Hitler's term for the years between 1920 and 1933. Most of the "party narratives" that introduced his speeches concerned this time.

Tripartite Pact: signed by Germany, Italy, and Japan on September 27, 1940. The treaty was an alliance between the European and Asian powers, directed against the United States in that there was a provision pledging mutual support for any power attacked by a power "not a belligerent at present."

Verdun: World War I had reached a stalemate by the end of 1915. The chief of the German general staff, General von Falkenhayn, suggested that attacking the ancient fortress city of Verdun might bleed dry the French army trying to defend it. For most of 1916, the German and French armies grappled over the city, with no short-term result and with debatable long-term results. In this struggle, approximately 420,000 soldiers, both French and German, died, and some 800,000 soldiers were seriously wounded. Verdun became a symbol of the futility of World War I operations.

Versailles, Treaty of: treaty ending World War I signed in 1919. This treaty declared the government of Germany guilty of starting the First World War and punished the German people with heavy reparations to repair war damage in France and Belgium; penalties for non-payment were harsh. In addition, Germany was essentially disarmed and could not develop new weapons. Further, the new Austrian Republic was forbidden to unite with the German Republic.

Volk: people, "folks"; a family, narrowly or widely understood.

Völkischer Beobachter: *People's Observer*, the official Nazi newspaper, full of racist propaganda.

Volksgemeinschaft: national or people's community. In Hitler's terms, the coordinated cooperative society of all true German people, united for national improvement.

Volksgenossen: "People" (i.e., the national family) + "racial comrades," Hitler's form of address to his fellow Germans.

Volksgerichtshof: people's courts, set up by the Nazis because they found legal formalities too time-consuming and concerned with individual rights.

Volkssturm: "people's storm," the Home Guard established in September 1944. It comprised all men between 16 and 60 not already serving.

Wehrmacht: "arms" + "power," the armed forces of Nazi Germany including the army, air force, and navy. At times loosely used of just the army.

Wolfsschanze: "Wolf's den," Hitler's headquarters in East Prussia.

Dates in Hitler's Life

1889 April 20	Adolf Hitler born in Braunau am Inn, Upper Austria.
1908	Hitler relocates to Vienna.
1913	Hitler moves to Munich, in Bavaria.
1914–1918	World War I, the "Great War."
1914	Hitler enlists in the Royal Bavarian Army and takes part in the First Battle of Ypres.
1918	Hitler is wounded during the Second Battle of the Marne and awarded the Iron Cross First Class.
1918 November 11	The Armistice: Germany capitulates.
1918–1919	Revolution in Germany; the Weimar Republic is formed. Imposition of Treaty of Versailles. Hitler returns to Munich and joins German Workers' Party.
1920	Founding of the National Socialist German Workers' Party (NSDAP *Nationalsozialistische Deutsche Arbeiterpartei*), the Nazi Party.
1923	The Beer-hall Putsch: Hitler attempts to seize power in Bavaria and march on Berlin, but his attempt fails.

1923–1929	Chancellor Gustav Stresemann ends hyperinflation and resolves some of Germany's problems. Nazis remain a minor party.
1924	Hitler is sentenced to five years' imprisonment for the Putsch, but serves only eight months; while in prison, he writes the better part of *Mein Kampf.*
1925	Reorganization of the Nazi Party.
1925	The Locarno Pacts: the powers reach an agreement on armament issues.
1929	Stresemann dies just as the Great Depression begins.
1930	In the Reichstag elections, the Nazis receive 18.3% of the votes, winning 107 seats out of 577.
1931	Unemployment reaches 5.6 million.
1932	Hitler defeated by von Hindenburg in the presidential election. Nevertheless, in the July Reichstag elections the Nazi share doubles to 37.4%. In the November election, it drops to 33.1%.
1933 January 30	President von Hindenburg appoints Hitler chancellor of a coalition government.
February 27	Reichstag fire, blamed on the Communists.
February 28	President von Hindenburg issues the decree "Protection of the People and State," suspending civil rights.
March 5	In the last multi-party Reichstag election, the Nazis receive 43% of the votes.

March 23	The Enabling Act is passed by the Reichstag, the legal foundation for the Nazi dictatorship.
May 2	All labor unions are banned.
July 14	All political parties except the Nazi Party are declared illegal.
October 14	Germany withdraws from the League of Nations.
November 12	In the first Reichstag elections under the Nazi regime, the Nazis receive 95.2% of the vote.

1934

January 30	Regional and local governments are suspended.
June 30	Night of the Long Knives: Hitler purges leaders of the storm troopers (SA) and many conservatives.
August 2	President von Hindenburg dies. Hitler, still chancellor, assumes the office of president.

1935

January 13	After a plebiscite the Saar is returned to Germany.
March 16	Military conscription begins.

1936

March 7	The German army enters the Rhineland.
August 1	The Olympic Games are held in Berlin.
November 25	Anti-Comintern Pact.

1937

January 30	Four-year extension of the Enabling Acts.

| November 5 | The Hossbach memorandum details plans for Nazi aggression. |

1938
| February | New command structure for the armed forces. |

| March 13 | The *Anschluss:* Austria is united with Germany. |

| September 29 | The Munich conference with Chamberlain: Hitler gains the Sudetenland from Czechoslovakia, supposedly his last territorial demand. |

| November 9 | *Kristallnacht*—a Nazi pogrom against the Jews throughout Germany. |

1939
| March 14–16 | In defiance of the Munich Accord, Germany declares the remaining Czech territory to be a "protectorate." |

| August 23 | The German-Soviet Non-Aggression Pact. |

| September 1 | Germany invades Poland and occupies Danzig. |

1940
| April | Germany invades Norway and occupies Denmark. |

| May–June | Germany invades Holland and Belgium and then France. |

| June 17 | France capitulates. |

| August–September | The Battle of Britain in the air. |

| December | Hitler finalizes plans to invade the Soviet Union (Operation Barbarossa). |

1941

April   Germany invades and occupies Yugoslavia and then Greece.

May 10   Rudolf Hess, the Führer's deputy, flies to Britain on a personal "peace mission." Hitler calls him "mad."

June 22   Germany attacks the Soviet Union in a "crusade" to eliminate Jews, Communists, and Gypsies and to enslave the Slavic peoples.

December 7   The *Nacht und Nebel* (Night and Fog) decree; the Japanese attack Pearl Harbor.

December 11   Hitler declares war on the United States.

1942

January   The Wannsee Conference plans the "Final Solution" to the "Jewish question."

November 19   Soviet forces attack and surround the German Sixth Army in Stalingrad.

1943

May 11   German and Italian forces surrender in Africa.

July 5–17   In Russia, the German center is shattered in the Battle of the Kursk Salient, the greatest tank battle in history.

July 10   Operation Husky: Allied forces land in Sicily.

July 25   Mussolini is deposed; Italy tries to leave the war.

September   The Germans occupy northern and central Italy.

1944

June 6   Operation Overlord: Allied landings in Normandy.

June 20	Massive Soviet offensive against Army Group Center.
July 20	Count Stauffenberg's attempt to kill Hitler and overthrow Nazi rule.
September 25	All men between sixteen and sixty are drafted into the *Volkssturm*.
December 16	German counterattack in Belgium, the Battle of the Bulge.
1945 January 30	Hitler's last speech to the German people, claiming that Germany will win the war.
March 7	The Americans cross the Rhine.
April 25	American and Soviet forces meet on the Elbe.
April 30	Hitler commits suicide in Berlin.
May 7	Germany surrenders unconditionally.

Maps

Concentration and Extermination Camps in Nazi Dominated Europe

SWEDEN

DENMARK

○ Jungenhof

Ostland

GERMAN

Treblinka ○

REICH

Mittelbau ✕

Buchenwald ✕

Majdanek ○

○ Sobibor

Ukraine

○ Belzec

✕ Theresienstadt

General-Government

Flossenburg ✕

○ Auschwitz

Protectorate

SLOVAKIA

Dachau ✕

HUNGARY

SWITZ.

ROMANIA

ITALY

CROATIA

SERBIA

BULGARIA

ALBANIA

0   100   200   300 MILES

© Bolchazy-Carducci Publishers, Inc.

Legend

✕   Main concentration camps in Germany

○   Extermination camps

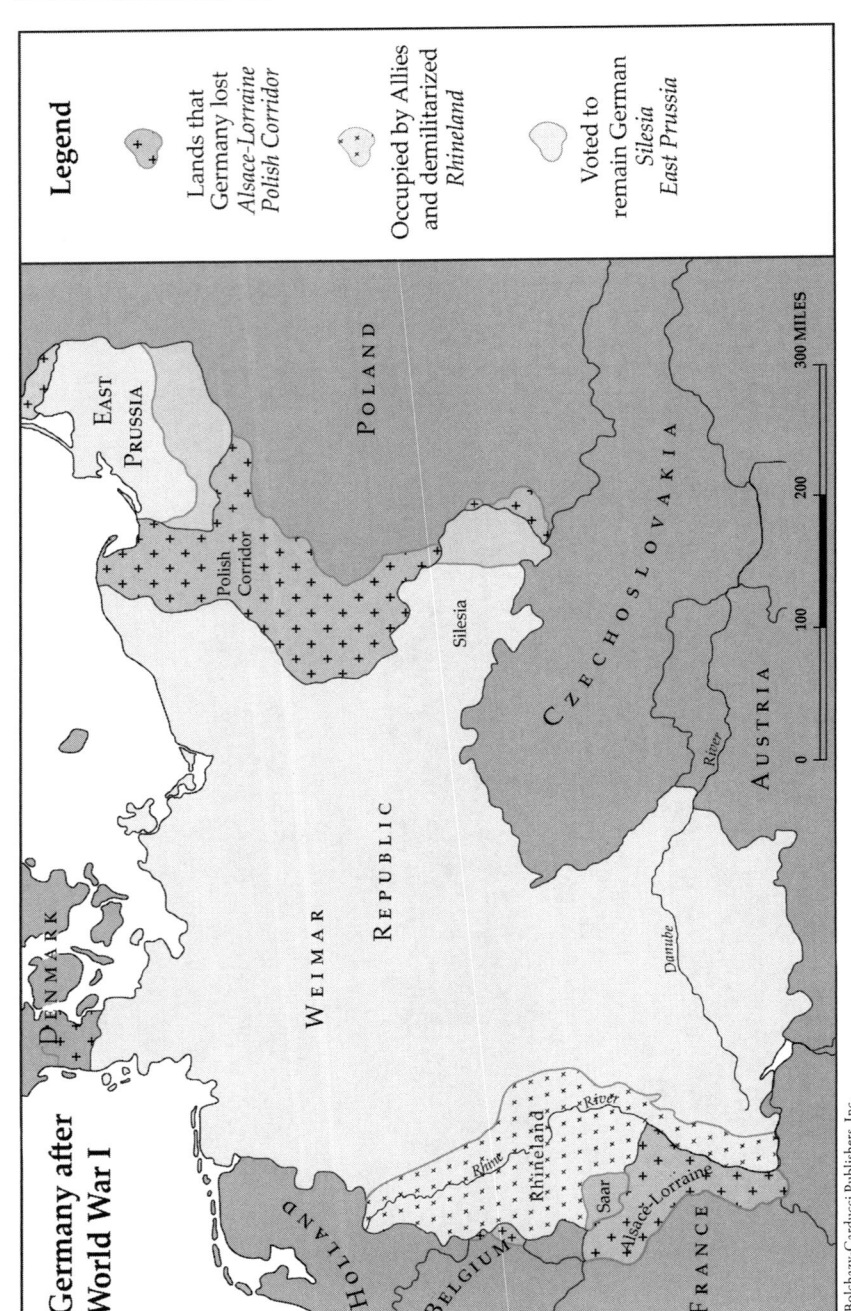

Germany after World War I

Legend

Lands that Germany lost
Alsace-Lorraine
Polish Corridor

Occupied by Allies and demilitarized
Rhineland

Voted to remain German
Silesia
East Prussia

DENMARK

EAST PRUSSIA

POLAND

Polish Corridor

Silesia

WEIMAR REPUBLIC

CZECHOSLOVAKIA

AUSTRIA

HOLLAND

BELGIUM

Rhineland

Rhine River

Saar

Alsace-Lorraine

FRANCE

Danube

River

0   100   200   300 MILES

© Bolchazy-Carducci Publishers, Inc.

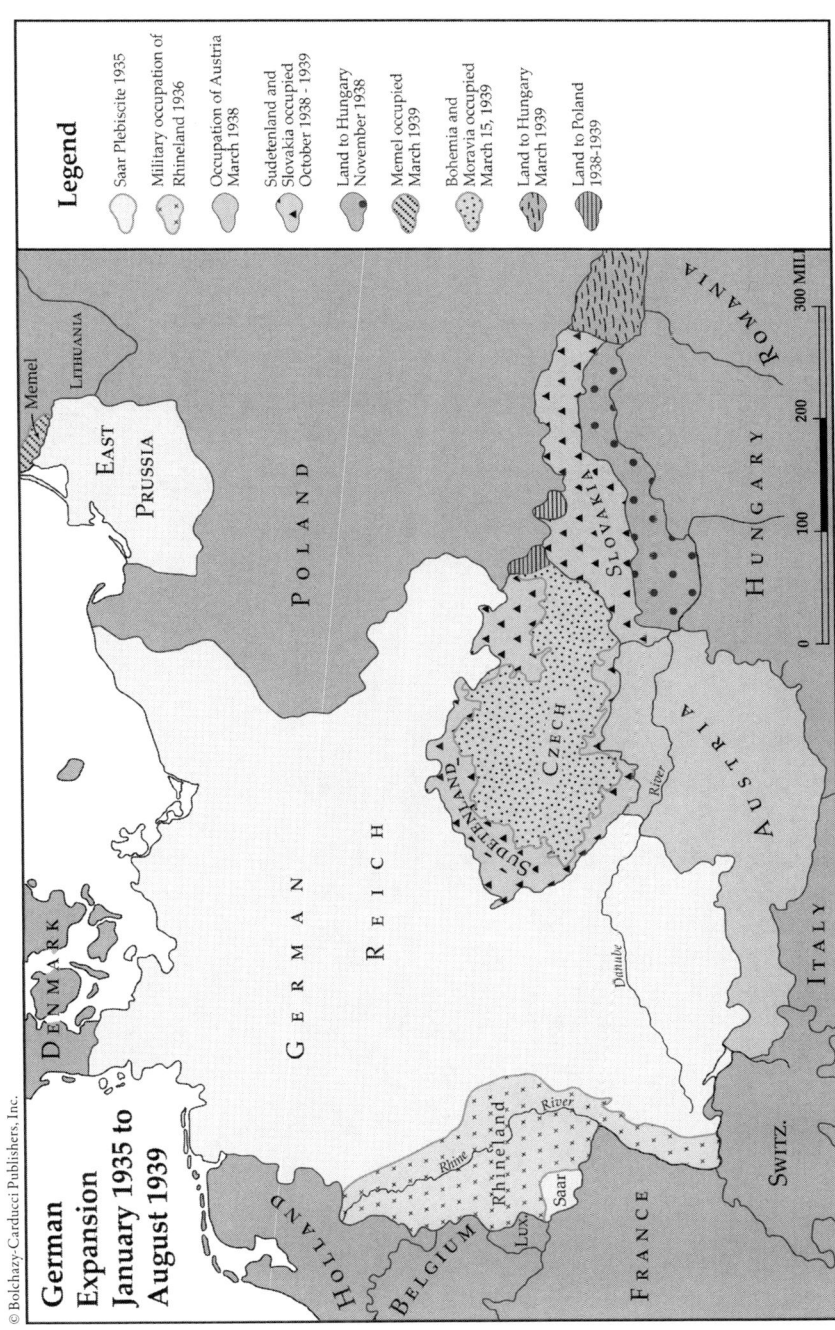

© Bolchazy-Carducci Publishers, Inc.

German Expansion January 1935 to August 1939

Legend

- Saar Plebiscite 1935
- Military occupation of Rhineland 1936
- Occupation of Austria March 1938
- Sudetenland and Slovakia occupied October 1938 - 1939
- Land to Hungary November 1938
- Memel occupied March 1939
- Bohemia and Moravia occupied March 15, 1939
- Land to Hungary March 1939
- Land to Poland 1938-1939

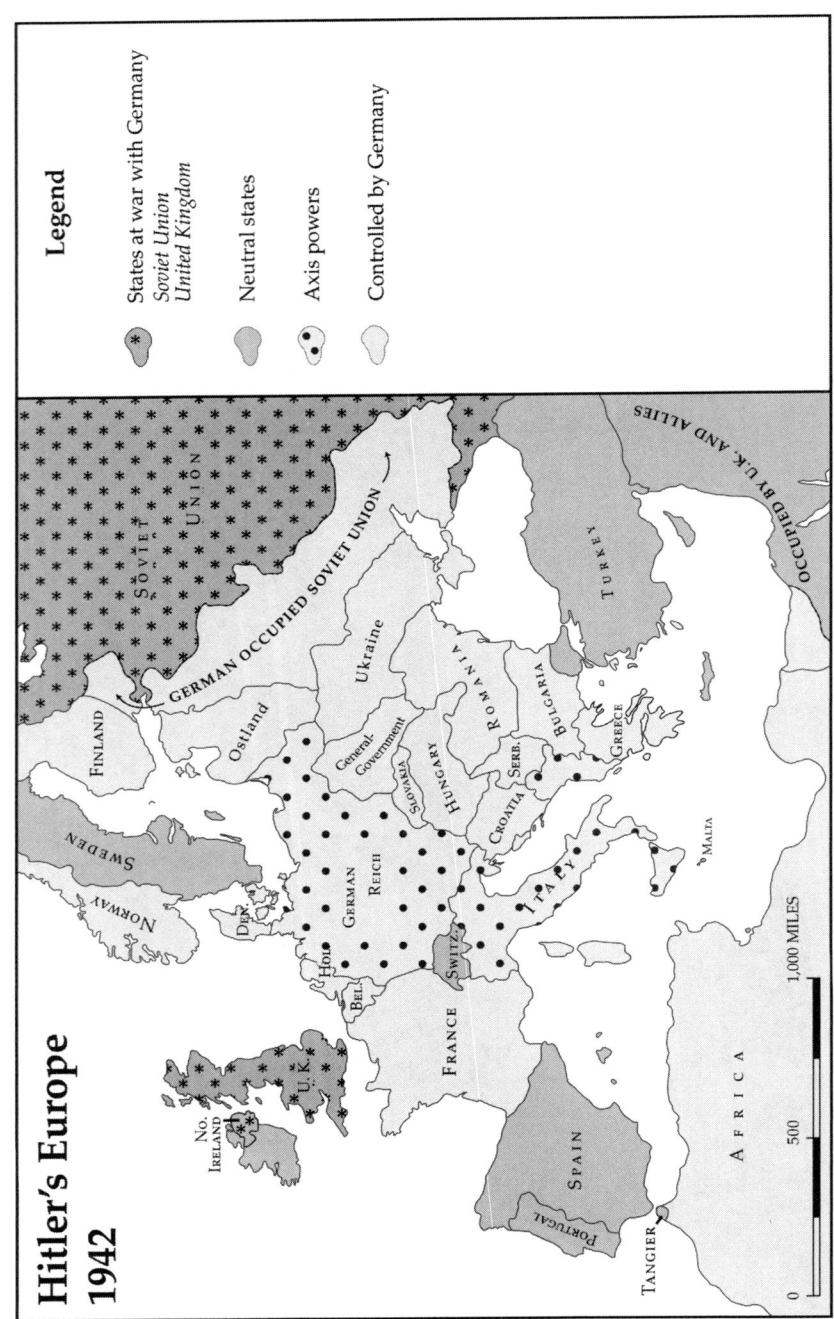

Hitler's Europe
1942

Legend

States at war with Germany
Soviet Union
United Kingdom

Neutral states

Axis powers

Controlled by Germany

© Bolchazy-Carducci Publishers, Inc.

Chronological Index of Speeches and Events

Sept 16, 1935
Hitler proclaimed the *Reichswehr* was now the *Wehrmacht*: 309

Nov 28, 1935
Interview with reporter Baillie: 555

Jan 19, 1936
Interview with Madame Titayna: 557

Feb 15, 1936
Hitler again talked about the automobile and the German people: 339

Mar 9, 1936
Interview with Ward Price: 562

Sept 11, 1936
Hitler spoke on the Volk and unity: 151

Sept 11, 1936
Hitler: children are the gift of women: 482

Oct 4, 1936
Hitler's currency reforms and efforts to achieve autarky: 346

Dec 1, 1936
All male youth to be part of the Hitler Youth: 466

Jan 30, 1937
Hitler's fourth anniversary of power: accomplishments of National Socialism: 178

Mar 15, 1937
Hitler: older men must keep fit: 474

May 20, 1937
Interview with Able Bonnard: 567

May 25, 1937
Hitler expressed his annoyance with Cardinal Mundelein: 431

June 6, 1937
Hitler emphasized his belief in God: 152

June 6, 1937
Hitler's belief in his "God sent mission" (repeat of above): 433

June 27, 1937
Hitler talked about the divine nature of the National Socialist movement: 153

July 19, 1937
Hitler spoke about degenerate art: 488

July 31, 1937
Hitler spoke about song and music: 497

Sept 7, 1937
Hitler spoke about "culture": 500

Sept 10, 1937
Hitler was the soul of the Nazi Party: 311

Sept 10, 1937
Hitler spoke about marriage: 483

Sept 13, 1937
Hitler explained how Germany was part of God's plan: 153

Sept 13, 1937
Hitler: Jewish Bolshevism and Jewish democracy were the same thing: 384

Oct 3, 1937
Hitler: The necessity of national unity and self-sacrifice: 154–55

Oct 5, 1937
Winter Relief was an insurance program: 155–56

Oct 31, 1937
Hitler kept part of his programs secret: 182

Nov 5, 1937
Hossbach Minutes: 603

Nov 19, 1937
Hitler talked about the use of force to gain *Lebensraum*: 184

Nov 22, 1937
Hitler presented his program for the future in a "secret speech": 312

Feb 20, 1938
Hitler talked about how the press misrepresented his actions, case in point—military personnel changes: 570

Nov 8, 1943
Hitler's continued obsession with
Jews: 413

Dec 20, 1943
Hitler anticipated the Allied invasion
in the West: 768

Mar 19, 1944
Hitler's last interview: 581

June 6, 1944
The invasion in the West: 771

July 7, 1944
The formation of the plot to remove
Hitler: 776

July 20, 1944
The attempt to kill Hitler failed: 777

July 21, 1944
Hitler launched massive retaliation
for the plot: 784

July 24, 1944
Hitler instituted "total war"
economy: 367

Aug 2, 1944
Retribution for the plot continued:
786

Dec 11, 1944
Hitler informed his army about his
plan to attack in the West: 791

Jan 1, 1945
Hitler's last New Year's
Proclamation: 416

Jan 22, 1945
Hitler still believed that the
"Bolshevik threat" would save him:
795

Mar 19, 1945
Speer and the Destruction Order:
369

Apr 13, 1945
The end of war was near: 797

Apr 29, 1945
Hitler married Eva Braun and wrote
his political and personal testaments:
802

Subject Index